Promoting Human Rights
Through Bills of Rights:
Comparative Perspectives

Promoting Human Rights Through Bills of Rights:

COMPARATIVE PERSPECTIVES

Edited by

Philip Alston

OXFORD

UNIVERSITY PRESS

OXFORD
UNIVERSITY PRESS

Great Clarendon Street, Oxford OX2 6DP

Oxford University Press is a department of the University of Oxford.
It furthers the University's objective of excellence in research, scholarship,
and education by publishing worldwide in

Oxford New York

Athens Auckland Bangkok Bogotá Buenos Aires Calcutta
Cape Town Chennai Dar es Salaam Delhi Florence Hong Kong Istanbul
Karachi Kuala Lumpur Madrid Melbourne Mexico City Mumbai
Nairobi Paris São Paulo Singapore Taipei Tokyo Toronto Warsaw

and associated companies in Berlin Ibadan

Oxford is a registered trade mark of Oxford University Press
in the UK and in certain other countries

Published in the United States
by Oxford University Press Inc., New York

British Library Cataloguing in Publication Data

Data available

Library of Congress Cataloging in Publication Data
Promoting human rights through bills of rights: comparative
perspectives/edited by Philip Alston.
p. cm.
Includes bibliographical references and index.
1. Civil rights. 2. International and municipal law.
3. Human rights. 4. Human rights. I. Alston, Philip.
K3240.6.P757 1999 341.4'81—dc—21 97–19746

ISBN 0–19–825822–4

1 3 5 7 9 10 8 6 4 2

Typeset by Hope Services (Abingdon) Ltd.
Printed in Great Britain
on acid-free paper by
Biddles Ltd.,
Guildford and King's Lynn

Preface

The French *Déclaration des droits de l'homme et du citoyen* of 1789 and the United States Bill of Rights of 1791 are by far the best known declarations of their type. But they are by no means alone. Today, many more countries have bills of rights than do not have them. Contrary to popular perception, this phenomenon is by no means a result of the end of the Cold War and the growing movement towards democracy in the world at large. Nor is it even a product of the great movement to recognize human rights that has gradually gained momentum since the adoption of the United Nations Charter in 1945. Even prior to the waves of new constitution-making that swept the world in the wake of the Second World War and the dramatic process of decolonization which it unleashed, bills of rights (defined as including dedicated chapters and such like in constitutions) were commonplace.

Nevertheless, the situation at the end of the twentieth century in relation to bills of rights is qualitatively different from anything that has gone before. Bills of rights are taken more seriously, their enforcement provisions are significantly more elaborate, far-reaching and potentially effective than ever before, and their relationship with the international normative regime that has been constructed in the human rights field gives them a coherence and a momentum which they have not had in previous eras. Yet despite these fundamental changes, bills of rights continue to be relatively neglected either as subjects of comparative constitutional law or in terms of their relationship with the international human rights regime. This volume is designed to contribute to the literature in both these respects. It is not a state of the art guide to the jurisprudence of each and every one of the world's major bills of rights. Such an aspiration would not only be impossible to meet but it would also have limited utility. Instead, this volume brings together a sampling of case studies which help to shed light on the key issues that arise in relation to bills of rights generally, while acknowledging that every situation is inevitably unique. Some of the chapters are of primarily historical importance, but they all contribute different elements which are essential to understanding the overall dynamics of bills of rights in general. Given that such bills are indeed now ubiquitous, and that various factors are conspiring to make them an important factor in international relations and no longer only in terms of domestic legal orders, such a broader focus is increasingly indispensable.

This volume has been long in the making, for various reasons. The first draft of some of the papers was presented at a conference organized by the

Centre for International and Public Law at the Australian National University in the second half of 1992. Since then, some of the contributions which had delayed publication at the time have failed to eventuate, a number of others have been added, and all of the original chapters have been updated. As a result, the range of country studies has evolved significantly from the time when the project was first conceived. Moreover, the decision to include a major concluding chapter was taken only late in the day on the advice of reviewers. The patience of all those concerned is deeply appreciated. Many debts have been incurred along the way and I am especially grateful to those who have assisted in various ways, including Mara Bustelo, Bridget Gilmour-Walsh, Mac Darrow, Claire Parkhill, Roslyn Walker, Libby Bunyan and Susan Garvin. Those responsible at Oxford University Press, including John Louth, Nigel Sleight and Myfanwy Milton, have been patient and encouraging throughout the process.

PHILIP ALSTON
European University Institute,
Florence.

Contents

Notes on Contributors

Philip Alston is Professor of International Law at the European University Institute in Florence, and visiting Global Law Professor at New York University.

Sir Gerard Brennan AC, KBE, has been Chief Justice of the High Court of Australia since 1995 and was previously Judge of the Australian Industrial Court and the Supreme Court of the Australian Capital Territory (1976–81), President of the Administrative Appeals Tribunal (1976–79), and Judge of the Federal Court of Australia (1977–81).

Andrew Byrnes is an associate professor of law and Director of the Centre for Comparative and Public Law in the Faculty of Law at the University of Hong Kong.

Martin Chanock is Professor of Legal Studies at La Trobe University, Melbourne.

Andrew Clapham is Associate Professor of Public International Law at the Graduate Institute of International Studies in Geneva and was previously the Representative of Amnesty International at the United Nations in New York.

Mac Darrow is a Research Associate at the European University Institute, Florence. He has previously worked in private legal practice and in the Human Rights Branch of the Australian Attorney-General's Department.

John J. Doyle is Chief Justice of the Supreme Court of South Australia, and was previously Solicitor-General from 1986 to 1995.

Mary Eberts practises law at Eberts Symes Street & Corbett in Toronto and teaches part-time at the Faculty of Law, University of Toronto.

Yash Ghai is Sir Y. K. Pao Professor of Public Law at the University of Hong Kong.

Philip Joseph is Associate Professor of Law, University of Canterbury.

David Kinley is a consultant to the Australian Human Rights and Equal

Opportunity Commission, and previously worked for the Australian Law Reform Commission.

David Kretzmer is Professor of Law at Hebrew University and a member of the Human Rights Committee established under the International Covenant on Civil and Political Rights.

Robert Sharpe is a Judge of the Ontario Court of Justice, in Toronto, and was previously Professor of Law and Dean of the Faculty of Law at the University of Toronto.

Belinda Wells is a Lecturer in Law at Flinders University, and previously worked as assistant to the Solicitor-General of South Australia.

Abbreviations

AC	Appeal Cases (Law Reports, UK)
AJIL	*American Journal of International Law*
All ER	All England Law Reports
ALJ	*Australian Law Journal*
ALR	Australian Law Reports
Alta. LR	*Alberta Law Review*
BCLR	British Columbia Reports (Law Reports, Canada)
BYIL	*British Yearbook of International Law*
Can. Bar Rev.	*Canadian Bar Review*
CAR	Conciliation and Arbitration Reports (Law Reports, Australia)
CCC	Canadian Criminal Cases
CCIL Bulletin	*Canadian Council of International Law Bulletin*
CERD	Committee on the Elimination of Racial Discrimination
CFA	Committee on Freedom of Association
Ch D	Chancery Division (Law Reports, UK)
CLR	Commonwealth Law Reports (Australia)
CML Rev.	*Common Market Law Review*
Co Rep	Coke Reports (Law Reports, UK)
CR	Criminal Reports (Law Reports, Canada)
CRNZ	Criminal Reports New Zealand
CRR	Canadian Rights Reporter
Cth	Commonwealth (Australia)
D. & R.	Decisions and Reports of the European Commission of Human Rights
DLR	Dominion Law Reports (Canada)
EA	East African Law Reports
EALJ	*East African Law Journal*
ECHR	European Convention on Human Rights
ECHR ser. A	Reports of the European Court of Human Rights
ECHR ser. B	Reports of the pleadings before the European Court of Human Rights
ECR	European Court Reports
EHRR	European Human Rights Reports
ER	English Reports (Law Reports, UK)
Fam LR	Family Law Reports (Australia)
Fed LR	*Federal Law Review* (Australia)
FFCC	Fact Finding and Conciliation Commission on Freedom of Association

HC Debates	House of Commons Parliamentary Debates
HKCLR	Hong Kong Criminal Law Reports
HKLJ	*Hong Kong Law Journal*
HKPLR	Hong Kong Public Law Reports
HL Debates	House of Lords Parliamentary Debates
HRLJ	*Human Rights Law Journal*
HRQ	*Human Rights Quarterly*
ICCPR	International Covenant on Civil and Political Rights
ICESCR	International Covenant on Economic, Social and Cultural Rights
ICLQ	*International and Comparative Law Quarterly*
ICR	Industrial Cases Reports (Law Reports, UK)
ILC	International Labour Committee
ILM	International Legal Materials
ILO	International Labour Organization
Imm AR	Immigration Appeal Reports (Law Reports, UK)
KLR	Kenya Law Reports
LQR	*Law Quarterly Review*
LRC (Const)	Law Reports of the Commonwealth: Constitutional and Administrative Law
MCLR	*Media and Communications Law Review* (Canada)
MLR	*Modern Law Review*
MULR	*Melbourne University Law Review*
NJCL	*National Journal of Constitutional Law* (Canada)
NLJ	*New Law Journal*
NR	National Reports (Law Reports, Canada)
NSCC	Nigeria Supreme Court Cases
NSR	Nova Scotia Reports (Law Reports, Canada)
NSWLR	*New South Wales Law Review*
NSWLR	New South Wales Law Reports (Australia)
NZAR	New Zealand Administrative Reports
NZLJ	*New Zealand Law Journal*
NZLR	New Zealand Law Reports
NZPD	New Zealand Parliamentary Debates
OR	Ontario Reports (Law Reports, Canada)
P 2d	Pacific Reporter 2nd series (Law Reports, USA)
PD	Probate Division (Law Reports, UK)
PL	*Public Law*
PLR	*Public Law Review*
QBD	Queens Bench Division (Law Reports, UK)
RUDH	*Revue universelle des droits de l'homme*
SA	South Australia
SASR	South Australian State Reports

SC	Session Cases (Law Reports, UK)
SCR	Supreme Court Reports (Law Reports, Canada)
SJ	*Solicitors Journal* (UK)
SLR	*Statute Law Review*
St Tr	State Trials (Law Reports, UK)
Syd LR	*Sydney Law Review*
TCL	*The Capital Letter* (New Zealand)
UBCLR	*University of British Columbia Law Review*
UNBLJ	*University of New Brunswick Law Journal*
UNTS	United Nations Treaty Series
US	United States Supreme Court Reports
UT Fac. L Rev.	*University of Toronto Faculty Law Review*
UTLJ	*University of Toronto Law Journal*
VR	Victorian Reports (Law Reports, Australia)
VUWLR	*Victoria University of Wellingtion Law Review*
Wheat.	Wheatons Reports (Law Reports, USA)
WLR	Weekly Law Reports (UK)
Yale JL Feminism	*Yale Journal of Law and Feminism*

1

A Framework for the Comparative Analysis of Bills of Rights

PHILIP ALSTON

Introduction*

In 1787 Thomas Jefferson wrote a letter from pre-revolutionary Paris to James Madison opining that 'a bill of rights is what the people are entitled to against every government on earth'.[1] In the intervening two centuries, a great many peoples have got what Jefferson considered to be their due. Moreover, within the course of the last decade alone, bills of rights have assumed particular and renewed importance in an extraordinary number of countries in all parts of the world. Whether proclaimed by constitutional assemblies, adopted by legislatures, incorporated on the basis of international treaties or discerned by judiciaries, not only their number but also their importance (in formal terms, at least) have increased very significantly.

One such example, the United Kingdom Human Rights Act of 1998, has attracted major attention within Western Europe, yet it is but a drop in the bucket in global terms. In Central and Eastern Europe alone, there have been more than twenty-five new or revised constitutions drafted since the end of the Cold War.[2] The situation is similar in Africa where the list of new or revised constitutions adopted since the end of the Cold War is equally impressive. It has even been characterized as a prolonged fit of 'constitutional fever'.[3] A

* Thanks to Gráinne de Búrca and James Heenan for helpful comments on a draft.
[1] Letter of 1787, in Ford (ed.), *Writings of Thomas Jefferson* (1892), vol.4, 477.
[2] They include: Albania (1993), Armenia (1995), Azerbaijan (1995), Belarus (1996), Bosnia-Herzegovina (1995), Bulgaria (1991), Croatia (1990), Czech Republic (1992), Estonia (1992), the Former Yugoslav Republic of Macedonia (1991), Georgia (1995), Hungary (1994), Kazakhstan (1995), Kyrgyz (1993), Latvia (1991), Lithuania (1992), Moldova (1994), Poland (1997), Romania (1991), Russian Federation (1993), Slovak Republic (1992), Slovenia (1991), Tajikistan (1994), Ukraine (1996), Uzbekistan (1992). All of these are available in English in Blaustein and Flanz (eds.), *Constitutions of the Countries of the World*, vols. I-XX and Supplement (1971 and regular updates). For analyses of these provisions see Henckaerts and van der Jeught, 'Human Rights Protection under the New Constitutions of Central Europe', (1998) 20 *Loyola of Los Angeles International and Comparative Law Journal* 475; Ludwikowski, '"Mixed" Constitutions—Product of an East-Central European Constitutional Melting Pot', (1998) 16 *Boston University International Law Journal* 1; and Verdussen (ed.), *La Justice constitutionnelle en Europe centrale* (1997).
[3] Glélé, cited in du Bois de Gaudusson, 'Introduction', in du Bois de Gaudusson, Conac, and Desouches (eds.), *Les Constitutions africaines publiés en langue française* (1998), vol. 2, 9.

recent compilation of the relevant constitutions published in French includes twenty since Benin and Guinea led the field in 1990.[4]

In addition, there have been regional and sub-regional initiatives which could be so characterized, depending on how we define a bill of rights, an issue to which we return below.[5] One such example is a 1997 initiative by twelve Caribbean states which resulted in the adoption of a 'Charter of Civil Society for the Caribbean Community'.[6] The document is not described by its title as a human rights charter although it is in fact overwhelmingly concerned with such rights and many of the formulations are drawn from the Constitutions of one or other of the Caribbean states. It was adopted, not by civil society as one might assume from its title, but by 'We the people of the Caribbean Community, acting through the assembled representatives of our Governments'.[7]

Virtually all of these constitutions contain a major set of human rights provisions and while their content differs, sometimes significantly, from one to the next, there is a core set of civil and political rights which is reflected almost without fail. This core includes: the right to life, freedom from torture, freedom from arbitrary arrest and detention, the right to be presumed innocent, the right to privacy, freedom of movement, the right to property, freedom of thought, conscience and religion, freedom of expression, freedom of asembly and association, and the right to participate in government.

In addition to these domestic constitutional provisions, there is a very strong tendency, perhaps most marked in the majority of the new constitutions of Central and Eastern Europe, to recognize international law as part of national law and, in many instances, to accord it a higher status than domestic legislation.[8]

This trend towards universal recognition of human rights in domestic constitutional law has been greeted enthusiastically by diverse groups within society, ranging from lawyers, judges and politicians through academic commentators to grassroots activists, trade union leaders, corporate officials and others. There is almost an element of triumphalism in some assessments. One study concludes that '[a]part from the ideal of democratic self-government

---

[4] They are: Benin (1990), Guinea (1990), Gabon (1991), Rwanda (1991), Mauritania (1991), Mali (1991), Burundi (1992), Congo (1992), Cape Verde (1992), Djibouti (1992), Madagascar (1992), Togo (1992), Seychelles (1993), Tunisia (1995), Cameroon (1996), Chad (1996), Niger (1996), Comoros (1996), Algeria (1996), and Burkina Faso (1997). *Ibid.*, (2 vols., 1998).

[5] See further below, 6–11.

[6] The Charter was adopted by the Conference of Heads of Government of the Caribbean Community at their Eighth Inter-sessional Meeting, in 1997. Available only in mimeo.

[7] First Preambular paragraph.

[8] See Stein, 'International Law in Internal Law: Toward Internationalization of Central-Eastern European Constitutions?', (1994) 88 *American Journal of International Law* 427; Schweisfurth and Alleweldt, 'The Position of International Law in the Domestic Legal Orders of Central and Eastern European Countries', in (1997) 40 *German Yearbook of International Law* 164; and Danilenko, 'Implementation of International Law in CIS States: Theory and Practice', (1999) 10 *European Journal of International Law* 51.

... there is no more universal feature of politics in the late twentieth century than rights'.[9] To a large extent, it is bills of rights which will prove or disprove the validity of such a claim. Yet it is by no means certain, in the case of a great number of them, that they will in fact prove to be successful.[10] Indeed, in various respects, the evidence would seem to warrant considerable caution in terms of prognoses.

It must be recalled that the enthusiastic endorsement of human rights within the context of constitutional instruments is not, in fact, without precedent. Indeed, even before the adoption of the Universal Declaration of Human Rights, 82 per cent of the national constitutions that had been drafted between 1788 and 1948 contained some form of protection for human rights. Thereafter, the percentage increased further so that 93 per cent of the constitutions drafted between 1949 and 1975 included human rights provisions.[11] Yet it would be a bold and optimistic observer who would characterize these periods of human rights-aware constitution-making as having been particularly successful. The historical record, in terms of the many bills which existed prior to the mid-1980s, is far from encouraging. Many of them were tokenistic concessions to normative decency which bore no relationship to the realities of the society and which were accompanied neither by the political will to take them seriously, nor accompanied by the institutional means which might have made them viable. They were, moreover, clearly lacking the support of civil society which seems so necessary but has too often been taken for granted in relation to bills of rights. In short, these bills of rights were often no more than facades presenting an image of legal and democratic legitimacy, which could actually have had a significant overall negative impact on respect for law and public perceptions of the utility of rights.[12] What is clear from the experience of earlier decades and earlier waves of constitutionalism is that there can be no sense of inevitability as to the effectiveness of bills of rights in guiding, channelling, or reinforcing the broader push towards democratization, respect for the rule of law, and the promotion of good governance, despite the extent to which such an association has tended, almost automatically, to be made.

There is no shortage of informed observers who would tell us that this failure was largely predictable and that the human rights endeavour, at least as it manifests itself through bills of rights and the international human rights

[9] Lacey and Haakonssen, 'Introduction: History, Historicism, and the Culture of Rights', in Lacey and Haakonssen (eds.), *A Culture of Rights: The Bill of Rights in Philosophy, Politics, and Law—1791 and 1991* (1991), 2.

[10] See, e.g., Bowring, 'Human Rights in Russia: Discourse of Emancipation or only a Mirage?', in Pogany (ed.), *Human Rights in Eastern Europe* (1995), 87.

[11] Van Maarseveen and van der Tang, *Written Constitutions: A Computerised Comparative Study* (1978), 191–5.

[12] The literature in this respect is vast. In relation to Africa, for example, see Gonidec, 'Constitutionnalismes africains', (1996) 50 *Revue juridique et politique* 23; and Ghai, 'Constitutions and Governance in Africa: A Prolegomenon', in Adelman and Paliwala (eds.), *Law and Crisis in the Third World* (1993), 51.

regime generally, is condemned to repeated failures until such time as it recognizes the specificity of every culture and the need for transformative strategies in different societies to be based upon what will often need to be radically different approaches. As Brown has noted, 'to overemphasise rights in isolation from their social context is counterproductive, potentially undermining the very factors which create the context in which rights are respected'.[13] A very different type of critique, but one which brings us to the same result, is that put forward by Lord Hoffman whose unfortunate claim to international recognition is as the judge whose casting vote in the first judgment given by the House of Lords in the Pinochet case[14] was subsequently nullified on the grounds that he had failed to disclose his links to Amnesty International, which had been permitted to intervene in the proceedings.[15] While rejecting any suggestion that his views reflect a 'vulgar Euroscepticism', he suggests that the United Kingdom has 'our own hierarchy of moral values, our own culturally determined sense of what is fair and unfair, and I think it would be unfair to submerge this under a pan-European jurisprudence of human rights'.[16] Any such assessment bodes ill for those who would expect that a bill of rights, adopted in the shadow of international pressures or of a desire to imitate what might today be represented as a 'politically correct' approach to constitutionalism, would have the potential to inculcate or reinforce a mentality that respects human rights.

The question that arises is whether there is reason to be more optimistic about the legacy of the proliferation of bills of rights resulting from the most recent burst of constitutionalism, in the late 1980s and the 1990s? At one level it is obvious that generalizations will be of limited utility in answering that question. Just as the forces that have initiated and facilitated such developments vary widely, so too will their prospects of success differ greatly from one country to another. This context-specific dimension is provided by the case studies presented in this volume.

The collection of essays that follows has two main aims. The first is to provide a survey of the type of approaches that have been adopted in different countries. Because of the very significant differences from one bill of rights to another, and because a meaningful appreciation of the role played by a particular bill can only be gained by seeing it in its broader constitutional, social and cultural context, individual case studies are indispensable.

[13] Brown, 'Universal Human Rights: A Critique', (1997) 1 *International Journal of Human Rights* 41.

[14] House of Lords, *R. v. Bartle and the Commissioner of Police for the Metropolis and Other, ex parte Pinochet (On Appeal from a Divisional Court of the Queen's Bench Division)*, judgment of 25 November 1998, (1998) 37 *International Legal Materials* 1302.

[15] House of Lords, *R. v. Bartle and the Commissioner of Police for the Metropolis and Other, ex parte Pinochet (On Appeal from a Divisional Court of the Queen's Bench Division)*, judgment of 24 March 1999, http://www.parliament.the-stationery-office.co.uk.

[16] Hoffman, 'Human Rights and the House of Lords', (1999) 62 *Modern Law Review* 159 at 165.

The second aim is to examine the impact which the evolution of the international human rights regime has had on the conception and functioning of bills of rights and how the increasing influence of that regime has affected, and in some respects transformed, many of the major debates which have traditionally surrounded bills of rights. Those debates have focused, for example, on the open-endedness—and thus the manipulability—of human rights norms, the extent to which bills of rights empower an unaccountable judiciary, the implications for the separation of powers of limitations upon the powers of both the executive and legislative branches, the compatibility of at least some types of bills with notions of the sovereignty of the people and the extent to which a conservative legal framework will usually stymie expectations that rights will be used to achieve a socially progressive agenda. In general, these and other arguments for and against the adoption of bills of rights are reviewed in the final chapter.

The volume as a whole provides an analysis of a cross-section of experiences of countries which have adopted different approaches to bills of rights. Its purpose is to shed some light on questions such as the following. How should we conceive of a bill of rights? What is its relationship to broader efforts to consolidate democratic forms of governance? How does it relate to the constitutional structure of a country? What is its impact upon theories of governmental legitimacy and the separation of powers? To what extent does it need to be linked to particular institutional arrangements? Is judicial interpretation and enforcement a necessary corollary of a bill of rights? What is its relationship to the country's obligations under international law? If it is rooted in them, what is its status in municipal law? If it is not overtly linked in any way to such obligations, what role, if any, do they play in the interpretation of the bill?

The volume does not seek to provide a guide to each of the world's principal bills of rights. Instead, the relatively few countries selected were chosen because they have something of specific interest to add to the overall picture of how bills of rights come into being, how they are designed, and how they function in practice. Because of this much broader objective, none of the chapters purports to provide a 'state of the art' analysis of current interpretations of particular provisions. Indeed, some of the analyses are of primarily historical importance, including those dealing with the Hong Kong Bill and that describing the concerns and values that shaped the approach to rights that led to the 1996 South African Constitution.

The most conspicuous omission from the volume is a chapter dealing with what is all too often referred to as 'the' Bill of Rights—that contained in the various amendments to the Constitution of the USA. There are several reasons for this omission. The first is that the American approach has already been the subject of innumerable analyses, assessments, critiques, evaluations, etc. There seemed to be little point in adding yet another, especially since it would be difficult to capture the essence of that experience in a single short chapter. The second is that the American Bill of Rights is, in many ways, *sui generis*. Because it is in a class of its own, experience under it offers fewer insights and less guidance than is usually assumed to those who are curious about the viability or optimal shape of bills of rights elsewhere in the world. A third reason is that the international human rights regime constitutes an important dimension of the study as a whole and the USA has had, and continues to have, a unique, and in many ways ambivalent, relationship with that regime.

It should also be made clear from the outset that there are no simple or consistent answers to many of the questions posed above, and that any recipes which might emerge from the individual country case studies are unlikely to be capable of easy application in relation to other situations. Nevertheless, there are strong reasons to conclude that the evolution of the international human rights regime has generated a variety of pressures which encourage convergence in relation to the approaches adopted to some of the central issues raised by the existence of a bill of rights. This conclusion is given concrete illustration in a number of the case studies contained in the present volume. Moreover, it may well be that this process of convergence can assist in overcoming some of the major problems which have justifiably been identified by those who are not convinced of the desirability of seeking to rely significantly upon bills of rights in order to provide adequate domestic protection of human rights.

Defining Bills of Rights

Michael Zander's book examining the pros and cons of incorporation of the European Convention on Human Rights into United Kingdom law is now in its fourth edition.[17] It is, by the standards in this area, a classic. Yet nowhere does it define what is meant by a bill of rights. Zander begins by stating that the European Convention could constitute a bill of rights for the United Kingdom. He then surveys a wide range of different approaches adopted in other countries, but at no point pauses to ask what exactly a bill of rights is. This approach is reasonably standard. As with the now omni-present term 'constitutionalism', there is no common definition of what constitutes a bill of rights. Even an article entitled 'What is a Bill of Rights . . . ' provides no answers.[18]

Dictionary definitions are hardly more helpful. The Oxford Dictionary lists three meanings for a bill of rights: (i) the English Bill of Rights of 1689; (ii) the

---

[17] *A Bill of Rights?* 4th ed. (1997).
[18] Goldwin, 'What is a Bill of Rights and What is it Good For?' in Licht and de Villiers (eds.), *South Africa's Crisis of Constitutional Democracy: Can the U.S. Constitution Help?* (1994), 143.

American Bill of Rights of 1791; and (iii) 'a statement of the rights of a class of people'.[19] The last, more generic category, is not easy to reconcile with historical practice unless the reference is to cases such as the post-First World War minorities treaties defined as bills of rights for the minority groups. Otherwise, it is revealing that there is no attempt to define a bill of rights by reference to its functions or other characteristics. Confining the definition by reference to the two main Anglo-Saxon historical precedents also excludes a great number of other bills and leaves no room for the more common usage which permits the use of this term in relation to a wide range of rights-related instruments.

An obvious alternative approach then is to infer the meaning of the term from a reasonable cross-section of examples. But as the contributions to this volume show, the term is applied in practice to a wide range of documents, from short manifestos detached from any particular institutional arrangements, through to detailed, constitutionally entrenched and legally enforceable charters. It is also used in reference to bundles (or even tiny packages) of norms or principles which are almost nowhere formally stated to constitute such a bill, but which are more typically to be found in constitutional chapters—of greatly varying length and content—under a heading such as 'fundamental rights'. The term is also often used in relation to much more general provisions which, in the view of the observer, are said to function in effect as bills of rights.[20] The philosophies underlying the different bills are diverse and their significance in practice varies from being unadulterated window-dressing to being the yardstick against which every governmental move is measured. In short, the practice seems to be so disparate that it provides few pointers to a satisfactory definition.

Perhaps it is only academics who feel the need for a definition? But even they have not offered definitions in significant numbers. One approach is that proposed below by David Kretzmer. He identifies three normative functions which can be fulfilled by a bill of rights in a legal system: (i) to define those basic rights that are recognized and protected; (ii) to delimit the scope of protection by setting standards against which to evaluate proposed restrictions; and (iii) to establish the constitutional status of the rights, by reference to those bodies authorized to invalidate inconsistent laws.[21] This is a useful approach, although one which leads more towards a typology of bills than to a definition. It also seems to omit a number of elements which are significant

---

[19] *Concise Oxford Dictionary* 9th ed. (1995), 127.

[20] Thus Marshall refers to Article 119 of the Treaty establishing the European Community (to become Article 141 after the entry into force of the Amsterdam Treaty) as an economic bill of rights for the United Kingdom. Marshall, 'Lions Around the Throne: The Expansion of Judicial Review in Britain', in Hesse and Johnson, *Constitutional Policy and Change in Europe* (1995), 178 at 191.

[21] See Kretzmer, 'Basic Laws as a Surrogate Bill of Rights: The Case of Israel', ch. 3 below.

for a broad-ranging inquiry into bills of rights in general. I will return to that issue below.

Another approach to definition is provided by Strauss who notes that, in the 1990s, the question of whether to adopt a bill of rights has become relevant for the first time for many people. He seeks to answer the question: What will they be adopting if they do so?[22] He identifies three different conceptions of the bill of rights. The first is as a code of relatively specific requirements and prohibitions. Its addressee is not crucial, although it may be the legislature and perhaps not the judiciary. The second is as a means of correcting structural deficiencies in representative government. It may, for example, impose limits on majoritarianism. The third is as a charter of fundamental human rights. But this analysis is, of course, based on 'the' American Bill of Rights. As a result, because the 'conceptualization' is so deeply rooted in one particular national experience, it actually has surprisingly little to offer in terms of a broad comparative approach.

Faced with the difficulty of avoiding an approach which is so country-specific, some commentators have opted instead for a rather minimalist approach. Thus for Demerieux it is '[s]elf-evidently . . . the purpose of a bill of rights . . . to secure protection and promotion of rights and their recognition by the state as part of the political package that is the Constitution'.[23] But does such an approach mean, for example, that no particular rights need be specified as long as one or two are? Is there no minimum list of 'fundamental' rights? Does the Constitution need to accord any particular status to those rights, or is it sufficient if they can be amended, abrogated or overridden without following any particular procedures, and without the government suffering any detriment as a result? Such minimalism is reminiscent of a definition of constitutionalism offered by Kommers who says that it 'means that branches and units of government will remain within their defined spheres of power, as defined by a written constitution'.[24] But this is purely descriptive and does not even mandate any particular degree of separation of powers, let alone spelling out any of the other elements commonly associated with the term.[25] As Okoth-Ogendo has commented in relation to Africa, this risks being constitutionality without the values of constitutionalism.[26]

[22] Strauss, 'The Role of a Bill of Rights', in Stone, Epstein and Sunstein (eds.), *The Bill of Rights in the Modern State* (1992), 539. The same volume was also published as (1992) 59 *University of Chicago Law Review* 1–583.

[23] Demerieux, *Fundamental Rights in Commonwealth Caribbean Constitutions* (1992), 34.

[24] Kommers, 'Procedures for the Protection of Human Rights in Diffuse Systems of Judicial Review', in European Commission for Democracy through Law, *The Protection of Fundamental Rights by the Constitutional Court* (1996), 97.

[25] See Murphy, 'Constitutions, Constitutionalism, and Democracy', in Greenberg *et al.*, (eds.), *Constitutionalism and Democracy: Transitions in the Contemporary World* (1993), 3.

[26] Okoth-Ogendo, 'Constitutions without Constitutionalism: Reflections on an African Political Paradox', in Greenberg *et al.*, n. 25 above, at 65.

A definition proposed by Jaconelli seeks to address at least part of this objection by requiring the bill to embody 'what are considered to be the fundamental moral rights . . . those which are considered the most important or those most at risk'. But he concedes that '[I]t will always be a moot point whether certain documents are bills of rights strictly so called'. For that purpose he suggest that the range of rights covered is the primary criterion with the normative status of the instrument *vis-à-vis* other sources of law being a secondary criterion.[27] But he lists no minimum requirement in relation to either criterion, thus rendering the discussion somewhat circular.

The definitional challenge is exacerbated when we talk of an unwritten bill of rights. How can we do so without falling prey to an oxymoron, albeit one that is widely accepted in relation to the situation that prevailed in the United Kingdom, at least up until 1998. After all, the word has distinct and unmistakable connotations of something written. None of us would wish to be offered an unwritten bill of exchange, bill of lading, bill of health, bill of goods, or bill of fare. But if we insist that there can be an unwritten bill of rights, then surely it is doubly important to establish criteria for what it can reasonably consist of? In other words, is there not some threshold beneath which a document, or even an unwritten bill, cannot be deemed adequate to warrant being called a bill of rights? If a tinpot dictator issues a decree proclaiming a bill of rights according to which 'all citizens shall be treated with respect and dignity except when the imperative of national security requires otherwise', can it be considered to be a bill of rights? If not, on the basis of what minimum criteria can we exclude it? Similarly, if a purported bill of rights goes well beyond any generally recognized listing of rights, thereby diluting or demeaning the latter with spurious provisions of the 'right to wear red socks' type, is there a point at which it overstretches the acceptable bounds of a bill of rights? This question has often been posed, but almost exclusively in the context of justifying the non-inclusion of economic, social and cultural rights.[28]

A closely related question is whether it is legitimate for a bill of rights to be seen not as a constitutional charter in the sense of a coherent set of fundamental principles capable of guiding the resolution of the most basic issues confronting the society, but rather as something resembling a 'bill of goods' in a descriptive, non-value oriented sense. Or as Dworkin puts it, as 'a document with the tone and texture of an insurance policy or a standard form of commercial lease'.[29]

---

[27] Jaconelli, *Enacting a Bill of Rights: The Legal Problems* (1980), 1 and n.1.

[28] Jaconelli, for example, notes that, in linguistic terms, 'any value which can be fitted into the "freedom to . . ." or "freedom from . . ." mould would seem to be a possible candidate for inclusion in the terms of a bill of rights' (*ibid.* at 6–7), but then rules out economic and social rights because they could not be implemented in the absence of a centrally planned economy.

[29] Dworkin, 'Unenumerated Rights: Whether and How *Roe* Should be Overruled', in Stone, Epstein and Sunstein, n. 22 above, at 384.

While there is no definitive answer that can be given to these questions, it may nevertheless be suggested that certain qualitative criteria against which to measure a purported bill of rights are now emerging as a result of the growing influence of the international human rights regime. These enable us to provide at least tentative answers to some of the definitional questions posed above; answers which would not have been helpful, or even credible, as recently as two decades or so ago. While there is still no set of standard minimum rules for bills of rights,[30] the list of non-derogable rights to be found in international treaties provides at least a minimum content.[31] In time, it might be possible to go further, and argue that any bill of rights worthy of the name should express some basic principles of equality, human dignity and non-discrimination, thus satisfying the concern that it should be capable of acting as a constitutional charter rather than a mere contractual list. The right to an effective remedy[32] is another element, although this falls short of requiring judicial supremacy or even requiring that the remedy should necessarily be provided by a judicial body. Similarly, while entrenchment *per se* cannot be demanded, in either a weak or strong form, an essential element would seem to be that procedures for derogation must be provided for, assuming that emergency measures are permitted at all.

In so far as there are some common characteristics of bills of rights which emerge from the principal precedents dealt with in the other chapters of this volume, we might conclude that a bill of rights is a formal commitment to the protection of those human rights which are considered, at that moment in history, to be of particular importance. It is, in principle, binding upon the government and can be overridden, if at all, only with significant difficulty. Some form of redress is provided in the event that violations occur.

By the same token, given the limitations of any such definition, it is probably better to offer a typology which seems likely to be of more use for analytical purposes than either a minimalist definition or a prediction of future requirements. It consists of the following elements which seek to identify the

---

[30] This is so, notwithstanding an effort to draw up such a model. In 1989 the Canadian Bar Association, in conjunction with the Cameroon Bar Council, adopted a 'Model Human Rights Charter for Developing Countries'. While the first Section invokes the principles of both the Universal Declaration and the African Charter on Human and Peoples' Rights, the model Charter is a rather bizarre hybrid of the Canadian Charter, economic and social rights, and a variety of measures apparently intended to reflect the particular problems facing developing countries. See Canadian Bar Association and the Cameroon Bar Council, *Model Human Rights Charter for Developing Countries* (1989); also printed in French in the same volume as *Charte type des droits de la personne des pays en développement*.

[31] There is, of course, an old question, which lurks not far beneath the surface of this proposition. It concerns the customary law status of such lists, and arises in so far as states are not parties to the relevant treaties. While the question is much beloved by international legal scholars, it is not of great practical significance in the present context. For an excellent comparative survey see Fitzpatrick, *Human Rights in Crisis: The International System for Protecting Rights During States of Emergency* (1994).

[32] See, for example, Article 2(3) of the International Covenant on Civil and Political Rights.

character of a given bill of rights. It reflects the great variation that currently exists in the world, rather than the minimum criteria approach proposed above.

(a) Status. What is the status of the bill *vis-à-vis* other laws? The possibilities range from the bill not being a law at all, through the status of ordinary legislation, to being constitutionally entrenched as superior to any other law.

(b) Scope. What rights are covered? To what extent are restrictions and derogation permitted? What criteria must such limitations satisfy?

(c) Functions. The functions performed can range from the symbolic (be it potent, fraudulent or in-between), through declaratory, to prescriptive or mandatory.

(d) Remedies. While judicial supremacy seems to be considered as an essential component by some commentators, a range of lesser remedies or procedures might be prescribed. They include political-level review, administrative review, judicial review of alleged violations, and anticipatory judicial review.

(e) Relationship to international law. While a bill of rights need have no direct relationship as such with international law, the reality is that most do have some such link, either as a result of their content or by the invocation of an international standard. But the nature of the indirect relationship, as determined by the status of international law obligations within municipal or domestic law, may be just as important in so far as those obligations are taken into account in the interpretation of the domestic bill of rights.

While any such typology inevitably has a number of weaknesses and limitations, its principal value is as a guide for comparative purposes.

Looking Ahead

The proliferation of bills of rights in recent years, especially in the countries of Africa, and Central and Eastern Europe, but also in the United Kingdom and elsewhere, will significantly accelerate a number of trends that are already under way. In the first place, the emergence of a genuinely comparative law of human rights should be a major outcome of the process. For many years, human rights advocates have sought to demonstrate that there were sufficient similarities between the provisions of various national constitutions and legal codes and those of the key international human rights treaties as to justify a quest to develop a code of human rights drawing upon a coherent corpus of jurisprudence.[33] Twenty years ago such an enterprise was appropriately looked upon with considerable scepticism. Today, however, the situation has

---

[33] In the introduction to his ground-breaking work, Paul Sieghart referred to both his aspiration to provide an 'annotated code' of human rights and of the emergence of a 'new corpus of [human rights] law': Sieghart, *The International Law of Human Rights* (1983), xxi and xix respectively.

changed dramatically as national courts consistently debate, and sometimes explicitly rely upon, interpretations adopted in cases decided in what would previously have been considered as at best exotic and at worst irrelevant and incomparable jurisdictions.[34] The change was nicely captured in comments made by a traditionalist member of the British House of Lords during debate over the adoption of the United Kingdom Human Rights Act 1998. In response to a survey seeking to show the increasing universality of human rights laws of this type, Lord Campbell observed that he was completely unable to understand 'why we have to be entertained for 20-something minutes with cases from here, there and everywhere'.[35] In the years ahead His Lordship is unlikely to be very happy as he surveys the extent to which cross-fertilization now characterizes the emerging human rights jurisprudence across a wide range of jurisdictions. As the Chief Justice of Zimbabwe recently noted, 'a judicial decision has greater legitimacy and will command more respect if it accords with international norms that have been accepted by many jurisdictions, than if it is based upon the parochial experience or foibles of a particular judge or court'.[36]

Secondly, this rapidly growing body of national jurisprudence will soon begin to 'bite the hand that feeds it' in the sense that there will be an increasing preparedness on the part of national courts to look less passively and more critically at the interpretations adopted by international bodies, whether they be the European or Inter-American Courts of Human Rights or the Human Rights Committee of the United Nations. Rather than undermining the authority or influence of these bodies, such interaction should have the effect of strengthening the overall body of jurisprudence and compelling greater rigour and clarity of reasoning.

Thirdly, the proliferation of bills of rights calls for much greater attention to be given to what might be termed the sociology of such bills. There is already an extensive literature on the dubious prospects of 'legal transplants' or laws or procedures that have been taken from one jurisdiction in which they had experienced a natural and balanced growth and are transplanted into a foreign jurisdiction which lacks the necessary social, cultural, religious, economic and legal context required to ensure that the plant will flourish as it had in its native environment. Scholars have long warned of the dangers involved in such undertakings and it is not difficult to characterize bills of rights as foreign transplants in many of the jurisdictions in which they have recently been implanted. In the past, judges in some jurisdictions have not been slow to echo such analyses. Thus, for example, a court in Guyana noted that the constraints

---

[34] 'These days, no Commonwealth judge, government lawyer, advocate, or human rights NGO can afford to ignore Commonwealth human rights case law': Lord Lester of Herne Hill, 'Introduction', [1996] 1 *Commonwealth Human Rights Law Digest* iii, vii.

[35] House of Lords Debates, vol. 583, cols. 827–8, 24 November 1997. Cited by Ewing, 'The Human Rights Act and Parliamentary Democracy', (1999) 62 *Modern Law Review* 79.

[36] Gubbay, 'Foreword', [1996] 1 *Commonwealth Human Rights Law Digest* i.

of public opinion and 'strong, deep-rooted, democratic, common law traditions' that apply in England, 'do not naturally prevail in other countries which have no such deep-rooted traditions and which face very different problems'.[37]

Moreover, the question is not just whether the transplant will wither on the vine, but also whether it can possibly develop into a plant whose fruit can usefully be compared to that grown on superficially similar vines in other countries. Alan Watson's writings have long stood as a warning to those who think comparisons can be made across legal cultures. As he notes, 'the differences in legal values may be so extreme as to render virtually meaningless the discovery that systems have the same or a different rule'.[38] Current trends will require human rights scholars to examine these issues much more closely in the future, not only with a view to improving comparative legal scholarship but also in order to identify measures that can be taken to improve the chances of the cross-cultural flourishing of bills of rights.

A fourth trend will be the rapidly diminishing importance of what has long been one of the staple foods of international legal analysis in the human rights area—the monism-dualism debate and the issue of modes of incorporation or alternatives to non-incorporation of human rights treaties.[39] This issue understandably assumed major importance at a time when international obligations were seen as the most promising avenue in most states for ensuring that domestic law was infused by human rights principles. Changes within states in terms of the growing and more diffuse influence of human rights norms, combined with the introduction of bills of rights either within new constitutions or as stand alone documents with special legal status of some sort, have made the old debates stale and far less interesting or relevant, at least in relation to civil and political rights. It remains the case, however, that there is still considerable life in the debate in terms of the domestic application of treaty norms in the economic, social and cultural rights domain.[40]

Finally, and perhaps most importantly, there will be a need for researchers to focus in a sustained and probing fashion on an issue which has so far attracted very little attention. That is the extent to which the evolving international human rights regime can serve to bring about a greater convergence

[37] *Ameerally and Bentham* v. *Attorney-General* (1978) 25 *West Indies Reports* 272, 291, cited in Demerieux, n. 23 above, at 37, n. 57.

[38] Watson, *Legal Transplants: An Approach to Comparative Law* (1974), 5.

[39] See especially Hunt, *Using Human Rights Law in English Courts* (1997), ch. 1.

[40] See General Comment No. 9 (1998) adopted by the United Nations Committee on Economic, Social and Cultural Rights on 1 December 1998, dealing with 'the domestic application of the Covenant' in which it observed that 'an analysis of State practice with respect to the Covenant shows that ... Some States have failed to do anything specific at all' in order to give domestic effect to the rights recognized in the Covenant: UN doc. E/CN.12/1998/24 (1998), para. 6. On the question to which this situation leads —whether economic and social rights should be accorded constitutional recognition—see Fabre, 'Constitutionalising Social Rights', (1998) 6 *Journal of Political Philosophy* 263.

in approaches across different domestic jurisdictions and how far such convergence could assist the bills of rights in their quest to become effective domestic tools for the promotion and protection of human rights. In particular, consideration will need to be given to convergence in terms of: the norms recognized and included in bills of rights, the legal status accorded to the norms, the means by which they are to be promoted and protected, the institutional framework designed to support them, and the interpretative approaches adopted by the courts and other authorities or groups which play a role in the on-going processes of applying, and thus often interpreting, the relevant norms.

If the international human rights regime can succeed in acting as a force for convergence, in much the same way as other developments act in an increasingly globalized world economy, the prospects that the many new bills of rights will not only survive but will flourish, should be greatly enhanced. Identifying ways of promoting such an impact will be one of the most important challenges facing the international human rights community in the years ahead.

I
National Level Protection of Human Rights Without a Bill of Rights

2

How Far Can The Common Law Go Towards Protecting Human Rights?*

JOHN DOYLE AND BELINDA WELLS

The common law has developed 'from case to case, like the ancient mariners, hugging the coast from point to point and avoiding the dangers of the open sea of system and science'.[1]

Constitutional law . . . is not at all a science, but applied politics, using the word in its noble sense.[2]

Introduction

There are two obvious limits to what the common law can achieve by way of protecting human rights. The first is a matter of law—the principle of Parliamentary supremacy. Any legislation can override rights recognised and protected by the common law. The second is a matter of technique and attitude. By and large the common law Courts have not reasoned from the premise of specific rights. Our boast, that we are free to do anything not prohibited by law, and that official action against our will must have the support of law, reflects the fact that our rights are residual—what is left after the law (and in particular, legislation) is exhausted. Our thinking does not proceed from rights to results—rather, our rights are the result.

We consider that both limits are of fundamental significance. All would accept this conclusion as to the first limit, but perhaps not as to the second. But we suggest that our accustomed methods of thought and our techniques of reasoning are significant. Change them and you may well begin to change the content of our law. Reasoning from and thinking in terms of an affirmative right can produce a different approach.

---

* This Chapter was originally presented as a conference paper in July 1992. At that stage, the High Court's decision in *Mabo* v. *Queensland (No 2)* was barely a week old, and judgment had not yet been delivered in the cases of *Dietrich* v. *R.*, *ACTV*, and *Nationwide News*. This Chapter was subsequently updated but its structure and emphases remain those reflected in the original analysis. In particular, the authors would now place greater emphasis upon the significance of the *Mabo* decision.

[1] Lord Wright, 'The Study of Law', 54 *LQR* (1938) 185 at 186.

[2] Frankfurter, 'The Zeitgeist and the Judiciary', a 1912 address reprinted in Macdeish and Prichard eds., *Law and Politics* (1962), 6.

The quotations which preface this article are relevant to two themes which we propose to develop.

The first is that whilst Australian Courts continue to develop law within the traditional parameters of Parliamentary supremacy and precedent, they have recently begun to strike out into the 'dangers of the open sea' by recognising and beginning to reason in terms of the human rights involved in the cases before them, and by attempting to balance in a principled way the public interests and values involved in reasoning in terms of those rights. In other words, the common law technique shows signs of changing to a focus on rights.

The second theme is that there appear to be ever-increasing opportunities for judicial activism—some would say 'politicisation'—in the protection of human rights. For some time now there have been signs of a challenge by the Courts to the absolute nature of the traditional approach to Parliamentary supremacy. Some judges[3] have asserted that there are rights which *are to be identified by the judges* and which are so fundamental that a Court may strike down a statute which is inconsistent with such rights.

More recently, a majority of the current High Court has been prepared to find in the Constitution the principle of representative government or representative democracy, which acts as the source of a wide freedom from legislative interference. Moreover, several members of the Court have viewed the Australian Constitution as concerned with the protection of various individual rights such as the right to equality under the law and before the Courts.

Each change offers great scope for judicial creativity. Together, they could provide radical change. In this article we will explore the appropriate limits of this creativity—not only how far the common law *can* go, but how far it *should* go.

Common Law Techniques

In these opening remarks we have taken the phrase 'common law' to mean judge-made law and judge-developed law in the broadest sense—and so including the interpretation of statutes and constitutional provisions. For present purposes that seems legitimate because our focus is on the judicial role in the protection of rights.

On this view, the common law has protected or can protect civil and political rights in various ways. First, the common law has, for a long time, recognised and protected various rights and freedoms which it has seen as 'fundamental' (but which cannot survive clear abrogation by statute). Secondly, the common law, responding to the avalanche of legislation which regulates our conduct, has developed rules of statutory construction which

---

[3] See, in particular, Murphy J. and Street C.J. in Australia, and Cooke P. in New Zealand.

reduce the degree of legislative encroachment on those rights and freedoms. These first two are well established, and their past development is not our main concern here. Our concern is whether a change in judicial technique in the first of these areas is producing or will produce a greater emphasis on and protection for rights. Thirdly, the High Court has in recent years begun to give new life to express guarantees in the Constitution and to expand the scope of the protection given to rights protected by those guarantees. However, we merely note that development, leaving it to others to expand on it. Fourthly, some judges have argued that there are limitations on the legislative competence of Parliament to enact legislation which contravenes fundamental rights: such limitations are, it is said, to be found in the 'peace, welfare and good government' formulae in the Commonwealth and State Constitutions, and in implications to be drawn from the structure of the Australian Constitution or from the free and democratic nature of Australian society. We will consider this topic because it raises the fundamental issue of the proper judicial role in the field of human rights.

We should also mention at the outset that this article is primarily concerned with those rights of individuals which are commonly referred to as 'civil and political rights', and which are set out in the International Covenant on Civil and Political Rights, 1966 ('the International Covenant') and in the European Convention for the Protection of Human Rights and Fundamental Freedoms, 1950 ('the European Convention').[4] We will refer only briefly to the protection of the rights set out in the International Covenant on Economic, Social and Cultural Rights, 1966.[5] It is unlikely that the common law will ever play a significant part in promoting and recognising most of these rights.

Judicial Law-Making—Signs of Change

Our Courts have rejected the 'oracular' theory of their function. They have acknowledged that they make law, rather than merely declare it. However it has only been relatively recently that the High Court has overcome its 'sensitivity to the separation of powers in a Parliamentary democracy'[6] and indicated a willingness to reassess areas of common law which are clearly established by precedent—but which do not accord with 'current social conditions'.[7] As McHugh J. has noted in an extra-judicial writing,[8] a series of decisions[9] between 1978 and 1980 indicated that the High Court 'would rarely

---

[4] G A Res. 2200A (XXI) (1966); and Council of Europe, Rome, 4.XI.1950 respectively.
[5] G A Res. 2200A(XXI) (1966) reprinted in United Nations, *Human Rights: A Compilation of International Instruments* (1994), 8–19.
[6] McHugh, 'The Law-making Function of the Judicial Process', 62 *ALJ* (1988 15 at 22).
[7] See *Jaensch* v. *Coffey* (1984) 155 CLR 549 at 599.   [8] See n. 6 above.
[9] *Dugan* v. *Mirror Newspapers Ltd* (1978) 142 CLR 538; *State Government Insurance*

depart from a rule if it was entrenched in the fabric of the law even when the Court had not previously considered the rule'.[10] Thus, for example, Gibbs C.J. emphasised that:

if the law is settled, it is our duty to apply it, not to abrogate it. It is for Parliament, whose members are elected representatives of the people, to change an established rule if they consider it to be undesirable, and not for judges, unelected and unrepresentative, to determine not what is, but what ought to be, the law.[11]

In the cases to which McHugh J.A. referred, Mason J (as he then was) took a somewhat less stringent view of the constraints imposed on the High Court by the doctrine of precedent. In *SGIC* v. *Trigwell* he said that: 'there are some cases in which an ultimate Court of Appeal can and should vary or modify what has been thought to be a settled rule or principle of the common law on the ground that it is ill-adapted to modern circumstances . . .'[12] However he warned of the dangers of such judicial law-making:

But there are very powerful reasons why the Court should be reluctant to engage in such an exercise. The Court is neither a legislature nor a law reform agency. Its responsibility is to decide cases by applying the law to the facts as found. The Court's facilities, techniques and procedures are adapted to that responsibility; they are not adapted to legislative functions or to law reform activities.[13]

Such judicial caution has diminished. In the last 10 years or so, the High Court has demonstrated an increased willingness to reassess well-established principles. *Trident* v. *McNiece*[14] and *Burnie Port Authority*,[15] for example, stand in marked contrast to *SGIC* v. *Trigwell*.[16] In *Jaensch* v. *Coffey* Deane J. acknowledged that in 'rare landmark case[s]', the Courts *must* reassess the content of a rule of law if 'the law is not to lose contact with the social needs which justify its existence and which it exists to serve'.[17] However, he urged caution, and stressed that 'the distinction between the judicial and legislative functions should never be forgotten'.[18]

In *Mabo*[19] Brennan J. (with whom Mason C.J. and McHugh J. agreed) cautioned against 'fracturing' the 'skeleton of principle' which underlies and informs the common law:

In discharging its duty to declare the common law of Australia, this Court is not free to adopt rules that accord with contemporary notions of justice and human rights if

---

Commission v. *Trigwell* (1979) 142 CLR 617; *Australian Conservation Foundation Inc* v. *Commonwealth* (1980) 146 CLR 493.

[10] See McHugh n. 6 above at 23.
[11] *Australian Conservation Foundation Inc* v. *Commonwealth* (1980) 146 CLR 493 at 529.
[12] (1979) 142 CLR 617 at 633.   [13] Ibid.   [14] (1988) 165 CLR 107.
[15] *Burnie Port Authority* v. *General Jones Pty Ltd* (1994) 120 ALR 42. Note, however, the dissenting opinion of McHugh J. at 94–6.
[16] See n. 12 above.   [17] (1984) 155 CLR 549 at 599–600.   [18] Ibid.
[19] *Eddie Mabo and Others* v. *Queensland* (1992) 175 CLR 1.

their adoption would fracture the skeleton of principle which gives the body of our law its shape and internal consistency.[20]

However, said Brennan J., a Court should question whether it must uphold a rule of the common law which 'seriously offends the values of justice and human rights (especially equality before the law) which are aspirations of the contemporary legal system'.[21] If a rule 'seriously offends those contemporary values', the Court must consider whether the rule is 'an essential doctrine of our legal system' and whether the disturbance that would be caused by over-turning it 'would be disproportionate to the benefit flowing from the over-turning'.[22]

As is evident from a case such as *Dietrich* v. *R*,[23] which we discuss below, judicial opinion will differ on the 'appropriate rate and subject matter of change' in the common law.[24] Nonetheless, the majority judgments in *Mabo* and *Dietrich* seem to represent a significant change in emphasis in the Court's attitude to judicial lawmaking. The judgments indicate a greater willingness to modify the law in response to changes in society which call for increased protection of human rights.[25]

Australian society has become an increasingly pluralistic society during the course of this century, and one in which individual rights are more often and more stridently asserted. As a whole we have probably become more tolerant of minority rights. These changes are making us a more rights-conscious and rights-centred society. A judiciary which adhered to a strict view of precedent and separation of powers and gave a narrow scope to its law-making function would be unable to react to these changes in society.

The need for the judiciary to develop the law to respond to these changes becomes evident if we accept that Parliament cannot protect the rights of all members of society. The legislature reacts to those who raise their voices most loudly, and who apply the most insistent pressure. It seems to us unrealistic to argue that the judiciary, being unelected, should play no part in developing the law in response to changes in society. Many important causes are not 'vote-winners' and are therefore neglected by the Executive, which has achieved an ascendancy over the Legislature.[26] In this climate, as McHugh J. has said:

---

[20] Ibid. at 30.　　　　　　[21] Ibid. See also ibid. at 109 per Deane and Gaudron J.J.

[22] Ibid. See discussion in the text pn p. 00.

[23] *Dietrich* v. *R*. (1992) 177 CLR 292.

[24] Ibid. at 320 per Brennan J. See discussion of Brennan J.'s dissenting judgment on p. 00.

[25] Of course, judicial responsiveness to change in society will not always result in an increased protection of individual rights. In times of war or other national emergency, the Courts may, in response to the prevailing view in society, place less emphasis on individual rights—and determine the legislative 'intention' or 'object' accordingly: e.g. *Liversidge* v. *Anderson* [1942] AC 206 at 218–9, 222, 251–2, 257–8 and 280 (Lord Atkin dissenting).

[26] This is one of the points made by Professor Zines in his second Chapter, 'The Entrenchment of Individual and Democratic Rights', in *Constitutional Change in the Commonwealth* (1991).

the judiciary has much to contribute to the democratic process . . . The Courts can protect individuals and groups denied real access to the political process. Judges enjoy immunity from political pressures . . . Judicial law-making is surely not as undemocratic as legislative inaction which fails to meet the need for law reform . . . The Courts, as much as the Legislatures, are in continuous contact with the concrete needs of the community.[27]

There are, of course, some inherent features of the common law which will generally impose limits on the Court's law-making role. First, the common law is opportunistic: the elaboration of a principle must wait until an appropriate case is presented to the Court. The Court will then typically—but not always—confine its reasoning to the case before it, avoiding broad statements of principle. The result is often patchy coverage of a particular area, and internal inconsistencies resulting from various segments of the area being settled by the Courts in different eras. In addition, the common law is incremental: new ground can only be claimed if it can be joined to the old.[28]

The developments in the law that do occur in areas involving rights will often turn on the judges' view of what is 'in the public interest'. This vague and apparently value-neutral term has been used to conceal the very different perceptions of society that may exist across a wide spectrum of political, social and economic views. The judiciary has traditionally been drawn from a narrow part of the spectrum, and has not been inculcated with the view that the protection of individual rights is a central part of its function.

However here again there are signs of change. Judges are more willing to acknowledge the value judgments and interests which underlie their decisions. In a paper presented in 1987, Sir Anthony Mason observed that the High Court was now 'less inclined to pursue [the] formal legal reasoning'[29] adopted by Sir Owen Dixon. Sir Owen Dixon's approach was essentially to arrive at a decision by 'close adherence to legal reasoning', without regard to the 'merits or demerits of the measure'.[30] Sir Anthony Mason espouses a very different approach. He says in his paper:

It is unrealistic to interpret any instrument . . . by reference to words alone, without any regard to fundamental values. By values I mean those that are accepted by the community rather than those personal to the judge. When the judge takes values into account, he should acknowledge and identify them . . . Unless disclosed, the decision cannot be correctly evaluated on appeal . . .[31]

One would expect that such a philosophy would be particularly appropriate

[27] See McHugh n. 6 above at 123–4.

[28] See McHugh n. 6 above at 120. McHugh J.A. (as he then was) also quotes Chief Justice Traynor of the Supreme Court of California, who pointed out that 'even if the judge finds a truly unprecedented case he must integrate it "in the often rewoven but always unbroken line with the past" '.

[29] Sir Anthony Mason, 'Future Directions in Australian Law', 13 *Monash University Law Review* (1987) 149 at 157.

[30] See (1951–2) 85 CLR xiv.   [31] See Mason n. 29 above at 158–9.

when a Court is considering issues involving human rights. Open identification of the rights involved in a case is likely to cause the reasoning of the Court to focus more on the advancement of those rights. We consider that a number of the cases mentioned in this article demonstrate that the High Court is increasingly reasoning in terms of rights which must be given adequate protection.

There is another important factor likely to contribute to change in the judiciary's role in protecting human rights. This is Australia's recent accession to the Optional Protocol to the International Covenant.[32] In *Mabo* Brennan J. acknowledged that this development brought 'to bear on the common law the powerful influence of the Covenant and the international standards it imports'.[33] We suspect that if, in time, a significant number of individual petitions is brought by Australians under the Optional Protocol, the Australian public—and our Government and judiciary—will experience the same 'flow-on' effects of greater exposure to human rights issues and jurisprudence as the United Kingdom has experienced since accepting the right of individual petition under the European Convention some 29 years ago. In the United Kingdom such heightened awareness of rights has resulted in judgments by the House of Lords which acknowledge that the European Convention is not incorporated into domestic law, but which nonetheless purport to apply the Convention's principles to cases before them.

In short, there are signs of changes which are likely to lead to a new emphasis on rights in judicial reasoning and in the development of the common law.

Nonetheless, Australian Courts are working within a system in which there is no entrenched Bill of Rights (as in Canada) or unentrenched Bill of Rights (as in New Zealand) to guide them. The International Covenant to which Australia has acceded is not incorporated into domestic law. Except in the case of the few express guarantees of rights in the Constitution, our Courts have no clear mandate to strike down legislation for contravening human rights. As such, their role in protecting human rights has, until recently, been confined largely to the first and second areas of protection mentioned above: that is, the areas of 'pure' common law and of statutory construction.

And so the issue is both how far the Courts can go, and how far they *should* go, in developing judge-made law in this area.

---

[32] Australia acceded to the Optional Protocol on 25 September 1991, and the Protocol came into effect on 25 December 1991. See Optional Protocol, Article 9(2).
[33] See *Mabo* n. 19 above at 42.

Parliamentary Supremacy

All of the potential for change mentioned above operates within the confines of the principle of Parliamentary supremacy. The principle has tended to limit the role that the Courts have played in protecting human rights.

As we have said, there have been some judicial challenges to this constraint. There has, since the 1970s, been a move in favour of extending the judicial function in the field of human rights—to allow the Courts to find in the Constitution various bases for implying rights and principles which are so fundamental they may override the will of Parliament. Other Chapters in this book consider this area in some detail, and we limit our discussion of it accordingly. However, this 'fourth' technique is of considerable interest and we will return to it later because it demonstrates the common law technique at its most creative—and thus involves a heightened tension between the functions of the elected Legislature, on the one hand, and the judiciary on the other. It raises the question of whether the public's respect for the judiciary could withstand a substantial increase in the judiciary's political power. We must ask ourselves whether we agree with Judge Learned Hand that judges should never have the power to discover 'fundamental rights' which are not expressed in the Constitution: 'For myself it would be most irksome to be ruled by a bevy of Platonic Guardians, even if I knew how to choose them, which I assuredly do not.'[34]

Aside from such challenges to Parliamentary supremacy, Dicey's principle still prevents judicial review on a rights basis of the content of Australian statutes. Subject to the limits on legislative power resulting from the federal Constitution, it is still true to say that no person or body has the 'right to override or set aside the legislation of Parliament'.[35] The Courts may, however, control Executive acts since we have also inherited from England the constitutional principle of 'the rule of law', which insists that coercive powers exercised by the State and its officers must be based upon 'authority conferred by law'.[36]

However, it is instructive to recall that there was a time in the seventeenth century—before the Courts finally conceded the notion of Parliamentary supremacy—when the idea that the common law contained fundamental precepts which could not be overridden by statute law could have taken hold. The idea was based upon Locke's theory of natural law, according to which a person's rights to liberty and property were sacred,[37] and it was reflected in a number of well-known dicta:

[34] Hand, *The Bill of Rights* (1958), 73–4.
[35] Dicey, *Introduction to the Study of the Constitution* (9th edn., 1939), 39–40.
[36] De Smith and Brazier, *Constitutional and Administrative Law* (6th edn., 1990), 18.
[37] Tremblay, 'Section 7 of the Charter: Substantive Due Process?', 18 *UBCLR* 201 at 240 (1984).

Lord Coke in *Dr. Bonham's* case:[38]

... when an Act of Parliament is against common right and reason or repugnant, or impossible to be performed, the common law will controul it and adjudge such Act to be void.

Hobart CJ in *Day* v. *Savadge:*[39]

... even an Act of Parliament, made against natural equity, as to make a man Judge in his own case, is void in itself ...

Holt CJ in *Callady* v. *Pilkington:*[40]

... if [an Act] give away the property of a subject, it ought not to be countenanced.

In England the idea that fundamental common law principles could take precedence over the clear will of the Legislature did not survive the seventeenth century.[41] However, as Professor Luc Tremblay has noted, in the USA the seventeenth and eighteenth century political theory 'that the people had certain inalienable rights with which no state could interfere' was preserved in the provisions of the American Constitution.[42] Professor Tremblay reminds us that: 'The theory was based on the philosophical principle that people had those rights in a state of nature (theory of natural law) and that when they agreed to come into society they created a government whose function was basically the protection of those rights (social compact theory).'[43]

Thus the Declaration of Independence refers to the 'self-evident truths' that all men are 'endowed by their Creator with certain inalienable Rights', among which are 'Life, Liberty and the pursuit of Happiness'.[44] No Legislature could remove these natural rights.

In England it was otherwise. From the eighteenth century a statute could not be declared unlawful—whatever its content—since it was regarded as 'the highest form of law that is known to this country'.[45] The Courts could do no more than create and apply rules of statutory construction which presume that in the absence of clear words, statutes do not intend to override fundamental common law principles. We have adhered to Dicey's view that:

---

[38] (1610) 8 Co Rep 107a at 118a; 77 ER 638 at 652.   [39] (1615) 80 ER 235 at 236.
[40] (1701) 88 ER 1485 at 1415.
[41] As Kirby P. remarked in *BLF* v. *Minister Industrial Relations* (1986) 7 NSWLR 372 at 403, 'it was generally believed that the notion did not survive the fundamental constitutional and political changes which followed the Glorious Revolution and the enactment of the Bill of Rights of 1688 and the Act of Settlement of 1700.' He noted that in the nineteenth and twentieth centuries there have been—at least until recently—only occasional exceptions to 'the Diceyan landscape'.
[42] See Tremblay n. 37 above at 214–5.   [43] Ibid.
[44] See also *Calder* v. *Bull* 3 US (3 Dall) 386, 388 (1798).
[45] *Cheney* v. *Conn* [1968] 1 WLR 242 at 247 per Ungoed-Thomas J.

There is no legal basis for the theory that judges, as exponents of morality, may over-rule Acts of Parliament. Language which might seem to imply this amounts in reality to nothing more than the assertion that the judges, when attempting to ascertain what is the meaning to be affixed to an Act of Parliament, will presume that Parliament did not intend to violate the ordinary rules of morality, or the principles of international law, and will therefore, whenever possible, give such an interpretation to a statutory enactment as may be consistent with the doctrines both of private and of international morality.[46]

And so, even today, the rules of statutory interpretation applied by the Courts 'embody in an attenuated form the ancient doctrine . . . that there was a sense in which the common law was fundamental'.[47] A Court cannot strike down a law which removes a common law right, but it can still say that there is a presumption against removal of the right.[48]

Judicial Recognition of Fundamental Common Law Rights ('the First Method')

We turn now to the first of the four methods of protecting human rights to which we referred above. This is the common law's recognition of fundamental rights in areas untouched by statute. In such areas, we suggest that the common law is playing and will play a greater role than previously because of an increased focus on rights by the judiciary. The Courts have in recent times been more concerned to identify and take into account the individual rights and the countervailing public interests involved in their decisions.

In Australia and England, fundamental common law rights such as the right to a fair trial and the right to freedom of speech are 'residual' rights: the individual is free 'to do what he will save to the extent that he is prevented from so doing by the law'.[49] The Government may remove the right by legislation, and a public authority may interfere with it if acting under lawful authority.

It has been pointed out that a distinction may be drawn between the residual nature of a 'freedom from interference except as provided by law' and the residual quality of the rights which have emanated from this freedom.[50] These rights are residual in the sense of being what is left after statutory intervention. However, increasingly the judiciary is giving them a positive value, so that in a 'pure' common law area they are 'perceived as a public interest or

---

[46] Dicey, *Introduction to the Study of the Law of the Constitution* (10th edn., 1959) as cited in the *BLF* case n. 41 above at 396 per Kirby P.

[47] Keir and Lawson, *Cases in Constitutional Law* (4th edn., 1967), 9.   [48] Ibid.

[49] *Wheeler* v. *Leicester City Council* [1985] AC 1054 at 1065 per Browne-Wilkinson L.J.

[50] Allan, 'Constitutional Rights and Common Law', 11 *Oxford Journal of Legal Studies* (1991) 453 at 457–8.

value entitled to independent weight'[51] in an argument; and in a case where it is claimed that a statute has the effect of encroaching upon one of them, the 'intrinsic importance of the freedom justif[ies] . . . a jealous and critical scrutiny'[52] of the claim.

Nonetheless, common law freedoms *are* 'residual' in the first sense. In some areas they have been all but extinguished by statute. For example, in eighteenth century cases such as *Entick* v. *Carrington*[53] the common law established the principle that it was unlawful for a person to enter another person's property except by consent or under statutory authority. This principle has recently been affirmed by the High Court in the cases of *Plenty* v. *Dillon*[54] and *Coco* v. *R.*[55]

However, these days entries and searches of premises are authorised by statute in many situations. Some of the statutes reflect the common law's concern with the invasion of individual rights. Section 10 of the Crimes Act 1910 (Cth) is an example. A Court construing and applying such provisions must bear in mind the common law background.[56] But other statutory provisions reverse much of what *Entick* v. *Carrington* stands for. Despite the common law's abhorrence for general warrants, provisions such as Sections 199, 200 and 214 of the Customs Act 1901 (Cth), and Section 67 of the Summary Offences Act 1953 (SA) have long enabled customs officers and the police to enter and search premises under the authority of general warrants issued to them at some earlier stage by their superiors.

The privilege against self-incrimination is another example which demonstrates the vulnerability of common law rights. The cases are full of dicta stressing the importance of this common law 'freedom'.[57] Nonetheless, an increasing number of statutes have expressly removed the common law right to claim the privilege.[58]

WHICH RIGHTS ARE PROTECTED BY THE COMMON LAW?

We have inherited from England the view that an entrenched Bill of Rights is unnecessary in common law countries, since the common law and the principle of Parliamentary supremacy will protect the fundamental rights listed in such documents.

However, when we look at the International Covenant, it is immediately evident that such a general assertion does not stand up to close scrutiny. We can recognise clauses which do reflect principles which have long been part of the

---

[51] Ibid. at 459.   [52] Ibid. at 458.   [53] (1765) 19 St Tr 1029; 95 ER 807.
[54] (1991) 171 CLR 635.   [55] (1993) 179 CLR 427.
[56] *George* v. *Rockett* (1990) 170 CLR 104 at 110–11.
[57] *Sorby* v. *Commonwealth* (1983) 152 CLR 281 at 294 per Gibbs C.J.
[58] For example, Trade Practices Act 1974 (Cth), ss 155(7) and 159(1); Corporations Law, s 597(12); Customs Act 1901 (Cth), s 214A(6); Royal Commissions Act 1902 (Cth), s 6A.

common law: for example, Articles 9 ('right to liberty and security of the person'), 14 ('right to a fair trial') and 19 ('right to freedom of expression').

On the other hand, it is clear that the common law has only rarely insisted on the protection of some of the other rights set out in the Covenant, such as the right to be free from torture and cruel, inhuman and degrading treatment (Article 7), the right of prisoners to be treated with humanity (Article 10), the right to freedom from arbitrary interference with privacy (Article 17), the right to peaceful assembly (Article 21), and the right of minorities to enjoy their culture, religion and language (Article 27). Such rights are only infrequently asserted before the Courts. The common law has not developed thorough jurisprudence in these areas.

In the area of economic, social and cultural rights the limited scope of common law protection of rights can be seen even more clearly. The Courts have not played a significant part in protecting rights set out in the International Covenant on Economic, Social and Cultural Rights, 1966: for example, rights to work (Article 6), to just and favourable conditions of work (Article 7), to social security (Article 9), to an adequate standard of living (Article 11), to the highest possible standard of physical and mental health (Article 12), to education (Article 13), and to participate freely in cultural and scientific pursuits (Article 15). In our view the Courts have, with some exceptions, rightly left the protection of such rights to the Legislature. Their protection invariably requires remedies and responses of a type beyond the powers of the courts.

At a general level then, the common law does not protect many aspects of the rights listed in the International Covenant. However, we will turn now to look at two examples of rights that the common law has recognised as important. A more detailed examination of these two rights—the right to a fair trial, and the right to freedom of speech—will illustrate the changes foreshadowed in the Introduction. The Courts are more inclined to decide cases by reference to these fundamental rights and are prepared to expand the scope of such rights.

Having considered these two particular rights in some detail, we will then look more generally at whether the Courts have in recent years become more conscious of rights; and whether they have recognised or are likely to recognise new rights as 'fundamental'.

The Right to a Fair Trial

The right to a fair trial involves more than just the rights of the accused. It is seen as conferring a power and a duty on Courts 'to mould the procedures of the trial to avoid or minimise prejudice to *either party*'[59]. The Court is required to have regard to not only the interests of the accused, but also the

---

[59] *Jago* v. *District Court (NSW)* (1989) 168 CLR 23 at 46–7 per Brennan J. (emphasis added).

interests of the other parties affected by the conduct of the trial (for example the Crown, and the general public), and the general interest in the 'administration of justice'.[60] As Dawson J said in *McKinney* v. *R*: 'A fair trial is one which is fair to both sides. It is for the trial judge to hold the scales so as to maintain an even balance . . .'[61]

In recent years the High Court has expanded the scope of the protection afforded to defendants by the right. The Court has indicated that a trial judge should insist on minimum standards of fairness during the course of a trial—such as compulsory warnings to the jury in relation to uncorroborated confessions—even if responsibility for ensuring that such standards are observed ultimately rests with the police, Parliament or the Executive. Secondly, the Court has acknowledged that in rare cases a trial judge's careful conduct of a trial will not be sufficient to provide an accused with a fair trial. In such instances the judge should be prepared to stay permanently the proceedings to prevent injustice—once again, even if responsibility for the injustice rests with one of the other institutions mentioned above. Lastly, the Court has insisted that a greater weight should be accorded to the right to a fair trial and the interest in the due administration of justice when considering claims by the Crown to public interest immunity in respect of certain documents.

These developments have occurred, we suggest, because a majority of the High Court has begun to take the right as its starting point. The Court is asserting that the individual may insist upon his or her right to a fair trial, and that the Court must do everything within its power to enforce it.

This is a change of focus, and has resulted in strong dissenting judgments from Brennan J. who, (with Dawson J.), continues to take the traditional approach to the right. The traditional approach tends to focus on the question of whether the jury's verdict should be set aside on one of the grounds for appeal set out in the relevant statutory provision.[62] It acknowledges that a Court must do its best to regulate its procedure in order to provide a fair trial, but does not reason from the right as a guarantee given to the individual. As a result, proponents of the traditional approach do not concede that the Court has an obligation to enforce the right to a fair trial, if to do so would interfere with the functions and responsibilities of the various organs of Government or the police.

The majority's focus on the right provides fertile ground for the recognition of new instances of unfairness. It offers significant potential for expanding the scope of the protection afforded by the right to a fair trial. The Court has

---

[60] See *McInnis* v. *R*. (1979) 143 CLR 575 at 579 per Barwick C.J.

[61] (1991) 171 CLR 468 at 488.

[62] For example, under the Criminal Law Consolidation Act 1935 (SA), s 353, an appeal against conviction may be allowed on the basis that the jury's verdict was 'unreasonable', or 'cannot be supported having regard to the evidence', or because the Court's judgment involved an error of law, or because there was a miscarriage of justice.

already moved from general assertions of the right, such as are found in *McKinney* v. *R*,[63] to acknowledging that 'undue delay', 'prejudicial publicity', and 'lack of legal representation' may be brought under its rubric as potential grounds of unfairness. In doing so, it has acknowledged the need to balance the right against countervailing public interests.

We begin with a brief reference to the traditional—uncontroversial— approach to the right to a fair trial. It is well accepted that the right imposes a duty on the Courts to regulate the *course of a trial* to ensure fairness to the parties. Various obstacles in the way of a fair trial may be encountered by a Court: for example, 'adverse publicity in the reporting of notorious crimes',[64] 'adverse revelations in a public inquiry',[65] 'absence of competent representation',[66] and 'the death or unavailability of a witness'.[67] When such an obstacle is encountered, the responsibility cast on a trial judge to avoid unfairness may be: 'discharged by controlling the procedures of the trial by adjournments or other interlocutory orders, by rulings on evidence and, especially, by directions to the jury designed to counteract any prejudice which the accused might otherwise suffer.'[68]

The technique which is most frequently used by the Courts to minimise unfairness to the accused is that of giving directions to the jury. Juries should be warned as to the weight that they should give to particular evidence if such a warning 'is necessary to avoid a perceptible risk of miscarriage of justice arising from the circumstances of [a] case'.[69] In some situations a warning should *always* be given. In *McKinney* v. *R*[70] four members of the High Court held that a jury should be warned of the dangers of convicting a person if 'the only [or substantially the only] basis for finding . . . guilt . . . is a confessional statement allegedly made whilst in police custody, the making of which is not reliably corroborated'[71] and if the accused person did not have access to a lawyer or to some other independent person to support his contention that he did not make the confession.

There are two interesting aspects to the majority's judgment in *McKinney*. The first is the indication of the shift in focus to a rights-centred approach. The majority asserted: 'The central thesis of the administration of criminal justice is the entitlement of an accused person to a fair trial according to the law.'

---

[63] (1991) 171 CLR 468.   [64] *Murphy* v. *R.* (1989) 167 CLR 94.

[65] *Victoria* v. *Australian Building Construction Employees' and Builders Labourers' Federation* (1982) 152 CLR 25.

[66] *McInnis* v. *R.* (1979) 143 CLR 573; *MacPherson* v. *R.* (1981) 147 CLR 512.

[67] These are the examples given by Brennan J. in *Jago* v. *District Court of New South Wales* (1989) 168 CLR 23 at 47.

[68] Ibid.

[69] *Longman* v. *R.* (1989) 168 CLR 79 at 86, as cited in *McKinney* v. *R.* (1991) 171 CLR 468 at 480 per Brennan J.

[70] See *McKinney* n. 63 above.   [71] Ibid. at 476.

From this, said the majority, it followed that the Court had a duty to lay down a rule of practice—since the absence of a warning in the circumstances described by them would '*prima facie* indicate that the requirement of fairness is unsatisfied and will give rise to the detriments of [a] miscarriage of justice and a need of a second trial . . .'.[72]

Secondly, the Court's focus on the right led it to lay down a rule the indirect effect of which will be to require the Executive to allocate further resources to criminal investigations. The Court said that because of 'the existence and increasing availability of reliable and accurate means of audiovisual recording',[73] the police no longer had any excuse for producing uncorroborated confessional evidence. The majority remarked: 'It is obvious that the content of the requirement of fairness may vary with changed social conditions, including developments in technology and increased access to means of mechanical corroboration.'[74]

The tension between this new emphasis on ensuring and promoting fairness on the one hand, and the traditional approach on the other, is evident in the judgment of Brennan J. in *McKinney*. Brennan J. took a narrow view of the judge's role in preventing unfairness. In some cases, he said, a trial judge should comment adversely on a failure by the investigating police officer to use available recording equipment. However, a warning to the jury would not be necessary in *all* cases (for example, where recording equipment was not available), and it was *not* the role of the Court to compel the police to use such equipment.

Brennan J. was in no doubt that in laying down such a general rule of practice, the majority had gone beyond the 'proper function of the Court' which is to 'mould the law' in order to 'enhance the administration of justice'.[75] He was emphatic in dissent:

To require judges to give a warning which reflects adversely on police confessional evidence because equipment for the electronic recording of police interviews is not provided is to unbalance the even-handed judicial administration of the law in order to induce an improvement in the administration of criminal justice for which the Executive Government is responsible. That is not the proper function of a Court. The majority hold the view, albeit its expression is *obiter*, that there should be a general rule of practice requiring the giving of a warning 'which will operate for the future'. With great respect, that phrase is more appropriate to the exercise of legislative power than it is to the exercise of judicial power.[76]

The High Court's focus on the right to a fair trial is, as we said earlier, already providing a fertile ground for the expansion of the right. The Court has recognised that in exceptional circumstances a trial judge may be obliged to grant a permanent stay of proceedings in order to prevent injustice. Such

---

[72] Ibid. at 478.   [73] Ibid. at 473.   [74] Ibid. at 478.   [75] Ibid. at 485–6.
[76] See *McKinney* at 486.

injustice may result from undue delay in bringing a matter to trial (as was asserted in *Jago*[77]); or from prejudicial publicity prior to the trial (as asserted in *Glennon*);[78] or from lack of legal representation (as asserted in *Dietrich*).[79] Once again, there has been strong dissent. Brennan J. (and probably also Dawson J.) has rejected the proposition that a Court may 'refuse to exercise [its] jurisdiction'[80] in order to prevent unfairness, and sees the majority's willingness to stay proceedings to prevent undue delay as another example of the Court wrongfully intruding onto the Executive's territory.

In *Jago* the accused argued that a stay of proceedings should have been ordered by the trial judge, since the trial took place after an unreasonable delay, some 8 to 10 years after the offences were alleged to have been committed. The High Court decided that there was not, at common law, 'a right to a speedy trial' which operated independently of any prejudice to the accused. The Court confirmed that whilst a trial judge did have a general power to prevent unfairness to an accused, this power operated only upon proof of actual prejudice or unfairness, rather than upon a concept of 'presumptive prejudice'.[81]

Nonetheless, the High Court recognised that a trial judge faced with allegations of undue delay had a power to ensure fairness, and that 'the test of fairness . . . involves a balancing process': 'the interests of the accused cannot be considered in isolation without regard to the community's right to expect that persons charged with criminal offences are brought to trial.'[82]

Each of the five judges except Brennan J. agreed that in an exceptional case of undue delay the appropriate remedy is to stay permanently the proceedings. The four judges differed only slightly as to the appropriate basis for a Court's power to grant such a remedy. They rejected the view that a stay of proceedings will only be available for the purpose of preventing an 'abuse of process' (a term traditionally reserved for oppressive or vexatious proceedings). They preferred to rely on the inherent power of the Courts 'to prevent their processes being used in a manner which gives rise to injustice',[83] or said that it was not necessary to decide between the two bases.[84] The four judges acknowledged that a Court would only be prepared to grant a permanent stay of criminal proceedings in exceptional circumstances, where there is: 'a fundamental defect which goes to the root of a [criminal] trial, of such a nature

---

[77] *Jago* v. *District Court of NSW* (1989–90) 168 CLR 23.
[78] *R* v. *Glennon* (1992) 173 CLR 592.   [79] *Dietrich* v. *R.* (1992) 177 CLR 292.
[80] See *Jago* n. 77 above at 47.   [81] Ibid. at 33 per Mason C.J.
[82] Ibid.
[83] Ibid. at 31 per Mason C.J. Mason C.J. and Toohey J. clearly prefer this basis (ibid. at 71–2). Deane J. appears to arrive at this view also (ibid. at 60). However he does indicate earlier in his judgment that the Court would be staying the proceedings pursuant to its power 'to prevent abuse of its process' (ibid. at 57–8).
[84] Ibid. at 74–5 per Gaudron J.

that nothing a trial judge can do in the conduct of the trial can relieve against its unfair consequences . . .'[85]

Mason J. considered that in such circumstances the Courts must act to prevent unfairness. He rejected arguments that 'the judge must keep out of the arena'[86] because it is for the Legislature to decide whether there should be a limitation period for bringing criminal proceedings, and for the Executive to decide whether to prosecute. He cited Lord Devlin in *Connelly* with approval:

Are the Courts to rely on the Executive to protect their process from abuse? Have they not themselves an inescapable duty to secure fair treatment for those who come or are brought before them? To questions of this sort there is only one possible answer. The Courts cannot contemplate for a moment the transference to the Executive of the responsibility for seeing that the process of law is not abused.[87]

Brennan J. saw the matter quite differently. He rejected the proposition that the Courts had an 'inescapable duty' to ensure fairness, and adhered to the traditional view that a Court may only grant a permanent stay of proceedings in the very rare situation where 'the prosecution amounts to an abuse of the process of the Court and is oppressive and vexatious . . .'.[88] He was against the Courts 'creat[ing] a form of artificial limitation period for criminal proceedings where it cannot truly be said that the due process of the criminal Courts is being used improperly to harass a defendant'.[89] In particular, the Courts could not grant a stay of proceedings on the basis of their powers to ensure a fair trial because the 'right to a fair trial' 'relates [only] to the process of the trial'[90]—to the conduct of the trial by the judge.

Brennan J.'s starting point is therefore 'the proper role that the Court should play', rather than 'the right'. He upholds the traditional role of the Court in controlling the procedures of the trial to prevent unfairness. Having done that, he says, the trial judge has discharged his responsibility. It follows from this, that 'unfairness occasioned by circumstances outside the Court's control does not make the trial a source of unfairness'.[91] Brennan J. gives the example of adverse media publicity. As in *McKinney* he considers that the Court is venturing beyond its proper domain:

The remedy . . . [of a permanent stay] marks the Court's disapproval of the failure of other branches of Government to furnish the resources necessary to cope with an

---

[85] *Barton* v. *R.* (1980) 147 CLR 75 at 111 per Wilson J. All or part of this passage is cited by Mason C.J. and Gaudron J. in *Jago* n. 77 above at 34 per Mason C.J., 75 per Gaudron J.

[86] Ibid. at 28.

[87] *Connelly* v. *DPP* [1964] AC 1254 at 1354, cited by Mason C.J. in *Jago* n. 77 above at 29.

[88] *DPP* v. *Humphreys* [1977] AC 1 at 46 per Lord Salmon, cited by Brennan J. in *Jago* n. 77 above at 51.

[89] *R* v. *Grays Justices, ex parte Graham* [1982] QB 1239 per May C.J. for the Divisional Court at 1247 cited in *Jago* n. 77 above at 54.

[90] *R.* v. *Sang* [1980] AC 402 at 455 per Scarman L.J. cited in *Jago* n. 77 above at 52.

[91] *R.* v. *Sang* [1980] AC 402 at 455 per Scarman L.J. cited in *Jago* n. 77 above at 47.

accumulation of criminal cases awaiting trial; it places pressure on Government to provide and to use the resources needed . . .[92]

The case of *Glennon*[93] involved the very situation of adverse media publicity referred to by Brennan J. in *Jago*. Here, five of the seven members of the High Court agreed that it would be appropriate for a Court to order a permanent stay of proceedings in extreme cases of prejudicial media publicity. Of the five, Deane, Gaudron and McHugh J.J. considered that the trial judge should have granted a stay of the prosecution against the defenant. Mason C.J. and Toohey J., on the other hand, did not regard a stay as appropriate in the instant case since the accused had shown no more than a possibility of prejudice on the part of a juror, and since sufficient weight should be given to 'the capacity of jurors to assess critically what they see and hear',[94] the effect of the trial judges' instructions to the jury, and 'the community's right to expect that a person accused of a serious criminal offence will be brought to trial'.[95] There was not a 'likelihood or substantial risk of prejudice arising from [the] pre-trial publication'.[96]

The majority thus took as its starting point the right of an accused to a fair trial, and then balanced that right against the community's interest, and considered what, if anything, a trial judge should have done to prevent unfairness. By contrast, Brennan J. (with whom Dawson J. agreed) proceeded from the assumption that a trial judge has only a limited obligation to apply certain safeguards during the course of a trial to prevent an appealable miscarriage of justice resulting. In his view the common law only guarantees an accused 'a trial conducted with all the safeguards that the Court can provide', and there can be 'no miscarriage of justice in a conviction after such a trial'.[97] Even if measures taken by a trial judge during the course of a trial are unlikely to be successful in countering the prejudice to an accused caused by pre-trial publicity, there is nothing more that a Court can do.

Finally, the case of *Dietrich* v. *R*[98] provides a further example of the Court's change in focus producing greater protection for an accused. The applicant's primary argument was that an accused person charged with a serious crime who cannot afford counsel 'has a right to be provided with counsel at the public expense'.[99] The Court rejected the argument that such an accused has a right to publicly-funded legal counsel.[100] However, a majority of the Court then directed its focus to the issue of whether the trial judge had done every-

[92] Ibid. at 49.   [93] *R.* v. *Glennon* n. 78 above.   [94] Ibid. at 603.
[95] Ibid. at 604–5.   [96] Ibid. at 605.   [97] Ibid. at 615.
[98] See *Dietrich* n. 23 above.   [99] Ibid. at 293.
[100] A majority of the Court considered that the Court's decision in the earlier case of *McInnis* v. *R.* did not preclude consideration of the existence of a right to publicly-funded legal counsel. Ibid at 303 per Mason C.J. and McHugh J., 331 per Deane J., 355 per Toohey J., 372 per Gaudron J.

thing possible, subject to countervailing interests, to protect the accused's 'right to a fair trial'.

Prior to the trial Mr Dietrich had exhausted all avenues for obtaining legal assistance. He had sought an adjournment until such time as he could obtain legal representation. The trial judge had refused his application. A majority of the High Court considered the particular circumstances of Mr Dietrich's trial—in particular, the weight of the prosecution evidence against him—and concluded that his trial had miscarried, and that he had been deprived of a real chance of acquittal.

The Court considered the earlier case of *McInnis* v. *R*,[101] in which the accused had also been denied an adjournment to enable him to obtain legal representation during his trial. There, the accused had likewise been convicted and had appealed. The High Court judges, with the exception of Murphy J., had held that the trial judge's refusal to adjourn had *not* resulted in a miscarriage of justice.

The two cases may well be distinguishable on their facts. In *McInnis*, for example, it was evident that a majority of the Court had regarded the Crown case against the accused as 'overwhelming'[102] or 'very strong indeed'.[103] In such circumstances, it was said, 'the absence of counsel cannot be said to have deprived the accused of a prospect of acquittal'.[104] In *Dietrich*, by contrast, all members of the majority (with the exception of Deane J.) examined aspects of the trial such as the strength of the prosecution case against the accused and decided that the accused *may* have been deprived of a prospect of acquittal.

However, more significantly for our purposes, the majority judgments in *Dietrich* reveal the change of emphasis referred to in relation to *McKinney* and *Jago*. The starting point taken by the majority was that a Court may adjourn or stay proceedings as 'an incident of the general power of a Court of Justice to ensure fairness'.[105] Consideration of the content of the requirement of a fair trial followed. As in *McKinney*, this resulted in the formulation of a general proposition. In *Dietrich*, a majority of the Court held that 'in the absence of exceptional circumstances,[106] a trial of an indigent person accused of a serious crime will be unfair if, by reason of lack of means and the unavailability of other assistance, he is denied legal representation'.[107]

---

[101] (1979) 143 CLR 575.   [102] Ibid. at 583 per Mason C.J.
[103] Ibid. at 580 per Barwick C.J.   [104] Ibid. at 583 per Mason C.J.
[105] *Jago* n. 77 above at 31 per Mason C.J., as cited by Toohey J. in *Dietrich* n. 23 above at 357. Deane and Gaudron J.J. found a further basis for the power in the exclusive vesting of the judicial power of the Commonwealth in the Courts designated by Chapter III of the Constitution, thus elevating the principle to the status of a constitutional right. See *Dietrich* ibid. at 326 per Deane J., 362 per Gaudron J.
[106] Or 'compelling circumstances'. Ibid. at 357 per Toohey J. The absolute position adopted by Murphy J. in *McInnis* was not followed.
[107] *Dietrich* n. 23 above at 337 per Deane J. There was little discussion on the issue of whether the trial of an unrepresented indigent person accused on a more trivial offence might also be 'unfair'.

The *Dietrich* principle directs a Court to examine the particular circumstances of each trial in order to determine whether there were (or are) in existence 'exceptional circumstances' which meant that the trial was fair despite
the absence of publicly-funded counsel. One possible example of such circumstances—an irrefutably strong prosecution case—has been mentioned
above. If such circumstances are not made out, it seems that the accused's
appeal against conviction will succeed. This is presumably on the basis that
the trial was unfair in that the accused had lost a 'real chance of acquittal'.[108]
Gaudron J., for example, explains that: 'What makes a trial without representation unfair is the possibility that representation might affect the outcome of
the case.'[109] As Toohey J. put it: 'It is the loss of a chance of acquittal fairly
open to an accused, rather than the unfairness of the trial itself, that leads to
a conviction being set aside'.[110]

In any event, in *Dietrich* five members of the Court have analysed one
aspect of the right to a fair trial and have formulated a generally consistent
'rule of practice' for the future guidance of trial judges. In doing so, they have
consciously developed the common law in a manner which they consider to be
consistent with the judicial role. Deane and Gaudron J.J., in particular,
emphasised the importance of the law maintaining contact with 'current
social conditions, standards and demands'[111] and 'community expectation'.[112]

This issue of the 'proper judicial role' is again at the heart of the dissenting
judgment of Brennan J. (It is also, of course, fundamental to understanding
the judgment of the other dissentient, Dawson J., but less explicitly so.) In a
judgment delivered soon after his judgment in *Mabo (No 2)*,[113] Brennan J.
again emphasised that whilst it is important for superior Courts to ensure that
judicial developments remain consistent with contemporary values, that role
must be balanced against the need for consistency and predicability in the
common law. Brennan J. referred to a continuous 'tension between legal development and legal certainty', and acknowledged that 'there is room for difference in opinion as to the appropriate rate and subject matter of change'.[114]

In *Dietrich*, Brennan J. again saw a limit on legal development in the form
of legislative and executive responsibility for matters external to court procedures. Both he and Dawson J. rejected the majority view that an adjournment
or stay of proceedings may be granted so as to prevent an unfair trial caused
by external factors (such as a refusal by a Legal Aid Commission to provide
legal representation). Brennan and Dawson J.J. regarded such a course of
action as improperly 'placing pressure upon . . . [the] authorities to reverse
their decision'.[115]

---

[108] Ibid. at 298.   [109] Ibid. at 375.   [110] Ibid. at 362 per Toohey J.
[111] Ibid. at 329 per Deane J.   [112] Ibid. at 372 per Gaudron J.
[113] See *Mabo* n. 19 above.   [114] *Dietrich* n. 23 above at 320–1.
[115] Ibid. at 340 per Dawson J. Presumably, an adjournment on the basis of other external

Nonetheless, in *Dietrich* a majority of the Court did not consider itself as constrained by the fact that ultimate responsibility for the means of ensuring fairness—here, legal aid schemes—rests with the Legislature and the Executive. The majority accepted that in most serious cases in which the accused has exhausted all possible means of obtaining legal aid, it will be necessary to adjourn or stay the proceedings to prevent injustice to the accused. The decision reflects the Court's new approach that it has a *duty* to prevent unfairness—regardless of whether its decisions put pressure on the Legislature or Executive to allocate further funds or change their procedures. The Court has given substance to the view expressed by Murphy J. in *McInnis* that: 'Courts should not allow the integrity of the judicial process to be undermined by the financial exigencies of legal aid schemes.'[116]

To summarise, a majority of the Court has taken the radical step of focusing on the right, and then asking what a trial judge could possibly have done to give it substance in the case before him or her. The change of focus offers fertile ground for future recognition of the right in relation to other types of unfairness. The fact that this is a major change of approach is underlined by the contrast provided by the judgments of Brennan J.

In recent times, the right to a fair trial has also assumed greater importance in a rather different area. This is the area of public interest immunity, previously referred to as Crown privilege. Only since *Conway* v. *Rimmer*[117] have our Courts even insisted that they must themselves evaluate claims that Government documents should be privileged from production for use in litigation. However since then—and especially since *Sankey* v. *Whitlam*[118]— Australian Courts have recognised that they must weigh up two competing considerations: on the one hand, all relevant evidence should be available so that justice can be done in the Courts; on the other hand, disclosure of the Government material may 'prejudice the national interest'.[119] In *Sankey* a majority of the Court conceded that the public interest in preventing interference with 'the course of justice'[120] may compel the disclosure of *any* class of Government documents—even Cabinet minutes, which had previously been automatically privileged from production.

The High Court in *Sankey* saw itself as giving recognition to the public

---

factors such as inadequate interpreter facilities or an inadequate venue would also be regarded in a similar light. See ibid. at 331 per Deane J., 363 per Gaudron J.

[116] See *McInnis* n. 101 above. It is, however, relevant to note that in *Dietrich* n. 23 above at 312, Mason C.J. and McHugh J. remarked that 'no argument was put to the Court that recognition of such a right for the provision of counsel at public expense would impose an unsustainable financial burden on Governments'.

[117] [1968] AC 910. The House of Lords declined to follow *Duncan* v. *Cammell Laird & Co Ltd* [1942] AC 624.

[118] *Sankey* (1979–1980) 142 CLR 1.

[119] Ibid. at 48 per Stephen J. (with whom Aickin J. agreed).

[120] Ibid. at 56 per Stephen J; cf. ibid. at 39 per Gibbs C.J.

interest in the due administration of justice. Perhaps because it was the prosecutor rather than the defendants who sought production of the documents,
the Court did not discuss the matter in terms of the right to a fair trial.
Stephen J. described the public interest in the case before him as:

the need that impartial justice should be done in the Courts of law, not least between
the citizen and Crown, and that a litigant who has a case to maintain should not be
deprived of the means of its proper presentation by anything less than a weighty public reason.[121]

However in *Alister* v. *R*,[122] where it was the defendants in a criminal trial
who sought production of Government documents, several of the judges
emphasised that the defendants' interest should be given considerable weight.
Brennan J. emphasised that a criminal court's power to compel production of
such documents, upon an accused's application, is a 'safeguard of individual
liberty'.[123] Murphy J. recognised that the case before him involved the general
public interest in 'the proper administration of justice',[124] but approached the
matter from the accused's perspective. Although he did not enunciate his reasons, Murphy J. held that if an accused was prevented, by reason of non-dis-
closure of material, from defending himself or herself properly, 'the proper
course may be to abandon the prosecution or for the Court to stay proceedings'.[125]

In light of the High Court's approach in *Jago*, *Glennon*, and *Dietrich*,[126] it
may be that if the present Court was faced with an application for production
by an accused which was resisted on the grounds of public interest immunity,
it would place a greater emphasis on the accused's rights, and on what the
court should do to protect them.

Freedom of Expression

When a Court focuses on the right as such, the need to balance other competing rights and interests becomes all the more apparent.[127] It is easier for a

---

[121] *Glasgow Corporation* v. *Central Land Board* 1956 SC (House of Lords) 1 at 18–19 per Lord
Radcliffe, cited in *Sankey* n. 118 above at 59.
[122] (1983–4) 154 CLR 404.   [123] Ibid. at 456.   [124] Ibid. at 431.   [125] Ibid.
[126] See *Jago* n. 77, *Glennon* n. 78 and *Dietrich* n. 23 above respectively.
[127] This Chapter was updated prior to delivery of the High Court's judgment in the case of
Theophanous v. *Herald & Weekly Times Ltd* (1994) 124 ALR 1. The discussion which follows
should be read in light of the Court's decision therein that '[at] the very least, development in the
common law must accord with . . . [the] content' of the implication of freedom of political communication which is derived from the principle of representative government or democracy
enshrined in the Constitution. Ibid. at 15 per Mason C.J., Toohey and Gaudron J.J. See, generally, n. 333 below and the text on pp. 00, 00. [Authors' note: But, more recently, in *McGinty* v.
Western Australia (1966) 134 ALR 289, a majority of the High Court held that the source of any
such freedom of political communication is sections 7 and 24 of the Constitution, and not an
'independent' principle of representative government enshrined in the Constitution. In view of

Court to ignore or pay little attention to these other interests if it is focusing only on a narrowly defined rule. However if the Court turns its focus to the basic right, it is forced to look at what we might colloquially describe as 'the big picture'.

In the cases involving the right to freedom of expression the Courts have in recent times generally considered 'the big picture'. Once again, the right itself has been accorded an independent value, to be weighed in the balance alongside other interests, rather than simply assuming a residual quality.[128] However, here the competing rights or interests are often perceived to be at least as important as the right to freedom of expression. The judge must engage in a balancing process which is difficult and which may produce a controversial result. We propose to refer to several of these cases to illustrate the fact that a closer focus on rights is likely to bring with it some new difficulties.

In the area of contempt of court concerned with prejudicial pre-trial publicity, for example, the High Court has decided that the right to a fair trial will generally prevail over the right to freedom of expression where there is a serious risk of interference with the former. Where the offence of contempt by 'scandalising the Court' is in issue, the judge must balance against freedom of expression the maintenance of public confidence in the administration of law. Where the disclosure of confidential Government information is under consideration, a Court must weigh up the importance of the right to freedom of expression against the public interest against disclosure: this may be based on reasons such as national security, relationships with foreign countries or because disclosure would restrain 'the ordinary business of Government'.[129]

The cases which follow provide examples of the balancing process, and its difficulties, in action. They also indicate that the Courts are placing greater emphasis on the right to freedom of expression in relation to confidential Government information, in relation to political and governmental matters generally, and probably also in relation to the dissemination of prejudicial pre-trial publicity.[130]

Two other issues are of interest here. The first is the issue raised by Lord Goff in the second *Spycatcher* case: in his view the balance adopted by the common law in relation to freedom of expression in 'pure' common law areas is consistent with that arrived at by the European Court of Human Rights

---

this change of approach, the Court may decide, in the forthcoming *Levy* and *Lange* decisions, that the freedom operates as a limit on Commonwealth legislative power, but not as a general guarantee to which all laws—including the common law—are subject.]

[128] We refer here to a residual quality in the second sense referred to above in the text on p. 00. The same observation could be made of the current position in Britain: see *Derbyshire County Council* v. *Times Newspapers Ltd* [1992] QB 770 (Court of Appeal); [1993] AC 534 (House of Lords).

[129] *Commonwealth* v. *John Fairfax and Sons Ltd* (1980) 147 CLR 39 at 52 per Mason J.

[130] See *Hinch* v. *Attorney-General of Victoria* (1987) 164 CLR 15.

when applying Article 10 of the European Convention.[131] This is not a contention that we have sufficient space to explore further.

Secondly, in this area we can see one of the main characteristics of the common law's approach to human rights generally: that of 'compartmentalisation'. In many areas of law, the common law has tended to categorise cases into various compartments—and has developed rules to apply to each compartment—rather than take an approach which identifies the underlying principles and attempts to apply those principles consistently across a broad range of cases. So, too, in the field of human rights. Australian and English Courts have not often attempted to reconcile the weight given to a particular right or interest in one area of the law, with the weight given to it in another context. Obviously the weight given to a right will differ according to the strength of the countervailing interests that it must be balanced against. However, some inconsistencies cannot be justified on this basis. For example, it may be difficult to reconcile the different weight accorded to the right of freedom of expression in the context of two different branches of the law of contempt, in the cases of *Hinch*[132] and *Gallagher*[133] respectively; or to justify the diminished importance given to the right to a fair trial in relation to fair and accurate reports of committal proceedings.

We will turn first to the part of the law of contempt which places some restrictions on freedom of expression in order to protect a defendant's right to receive a fair trial of the criminal charges against him. It is well established at common law that a person who publishes material likely to influence jury members and thus likely to prejudice a defendant's chances of an acquittal may be guilty of contempt of court. This is because:

the law regards as fundamental to the preservation of the rights and freedoms necessary for the maintenance of an open and democratic society that a person should not be convicted of a serious criminal offence save by the verdict of a jury given after a fair trial upon the evidence presented at that trial.[134]

However, the Courts have recognised that they must balance against this the competing public interest in freedom of speech and discussion, which

---

[131] *Attorney-General* v. *Guardian Newspapers Ltd and Others (No .2)* [1990] 1 AC 109 at 282–4. See also Sir John Donaldson MR at 178 (Court of Appeal), and *Derbyshire County Council* v. *Times Newspapers Ltd* [1992] QC 770 at 810–13, 822–3 and 829–30 (Court of Appeal). In *Derbyshire*, each of the three members of the Court of Appeal cited, and relied upon, this passage from Lord Goff's speech in *Spycatcher*. The passage has been endorsed by the Court of Appeal in *Rantzen* v. *Mirror Group Newspapers (1986) Ltd* [1994] QB 670 at 691–2, and by the House of Lords in *Derbyshire* [1993] AC 534. Note, however, that in the latter case the House of Lords placed less emphasis than the Court of Appeal upon the guiding role of the European Convention. Lord Keith (with whom the other judges agreed) said that he, by contrast, had reached his conclusion 'upon the common law of England without finding any need to rely upon the European Convention'. Ibid. at 551.

[132] See *Hinch* n. 130 above.   [133] *Gallagher* v. *Durack* (1983) 152 CLR 238.

[134] *Hinch* n. 130 above at 408 per Gaudron J.

encompasses the public's right to be informed on matters of public importance. In the recent case of *Hinch*[135] the High Court agreed that in those cases
in which there is no intention to interfere with the administration of justice a
two-limb test should be applied. Publication of material will constitute a contempt of court where:

(a) the publication creates a 'real risk of serious prejudice to a fair trial'[136]
(or another similar formulation); and

(b) the detriment of this risk 'is not outweighed by the combination of the
abstract public interest in freedom of discussion and any specific public
benefits of such discussion in the circumstances of the particular
case'.[137]

The Court emphasised that both of the two competing interests must be taken
into account: it rejected the contention of Gibbs C.J. (in an earlier case) that
there will be a contempt of court whenever the first limb of the test is satisfied.[138]

In *Hinch* the Court emphasised that freedom of expression is an important
interest in the balancing exercise, and should only be restricted in limited circumstances:

Freedom of public discussion of matters of legitimate concern is, in itself, an ideal of
our society . . . Matters of importance or concern or interest to the nation, to a particular section of the community or to particular individuals are commonly involved in
judicial proceedings and it would be oppressive and futile to adopt the approach that
the mere fact that they are so involved should automatically remove them from the
public domain.[139]

All the same, it recognised that certain types of interference with the criminal
process are so serious that they can virtually never be justified: for example,
where 'the media prejudges issues to be litigated in a proceeding . . . or can-
vasses the evidence so as to engage in a trial by media',[140] or where it exposes
the criminal record of an accused prior to trial. In the view of some of the
judges where, as in the instant case:

the publication is in the mass media and is directed solely to the merits of the very issue
to be determined in the pending proceedings (e.g. the guilt or innocence of an accused),

---

[135] Ibid.   [136] Ibid. at 28 per Mason C.J.

[137] Ibid. at 57 per Deane J.

[138] In *Victoria* v. *Building Construction Employees' and Builders Labourers' Federation* (1982)
152 CLR 25 at 56 Gibbs C.J. said: '[t]he law strikes a balance; in the interest of the due administration of justice it will curb freedom of speech, but only to the extent that it is necessary to prevent a real and substantial prejudice to the administration of justice.' In one way or another, the
various members of the Court in *Hinch* recognised that it would be more difficult to establish a
public interest justification where the subject matter of the discussion was pending criminal proceedings. Deane J., for example, acknowledged the attraction of Gibbs C.J.'s view in relation to
such proceedings, before rejecting it. See *Hinch* n. 130 above at 48.

[139] Ibid. at 57.   [140] Ibid. at 43 per Wilson J.

there would be no countervailing public interest consideration which might effectively outweigh the detriment of a clear tendency to prejudice the due administration of justice . . .[141]

On the other hand, most members of the Court in *Hinch* specifically mentioned that in certain instances the public interest in open discussion will prevail—notwithstanding the fact that pending criminal proceedings are a central (rather than an incidental) subject of the discussion, and that the discussion creates a considerable risk of interference with those proceedings. In such instances, the first limb of the test is made out, but the risk of prejudice to the accused is said to be outweighed by a 'superior' public interest. Mason C.J. gave a number of examples of circumstances in which material may legitimately be published despite the fact that it may 'have a strong tendency to induce readers and viewers to conclude that the accused is guilty of the offence charged'.[142] He referred to the common law view that fair and accurate reports of Court proceedings (including committal proceedings) and of proceedings in Parliament, when made in good faith, do not amount to a contempt of court. He gave as other instances '[t]he discussion of a major constitutional crisis or of an imminent threat of nuclear disaster'.[143]

The judgments in *Hinch* indicate that the Court is prepared to identify the rights and interests involved in cases before them, and to balance them according to the circumstances of the case. They also illustrate the difficulties in doing so. In addition, it seems to us that the law of contempt exhibits the feature of 'compartmentalism' which is typical of the common law approach to rights generally.

Of course, the weight that a Court gives to a particular right will depend upon the strength of other countervailing public interests. It seems to us that despite the oddity of the result the High Court has valid reasons for distinguishing between the weight to be accorded to the right to a fair trial in the context of a particular trial, and the weight that the right is to be given in the context of contempt proceedings arising out of prejudicial publicity. The cases of *Hinch*[144] (contempt) and *Glennon*[145] (right to a fair trial) illustrate the point: in each case the High Court was considering the possible prejudicial effects of the same pre-trial publicity, but after carefully considering the weight to be given to the competing interests, and the purpose of judicial intervention, the Court applied different tests of intervention.

We have already summarised what the Court decided in *Hinch*. *Glennon* suggests that a Court is more likely to punish for contempt than it is to stay permanently proceedings because of unfair publicity. In *Glennon* the majority judges focused on the particular trial before them and emphasised the powers

---

[141] Ibid. at 52 per Deane J.
[143] Ibid. at 26 per Mason C.J.
[145] See *Glennon* n. 78 above.
[142] Ibid. at 25.
[144] Ibid.

of the trial judge to give directions which overcome the prejudice, and 'the community's right to expect that a person accused of a serious criminal offence will be brought to trial'.[146] As a result they came up with a much narrower test of intervention: 'a permanent stay will only be ordered in an extreme case . . . and there must be a fundamental defect 'of such a nature that nothing that a trial judge can do in the conduct of the trial can relieve against its unfair consequences . . .'[147]

It remains to be seen whether the High Court will take a consistent and principled approach to upholding 'freedom of expression'[148] in different contexts. We mention this because the Court's emphasis in *Hinch* on the importance of this right seems inconsistent with the approach taken by the Court some 4 years earlier in *Gallagher* v. *Durack*.[149] *Gallagher* involved a different branch of the law of contempt of court: that of 'scandalising the Court' by making 'imputations on Courts or judges which are calculated to bring the Court into contempt or lower its authority'.[150] Four members of the five member Court held that in this area the law must reconcile two principles, 'each of which is of cardinal importance': one, that 'speech should be free, so that everyone has the right to comment in good faith on matters of public importance, including the administration of justice, even if the comment is outspoken, mistaken or wrong-headed';[151] the other, that 'it is necessary for the purpose of maintaining public confidence in the administration of law that there should be some certain and immediate method of repressing imputations upon Courts of Justice which, if continued, are likely to impair their authority'.[152] The majority did not appear to consider that a Court should make a finding of contempt only in exceptional cases.

Murphy J., on the other hand, emphasised that the offence of contempt by 'scandalising the Court' is 'a limitation on that freedom of expression which is essential to the achievement and maintenance of a democratic society' and held that a 'clear and present danger to judicial administration', rather than a 'mere tendency to detract from' judicial administration, represented a 'better balance between the conflicting interests of free speech and of integrity of the judicial system'.[153] In his view the power of a Court to punish for 'scandalising' 'should be strictly confined'.[154] Given the emphasis placed by the High

---

[146] See *Hinch* n. 130 above at 350 per Mason C.J. and Toohey J.

[147] Ibid. Deane, Gaudron and McHugh J.J. agree that a permanent stay of proceedings should only be ordered in an 'extreme' or 'singular' case. Ibid. at 358.

[148] As distinct from the freedom of political communication necessary for an effective system of representative government. See discussion of *Australian Capital Television Pty Ltd* v. *Commonwealth* (1992) 177 CLR 106 and *Nationwide News* v. *Wills* (1992) 177 CLR 1 in the text on p. 00. See also n. 127 above.

[149] See *Gallagher* v. *Durack* n. 133 above.

[150] Ibid. at 243 per Gibbs C.J., Mason, Wilson and Brennan J.J.   [151] Ibid.

[152] Ibid. citing Dixon J. in *R. v. Dunbabin, ex parte Williams* (1935) 53 CLR 434 at 447.

[153] *Gallagher* v. *Durack* n. 133 above at 246.   [154] Ibid. at 249.

Court in *Hinch*[155] on the importance of the right to free speech and, in the recent cases of *ACTV*[156] and *Nationwide News*,[157] on the public's right to discuss and be informed on matters of public importance, it must be regarded as a reasonable possibility that the High Court will in future confine the scope of the offence of 'scandalising the Court'—at least where the subject of discussion is considered to be of public interest.[158]

Finally, we note in passing that since Mason J.'s decision in *Commonwealth v. John Fairfax*[159] the common law has accorded greater weight to the 'public's right to know' in the context of Government claims for protection of confidential information—and thus has again involved the Courts in difficult assessments of the relative weights to be given to different public interests.[160]

COMMON LAW RIGHTS—GENERAL OBSERVATIONS

On a more general level, we propose to look at a variety of cases which illustrate certain characteristics of the common law's protection of human rights. Our first point is that a majority of the High Court now regards infringement of common law rights as relevant to the process of characterisation involved when considering whether a law is supported by the implied incidental power under the Constitution. Secondly, we will examine the extent to which the Courts may be prepared to overrule previous decisions in areas involving human rights issues. Thirdly, we suggest that the English Courts' attitude to creating a new right of privacy indicates a judicial reluctance to recognise new rights. Finally we will focus on several aspects of the High Court's decisions in *Mabo* and *Dietrich*, including Brennan J.'s statement in *Mabo* that the International Covenant is 'an important influence on the development of the common law'.[161]

We turn to the first issue: the relevance of common law rights in the characterisation process. As a result of the High Court decisions in the cases of *Davis v. Commonwealth*[162] and *Nationwide News*,[163] it is now evident that the impact of a particular law on a right traditionally recognised by the common law will be a relevant consideration when determining whether the law can be characterised as falling within the scope of the implied incidental power.

---

[155] See *Hinch* n. 130 above.
[156] *Australian Capital Television Pty Ltd* v. *Commonwealth* (1992) 177 CLR 106.
[157] *Nationwide News Pty Ltd* v. *Wills* (1992) 177 CLR 1. However, see n. 173 below and accompanying text.
[158] For example, the distribution of the drug thalidomide. See *Sunday Times* v. *United Kingdom* (1979) 2 EHRR 245, a decision of the European Court of Human Rights at Strasbourg.
[159] See *John Fairfax and Sons Ltd* n. 129 above.
[160] See, for example, the second *Spycatcher* case n. 131 above.
[161] *Mabo* n. 19 above at 422.   [162] (1988) 166 CLR 79.
[163] *Nationwide News* n. 157 above.

In *Davis*, the Court was required to decide (amongst other matters) whether the Commonwealth Parliament had power to enact Section 22 of the Australian Bicentennial Authority Act 1980 (Cth). Section 22 made it an offence for a person to use various prescribed expressions in connection with a business or trade or the supply or use of goods, except with the consent of the Bicentennial Authority.

The Court decided the question of the validity of the provision by characterising the scope of the Commonwealth's legislative power. The Court held that although the Executive power (Section 61 of the Constitution), operating in conjunction with the incidental power, authorised laws which protected the integrity of the commemoration of the Bicentenary, the restrictions imposed by Section 22 of the Act on the use of certain expressions did not 'contribute' to this purpose. Some of the restrictions could not be supported by either the express incidental power or any other head of legislative power. Mason CJ, Deane and Gaudron J.J. said:

In arming the Authority with this extraordinary power the Act provides for a regime of protection which is grossly disproportionate to the need to protect the commemoration and the Authority . . . Although the statutory regime may be related to a constitutionally legitimate end, the provisions in question reach too far.[164]

Their judgment could have left it at that: the provisions reached 'far beyond the legitimate objects sought to be achieved'.[165] Instead, the judgment mentioned a further factor. The framework of regulation, said the three judges, also:

impinges on freedom of expression by enabling the Authority to regulate the use of common expressions and by making unauthorised use a criminal offence . . . This extraordinary intrusion into freedom of expression is not reasonably and appropriately adapted to achieve the ends that lie within the limits of constitutional power.[166]

The judgment appears to leave the role of freedom of expression in the matter somewhat unclear. It seems that the judges saw the intrusion on freedom of expression as providing an indication as to whether the legislation was 'appropriately adapted' or not. If the legislation resulted in a considerable intrusion into freedom of expression, then this was less likely to be the case: such a case would call for strict scrutiny of the means employed by Parliament to achieve its object. This seems to have been Brennan J.'s point also: he examined the law carefully to see whether it was a law supported by Section 51(xxxix) of the Constitution and concluded that it was 'not a law which protects the efficacy of what the Executive Government has done or may do in organising the commemoration':[167] 'freedom of speech can hardly

---

[164] Ibid. at 100.   [165] Ibid.   [166] Ibid.
[167] *Nationwide News* n. 157 above at 116.

be an incidental casualty of an activity undertaken by the Executive Government to advance a nation which boasts of its freedom.'[168]

The process of characterisation employed in *Davis* was explained further by Mason C.J. and McHugh J. in the subsequent case of *Nationwide News*.[169] Here, the Court was considering the validity of Section 299(1)(d)(ii) of the Industrial Relations Act 1988 (Cth). The section made it an offence by writing or speech to use words 'calculated . . . to bring a member of the [Industrial Relations] Commission or the Commission into disrepute'. Mason CJ, McHugh J and Dawson J ultimately decided that the provision was not supported by the incidental scope of the power in Section 51(xxxv) of the Constitution. Each regarded it as relevant to consider the extent to which the common law had accorded protection to Courts in the context of the contempt of court jurisdiction.

Dawson J. made no reference to the competing interests involved in such an area. However, the tests of characterisation formulated by Mason C.J. and McHugh J. emphasise the major role now accorded to common law rights in this context. Mason C.J. relied upon the decision in *Davis*. He held that a law:

will not fall within the scope of what is incidental to the substantive power unless it is reasonably and appropriately adapted to the pursuit of an end within power, i.e., unless it is capable of being considered to be reasonably proportionate to the pursuit of that end.[170]

Secondly, he said, in determining whether this requirement is satisfied:

it is material to ascertain whether . . . [the law] causes adverse consequences unrelated to the achievement of the legitimate object, which . . . result in any infringement of fundamental values traditionally protected by the common law, such as freedom of expression.[171]

McHugh J. also focused on the impugned provision's impact on a common law right. His starting point was the conclusion that Section 299(1)(d)(ii) 'constitutes a far reaching interference with the common law right of members of the public to make fair comments on matters of public interest'.[172] Both judges then proceeded to analyse the weight to be given to the competing public interest of upholding the authority of government institutions like the Industrial Relations Commission. In our view, both judgments deferred considerably to the balance regarded as appropriate within the common law on contempt of court.[173]

---

[168] Ibid.   [169] Ibid. per Mason C.J. and McHugh J.
[170] Ibid. at 30.
[171] Ibid. at 31. See also Mason C.J.'s emphasis on 'the paramount importance of freedom of expression'. Ibid. at 34.
[172] Ibid. at 103.
[173] See, in particular, ibid. at 33, second paragraph per Mason C.J. See also ibid. at 105 per McHugh J., 91 per Dawson J.

The questions for Mason C.J., Deane, Gaudron and Brennan J.J. in *Davis* and for Mason C.J. and McHugh J. in *Nationwide News* were questions of characterisation. Nonetheless, the common law right of freedom of expression was perceived to be relevant to the decision. In our view, the cases indicate that although in this context the High Court will now identify the rights involved in its decisions, it may still refrain from a full analysis of the scope and application of the rights. It seems likely that it will on occasion adopt, without extensive discussion, the balance between the relevant rights and interests arrived at in the common law.

When a Court does focus on, and fully analyse, the rights and interests involved in a case before it, to what extent will it be prepared to further develop or change the existing law on the matter? A good example of the common law's capabilities, and its possible limitations, is to be found in Lord Scarman's judgment on the law of blasphemy in *R*. v. *Lemon*; *R*. v. *Gay News*.[174] Lord Scarman focuses his full attention on the various rights involved in the area, and takes into account the weight given to the rights in other contexts. He is prepared to use his analysis to decide an uncertain point of law in a way which is principled and which reflects contemporary values. However his judgment also demonstrates the potential conservatism of the common law when faced with a clear and long-standing line of authority.

The main issue before the Court was whether the *mens rea* of the offence of blasphemous libel was constituted by an intention to publish material which was in fact blasphemous; or whether it was necessary for the prosecution to prove, in addition, that the defendant intended to blaspheme. A majority of the Court held that the second aspect was not a necessary component of the offence. Lord Scarman stated firmly that, whatever the historical position, '[t]he issue is . . . one of legal policy in the society of today'.[175] He conceived it to be his duty to state 'the existing law in a form conducive to the social conditions of the late twentieth century',[176] and emphasised that he was concerned with what 'makes legal sense in a plural society which recognises the human rights and fundamental freedoms of the European Convention'.[177] He considered the implications of Article 9 ('the right to freedom of religion') and Article 10 ('the right to freedom of expression') of the Convention. In his view Article 9 necessarily implies that there is 'a duty on all of us to refrain from insulting or outraging the religious feelings of others'.[178] He noted that the

---

[174] *R*. v. *Gay News* [1979] AC 617.   [175] Ibid. at 664.

[176] Ibid. at 658–9. He cited Lord Sumner's speech in *Bowman* v. *Secular Society Ltd* [1917] AC 406 at 466–7, which begins as follows: 'The words, as well as the acts, which tend to endanger society differ from time to time in proportion as society is stable or insecure in fact, or is believed by its reasonable members to be open to assault.' Lord Sumner concluded: 'there is nothing in the general rules as to blasphemy and irreligion, as known to the law, which prevents us from varying their application to the particular circumstances of our time in accordance with that experience.'

[177] *R*. v. *Gay News* n. 174 above at 665.   [178] Ibid.

right covered by Article 10 is expressly stated to be subject to such restrictions as are prescribed by law and necessary to protect the rights of others. Having analysed the competing rights involved, Lord Scarman struck a balance between the two which enabled him to decide the question of the appropriate mens rea for the offence of blasphemy. In his view:

It would be intolerable if by allowing an author or publisher to plead the excellence of his motives and the right of free speech he could evade the penalties of the law even though his words were blasphemous in the sense of constituting an outrage on the religious feelings of his fellow citizens. This is no way forward for a successful plural society. Accordingly . . . [as with the test for obscenity] the character of the words published matters, but not the motive of the author or publisher.[179]

All of this indicated that Lord Scarman was prepared to take a flexible approach to the content of the law of blasphemy, to model it so that it performed a useful purpose in twentieth century Britain. However, on closer inspection of the judgment it seems that all this flexibility was contingent upon Lord Scarman's finding that the present legal position on the mens rea of the offence was unclear. When faced with another possible extension of the scope of the offence, he baulked—presumably because the common law on this point was long settled.

The second issue as to the scope of the common law offence—raised only by Lord Scarman—was whether the offence should be extended to protect the religious feelings of non-Christians. It was well settled that as a matter of history it had never done so. Lord Scarman was receptive to the idea of widening the scope of the offence in this way. He believed that modern Britain is 'an increasingly plural society' in which 'it is necessary not only to respect the differing religious beliefs, feelings and practices of all but also to protect them from scurrility, vilification, ridicule and contempt'.[180] He recognised that the offence of blasphemous libel would not fully serve this purpose unless it was extended to protect not only the religious beliefs and feelings of Christians (as was presently the case), but also those of non-Christians. He saw the offence as being 'not sufficiently comprehensive' because 'it is shackled by the chains of history'.[181] Nonetheless, Lord Scarman held that it was 'not open' to him to make by judicial decision the comprehensive reform of the law which he believed to be beneficial.[182] Legislation was needed to effect the change.

More recently, the Divisional Court in England has agreed with him. In Choudhury[183] Watkins L.J. (with Stuart-Smith L.J. and Roch J.) held that the common law offence of blasphemy was clearly restricted to a scurrilous vilification of the Christian religion. As a result, it was 'not open' to the Court to extend its scope,[184] and it was 'not necessary to pay any regard to the

---

[179] Ibid.   [180] Ibid. at 658.   [181] Ibid.   [182] Ibid.
[183] R. v. Chief Metropolitan Stipendiary Magistrate, ex parte Choudhury [1991] 1 QB 429.
[184] Ibid. at 447.

(European) Convention'.[185] In relation to the first of these propositions the Court said: 'The mere fact that the law is anomalous or even unjust does not, in our view, justify the Court in changing it, if it is clear.'[186]

As we have seen, the common law is not uniformly resistant to change. Nonetheless, these speeches by Lord Scarman and Watkins LJ indicate that the judges' perception of their role in changing the common law will sometimes operate as a constraint.

In addition, it seems unlikely that the Courts will be prepared to recognise new fundamental rights capable of affecting the result in a particular case. This is suggested by the Courts' attitude to arguments that the common law should recognise a general right or tort of privacy.[187] In *Malone* v. *Commissioner of Police*,[188] for example, Sir Robert Megarry V-C rejected a contention that there is a right to hold a telephone conversation in the privacy of one's home without being subjected to wire-tapping. In his view: 'No new right in the law, fully-fledged with all the appropriate safeguards, can spring from the head of a judge deciding a particular case: only Parliament can create such a right.'[189] He added: 'The wider and more indefinite the right claimed, the greater the undesirability of holding that such a right exists.'[190]

The English Court of Appeal has subsequently confirmed that English law does not recognise a right or tort of privacy.[191] Each of the judges condemned the failure of the law to provide protection for a person subjected to the sort of intrusion by the media that the plaintiff had suffered; for example, Bingham L.J. said: 'This case . . . highlights, yet again, the failure of both the common law of England and statute to protect in an effective way the personal privacy of individual citizens.'[192] Nonetheless the Court did not contemplate rectifying the omission itself by introducing a new common law right of privacy.[193] Instead, it appealed to Parliament to take up the matter.

---

[185] Ibid. at 449. The Court appears to have accepted Mr Lester QC's argument on this point. However the Court (perhaps rather surprisingly) then went on to consider whether the United Kingdom was in breach of the European Convention. It accepted Mr Lester QC's arguments that it was not.

[186] Ibid. at 447.

[187] The common law has long recognised a 'right to personal inviolability'. See, for example, *Department of Health and Community Services (NT)* v. *JWB and SMB ('Re Marion')* (1992) 175 CLR 218 (High Court). However this right does not provide any assistance to defendants affected by non-physical attacks: for example, intrusions by the media.

[188] *Malone* v. *Commissioner of Police of the Metropolis* (No 2) [1979] Ch 344.

[189] Ibid. at 372. [190] Ibid.

[191] *Gordon Kaye (by Peter Froggatt his next friend)* v. *Andrew Robertson and Sport Newspapers*, unreported, judgment delivered on 23 February 1990. This is also true of Australian law: see the majority view in *Victoria Park Racing and Recreation Ground Co Ltd* v. *Taylor* (1937) 58 CLR 479.

[192] *Victoria Park Racing and Recreation Ground Co Ltd* v. *Taylor* (1937) 58 CLR 479. See also the rather similar facts in *Ettingshausen* v. *Australian Consolidated Press Ltd* (1990–91) 23 NSWLR 443 in which the plaintiff claimed in defamation.

[193] The plaintiff was obliged to base his claim on various well-established rights of action (libel, malicious falsehood, trespass to the person, and passing off) which are, of course, themselves common law creations.

However, as is evident from recent cases in areas such as 'the right to a fair trial', the common law is generally playing an increasing role in the protection of human rights in areas unaffected by statute or constitutional law. It is really only necessary to refer to the High Court's decision in *Mabo*[194] to illustrate this point.

The judgments in *Mabo* are significant in a number of respects. We will highlight two of these matters. First and foremost, the High Court decided to overturn a well-established line of authority denying 'native title', on the basis that the previous doctrine was founded on an attitude of racial discrimination and resulted in injustice. Secondly, the International Covenant was recognised as an important influence on the development of the common law.

In *Mabo* the Court effected an extraordinarily important change in the law, rejecting legal propositions that had survived for more than 150 years. In doing so, it removed assumptions which had allowed federal Governments to ignore calls for a fundamental reassessment of Aboriginal and Torres Strait Islander land rights. A majority of the Court did not envisage the righting of past wrongs, but did provide a foundation upon which future land claims might be dealt with more fairly.

Six members of the Court rejected the two propositions that 'the territory of New South Wales was, in 1788, *terra nullius* in the sense of unoccupied or uninhabited for legal purposes' and that, upon settlement by the British, 'full legal and beneficial ownership of all lands of the Colony vested in the Crown, unaffected by any claims of the Aboriginal inhabitants'.[195] Instead, they declared that 'the common law of this country recognises a form of native title which, in the cases where it has not been extinguished, reflects the entitlement of the indigenous inhabitants, in accordance with their laws and customs, to their traditional lands. . .'[196]

Deane and Gaudron J.J. spoke in 'unusually emotive'[197] terms of the acts of dispossession and oppression of the Aboriginal people which have been the practical result of the legal propositions mentioned above. In these 'unique' circumstances, they said, 'the Court is under a clear duty to re-examine the two propositions'.[198]

Brennan J. (with Mason C.J. and McHugh J.) agreed that a re-examination was called for. He declared that the long settled doctrine of *terra nullius* must be rejected because it was predicated upon an assumption that the Aboriginal people were 'low in the scale of social organisation'—an assumption that was not only 'false in fact' but also manifestly discriminatory.[199] Brennan J. pointed out that the doctrine did not accord with either 'the expectations of the international community' or 'the contemporary values of the Australian

---

[194] *Mabo* n. 19 above.
[195] Ibid. at 108 per Deane and Gaudron J.J.
[196] Ibid. at 15 per Mason C.J. and McHugh J.
[197] Ibid. at 120 per Deane and Gaudron J.J.
[198] Ibid. at 109.
[199] Ibid. at 39–40.

people',[200] and said: '[I]t is imperative in today's world that the common law should neither be nor be seen to be frozen in an age of racial discrimination.'[201]

Nonetheless, both of these majority judgments emphasised that the Courts did not possess unlimited power to re-open long-settled 'fundamental propositions'.[202] As mentioned earlier, Brennan J. took the view that the common law could only adopt changes which would not 'fracture a skeletal principle of [the] legal system'.[203] He found, however, that the recognition of indigenous rights and interests in land did not have this effect.

Dawson J. (in dissent) adopted the traditional stance against judicial law-making. His judgment highlights the radical nature of the approach taken by the other six judges. In Dawson J.'s view, a change in the political policy which lies behind the legal regime on land rights does not necessitate a change in the law:

It requires the implementation of a new policy to do that and that is a matter for Government rather than the Courts. In the meantime it would be wrong to attempt to revise history or to fail to recognise its legal impact, however unpalatable it may now seem. To do so would be to impugn the foundations of the legal system.[204]

Another significant feature of *Mabo* is Brennan J.'s emphasis on the importance of the principles set out in the International Covenant. This emphasis is unprecedented for a High Court judge. In Brennan J.'s view:

The opening up of international remedies to individuals pursuant to Australia's accession to the Optional Protocol to the International Covenant on Civil and Political Rights brings to bear on the common law the powerful influence of the Covenant and the international standards it imports. The common law does not necessarily conform with international law, but international law is a legitimate and important influence on the development of the common law, especially when international law declares the existence of universal human rights. A common law doctrine founded on unjust discrimination in the enjoyment of civil and political rights demands reconsideration.[205]

This is a major step forward. Brennan J. (with whom Mason C.J. and McHugh J. agreed) insisted that the common law *must* keep in step with international law's condemnation of doctrines based on racial discrimination.[206] The Court must uphold the principle of 'the equality of all Australian citizens before the law', even if that would involve overruling previous decisions.[207]

Until *Mabo*, the focus of the Courts had been on the degree to which international Covenants could be used as a source to 'fill . . . a lacuna in the

---

[200] Ibid. at 42.   [201] Ibid. at 41–2.
[202] Ibid. at 109 per Deane and Gaudron J.J. Toohey J.'s judgment (the other majority judgment) does not focus on this issue.
[203] Ibid. at 43. See discussion in the text on p. 00.   [204] Ibid. at 145.
[205] *Mabo* n. 19 above at 42. Note also Toohey J.'s reference, ibid. at 215, to Article 5 of the International Convention on the Elimination of All Forms of Racial Discrimination.
[206] *Mabo* n. 19 above at 42.   [207] Ibid. at 58.

common law'[208] and to provide guidance whenever 'the inherited common law is uncertain'.[209] There had been no question of a Covenant being relied upon as a basis for overruling well-established authority. The use of international treaties had been taken furthest by Kirby P. in the NSW Court of Appeal, and Nicholson C.J. in the Family Court.[210] In *Jago* v. *District Court of New South Wales*,[211] for example, the Court was required to decide whether the common law recognised a 'right to a speedy trial'. Kirby P referred disparagingly to the use of 'disputable antiquarian research concerning the procedures which may or may not have been adopted by the itinerant justices in eyre in parts of England in the reign of King Henry II'.[212] He said:

where the inherited common law is uncertain, Australian judges, after the Australia Act 1986 (Cth) at least, do well to look for more reliable and modern sources for the statement and development of the common law. One such reference point may be an international treaty which Australia has ratified and which now states international law.[213]

Brennan J.'s statements in *Mabo* can be seen as embracing Kirby P's view, and as extending its application in exceptional cases to long-settled areas of the common law. However there is no indication in the judgment of Brennan J. that international instruments are to be used as anything more than sources of law for the Court to dip into at will.[214] There is no suggestion that the Court will adopt the approach taken by Nicholson C.J. in *Re Marion*.[215] There, Nicholson C.J. recanted his view in *Re Jane*,[216] and said that it was 'strongly arguable' that various provisions of the Human Rights and Equal Opportunity Commission Act 1986 (Cth) ('HREOC Act'), and the scheduling to the Act of international instruments, implied that the rights and principles set out in the instruments are incorporated into Australian domestic law.[217]

The High Court gave judgment in the appeal[218] from *Re Marion* at much the same time as it handed down judgment in *Mabo*. With the exception of Brennan J., the judges did not refer to the various international instruments which had been considered by the Full Family Court below, and which were

---

[208] *Cachia* v. *Hanes* (1991) 23 NSWLR 304 at 313 per Kirby P.

[209] *Jago* v. *District Court of NSW* (1988) 12 NSWLR 558. In addition, international instruments have been used to lend support to well-recognised common law rights. e.g. *J* v. *Lieschke* (1986–87) 162 CLR 447 at 463 per Deane J.

[210] See *Re Marion* (1991) 14 Fam LR 427 at 449–51.   [211] See *Jago* n. 209 above.

[212] Ibid. at 569.   [213] Ibid.

[214] 'The common law does not necessarily conform with international law . . .' *Mabo* n. 19 above at 42 per Brennan J.

[215] *Re Marion* n. 210 above.

[216] *Re Jane* (1988–89) 85 ALR 409 at 425. Nicholson C.J. supported the approach taken by Samuels J.A. in *Jago* n. 209 above at 582.

[217] *Re Marion* n. 210 above at 449. Nicholson C.J. did not, however, clearly spell out the consequences which flowed from this position.

[218] *Department of Health and Community Services (NT)* v. *JWB and SMB* n. 187 above.

relevant to the question before the Court of whether parents may authorise the sterilisation of mentally disabled children. Clearly the judges considered that they were under no obligation to do so—even though they were considering an area in which the law was uncertain.[219]

It seems to us that the case of *Dietrich* v. *R*[220] typifies current judicial attitudes to the use of the International Covenant in developing the common law. A number of the judges appeared to accept the proposition that an international instrument may provide guidance where the common law is unclear.[221] It is less obvious whether this will also be the case in circumstances involving a lacuna in domestic law.[222] In any event, the main impression is that of a Court intent on taking its own measure of what constitute the 'prevailing social values' of Australia, on the basis that the common law must 'keep in step' with such values. Whilst the International Covenant is cited in support of the judges' primary findings, it does not mark the starting point of their analyses.

Nonetheless, Brennan J.'s remarks in *Mabo* do suggest that in future the High Court may more frequently refer to international human rights standards as sources of domestic law. There are probably a number of factors which have in the past combined to dissuade the Court from taking such an approach. These include the doctrine that international treaties are not incorporated into Australian domestic law, and parochialism. However another cogent reason has been the Court's uncertainty as to the content of the broad statements of rights and principles set out in such treaties:

[W]hat are the principles sought to be thus incorporated? Most international human rights law is treaty based, and therefore referable to specific words. But they are not usually precise, or necessarily tailored to local conditions: precision and adaptation may need to be effected locally by the appropriate organ. . .There is no international Court with hierarchical authority to pronounce human rights law for the use of Australian Courts.[223]

The last point can no longer be made with the same force—at least in relation to the International Covenant. Since Australia acceded to the First Optional Protocol to the Covenant in 1991, there *has* been a body (the UN Human Rights Committee) which, although not a Court, has been authorised

---

[219] Compare the English approach referred to on p. 49.

[220] See *Dietrich* n. 23 above.

[221] For example, Toohey J. in ibid. at 360, Mason C.J. and McHugh J. in ibid. at 306 ('assuming, without deciding' the matter), and Brennan J. who did not regard the influence of the International Covenant as limited to those situations in which the common law is unclear. Cf. Dawson J. in ibid. at 349.

[222] Ibid. at 360 per Toohey J. This issue was not explicitly discussed by the other judges.

[223] Anderson and Rowe, 'Human Rights in Australia: National and International Perspectives', 24 *Archiv Des Volkerrechts* (1986) 56 at 83, as cited by Nicholson C.J. in *Re Jane* (1988–89) 85 ALR 409 at 424–5.

to express its views on whether Australia has contravened rights set out in the Covenant. Australian individuals may now submit to the Committee communications alleging violations of these rights.[224] If reasonably frequent use is made of this procedure, this is likely to heighten the Australian judiciary's awareness of both the Covenant and the Committee's jurisprudence.[225] It is already evident in cases such as *Dietrich* that the High Court is increasingly willing to have regard to comparative material such as the more developed jurisprudence of the European Human Rights Commission and Court, the Canadian Supreme Court and the United States Supreme Court.

Statutory Interpretation ('the Second Method')

The Courts use statutory interpretation to protect rights in two ways: first, by interpreting 'value-laden' expressions in statutes so as to protect rights; secondly, by the use of presumptions.

As to the first of these, we are referring particularly to expressions in statutes which indicate that a certain standard of morality is required by society. For example, there are (or have been) statutory offences of behaving in an offensive manner,[226] publishing obscene and indecent material,[227] and posting material which has on it words or marks of an 'indecent, obscene, blasphemous, libellous or grossly offensive character'.[228] We have already referred to Lord Scarman's consideration of the common law offence of blasphemy. In addition, there are or have recently been a number of statutory offences of blasphemy in State Acts, and offences relating to 'blasphemous' material in Commonwealth statutes.[229]

Generally the statutes do not indicate the scope that is to be given to these expressions. Nor has the common law provided significant assistance to trial

---

[224] The First Optional Protocol to the International Covenant on Civil and Political Rights, Article 2. To date, the Human Rights Committee has delivered its views in relation to only one such communication: that of *Toonen* v. *Australia* (delivered 31 March 1994). The Committee's views are awaited in relation to the communication submitted on behalf of a Cambodian applicant for refugee status who has been held in detention since arriving in Australia.

[225] See text on p. 49 for a reference to the English Courts' approach to the application of the European Convention on Human Rights. For a discussion of the influence of the European Convention on English law, as against the likely influence of the Covenant on the protection of rights in Australia, see Jones, 'Legal Protection for Fundamental Rights and Freedoms: European Lessons for Australia?', 22 Fed LR (1994) 57 at 84–8.

[226] Summary Offences Act 1953–1985 (SA). See *Khan* v. *Bazeley* [1986] 40 SASR 481.

[227] Obscene and Indecent Publications Act 1901–1955 (NSW), s 16(d). See *Crowe* v. *Graham* [1969] 121 CLR 375.

[228] Post and Telegraph Act 1901–1970 (Cth), s 107. See *Romeyko* v. *Samuels* [1972] 2 SASR 529.

[229] For example, the Broadcasting Act 1942 (Cth), s 118, and various regulations under the Customs Act 1901 (Cth).

judges: for example, a thing has been said to be 'obscene' if it is 'offensive to current standards of decency'.[230] Generally speaking, a Court undertaking the task of 'interpreting' and applying these expressions must make a value judgment about the weight that contemporary society ascribes to certain values. The making of that value judgment is fertile ground into which to plant a more rights-focused approach.

Since prosecutions for these offences are now relatively rare, we have to go back to *Crowe* v. *Graham*[231] to find a High Court authority on 'obscenity' and 'indecency'. In the present context, the judgment of Windeyer J. is of interest. Windeyer J. took the view that a judge should not get side-tracked into abstract arguments about the weight that society gives to certain rights and values; for example, the right to freedom of expression on the one hand, and the interest in protecting members of the public from exposure to offensive acts or publications on the other. He rejected the NSW Court of Appeal's references to American authorities (and to the First and Fourteenth Amendments upon which they were based) as 'only remotely relevant', and stated firmly: 'their Honours were wrong in invoking considerations of 'private liberty as a basic right and need of modern man' as an aid for the interpretation of a statute of the Parliament of New South Wales dealing with obscenity and indecency.'[232]

In view of the greater emphasis now placed by the High Court on identifying and applying rights such as freedom of expression, we doubt whether this criticism would be made today. We suggest that we will instead see greater reference to rights when courts are interpreting value-laden expressions.

Secondly, the Courts have developed various presumptions which are to be applied when interpreting legislation. These common law presumptions are not generally used for the sole or even the main purpose of ascertaining Parliamentary intention; rather, the Courts *presume* that Parliament had a certain intent except when the provision makes it unequivocally clear that this was not the case:

even where Parliament confessedly possesses plenary power within its own territory, the full literal intention will not ordinarily be ascribed to general words where that would conflict with recognised principles that Parliament would be *prima facie* expected to respect. Something unequivocal must be found, either in the context or the circumstances, to overcome the presumption.[233]

Thus, the presumptions have traditionally been applied in such a way that they 'no longer have anything to do with the intent of the Legislature; they are

---

[230] *R.* v. *Close* [1948] VLR 445 at 463 per Fullagar J., cited with approval by Windeyer J. in *Crowe* v. *Graham* (1969) 121 CLR 375 at 393.
[231] (1969) 121 CLR 375.   [232] Ibid. at 398–9.
[233] *Ex parte Walsh and Johnson: Re Yates* (1925) 37 CLR 36 at 93 per Isaacs J.

a means of controlling that intent'.[234] They are sometimes referred to as forming a common law Bill of Rights.[235]

So what are the 'recognised principles' that the Courts strive to uphold? There are, of course, many such principles and rights, and we refer to Pearce and Geddes *Statutory Interpretation* (3rd edn. 1988) for a more exhaustive coverage than we can provide here.[236] Nonetheless, we will touch on some of the most significant areas in which the Courts have used presumptions to protect civil and political rights.

Not all of the presumptions are subcategories of the presumption not to invade common law rights. A Court interpreting a statute will, if relevant and unless there is clear indication to the contrary, presume that Parliament did not intend to violate international law (including Conventions that Australia has acceded to), did not intend to interfere with vested proprietary interests (or to alienate them without adequate compensation), and did not intend to oust the jurisdiction of the Courts.[237] The Court will presume that a statute does not have a retrospective operation 'unless the intention appears with reasonable certainty'.[238] It will assume that mens rea is an essential ingredient of an offence in a penal provision unless there are indications that Parliament intended otherwise.[239]

The presumption against invasion of common law rights has been invoked to uphold a wide range of rights. The presumption is currently described as: 'the general principle that a statute will not be construed to take away a common law right unless the legislative intent to do so clearly emerges, whether by express words or by necessary implication.'[240]

The Courts have for a long time inclined against finding that there are express words or a necessary implication which remove a right. The usual approach has been that enunciated by O'Connor J. in *Sargood Bros* v. *Commonwealth*: 'an Act will never be construed as taking away an existing right *unless its language is reasonably capable of no other construction.*'[241]

Similarly, in *Melbourne Corporation* v. *Barry*[242] Higgins J. observed that 'any interference with a common law right cannot be justified except by statute—by express words or necessary implication'—and then construed that

---

[234] Tremblay n. 37 above at 242.

[235] Ibid. See also Pearce and Geddes, *Statutory Interpretation* (3rd edn., 1988), 97.

[236] Pearce and Geddes, ibid. As will become apparent, we derived considerable assistance from this book when preparing this part of the Chapter. See also *Wentworth* v. *NSW Bar Association* (1992) 176 CLR 239 at 252.

[237] See Pearce and Geddes n. 235 above, ch. 5.

[238] *Maxwell* v. *Murphy* (1957) 96 CLR 261 at 267 per Dixon C.J.

[239] See *Sweet* v. *Parsley* [1970] AC 132 and *He Kaw Teh* v. *R.* (1985) 157 CLR 523.

[240] *Pyneboard Pty Ltd* v. *Trade Practices Commission* (1982–3) 152 CLR 328 at 341 per Mason C.J., Wilson and Dawson J.J.

[241] (1910) 11 CLR 258 at 279.

[242] *Melbourne Corporatioin* v. *Barry* (1922) 31 CLR 174 at 206 in relation to the common law 'right' to take part in processions.

test as meaning that: 'If a statute is capable of being interpreted without sup-
posing that it interferes with the common law right, it should be so interpreted.'[243]

In more recent cases, the Courts have usually adhered to this strict
approach against statutory interference with common law rights. For example, in *Tassell* v. *Hayes* Mason, Wilson and Dawson J.J. stated firmly that the
right of a defendant in a criminal case to be tried by jury should 'not be diminished save by language which is reasonably capable of no other construction'.[244] Deane J. said that legislative provisions modifying or abolishing the
right 'should be strictly construed in favour of the accused'.[245] And recently
in *Coco* v. *R.* the High Court emphasised that a common law right such as the
right to exclude all unauthorised persons from premises may only be abrogated or curtailed by 'unmistakable and unambiguous language'.[246]

Even the weight to be given to second reading speeches—to Parliament's
spoken intention—may be slight when compared to the power of the presumption against invasion of common law rights. Mason C.J., Wilson and
Dawson J.J. took this view in a fascinating judgment in *Re Bolton, ex parte
Beane*.[247] In that case the Court was asked to decide whether Section 19 of the
Defence (Visiting Forces) Act 1963 (Cth) authorised the arrest in Australia of
a deserter or absentee without leave from the armed forces of the USA—
where the deserting or absenting had occurred outside Australia. Mason C.J.,
Wilson and Dawson J.J. agreed that since Section 19 was ambiguous as to the
latter point, consideration should be given to the second reading speech:
Section 15AB of the Acts Interpretation Act 1901 (Cth) said so. The speech,
they conceded, 'unambiguously asserts that [the relevant provision] . . . relates
to deserters and absentees whether or not they are from a visiting force'.[248]
Nonetheless, in their judgment, the second reading speech whilst 'available as
an aid to interpretation',[249] could not of itself be determinative. That was
because in a case in which one interpretation of a statute would invade a common law right, the Court's task was to apply the presumption against invasion
to the express words before them—*not* to inquire into what Parliament actually intended (even when this intention was clear from extrinsic material):

The words of a Minister must not be substituted for the text of the law. Particularly
is this so when the intention stated by the Minister but unexpressed in the law is

---

[243] Ibid. See also *R.* v. *Snow* (1915) 20 CLR 315 at 322 where Griffith C.J. stated that
only 'the clearest language' in a statute could displace 'the common law effect of a verdict of
acquittal'.
[244] (1987) 163 CLR 34 at 41. The majority cited *Sargood Bros* n. 241 above at 279 per
O'Connor J.
[245] *Tassell* v. *Hayes Mason* n. 244 above at 50.
[246] *Coco* v. *R.* n. 55 above at 436–8 per Mason C.J., Brennan, Gaudron and McHugh J.J., 446
per Deane and Dawson J.J.
[247] (1987) 162 CLR 514.
[248] (1987) 162 CLR 514 at 518.   [249] Ibid.

restrictive of the liberty of the individual . . . The function of the Court is to *give effect to the will of Parliament as expressed in the law.*[250]

Brennan J. and Deane J. took the same approach in their judgments: in summary, if no clear legislative intent to derogate from a fundamental right or freedom is evident from the provisions of the Act, then, 'notwithstanding Section 15AB of the Acts Interpretation Act, the second reading speech of the responsible Minister cannot supply the deficiency'.[251]

However, it seems to us that in the area of the privilege against self-incrimination, the High Court has been more willing to find that a statute evinces a clear intention on the part of Parliament to abrogate a common law right. In *Pyneboard*[252] Mason A.C.J., Wilson and Dawson J.J. held that the presumption against removal of the privilege would be overridden where 'it appears from the character and purpose of the provision'[253] that Parliament intended to impose on a witness an unqualified obligation to answer questions. Their Honours considered that such a legislative intention is clear:

when the object of imposing the obligation is to ensure the full investigation in the public interest of matters involving the possible commission of offences which lie peculiarly within the knowledge of persons who cannot reasonably be expected to make their knowledge available otherwise than under a statutory obligation.[254]

This approach of inquiring into the 'object' of the provision seems to depart from the strict approach usually taken by the courts when applying the presumption against removal of common law rights. *Pyneboard* indicates that in the absence of express words the privilege against self-incrimination will be abrogated when the Court considers that Parliament *must have* intended such abrogation—even though the converse argument is also plausible. This takes the concept of 'necessary implication' further than it has been taken before. A provision which imposes an obligation on a witness to answer questions does not, in our view, *necessarily* oust a right to rely on the privilege against self-incrimination in relation to incriminatory questions—since the provision is 'reasonably capable' of being interpreted as imposing an obligation which is subject to the privilege.

In relation to the privilege against self-incrimination, therefore, the High Court seems to have turned its focus to identifying the mischief that the legislation was designed to avoid. We suspect that this focus is confined to this area, since *Tassell* v. *Hayes*,[255] *Re Bolton, ex parte Beane*,[256] and *Coco* v. *R*[257]

---

[250] Ibid. (emphasis added).

[251] Ibid. at 532 per Deane J. The 'fundamental principle relating to the freedom of the subject' was that 'subject to extradition and migration legislation, every person coming from abroad, as soon as he sets foot in Australia, without breach of Australian law, is free'. Ibid. at 532.

[252] *Pyneboard Pty Ltd* v. *Trade Practices Commission* (1983) 152 CLR 328.

[253] Ibid. at 341.   [254] Ibid.

[255] *Tassell* v. *Hayes-Mason* n. 244 above.

[256] *Re Bolton, ex parte Beane* n. 247 above.   [257] *Coco* v. *R.* n. 55 above.

are later cases. Perhaps the Court is applying a different standard to the protection of rights—and in weighing the importance of the countervailing public interests—when such issues arise within the context of corporate regulation. In any event, the end result of such attempts by the Courts to divine Parliamentary intent may be a loss in predicability, an increased uncertainty as to the way in which the Courts will interpret a particular statute.

The final issue that we will mention in the context of statutory interpretation is that of the Courts' use of treaties such as the International Covenant. We have said that there is a presumption against violation of international law:[258] nonetheless, 'the Courts are bound by the statute law of [the] . . . country, even if that law should violate a rule of international law'.[259]

A number of Australian judges have acknowledged that the Courts may refer to international instruments to assist them in resolving statutory ambiguities.[260] Certainly, the English courts have now accepted this as a legitimate—even an obligatory—area of influence for the European Convention. Whilst reference to the Convention is regarded as 'unnecessary or inappropriate' where the common law or statutory provision under consideration is 'clear and unambiguous', the English courts have recently accepted that they should apply Convention principles and case law where the law is ambiguous, 'otherwise unclear', or 'undeclared by an appellate Court'.[261]

Since Brennan J.'s emphasis in *Mabo* on the influence of international law on the common law,[262] it seems likely that our Courts will more frequently turn to the principles set out in the International Covenant to help them resolve uncertainties in both the common law and statute law. However, if

---

[258] '[E]very statute is to be so interpreted and applied, as far as its language admits, as not to be inconsistent with the comity of nations or with the established rules of international law.' *Polites* v. *Commonwealth* (1945) 70 CLR 60 at 69 per Latham C.J. See also *Daemar* v. *Industrial Commission of New South Wales* (1988) 79 ALR 591 at 599 per Kirby P.

[259] *Polites* v. *Commonwealth* (1945) 70 CLR 60.

[260] For example, see *Jago* n. 209 above at 582 per Samuels J.A. (cited with approval in *Re Jane* (1988–89) 85 ALR 409 at 42 per Nicholson L.J.); *Cachia* v. *Hanes*, n. 208 above at 313 per Kirby P; *Dietrich* v. *R.* n. 23 above at 348–9 per Dawson J., 306 per Mason C.J. and McHugh J. ('assuming, without deciding'); *Lim and Others* v. *Minister for Immigration, Local Government and Ethnic Affairs and Another* (1992) 172 CLR 1 at 38 per Brennan, Deane and Dawson J.J.

[261] *Derbyshire County Council* v. *Times Newspapers Ltd* [1992] QB 770 at 830 per Butler-Sloss L.J. (Court of Appeal). See also *Re M and H* [1990] 1 AC 686 at 721 per Lord Brandon in relation to the first point, and R. v. *Secretary of State for the Home Department, ex parte Brind* [1991] 1 AC 696 at 718 per Donaldson MR (Court of Appeal), 747–8 per Lord Bridge (House of Lords) in relation to the second point. In addition, the Court of Appeal has recently decided that it should 'give proper weight' to jurisprudence on Article 10 of the European Convention when exercising its statutory discretion to interfere with excessive or inadequate awards of damages by juries: *Rantzen* v. *Mirror Group Newspapers (1986) Ltd* [1994] QB 670 at 692. However, note also the ambivalent attitude of Lord Keith (with whom the other judges concurred)—at least in relation to reliance upon the Convention in developing the *common* law—in *Derbyshire County Council* v. *Times Newspapers* [1993] AC 534 at 551.

[262] *Mabo* n. 19 above at 42.

English case law is any indication,[263] they may continue to assert that an administrative decision-maker is not under any obligation to have regard to the principles expressed in international treaties when exercising his or her discretion. This would be so whether or not the decision-maker was exercising the discretion under statute.

It is of course well established at common law that treaties, being made by the Executive, are not self-executing: 'they do not give rights or impose duties on members of the Australian community unless their provisions are given effect by statute'.[264] In *Kioa*[265] it was argued that a decision-maker exercising discretion under a statute (such as the Migration Act 1958 (Cth)) was nevertheless obliged to consider the provisions of the International Covenant, since the preamble to the Human Rights Commission Act 1981 (Cth) stated that:

it is desirable that the laws of the Commonwealth and the conduct of persons administering those laws should conform with the provisions of the International Covenant on Civil and Political Rights, the Declaration of the Rights of the Child . . . and other international instruments relating to human rights and freedoms.

However the argument was decisively rejected. Gibbs C.J., Wilson and Brennan J.J. reaffirmed the principle that 'treaties do not have the force of law unless they are given that effect by statute',[266] and decided that the words of the preamble to the Act 'did not have the effect of making the Covenant and the Declaration part of Australian municipal law'.[267] As a result, there was no legal obligation on the part of the decision-maker to ensure that the decision conformed with the Covenant or the Declaration.[268]

Nonetheless, it is probably fair to say that as Australian Courts become more conscious of the importance of the rights and principles set out in the International Covenant and other treaties, these principles cannot be 'safely

---

[263] *Brind*, n. 261 above at 718 per Lord Donaldson M.R., and in the House of Lords at 748 per Lord Bridge, 761–2 per Lord Ackner.

[264] *Koowarta* v. *Bjelke-Petersen* (1982) 153 CLR 168 per Gibbs C.J.

[265] *Kioa* v. *West* (1985) 159 CLR 550.   [266] Ibid. at 570 per Gibbs C.J.

[267] Ibid. In relation to the Human Rights and Equal Opportunity Commission Act 1986 (Cth) ('HREOC Act') which is now in force—and which does not contain such a preamble—Nicholson C.J. initially remarked: 'If there ever was an opportunity to expressly incorporate these instruments into domestic law, it was presented by the Human Rights and Equal Opportunity Commission Act and Parliament chose not to do so.' *Re Jane* (1988–89) 85 ALR 409 at 425. As mentioned above, a year or so later in *Re Marion* n. 210 at above 449–51 Nicholson C.J. recanted and instead considered that it was 'strongly arguable' that the HREOC Act and its schedules implied that the rights and principles set out in the scheduled instruments are incorporated into Australian law. The High Court did not discuss the issue on appeal; see n. 187 above. However, it is clear from the judgments in *Dietrich* v. *R.* that the Court does not subscribe to this view. See *Dietrich* n. 23 above at 305 per Mason C.J. and McHugh J., 321 per Brennan J., 348 per Dawson J., 360 per Toohey J.

[268] *Kioa* v. *West* n. 265 above at 570 per Gibbs C.J., 630 per Brennan J. However see *Sezdirmezoglu* v. *Acting Minister for Immigration & Ethnic Affairs* (1983–4) 51 ALR 575 at 578 per Smithers J.

... ignored by a decision-maker'.[269] Whilst the High Court judges in *Kioa* rejected the notion that there was an *obligation* on the decision-maker to take the Covenant into account, they nonetheless paused to consider the application of the relevant principles to the case before them. And in the recent case of *Teoh*, the Federal Court came close to (but avoided) deciding that an administrative decision-maker has an obligation to apply such principles.[270] The Court held that parents and children have a legitimate expectation that a decision-maker, when exercising administrative powers which affect children, will apply or take into account the provisions of the United Nations Convention on the Rights of the Child which has been ratified by Australia.[271] Further, it held that where a decision-maker has failed to meet that legitimate expectation, his or her decision may be set aside on the basis that there has been a failure to accord procedural fairness, or some other error of law.

Express Constitutional Protection ('the Third Method')

There are a handful of provisions in the Commonwealth Constitution which would seem, on their face, to offer some protection to the civil and political rights of individuals. However the High Court has tended in the past to impose a narrow construction on provisions such as Sections 80, 116 and 117. (Section 51(xxxi), being concerned with property rights, has been interpreted widely.) As a result the protection afforded by the provisions has often been 'in truth illusory'.[272]

The Court's interpretation of Section 80 provides a remarkable illustration of this restrictive approach which 'ignor[es] substance in favour of form'.[273] Section 80 provides that the trial on indictment of any Commonwealth offence 'shall be by jury'. Although the common law has traditionally contemplated that a person who is charged with a serious offence will be tried on indictment, in *Kingswell* v. *R*[274] a majority of the Court adhered to the view

---

[269] *Lebanese Moslem Association* v. *Minister for Immigration and Ethnic Affairs* (1986) 67 ALR 195 at 205 per Pincus J. Nicholson C.J. seems to have been referring to public decision-makers when he said in *Re Jane* n. 267 above at 425, in relation to treaties like the International Covenant, that it is 'permissible' and 'useful to have regard to them in considering the exercise of discretion'.

[270] *Teoh* v. *Minister for Immigration, Local Government and Ethnic Affairs* (1994) 121 ALR 436. Carr J. described the ratification by Australia of the United Nations Convention on the Rights of the Child as 'part of the context in which Australian decision-makers have to determine how to carry out their duty to act fairly'. Ibid. at 466. See also ibid. at 443 per Black C.J., 450 per Lee J.

[271] Ibid. at 449–50 per Lee J., 466 per Carr J. See also ibid. at 443 per Black C.J. [Authors' note. This approach was endorsed by the High Court on appeal: see *Minister for Immigration and Ethnic Affairs* v. *Teoh* (1995) 128 ALR 353.]

[272] *R.* v. *Federal Court of Bankruptcy, ex parte Lowenstein* (1938) 59 CLR 556 at 582 per Dixon and Evatt J.J.

[273] *Street* v. *Queensland Bar Association* (1989–90) 168 CLR 461 at 523 per Deane J.

[274] (1985) 159 CLR 264.

taken in previous cases that 'there is nothing to compel procedure by indict-ment'.[275] As a result, the guarantee of trial by jury may be easily avoided.

Nonetheless, it seems that there is some prospect of the High Court taking a wider view of Sections 80, 116 and 117 of the Constitution in the future. In the past 5 or 10 years, the High Court has, as we have said, increasingly indi-cated a desire to make decisions which accord with contemporary values, including a greater respect for human rights and tolerance for the beliefs and practices of others. Mason A.C.J. and Brennan J.'s discussion of freedom of religion in *Church of the New Faith*, for example, emphasises that the guaran-tee in Section 116 is a 'bastion of freedom' which should protect a very wide range of beliefs and conduct.[276]

All the same, it is difficult to predict how well the Court will manage the sen-sitive balancing exercise which will be required when evaluating the validity of a law which obviously places restrictions on conduct which forms part of an individual's beliefs. In *Church of the New Faith* Mason A.C.J. and Brennan J. were not actually required to apply Section 116; nonetheless they formulated a test of invalidity which seems to require a Court to decide whether a partic-ular law can be characterised as a law about religion, rather than to engage in a balancing exercise which involves consideration of whether the restrictions imposed by a law are reasonable in our society.[277]

Secondly, the High Court's recent judgments indicate a new desire to isolate and give meaning to the object of constitutional provisions. This approach has given new life to Section 117 of the Constitution, which protects individuals from discrimination based upon residence in a particular State.[278] It seems to us that if such an object-based approach was applied to Section 80, the pro-tection afforded to the individual by that provision would also be widened. This would be so even if the Court continued to distinguish Section 117 from the other constitutional provisions on the basis that Section 117 is expressed as an individual guarantee whereas the other provisions are expressed as lim-itations on the powers of the Commonwealth or the States.[279]

---

[275] *R* v. *Archdall and Roskruge, ex parte Carrigan and Brown* (1928) 41 CLR 128 at 139–40 per Higgins J. This view was not challenged by the Court in *Brown* v. *R.* (1986) 160 CLR 171.

[276] *Church of the New Faith* v. *Commissioner for Payroll Tax (Vic)* (1982–83) 154 CLR 120 at 131–2.

[277] Ibid. at 136. See also the Court's failure to fully analyse the bases on which freedom of expression may be restricted in *Adelaide Company of Jehovah's Witnesses Inc* v. *Commonwealth* (1943) 67 CLR 116.

[278] In *Street* v. *Queensland Bar Association* (1989) 168 CLR 461 the Court overruled *Henry* v. *Boehm* (1973) 128 CLR 482. See also *Goryl* v. *Greyhound Australia Pty Ltd* (1993–94) 179 CLR 463. It remains to be seen whether Section 117 will, in the future, be interpreted as binding the Commonwealth as well as the States. In *Leeth* v. *Commonwealth* (1992) 174 CLR 455 the High Court found it unnecessary to decide this question.

[279] As Professor Zines points out in *The High Court and the Constitution* (3rd edn., 1992), 330, several of the judges in *Street* n. 278 above remarked on this difference in the way that Section 117 is expressed.

Other Constitutional Limitations on Legislative Power ('the Fourth Method')

Aside from the constitutional implication of freedom of political communication discussed below, the express constitutional guarantees are still the only means by which Australian Courts have invalidated legislative provisions on the basis that they infringe fundamental human rights. If an Australian Court was faced with a State law which took up Leslie Stephen's example and provided that 'all blue-eyed babies should be murdered',[280] it is unlikely that the Court would rely on the moral repugnance of the law to declare it invalid.[281]

Nonetheless, possible sources of limitation on legislative competence have been raised in various quarters. The dicta may be divided into two categories. The first category relates to the limitations imposed by the 'peace, welfare and good government' and 'peace, order and good government' formulae in the State and Commonwealth Constitutions. The second category of judicial dicta asserts that there are fundamental principles implicit in the Commonwealth Constitution or in our 'free and democratic society', or which are common law rights which 'lie so deep that even Parliament . . . [can] not override them'.[282]

The first possibility achieved a brief prominence after the NSW Court of Appeal gave judgment in the *BLF* case. Street C.J. took the view that the New South Wales Parliament has 'plenary or sovereign'[283] powers to legislate, but that its powers 'are circumscribed or limited by the requirement of the peace, welfare and good government of New South Wales'.[284] He said:

The limit may be wide and extensive. Ultimately, however, it is a binding limit. Laws inimical to, or which do not serve, the peace, welfare and good government of our parliamentary democracy, perceived in the sense that I have previously indicated, will be struck down by the Courts as unconstitutional.[285]

Street C.J. seems to be referring back to his statement that universal suffrage and 'fundamental constitutional principles' such as the independence of the judiciary are 'inherent . . . in the very substance of our parliamentary democracy'.[286] Presumably he would consider invalid any law which contravened such principles. Street C.J. gained some support for his view from Priestley J.A. who referred to Leslie Stephen's example of a morally repugnant statute, and said:

it is at least arguable that if a statute were ever passed of the kind referred to by Stephen then it would be open to a Court to hold that it was so manifestly not for the peace,

---

[280] Stephen, *Science of Ethics* (1882), 143 as cited in Dicey, *Introduction to the Study of the Law of the Constitution* (9th edn., 1948), 81.

[281] Cf. *BLF* case (1986) 7 NSWLR 372 at 420 per Priestley J.A. See also *Nationwide News Pty Ltd* v. *Wills* n. 157 above at 48 per Brennan J.

[282] *Taylor* v. *New Zealand Poultry Board* [1984] 1 NZLR 394 at 398 per Cooke J. as cited in the *BLF* case n. 281 above at 386 per Street C.J.

[283] Ibid. at 384. [284] Ibid. [285] Ibid. [286] Ibid. at 382–3.

order and good government of the State as to be ultra vires the written authority of the Parliament to make laws . . . [T]here is arguably greater scope for judges here to make a declaration of invalidity than would be open to judges in England.[287]

However, Mahoney J.A. rejected the argument that the 'peace order and good government' formulae represented a limitation on legislative power, Kirby P. doubted it, and Glass J.A. preferred to 'reserve his position' on the question.

In any event, the argument was short-lived. A unanimous full bench of the High Court declared in *Union Steamship* v. *King* that:

the words 'for the peace, order and good government' are not words of limitation. They . . . do not confer on the Courts of a State, jurisdiction to strike down legislation on the ground that, in the opinion of a Court, the legislation does not promote or secure the peace, order and good government of the colony . . . [T]he exercise of its legislative power by the Parliament of New South Wales is not susceptible to political review on that score.[288]

Nevertheless, the sentence which followed this passage in their Honours' judgment is of great interest. The Court continued: 'Whether the exercise of that legislative power is subject to some restraints by reference to rights deeply rooted in our democratic system of government and the common law . . . a view which Lord Reid firmly rejected in *Pickin* v. *British Railways Board*,[289] is another question. . .'[290]

The Court did not need to discuss that question. It referred to the various New Zealand cases in which Cooke P. had queried whether there are some common law rights which go 'so deep that even Parliament cannot be accepted by the Courts to have destroyed them'.[291] It then turned to consider another issue.

The remarkable thing is that the Court did not dismiss this possibility out of hand.[292] Such a suggestion would require a reconsideration of the long-accepted principle of Parliamentary supremacy. Nonetheless, thus far the cases have not shown the High Court to be receptive to such arguments.

Until recently, the High Court judges, with the exception of Murphy J., have not generally seen the Constitution as including implied freedoms or guarantees of individual rights.[293] The Court's theory that Section 92 guaranteed

---

[287] Ibid. at 421–2.   [288] (1988) 166 CLR 1 at 10.

[289] [1974] AC 765 at 782.   [290] *Union Steamship* v. *King* n. 288 above.

[291] *Fraser* v. *State Services Commission* [1984] 1 NZLR 116 at 121. See also the judgments of Cooke J. referred to in the *BLF* case n. 281 above at 404 per Kirby P.

[292] This issue of a possible non-constitutional source of limitation is discussed briefly in Zines, 'A Judicially Created Bill of Rights?', 16 Syd LR (1994) 166 at 180.

[293] One early exception, which was not taken up and applied by later Courts, was the implication of political access and communication recognised by Griffith C.J. and Barton J. in *R.* v. *Smithers, ex parte Benson* (1912) 16 CLR 99. Barton J., ibid. at 109–10 stated: 'the creation of a federal union with one Government and one Legislature in respect of national affairs assures to every free citizen the right of access to the institutions, and of due participation in the activities of the nation.'

'individual rights' was an exception to this trend, since the Court grafted an individual right onto the express words of that constitutional provision.[294] With *Cole* v. *Whitfield*[295] that theory has, of course, disappeared.

A new source of constitutional protection has, however, opened. In *Australian Capital Television Pty Ltd* v. *Commonwealth* ('ACTV')[296] and in *Nationwide News Pty Ltd* v. *Wills* ('*Nationwide News*')[297] a majority of the Court recognised that the principle of representative government (or representative democracy) which underlies and is recognised in the terms of the Constitution presupposes a freedom of communication in relation to political matters, at least during an election period and probably generally.[298]

In discerning an implication of representative government or representative democracy in the Constitution, most of the judges relied not only upon specific provisions in the Constitution,[299] but also upon those common law principles which form 'the fabric on which the written words of the Constitution are superimposed'.[300] Secondly, the judgments acknowledged that it was the common law which both 'informed' the Court that a reasonable degree of freedom of political communication was necessary for the effective operation of a system of representative government, and which provided guidance as to the extent of permissible limitations on the freedom.

As to the first point, the Court drew upon Australian, United Kingdom[301]

[294] It is apposite to recall Murphy J.'s criticism in *Buck* v. *Bavone* (1975–76) 135 CLR 10 at 132–3 of the dangers of a Court imposing its own economic or political philosophy in the absence of clear guidance by a constitutional provision. He quoted Lord Wright: 'The idea of Section 92 as a power in the air brooding and ready in the name of freedom to crush and destroy social and industrial or political experiments in Australian life ought, I think, to be exploded . . .'. Wright, 'Section 92—A Problem Piece', 1 Syd LR 146 at 157 (1954).

[295] (1988) 165 CLR 360.   [296] *ACTV* n. 148 above.

[297] *Nationwide News* n. 148 above.

[298] A majority of the Court appeared to consider that the Australian Constitution contains an 'independent' principle of representative government, from which other implications—such as an implied freedom of political communication—can be drawn. Dawson and McHugh JJ, on the other hand, regarded the provisions of the Constitution (in particular, sections 7 and 24), interpreted in light of background doctrines such as representative government, as the sole source of protection of communication for the purpose of the electoral process. The potential impact of the implied freedom recognised by the majority remains unclear. Brennan J put forward the following view: '[U]nlike freedoms conferred by a Bill of Rights in the American model, the freedom cannot be understood as a personal right the scope of which must be ascertained in order to discover what is left for legislative regulation; rather, it is a freedom of the kind for which Section 92 of the Constitution provides: an immunity consequent on a limitation of legislative power.' See *ACTV* n. 148 above at 150. [Authors' note: but see note 127 above.]

[299] Most notably, Sections 7 and 24 of the Constitution.

[300] *Commonwealth* v. *Kreglinger & Fernau Ltd & Barnsley* (1926) 37 CLR 393 at 413 per Isaacs J., as cited by Mason C.J. in *ACTV* n. 148 above at 135. Brennan J. in *Nationwide News* n. 148 above at 45 and Gaudron J. in *ACTV* n. 148 above at 209 cited the statement made by Sir Owen Dixon that 'constitutional questions should be considered and resolved in the context of the whole law, of which the common law . . . forms not the least essential part'. See Dixon 'The Common Law as an Ultimate Constitutional Foundation', 31 ALJ 240 at 245 (1957) reprinted in Dixon, *Jesting Pilate* (1965), 203 at 212–13.

[301] Most of the judges cited Lord Simon of Glaisdale in *Attorney-General* v. *Times Newspapers* [1974] AC 273 at 315.

and Canadian authorities in asserting that freedom of public discussion of political matters is essential to sustain a representative democracy. It held that such freedom must extend not only to communications between the electors and political candidates or representatives, but also to communications amongst members of society and by the media. With one exception,[302] it was not thought necessary to decide whether the principle of representative government also entails other freedoms, such as freedom of movement, freedom of association, and freedom of speech generally.[303]

Secondly, existing jurisprudence on the permissible limitations on freedom of speech generally was influential in many of the judgments in *ACTV* and *Nationwide News*. Each of the judges who recognised the existence of the implied freedom emphasised that the freedom was not absolute. As Mason C.J. put it, in all jurisdictions the guarantee of freedom of expression has been recognised as: 'but one element, though an essential element, in the constitution of "an ordered society", or a "society organised under and controlled by law'.'[304]

All recognised that it was 'necessary to weigh the competing public interests'.[305] Some proposed two levels of scrutiny of an impugned law, so that only those laws which could be characterised as targeting information and ideas generally, or political communications, would receive a high level of scrutiny. In the view of Mason C.J., legislation which fell into this category could only be upheld if the restriction on the freedom was based upon a 'compelling justification' and was 'reasonably necessary to achieve the competing public interest'.[306] McHugh J. also propounded a test of 'compelling justification' but did not explain how it was to be applied. He did, however, conclude in *ACTV* that Parliament could have adopted means which were 'less drastic' in order to achieve the public interest of eradicating undue influence in the political process. Gaudron J.'s test of infringement was more precise: she asked whether the law regulating political discourse was 'reasonably and appropriately adapted to achieve some end within the limits of' the head of power.[307] Brennan J. seemed to be advocating a lower level of Court supervision; in his view, the role of the Court is to declare 'whether a balance struck by Parliament is within or without the range of legitimate legislative choice'.[308]

By contrast, the test laid down by Deane and Toohey J.J. appears to lie at the other end of the spectrum of scrutiny, and to inject a greater level of subjectivity into the process of determining the permissibility of a restriction on freedom of political communication. Deane and Toohey J.J. took the view that legislation which falls within the 'stricter scrutiny' category will only be

---

[302] McHugh J. stated that a constitutional right of freedom of association was implicit in Sections 7 and 24 of the Constitution.

[303] See *ACTV* n. 148 above at 212 per Gaudron J. This was not discussed by the other judges.

[304] Ibid. at 142 per Mason C.J.   [305] Ibid. at 143.   [306] Ibid.

[307] Ibid. at 218.   [308] *Nationwide News* n. 148 above at 52.

upheld[309] if it is justified as being in the public interest for various reasons including the reasons that it does 'not go beyond what is reasonably necessary for the preservation of an ordered society or for the protection or vindication of the legitimate claims of individuals to live peacefully and with dignity in such a society'.[310] Like the tests applied by Mason C.J. and McHugh J., it is an approach which appears to scrutinise carefully not only the proportionality of the *means* of achieving the public interest asserted by Parliament, but also the legitimacy of the interest itself.

In any event, the issue raised by all of these tests is how a Court is to assess *whether* there is a competing public interest which may justify a restriction on the freedom, and what the *weight* and *scope* of that public interest may be. Here we must consider the impact of the common law background upon the application of the constitutional freedom.

One of the judgments in *ACTV* is particularly clear on this point. Gaudron J. said:

As the implied freedom is one that depends substantially on the general law, its limits are also marked out by the general law. Thus, in general terms, the laws which have developed to regulate speech, including the laws with respect to defamation, sedition, blasphemy, obscenity and offensive language, will indicate the kind of regulation that is consistent with the freedom of political discourse.[311]

McHugh J. agreed that such restrictive laws may be based upon a 'compelling justification'.[312] And in *Nationwide News* Brennan J. asserted that laws such as those on defamation and sedition 'strike an appropriate balance between the postulated freedom of discussion and the private or public interest which is protected by the curtailing of the freedom'.[313]

Mason, Deane and Toohey J.J. did not state a view on the matter. It is evident, however, that in relation to the particular legislation under consideration in *Nationwide News*, Deane and Toohey J.J. were in fact influenced by the balance of interests considered appropriate by the common law in the area of contempt of court. Nonetheless, they cautioned—wisely in our view—that it 'would be unwise and impracticable to seek to identify in advance the precise categories of prohibition or control which are consistent with the implication' of freedom of political communication.[314] In our view this is particularly so given that in Australia and the United Kingdom few statutory or common law rules restricting communication have ever been challenged on the ground of constituting an impermissible restriction on free speech, and none have ever been tested against the degree of political communication necessary for the operation of an effective representative democracy.

---

[309] Subject to their comments on the 'prima facie scope' of the implication: ibid. at 77.
[310] Ibid. at 77.
[311] *ACTV* n. 148 above at 217.
[312] Ibid. at 236.
[313] *Nationwide News* n. 148 above at 52.
[314] Ibid. at 76.

Other than the High Court's recent acceptance of an implied freedom of political communication, there have been only isolated judicial references to fundamental rights and principles 'implicit' in the Constitution. However some members of the High Court have indicated that they envisage the Constitution playing a greater role in protecting individual rights; for example in 1984 Deane J. asserted that: 'the provisions of the Constitution should properly be viewed as ultimately concerned with the governance and protection of the people from whom the artificial entities called Commonwealth and States derive their authority.'[315]

Deane J. and other members of the Court have said that one of the functions of Section 109 is to 'protect . . . the individual from the injustice of being subjected to the requirements of valid and inconsistent law of the Commonwealth and State Parliaments on the same subject'.[316] Linking Section 109 to the protection of individuals has added a new perspective to a long-standing body of law.

In the recent case of *Leeth* v. *Commonwealth*[317] Deane and Toohey J.J. took this theme of constitutional protection for individuals further. Referring to the well-known implication set out in *Queensland Electricity Commission* v. *Commonwealth*,[318] which prevents Commonwealth laws from discriminating against the States, they said:

[I]t would be somewhat surprising if the Constitution, which is concerned with matters of substance, embodied a general principle which protected the States and their instrumentalities from being singled out by Commonwealth laws for discriminatory treatment but provided no similar protection of the people who constitute the Commonwealth and the States.[319]

Deane and Toohey J.J. went on to find that the 'equality of all persons under the law and before the Courts' was a fundamental doctrine of the common law which existed and was fully recognised at the time that the Constitution was passed.[320] In their view various provisions in the Constitution supported the conclusion that the Constitution adopted this doctrine of legal equality 'as a matter of necessary implication'.[321] For example, the existence of a number of specific provisions preventing discrimination in certain contexts made 'manifest rather than undermine[d] the status of [the] doctrine as an underlying principle of the Constitution as a whole'.[322]

However, with the possible exception of Brennan J, the other members of

---

[315] *University of Wollongong* v. *Metwally* (1984) 158 CLR 447 at 477.
[316] Ibid.   [317] *Leeth* v. *Commonwealth* (1992) 174 CLR 455.
[318] (1985) 159 CLR 192.   [319] *Leeth* n. 317 above at 484.
[320] Ibid. at 486. See discussion of their judgment in Zines n. 292 above at 181–3.
[321] *Leeth* n. 317 above.
[322] Ibid. at 28. For example, Sections 86, 88, 90, 51(ii), 51(iii), 99, 92, 24, 25 and 67 of the Constitution. In their view, it was inappropriate here to invoke the rule of *expressio unius exclusio alterius*.

the Court in *Leeth* did not favour a general implication of 'equal protection under the law'. In a joint judgment Mason C.J., Dawson J. and McHugh J. stated firmly that no general implication could be drawn from the Constitution 'that Commonwealth laws must not be discriminatory or must operate uniformly throughout the Commonwealth'.[323]

Brennan J.'s judgment, on the other hand, included examples of impermissible discrimination which indicated that he had some sympathy for a constitutional implication.[324] However his judgment was more concerned with the practicalities of handling federal offenders in State Courts and State prisons—practicalities which would often justify discrimination. Gaudron J. did not consider whether there is a general implication of legal equality. Instead she decided that the law under consideration was invalid because it required a Court exercising federal jurisdiction under Section 71 of the Constitution to treat people unequally and thus to do something which was not part of the judicial power of the Commonwealth. In her view a Court exercising that judicial power must apply 'the concept of equal justice'.[325]

And so, *Leeth* has pushed the frontiers further towards a more 'individual rights' focus to constitutional interpretation—but has left in a state of some uncertainty the specific issue of whether the Constitution is subject to an underlying implication of 'equal protection under the law'. On the latter issue, Deane and Toohey J.J. took the opportunity to more fully develop remarks made by them in earlier cases.[326] Together with Brennan J. and Gaudron J., they relied upon various provisions in the Constitution (or, in Brennan J.'s case, its preamble), to support restrictive implications of various types. Mason C.J., Dawson J. and McHugh J., on the other hand, countered that the specific provisions of the Constitution do not support any general implication against discrimination in the application of Commonwealth laws.

To summarise, it seems likely at this stage that a majority of the High Court takes the view that constitutional implications should only be derived from the 'frame' or 'structure' of the Constitution (in addition to the text of the Constitution) where the implication is a doctrine of government which is 'logically or practically necessary for the preservation of the integrity of that structure'.[327] The main doctrines of this type are perceived to be the principles of responsible government, representative government or representative democracy, a federal system, and the separation of legislative, executive and

---

[323] Ibid. at 7 and 8.   [324] Ibid. at 16.

[325] Leeth n. 317 above 44 and 45.

[326] In *Queensland Electricity* n. 318 above at 247–8, Deane J. said that the words of the Constitution may contain an implication of the 'underlying equality of the people of the Commonwealth under the law of the Constitution'. In *Street* n. 278 above at 554, Toohey J. interpreted Section 117 of the Constitution as indicating that Australia's laws are 'to apply equally to all its citizens'. These statements by Deane J. and Toohey J. are noted by Zines n. 279 above at 335.

[327] *ACTV* n. 148 above per Mason C.J. at 135.

judicial powers.[328] They are not perceived to include guarantees of individual rights.

In our view, most members of the Court would agree with Mason C.J. that:

it is difficult, if not impossible, to establish a foundation for the implication of general guarantees of fundamental rights and freedoms. To make such an implication would run counter to the prevailing sentiment of the framers that there was no need to incorporate a comprehensive Bill of Rights in order to protect the rights and freedoms of citizens.[329]

The Court has not adopted the view taken by Murphy J. that other constitutional implications which are 'at least as important' as the doctrines of government mentioned above arise 'from the nature of Australian society'.[330] Murphy J. regarded the Court as having the power to strike down legislation which contravened implied rights such as freedom of speech and movement, and implied prohibitions on slavery and serfdom, and on cruel and unusual punishment.[331] The High Court denied the existence of these rights in *Miller* v. *TCN Channel Nine*,[332] decided in 1986.

Nonetheless, the decisions in *ACTV* and *Nationwide News* have opened up a significant area for future development of rights and freedoms. Whilst the Court has not embraced Murphy J.'s approach to constitutional implications, it has emphasised the importance of protecting those rights which are necessary to the effective operation of a system of representative government. On the facts in *ACTV* and *Nationwide News* the Court was able to confine its attention to the rights of political communication necessary for an election process, and to the right to criticise Government processes and institutions (including the judiciary). However, it is evident from some of the judgments that the implication of representative government or democracy may carry with it other rights: 'The notion of a free society governed in accordance with the principles of representative parliamentary democracy may entail freedom of movement, freedom of association and, perhaps, freedom of speech generally.'[333]

And so we have witnessed, during the past few years, the emergence of this

---

[328] Ibid. See also *Nationwide News* n. 148 above at 69–70 per Deane J.

[329] *ACTV* n. 148 above at 136. A number of the judgments in *ACTV* and *Nationwide News* cite the following passage written by Professor Harrison Moore in 1901 in relation to the Constitution: 'The great underlying principle is, that the rights of individuals are sufficiently secured by ensuring, as far as possible, to each a share, and an equal share, in political power'. See Moore, *The Constitution of the Commonwealth of Australia* (1st edn., 1902), 329.

[330] *Australian Communist Party* v. *Commonwealth* (1951) 83 CLR 1 at 193, as cited by Murphy J. in *Miller* v. *TCN Channel Nine* (1986) 161 CLR 556 at 581.

[331] See *McGraw-Hinds (Aust) Pty Ltd* v. *Smith* (1979) 144 CLR 633 at 670 per Murphy J. and *Miller* v. *TCN Channel Nine* (1986) 161 CLR 556 at 581.

[332] (1986) 161 CLR 556.

[333] *ACTV* n. 148 above at 212 per Gaudron J. See also ibid. at 227 per McHugh J: 'the proper conclusion to be drawn from the terms of ss. 7 and 24 of the Constitution is that the people of Australia have constitutional rights of freedom of participation, association and communication

new area of constitutional protection, together with a recognition by some judges that the common law rights to a fair trial and to 'equality under the law' should be afforded constitutional protection. In our view we are witnessing a significant change in the High Court's attitude towards its ability to protect common law rights.

There are many points to be made about the issues of whether the courts *should* strike down legislation for contravening rights which they see as 'fundamental', and whether accession to international treaties guaranteeing rights should make a difference. This article does not attempt to survey the various arguments, many of which are addressed in other chapters in this volume. However we want to say something about these matters because of the degree of judicial creativity that would be involved if the Courts were to take on the role of identifying which rights were 'fundamental' in this sense.

First, it is rather remarkable to find that there are judges in Australia and New Zealand who are willing to challenge the doctrine of Parliamentary supremacy, despite the fact that the doctrine has been accepted almost without exception for nearly 300 years. This represents a very significant change in judicial attitude. In the *BLF* case,[334] for example, each of the five judges gave due consideration to the arguments put to them which challenged the doctrine. Street C.J. (and perhaps also Priestly J.A.) agreed with the 'peace, order and good government' argument. Yet, as one writer has pointed out, '20 years ago any counsel daring to make such a submission would have got short shrift from the Court'.[335]

The High Court in *Union Steamship*[336] rejected outright any possibility of reliance on the 'peace, order and good government' formulae. Nonetheless, as we have said, it did not reject out of hand the suggestion that the exercise of legislative power is subject to constraints imposed by 'rights deeply rooted in our democratic system of government and the common law'.[337] On the other hand, only Murphy J. in Australia and Cooke P. in New Zealand have sustained arguments *in* favour of such a contention.

Secondly, it is interesting to consider *why* our judges have become more receptive both to challenges to the doctrine of Parliamentary supremacy, and to the idea of finding in the Constitution new sources of rights and freedoms. It seems to us that there is a variety of reasons. We have already mentioned them as reasons for changes in the Courts' attitude to protecting rights generally. In brief, the judiciary is more conscious of rights, and more willing to give

in relation to federal elections.' Note that this Chapter was revised prior to delivery of the High Court's judgments in the cases of *Theophanous* v. *Herald and Weekly Times*, *Stephens* v. *WA Newspapers Ltd*, and *Cunliffe* v. *Commonwealth*. These judgments provide further indications of the scope of the constitutional protection that may be implicit in the doctrines of representative government and representative democracy. The judgments are reported at (1994) 124 ALR 1, (1994) 124 ALR 80 and (1994) 124 ALR 120 respectively.

[334] See *BLF* case n. 281 above.
[335] Zines n. 26 above at 49.
[336] See *Union Steamship* n. 288 above.
[337] Ibid.

effect to them where possible. It is more aware of the articles of the International Convention and of the way in which rights are protected in other systems of law. Perhaps some judges are reacting to the political reality of power being concentrated in the hands of the Executive rather than in the Legislature,[338] and some are recognising that even the Legislature in a democratic society does not aim to protect the rights of all individuals in that society.

The fundamental issue is, *should* the Courts have power to identify (or create) rights which are 'fundamental', and to invalidate legislation which contravenes them? Our hesitation in accepting that they should is not because we agree with the suggestion that the individual's recourse to the ballot-box—the 'democratic nature of our Parliamentary institutions'—and the Courts' techniques of statutory interpretation, sufficiently protect the individual 'from an oppressive majority in Parliament'.[339] We hesitate because in Australia not only is there no mandate from the people to strike down legislation on this basis, but also there are no democratically sanctioned guidelines (such as a Bill of Rights) which would indicate to a Court the rights that are to be protected in this way. We share Professor Zines' concern that judges should not, in this respect, 'be given . . . a blank cheque',[340] because:

[t]o accept only 'peace, welfare and good government' (as Street CJ does) or 'a free and democratic society' (as Murphy J did) or 'deeply held common law principles' (as Cooke P does) as the starting point in reasoning is to invite a judge to discover in the Constitution his or her own broad political philosophy.[341]

Parallels may be drawn between a judge in Australia performing such a role, and the role played by the United States Supreme Court in identifying as 'fundamental' various rights which are not set out in the American Constitution.[342] For example, criticism has been levelled at the United States Supreme Court for its decisions in *Griswold* and *Roe* v. *Wade*.[343] In these

---

[338] Zines n. 26 above at 35. This point has particular force in the 'Executive paradise' of New Zealand: Zines ibid. at 47.

[339] See *BLF* case n. 281 above at 405 per Kirby P.

[340] Zines n. 26 above at 52. See also *Grace Bible Church* v. *Reedman* (1984) 36 SASR 376 at 386 per White J: 'If the Court could substitute its own opinion for the Parliament's opinion as to what is a law for the peace, welfare and good government of the State (or if a judge could uphold every man's opinion that a particular law was invalid because it was not a good law) we would not be living under the rule of law but in a state of chaos.'

[341] Ibid. Note also the distinction that Professor Zines draws between implications of 'federalism' and 'responsible government', on the one hand, and those of 'fundamental rights' on the other. See Zines n. 279 above at 338–9.

[342] Zines n. 26 above at 52–3 makes this point, and mentions *Lochner* v. *New York* 198 US (105). It seems to us that the real issue for Holmes J. (dissenting) in that case was not his point that the majority had decided the case 'upon an economic theory which a large part of the country [did] . . . not entertain', but the issue of 'whether judges should engage in any search for fundamental rights, even if what they find *does* reflect a popular consensus'. Shattuck, *Rights of Privacy* (1977), 95.

[343] *Griswold* v. *Connecticut* 381 US 479 (1965); *Roe* v. *Wade* 410 US 113 (1973).

cases, a majority of the Court recognised a right of personal privacy—despite the fact that the American Constitution 'does not explicitly mention any right of privacy'.[344] Of course any Court charged with the task of applying an entrenched Bill of Rights must strike courageously out into the ocean of principle, and will be required to make constant value judgments about what is encompassed by each right. Such a Court is seen much more clearly as an integral part of the overall political process. Nonetheless, even here there are cogent arguments for limiting the scope of the Court's powers. That limitation is to be found in the express words of the democratically-sanctioned Bill of Rights. In the view of Judge Learned Hand a judge should not go further and take on the role of 'communal mentor' in the belief that the 'Courts may light the way to a saner world'.[345]

Conclusion

Despite our excursion into the creative realm of implied constitutional (and other) limitations, the focus of this article has been not on this area or on express constitutional guarantees. The focus has been on the first two methods by which the common law protects human rights: that is, its recognition of rights in 'pure' common law areas, and its rules of statutory interpretation.

In the 'pure' common law areas the High Court has indicated in recent times both that it is generally more 'rights conscious', and also that it is increasingly willing to expand the content of established rights. On the other hand, the Court so far seems unlikely to take on the role of discovering new rights such as a right of privacy. Nonetheless the Court's attitude in *Mabo* indicates that significant change is in the air: three members of the Court emphasised the importance of the rights set out in the International Covenant,[346] and at least five of the judges would seem to agree with Brennan J. that: 'no case can command unquestioning adherence if the rule it expresses seriously offends the values of justice and human rights . . . which are aspirations of the contemporary Australian legal system.'[347]

There are limits to how far the common law can go. Insofar as such limits are a matter of attitude and traditions of reasoning, there are clear signs of change. We believe that most would regard this as a change for the good. However, other limits are posed by the principle of Parliamentary supremacy, and by the constraints on judicial law-making involved in interpreting a written

---

[344] *Roe* v. *Wade*, ibid.
[345] Hand n. 34 above at 70–1.
[346] Brennan J., with whom Mason C.J. and McHugh J. agreed.
[347] *Mabo* n. 19 above at 30 per Brennan J. (with whom Mason C.J. and McHugh J. agreed). See also ibid. at 109 and 120 per Deane and Gaudron J.J.; cf. ibid. at 145 per Dawson J.

Constitution. Here too, there are signs of change, but this is change which raises fundamental issues about the role of the judiciary in our society.

We have no doubt that the common law can and will go further than it has, and can do so in an evolutionary manner reflecting changes in our society. But we now also need to resolve the issue of whether our Courts are to take us along a more radical path which leads to the Courts identifying fundamental rights or freedoms which can invalidate legislation.

We conclude with one final point. The role of the common law in protecting human rights is very much in the hands of lawyers, since the development of the common law generally is uniquely dominated by lawyers. This does not imply that contributions from non-lawyers are not welcomed or, indeed, essential for healthy growth. However it is the lawyers in the Courts who argue the law and declare the law. If the common law is to retain its relevance to the society in which it operates by actively protecting human rights, then the training and patterns of thought of our lawyers require some reconsideration, so that they may be better equipped to think, reason and argue in terms of rights.

3

Basic Laws as a Surrogate Bill of Rights: The Case of Israel

DAVID KRETZMER

A. Background

Israel was for a long time regarded as one of the few countries which, like the United Kingdom, had neither a formal constitution nor a bill of rights. The 1948 Declaration of Independence announced that the new state's constitution would be drawn up by an elected constituent assembly. After its election, however, the Assembly transformed itself into the Knesset, Israel's Parliament, and adoption of the constitution was delayed. Under a Knesset resolution of 1950 it was decided that the state's formal constitution would be drawn up on the basis of a series of basic laws. Pursuant to this resolution, basic laws were enacted, covering virtually all aspects of Israel's system of government. But until 1992 a basic law on civil liberties or human rights was not included among them.

Lack of a basic law on human rights was by no means an oversight. Attempts made over the years by members of the Knesset, the Knesset Constitution and Law Committee, and Ministers of Justice to facilitate passage of such a basic law met with political opposition, mainly from the religious political parties. These parties, which have held the balance of power in Israel's coalition system almost without interruption since independence, feared that a bill of rights would open the way to judicial review of legislation which enforced religious norms at the expense of individual freedoms and rights. The principal examples of such legislation are laws regarding religious marriage and Sabbath observance.

In the final session of the outgoing Knesset prior to the 1992 elections, two basic laws concerning human rights were finally adopted: the Basic Law—Freedom of Occupation, and the Basic Law—Human Dignity and Liberty.[1] The impetus for these Basic Laws emerged from the realization that, while enactment of a general bill of rights may be impossible for political reasons, it might be feasible to pass a bill covering those rights that are not considered politically controversial. Thus, the first basic law on human rights introduced in Israel concerns a right that is not specifically referred to in many constitutions and human rights instruments, namely the 'freedom of occupation' or,

---

[1] A translation of the Basic Laws appears at the end of this chapter.

in other words, the freedom to pursue the vocation of one's choosing. The second basic law concerns a range of rights under the general rubric of 'human dignity and liberty'.

The assumption that the issues raised by the right to freedom of occupation are not controversial, especially when it comes to the relationship between State and religion, did not stand the test of time. Shortly after enactment of the original version of the Basic Law—Freedom of Occupation, the Supreme Court ruled that import restrictions on meat on the grounds of *kashrut* (i.e., that the meat fails to comply with the dietary laws of the Jewish religion) violated the freedom of occupation.[2] Demands by religious parties for a 'remedy' to the situation, through the introduction of ordinary legislation, were blocked by this Basic Law. The political solution was to re-enact the Basic Law, enabling inclusion of a provision that would allow for a parliamentary override of its restrictions. Additional amendments were introduced during this process, not only to the Basic Law—Freedom of Occupation, but also to the Basic Law—Human Dignity and Liberty. Paradoxically, these amendments may strengthen the arguments in favour of a judicial interpretation of the Basic Laws, thus extending their application to rights that were intentionally omitted.

B. The Status of Human Rights Prior to the Basic Laws

A bill of rights fulfils at least one of three normative functions in a legal system. Its first, and most obvious, function is to define those basic rights that are recognized and protected by the system. The second is to delimit the scope of protection of recognized rights by setting standards for decisions on whether, and when, they may legitimately be restricted. The final function is to establish the constitutional status of the recognized rights, by determining whether legislation that is inconsistent with specific rights may be invalidated by a court or other constitutional bodies.

The lack of a formal constitution or bill of rights does not mean that human rights had no status in Israel's legal system prior to enactment of these Basic Laws. In a long line of decisions, starting with Justice Agranat's landmark decision in the *Kol Ha'am* case,[3] the Supreme Court created what may be terms a 'judicial bill of rights'. Fundamental rights, as recognized in other democratic countries, enjoy the status of 'soft legal principles', as the author has elsewhere termed them.[4] They are *legal* principles because government authorities cannot restrict them without express statutory authority, all authorities must be guided by them in interpretation of statutes, and because

---

[2] See *Mitrael Ltd.* v. *Minister of Commerce and Industry* (1993) 27 P.D.(i) 521.
[3] See *Kol Ha'am* v. *Minister of Interior* (1953) 7 P.D. 871.
[4] See Kretzmer, 'Demonstrations and the Law' (1984) 19 *Israel LR.* 47.

government authorities must give them appropriate weight when exercising administrative discretion. They are *soft* principles because they do not limit the legislative power of the Knesset. The Supreme Court has refused to invalidate primary legislation that places restrictions on those basic rights recognized as legal principles.[5]

Given the central position that fundamental rights hold in judicial decision-making in Israel, a bill of rights was not needed to fulfil the first of these normative functions. Most of the civil and political rights included in the International Covenant on Civil and Political Rights have been recognized as protected rights by the Supreme Court. Freedom of occupation, the concern of one of the Basic Laws, was described in an early Supreme Court decision as one of the natural rights of man,[6] and has since been referred to in dozens of decisions.

The Supreme Court has also developed an extensive jurisprudence on the scope of protection of recognized rights and on the tests to be employed to balance those rights with other rights or interests.[7]

The main contribution of a bill of rights to Israel's constitutional system would therefore be to enhance the *status* of basic rights, both by placing limits on the Knesset's legislative power to restrict rights and by allowing for judicial review to ensure that those limits are respected.

C. The Basic Laws, Legislative Supremacy, and Judicial Review

Although basic laws were intended to be chapters in Israel's evolving constitution, the Supreme Court held in the past that such laws were not inherently superior to ordinary legislation.[8] Thus, the Court maintained that in the case of a clash between a special provision in ordinary Knesset legislation and a general provision in a basic law, the former was to prevail.[9] It also held that the Knesset may amend a provision in a basic law by means of ordinary legislation passed by a simple majority.[10] On the other hand, the Court has recognized that the Knesset is bound by an express entrenched provision in the

---

[5] See, e.g., *Rogozinsky* v. *State of Israel* (1972) 26 P.D. (i) 129; *Tnuat Laor* v. *Speaker of the Knesset* (1990) 33 P.D. (iii) 529.

[6] See *Bejarano* v. *Minister of Police* (1949) 2 P.D. 80, at 82.

[7] The decisions are too numerous to mention here. But see, e.g., *Kol Ha'am* v. *Minister of Interior*, above n. 3; *Kahane* v. *Broadcasting Authority* (1987) 41 P.D. (iii) 244 (freedom of speech); *Dahaar* v. *Minister of Interior* (1986) 40 P.D. (ii) 701 (right to travel abroad); *Poraz* v. *Mayor of Tel Aviv* (1988) 42 P.D. (ii) 309 (equality).

[8] See *Kaniel* v. *Minister of Justice* (1973) 27 P.D. (i) 794; *Ressler* v. *Chairman of the Central Elections Committee* (1977) 31 P.D.(ii) 556. For a discussion of the status of the basic laws see Kretzmer, 'Judicial Review of Knesset Decisions', (1988) 8 *Tel. Aviv. Uni. Studies in Law* 95.

[9] See *Negev* v. *State of Israel* (1974) 28 P.D. (i) 640.

[10] See Rubinstein, *The Constitutional Law of the State of Israel* (4th edn., 1991), 459–60.

Basic Law—The Knesset,[11] and has invalidated legislation that was not enacted with the special majority required by that provision.[12]

Section 7 of the Basic Law—Freedom of Occupation expressly states that it may not be changed 'except by a Basic Law passed by a majority of the members of the Knesset'. Requirement not only of an absolute majority, but also of adoption of a new basic law, in order to effect change in this Basic Law makes the entrenchment stronger than that in section 4 of the Basic Law—The *Knesset*.[13] According to the approach taken by the Supreme Court, the entrenched clause in that Basic Law may be modified by an ordinary law, provided that it is passed with a special majority.[14]

In contrast to the Basic Law—Freedom of Occupation, the Basic Law—Human Dignity and Liberty does not contain an explicit entrenchment clause. Such a clause was included in the bill, but was dropped at the second-reading stage. This has caused some interesting anomalies. Thus, section 1a, which was drafted on the assumption that the entrenchment clause incorporated in the original bill would remain, declares that the purpose of the law is to *entrench* human dignity and liberty in a basic law. Comparison of these two new Basic Laws would seem to imply that freedom of occupation is more important than such fundamental rights as the right to life, bodily integrity, dignity, and personal liberty of the individual.

Section 11 of the Basic Law—Human Dignity and Liberty states that all governmental authorities are bound to respect the rights protected under that law. Furthermore, section 8 declares that no restrictions may be placed on protected rights, except by a law that meets defined substantive standards. These provisions would seem to leave little room for doubt that the Basic Law is intended to place restrictions on the legislative power of the Knesset. Nevertheless, given the existing jurisprudence of the Supreme Court regarding the status of basic laws, and the lack of an express entrenchment clause, questions were raised as to whether legislation that failed to meet the demands of the Basic Law—Human Dignity and Liberty would be regarded as invalid.

---

[11] See section 4 of the Basic Law—The Knesset which provides: 'The Knesset shall be elected in general, national, direct, equal, secret and proportional elections, according to the Knesset Elections Law; this section may not be amended, except by a majority of Knesset members'.

The majority referred to is an absolute majority of Knesset members (i.e., at least 61 of the 120 members) in all three readings of the bill. The general rule in Knesset voting is that a simple majority of those voting for or against a bill is sufficient.

[12] See *Bergman* v. *Minister of Finance* (1969) 23 P.D. (i) 693; *Agudat Derech Eretz* v. *Broadcasting Authority* (1981) 35 P.D. (iv) 1; *Rubinstein* v. *Speaker of the Knesset* (1983) 37 P.D. (iii) 141; *Tnuat Laor* v. *Speaker of the Knesset*, above n. 5.

[13] It should be mentioned, however, that under the present system a basic law is enacted by the Knesset itself according to the same procedure followed for the introduction of ordinary legislation.

[14] See *Kaniel* v. *Minister of Justice*, above n. 8; *Ressler* v. *Chairman of the Central Elections Committee*, above n. 8.

These doubts were dispelled in a decision handed down by an expanded bench of nine justices of the Supreme Court in November 1995.[15] This decision relates to legislation affecting the right of creditors to collect debts against agricultural settlements. Creditors argued that the said legislation violated their property right, protected under section 3 of the Basic Law, and that it did not meet the requirements of section 8. The Court was unanimous in holding that the property rights of creditors were indeed violated by the legislation, but that it met the requirements of section 8. It could therefore easily have avoided addressing questions relating to the binding force of the Basic Law and the power of judicial review over incompatible legislation. Nonetheless, some of the justices dealt with these questions at great length.

The majority of judges on the Court held that the Basic Law—Human Dignity and Liberty and the Basic Law—Freedom of Occupation have formal constitutional status, which is thus superior to that of ordinary legislation.[16] All legislation passed after the entry into force of these Basic Laws must therefore respect the rights guaranteed under them. Furthermore, the courts have the power to review legislation in order to determine whether it does indeed meet those standards, and to invalidate legislation that fails to do so. Only one of the judges on the Court refused to recognize the power of the Knesset to give legislation superior constitutional status, or to bind its legislative power so that it exceeds the majority rule in a parliamentary democracy.[17]

D. The Protected Rights

The Basic Law—Freedom of Occupation protects one specific right: the right of all citizens or residents to engage in any occupation, profession, or trade. The Basic Law—Human Dignity and Liberty covers a number of fundamental rights: the right to life, body, and dignity, and to the protection of these

---

[15] See *United Mizrachi Bank Ltd.* v. *Migdal Co-operative Village* (1993) 49 P.D. (iv) 221.

[16] There was some difference of opinion among the judges regarding the theoretical basis for the power of the Knesset to pass constitutional laws that have a superior status to ordinary legislation. Barak J relied on the theory, rejected in the past by the Court, according to which the Knesset possesses both legislative and constituent power. When enacting a basic law, the Knesset is exercising its constituent power. It may therefore place restrictions on the use of legislative power. This view appealed to three of the other justices on the bench. Shamgar J rejected the constituent power theory, but held that as a sovereign legislative body the Knesset could ascribe constitutional status to basic laws and could also place binding constraints on itself.

[17] Mishael Cheshin J took the view that the Knesset may regulate the *type* of majority required for given decisions or legislation. It may thus stipulate that in ordinary cases a simple majority is sufficient, while in special cases an absolute majority of its members is required. However, the Knesset does not have the power to entrench a statute by a requirement that exceeds an absolute majority. Cheshin J also expressed the view that the Knesset could overcome the demands of section 8 of the Basic Law—Human Dignity and Liberty by including a provision in subsequent legislation that such legislation would be valid notwithstanding the provisions of the Basic Law.

(sections 2 and 4); the right to protection of property (section 3); liberty of the individual (section 5); the right to leave and enter the country (section 6); and the right to privacy and personal confidentiality (section 7).

It was not a coincidence that certain fundamental rights protected both by international human rights instruments and by modern constitutions are not specified in the Basic Laws. As noted earlier, the notion of a series of basic laws on human rights was intended to overcome opposition by the religious parties to entrenchment of those rights that are affected by religiously motivated legislation. The most politically sensitive rights in this respect are the freedom of religion and conscience and the right to equality. The former is affected by the lack of civil marriage in Israel. The jurisdiction granted to the religious courts in matters of marriage and divorce, in as much as the law applied by both the Jewish Rabbinical and Muslim courts may be regarded as discriminatory towards women, clearly affects the right to equality.

Despite the fact that no explicit mention is made of certain rights expressly detailed in international human rights covenants and charters, some of these may be seen as inherent to the rights specified in the Basic Law—Human Dignity and Liberty. Thus, for example, the prohibitions against slavery, torture, and cruel, inhuman, and degrading treatment or punishment are covered by the right to human dignity; the right to due process is bound to the right to liberty of the person. The question at issue is whether the principle of human dignity should be extended to include those rights, such as the right to equality, freedom of religion, and freedom of expression, that were intentionally excluded from the Basic Law.

Indeed, in a number of decisions handed down by justices of the Supreme Court, the view is taken that certain fundamental rights not explicitly mentioned in the Basic Laws, such as the right to equality and freedom of expression, are protected under the umbrella of human dignity.[18] Furthermore, in his extra-judicial writings, Barak J, now President of the Court, has dismissed the idea that original intent should be the guiding principle in interpreting the Basic Laws that are part of Israel's developing formal constitution.[19] According to Barak J's general theory of interpretation, the concept of human dignity must be interpreted in the light of its 'objective purpose', which can be deciphered from its meaning in international human rights instruments and other democratic constitutions. In the final analysis, it must include 'all those human rights that have a close substantive connection to human dignity and liberty according to prevailing concepts among the enlightened public in

---

[18] See, e.g., *Re'em Engineers Ltd.* v. *Municipality of Nazareth Elite* (1992) 47 P.D. (v) 189, 201; *Dayan* v. *Commander of Jerusalem Police* (1993) 48 P.D. (ii) 456, 468; *Hupert* v. *Yad Vashem* (1995) 48 P.D. (iii) 353, 360–3; *El Al Airlines* v. *Danilewitz* (1994) 48 P.D. (v) 749; *Women's Network* v. *Minister of Transport* (1994) 48 P.D. (v) 501.

[19] See Barak, *Interpretation in Law, Volume III, Constitutional Interpretation* (1994) 149 *et seq; idem*, 'Human Dignity as a Basic Right', *Ha'aretz*, 3 June 1994, b5.

Israel'.[20] Following this approach, it is almost self-evident that the concept of human dignity includes both equality and freedom of religion.

A broad view of the concept of human dignity was reinforced by an amendment to the Basic Law—Human Dignity and Liberty, introduced with the revision of the Basic Law—Freedom of Occupation. Section 1 of both Basic Laws now states:

Basic human rights in Israel are based on the recognition of the value of the human being, and the sanctity of his life and his freedom, and these will be respected in the spirit of the principles of the Declaration of Independence of the State of Israel.

The principles set forth in the Declaration on the Establishment of the State of Israel include 'complete equality of political and social rights, irrespective of race, religion or sex' and freedom of religion and conscience. The argument that these rights are incorporated in 'human dignity' may now be based not only on reference to international instruments but also on interpretation of this concept in the spirit of these principles. Nevertheless, given the structure of the Basic Laws, which refer to some—but not all—specific rights, together with the clear political desire not to 'constitutionalize' all fundamental rights protected in other constitutions and international instruments, the Court may well develop a jurisprudence that allows for resort to the notion of 'human dignity' to address gross violations of rights not specifically listed but that, at the same time, does not turn this notion into a catch-all concept for restrictions on rights that were intentionally omitted from the Basic Laws. This approach has recently been adopted by Dorner J in two cases, one dealing with equality[21] and the other with freedom of expression.[22]

E. Scope of Protection

Under accepted standards of international law, certain rights, among which the right to freedom from torture and slavery, enjoy absolute protection. Such rights may not be restricted, even in the event of a clash with other rights or with the interests of state security or public order. In contrast, the protection extended to most rights is relative; these rights may be subject to legitimate restrictions on the grounds of need for protection of other rights or interests.

[20] See Barak, *Interpretation in the Law*, above n. 19 at 416 and *Vickselbaum* v. *Minister of Defence* (1993) 47 P.D. (ii) 812.

[21] See *Alice Miller* v. *Minister of Defence* (1994) 49 P.D. (iv) 94. This case dealt with gender discrimination in accepting candidates for pilot training in the Israel Air Force. Dorner J was of the opinion that discrimination on some grounds may not be degrading and would therefore not be covered by the concept of human dignity. She held, however, that discrimination on grounds of race or gender always degrades the individual and therefore constitutes a violation of his or her right to human dignity.

[22] See *Golan* v. *Prisons Authority* (1994, not yet reported).

Three approaches may be taken to the obvious need to balance relative rights with other rights and interests. The first, as in the Constitution of the USA, is to ignore the issue in the constitution itself, which merely defines the protected rights. The creation of balancing principles is left to the courts, whose role includes interpretation of the constitution and examination of allegations that the government has exceeded its constitutional authority. The second approach, prevalent in human rights instruments, including the European Convention on Human Rights, favours the incorporation of provisions which define the legitimate restrictions on specific rights. Under the third approach, adopted in the Canadian Charter of Rights and Freedoms, one general balancing test is provided to judge the legitimacy of restrictions on all the protected rights.

The Israeli Basic Laws follow the Canadian model. The individual rights themselves are cast in absolute terms, but the Basic Laws provide a general balancing test that must be applied in all cases. Section 8 of the Basic Law—Human Dignity and Liberty states this test in the following terms:

There shall be no violation of rights under this Basic Law except by a Law fitting the values of the State of Israel, designed for a proper purpose, and to an extent no greater than required or by such a law enacted with explicit authorization therein.

Questions of purpose and the extent of change required to have arisen in other jurisdictions, and the Israeli courts will be able to look to them for guidance. The Supreme Court has already turned to Canadian and German jurisprudence and has thus far favoured an interpretation of the necessary 'extent' requirement similar to the proportionality test developed by the courts in those countries.

More problematical is the reference to 'a Law fitting the values of the State of Israel'. This phrase must be read together with section 1(a) of the Basic Law—Human Dignity and Liberty, which refers to the 'values of the State of Israel as a Jewish and democratic state'.[23] It merits separate attention.

F. A Jewish and Democratic State

Israel's constitutional system is based on two fundamental tenets: that the state is democratic and that it is also Jewish. The first of these principles provided the original rationale for the incorporation of basic civil rights, such as freedom of speech, in the legal system, even though they were not directly indicated in any written law.[24] The second formed the initial legal basis for excluding a political list from participation in the Knesset elections, despite

[23] A parallel provision also appears in section 2 of the Basic Law—Freedom of Occupation.
[24] See *Kol Ha'am* v. *Minister of Interior*, above n. 3.

the fact that no legislation provided for such exclusion.[25] The constitutional challenge facing the State of Israel is to create a synthesis between these two principles.

The significance of Israel as a Jewish state has been the subject of major debate. On the ideological level, views have ranged from those of the minimalists, who believe that the right of all Jews to immigrate to Israel constitutes the only necessary element in its definition as a Jewish state, to those who would ascribe a Messianic mission to the state itself. While the issue remained rather vague for a long time, a 1985 amendment to the Basic Law—The Knesset, adopted a highly controversial definition which served only to fuel the tension between these two tenets. According to section 7A of the Basic Law—The Knesset, introduced by the said amendment, a political list may not participate in the Knesset elections if, by its aims or actions, it expressly or by implication 'negates the State of Israel as the state of the Jewish people'.[26]

The definition in section 7A ignores the status of Israel's non-Jewish citizens, who comprise 18 per cent of the population. It would seem to imply that contrary to the democratic notion of the state as the state of all its citizens, the State of Israel is not the state of its non-Jewish citizens.[27] The implications of this particularistic approach were most clearly articulated in the opinion of Dov Levin J in his dissent in *Ben-Shalom* v. *Central Elections Committee for the Twelfth Knesset*.[28] Levin J took the view that a list demanding total equality between Jews and Arabs in Israel, on the group as well as individual level, should be excluded under section 7A.

The definition adopted in section 1a of the Basic Law—Human Dignity and Liberty and section 2 of the Basic Law—Freedom of Occupation is thus a welcome change. Use of the term 'Jewish and democratic state' would seem to imply that there can be no contradiction between the two tenets and that some form of synthesis must therefore be found. According to these two Basic Laws, a conception of the Jewish state that is inconsistent with democratic values must be rejected.

Definitions of the expression 'Jewish and democratic state' have already cropped up in decisions of the Supreme Court, with controversial repercussions between two leading justices. According to Elon J, in cases where various approaches to an issue are compatible with democratic values, the Court must look to the tradition of Jewish law. By favouring the approach consistent with that tradition, a synthesis may be created between the notions of a

---

[25] See the opinion of Agranat J in *Yardor* v. *Chairman of Knesset Elections Committee* (1965) 19 P.D. (iii) 365.

[26] The said section also includes two further grounds for excluding lists from participation in Knesset elections: that the list negates the democratic nature of the state or that it incites racism.

[27] The author has discussed this issue elsewhere; see Kretzmer, *The Legal Status of the Arabs in Israel* (1990), Ch. 2.

[28] (1989) 43 P.D. (iv) 221.

democratic and Jewish state.[29] Barak J, on the other hand, has written that 'the values of the State of Israel as a Jewish state are those universal values that are common to members of democratic societies and which grew out of Jewish tradition and history'.[30]

The notion of restrictions on rights 'necessary in a democratic society' has been developed in the jurisprudence of the European Court of Human Rights. Similarly, the Supreme Court of Canada has given close attention to the question of whether restrictions on basic rights may be 'demonstrably justified in a free and democratic society'. The question requiring the attention of the Israeli courts is whether the notion of a 'Jewish and democratic state' leads to different result from those adopted in European and Canadian decisions.

G. The Basic Laws and the ICCPR

The same impetus that led to enactment of the human rights-related Basic Laws had brought about ratification, 6 months earlier, of the International Covenant on Civil and Political Rights (ICCPR) by the Government of Israel.[31] Under the rule of British law followed in Israel, international treaties and conventions ratified by the government do not become part of domestic law unless they are incorporated by Knesset legislation. No legislation incorporating the ICCPR was enacted. While the Basic Laws were not instituted with the specific intention of giving constitutional status to the rights protected under the ICCPR, Article 2 of this Covenant requires State Parties 'to adopt such legislative or other measures as may be necessary to give effect to the rights recognized in the present Covenant'. To what extent do the Basic Laws enable Israel to meet this obligation?

As explained above, the two Basic Laws do not purport to cover all the fundamental rights protected under the ICCPR or by modern bills of rights. A number of bills dealing with other rights, such as freedom of expression, freedom of association, and the right to fair trial were in various stages of the legislative process when the Knesset was dissolved prior to the May 1996 elections. At the time of writing, they had not been revived for debate by the new Knesset. Unless additional basic laws are enacted, those rights included in the ICCPR, but which remain outside the scope of the two Basic Laws, will only be able to command the weaker protection of judge-made case law, leaving them vulnerable to restriction by Knesset legislation.

---

[29] See *Chevra Kadisha Kehilat Yerushalayim* v. *Kastenbaum* (1991) 46 P.D. (ii) 464; *Shefer* v. *State of Israel* (1988) 48 P.D. (i) 87.

[30] See Barak, 'The Constitutional Revolution: Protected Human Rights', (1992) 1 *Mishpat Umimshal* 9 at 31.

[31] It also ratified the International Covenant on Economic, Social and Cultural Rights. Israel is now a party to all six of the universal human rights treaties.

While the ICCPR cannot be applied directly by the courts in such a way as to override domestic legislation, Israeli courts are bound to interpret legislation in a manner consistent with Israel's treaty obligations. This may become relevant in interpreting the scope of concepts such as human dignity so as to include rights protected under the ICCPR, including protection against torture and cruel, inhuman, or degrading treatment or punishment. It may also be relevant in interpreting the scope of the balancing tests laid down in the Basic Laws in order to prevent the introduction of restrictions on basic rights that exceed those permitted under the ICCPR.

Section 12 of the Basic Law—Human Dignity and Liberty provides that during a state of emergency, the government may institute emergency legislation that limits basic rights, provided that such limits are for a worthy purpose and that they do not exceed the period of time or the extent of change necessary.[32] As this provision makes no distinction between those rights which may or may not be limited by emergency legislation, it would appear to be incompatible with Article 4(2) of the ICCPR, which specifies that derogation may not be made from specified provisions, even in a state of emergency.[33] However, the Basic Law—The Government, adopted the day after enactment of the Basic Law—Human Dignity and Liberty, restricts the emergency powers of the government. Section 50(e) of that Basic Law states that the measures provided for in emergency legislation may not exceed those demanded by the emergency situation. Furthermore, its section 50(d) stipulates that emergency legislation may not restrict access to the courts, nor can it provide for retroactive punishment, or permit violation of human dignity. Interpretation of these provisions so as to ensure compliance with Israel's obligations under international law should lead to the conclusion that adoption of emergency measures inconsistent with Article 4 of the ICCPR would be unconstitutional.

H. Judicial Review and Prior Legislation

Introduction of judicial review of Knesset legislation raises the question whether all legislation in force at the time the Basic Laws were adopted meets their standards. This always provided a bone of contention in debates over a bill of rights for Israel. Concern was expressed by the religious parties, which feared that legislation enforcing religious norms would not stand up to review. But even greater apprehension was shown by the defence establishment, which

[32] Under Israeli law, the government has the power, during a state of emergency, to promulgate temporary emergency legislation in order to defend the state, public security, and maintenance of supplies and essential services.

[33] The rights stipulated are the right to life (Art. 6); the right to freedom from torture (Art. 7) or slavery (Art. 8); non-imprisonment for contractual debt (Art. 11); non-retroactivity of criminal offences (Art. 15); right to recognition as a person before the law (Art. 16) and freedom of thought, conscience and religion (Art. 18).

was aware that much of the British Mandatory emergency legislation still in force would not meet those standards. Thus, for instance, the Supreme Court itself has described regulation 94 of the Emergency Regulations (Defence) 1945, which deals with licensing of the press, as a provision 'that is inimical to basic conceptions of freedom of speech and expression in a democratic society'.[34]

The question of prior legislation has been dealt with in different ways by the two Basic Laws. As the issue of freedom of occupation was not regarded as politically sensitive or threatening to existing security powers, the original version of the Basic Law—Freedom of Occupation, adopted in February 1992, allowed a 2-year period of grace for existing legislation, after which it would be subject to review under the exacting standards of the Basic Law. This period of grace has, however, since been extended twice for further periods of 2 years.

The rights ensured in the Basic Law—Human Dignity and Liberty are considered far more problematical. Many of them are regulated by emergency legislation. There are, for instance, emergency laws in Israel which provide for administrative detention and other restrictions on freedom of movement, including the right of citizens to travel abroad. These restrictions clearly violate the right protected in section 6(a) of the Basic Law.[35] While it was to be hoped that these laws could have been dealt with by means of a similar approach to that taken with the Basic Law—Freedom of Occupation, such a proposal was rejected. Instead, section 10 declares that 'the Basic Law shall not affect the validity of any law in force prior to the commencement of the Basic Law'.

This immunity from review granted to prior legislation greatly weakens the import of the Basic Law—Human Dignity and Liberty. The refusal to allow such review according to the standards of the Basic Law would seem to reveal a lack of confidence in the legitimacy of that legislation, even in the light of Israel's critical security situation.

Despite the fact that the courts cannot invalidate already existing legislation that is inconsistent with the terms of the Basic Law—Human Dignity and Liberty, some justices on the Supreme Court have taken the view that adoption of the Basic Laws has changed the status of the rights protected therein.[36] As *constitutionally* protected rights, they now carry a greater weight than was the case in the past. In their opinion, the courts should reconsider interpretations of legislation accordingly. If this approach were followed, the Basic

---

[34] See *Al-Assad* v. *Minister of Interior* (1980) 34 P.D. (i) 505, 513.

[35] Upon acceding to the ICCPR, Israel submitted a declaration under Article 4 that a state of emergency exists in the country, and that in so far as emergency measures are inconsistent with Article 9 of the Covenant, Israel derogates from its obligations under that provision.

[36] See the opinions of the majority in the case of *Ganimat* v. *State of Israel*, (1995) 49 P.D. (iii) 355, and the opinion of Dorner J in *Alice Miller* v. *Minister of Defence*, above n. 21.

Law—Human Dignity and Liberty could influence the interpretation of prior legislation, even though such legislation cannot be declared invalid on the ground of incompatibility with the rights safeguarded under the Basic Law.

I. The Override Clause

Unlike the Basic Law—Human Dignity and Liberty, changes cannot be introduced to the Basic Law—Freedom of Occupation 'except by a Basic Law passed by a majority of the members of the Knesset (section 7). However, under section 8 of the revised Basic Law, the Knesset retains the power to include an override clause in legislation. Such legislation will be valid, even if it limits the freedom of occupation in a manner inconsistent with the balancing provision, provided that two conditions are met: (i) that the legislation is passed by an absolute majority of Knesset members, and (ii) that express statement is made in the legislation that it will take effect notwithstanding the provisions of the Basic Law. Any such laws will automatically expire four years after adoption, unless the law itself provides for a shorter duration. The Knesset made hasty use of this override provision, as soon as the revised Basic Law was published, with enactment of the Import of Frozen Meat Law 1994. This law prohibits the importation of meat that has not been certified as kosher. This is the only instance to date of recourse to the override provision.

The Canadian Charter once again provided the model for the override clause in this Basic Law. However, there are significant differences between the provision as it appears in section 33 of the Canadian Charter and section 8 of the Israeli Basic Law. The relevant section of the Canadian Charter provides that such declaration, notwithstanding that it restricts a basic right, shall hold effect for 5 years after it comes into force or until an earlier date as specified. Section 8 of the Basic Law, on the other hand, stipulates that the overriding law itself shall expire after 4 years or on an earlier date as set down.

Furthermore, the Canadian Charter explicitly states that the legislature that adopted an overriding statute may re-enact the declaration at the end of the 5-year period. The Israeli law contains no parallel provision. It remains to be seen whether the courts will take this as implying that such a provision may not be re-enacted after expiry.

J. Conclusion

Adoption of the Basic Law—Human Dignity and Liberty and the Basic Law—Freedom of Occupation has brought about a mini-revolution in Israel's constitutional system. The introduction of judicial review of parliamentary legislation has reduced the vulnerability of fundamental rights. Nevertheless, the system itself continues to suffer a number of deficiencies that limit the impact of this constitutional revolution.

In the first place, the Basic Laws themselves are subject to modification by the Knesset. While amendments to the Basic Law—Freedom of Occupation require an absolute majority, the Basic Law—Human Dignity and Liberty may be altered by simple majority. Secondly, the Basic Laws do not give specific mention to several fundamental rights, including freedom of religion and conscience, the right to equality, and freedom of expression. The Supreme Court will most likely interpret the principle of 'human dignity' so as to take in violations of rights not explicitly referred to, but will refrain from extending full protection to rights that were intentionally omitted from the Basic Laws. Finally, the Basic Laws do not allow for judicial review of primary legislation that was in force at the time of enactment. As noted earlier, under the Basic Law—Freedom of Occupation, prior legislation was to be subject to judicial review after a period of grace that was to have elapsed in 1994, but that period has been twice extended. To date, judicial review under both Basic Laws has been limited to legislation introduced after their coming into force.

The Basic Laws lay down a general balancing test for examining the legitimacy of restrictions on protected rights. As in most systems which provide for judicial review of the constitutionality of legislation, the scope of the rights protected under the Basic Laws will largely depend on the way the Supreme Court interprets both the rights themselves and the balancing test. There continues to be significant resistance in the political arena to judicial review of parliamentary legislation, especially when the legislation in question is to give effect to religious norms. In this political climate, the Supreme Court of Israel will have to tread carefully, lest an over-activist approach should spur those political forces that oppose judicial review not only to check attempts to extend the rights covered, but even to press for revocation or a watering down of the modest restrictions on parliamentary legislation imposed by the Basic Laws.

Text of the Basic Laws[37]

Basic Law—Human Dignity and Liberty[38]

Basic principles

1.   Fundamental human rights in Israel are founded upon recognition of the value of the human being, the sanctity of human life, and the principle that

[37] This version of the two Basic Laws is an English language translation taken from the website of the Israel Ministry of Foreign Affairs: (http://www.israel.org/gov/laws/basiclaw.html).
[38] Passed by the Knesset on 17 March 1992 and published in *Sefer Ha-Chukkim* No. 1391 of 25 March 1992; as amended by the Knesset on 9 March 1994 and published in *Sefer Ha-Chukkim* No. 1454 of 10 March 1994.

all persons are free; these rights shall be upheld in the spirit of the principles set forth in the Declaration of the Establishment of the State of Israel.

Purpose

1a. The purpose of this Basic Law is to protect human dignity and liberty, in order to establish in a Basic Law the values of the State of Israel as a Jewish and democratic state.

Preservation of life, body and dignity

2. There shall be no violation of the life, body or dignity of any person as such.

Protection of property

3. There shall be no violation of the property of a person.

Protection of life, body and dignity

4. All persons are entitled to protection of their life, body and dignity.

Personal liberty

5. There shall be no deprivation or restriction of the liberty of a person by imprisonment, arrest, extradition or otherwise.

Leaving and entering Israel

6. (a) All persons are free to leave Israel.

(b) Every Israel national has the right of entry into Israel from abroad.

Privacy

7. (a) All persons have the right to privacy and to intimacy.

(b) There shall be no entry into the private premises of a person who has not consented thereto.

(c) No search shall be conducted on the private premises of a person, nor in the body or personal effects.

(d) There shall be no violation of the confidentiality of conversation, or of the writings or records of a person.

Violation of rights

8. There shall be no violation of rights under this Basic Law except by a law befitting the values of the State of Israel, enacted for a proper purpose, and to an extent no greater than is required, or by regulation enacted by virtue of express authorization in such law.

Reservation regarding security forces

9. There shall be no restriction of rights under this Basic Law held by persons serving in the Israel Defence Forces, the Israel Police, the Prisons Service and other security organizations of the State, nor shall such rights be subject to conditions, except by virtue of a law, or by regulation enacted by virtue of a law, and to an extent no greater than is required by the nature and character of the service.

Validity of laws

10. This Basic Law shall not affect the validity of any law (din) in force prior to the commencement of the Basic Law.

Application

11. All governmental authorities are bound to respect the rights under this Basic Law.

Stability

12. This Basic Law cannot be varied, suspended or made subject to conditions by emergency regulations; notwithstanding, when a state of emergency exists, by virtue of a declaration under section 9 of the Law and Administration Ordinance, 5708–1948, emergency regulations may be enacted by virtue of said section to deny or restrict rights under this Basic Law, provided the denial or restriction shall be for a proper purpose and for a period and extent no greater than is required.

BASIC LAW—FREEDOM OF OCCUPATION[39]

Basic principles

1. Fundamental human rights in Israel are founded upon recognition of the value of the human being, the sanctity of human life, and the principle that

[39] Passed by the Knesset on 9 March 1994 and published in *Sefer Ha-Chukkim* No. 1454 of 10 March 1994, p. 90.

all persons are free; these rights shall be upheld in the spirit of the principles set forth in the Declaration of the Establishment of the State of Israel.

Purpose

2. The purpose of this Basic Law is to protect freedom of occupation, in order to establish in a Basic Law the values of the State of Israel as a Jewish and democratic state.

Freedom of occupation

3. Every Israel national or resident has the right to engage in any occupation, profession or trade.

Violation of freedom of occupation

4. There shall be no violation of freedom of occupation except by a law befitting the values of the State of Israel, enacted for a proper purpose, and to an extent no greater than is required, or by regulation enacted by virtue of express authorisation in such law.

Application

5. All governmental authorities are bound to respect the freedom of occupation of all Israel nationals and residents.

Stability

6. This Basic Law shall not be varied, suspended or made subject to conditions by emergency regulations.

Enactment

7. This Basic Law shall not be varied except by a Basic Law passed by a majority of the members of the Knesset.

Effect of non-conforming law

8. A provision of a law that violates freedom of occupation shall be of effect, even though not in accordance with section 4, if it has been included in a law passed by a majority of the members of the Knesset, which expressly states that it shall be of effect, notwithstanding the provisions of this Basic

Law; such law shall expire four years from its commencement unless a shorter duration has been stated therein.

Repeal

9. Basic Law: Freedom of Occupation[40] is hereby repealed.

Provisional

10. The provisions of any enactment which, immediately prior to this Basic Law would have been of effect but for this Basic Law or the Basic Law repealed in section 9, shall remain in effect two years from the commencement of this Basic Law, unless repealed earlier; however, such provisions shall be construed in the spirit of the provisions of this Basic Law.

---

[40] This Basic Law—Freedom of Occupation repeals and replaces the former Basic Law on Freedom of Occupation, enacted in 1992.

II
The Role of International Norms in the Absence of a Bill of Rights

4

The European Convention on Human Rights in the British Courts: Problems Associated with the Incorporation of International Human Rights

ANDREW CLAPHAM

The aim of this Chapter is to show three things. First, that the European Convention on Human Rights ('ECHR') has, to some extent, already been used by judges in the United Kingdom prior to the entry into force on 2 October 2000 of the main provisions of the Human Rights Act 1998. Second, that incorporating an international treaty need not involve a complete abdication of sovereignty to the judiciary. Third, that if one does consider incorporating an international human rights instrument there are a number of pitfalls which ought to be addressed in the incorporating legislation.

The Relevance of the Convention in British Courts

The United Kingdom was one of the key actors in the drafting of the European Convention on Human Rights, was one of the original signatories on 5 November 1950, and on 8 March 1951 was the first State to ratify the Convention.

Although the Convention has not been incorporated into domestic law it is surprisingly relevant in the domestic Courts of the United Kingdom. The Convention may be relevant in the following situations:

(a) as an aid to statutory interpretation;
(b) as part of the common law;
(c) as a factor to be taken into consideration by administrative bodies when exercising their discretion;
(d) as part of European Community law;
(e) due to a pending application in Strasbourg;
(f) due to the case law of the European Court of Human Rights; and
(g) due to a 'friendly settlement' under the Convention.

Only the first three categories will be dealt with here.[1] It would seem that the situation in most common law countries regarding judicial interpretation of international treaties is no different from the current situation in the United Kingdom.[2] Where the situation is analogous, comparisons can be made between the fact of a procedure before the European Commission and Court of Human Rights, and the possibility of complaints against the Government concerned under the Optional Protocol to the International Covenant on Civil and Political Rights (assuming that it is a party thereto).

AS AN AID TO STATUTORY INTERPRETATION

In 1974 the House of Lords first used the Convention as an aid to statutory interpretation. In *R.* v. *Miah* Lord Reid, who delivered the only opinion, relied on Article 11(2) of the Universal Declaration of Human Rights, and Article 7 of the European Convention on Human Rights, to demonstrate that it was 'hardly credible that any Government department would promote, or that Parliament would pass, retrospective criminal legislation'.[3]

This conclusion stemmed from the general principle that, so far as the language permits, Parliament is presumed to legislate in accordance with international law.[4] Where the rule of international law is straightforward, as it was in this case—States may not create retroactive criminal offences—then the solution is relatively easy.[5] But other human rights are more problematic, and their ambit depends to a large extent on how much recognition is given to the individual right by any one Court or judge.

A second case illustrates how different judges are prepared to give different emphases to the right in question. Article 9(1) of the Convention states that everyone has the right to freedom of religion, but this right can be restricted in order to protect the rights and freedoms of others (Article 9(2)). When the Court of Appeal in *Ahmed* v. *Inner London Education Authority*[6] was asked to

---

[1] A detailed examination of all the categories can be found in Clapham, *Human Rights in the Private Sphere* (1993) at 1–66.

[2] Kirby, 'The Role of the Judge in Advancing Human Rights by Reference to International Human Rights Norms', 62 ALJ (1988) 514 at 515; Bayne, 'Administrative Law, Human Rights and International Humanitarian Law', 64 ALJ (1990) 203; Starke, 'Durability of the Bill of Rights 1688 as Part of Australian Law', 65 ALJ (1991) 695.

[3] [1974] 1 WLR 683 at 698.

[4] *Bloxham* v. *Favre* [1883] 8 PD 101 per Sir James Hannen P.

[5] Similarly, in *R.* v. *Deery*, 20 *Yearbook of the European Convention on Human Rights* (1977) 827, Article 7 was used to decide that the Firearms Regulations Amendment Order 1976 (NI), which increased the maximum term of imprisonment from 5 to 10 years in Northern Ireland, did not operate retroactively. So a sentence of 6 years passed on Deery for an offence committed before the Order, was an error. However, it was stated that should a Statute *clearly* suggest retroactive penalties, then the Court must follow the Statute and that the presumption of adherence to treaty obligations would be rebutted.

[6] *Ahmed* v. *ILEA* [1978] 1 All ER 574.

consider Section 30 of the Education Act 1944 in the light of Article 9, it was divided as to the weight which should be given to freedom of religion.

The case concerned a Muslim schoolteacher with a contract to teach 5 days a week. The contract provided for a lunch break from 12.30 a.m. to 1.30 p.m. Mr Ahmed, as a devout Muslim, had a duty to attend Friday prayers, unless he had an excuse, as defined in the Koran. The prayers at the nearest mosque were from 1 p.m. to 2 p.m. This meant he missed about 45 minutes of teaching each Friday. The Inner London Education Authority proposed to vary his contract to a 4½ week and Mr Ahmed resigned. The case arose out of a claim for unfair dismissal.

The case turned on an interpretation of Article 30 of the Education Act 1944, the relevant part of which reads as follows: '[N]o teacher . . . shall . . . receive any less emolument or be deprived of or disqualified for any promotion or any other advantage by reason of . . . his religious opinions or his attending or omitting to attend religious worship.'

Lord Denning read this as subject to the implied phrase 'so long as the school time-table allows'. He dismissed the European Convention as 'drawn in such vague terms that it can be used for all sorts of unreasonable claims and provoke all sorts of litigation'.[7] He continued, 'as so often happens with high-sounding principles, they have to be brought down to earth. They have to be applied in a work-a-day world'.[8] Lord Denning determined that Mr Ahmed's right to manifest his religion was subject to the rights of others, namely, the Education Authority and 'the children whom he is paid to teach', and concluded: 'I see nothing in the European Convention to give Mr Ahmed any right to manifest his religion on Friday afternoons in derogation of his contract of employment, and certainly not on full pay.'[9] The Court of Appeal found against Mr Ahmed.

Scarman LJ (as he then was) dissented. He took a rather different approach to the interpretation of Section 30:

there were until recently no substantial religious groupings in our country which fell outside the broad categories of Christian and Jew. So long as there was no discrimination between them no problem was likely to arise. The 5-day school week, of course, takes care of the Sabbath and of Sunday as days of special religious observance. But with the advent of new religious groups in our society Section 30 assumes a new importance . . . society has changed since 1944; so also has the legal background. Religions such as Islam and Buddhism have substantial followings among our people. Room has to be found for teachers and pupils of the new religions in the educational system, if discrimination is to be avoided. This calls not for a policy of the blind eye but one of understanding. The system must be made sufficiently flexible to accommodate their beliefs and their observances, otherwise they will suffer discrimination, a consequence contrary to the spirit of Section 30, whatever the letter of that law.[10]

---

[7] Ibid. at 577.　　　　　　　　　　[8] Ibid.　　　　　　　　　　[9] Ibid. at 578.
[10] *Ahmed* v. *ILEA* [1978] 1 All ER 574 at 583.

Scarman LJ then listed the legal changes which had occurred since 1944, including the United Kingdom's international obligations under the European Convention and the Charter of the United Nations. He continued:

Today therefore, we have to construe and apply Section 30 not against a background of the law and society of 1944 but in a multi-racial society which has accepted international obligations and enacted statutes designed to eliminate discrimination on grounds of race, religion, colour or sex.[11]

A number of points arise out of these two very different approaches. First, the use of the Convention in the Court of Appeal, which for most practical purposes, is the final court of appeal,[12] depended not so much on its precise legal *status* as an aid to interpretation but on the willingness of the individual judges to take the Convention into account, not only its provisions but also the philosophy and practice behind it.

Secondly, the rule which is generally supposed to legitimize the use of the Convention as an aid to statutory interpretation—*that the Legislature is presumed to legislate in accordance with international obligations*—is not relied on as such. Clearly 'Parliament in 1944 never addressed its mind to the problems of this case'.[13] Indeed in most cases of statutory interpretation in accordance with international human rights obligations, it is unlikely that the facts of the case will have been foreseen when Parliament debated the Act. One could go further and say that even if they were foreseen, the Act was probably deliberately left ambiguous due to compromises and amendments incorporated during the legislative process. The strength of a judicially enforceable human rights instrument, such as the European Convention on Human Rights, lies in the fact that unforeseen situations can be resolved without always having to implement new legislation. Problems can be resolved by virtue of the dynamic nature of the Convention, according to changing perceptions of morals and society.

The European Court of Human Rights itself, in a case concerning laws on homosexuality in Northern Ireland, stated in *Dudgeon* v. *United Kingdom*:[14]

As compared with the era when that legislation was enacted, there is now a better understanding, and in consequence an increased tolerance, of homosexual behaviour to the extent that in the great majority of the Member States of the Council of Europe it is no longer considered to be necessary or appropriate to treat homosexual practices of the kind now in question as in themselves a matter to which the sanctions of the criminal law should be applied.

---

[11] Ibid.
[12] See the comment of Donaldson MR: 'So in practical terms of the everyday life of this country this Court is the final court of appeal and must always be the final court of appeal in circumstances of real urgency': *C* v. *S* [1987] 2 WLR 1108 at 1123.
[13] *Ahmed* v. *ILEA* n. 6 above at 585 per Scarman L.J.
[14] *Dudgeon* v. *United Kingdom* (1982) 45 ECHR ser. A at 24.

But, theoretically, the question of Parliament's intention remains. In 1977, the Northern Ireland Standing Advisory Commission on Human Rights[15] felt it was not clear whether the presumption of conformity with the Convention applies only to legislation enacted *after* ratification of the Convention.[16]

The case which is generally relied on as a precedent that it is legitimate to refer to a treaty in order to construe legislation is *Salomon v. Commissioners for Customs and Excise.*[17] In that case Diplock LJ stated that there was 'a prima facie presumption that Parliament does not intend to act in breach of international law, including therein treaty obligations'. But he was in that case construing an Act, which although it did not say so, was deliberately intended to carry out the terms of a treaty,[18]—a treaty, incidentally, which was ratified *after* the royal assent of the Act which had implemented its terms into domestic law! Diplock LJ suggested that Courts may refer to treaties where 'extrinsic evidence' makes it plain that the legislation 'was intended to fulfil Her Majesty's Government's obligations under a particular convention',[19] even if the statute does not expressly refer to the Convention. The judgment of Diplock LJ would seem to suggest that only legislation which was passed with the intention of fulfilling obligations under the European Convention on Human Rights can be interpreted with respect to the Convention. He even warns: 'Of course the Court must not merely guess that the statute was intended to give effect to a particular Convention. The intrinsic evidence of the connection must be cogent.'[20]

However, future references to this passage by Lord Diplock seem to have ignored the need for such 'linkage' and the rule of construction now seems to be that 'in the absence of very clear words indicating the contrary . . . [there is] a presumption that Parliament has legislated in a manner consistent, rather than inconsistent, with the United Kingdom's treaty obligations'.[21]

For the reasons already given, it is suggested that the concept of giving effect to the intentions of Parliament is an unhelpful one. A better justification for using the Convention as an aid to statutory interpretation is that all statutes *ought* to be interpreted 'so as to be in conformity with international law'.[22] This is not, however, the attitude which was taken by the House of

---

[15] *The Protection of Human Rights by Law in Northern Ireland* (Cmnd. 7009, 1977), para. 5.25.
[16] The Convention was ratified by the United Kingdom on 22 February 1951.
[17] [1967] 2 QB 116 at 143.
[18] Convention on the Valuation of Goods for Customs Purposes 1950 (Cmnd. 9233), and Customs and Excise Act 1952 (UK).
[19] *Salomon v. Commissioners for Customs and Excise* n. 17 above at 143. [20] Ibid.
[21] Donaldson M.R. in *R. v. Secretary of State for the Home Department, ex parte Brind* [1990] 1 All ER 469 at 477; and see the judgment of the House of Lords in this case [1991] 1 All ER 720 where Lord Ackner affirmed this view.
[22] Diplock L.J. in *Salomon v. Commissioners for Customs and Excise* n. 17 above at 141: 'I think we are entitled to look at it, because it is an instrument which is binding in international law: and we ought always to interpret our Statutes so as to be in conformity with international law. Our

Lords Select Committee on a Bill of Rights in 1978,[23] but there is some evidence that judges are now prepared to take this broad brush approach.

Lord Scarman, after stating that neither the European Convention nor the decision of the European Court of Human Rights in *Sunday Times* v. *United Kingdom* were part of the law of the United Kingdom, went on to justify his reference to the Convention:

I do not doubt that, in considering how far we should extend the application of contempt of court, we must bear in mind the impact of whatever decision we may be minded to make on the international obligations assumed by the United Kingdom under the European Convention. If the issue should ultimately be, as I think in this case it is, a question of legal policy, we must have regard to the country's international obligation to observe the European Convention as interpreted by the European Court of Human Rights.[24]

This seems to be a more 'honest' approach to the use of the Convention, as no reference is made to the implied intention of the framers of the secondary legislation under consideration.[25] It could however be challenged on the grounds that it denies the 'transformation' tradition of English law. This states that treaties ratified by the Executive are not part of the law until *transformed* by Parliament through legislation into domestic laws.[26] It is suggested that this challenge fails. It fails due to the special nature of the European Convention on Human Rights and other relevant human rights instruments. The Convention declares *principles*; these principles can be legitimately used to interpret statutes where there is evidence of an intention by the Legislature to give effect to those principles, either in the statute under consideration or in *another* statute. So, in this way, when Scarman LJ (in *Ahmed* v. *ILEA*)

Statute does not in terms incorporate the Convention nor refer to it. But that does not matter. We can look at it.' He is, of course, referring to the Convention on the Valuation of Goods for Customs Purposes.

[23] *Report of the Select Committee on a Bill of Rights*, House of Lords paper No. 176 (1978), 28: 'Furthermore there is a case for saying that even the tenuous influence the Convention does have on the construction of Acts of Parliament is confined to Acts passed since we ratified the Convention . . . The justification for invoking the terms of a treaty to construe an Act seems to be that Parliament must be taken to be aware of our international obligations when it passed the Act.'

[24] *Attorney-General* v. *BBC* [1980] 3 WLR 109 at 130.

[25] The Court here had to decide if a local valuation Court was a 'Court' for the purposes of RSC Order 52 rule 1(2) relating to contempt of court.

[26] See *The Parlement Belge* [1879] 4 PD 129. Ott has noted that in this case the judge, Sir Robert Phillimore, was concerned not to deprive British subjects of their rights of action under common law without their consent. Phillimore held that private rights could not be removed without an Act of Parliament. The judgment can therefore be seen as an incidence of the Court's protecting the citizen from the Executive and insisting on the necessity of Parliamentary legislation. The precedent need not prevent the Courts from interpreting enactments so that they conform to the international protection which the Executive has decided to guarantee citizens under its jurisdiction. See Ott, *Public International Law in the Modern World* (1987), 39. For a number of suggestions relating to policy reasons for *not* automatically applying international law see Jackson, 'Status of Treaties in Domestic Legal Systems: A Policy Analysis', 86 AJIL (1992) 310.

referred to the Convention he referred to it in the context of other legislation dealing with discrimination: the sex discrimination and race relations Acts, and also the Trade Union and Labour Relations Act 1974.[27]

It remains to be seen to what extent the Convention will be used in cases involving statutes passed before the United Kingdom's ratification of the Convention. But the approach of the House of Lords Select Committee on a Bill of Rights is difficult to justify, resting as it does on an implied intent at a particular point in time.[28]

A Direct Clash Between a Statute and the European Convention

Before leaving the area of statutory interpretation mention should be made of the situation where there is a perceived *clash* between a statute and the Convention. Of course, it is not clear at what point it is no longer possible to interpret a statute so as to be in conformity with the Convention, so that a judge is obliged to find the two in irreconcilable opposition. In the United Kingdom, when a statute is in opposition to a treaty, the statute must prevail.[29] However, in the context of the European Convention on Human Rights, Lord Denning felt able to depart from this orthodoxy. In *Birdie* v.

[27] This is not dissimilar to Ronald Dworkin's account of Judge Earl's theory of legislation: 'He said that Statutes should be constructed from texts not in historical isolation but against a background of what he called general principles of law: he meant that judges should construct a Statute so as to make it conform as closely as possible to principles of justice assumed elsewhere in the law. He offered two reasons. First, it is sensible to assume that legislators have a general and diffuse intention to respect traditional principles of justice unless they clearly indicate the contrary. Secondly, since a Statute is part of a larger intellectual system, the law as a whole, it should be constructed so as to make that larger system coherent in principle': Dworkin, *Law's Empire* (1986), 19–20.

[28] It has been suggested that the use of the Convention as an aid to statutory interpretation for Statutes passed before the Convention's ratification can still be rationalized in terms of 'Parliament's intention . . . if one regards the parliamentary intention on which the presumption is based as being that the Courts will interpret legislation in accordance with the developing international obligations of the United Kingdom'. See Duffy, 'The European Convention on Human Rights in English Law', 29 *ICLQ* (1980) 585. The problem with this approach is that often the developing international obligations are strongly resisted by the United Kingdom Government, as evidenced by the numerous failures to achieve 'friendly settlements' in Strasbourg in cases involving the United Kingdom. So, it has to be admitted that it is unlikely that the Legislature intended the Courts to interpret legislation in accordance with the evolving obligations *imposed* on the United Kingdom; but more in accordance with how the Government perceived those obligations. Another argument against such an approach is that international obligations may oblige States to take *positive* measures to ease discrimination. This is apparent not only from the Court's decision in the *Marckx* case (1980) 31 ECHR ser. A, but also from the comments of the Commission when considering Mr Ahmed's application to them: 'the Commission further observes that the object of Article 9 is essentially that of protecting the individual against unjustified interference by the State, but that there may also be positive obligations inherent in the effective 'respect' for the individual's freedom of religion'. *X* v. *UK* 22 D. & R. 27 at 33.

Therefore on the intention theory we have to conclude that if Parliament intends to comply with the obligation to take positive measures, then it will have already taken these measures to a sufficient degree, and so there can be no justification for judicial interference.

[29] *Mortenson* v. *Peters* [1906] 14 Scots LTR 227; *The Parlement Belge* [1879] 4 PD 129.

Secretary of State for Home Affairs[30] Lord Denning MR stated that 'if an Act of Parliament did not conform to the Convention I might be inclined to hold it invalid'.[31] This surprising statement was repudiated in a later case in the same year, when Lord Denning returned to the orthodox view: that treaties do not become part of the law until made so by Parliament, and that 'if an Act of Parliament contained any provisions contrary to the Convention, the Act of Parliament must prevail'.[32] He continued '[b]ut I hope that no Act ever will be contrary to the Convention. So the problem should not arise'.

The point did arise for Lord Denning in *Taylor* v. *Co-op. Retail Services*.[33] After examining the case of *Young, James and Webster*[34] decided by the European Court of Human Rights in Strasbourg he concluded:

Mr Taylor was subjected to a degree of compulsion which was contrary to the freedom guaranteed by the European Convention on Human Rights. He was dismissed by his employers because he refused to join a 'closed shop'. He cannot recover any compensation from his employers under English law because under the Acts of 1974 and 1976, his dismissal is to be regarded as fair. But those Acts themselves are inconsistent with the freedom guaranteed by the European Convention. The United Kingdom Government is responsible for passing those Acts and should pay him compensation. He can recover it by applying to the European Commission, and thence to the European Court of Human Rights.

Similarly, Fox LJ found that the 'Convention is not part of the law of England and it cannot be used in the English Courts to displace the provisions of an English statute'.

More recently, in *Re M and H*, Lord Brandon affirmed that in the event of a conflict between an unambiguous statute and the Convention the Courts are bound to give effect to the statute.[35]

THE CONVENTION AS PART OF THE COMMON LAW

The Convention has been used mostly to buttress the principles already contained in the common law. So in one of the first references to it, Lord Kilbrandon, in the House of Lords, stated (in the context of a libel action): 'one must be watchful against holding the profit motive to be sufficient to justify punitive damages: to do so would be seriously to hamper what must be

---

[30] [1975] 119 SJ 322.

[31] See Carter, 'Decisions of British Courts During 1974–75 Involving Questions of Public and Private International Law', XLVII BYIL (1975) 341 at 359.

[32] *R.* v. *Secretary of State for Home Affairs, ex parte Bahjan Singh* [1976] QB 198 at 207.

[33] [1982] ICR 600.

[34] (1981) 44 ECHR ser. A.

[35] House of Lords, [1988] 3 WLR 485 at 498: 'I am, however, willing to assume, for the purposes of dealing with the contention of counsel for the father, that the denial to him of the right

regarded, at least since the European Convention was ratified, as a constitutional right to free speech.'[36]

Similarly, the right to public assembly, a common law right, is according to Forbes J 'in fact, specifically mentioned in Article 11 of the European Convention on Human Rights'.[37] Despite such deference to the Convention's norms, the Convention had no real bearing on the outcome of these or other cases where it was referred to in the same way.[38]

These references have made little impact and are no cause for surprise. Two cases which are more startling in relation to the Convention are *Cheall* v. *Apex*[39] and *UKAPE* v. *ACAS*.[40] In these cases Lord Denning found two 'common law rights' which had been confirmed by the European Court of Human Rights, and therefore, it was the duty of the Court of Appeal to give effect to these rights. The rights, respectively, were:

(a) the right to be a member of a trade union of one's choice; and
(b) the right to have one's union recognized for collective bargaining.

Lord Denning had recourse to the first right in *Cheall* v. *APEX*. He relied on the case of *Young, James and Webster* v. *United Kingdom*,[41] a judgment of the European Court of Human Rights. Without going into a detailed examination of this judgment of the European Court of Human Rights we might still comment on Lord Denning's use of this case law. Lord Denning's interpretation of the Convention in this context can be criticized on a number of grounds.

First, the European Court specifically limited this decision to the facts of the case and to employees who are employed *before* the implementation of the 'closed shop' agreement; the facts of *Cheall* were completely different.

Secondly, Mr Cheall wanted to *move* from one union ('ACTSS') to another

referred to above constitutes a breach of Articles 6 and 8 of the Convention. Even on that assumption it seems to me that counsel's contention is founded on a misapprehension as to the status of the Convention in relation to English law. Although the United Kingdom is a party to the Convention, Parliament has not so far seen fit to make it a part of our country's domestic law. This means that English Courts are under no duty to apply its provisions directly. Further, while English Courts will strive when they can to interpret Statutes as conforming with the obligations of the United Kingdom under the Convention, they are nevertheless bound to give effect to Statutes which are free from ambiguity in accordance with their terms, even if those Statutes may be in conflict with the Convention.'

[36] *Broome* v. *Cassell & Co* [1972] AC 1027 at 1133.
[37] Forbes J. in *Hubbard* v. *Pitt* [1976] QB 143 at 156, although he later found justifications for limiting this right.
[38] See the House of Lords case, *Gleaves* v. *Deakin* [1979] 2 All ER 497, where Lord Diplock referred to the Convention when making the suggestion that in future, private actions for criminal libel should be brought only with the consent of the Attorney-General. The Libel Act 1843 creates an offence even where the 'libellous' statement is true, unless the *defendant* can show it was for the public interest!
[39] [1982] 3 All ER 855.   [40] [1979] ICR 303.
[41] (1981) 44 ECHR ser. A.

('APEX'). Article 11 guarantees the right to join a union for the protection of
one's interests. Mr Cheall's interests would also have been served by membership of the original union.

Thirdly, Mr Cheall had been expelled from APEX in accordance with the
Bridlington Principles (which are the rules which the Trade Union Disputes
Committee employ when regulating inter-union disputes). It was put to Lord
Denning that these rules were necessary to keep order in industrial relations,
and that an invalidation of the rules would lead to industrial chaos. In the language of the Convention: Article 11(2) allows for restrictions on Article 11(1)
where they are necessary in a democratic society, for the protection of the
rights and freedoms of others (here the employers and union members). Lord
Denning construed Article 11 as a right without limitations, and ignored the
collective rights of the individuals already in the collective:

I take my stand on something more fundamental. It is the freedom of the individual to
join a trade union of his choice . . . Even though it should result in industrial chaos,
nevertheless the freedom of each man should prevail over it. There comes a time in
peace as in war, as recent events show,[42] when a stand must be made on principle, whatever the consequences. Such a stand should be made here today.[43]

Fourthly, Lord Denning may have overestimated Mr Cheall's chances of
success in Strasbourg. As a justification for the decision Lord Denning stated
that he wanted to save Mr Cheall the time and expense of a trip to Strasbourg.
But only States can be respondents in Strasbourg. This was a case involving
the rules of a union and their relation to an individual; it was not apparent
that the United Kingdom would be held to have violated the Convention, nor
indeed was it.[44]

The decision of the Court of Appeal (with Lord Denning in the majority)
was overruled by the House of Lords.[45] Lord Diplock (who gave the only
opinion) dismissed the 'supposed rule of public policy'[46] reinforced by Article
11 in the following terms: 'Freedom of association can only be mutual; there
can be no right of an individual to associate with other individuals who are
not willing to associate with him'.

Lord Denning's second 'common law right', supposedly reinforced by the
Convention, arose in the case of *UKAPE* v. *ACAS*. Although less weight was
given to the Convention in this case than in *Cheall*, the case is interesting as
no reference is made to the judgments[47] of the European Court of Human
Rights. For instance in the *National Union of Belgian Police Case*[48] the Court

[42] Lord Denning was speaking just after the Falklands War.   [43] [1982] ICR 557.
[44] *Cheall* v. *United Kingdom* [1986] 8 EHRR 76.
[45] *Cheall* v. *APEX* [1983] 2 WLR 679.
[46] That an individual has a right to join and remain a member of the union of his or her choice.
[47] *National Union of Belgian Police Case* (1976) 19 ECHR ser. A; *Swedish Engine Drivers'
Union Case* (1976) 20 ECHR ser. A; *Schmidt and Dahlstrom Case* (1976) 21 ECHR ser. A.
[48] (1976) 19 ECHR ser. A.

held, inter alia, that Article 11 contained *no* implied right to consultation, for the purposes of collective bargaining.

The Court of Appeal was again overruled by the House of Lords.[49] Lord Scarman referred to the point on the European Convention and rejected the idea that Article 11 included a right for *every* trade union to recognition for the purposes of collective bargaining. He continued: 'Until such time as the statute is amended or the Convention both becomes part of our law and is interpreted in the way proposed by Lord Denning MR, the point is a bad one.'[50]

These last two cases lead to the conclusion that the use of the Convention as part of the common law may depend entirely on the enthusiasm with which any one judge is prepared to embrace it.[51] It does not really follow the developments in Strasbourg and is in danger of polarizing opinion as to the validity of the Convention. The blame for this could be laid:

(a) on the shoulders of practising barristers[52] for failing to bring to the attention of the Bench the relevant case law; or

(b) on Parliament and Government for failing to give the Convention a defined status and priority.[53]

Other factors which have led to this situation are:

(c) the absence of a suitable body such as a 'Human Rights Commission' to co-ordinate and assist complaints in the United Kingdom Courts based on the Convention;[54]

(d) on the lack of familiarity of a good proportion of the legal profession with the European dimension in United Kingdom law; and

---

[49] [1981] AC 424 where there was no argument on the Convention, nor was there reference to the pertinent Strasbourg cases.

[50] *UKAPE* v. *ACAS* n. 49 above at 446.

[51] See Lord Denning's comments on the Convention when interviewed on the radio. 'Asked whether he approved of the Convention he said "yes". Asked whether he wanted it introduced into our law he said "No, I prefer it as it is. I can look at it when I like and I don't have to look at it when I don't like".' Quoted by Lord Scarman in 'The ECHR: Two New Directions, EEC—UK', British Institute of Human Rights Conference held at King's College, London, 15 February 1980.

Also note the lack of reference to the Convention when Lord Denning was faced with a large militant Union demanding recognition from the Post Office: *R.* v. *Post Office, ex parte ASTMS* [1981] ICR 76.

[52] See Warbrick, 'European Convention of Human Rights and English Law', 130 *NLJ* (1980) 852; and also in 'The ECHR: Two New Directions EEC—UK', n. 51 above at 43.

[53] In particular, see articles by Lester, 'The Constitution, Decline and Renewal' in Jowell and Oliver eds., *The Changing Constitution* (1985), 273 and 'Fundamental Rights: The United Kingdom Isolated?', *PL* (1984) 46, and comments in 'The ECHR: Two New Directions EEC—UK', n. 51 above at 33.

[54] See p. 135.

(e) a mistrust of 'the chaps at Strasbourg',[55] and 'those people over there'.[56]

The Use of the Convention to Create or 'Discover' the Common Law

Only a few of the decided cases will be discussed here. The first, *Malone* v. *Commissioner of Police for the Metropolis (No. 2)*[57] is decisive authority for the rule that the Courts have no authority to make a *declaration* solely on the grounds that a Convention right has been violated. The case is important as it reveals to some extent the very English conception of a 'right'.

Included in Mr Malone's claim, was a request for a declaration that the interception and monitoring of his telephone lines violated Article 8 of the Convention (respect for private and family life, home, and correspondence). Under Order 15 rule 16 of the Rules of the Supreme Court: 'No action or other proceedings shall be open to objection on the ground that a merely declaratory judgment or order is sought thereby, and the Court may make binding declarations of right whether or not any consequential relief is or could be claimed.'

According to the argument of Mr Malone, this meant the Court could give a declaration not only as regards *legal rights* but also as to *moral* and *international obligations*. After very careful consideration by Sir Robert Megarry VC, this argument was rejected:

I can see nothing in RSC Ord 15 r 16 to open the doors to the making of declarations on a wide range of extra-legal issues . . . declarations will only be made in respect of matters justiciable in the Courts; treaties are not justiciable in this way; the Convention is a treaty with nothing in it that takes it out of that category for this purpose; and I therefore have no power to make the declaration claimed.[58]

A declaration then, can only be claimed in respect of a legally justiciable 'right' in the United Kingdom. The nature of this 'right' is far removed from the tradition of civil or human rights but contains the notion of a remedy or relief. The relationship between the individual and the State or law-making body is in the following terms: 'England is not a country where everything is forbidden except that which is expressly permitted'.[59]

Put another way this means that *anyone* can do *anything* unless it is

---

[55] Lord Hailsham (former Lord Chancellor) in a radio interview on the question of incorporation of the European Convention: 'Would a Bill of Rights Politicize the British Judges?', *The Listener* (12 February 1987) 16.

[56] Lord Denning in the debate on the Human Rights and Fundamental Freedoms Bill in the House of Lords. See HL Debates, vol. 473 (9 April 1986) at column 268. (Lord Denning had moved an amendment to the Bill which was intended to end the right of individual petition to Strasbourg.)

[57] [1979] 2 All ER 620.

[58] *Malone* n. 57 above at 628 per Megarry V-C.   [59] Ibid. at 630 per Megarry V-C.

expressly prohibited. So, when it was put to Sir Robert Megarry VC that the power to tap telephones had to be given, either by statute or by the common law, he replied that no positive authority was given by the law to permit people to smoke. Both telephone tapping and smoking were an invasion of other people's privacy.

This comparison is only valid due to the English tradition that no difference should be made regarding the standards that are imposed on individuals and public servants. With no theoretical 'public law' structure, this means that the police or any other public authority are free to do anything, unless it has been previously expressly outlawed.

Sir Robert Megarry VC was certain that this situation was not in conformity with the Convention as interpreted by the European Court of Human Rights in the *Klass* case and pointed out that 'telephone tapping is a subject which cries out for legislation'.[60]

So, although the Convention was admittedly violated, no common law 'right' existed.[61] And, although the Convention was extensively examined, it was felt that, even if the Convention had been a legitimate source of a right, it would not have been used in this context to find for the plaintiff, as its terms were too general to be appropriate to regulate a matter as complex as telephone tapping.

This case may have decided that Articles of the Convention, on their own, are incapable of creating rights in the United Kingdom Courts, but some judges have since relied on the Convention when deciding which direction the common law should take. In *Harman* v. *Home Office*[62] it was argued that when English law is unclear it should be interpreted in accordance with international obligations and that this was so even when it was the common law which was unclear.[63]

The case involved an appeal against a finding for contempt of court against Harriet Harman, a solicitor and then a legal officer for the National Council for Civil Liberties. Ms Harman had been acting for a prisoner who had alleged, inter alia, 'cruel and unusual punishments' contrary to the Bill of Rights 1688, arising out of his treatment in an experimental 'control unit' in

---

[60] Ibid. at 649. Since this decision the European Court of Human Rights has found in favour of Mr Malone (*Malone* v. *United Kingdom* (1985) 95 ECHR ser. A) and Parliament has passed the Interception of Telecommunications Act 1986. The *Klass* case is reported in (1978) 28 ECHR ser. A.

[61] Note, Megarry V-C refused to '*discover*' that the common law (buttressed by Article 8) had always protected the home and family life: 'It seems to me that where Parliament has abstained from legislating on a point that is plainly suitable for legislation, it is indeed difficult for the Court to lay down new rules of common law or equity that will carry out the Crown's treaty obligations, or discover for the first time that such rules have always existed': [1979] 2 All ER 620 at 647.

[62] [1983] AC 280.

[63] See also *R.* v. *Lemon* [1979] AC 617 at 655 (House of Lords), *Broome* v. *Cassell and Co. Ltd* [1972] AC 1027 at 1135 (House of Lords) and *Blathwayt* v. *Baron Cawley* [1976] AC 397 at 426 (House of Lords).

prison.[64] After an order for discovery had been granted in relation to certain documents,[65] these documents were read out in open court. A few days later Ms Harman allowed a journalist, who had been absent from part of the hearing, to have access to the documents which had been read out. The journalist wrote an article critical of the Home Office Ministers and civil servants, and the Home Office brought an action against Ms Harman alleging contempt of court, on the grounds that she was in breach of her obligation only to use the discovered documents for the purposes of the case.

It was undisputed that had this, or any other, journalist taken a shorthand note of the proceedings or ordered a transcript of the case, and then written an article based on such information, there could have been no action for contempt of court. The sole issue was whether the circumstances of the 'short cut' taken by the journalist constituted a contempt of court by the solicitor, Ms Harman.

Lord Diplock stated at the beginning of his opinion that the case was '*not* about freedom of speech, [or] freedom of the press', and that it did not 'call for consideration of any of those human rights and fundamental freedoms which in the European Convention on Human Rights are contained in separate articles each starting with a statement in absolute terms but followed immediately by very broadly-stated exceptions'.[66] The majority dismissed the appeal and found Ms Harman to be in contempt of court.[67]

Lords Scarman and Simon, in a joint dissenting opinion, referred to the case law of the European Court of Human Rights,[68] and pointed out that the exceptions to Article 10 (of the Convention) 'must be narrowly interpreted' in the words of the Strasbourg Court, and that according to that Court the exceptions were limited to those situations which demonstrated a 'real pressing need' and no such need existed here.

Clearly the use of the Convention was not outlawed in this situation, but different perceptions of its purpose led to opposite conclusions. Lord Diplock saw the exceptions to the right to free speech as 'broadly-stated'. Lords Scarman and Simon referred to the Strasbourg interpretation of the right to free speech and found that the exceptions had to be 'narrowly interpreted'.

In 1987 the House of Lords made reference to the Convention in three sep-

---

[64] *Williams* v. *Home Office (No 2)* [1981] 1 All ER 1151 (High Court); 1211 (Court of Appeal).

[65] Which contained details of the nature of the control units regime and the method by which prisoners were selected for it.

[66] *Harman* n. 62 above at 299. Cf. Lord Oliver in *Re B (A Minor)* [1987] 2 WLR 1213 at 1224, a case involving the sterilization of a mentally handicapped girl of 17: 'this case is not about eugenics; it is not about the convenience of those whose task it is to care for the ward or the anxieties of her family; and it involves no general principle of public policy'.

[67] Ms Harman took her case to Strasbourg where it ended in a 'friendly settlement' and an undertaking by the United Kingdom Government to change the Rules of the Supreme Court (application 10038/82, (1984) 7 EHRR 146).

[68] *Handyside Case* (1976) 24 ECHR ser. A; *Sunday Times* case (1979) 30 ECHR ser. A.

arate cases.[69] This has clearly established its legitimacy as a source of princi-ple when interpreting the common law. And by 1988 the general logic of the Convention had 'infiltrated' a number of judgments concerning confidential-ity; yet the approach of the Convention was still held to do no more than mir-ror the common law method. Lord Donaldson MR stated this in the second *Spycatcher* case in the following way:

The starting point of our domestic law is that every citizen has a right to do what he likes, unless restrained by the common law, including the law of contract, or by statute. If therefore, someone wishes to assert a right to confidentiality, the initial burden of establishing circumstances giving rise to this right lies on him. The substantive right to freedom of expression contained in Article 10 is subsumed in our domestic law in this universal freedom of action. Thereafter, both under our domestic law and under the Convention, the Courts have the power and the duty to assess the 'pressing social need' for the maintenance of confidentiality 'proportionate to the legitimate aim pursued' against the basic right to freedom of expression and all other relevant factors. In so doing they are free to apply 'a margin of appreciation' based on local knowledge of the needs of the society to which they belong: see *Sunday Times* v. *United Kingdom* (1979) 2 EHRR 245 and *Lingens* v. *Austria* (1986) 8 EHRR 407. For my part I detect no inconsistency between our domestic law and the convention. Neither adopts an absolute attitude for or against the maintenance of confidentiality. Both contemplate a balancing of private and public attitudes.[70]

The impact of the incorporation of phrases such as 'pressing social need', 'proportionality' and 'margin of appreciation' should not be underestimated as they evoke the case law of the Strasbourg organs. It is interesting that Lord Donaldson accepts the proportionality test in this context while it was expressly ruled out as unworkable when invoked as a ground for judicial review of administrative action (see p. 000 below). Nowhere is the logic of the Convention more evident than in the judgment of Scott J in the Divisional Court. 'I can see no "pressing social need" that is offended by these articles. The claim for an injunction against these two newspapers in June 1986 was not, in my opinion, "proportionate to the legitimate aim pursued".'[71] Nevertheless, Lord Donaldson, although he accepted the method, found him-self in 'profound disagreement with the judge' on this particular point. He found that the public interest in the due administration of justice outweighed the public interest in publication.[72]

[69] *Hone* v. *Maze Prison Board of Visitors* [1988] 1 All ER 321; *Re KD (A Minor) (Ward: Termination of Access)* [1988] 1 All ER 577; *Attorney-General* v. *Guardian Newspapers Ltd* [1987] 3 All ER 316.

[70] *Attorney-General* v. *Guardian (No 2)* [1988] 3 All ER 594 at 596, and see also Dillon L.J. at 615, and Brightman L.J. at 627–8 and 637 (reference to 'duties and responsibilities' in Article 10(2)). Similarly, see the opinions of Lord Griffiths at 652, and Lord Goff at 660 and 666 in the House of Lords.

[71] [1988] 3 All ER 545 at 587.

[72] Perhaps it is worth very briefly outlining some of the background to this case. The *Guardian* and *The Observer* had published reports of the forthcoming trial in Australia concerning the

But the last word in this section has to be from the case of *Derbyshire County Council* v. *Times Newspapers Ltd and Others*.[73] In this case the Court of Appeal had to define the extent of of the common law tort of libel. The *Sunday Times* had published two articles questioning the propriety of certain investments made by the Council. The articles had headings such as '[b]izarre deals of a council leader and media tycoon'. The judgment concedes that full use should be made of Article 10 to resolve an uncertainty in municipal law. The Court found that to allow a local authority to sue for libel was not necessary in a democratic society. It was an unjustifiable restriction on freedom of expression. The case really turns on proportionality, as the Court considered that the other options open to the local authority—actions for criminal libel or malicious falsehood—might be legitimate restrictions on freedom of expression where the reputation of the local authority might be damaged so as to impair its function for the public good. It was the existence of alternative, less intrusive measures which made the possibility of a civil libel action disproportionate and unnecessary.

In summary, it can be said that the use of the Convention is now an established component in decisions determining the scope of the common law. Nevertheless, the history of this aspect of the Convention's use by the British courts suggests that British judges still have some way to go before the human rights in the Convention are vigorously protected as part of the common law.

As a Factor to be Taken into Account by Administrative Bodies when Exercising their Discretion

In an early case of judicial review, *R.* v. *Secretary of State for Home Affairs, ex parte Bhajan Singh*,[74] Lord Denning held that:

immigration officers and the Secretary of State in exercising their duties ought to bear in mind the principles stated in the Convention. They ought, consciously or subconsciously, to have regard to the principles in it—because after all, the principles in the Convention are only a statement of the principles of fair dealing; and it is their duty to act fairly.[75]

Attorney-General's attempts to obtain injunctions to restrain publication of the book *Spycatcher*. The Attorney-General obtained interlocutory injunctions against these newspapers and it was these injunctions which Scott J. was referring to when he invoked the Convention's logic. Scott J. took into consideration two allegations in the newspaper reports which were of particular public interest. The first concerned a plot by the British Secret Service to assassinate President Nassar of Egypt, the second related to a plot by MI5 officers to destabilize the Wilson Government.

In the end, the European Court of Human Rights found that the United Kingdom had violated the Convention: *Case of The Sunday Times* v. *The United Kingdom (No. 2)* (1991) 217 ECHR ser. A; *Case of the Observer and Guardian* v. *United Kingdom* (1991) 216 ECHR ser. A.

73 [1992] All ER 65; [1993] AC 534 (HL).
74 [1975] 2 All ER 1081.   75 *Bhajan Singh* n. 74 above at 1083.

However in a later case, *R.* v. *Chief Immigration Officer, ex parte Salamat Bibi*,[76] he significantly changed his position, and the status of the Convention in this context, finding the Convention to be 'indigestible':

I desire, however, to amend one of the statements I made in *R.* v. *Secretary of State for Home Affairs, ex parte Bhajan Singh*. I said then that the immigration officers ought to bear in mind the principles stated in the Convention. I think that would be asking too much of the immigration officers. They cannot be expected to know or apply the Convention. They must go simply by the immigration rules laid down by the Secretary of State and not by the Convention. I may also add this. The Convention is drafted in a style very different from the way which we are used to in legislation. It contains wide general statements of principle. They are apt to lead to much difficulty in application; because they give rise to much uncertainty. They are not the sort of thing which we can easily digest. Article 8 is an example. It is so wide as to be incapable of practical application. So it is much better for us to stick to our own statutes and principles, and only look to the Convention for guidance in case of doubt.[77]

Lord Denning was not alone in taking this stance. Roskill LJ (as he then was) in his concurring judgment stated: 'there are no grounds for imposing on those who have the difficult task, which immigration officers have, to perform the additional burden of considering, on every occasion, the application of the Convention'.[78] Similarly, Geoffrey Lane LJ stated: 'One only has to read the article in question, Article 8(2), to realize that it would be an impossibility for any immigration officer to apply a discretion based on terms as wide and as vague as those in Article 8(2).'

It is important to note that these judgments are based on the *practicality* of asking immigration officers to consider Article 8 (the right to respect for family life, etc.) when deciding individual immigration cases. If the rationale for the irrelevance of the Convention in this area is the intolerable burden it would place on busy immigration officers, who are ill-equipped to apply 'general statements of principle', then the questions arise: is it relevant for other public bodies such as Ministers, local authorities or other bodies acting in a judicial way? And may other articles be distinguished as less difficult? For example, Article 3 (prohibition of torture, inhuman or degrading treatment) has no limitation clause and is arguably more capable of 'practical application'.

In *R.* v. *Secretary of State for the Home Department, ex parte Fernandes*[79] the Court of Appeal, relying on the *Bibi* case, held that the Secretary of State was under no obligation to consider whether his actions were in contravention

---

[76] [1976] 3 All ER 843. [77] *Salamat Bibi* n. 76 above at 847.
[78] Ibid. at 849; he also felt that the dictum of Scarman L.J. (as he then was) in *R.* v. *Secretary of State for the Home Department, ex parte Phansopkar* [1975] 3 WLR 225 to the effect that it was the duty of public authorities in administering the law to have regard to the Convention, was too wide.
[79] [1981] Imm AR 1, and *Times* (20 November 1980).

of the Convention. Again, this was in the context of deportation of immigrants and the interpretation of Article 8.

It is suggested that this was an unfortunate extension of the rule in *Bibi* which was based on the impracticability of immigration officers balancing the various factors involved in Article 8. The same argument cannot be applied to decisions of the Secretary of State who should be able to consider and evaluate the provisions of the Convention and even its case law. Although the Convention does not give rise to enforceable *rights* as it is not part of the law, the Treaty was entered into by the Executive and, as such, produces international obligations on the Crown. As a member of the Executive and a Crown employee it is surely not illogical that the Secretary of State should at least take into account these obligations when making decisions, even if technically not bound by them in national law.

The inability of the Courts to examine the Secretary of State's actions for conformity with human rights is highlighted by several cases concerning deportations.

Mr Cheblak was a Lebanese citizen who worked as an academic and was employed by the Arab League in London as a senior research officer. Shortly after the beginning of the war against Iraq in 1991 he was arrested and informed of the Home Secretary's intention to deport him 'for reasons of national security'.[80] The Court of Appeal reaffirmed that the nature of national security meant that they would not, and could not, demand further details regarding the necessity of this decision. They also reaffirmed that, as long as the decision could not be said to be 'irrational' it would not be reviewed. Lord Donaldson even offered a rationale for the 'surprising' decision of the Secretary of State: 'Those who are able most effectively to undermine national security are those who least appear to constitute any risk to it.'[81]

There may still be scope left for the argument that, where the decision is made due to authority given by statute or in consequence of an interpretation of a statute, then the Convention is a relevant factor to be taken into account by the body taking the decision. This would be so due to the principle that, wherever possible, statutes have to be interpreted in accordance with the Convention.

Although judicial review of administrative action will often be a case of interpreting the empowering statute to find out if the decision was ultra vires or not, some of the most important cases of judicial review will now involve administrative decisions where no empowering statute falls to be considered. In *Council of Civil Service Unions* v. *Minister for the Civil Service*[82] the Prime

---

[80] *R.* v. *Secretary of State for the Home Department, ex parte Cheblek* [1991] 2 All ER 319. For the non-judicial safeguards surrounding such a decision see ibid. at 329–33.

[81] Ibid. at 333.   [82] [1985] AC 374.

Minister had issued an instruction that the staff at Government Communications Headquarters (GCHQ) would no longer be permitted to belong to national trade unions. The House of Lords found that even though this instruction was issued under a prerogative power it was still reviewable as if it had been empowered by statute. Similarly, in *R. v. Panel for Take Overs and Mergers, ex parte Prudential Bache Inc.*[83] the self-regulating panel was set up neither by statute nor by the prerogative but the supervisory jurisdiction of the High Court extended to cover the decisions of this body due to their public law nature. To some extent, judges may feel they are justified in ignoring the Convention when deciding on the *reasonableness*[84] of administrative action, as the rules of statutory interpretation may be irrelevant due to the absence of any sort of ambiguity contained in a statute.

[83] [1987] 2 WLR 699.

[84] Lord Diplock in *CCSU v. Minister for Civil Service* [1985] AC 374 took the opportunity to redefine the heads of judicial review as (1) illegality; (2) irrationality; and (3) procedural impropriety, which includes failure to observe the basic rules of natural justice. Should the rules of natural justice come to include, say, Article 6 of the Convention then it may be that the Convention could be given more attention. Lord Diplock also suggested that a further head may be adopted in the future, that of 'proportionality'; and he specifically referred to the fact that this is 'recognised in the administrative law of several of our fellow members of the EEC'. It should be noted that the concept of proportionality has also gained favour with the European Commission of Human Rights, where it has been referred to as 'inherent in the exception clause of Article 10(2)' (and presumably similar articles): see *Gay News Ltd and Denis Lemon v. United Kingdom* (1982) 5 EHRR 123. Also in the *Dudgeon* case (1981) 45 ECHR ser. A, para. 60, the European Court of Human Rights used 'proportionality' to conclude that the justifications for retaining the law on homosexuality were outweighed by the effect such legislation had on individuals. If these new heads of judicial review are embraced by the Courts then it may be that elucidation of terms such as 'natural justice' and 'proportionality' will require reference to the Convention or even to the case law of the European Court of Justice in Luxembourg. For the way that this Court has developed this field see Schwarze, 'The Administrative Law of the Community and the Protection of Human Rights', 23 CML Rev. (1986) 401. In an article ('Beyond *Wednesbury*: Substantive Principles of Administrative Law', PL (1987) 368 at 374–81 advocating new heads of judicial review rather than the *Wednesbury* reasonable tests, Jowell and Lester suggest that the following principles be applied: proportionality, legal certainty, consistency, and fundamental human rights. All these principles emerge from EC or Convention law. Should English administrative law develop along these lines the Convention and its jurisprudence will become more relevant, even in the absence of the *formal* incorporation of the substantive rights contained therein. Most recently the Court of Appeal has clearly stated that proportionality *cannot* be considered a separate head of review but is one aspect of reasonableness: *R. v. Secretary of State for the Home Department ex parte Brind* [1990] 1 All ER 469; see also *Colman v. General Medical Council* [1989] 1 Medical Law Reports 23 (QBD), and [1990] 1 All ER 489 (Court of Appeal). It should be noted that one can not conclude that proportionality (as understood in EC law and in several other Member States) is therefore established in English law. The reason that the Courts did not accept proportionality is exactly because it was not considered part of English law and its inclusion could 'create a monster that could quickly get out of control and cause widespread disruption of many administrative processes that might attract its application': *Colman* [1989] 1 Medical Law Reports 23 at 30 per Auld J. Further, '[i]n our opinion the application of such a concept of proportionality would result in the Courts substituting their own decisions for that of the Minister and that is something which the Courts of this country have consistently declined to do. The Courts will not abrogate to themselves executive or administrative decisions which should be taken by executive or administrative bodies': Watkins L.J. cited by Donaldson MR in *Brind* [1990] 1 All ER 469 at 479. For the extent that these cases deal with the Convention see below.

This was deemed to be the situation in *R*. v. *Secretary of State for the Home Department, ex parte Brind*.[85] This case concerned directives issued by the Home Secretary to the British Broadcasting Corporation (BBC) and the Independent Broadcasting Authority (IBA) prohibiting the broadcasting of direct statements by representatives of proscribed organizations in Northern Ireland. A number of journalists together with a union official from the National Union of Journalists applied for judicial review of the Minister's decision on the grounds, inter alia, that the directives were unlawful in that they were in breach of Article 10 of the Convention.

The Convention was 'at the forefront' of the applicant's argument and Lord Donaldson, MR, dealt with the status of the Convention in some detail. His judgment clarifies a number of issues. Having recalled that the principles in the Convention are difficult to distinguish from the English common law ('at least if the Convention is viewed through English judicial eyes'[86]), and that the Convention is an international treaty which has not been incorporated into English law, even though there are 'well-informed supporters of this course', he confirmed that the 'duty of the English Courts is to decide disputes in accordance with English domestic law as it is, and not as it would be if full effect were given to this country's obligations under the Treaty, assuming that there is a difference between the two'.[87] He continued as follows:

It follows from this that in most cases the English Courts will be wholly unconcerned with the terms of the convention. The sole exception is when the terms of primary legislation are fairly capable of bearing two or more meanings and the Court, in pursuance of its duty to apply domestic law, is concerned to divine and define its true and only meaning. In that situation various prima facie rules of construction have to be applied, such as that, in the absence of very clear words indicating the contrary, legislation is not retrospective or penal in effect. To these can be added, in appropriate cases, a presumption that Parliament has legislated in a manner consistent, rather than inconsistent, with the United Kingdom's treaty obligations . . .[88]

Thus far I have referred only to primary legislation, but it is also necessary to consider subordinate legislation and Executive action, whether it be under the authority of primary or secondary legislation. Counsel for the applicants submits that, where there is any ambiguity in primary legislation and it may accordingly be appropriate to consider the terms of the Convention, the ambiguity may sometimes be resolved by imputing an intention to Parliament that the delegated power to legislate or, as the case may be,

---

[85] [1990] 1 All ER 469 (Court of Appeal); [1991] 1 All ER 720 (House of Lords). For a comment on the Court of Appeal judgment see Jowell, 'Broadcasting and Terrorism, Human Rights and Proportionality', PL (1990) 149. See also *R*. v. *General Medical Council, ex parte Colman* [1990] 1 All ER 489.

[86] Ibid. at 477.   [87] Ibid.

[88] Lord Donaldson refers to Diplock L.J.'s judgment in *Salomon* v. *Customs and Excise Commissioners* [1966] 3 All ER 871 at 875 (see p. 99), the passage in *Chundawadra* v. *Immigration Appeal Tribunal* [1988] Imm AR 161 at 173 (which repeats the Diplock judgment verbatim), and the passage by Lord Diplock in *Garland* v. *British Rail Engineering Ltd* [1982] 2 All ER 402 at 415.

the authority to take Executive action, shall be subject to the limitation that it be consistent with the terms of the Convention. This I unhesitatingly and unreservedly reject, because it imputes to Parliament an intention to import the Convention into domestic law by the back door, when it has quite clearly refrained from doing so by the front door.[89]

Lord Donaldson then asserted that the empowering legislation was in no way ambiguous and:

It follows that whilst the Home Secretary, in deciding whether or not to issue a directive and the terms of that directive, is free to take into account the terms of the Convention, as at some stage he undoubtedly did, he was under no obligation to do so. It also follows that the terms of the Convention are quite irrelevant to our decision and that the Divisional Court erred in considering them, even though in the end it concluded that it derived no assistance from this consideration.[90]

Gibson LJ also considered Articles 10, 1, and 13 of the Convention and the argument that the Convention had not been incorporated precisely because successive Governments considered that there already existed the necessary arrangements within the domestic order for compliance. He considered that the principle of interpretation existing in the common law meant that the Convention was relevant when construing legislation, when declaring and applying the common law and when reviewing the exercise of administrative discretion. Nevertheless, he confirmed that although it was correct to use the Convention to construe an Act of Parliament passed *after* the Treaty had been signed, the Convention could *not* be used to review the substantial validity of the *action of the Minister*.[91]

Watkins LJ in the Divisional Court had come to the opposite conclusion: '[W]here Parliament has created for a Minister a statutory power in terms

---

[89] *Brind* n. 85 above at 477–8.   [90] Ibid.

[91] Professor Eric Barendt has criticized the Court of Appeal's reasoning in this case. He relies on the broad terms of the opinion of Lord Diplock in *Garland* v. *British Rail Engineering Ltd* [1983] 2 AC 751 at 771: 'It is a principle of construction of United Kingdom Statutes, now too well established to call for citation of authority, that the words of a Statute passed after the treaty has been signed and dealing with the subject matter of the international obligation of the United Kingdom, are to be construed, if they are reasonably capable of bearing such a meaning, as intended to carry out the obligation and not to be inconsistent with it.' Barendt suggests that it is clear that this applies equally to the Convention and therefore the Convention should be used to construe the legislation which delegates the relevant power 'as only conferring authority to issue directives in conformity with the Convention, at least where the text of the statute makes that interpretation possible': Barendt, 'Broadcasting Censorship', 106 LQR (1990) 354 at 357. For discussion as to the possible necessity of some sort of 'linkage' between the Statute 'dealing with the same subject matter' and the Treaty see pp. 000–00. The question does not really seem to be whether the Court accepts that Parliament intended power to be exercised in conformity with Article 10 or any other international obligation, but rather whether parliament could be said to have intended that the Courts should be able to review the Minister's actions for conformity with the international norms. It is presumably a reluctance to impute this last intention which led the Court of Appeal and the House of Lords to reject the relevance of the Convention as well as the doctrine of proportionality.

which place no limitation on that power, then reference must be made to Article 10 by a Court when deciding what are the limitations to be placed on the use of that power.'[92] However, this was expressly overruled in the Court of Appeal.

The appeal to the House of Lords concerned two points: the relevance of the Convention and the proportionality principle. Most of the opinions affirm that the Secretary of State's action cannot be reviewed by the Courts for conformity with the Convention.[93] It was affirmed that because Parliament has *not* incorporated the Convention and because Parliament:

has been content for so long to leave those who complain that their Convention rights have been infringed to seek their remedy in Strasbourg, it would be surprising suddenly to find that the judiciary had, without Parliament's aid, the means to incorporate the Convention into such an important area of domestic law and I cannot escape the conclusion that this would be a judicial usurpation of the legislative function.[94]

The judgment does not represent an anti-human rights, or even an anti-European stance. What the majority of the House of Lords reaffirmed was that the Courts have no authority to review Ministerial decisions unless they are 'unreasonable' in the narrow sense defined in *Associated Provincial Picture Houses* v. *Wednesbury Corporation*. According to their Lordships the judgment would have to be 'perverse', or 'irrational'. They referred to passages of Lord Diplock's opinion in the *CCSU* v. *Minister for the Civil Service* case, where he likened an irrational decision to 'a decision which is so outrageous in its defence of logic or of accepted moral standards that no sensible person who had applied his mind to the question to be decided could have arrived at it'.[95]

It is worth noting in parenthesis that, if the judges had had the benefit of a Bill of Rights, in the form of the Convention, it would seem that they would nevertheless have found that the Ministerial directives were not in breach of Article 10. All the speeches suggest that the object of the Minister's action was legitimate and the action taken proportionate to the aim to be achieved.

The proportionality test was also rejected by most of their Lordships.[96]

---

[92] *Brind* n. 85 above at 485 cited by McCowan L.J. who disagreed on this aspect.

[93] Lord Templeman was prepared to go beyond the *Wednesbury* principles of unreasonableness, which he thought were inappropriate due to their subject matter and date. He embraced the language of the European Court of Human Rights and asked whether the interference with freedom of expression was justifiable as necessary and proportionate to the damage which the restriction is designed to prevent. He acknowledged that the Secretary of State must be afforded a margin of appreciation and concluded that there had been no abuse of power.

[94] *Brind* n. 85 above at 723 per Lord Bridge; see also ibid. at 734–5 per Lord Ackner: 'If the Secretary of State was obliged to have proper regard to the Convention, i.e. to conform to Article 10, this inevitably would result in incorporating the Convention into English law by the back door.'

[95] [1985] AC 374 at 410.

[96] Although Lord Templeman seems to have applied the proportionality doctrine to the case (see above).

Lord Ackner said that the doctrine could not be followed until the Convention is incorporated by Parliament. Lord Lowry found the idea impractical, likely to give rise to uncertainty and prolonged decisions, as well as taking up the Courts' time 'which could otherwise be devoted to other matters'.[97] Lord Roskill was not prepared to apply the principle in the present case but did not 'exclude the possible future development of the law in this respect, a possibility which has been canvassed in some academic writings'.[98]

It is difficult to see why this result is not a violation of Article 13 of the Convention. Clearly, there is no access to a national tribunal for the determination of whether there has been a violation under Article 10.[99]

This case is important not only because it gives the clearest statement so far by the House of Lords concerning the applicability of the Convention in the English Courts, but also because it deals with exactly the sort of subject matter which some people argue should be decided by judges using the Convention and which others argue is a matter of policy and Executive discretion better left to elected politicians. The latter group are unwilling to see the Courts engage in balancing acts weighing the public interest or national security against individual rights as defined by a European Court.

Incorporation of the European Convention into Domestic Law, Either as a Bill of Rights or as an Interpretation Act

In 1990 this issue was debated twice in the House of Lords,[100] and in 1986 and 1987 there were two separate attempts to incorporate the European Convention on Human Rights into the law of the United Kingdom.[101] The first attempt was the Human Rights and Fundamental Freedoms Bill, introduced as a private member's Bill in the House of Lords. This Bill passed through all stages in the House of Lords, but was given no time by the Government in the House of Commons.

The second attempt was the Human Rights Bill, another private member's

---

[97] *CCSU* n. 95 above at 739.   [98] Ibid. at 725; and see Jowell and Lester n. above 84.

[99] The decision of the House of Lords has also been applied in the context of judicial review of the Secretary of State's discretion on whether to surrender an applicant to the USA under Article V(2) of the United States of America (Extradition) Order 1976. See *R. v. Secretary of State for the Home Department ex parte Chinoy*, judgment of 10 April 1991, *Times*, law reports (14 April 1991), 28.

[100] Motion entitled 'Debate to call attention to the state of civil liberties under this Administration', HL Debates, vol. 519 (23 May 1990) at columns 904–35; Early Day Motion on incorporation of the European Convention on Human Rights, introduced by Lord Holme of Cheltenham, HL Debates. vol. 524 (5 December 1990) at column 185: see Hudson, 'ECHR and a Bill of Rights', 140 NLJ (1990) 1757.

[101] For the background *see* Blackburn, 'Legal and Political Arguments for a United Kingdom Bill of Rights' in Blackburn and Taylor eds., *Human Rights for the 1990s* (1991), 109; and Blackburn, 'Parliamentary Opinion on a new Bill of Rights', *Political Quarterly* (1989) 469.

Bill, with support from all parties, but not backed by the Government. On 6 February 1987, at the second reading of the Bill, ninety-six Members of Parliament voted in favour of the Bill and sixteen voted against. However, due to a procedural rule requiring at least 100 votes in favour, the Bill proceeded no further.

Although there have been several similar attempts in the past to incorporate the European Convention,[102] it seems that the form that such a Bill may take is becoming more settled. The latest proposed clause on entrenchment means that the old arguments on the sovereignty of Parliament do not arise in the same way. As Parliament retains the power to pass any Act even after an adverse judgment by the Courts, accusations of 'government by the judges' or 'the spectre of a judicial super-Legislature' do not have the same relevance.

ENTRENCHMENT

Some of the proposals regarding entrenchment can be briefly explained as follows. When the Bill went through the House of Lords in 1985, the original proposal was for a Bill of Rights which would entrench the Convention,[103] to the extent that a *future* Act of Parliament would have to expressly state that it was to operate *notwithstanding* the Bill of Rights/Human Rights Act.[104]

However, at the second reading in the House of Lords, this clause was amended after objections that it: '[F]lies in the teeth of a well-established constitutional doctrine that one Parliament can not bind a subsequent Parliament. That principle is intrinsic to the doctrine of the sovereignty of Parliament in this country and has prevailed for many centuries.'[105]

The amended clause provided that no provisions of future Acts are to be construed as authorizing acts contrary to the Convention, unless such a construction is unavoidable in order to give effect to the Act.[106]

This amendment changes what could be described as a 'Bill of Rights' (with an express derogation clause) into an Interpretation Act. In other words,

---

[102] For the details of these attempts see Zander, *A Bill of Rights?* (3rd edn., 1985).

[103] Articles 2–12, 14, and the First Protocol including the United Kingdom's reservation.

[104] 'Save in so far as such enactment is an Act which expressly directs that this subsection shall not apply to the doing of the act in question, or is made pursuant to a power which expressly so directs'; part of Clause 4(2) of the Human Rights and Fundamental Freedoms Bill (HL) No. 21 (1985).

[105] Lord Lloyd of Hampstead, Debate on the Human Rights and Fundamental Freedoms Bill, HL Debates, vol. 473 (9 April 1986) at column 271.

[106] In full, cl 4(2) reads: 'No provision of an Act passed after the passing of this Act shall be construed as authorising or requiring the doing of an act that infringes any of the fundamental rights and freedoms, or as conferring power to make any subordinate instrument authorising or requiring the doing of any such act, unless such a construction is unavoidable if effect is to be given to that provision and to the other provisions of the Act.' This formula was adopted in the Human Rights Bill (House of Commons), Bill No. 19 (10 December 1986).

under the first version, should a Court be faced with a statute passed by Parliament[107] which contravened the Convention (as interpreted by the national Court), then that Court would give the Convention priority and hold the Act invalid. Under the second version, if the effectiveness of the Act requires an interpretation which contravenes the Convention, the Court has to give priority to the Act of Parliament.

There is, therefore, a big difference between the two in terms of constitutional theory. However, one should not be considered a 'stronger' version than the other. It is quite possible that the Legislature would choose, in some circumstances, to include a 'notwithstanding clause'. If evidence is needed for this proposition, it can be found in the clauses used to oust the jurisdiction of the Courts: for example the Interception of Communications Act 1985[108] creates a new Tribunal and then specifically disallows any review of the Tribunal's decision by the Courts,[109] and the Local Government Finance Act 1987 reads in part 'This section shall have effect notwithstanding any decision of a Court purporting to have contrary effect'.

Similarly, in Canada, where the new Charter for Fundamental Rights and Freedoms 1982 (which surplants the Canadian Bill of Rights), has been enacted, the Quebec Legislature has already passed legislation[110] ensuring that all Acts passed before the Charter are 'to operate notwithstanding the Canadian Charter of Rights and Freedoms'. Although the motives for such action are primarily linked to this Province's political objections to the manner of adoption of the Charter, the 'notwithstanding' formula has been used by the Quebec Legislature in new legislation passed since the Charter was adopted.[111] In the past, even the Federal Legislature had recourse to the formula when it passed an Act wherein 'it is hereby declared that this Act shall operate notwithstanding the Canadian Bill of Rights'.[112]

Moreover, under the Bill of Rights version the implication is that judges can be asked to hold a whole Act of Parliament invalid. This, they will clearly be reluctant to do, and in a borderline case may choose to uphold the whole Act. Under the Interpretation Act variant, the emphasis is on interpreting provisions of Acts so as to be in conformity with the Convention.

---

[107] Passed after the 'Human Rights Act' and not *expressly* stating that it was to take effect notwithstanding the Human Rights Act.

[108] Enacted as a result of the judgment of the European Court of Human Rights in the *Malone* case (telephone tapping). For an appraisal and criticism of this Act, and its failure to really comply with the spirit of the *Malone* judgment, see Fitzgerald, and Leopold, *Stranger on the Line: The Secret History of Phone Tapping* (1987), 133–54.

[109] Section 7(8) reads: 'The decisions of the Tribunal (including any decisions as to their jurisdiction) shall not be subject to appeal or liable to be questioned in any Court.'

[110] An Act Respecting the Constitution (Act 1982 SQ 1982), Section 1 (Quebec).

[111] See Tarnopolski, 'The New Canadian Charter of Rights and Freedoms as Compared and Contrasted with the American Bill of Rights', 5 HRQ (1983) 227.

[112] Canadian Public Order Act 1970, s 12(1).

This issue of future Acts of Parliament and their validity is not so important in practice. As has been seen in the previous two sections, the vast majority of human rights cases coming before the Courts concern administrative practices and rules, together with old statutory and common law offences.

METHOD OF JUDICIAL REVIEW

Most proposals for incorporation of the European Convention include, not only methods of judicial review of legislation, but also the imperative that 'no person shall do any act . . . which infringes any of the fundamental rights and freedoms of any other person'.[113] The judicial review which is proposed can usefully be described using the terminology developed by Professor Cappelletti in *Judicial Review in the Contemporary World*.[114]

The review would be 'decentralized'. This means that any Court could apply the 'higher law' of the European Convention, to construe provisions or decisions so as to be in conformity with the Convention. Also *any* Court could prohibit or declare invalid action which contravened the rights set out in the Convention. This means that the Convention would not only be used by the highest Court when contemplating the validity of Acts of Parliament,[115] but also by the lower Courts when deciding questions as diverse as: the legality of a street protester's obstruction of the highway; whether to grant an injunction to prevent publication; sexually discriminatory retirement ages; or even dismissal on the grounds of homosexuality. In this way, the vocabulary of the Convention would become part of the legal culture at all levels and not only relevant to decide major constitutional issues.[116]

The review would be 'incidenter'. This means that the Convention would normally be raised as an additional argument in the context of a legal conflict, rather than relied on to initiate an action. This would mean that knowledge of the Convention and its practice would be dispersed through the widest community possible. In countries where constitutional matters can only be raised in a special context and only in a central Court or council, only a few specialists are familiar with the Constitutions's provisions and philosophy; not only does this mean that there is restricted access to arguments based on constitutional-type rights, but it considerably diminishes the educative effect of such a codification of fundamental rights and duties. For the Convention to become

---

[113] Human Rights Bill 1986, cl 3(1).   [114] (1971).

[115] It is assumed that actually holding invalid an Act of Parliament or even delegated legislation would be for the highest Court to finally determine. Note that two detailed proposals for a British Bill of Rights both include a provision allowing for a speedy review process by the higher Courts. See Institute for Public Policy Research, *A British Bill of Rights* (1990) and Liberty, *A People's Charter* (1991).

[116] It might be added that there would be an element of centralization because the Strasbourg organs would usually deliver the authoritative interpretation of the Convention.

a living code, rather than a dead letter, it must be debated and considered in different contexts in every Court and tribunal, and not just by the 'great and the good' sitting in judgment. It is suggested that this 'decentralized/incidenter' version is the most appropriate in the context of incorporation of the Convention into United Kingdom law.[117]

EFFECT OF INCORPORATION

At this point it is submitted that the Convention could have an enormous impact on administrative practices and the decisions of the lower Courts, should it be incorporated. Whether or not the decisions of the Court of Appeal or the House of Lords would be radically different is difficult to guess. It may be worth returning briefly to some of the decisions which were examined earlier.

In *Re the Council of Civil Service Unions*[118] all the judges in the House of Lords accepted the argument that the 'national security issue' meant they had no authority to review the Prime Minister's decision to ban trade union membership at GCHQ. It might therefore be suggested that the incorporation of the European Convention on Human Rights, allowing as it does for restrictions in the interests of national security, would have made no difference to the result achieved with the present law. This may be so, but the case law of the European Court of Human Rights requires that the rights take effect with limited restrictions. This means that it would be for the Crown to show *evidence* of the restriction being necessary in the interests of national security. It is debatable whether this shift in the burden of proof would make any difference to the outcome, but what is clear is that the job which the Court is doing would be exposed: the judges would be faced with a clear choice between the right to join and form trade unions, as found in Article 11(1), and the Minister's objection that it was *necessary* to restrict this right on the grounds of national security.

After failing in the House of Lords the unions took the case to Strasbourg

---

[117] When Lester suggested a sort of Constitutional Council in 1968 this may have been meant as a preliminary step or compromise: *Democracy and Human Rights Fabian Tract No. 390* (1968). His more recent suggestions refer to incorporation along the lines outlined above (Lester articles, n. 53 above; Jowell and Lester, n. 84 above); similarly, the proposal of Sir Leslie Scarman (as he then was) for a Supreme Court *(English Law—The New Dimension* (1974), 77–82) have been dropped in favour of the Bill described above, which he helped to draft. For Lord Scarman's later proposals see Scarman, 'Britain and the Protection of Human Rights', 15 Cambrian Law Review (1984) 5. However, the issue of a separate constitutional council has been revived by Lee, 'Arguments against a Bill of Rights', in Neuberger ed., *Freedom of Information . . . Freedom of the Individual* (1987). See also two proposals for Bills of Rights which go beyond the Convention: Lester et al., *A British Bill of Rights* (1990); Liberty, n. 115 above, which both stress the role of the High Court and the judicial review process.

[118] [1984] 3 All ER 935.

where the Commission declared the application inadmissible.[119] From the perspective of the disappointed applicants there are two relevant reactions to such an outcome:

(1) The restrictions which are allowed are so wide, that the core of the right becomes meaningless—incorporation of the Convention would have made no difference in this particular case.[120]

(2) Despite many progressive decisions by the Commission in the past, their make-up now reflects an increasingly 'Conservative Europe', and having considerably expanded the scope of the Convention, the Commissioners are now treading much more carefully. It is perhaps possible that an English Bench might have been less wary of finding a violation of Article 11. In any case, the Commissioner's decision shows the necessity of 'repatriating' this Bill of Rights.[121]

There is no way of accurately stating what would have happened if the Convention had been part of domestic law. A realistic approach must consider the long term effects of incorporation—even if different decisions cannot be foreseen in the immediate future, the educative impact of the rights discourse would eventually have some influence. It is sometimes suggested that such a rights discourse would only exacerbate the problems encountered by collectives in their attempts to assert their rights. As we saw above, judges sometimes naturally gravitate to awarding individuals rights over their colleagues in the collective. This can undermine the effectiveness of the collective and weaken its power to organize. So far, the collective right to associate has not been given much priority either at the national or international level.

Nevertheless, the Convention, while stressing a rights approach, need not give rise to a culture based around individual rights holders. The framework of the Convention is capable of supporting a reasoned approach to the clash of interests between individuals and collective organizations. On balance, it is suggested that using the Convention would be more likely to stimulate a democratic debate about the nature and purpose of the rights being claimed. Ignoring the Convention leaves the debate exclusively in the hands of lawyers

---

[119] *Council of Civil Service Unions and Others* v. *United Kingdom* (application 11603/85) 50 D. & R. 228). The Commission found that the workers at GCHQ could be considered as 'members . . . of the administration of the State' under Article 11(2) and that the restrictions were 'lawful' in the narrow sense (in accordance with the law) and in the wider sense (proportionate to the aim to be achieved).

[120] For an example of this approach see Mr N. Brown, Labour Party spokesman in the debate on the Human Rights Bill, HC Debates, vol. 109 (6th) (6 February 1987) at column 1278.

[121] These sentiments were variously expressed at the conference 'A Bill of Rights for the U.K.?', (conference on the incorporation of the ECHR, organized by the NCCL and the Cobden Trust and held in London, 29 January 1987), by some of those who had been involved in this application to the Commission.

who are the only ones entitled to 'divine and define' ancient common law rights.

In fact, the current situation, whereby the Convention is only debated in Strasbourg, means that the clash of rights is not debated at all in the domestic arena. When the issue arises at the international level, the conflict is handed over to an even more select set of lawyers, debated in a foreign land, and possibly eventually determined by a panel of judges, most of whom will be unfamiliar with the balance of industrial relations in the United Kingdom.

We might also return to the first *Spycatcher* case—*Attorney-General* v. *Guardian Newspapers Ltd.*[122] In this judgment the restrictions in the Convention were relied on by one of the majority judges, Lord Templeman, to uphold an injunction *against* the newspapers. Such a restriction on the 'fundamental principle of freedom of the press' was legitimated by reference to the restrictions permitted in the Convention by Article 10(2). In *Lord Advocate* v. *Scotsman Publications Ltd and Others* Lord Templeman developed his approach to paragraph 2 of Article 10 and stated: 'In my opinion it is for Parliament to determine the restraints on freedom of expression which are necessary in a democratic society.'[123] However, it may be that had the Convention had the effect of law rather than its present rather confused status, the majority of their Lordships may have chosen freedom of expression over the common law concepts of 'confidentiality' and 'breach of contract'. Most pertinent is the fact that if the case had revolved around an interpretation of the European Convention, the Court would have had to consider in depth the case law of the European Commission and Court of Human Rights.[124]

This case law includes two decisions of the European Court of Human Rights, where paramount consideration was given to the freedom of the press, and where it was stated that 'freedom of expression constitutes one of the essential foundations of a democratic society'.[125] It also includes the decision

---

[122] [1987] 3 All ER 316.

[123] [1989] 2 All ER 852 at 859. See Walker, 'Spycatchers Scottish Sequel', PL (1990) 354 at 368. Walker, ibid. at 370 warns that: 'Viewed in the context of the debate over reception of the Convention in our domestic Courts, this novel doctrine might, in the face of appropriately crafted legislative initiatives, accord Government such extensive control over its own 'margin of appreciation' as to empty the Convention of effective content in respect of the development of cognate areas of common law.'

[124] Note, cl 6 of the proposed 'Human Rights Bill' reads: 'For the purpose of this Act judicial notice shall be taken of the Convention and the Protocols thereto to which the United Kingdom is signatory and of all published judgments of the European Court of Human Rights and of all published reports and decisions of the European Commission of Human Rights established by the Convention.'

In fact, the case law of the Court was eventually referred to in the proceedings of the main action: see Lord Donaldson MR in *Attorney-General* v. *Guardian (No. 2)* [1988] 3 All ER 595 at 596.

[125] *Sunday Times* case (1979) 30 ECHR ser. A, para. 65, and *Lingen's Case* (1986) 103 ECHR ser. A, para. 41; of course, the case law also includes the *Handyside Case*, 21 ECHR ser. A, where

of the Commission in *Harman* v. *United Kingdom*[126] which ended in a friendly settlement, but arose out of a finding of contempt of court concerning publication of documents read out in open court. As the House of Lords in the interim proceedings in the *Spycatcher* case imposed a ban on reporting proceedings in *open court* in Australia, the spirit of the *Harman* v. *UK* decision could have been of particular relevance, especially as it came after a House of Lords decision[127] in which the majority had eschewed the Convention as irrelevant.

It seems clear that incorporation of the Convention will not automatically lead the judges to different conclusions,[128] indeed the judge at first instance, all three judges in the Court of Appeal, and two members of the House of Lords in the trial of the substantive issues in the *Spycatcher* case,[129] referred to Article 10 of the Convention and occasionally used its language in their judgments and opinions—despite the fact that the Convention is *not* at present incorporated into the law. However, it must be stated that the Convention, and more importantly the case law of the Strasbourg bodies, would have an educative effect in cases which touch on issues raised by the Convention.

The potential educative effect of the Convention is already clear from the way that critics of Government action now frequently phrase their attacks on the administration in terms of the rights contained in the Convention. Some critics have gone on to speculate what would have happened if the Convention had been law, and then call for its enactment.[130]

---

the Court allowed a 'margin of appreciation' to the United Kingdom, and upheld the ban on *The Little Red Schoolbook*. (This case was distinguished in the *Sunday Times Case* as one which turned on a question of morals and thus merited less interference from a supranational Court than cases where the restriction is justified in order to protect the authority of the judiciary.)

[126] Application 10038/82, 38 D. & R. 53 (11 May 1984) (admissibility); report of the Commission, adopted 15 May 1986, see Council of Europe, *Information Sheet No. 20* (Strasbourg, 1987) 42. The friendly settlement contained an undertaking by the United Kingdom Government to amend the rules concerning disclosure of documents, and compensation for Ms. Harman (legal expenses) of £36,360 (46 D. & R. 57).

[127] *Harman* v. *Home Office* [1983] AC 280 (discussed earlier on p. 000).

[128] Note that in *Malone* Megarry V-C commented that even if he had felt that he could 'incorporate' the Convention into the common law, he would not have attempted to 'legislate' judicially in such a complex field. In *Harman* the majority of the House of Lords found that the Convention was not relevant to the main issue which they felt was a construction of the rules of discovery of documents. It was only the minority who thought the case raised questions concerning freedom of expression.

[129] *Attorney-General* v. *Guardian (No. 2)* [1988] 3 All ER 545 (Chancery Division); 594 (Court of Appeal); 638 (House of Lords).

[130] 'The real case for a Bill of Rights', *The Observer* (1 February 1987), 11; 'Win one for civil liberties', *The Guardian* (3 February 1987), 12; 'Relentless hounds in the pursuit of freedom', *The Guardian* (3 February 1987), 25; 'How to take the wrong attitude to citizen's rights', *The Guardian* (5 February 1987), 19; 'Writing Civil Liberties into Law', *The Financial Times* (2 February 1987); 'Spycatcher Shambles', *The Economist* (8 August 1987), 14; 'Civil Liberties: overcoming the SEJ factor' (Peter Kelner), *New Statesman* (6 February 1987), 3; 'Human Rights under the Law' (Lord Gifford) *New Statesman* (6 February 1987), 12.

For example, in January 1987 the Special Branch carried out a raid on the offices of the *New Statesman*. This raid lasted for 4 days without a break; other raids took place at the offices of the BBC, and at the houses of the journalist Duncan Campbell, and the television producer, Brian Barr. This prompted considerable criticism of the Government, but most interesting for present purposes is the fact that opponents of the Government phrased their attacks in terms of the Convention: David Owen stated that this raid 'shows the need for a Bill of Rights',[131] and Peter Kelner in the *New Statesman* constructed a scenario where the Interpretation Act (referred to above) was already part of the law:

Let us imagine that Sir Edward's Bill was already on the statute book. The Special Branch arrive at the BBC's Scottish headquarters in Glasgow. They produce their warrant in conformity with the Official Secrets Act and the Police and Criminal Evidence Act. Under the Human Rights Act the BBC's lawyers would be able to test the warrant in a far more fundamental way than they were able to do last Saturday.

Kelner went on to quote Article 10 of the Convention which provides that: 'Everyone has the right to freedom of expression. This right shall include freedom to hold opinions and to receive and impart information and ideas without interference by public authority and regardless of frontiers . . .'.

In Kelner's view, the raid on the BBC had violated its right to receive as well as its righ to impart information. By removing the transmission copies of *all* of Duncan Campbell's films (and not just the one on the Zircon Project), it violated the BBC's right to impart information.

He suggested that if the lawyers representing the BBC had sought an injunction on the basis of Article 10(1) the response on behalf of the Special Branch would have invoked the provisions of Article 10(2) according to which: 'The exercise of these freedoms, since it carries with it duties and responsibilities, may be subject to such formalities, conditions, restrictions or penalties as are prescribed by law and are necessary in a democratic society, in the interests of national security, territorial integrity or public safety . . .'.

Kelner then continued in the following vein:

'The interests of national security': upon those five words would the State seek to uphold its right to raid offices at weekends, wake up film technicians in the middle of the night and take away boxloads of films and papers. Doubtless the Security Services' lawyers would argue that the mere statement that 'the interests of national security were at stake' should be sufficient: it would be unnecessary to *prove* that national security were in jeopardy.

But wait. Article 10 does not leave the concept of 'national security' unqualified. It refers to 'formalities, conditions, restrictions or penalties as are prescribed by law *and are necessary in a democratic society*' (emphasis added). In other words, it is not enough for the State to say 'national security is at stake', or even 'national security is

---

[131] *The Guardian* (2 February 1987), 6.

at stake and we've got the Official Secrets Act to back us up m'lud'. A judge, hearing the BBC's application for an injunction against the Special Branch, would have to be satisfied that the violation of human rights indicated by the warrant was based on rules that were 'necessary in a democratic society'.

If the BBC were to have fought last Saturday's warrant on those grounds under a Human Rights Act, a judge would have had three options. He could have held an immediate hearing and found for the Special Branch; or held an immediate hearing and held for the BBC; or stopped the search, ordered the BBC not to move or destroy any of the material relating to Campbell's programmes, and ordered a full scale hearing of the issue of whether the search was lawful.[132]

This passage is important as it shows two things: first, the Convention has entered into the vocabulary and imagination of those who want to hold the Government accountable; and secondly, it is not the result of the scenario which is of immediate significance, but the *possibility of it taking place*. In this way it may be that some alleged violations (whether or not they might actually be justified in the Courts later on) might be prevented; this is because their perpetrators may fear having their action scrutinized in the light of the Convention.

Another call for the incorporation of provisions of the Convention has come from G. McCormack[133] after the shooting of three Irish Republican Army (IRA) members in Gibraltar. McCormack compares the Criminal Law Act 1967 which provides in Section 3 that 'a person may use such force as is reasonable in the circumstances in the prevention of crime or in effecting or assisting in the lawful arrest of offenders or suspected offenders or of persons unlawfully at large' with Article 2 of the Convention which states in paragraph 2 that the Article is not violated if the use of force was no more than absolutely necessary:

(a) in defence of any person from unlawful violence;
(b) in order to effect a lawful arrest or to prevent the escape of a person lawfully detained;
(c) in action lawfully taken for the purposes of quelling a riot or insurrection.

He suggests that Article 2 presents a clearer test. In effect, this would mean that a killing by a member of the Security Services or police force would contravene Article 2 unless it could be shown that the death was *absolutely necessary*; this is, in effect, just a question of a higher burden of proof, since under the criminal law now in force it is for the prosecution to show 'beyond

---

[132] *New Statesman* (6 February 1987), 3.
[133] 'Lack of Clarity on Lethal Force', *Independent* (25 March 1988), 10. See now *McCann* v. *United Kingdom* (1995) 324 ECHR ser. A.

reasonable doubt that the [soldier's] act of shooting constituted, in the circumstances, unreasonable force',[134] this being a question of fact.

Such a change in the burden of proof may also make a difference in a claim based on civil law. In *Farrell* v. *Secretary of State for Defence*[135] the widow of a man, who was shot dead by soldiers while he was robbing a bank, sued the Government for compensation. However, the jury found that the soldiers had reasonable cause to suspect a bomb, and that it was reasonable to shoot-to-kill, and that such shooting was not out of proportion to the occasion. So the widow lost her case. She made an application to the European Commission of Human Rights which was declared admissible, as the Commission felt that the case raised the issue as to whether 'the use of force was no more than absolutely necessary to effect a lawful arrest'[136] (Article 2(2)(b)). However, the case ended in a friendly settlement,[137] with Mrs Farrell accepting the £37,000 offered to her by the Government. We can not infer from this that the test under the Convention is more favorable to the widow than the test under the Criminal Law Act (Northern Ireland) 1967. We can only conclude that the Government was prepared to act on 'compassionate grounds and in order to terminate'[138] the proceedings before the Commission; whereas a jury in Northern Ireland were satisfied that the shooting was reasonable.[139]

These detailed comparisons of the different laws applicable in the United Kingdom Courts and in the bodies of the Council of Europe in Strasbourg show some of the differences that incorporation of the Convention would make, yet they also demonstrate the usefulness of an international forum for challenging various State practices.[140]

---

[134] *Attorney-General for Northern Ireland's Reference (No. 1 of 1975)* [1977] AC 105 at 139.

[135] [1980] 1 All ER 166.

[136] *Farrell* v. *United Kingdom* (application 9013/80) 30 D. & R. 96 at 102 (11 December 1982).

[137] *Farrell* v. *United Kingdom* (application 9013/80) 38 D. & R. 44 (2 October 1984).

[138] Extract from a letter of the United Kingdom Government, quoted in 38 D. & R. 47.

[139] In another case, *Stewart* v. *United Kingdom* (application 10044/82) 39 D. & R. 162 (10 July 1984), which involved an application by the mother of a 13-year old boy killed by a plastic bullet fired by a British soldier, the Commission found that the use of force had been proportionate to the aim pursued—preventing serious injury in a 'riot' situation.

[140] Of course, it could be argued that incorporation of the Convention would make it more difficult to obtain relief in Strasbourg, as it would take longer and be more expensive to exhaust domestic remedies as required by Article 26. Also it might be argued that the scope allowed for claims under Article 13 (complaints of no effective national remedy) would be reduced; similarly, it could be said that incorporation would mean that the Commission would allow a larger margin of appreciation, as it would be unwilling to act as a 'fourth instance'; none of these arguments are borne out in practice, for example in none of the countries where the Convention has been incorporated has there been a significant drop in the number of applications declared admissible by the Commission. See Kerridge, 'Incorporation of the European Convention on Human Rights into United Kingdom Domestic Law', in Furmston et al. eds., *The Effect on English Domestic Law of Membership to the European Communities and of Ratification of the European Convention on Human Rights* (1983), 247 at 272. Further evidence is provided by the *Sunday Times Case*, n. 68 above, where the European Court of Human Rights effectively reviewed the way that the House of Lords had balanced the right to free speech against the right to a fair trial and, in a way, 'overruled' them. Although it might be true that some cases would take longer to complete their

We should be wary of those who argue that all questions of human rights should be decided at home.[141] It is not always a case of plaintiffs having to take the long and costly road to Strasbourg, but sometimes more a question of airing a difficult issue in an international forum.[142] Indeed, the most repeated argument in favour of incorporation of the Convention refers to the existing situation where the United Kingdom's 'dirty laundry is washed in public' and argues that these issues should be decided privately at home in the United Kingdom. However, an essential part of laundering dirty washing is airing it. Often a case in Strasbourg creates the opportunity to air grievances which might otherwise receive less attention.

Jury Trials

The rights contained in the Convention could have a significant effect on the outcome of *jury trials* where the provisions of the Convention would have superior status to domestic laws. This means that someone arrested for offences under the Public Order Act 1986 could plead in their defence the right to freedom of peaceful assembly and freedom of association. This could make a considerable impression on a jury. Similarly, in trials concerning official secrets, a defendant could rely on the right to freedom of expression, including the right to hold opinions and to receive and impart ideas. Of course, all these rights are subject to restrictions in the interests of national security, public safety, and the prevention of disorder and crime, but the important point is that the *right* would be part of the law and therefore could be argued. It is not enough that the restriction exists in law, it has to be implemented 'in proportion' to the aim to be achieved.

Discretionary Decisions

It is further suggested that the provisions of the Convention would have their greatest significance where discretionary decisions are taken. If the Convention were part of domestic law, its provisions would have to be considered not only in the Courts but also when a discretionary power is exercised. Some of the most important cases which reach the Strasbourg Court

domestic stage, this might be offset by the case subsequently being better prepared by the time it arrived at Strasbourg and therefore likely to pass more quickly through the various stages there. See Kerridge, ibid. at 271–3).

[141] e.g. Lord Hailsham (formerly Lord Chancellor), 'What we have done is put ourselves in the hands of judges at Strasbourg, instead of putting ourselves in the hands of judges in Westminster or Edinburgh'. *The Listener* 'Would a Bill of Rights politicize British judges?' (12 February 1987), 16.

[142] See especially *Tyrer* v. *United Kingdom* (1978) 26 ECHR Ser. A (judicial birching in the Isle of Man), and *Dudgeon* v. *United Kingdom*, n. 14 above (prohibition on homosexual sex in Northern Ireland). In both these cases local opinion was in favour of laws which were eventually found to be incompatible with the Convention.

and Commission, having originated in the United Kingdom, involve discretionary decisions in prisons and mental hospitals. To these can be added the cases which involve the decisions of the Secretary of State as well as decisions taken by the police and immigration officers. Should the Convention come to be considered in this way so that violations of human rights were *prevented* rather than *compensated*, the effective protection of human rights could be greatly enhanced.

For example, Section 14 of the Public Order Act 1986 concerns public assemblies of 20 or more people in a public place. It grants the police the power to impose restrictions on the size, location, or duration of the assembly, if the police reasonably believe that the assembly may result in 'serious disruption to the life of the community'. Should the police use this power unreasonably, the decisions could be challenged by means of judicial review after the event, and the European Convention would be relevant. But even if the judiciary were to find *against* the police, the right of assembly would nevertheless still have been seriously violated. The real strength of the Convention in this context lies in the fact that there would be an overriding right to assembly, and this would have to be taken into account by the police *before* exercising the discretion to impose restrictions. It would not only be the threat of judicial review which would ensure consideration of the Convention but also the fact that those who were arrested in defiance of the restrictions would be able to rely on the right to assembly at their criminal trial before a jury.

That the provisions of the Convention have a part to play in situations such as these is quite clear, and it is worth noting that the Government has already sent a circular to the Chief Officer of Police and various Clerks to the Magistrates and Crown Courts pointing out that the provisions in the Public Order Act 1986 should be implemented in such a way that the provisions of the European Convention on Human Rights are not contravened.[143]

The Judges

The arguments against incorporation have usually revolved around the question of who should have the final word in such cases: the judges or the elected Legislature? Opponents of incorporation in the past have pointed to the fact that judges can not be voted out of office nor are they particularly representative of the community in terms of their education, class, sex, colour, age, and

---

[143] See Home Office Circular No. 11/1987 ref. QPE/86 5/19/2 of 23 February 1987, para. 11: 'The right to assemble, demonstrate and protest peacefully within the law is fundamental to our democratic way of life. Senior police officers responsible for the policing of assemblies and demonstrations will no doubt continue to have regard to the need to protect these rights within the framework provided by the law, including Part II of this Act. Under Articles 10 and 11 of the European Convention on Human Rights (to which the United Kingdom is a signatory) everyone has the right to freedom of expression and to assemble peacefully and associate with others.'

social interests.[144] Also, it is often said that a Bill of Rights would politicize the judges, in that their appointment would become a matter of great political importance to the Government of the day.[145] All these arguments lose some of their force when the proposals involve an Interpretation Act, rather than a Bill of Rights, as in this case the Government still has the final say, and the risks of a head-on clash between the Government and the judges are considerably reduced.

From the previous sections it is clear that the judiciary already decides cases which raise issues under the Convention. Incorporation of the Convention would *expose* many of the choices which judges make as 'judgments' between competing claims; in this sense they would be more political, but it is suggested that little would change as regards their appointment. Indeed, if the presence of the European Convention as part of the law of the United Kingdom acted as a catalyst for instigating a considered system of judicial appointment and retirement, the 'legitimacy' of judicial review would be slightly enhanced. The importance of judicial representativity is underlined by D. Pannick in his book, *Judges*:

If it would not result in an unacceptable diminution in the quality of our judges, basic principles of representative government suggest that the judiciary should cease to reflect the values, background, and interests of so narrow a slice of society. One important way to encourage respect for the law is to show those whose behaviour it regulates that the law is made by those whom it binds, not by a remote group whose attitudes and ideals are foreign to those of ordinary people. The judiciary can claim many virtues. But it can not pretend to be representative of the populace. A broadening of the judicial base would do much to strengthen the rule of law.[146]

Although historically it would have been nearly impossible for ordinary people to become lawyers, some barriers have been removed, but in many ways the profession, and particularly the Bar, remains unattractive to representatives of those groups most oppressed under the law. At this point, perhaps, we should take a different perspective, and ask whether, if the law came to include the European Convention, so that questions of dignity, discrimination, and democracy were openly debated in the Courts by lawyers, in the vocabulary of human rights—would practitioners from a wider base be attracted to the law?[147] Of course, the judiciary should be more representative than it is at present—not only would this make the system *seem* fairer, but it

---

[144] See Griffith, 'The Political Constitution', 42 MLR (1979) 17, and also Griffith, *The Politics of the Judiciary* (3rd edn., 1985). For a survey of the background of the judiciary, see 'Judges on Trial', *Labour Research* 9 (January 1987).

[145] See Lord Lloyd of Hampstead, 'Do We Need A Bill of Rights?', 40 MLR (1977) 121.

[146] (1987).

[147] This is not to say that there are *no* representative barristers in the United Kingdom: see the research by Scheingold, 'Radical Lawyers and Socialist Ideas', 15 *Journal of Law & Society* (1988) 122. It is worth noting the emphasis which is placed on a *rights* strategy. Ibid. at 122, 125. Dworkin argues that the legal profession changed in the USA due to a 'rights conception of the

would also allow a much wider range of experiences to be brought into the decision-making process. However, the real question to be addressed is: should the judiciary, whatever its composition, be allowed to review the acts of the Legislature in this way?

The Legitimacy of Judicial Review

At the theoretical level it is hard to make a case for giving judges the power to annul provisions contained in legislation or even subordinate legislation. However, if we examine this power in the context of the United Kingdom and the European Convention on Human Rights, it emerges that, so far, the major beneficiaries of the judicial decisions in Strasbourg based on the Convention have been: prisoners,[148] mental patients,[149] immigrants,[150] and children.[151]

In most cases these beneficiaries do not have the right to vote.[152] So it can be argued that, as they have no power through the ballot box, it is legitimate to protect their 'interests' (rights) with a supra-legislative norm or Convention. To legitimate generally the institution of judicial review of legislation is more problematic.[153]

For example, Article 1 of Protocol 1 concerns respect for possessions. So it would seem that the Convention is a potential tool, in the hands of those with property, against a Government trying to redistribute wealth. But Article 1 of the First Protocol contains paragraph (2) which allows for deprivation of possessions in the 'public interest'. It is important to note that the European

rule of law': see Dworkin, 'Political Judges and the Rule of Law', in *A Matter of Principle*, (1985) 9 at 31.

[148] *Ireland* v. *United Kingdom* (1978) 25 ECHR ser. A; *Golder* v. *United Kingdom* (1975) 18 ECHR ser. A; *Silver* v. *United Kingdom* (1983)61 ECHR vol. A; *Weeks* v. *United Kingdom* (1987) 145 ECHR ser. A; and also the numerous findings and settlements of the Commission.

[149] *X* v. *United Kingdom* (1981) (application no. 9444/81) and also note the changes made in the United Kingdom in the light of findings against other countries by the Strasbourg organs.

[150] *Abdulaziz, Cabales and Balkandali* (1985) 94 ECHR ser. A (judgment 28 May 1985); *Alam and Kahn* v. *United Kingdom*, 10 *Yearbook of the European Convention on Human Rights* (1967) 788. This friendly settlement stimulated changes in the *United Kingdom* appeals legislation in the field of immigration.

[151] *Campbell and Cosans* v. *United Kingdom* (1982) 48 ECHR ser. A; *Tyrer* v. *United Kingdom* (1979) 26 ECHR ser. A.

[152] See Representation of the People Act 1983; prisoners: s 3(1); mental patients: s 7(1); and children: (under 18) s 1(1)(c).

[153] For one suggestion see Cappelletti in Favoreu and Jolowicz eds., *Contrôle juridictionnel des lois* (1986), at 314 where he concludes that: 'As long as constitutional judges act with this very purpose in mind—to reinforce fundamental freedoms—the democratic legitimacy of judicial review can hardly be denied'.

See also Tribe 'The Futile Search for Legitimacy', in *Constitutional Choices* (1985) ch. 1 especially at 6–7. For a philosophical approach to this question see O'Hagan, *The End of Law?* (1984), who, having dealt with aspects of Hegel, Marx, Tönnies, and Habermas, argues for a philosophy of law which gives a central place to judicial review, and in particular to the civil rights found in the Convention.

Court of Human Rights has held (in the *Lithgow* case which was brought by shareholders complaining about the Labour Government's nationalization legislation of 1977) that they will allow a large 'margin of appreciation' as regards nationalization, and that the Court would respect the legislature's judgment for future legislation.[154]

Similarly, in the *Case of James and Others*,[155] where the Duke of Westminster complained of a breach of Article 1 of the First Protocol, due to the operation of the Leasehold Reform Act 1967 (as amended), which grants in certain circumstances to a tenant (under a long lease) the right to buy the freehold of the property, the Strasbourg Court held that the national legislature was to enjoy a wide margin of appreciation in interpreting social and economic policies.

If the Court had held that the Convention protected the wealth of landlords and shareholders against the reforms of an elected Legislature, it would have suggested to many that the rhetoric of 'human rights' was another device to entrench the values of liberal individualism against periodic tides of 'reformist' socialism.

Although it is quite possible that a British Court could have interpreted the same Article and come to the opposite result—and found in favour of the shareholders/landlords—under the present doctrine of Parliamentary sovereignty, Parliament (or in reality the Government) would be able to pass legislation which reversed the Court's decision. There are several examples of legislation with this effect. For example, after the Secretary of State's direction concerning the takeover of Lambeth Council by Commissioners was held invalid by the Courts,[156] the Government passed the National Health Service (Invalid Direction) Act 1980 which declares the 'invalid' direction to take effect as if it had been valid.

Obviously a judicial ruling that nationalization legislation was invalid could prove embarrassing for a Government committed to the 'rule of law', but it must be emphasized that the possibility of such a ruling has been much diminished by the *Lithgow* judgment in Strasbourg, and, in any event, such a ruling would hardly deter any government committed to radical change.

CONCLUSION ON THE DESIRABILITY OF A BILL OF RIGHTS

If the 'big cases' in the House of Lords are unlikely to be decided differently (especially where the issue of 'national security' is raised by the Government), and judicial decisions are liable to be reversed by retrospective legislation, it

---

[154] *Case of Lithgow and Others* (1986) 102 ECHR ser. A (8 July 1986).
[155] (1986) 98 ECHR ser. A.
[156] *Lambeth Council* v. *Secretary of State for Social Services* (1980) 79 LGR 61.

might be said that the present proposals for a Bill of Rights (Interpretation Act) would change very little.

While in no way suggesting that a Bill of Rights would solve all the inequalities and injustices which exist, it is suggested that its introduction could have at least an important *educative* impact. It could have an impact in different spheres in the following ways:

(1) It could have an effect on the judges and legal profession who would be called on to examine both the Convention and the case law of the European Commission and Court of Human Rights.

(2) It would provide some sort of accessible code for ordinary people as to some of their principal rights on arrest,[157] and after of detention,[158] and could be particularly important for groups such as prisoners and refugees, where not only are minimum 'European Standards' emerging, but they are also already becoming increasingly familiar to groups such as the prisoners themselves. The Convention has sometimes formed a focal point for certain interest groups in the United Kingdom,[159] including: MIND (National Association for Mental Health); STOPP (Society of Teachers Opposed to Physical Punishment); NIGRA (Northern Ireland Gay Rights Association); NCCL (National Council for Civil Liberties) now renamed 'Liberty'; JUSTICE (British Section of International Commission of Jurists); CAJ (Committee on the Administration of Justice); PROP (Preservation of the Rights of Prisoners); and JCWI (Joint Council for the Welfare of Immigrants). This is a phenomenon particular to the United Kingdom,[160] but it is of increasing relevance at the European level in Strasbourg now that there are greater rights of audience before the Court, and that the procedure for intervention by interested 'third parties' is more familiar. What is most relevant to the present discussion is the fact that there exists a certain amount of expertise and experience at the national level.

(3) Public authorities, or rather their officers, would be obliged to consider the Convention and its jurisprudence when exercising their discretion. In this way not only would there be remedies for failure to consider the Convention, but it may also be that, in some circumstances, violations would be avoided.

(4) It may be that the *principles* contained in the Convention may become persuasive generally. For example, Article 14 states that the rights in the

---

[157] Article 6(3).   [158] Article 5.

[159] For the tactics involved in these campaigns see Grosz and Hulton, 'Using the European Convention on Human Rights', in Cooper and Dhavan eds., *Public Interest Law* (1986), 138.

[160] The late Judge Wiarda, former President and one of the longest serving judges at the European Court of Human Rights, suggested that this in some part explains the disproportionate number of cases against the United Kingdom which end in hearings before the Court of Human Rights. See Council of Europe (1/85) *Forum* at 2.

Convention 'shall be secured without discrimination on any ground such as sex, race, colour, language, religion, political or other opinion, national or social origin, association with a national minority, property, birth or other status'.[161] The strength of such wide Articles lies in their capacity to fill gaps where legislation has not been enacted, either through lack of foresight or enthusiasm.

Some Problems Associated with Incorporation of International Treaties as National Bills of Rights

This part of the Chapter assumes that non-European countries without a Bill of Rights might consider incorporating the International Civil and Political Rights Covenant as a Bill of Rights or Interpretation Act. It attempts to point to some of the pitfalls experienced in the United Kingdom-Convention dynamic and to make some suggestions as to how these could be avoided. Of course, one should not suggest that the work of the European Commission and Court of Human Rights in Strasbourg is the same as the work of the United Nation Human Rights Committee under the Optional Protocol to the Covenant. But some of the problems of incorporation deserve discussion and the two systems are in some ways similar.

A CEILING OF MINIMUM INTERNATIONAL STANDARDS OR A FLOOR FOR NATIONAL ACTION?

One problem associated with the incorporation of international human rights is that the authoritative guiding interpretation remains with the international body entrusted with the interpretation of the relevant instrument. Where this involves a progressive standard this has obvious advantages for victims and future victims of violations. However, often no international consensus emerges regarding the standard to be applied. Examples in the European context which have involved comparative inquiries have involved questions such as the age of consent for homosexual relations, the rights of transsexuals to have their documents amended to reflect their current sex, the rights to family reunification in immigration cases, the rights of illegitimate children, the right to divorce, the rights of transsexuals to marry, the rights of individual trade union members with regard to the closed shop, and the length of detention of terrorists without charge. Although judgments are liable to review in the light of an emerging European consensus, the problem is that judges or

---

[161] Although the Article refers to the other Articles in the Convention, it is not necessary to show that one of the other Articles has been violated, it is enough that the matter is covered by one of the other Articles. See *Belgian Linguistics Case* (1967) 6 ECHR ser. A.

Governments may be tempted to point to such minimum standards as evidence of the limits of the human rights at stake. The challenge is to ensure that national Courts treat the international human rights as part of their national heritage and interpret them in the national context so as to give the appropriate maximum protection at the national level.

The divergence of opinion at the international level may have been due to different religious considerations, different legal systems, different industrial relations systems or differing perceptions of the danger caused by threats from terrorism. It is important that national Courts have the autonomy to interpret the relevant international human rights so as to make them appropriate to the national culture. The Courts need not fear censure from the United Nations Human Rights Committee for breaking ranks and giving over-generous interpretations of the Covenant. Should the Government lose before a national Court the Government can not 'appeal' to the Committee. Only individuals who lose before the national courts have the right to petition the Committee.

If the incorporated Bill of Rights is to be domesticated to good effect there may be a real role for a national institution to promote and explore the application of the Bill of Rights in the national context. In this way there can be some democratic input into delicate national questions which are not easily solved by reference to international jurisprudence. Moreover, complex questions such as surrogacy, artificial insemination, and sexual life can not be left to national and international judges armed only with a Bill of Rights operating as a higher law.

In the United Kingdom context Human Rights Commissions have been suggested in the past and are now being suggested as essential components to new Bills of Rights based on the International Covenant on Civil and Political Rights (1966), the European Convention (1950), and a number of other rights not covered by these treaties.[162]

---

[162] Institute for Public Policy Research n. 115 above which foresees the following functions for such a Commission (modelled on the Commission for Racial Equality and the Equal Opportunities Commission): to bring proceedings in its own name, to assist individual complainants, to investigate practices and procedures which appeared to be incompatible with the Bill of Rights, to appear (at the request of the Court) as a friend of the Court to provide information and argument, and to act in an advisory capacity to Parliament.

In drawing up proposals for a British Bill of Rights the civil liberties organization, Liberty, *A People's Charter* (1991) included a number of rights which went beyond the Convention and Covenant. In order to highlight the limitations of the Covenant as a model for a Bill of Rights a few of Liberty's suggestions are listed below.
  (a) No one to be subjected without their express consent to medical or scientific experimentation, testing or research.
  (b) Everyone charged with a criminal offence to have the right to be tried by a jury of their peers in all cases involving potential loss of liberty.
  (c) Anyone affected by inaccurate statements disseminated to the public in general by any medium of communication has the right to reply or make a correction using the same communication outlet under such conditions as the law may establish.
  (d) Rights concerning anti-union discrimination and the right to strike.   *cont./*

Whether or not existing human rights Commissions could or should be adapted to carry out such a function may depend on the extent to which an incorporated Bill of Rights actually supplants the current work of such Commissions. Interestingly, when the civil liberties organization Liberty put forward its suggestions for a Human Rights Commission in the United Kingdom as part of a constitutional settlement involving a Bill of Rights, they stated that the suggested powers were partly based on powers contained in the provisions of Australia's Human Rights Commission Act 1981.[163] Liberty's proposed United Kingdom Human Rights Commission would report to a new Human Rights Scrutiny Committee (members of Parliament elected by Parliament according to the proportion of votes cast at the General Election). This Committee would have special powers regarding derogation and amendment to legislation with respect to the Bill of Rights.

The suggested composition of the Commission is equal proportions of: members of the legal profession (including academics and judges), human rights organizations, and lay members of the community (reflecting where possible those categories against whom discrimination is forbidden under the Bill of Rights: gender, national or social origin, nationality or citizenship, mental or physical disability or illness, sexual orientation, gender identity, age, marital, economic, or other status).

Because many of the questions which now arise under the rubric of human rights will relate to changing cultural mores, it is surely desirable to obtain Parliamentary input since this can add a sort of legitimacy to judicial interpretations. Of course, suggestions that judges always have to defer to authorative Parliamentary interpretations would undermine the whole point of having a Bill of Rights. But judges dealing with human rights questions may need to refer to positions of principle determined in the domain of public debate rather than plucking interpretations from the air.

Two examples of the way in which judges benefited from such assistance can be found in the area of sexual rights. The first example concerns the Canadian Charter of Rights and Freedoms and the way in which the Canadian Court of Appeal has interpreted the equality provision of the Charter so as to cover discrimination on the grounds of sexual orientation. In order to bolster their

---

(e) The right to marry for everyone (this would include gays, lesbians, and transsexuals).
(f) Everyone of marriageable age to have the right to found a family (this would include single women seeking fertility treatment).
(g) Equal rights for children born inside and outside wedlock.
(h) Freedom from discrimination for categories not included in Article 26 of the Covenant: ethnic origin, nationality, or citizenship, mental or physical disability, or illness, sexual orientation, gender identity, age, and marital status.
(i) Education rights.
(j) Rights to asylum.
(k) Rights not to be extradited without adequate safeguards.

[163] Liberty, ibid. at 100.

argument, the judges referred to Parliamentary debates which had suggested that the Canadian Human Rights Code should be amended in this way.[164]

The second example relates to the rights of transsexuals. The European Court of Human Rights has referred to resolutions of the Council of Europe's Consultative Assembly and the Community's European Parliament which specifically call on States to make the appropriate changes in transsexuals' civil status records.[165] Although not determinative, such resolutions give some indication as to which limitations on rights are really 'necessary in a democratic society'. Or, in other words, whether the Governmental restrictions really respond to a 'pressing social need'.[166]

One problem with incorporation of the Covenant is that recourse to the *travaux préparatoires* will not resolve the dilemmas faced by judges in the modern world. Nor will reference to resolutions of United Nations bodies (such as the General Assembly) enable judges at the national level to make informed decisions on the sort of questions likely to arise in the domestic Courts should the Covenant be incorporated.

It is not only a question of taking the temperature in the country concerned rather than at the international level which poses a challenge, however. If fundamental decisions about society are to be placed in the hands of the judiciary there needs to be a way for all interests to be represented, and for judges to be able to take this decision in something approaching an 'ideal speech situation'.

THE NEED FOR ALL INTERESTED PARTIES TO BE REPRESENTED AND INFORM THE PROCESS

One problem with addressing fundamental questions through two parties before a judge or judges is that the Court may not be informed of all the interests affected by its decision. The procedure for applications under the European Convention on Human Rights and its interpretation by the European Court of Human Rights makes provision for third party submissions. Often these submissions will merely add comparative evidence of an evolving norm in order to assist the applicant's case. Sometimes, however, it may be necessary purely to represent another set of interests. For example, in

---

[164] *Versey* v. *Canada (Correctional Service)* (1989) 44 CRR 364 (FFTD); Federal Court of Appeal (1990) 109 NR 300.

[165] *Cossey* v. *United Kingdom*, 184 ECHR ser. A, para. 41; note also the more recent case of *B.* v. *France*, 232–C ECHR ser. A, para. 46 (judgment 25 March 1992), where, unlike *Cossey*, the applicant was successful.

[166] For an example of how the European Court of Human Rights reviews national decisions to see if they were really necessary in a democratic society to meet a pressing social need and whether the restriction was 'proportionate to the legitimate aim pursued' and whether the reasons adduced by the national authorities to justify it are 'relevant and sufficient' see *Case of the Observer and Guardian* v. *United Kingdom* (1991) 216 ECHR ser. A, para. 59 et seq. (judgment 26 November 1991).

Young, James and Webster v. *United Kingdom*[167] the Trades Union Congress (TUC) submitted a long brief explaining the purposes of the closed shop. In this case the three applicants were arguing that the requirement that they join the relevant trade union violated their human rights. The respondent Conservative Government was basically sympathetic to the applicants' case and did not argue that the previous Labour Government's legislation was necessary in a democratic society for the protection of the rights of others. The interests of the trade union movement and their members would have remained unrepresented had there been no provision for such briefs as the one eventually submitted by the TUC.

In the European system there are some additional built-in safeguards in that the Commission of Human Rights is entrusted to represent the public interest before the European Court of Human Rights. No such provisions exist in the context of the supervision of the International Covenant on Civil and Political Rights. A challenge facing any country considering the incorporation of the Covenant as a judicially enforceable Bill of Rights must be how to ensure that the national judicial forum is fully informed. It may not be appropriate to leave the public interest to be represented by a Governmental office such as the Attorney-General.

Clearly, individuals will not always have the means to prepare complex briefs outlining the implications of the decision and there is an obvious role here for a national human rights Commission (see above). In addition, there will be some cases where vital interests in society could remain unrepresented unless procedural provisions are foreseen at the time of incorporation.

RETROACTIVE EFFECT

When the European Court of Human Rights or even the European Court of Justice of the European Communities gives a judgment regarding English law it may be actually questioning the validity of a piece of domestic legislation. However, this sort of international judicial review does not really overturn or invalidate such legislation. Rather, it allows the national authorities time to remedy the situation. Where the judgments of these courts have had potentially far-reaching economic or organizational consequences, the Courts have been careful to limit their judgments so that they only operate prospectively.[168]

---

[167] (1981) 44 ECHR ser. A.

[168] See *Lueicke, Betkacem and Koç* v. *Federal Republic of Germany* (1978) 29 ECHR ser. A (judgment 28 November 1978) (applicants charged the costs of interpretation contrary to ECHR Article 6(3)(e)); *Defrenne* v. *Sabena* [1979] ECR 480 (equal pay for men and women—EEC Article 119); *Vermeire* v. *Belgium* (1991) 214–C ECHR ser. A (judgment 29 November 1991) (exclusion of granddaughter from the estate of her deceased grandparents due to her being 'illegitimate'— violation of ECHR Article 14 in conjunction with Article 8).

On the other hand, when a domestic Court has to grapple with the conformity of legislation or administrative practices with a Bill of Rights, that Court
may be faced with the choice of simply declaring the whole piece of legislation
valid or void. Where such a decision relates to matters such as equal pay,
retirement ages, or social security benefits, the resulting economic strain on
the public and private spheres could result in chaos. So far, the European
Courts mentioned above have had to temper their quest for justice with practical limitations so as to make at least some progress. But, as yet, domestic
Courts in the United Kingdom have not had to face such questions (although
these issues are likely to arise more and more frequently in the context of EC
law). British judges can rely on the discretionary technique of refusing to
review administrative provisions and decisions unless they are completely
irrational. In addition, they may refuse to offer a remedy where administrative
chaos may result.

Should an international treaty be incorporated into domestic law so as to
enable national judges to decide the issues dealt with at the national level, then
some attention may need to be given to the possibility of allowing for a certain flexibility in the actual effect which the judgments are to have. This problem is particularly acute for the common law judge where there is no special
provision for a constitutional Court or a special administrative council.

Application to the Private Sphere

A tricky question now facing constitution builders in the 1990s is to what
extent the Bill of Rights should bind non-State actors. Is it only public officials
and Government which have an enforceable duty to respect human rights?

Although administrative law has developed as a separate field in the United
Kingdom, Dicey's adherence to equal application of the law to public as well
as private actors lives on.

The division in other countries between public and private law has rather
obscure origins. The continental division between public and private law can
be traced to a number of factors including Justinian's separation of the
Institutes from the *Corpus Iuris*, a mistrust by the French revolutionaries of
the *parlements*, and a timidity on the part of jurists to challenge the authority
of the State.[169] However, it was never intended to remove the sphere of private
law from the rule of law; rather the intention was to remove the sphere of public law from the judges.

Rather than reflecting on the question in civil law countries generally, or in

---

[169] See Watson, *The Making of the Civil Law* (1981), 144 *et seq.*; David and Brierley, *Major
Legal Systems of the World Today* (1985), 60 et seq.

the USA and Canada, I shall briefly mention aspects of the debate as it has
evolved in the United Kingdom.

The Protection of Human Rights Bill (1971)

It is worth examining this initiative by Sam Silkin in the House of Commons
because the Bill specifically accommodated threats to human rights from private bodies. The purpose of the Bill was explained by Silkin as follows:

The Bill would enable the humblest of our citizens and those who visit our shores to
complain to a new tribunal, the National Tribunal of Human Rights, of the violation,
whether by public authority *or by private organisation*, of those rights and freedoms
which society believes should be protected but which remain, for the time being, outside the protection of the law.[170]

What the brief debate actually illustrates is that one of the main aims of the
Bill seems to have been to curb *private power*. This may have been partly in
order to score political points in an ideological battle—Conservative support
for the introduction of a Bill of Rights at this time seems to have been aimed
at the programme of the Labour Party in Government. Parliament was considered by some Conservatives to be 'virtually an elective dictatorship'.[171] On
the other hand, Sam Silkin and Peter Archer (both Labour, and at the time in
Opposition)[172] were seeking to control the press, advertisers, employers,
neighbours, landlords, property companies, and the people who control individuals' lives in a technological age. Peter Archer's speech makes this quite
clear, even if the images are more evocative of a 1920s silent film than the
dawning of the computer age.

There are times when we all have the feeling of being lashed to a railway track in the
path of an on-rushing train. As my Honourable and learned friend said, it may be that
this is one of the prices that we have to pay for the privilege of living in a technological
age. It is undoubtedly a privilege, because few people would want to put the clock back
to the simpler days before the age of technology . . .

We on this side of the House take the view that there are other relationships, not only
relationships between the individual and Government, which can also blight lives, and
which, for many individuals can result in tragedy. Very serious distress can be caused
by an employer, by a landlord, or by a neighbour. Not all wrecked lives are wrecked by
Governments. Sometimes to safeguard individuals from this kind of danger may entail
giving more power to Governmental officials . . .

[W]ith modern communications, people are governed and dealt with and related [to]

---

[170] HC Debates, vol. 814 (5th) (2 April 1971) at column 1854, emphasis added.
[171] Hogg (later Lord Chancellor, Lord Hailsham), *New Charter*: Some Proposals for
Constitutional Reform (1969), 7; Lord Hailsham returned to this line of approach after the
Labour Party had been returned to power in 1974 again claiming that the Executive had too much
power within Parliament: Zander, n. 102 above at 11.
[172] They went on to become Attorney-General and Solicitor-General respectively.

in much larger units than previously. So it is inevitable that their lives are governed by decisions taken by people whose faces they do not know and often whose very names and identities are unknown to them . . .

This becomes more frightening for individuals. The wicked landlord of Victorian melodrama was a frightening enough individual, but at least the heroine could talk to him, and, in the last resort, could appeal to his better nature. These days the tenant who seeks to obtain the reversal of a decision from his landlord will be lucky indeed if he can find anyone who admits to having the power to alter such a decision, because usually it is a big property company.[173]

In the 1990s there is similar anxiety. In particular, the legal frameworks for the control of the newly privatized monopolies would not seem to offer the same accountability as the regime which operated when they were 'public' bodies.[174] Private prisons, universities, and mental hospitals are now integral parts of civil society.

Where electricity, gas, or water companies take action against individuals the results can be dramatic. In fact, following a recent admissibility decision by the European Commission of Human Rights, Professors Antonio Cassese and Frédéric Sudre have individually suggested that, in some circumstances, cutting off the power supply to someone's residence could lead to a violation of Article 3 of the Convention (inhuman and degrading treatment).[175] The 'private world of commerce' cannot be easily divorced from the 'public world of human rights'.

The Home Office Discussion Document (1976)[176]

This report presented a thorough examination of the advantages and disadvantages of incorporation of the Convention or a Bill of Rights. The conclusions of the working group concerning 'rights against individuals' are summarized in their report in the following way:

On the one hand:

---

[173] HC Debates, vol. 814 (5th) (2 April 1971) at columns 1861–2. The debate was curtailed due to there being less than forty members present and the Bill was never resurrected. I hope the reader will forgive the licence which has been taken in splicing these passages together. The gist of the speech has only been *slightly* distorted.

[174] See Garner, 'After Privatisation: Quis Custodiet Ipsos Custodes?', PL (1990) 329; Prosser, 'Constitutions and Political Economy: The Privatisation of Public Enterprises in France and Great Britain', 53 MLR (1990) 304.

[175] See Cassese, 'Can the Notion of Inhuman and Degrading Treatment Apply to Socio-Economic Conditions?', *European Journal of International Law*, (EJIL (1991) 141–5); Sudre, 'La première décision 'quart-monde' de la Commission européenne des droits de l'homme: Une 'bavure' dans une jurisprudence dynamique/Affaire Van Volsem', RUDH (1990) 349. The decision of the Commission with which these two articles are concerned is reported in RUDH 384 (1990).

[176] Home Office, *Legislation on Human Rights with Particular Reference to the European Convention: A Discussion Document* (1976).

a. Our legal system makes no distinction between public and private law. Any attempt to introduce such a distinction might have anomalous and artificial consequences.
b. A limitation to public or quasi-public authorities might be difficult to defend, especially in modern conditions where people feel no less threatened by powerful private organisations.
On the other hand
a. Constitutional guarantees of fundamental rights are usually regarded as protecting the individual against public authorities rather than other individuals or private bodies.
b. Making the guaranteed rights avail against private persons and organisations would greatly extend the likely area of controversy.

The report put forward the suggestion that the Bill of Rights could be drafted so that it applied to 'State action'. In this way it could be applied to 'non-governmental bodies of a quasi public character'. The report also suggests that the concept of 'State action' would allow Courts to 'hold the State responsible for not ensuring (by legislation or otherwise) that a citizen's rights were adequately protected from infringement by anybody, whether by a public authority or by another citizen or by private organisation'.[177] The working group also foresaw that the 'general evolutionary approach in Strasbourg' could mean that the Commission and Court might come to adopt 'a wider interpretation' than the original intention of the framers of the Treaty.

This far-sighted approach to the problem has the merit that it would replicate in the United Kingdom's Courts what is currently done in Strasbourg. It also openly admits the existence of a grey zone of quasi-governmental activity. Nevertheless, the working group recognized the dangers of allowing the Courts 'room for manoeuvre'. They foresaw that the problem would not disappear, and that it would have to be tackled head-on as 'there would be objections to leaving the effect of the Bill imprecise, particularly about its application to politically controversial areas'.[178]

The Human Rights Bill (1986) and the Continuing Debate

Clauses 1, 2, and 3 of the 1986 Human Rights Bill[179] imply that the 'Bill of Rights' is to be used only against the organs of the State. Liability is imposed on 'the Crown', 'Ministers of the Crown', 'a person holding statutory office', 'a public body', and 'a person holding public office'. However, 'public body' is defined as 'a body of persons, whether corporate or unincorporate, carrying on a service or undertaking of a public nature'.[180]

Such a public/private distinction allows the Convention to be disregarded in those cases where it may be especially relevant. Arguably it is also a retrograde step in that it would remove consideration of the Convention from

---

[177] Ibid. para. 2.19 (emphasis added).   [178] Ibid. para. 2.19.
[179] Bill 19, House of Commons (10 December 1986).   [180] Ibid. cl 1.

certain types of cases where it is currently considered to be relevant. Is *Gay News* a public body under this definition? Lord Scarman held they had duties under the Convention. Is Salman Rushdie a public body? Are trade unions public bodies? Do they become more public when they operate a 'closed shop' or 'unreasonable rules'? It was suggested by the Commission, and hinted at in the House of Lords, that the Convention comes into play at this point. Are foster parents offering a public service? Are adoptive parents a public body? Are the privatized electricity, gas, and water boards obliged to act so that Convention rights are respected?

Furthermore, the Bill does not seem to allow for Courts to 'hold the State responsible for not ensuring (by legislation or otherwise) that a citizen's rights were adequately protected from infringement by anybody, whether a public authority or by another citizen or by a private organization'.[181] The Bill prohibits 'acts' which infringe fundamental rights and freedoms and defines an 'act' as including a *deliberate* omission.[182] It is unlikely that a United Kingdom court would find a failure to legislate to close a loophole in the law, a *deliberate* omission by a Minister, public body, etc.

The debates in 1986 and 1987 concerning these attempts to incorporate the Convention did not address the public/private dichotomy, nor did the 1990 debates on incorporation in the House of Lords.[183] Increasingly, the issue of incorporation has been presented as a question of 'repatriating' or 'domesticating' the Convention.[184] In December 1990, when the question of incorporation was debated in Parliament, the idea of incorporation was 'simply to take the European Convention and make it part of British law so that British

---

[181] Home Office Discussion Document n. 176 above at para. 2.19, the 'State Action' approach.

[182] Bill 19 n. 179 above, cl 1(2).

[183] Debate on the Human Rights and Fundamental Freedoms Bill, HL Debates, vol. 473 (9 April 1986) at column 267 et seq.; debate on the Human Rights Bill, HC Debates, vol. 109 (6 February 1987) at column 1223 et seq. (Sir Ian Percival seems to have foreseen that in a rerun of the *Young, James and Webster* case it would be for the Courts to decide in a case of judicial review whether the legislation was necessary in a democratic society: 'The Bill does not give everybody the right to take proceedings against everybody else who is thought to be in breach of its terms. It gives the right to take proceedings against public authorities' (ibid. at column 1235)); Debate to call attention to the state of civil liberties under this Administration, HL Debates, vol. 519 (23 May 1990) at column 904; Early Day Motion to call attention to the case for the incorporation of the European Convention on Human Rights into United Kingdom law as a Bill of Rights, HL Debates, vol. 524 (5 December 1990) at column 185.

[184] See e.g. Holme (later Lord Holme and mover of the motion on incorporation in the House of Lords on 5 December 1990), 'How to keep out of Strasbourg', *Times* (12 August 1988), and 'Put Britain on the Rights Road', *Times* (8 January 1985); Lord Broxbourne (sponsor of the 1986 Bill), 'Bringing Our Rights Home', *The Sunday Times* (8 December 1985); 'An imported Magna Carta: Britain's citizens should not need to go to Strasbourg to protect their human rights', *The Economist*, editorial (29 June 1985); Robertson 'Repatriating a Bill of Rights', *New Statesman* (6 December 1985); Alexander, R. (now Lord Alexander), 'Bringing Strasbourg Home', *Counsel—The Journal of the Bar of England and Wales* (1987), 40 and 'Human Rights: trust our judges', *Times* (10 December 1985).

citizens in British Courts may have access to the rights for which at present they have to travel a long, expensive and weary road to Strasbourg'.[185]

It is now clear, however, that the sphere of relations between individuals may be considered in Strasbourg. It is possible that the Commission may find the rules of a trade union unreasonable and hence a violation of the Convention.[186] Questions of sexual assault, terrorist threats, private corporal punishment, media concentrations, offensive publications, and discriminatory dismissal have all been considered justiciable in Strasbourg even though all the action at the national level took place between private actors (in the private sphere).[187] If incorporation is designed to save victims 'the long 5 year trek to Strasbourg, supported by lawyers who largely take no fee',[188] then it ought to cover cases in the sphere of relations between individuals.

Conclusions on Incorporation and the Question of Rights Against Private Power

It would be presumptuous to suggest a formula to address the public/private question for incorporation in any future Bill of Rights. What is suggested is that formulae which allow for cases to be declared outside the scope of the Bill due to the 'private' nature of the conflict or the respondent will mean that Courts may be tempted to transfer substantive questions into jurisdictional questions about the boundaries of the public and private sectors. The labels 'public' and 'private' are more like tactical weapons than descriptive labels. This is not surprising because in the human rights context 'private' quickly becomes 'privacy' and hence inviolable. For example, in the 1970s when the issue of racial discrimination in working men's clubs arose, the Labour Party argued that these clubs should be covered by the law on discrimination because of their public nature; in the 1990s the Labour Party protested about legislation allowing police to enter these same clubs, arguing that such clubs are private places. There is no contradiction in such statements.[189] They only

[185] Lord Holme of Cheltenham, author of the motion calling for attention to be paid to the case for incorporation of the European Convention on Human Rights, HL Debates, vol. 524 (5 December 1990) at column 187.

[186] See *Cheall* v. *United Kingdom*, n. 44 above.

[187] See generally Clapham n. 1 above at ch. 7.

[188] Lord Hutchinson, HL Debates, vol. 524 (5 December 1990) at column 197.

[189] Cf. Lord Hutchinson of Lullington: 'It was amusing to hear the vehemence with which noble Lords on the Labour Benches opposed that part of the Law Reform (Miscellaneous Provisions) (Scotland) Bill giving police the right of almost unfettered entry to clubs, arguing as they did that clubs, particularly working men's clubs, were essentially private places. As the noble and learned Lord, Lord Hailsham, will remember, that is almost precisely the opposite of the stance that Labour took when in power. In 1976 the Labour Government took precisely the opposite line, arguing that clubs, and in particular working men's clubs, were essentially public places and must therefore be subject to the restrictions and obligations of race relations legislation.' (House of Lords Debate on Civil Liberties, in HL Debates, vol. 519 (23 May 1990) at column 917).

go to show that the choice of label 'public' or 'private' may depend on the harm sought to be avoided.

One solution may be to leave any incorporation Bill silent on the application of rights against private parties. This is the solution adopted in the new Dutch Constitution, and it was advocated in the context of proposals for a Bill of Rights in New Zealand.[190] However, the Bill of Rights as adopted in September 1990 included the following section:

3. Application
This Bill of Rights applies only to acts done -
(a) by the legislative, executive, or judicial branches of the government of New Zealand; or
(b) by any person or body in the performance of any public function, power, or duty conferred or imposed on that person or body pursuant to law.

At first glance this would seem to limit the scope of application to the public sphere. However, the Section specifically mentions the judiciary, and therefore seems to bind it in its determination of disputes concerning private actors. In this way, human rights principles become relevant for the determination of conflicts in the private sphere. Human rights need not be relegated to an exclusive zone on the public side of the public/private divide. What the New Zealand formula does not permit is for one party to bring the case before the Courts by claiming a remedy against a non-governmental body solely basing the case on the rights contained in the Bill of Rights. The Bill of Rights only comes into play once the case is before the judge.[191]

Returning to the question of incorporation of the European Convention

[190] See Elkind and Shaw, *A Standard for Justice* (1986). For the actual formulation adopted see below. Note the draft 'Basic Law' for Hong Kong specifically allowed for protection from individual's interferences with privacy in Article 30. However, the Hong Kong Bill of Rights Ordinance 1991, enacted on 8 June 1991, contains a new formula in its Section 7: (1) This Ordinance binds only—(a) the Government and all public authorities; and (b) any person acting on behalf of the Government or a public authority . . .

This Bill of Rights incorporates rights from the Civil and Political Rights Covenant, and there is considerable authority (including the General Comments of the United Nations Human Rights Committee) to suggest that some of the rights in the Covenant should be interpreted to cover private activity. Other Articles do not exclude private actors from their scope. Comparisons with other European jurisdictions where the Convention has the status of domestic law are not particularly helpful. This is because the Convention will nearly always take second place to an examination of the domestic constitution. Even where the Convention has been specifically incorporated through a separate Act of Parliament, such as the European Convention Act (Act No. XIV of 1987) in Malta, a case concerning private individuals came to be determined by an application of the *Constitutional right* prohibiting inhuman and degrading treatment and not the *Convention right* which was held not to give rise to a *remedy* in national law. See *Buttigieg* v. *Air Malta* (Constitutional Court of Malta, 9 October 1989).

[191] Note the proposals by Liberty for a Bill of Rights in the United Kingdom to adopt a similar formula. Article 22 of their proposal states that an individual within the jurisdiction of the United Kingdom shall enjoy the rights contained in the Bill against: (a) any act or omission by the legislative, executive, judiciary or Crown; and (b) any act or omission by any individual or body in the performance of any public function.

into United Kingdom law, it is clear that the main purpose of such a step would be in order to reinforce its role as an aid to interpretation. Considering that British judges already defer to the Convention in 'private law' cases,[192] the New Zealand formula would therefore seem relatively appropriate. Even if it excludes relying on Convention Articles to found a claim, this is not necessarily disadvantageous. Most situations will be covered by some sort of domestic legislation. Where no remedy exists, one could foresee claims at the national level against the State for a failure to provide a remedy. Those situations where plaintiffs cannot put their complaints before the Courts may even constitute a violation of the 'right to a remedy' under Article 13 of the European Convention on Human Rights and can be dealt with by the European Commission and Court of Human Rights as a failure by the State to provide domestic legislation in this field. The actual legislation can then be enacted and debated in Parliament and civil society. This solution defuses two of the most powerful arguments against human rights in the private sphere: first, that allowing everyone to claim violations of human rights against everyone else would clog up the Courts and dilute the notion of human rights; and secondly, that complex conflicts of interests between different sectors of civil society are better dealt with by democratically enacted legislation than by recourse to abstract conflicting principles such as 'freedom of expression' or 'privacy'.

On the other hand, it ensures that human rights principles are applied by judges in all cases and that some spheres are not excluded arbitrarily from the public world of the Bill of Rights.[193] Domestic violence, discrimination at work or in housing, and invasions of privacy are not primarily instigated by State agents. If a Bill of Rights is to have a really educative and preventive function, then everyone should feel bound by its norms—whether or not they perceive themselves as carrying out a public function. To create a culture of human rights means going beyond instructing officials that there are annoying limits on Government action. The challenge must be to allow everyone to feel that such principles and rules contribute to greater respect for people's dignity, and that it is respect for these rights which enables better participation in civil society and political decision-making.

---

[192] See *Cheall* n. 44 above; *Blathwayt* v. *Lord Cawley* [1976] AC 397 at 426; *R.* v. *Bow St. Ct., ex parte Choudhury* [1990] 3 WLR 986.

[193] For details of how the public/private divide has operated under the Canadian Charter of Rights and Freedoms so as to disadvantage women's groups and organized labour see Fudge, 'The Public/Private Distinction: The Possibilities of and the Limits to the Use of Charter Litigation to Further Feminist Struggles', 25 O*sgoode Hall Law Journal* (1987) 485, and Mandel, *The Charter of Rights and the Legalization of Politics in Canada* (1989).

Summary

Even in a common law country which has not incorporated the relevant international human rights instrument, there are ample possibilities for the judiciary to use the rights and principles contained in such an instrument. The area where non-incorporation has left the individual stranded without recourse to the Courts has been in the field of judicial review of Ministerial discretionary decisions. The judicial reticence in this area is related more to traditional views about the questionable legitimacy of usurping the role of Ministers than an antipathy to human rights. However, it may be possible for judges to reorientate their approach to judicial review by looking for the source of the discretionary power rather than waiting for a Bill of Rights. Alternatively, proportionality may yet come to be accepted as a ground for review of discretionary decisions as part of the traditional resonableness test.

It could be said that a Bill of Rights is the ideal, but sometimes it seems that campaigning for such a step actually dissuades judges from using legitimate methods of interpretation. There may exist a fear that to refer to human rights treaties is to introduce a Bill of Rights through the back door thus thwarting the democratic process.

A fully entrenched Bill of Rights presents two acute problems. First, how can Parliament be left the option of amending the Bill without destroying the fundamental and restraining purpose of the Bill? Secondly, can Parliament overrule specific judicial decisions of which it dissapproves? What if the judiciary gives a restrictive interpretation which actually unreasonably limits rights? The balance to be achieved in the incorporating legislation will depend on the trust which the judiciary enjoys in the particular national context. It may also depend on the possibility of a final review by an international Court or committee.

Where the Bill of Rights is actually cloned from one or more international instruments there ought to be institutional possibilities to ensure that the human rights debate remains a lively national one. If human rights dilemmas are easily exported to far-away international tribunals one loses the chance to make Governments accountable and have a real democratic debate in society.

Various national institutions, such as Commissions or Parliamentary committees, may be employed to encourage a human rights senstitive approach to legislation before it is adopted. In addition, a Human Rights Commission can play an essential role in assisting individuals or groups to present their cases. In some cases there will be a role for such a Commission (or another body) to present an *amicus curiae* brief to the Court. If one asks the judiciary to solve fundamental societal dilemmas on human rights principles, then one has to ensure that the whole of society's interests are represented in that forum.

At the international level States are sometimes responsible for ensuring that the human rights contained in the international instruments are protected even against private abuses of power. Of course, it is the State which is held responsible for failing to provide a remedy. The non-State actor who committed the abuse is not a party at the international level. When this issue arises at the national level the national judges have no procedural defence that only States may appear as respondents at the international level. Every day, national judges are deciding cases and controversies between private parties. Fundamental rights principles may be relevant if not decisive for a resolution of these conflicts. If one tries to erect a public/private barrier one risks relegating certain issues to the realm of the domestic or private sphere and recreating the sort of inequality which Bills of Rights are supposed to address.

The challenge when incorporating an international set of human rights must be to make the Bill or Charter a living instrument which focuses and stimulates debate rather than fossilizing and stifling it.

Afterword: Human Rights Act 1998

After 1997 the debate over incorporation of the European Convention on Human Rights into the domestic law of the United Kingdom moved into a new phase. In May 1997 a Labour Government was elected and moved to fulfil their election promise to incorporate the Convention.[194] Although British judges have become more comfortable with the Convention and have referred to it in an increasing number of cases,[195] incorporation continued to raise a number of problems. Three of the topics discussed in this Chapter were the focus of much debate in the lead-up to the adoption of the Human Rights Act 1998.[196] Although much of the debate concerned particular features of the United Kingdom legal system, these three issues will surface in any situation where a government is considering incorporation of an international human rights treaty into domestic law.

First, there were different views as to whether the United Kingdom should have an 'interpretation act' or a 'Bill of Rights'.[197] As we saw above, under the

---

[194] For details of the Labour Party's proposal for incorporation made whilst in opposition see Straw and Boateng 'Bringing Rights Home: Labour's Plans to Incorporate the European Convention on Human Rights in U.K. Law' (1997) *European Human Rights Law Review* 71–80. The Human Rights Bill, HL Bill 38, was presented to Parliament along with a White Paper, *Rights Brought Home: the Human Rights Bill* (Cm 3782) in October 1997.

[194] See Beloff and Mountfield, 'England and Wales; Unconventional Behaviour?', Dickson, 'The Convention in Northern Irish Courts'; Grotian, 'The European Convention: A Scottish Perspective', all in (1996) *European Human Rights Law Review* at 467–95, 496–510, and 511–23.

[196] See www.hmso.gov.uk/cgi-bin/ht...gov.uk/acts/acts1998/19980042.htm. The Act received the Royal Assent on 9 November 1998 and certain of its provisions came into force on that date. The principal provisions will not enter into force, however, until 2 October 2000, although there is provision for retrospective effect of parts of the Act as from that date.

[197] See generally Murray Hunt, *Using Human Rights Law in English Courts* (1997); Lord Irvine, 'The Development of Human Rights in Britain under an Incorporated Convention on Human Rights' [1998] *Public Law* 221; Markesinis (ed.), *The Impact of the Human Rights Bill on*

first model (sometimes known as the 'New Zealand Model') the judges cannot actually strike down an Act of Parliament as invalid. Those who advocated a Bill of Rights (or something closer to the Canadian model) argued that British judges, who understand the national legal culture, should have a say in determining the conformity of legislation with the Convention and that this should not remain 'the sole prerogative of European judges'.[198] Although this view challenges the rhetoric of those who claim that incorporation will 'bring rights home' or 'repatriate' the Convention, to allow judges to strike down legislation suggests a radical reorganization of the relationship between Parliament and the judges. It also implies a special constitutional court which would specialize in dealing with the validity of primary legislation. Although many countries have such judicial review of parliamentary action, the climate in the United Kingdom proved not to be ripe for such an abdication of power by elected representatives. Furthermore the situation was complicated by the fact that the supreme law would not be a home-grown Constitution such as those found in South Africa, Germany and the USA, but rather a European treaty. Lord Lester, who agreed in principle that the judges should be able to 'disapply primary legislation that is in conflict with directly effective Convention rights and duties', admits that 'in the current climate of concern about parliamentary sovereignty from the supremacy of European law, such a measure would provoke strong opposition in the House of Commons and beyond. Furthermore the senior judges, so far from being guilty of judicial imperialism, have no enthusiasm for new powers that would put them so directly at odds with the elected branch of parliamentary government'.[199]

Different models suit different polities at different times. The European Convention has historically been seen as a cloak of protection for detainees, prisoners, asylum-seekers, mental patients, homosexuals, and the media. But

English Law (1998); and Ewing, 'The Human Rights Act and Parliamentary Democracy' (1999) 62 *Modern Law Review* 79.

[198] See Emmerson, 'Opinion: This Year's Model—The Options for Incorporation' (1997) *European Human Rights Law Review* 313–28 at 317. Emmerson points to the binding nature of a judgment issued by the European Court of Human Rights under Article 52 of the European Convention and states that when the Court declares that an Act of Parliament has violated an individual's rights, 'Parliament almost invariably amends the relevant legislation. Although the ultimate decision is for Parliament to take, the political reality is that there is usually no choice. Member States of the Council of Europe are effectively obliged to abide by the rules of the club. Viewed in this way, the issue confronting the Government is not whether judges should have the power to declare legislation inconsistent with the Convention. That is a power that already exists. The real issue is whether it should remain the sole prerogative of European judges, or should be extended to British judges who have some measure of familiarity with the domestic legal system': at 317. See also 'Human Rights are no threat to Parliament'; *The Times,* 22 July 1997, at 35.

[199] Lester, 'First Steps Towards a Constitutional Bill of Rights' (1997) *European Human Rights Law Review* 124–31, see also the other articles in the same issue: Sir Nicholas Lyell 'Whither Strasbourg? Why Britain Should Think Long and Hard Before Incorporating the European Convention on Human Rights' at 132–40; Wadham, 'Bringing Rights Half-way Home' at 141–45; and Ewing and Gearty, 'Rocky Foundations for Labour's New Rights' at 146–51.

its provisions can also be invoked to protect landlords, shareholders, tobacco advertisers, multinationals, anti-union employers, foetuses, and racist organizations. Even if a major clash is only likely to arise every few years,[200] the fundamental question remains: who do we trust with the last word over how to balance conflicts of rights?

The Human Rights Act passed by the Parliament in 1998 (hereinafter the 'Act') has devised a delicate system of checks and balances to allow judges to pronounce on the compatibility of primary legislation without actually reversing the balance of power between Parliament and the judiciary. In this way, judgments concerning the conformity of primary legislation will not remain the 'sole prerogative of European judges'.

The Act provides in section 4 for certain courts of review to make a declaration of incompatibility of primary legislation with certain of the Convention rights.[201] A declaration of incompatibility may also be made in relation to subordinate legislation where the primary legislation concerned prevents the removal of the incompatibility. The 'declaration of incompatibility' does not affect the validity, continuing operation or enforcement of the provision in respect of which it is given and is not binding on the parties to the proceedings in which it is made.[202]

This new declaratory power preserves the distinct spheres of operation of national and international law at the same time as emphasizing the similar nature of the obligations arising at the national and international levels. While European Court judgments remain binding only in international law, the political advisability of compliance with this international obligation is enhanced beyond the need to remain in step with the Council of Europe.[203] In the words of the White Paper, such a declaration will: 'almost certainly prompt the Government and Parliament to change the law'.[204] As if to emphasize the similar nature of the obligations arising from a declaration or

---

[200] Francesca Klug's comparative summary of the Canadian and New Zealand practice leads her to conclude that even if courts do not often overturn statutes on hotly disputed issues, nevertheless when they do they 'have the potential to discredit the very idea of Bills of Rights by the ousting of the democratic process from what many would see as legitimate democratic debate': 'A Bill of Rights for the United Kingdom: A Comparative Summary' (1997) *European Human Rights Law Review* 501–7 at 502.

[201] Section 4 (4). For the purposes of the Act, 'Convention rights' are defined in section 1 to mean Articles 2 to 12 and 14 of the Convention, Articles 1 to 3 of the First Protocol, Articles 1 and 2 of the Sixth Protocol, as read with Articles 16 to 18 of the Convention.

[202] Section 4(6).

[203] See Emmerson n. 198 above. The White Paper asserts: 'A Finding by the European Court of Human Rights of a violation of a Convention right does not have the effect of automatically changing United Kingdom law and practice: that is a matter for the United Kingdom and Parliament. But the United Kingdom, like all other States who are parties to the Convention, has agreed to abide by the decisions of the Court or (where the case has not been referred to the Court) the Committee of Ministers. It follows that, in cases where a violation has been found, the State concerned must ensure that any deficiency in its internal laws is rectified so as to bring them into line with the Convention': at para. 1.10.

[204] White Paper n. 194 above at para. 2.10.

judgment on incompatibility with the Convention at the national and international levels, the Act provides for a 'fast-track procedure' for changing
legislation.

Section 10 empowers a Minister of the Crown or Her Majesty in Council
(depending on the nature of the legislation) to amend legislation by 'remedial
order' in response to a national judicial 'declaration of incompatibility' or a
finding of the European Court of Human Rights where he or she considers
there are compelling reasons for so doing. Remedial orders made under this
section can have retroactive effect.[205] The Act requires that remedial orders be
approved by both Houses of Parliament and sets out a two-stage procedure to
this end. To allow for consultation and debate, a draft of the proposed order,
together with an explanation of the incompatibility which the draft order seeks
to remove, the reasons for proceeding under section 10 and the reasons of the
terms of the draft order, must be laid before Parliament for a period of 60
days.[206] After this period, the draft order may be returned to Parliament for a
second time, together with a summary of any representations and details of
consequential changes. After a period of 60 days, the draft may then be
approved by a resolution of both Houses of Parliament.[207] In urgent cases, a
remedial order may be made without being approved in draft. In these cases,
the order must be approved by the Parliament within a 120-day period after the
original order was made.[208] Urgent orders must also include a statement of the
reasons for the urgency of the matter.[209] This procedure means that, theoretically, findings of incompatibility at either the national or the international level
could result in changes in the law sooner than would otherwise be the case.

The declaration of incompatibility, combined with the possibility of remedial action, is a bold device for incorporating international human rights into
national law and neatly avoids any impression that national and international
decisions have a different hierarchical status. Taken together with sections 2
and 3, this model for incorporation goes beyond most attempts to incorporate
international human rights treaties into national law. Section 2 states that a
court or tribunal dealing with a question arising under the Bill in connection
with a Convention right 'must' take into account judgments, decisions, and
opinions of the European Commission and Court of Human Rights, as well
as the Committee of Ministers; and section 3 states that 'So far as it is possible to do so, primary legislation and subordinate legislation must be read in a
way which is compatible with the Convention rights'. However, the Act cannot really claim to have completely 'brought rights home'. Some issues will
remain the 'sole prerogative of European judges'.

[205] Section 1(1)(b) of Schedule 2 to the Act.
[206] Section 3(1) of Schedule 2 to the Act.
[207] Sections 2(a) and 3(2) of Schedule 2 to the Act.
[208] The procedure is set out in section 4 of Schedule 2 to the Act.
[209] Section 2(b) of Schedule 2 to the Act.

Section 6(6) excludes failure to legislate from the purview of the judicial control over the Convention at the national level. Complaints about the lack of legislation or even a failure to enact a remedial order following a 'declaration of incompatibility' will have to be taken to the European Court of Human Rights in Strasbourg where they will remain justiciable. This Court has in the past pointed to important lacunae in the legislative framework and has deemed the failure to legislate to represent a breach of Convention obligations. The failure to legislate arises particularly where the complaint is essentially against harm emanating from private actors and the State has taken no measures to attempt to prevent or punish such infringements on the enjoyment of Convention rights.[210] We are therefore faced with an imbalance. Where the government has chosen to enact legislation to protect individuals and groups then that legislation can be challenged for compatibility. Where a government has failed to legislate there is no possibility of challenge. There is a temptation to see human rights issues as simply claims by an aggrieved individual against the overbearing apparatus of the State. But, as suggested above, human rights legislation can be seized on by powerful actors to protect their interests. Allowing judges to question the validity of legislation enacted by a legislator committed to social justice may be not only anti-democratic, it may also end up in a net reduction of human rights protection. This leads us to a second question addressed above: should the incorporated Treaty also bind private actors at the national level?

As we saw, different suggestions regarding the application of a Bill of Rights to the private sphere have been made in the United Kingdom context. The most recent ones tend to deny direct 'horizontal application'.[211] Interestingly, the 1996 Labour Party discussion document had suggested that individuals would be able to bring cases against the State for failure to 'protect them against abuse of human rights by private bodies or individuals'.[212]

---

[210] See Clapham, *Human Rights and the Private Sphere* (1993), ch. 7, and more recently *Osman* v. *United Kingdom,* Application No. 23452/94, Opinion of the European Commission of Human Rights, 1 July 1997.

[211] Lord Lester's 1997 Human Rights Bill received an unopposed second reading in the House of Lords and does not allow for application against private bodies. However, he suggests it would have indirect horizontal effect as judges adapt the common law. 'The Bill would apply to acts done by or on behalf of a Minister of the Crown or by any person or body discharging public functions. This would ensure that its provisions did not have "horizontal effect" to create new torts in the private sphere. The protection given by the Bill is against contravention of Convention rights by the State or by some other public authority endowed by law with coercive powers. The Bill is concerned with public law, not private law. However, the definition of public bodies is sufficiently broad to enable the courts to include any body whose decisions are subject to judicial review, including "private governments", like privatized prisons, or the City Takeover Panel or the Advertising Standards Authority. Moreover as the *Derbyshire* case indicates, the Bill would have indirect horizontal effect where private law rights and duties needed to be adopted to accommodate Convention rights: 'First Steps Towards a Constitutional Bill of Rights' n. 199 above at 127.

[212] See Straw and Boateng n. 194 above at 76: 'We take the view that the central purpose of the ECHR is to protect individuals against the misuse of power by the state. The Convention imposes obligations on states, not individuals, and it can not be relied upon to bring a case against private

However, as explained above, this promise seems to have been reneged on in the Act which explicitly excludes failure to legislate from judicial control. If parliamentary sovereignty can be preserved by allowing the courts to issue non-binding 'declarations of incompatibility' with regard to primary legislation, it is hard to see why a similar arrangement could not be made for failure to legislate to protect from abuse by private bodies. A declaration of legislative failure could alert Parliament to its failure to act and would allow the national judges to do what is already done by the judges of the European Court of Human Rights. In some circumstances remedial orders could probably be made so as to adjust related primary legislation to fill the gap.

For all the reasons given in the earlier part of this chapter it seems inexplicably traditional to deny the application of the Convention to the legal relationship between individuals. If one admits that private power and individuals can abuse human rights, then its seems almost negligent to deny a direct remedy to individuals in the private spheres of the family, the home, and the workplace. The Act does offer a nod in the direction of the absurdity of delimiting a private/public border. However, the wording in the legislation simply leaves a happy hunting ground for legal eagles. The Act states in section 6 that it is unlawful for a 'public authority' to act in a way which is incompatible with a Convention right as defined. It goes on in subsection 3(b) to define 'public authority' as including 'any person certain of whose functions are functions of a public nature'.[213] And then it clarifies this by adding in subsection 5 that 'In relation to a particular act, a person is not a public authority by virtue only of subsection (3)(b) if the nature of the act is private'.

It seems from the White Paper that the intention here is to ensure that privatized utilities are covered. So electricity boards, the railways and British Telecom would probably be covered. The White Paper stated in para. 2.2:

The definition of what constitutes a public authority is in wide terms. Examples of persons or organizations whose acts or omissions it is intended should be able to be challenged include central government (including executive agencies); local government; the police; immigration officers; prisons; courts and tribunals themselves; and to the extent that they are exercising public functions, companies responsible for areas of activity which were previously within the public sector, such as privatised utilities. The actions of Parliament, however, are excluded.

persons. For this reason we consider that it should apply only to public authorities—government departments, executive agencies, quangos, local authorities and other public services. An appropriate definition would be included in the new legislation and this might be framed in terms of bodies performing a public function. We would welcome views on this. Individuals would in certain circumstances be able to use the new Act to seek to secure effective action by public authorities to protect them against abuse of human rights by private bodies or individuals. Nevertheless this new legislation is not intended to alter existing legal relationships between individuals'.

[213] Notably, the Act excludes both Houses of Parliament and persons exercising functions in connection with Parliamentary proceedings: section 6(2) of the Act.

We saw above that in the past this issue turned on the extent to which it is thought the Convention might be used against trade unions. The issue has again been politicized but this time the concern is the extent to which the Convention might be used to elaborate a law of privacy that could be used against the media. As the Act stands, it could cover violations of privacy by the media in any of three ways. First, because the Act aims to give 'further effect'[214] to the rights and freedoms in the Convention, the duty of the courts to defer to the Convention when the common law is ambiguous or developing is surely strengthened. Cases involving, say, breach of confidence would have to be resolved with full respect for the Convention as it has been interpreted by the European Court of Human Rights. Secondly, the courts could find themselves bound, in answering a request for an injunction, to follow the demands of the Convention as the courts themselves are a 'public authority' under the terms of the Act (section 6(3)). Should the courts take this approach, this would in effect resolve the problem of ensuring the Convention is applied in cases involving private parties as long as some law exists to enable one party to bring the cause of action. Thirdly, following an unsuccessful complaint to the Press Complaints Commission, an action could then be brought against that Commission arguing that it was a 'public authority'.[215] But even if privacy cases are not beyond the scope of the Act it is unfortunate that future issues could be ruled outside its scope. Failure to regulate certain aspects of the Internet or to provide effective anti-stalking legislation might be relegated to a private sphere beyond the reach of the Act. Judicial protection of human rights in the private sphere is not as impossible as the Act pretends. Other jurisdictions have resolved the problems with some care.

There was a fierce debate on this subject in South Africa and the 1996 Constitution in fact allows for human rights claims against private actors. The language in the Constitution suggests that judicial caution may be necessary in this field but the possibility of a human rights claim against a non-State actor remains:[216]

Application
    8. (1)   The Bill of Right applies to all law and binds the legislature, the executive, the judiciary and all organs of the state.

[214] Preamble to the Act.

[215] Whether the PCC is a public authority has become a politicized question in the context of the Human Rights Bill debate: William Hague, 'Bound and Gagged', *The Guardian* 9 December 1997 at p. 9. But see the letters page of the same day 'Freedom of the press' which point out that the PCC should be treated like any other public authority and is already subject to judicial review. See also 'Secret move to shield royals from press' and 'Irvine says freedom of the press will be safe with British judges', *The Guardian,* 4 November 1997 at pp.1 and 4.

[216] As adopted on 8 May 1996 and amended on 11 October 1996 by the Constitutional Assembly and signed into law on 10 December 1996. For the Constitutional Court's defence of the importance of applying constitutional rights in a horizontal fashion see their judgment of 6 September 1996 in Case CCT 23/96: Certification of the Constitution of the Republic of South Africa, 1996, paras 53–58, Internet address http://www.polity.org.za/govdocs/misc/cert.html#3A.

(2)   A provision of the Bill of Rights binds a natural or a juristic person if, and to the extent that, it is applicable, taking into account the nature of the rights and of any duty imposed by the right.

(3)   In applying a provision of the Bill of Rights to a natural or juristic person in terms of subsection (2), a court—

(a)   in order to give effect to a right in the Bill, must apply or if necessary develop, develop the common law to the extent that legislation does not give effect to that right; and

(b)   may develop rules of the common law to limit the right, provided that the limitation is in accordance with section 36(1).

(4)   A juristic person is entitled to the rights in the Bill of Rights to the extent required by the nature of the rights and of the juristic persons.

Section 36(1) reads:

36(1) The rights in the Bill of Rights may be limited only in terms of law of general application to the extent that the limitation is reasonable and justifiable in an open and democratic society based on human dignity, equality and freedom, taking into account all relevant factors including—

(a)   the nature of the right;
(b)   the importance of the purpose of the limitation;
(c)   the nature and extent of the limitation;
(d)   the relation between the limitation and its purpose; and
(e)   less restrictive means to achieve the purpose.

These sections of the South African Constitution represent a detailed guide for the judiciary on how to apply human rights in the private sphere. These are the sorts of steps that the European Court of Human Rights in Strasbourg would apply when considering whether the United Kingdom has failed to fulfil its international obligations to protect human rights in the sphere of relations between individuals.

The issue of the judicial application of human rights in relations between private actors is closely bound up with the previous discussion of who has the ultimate right to legislate. If the judges are to be given the power to disapply legislation, or even declare it invalid and void, then allowing unguided judicial supra-legislation over private relations could potentially lead to considerable uncertainty in a number of fields, with reduced possibilities for the legislature to intervene or reverse decisions through legislation. Although the European Court will still have the final say concerning the interpretation of the Convention, that Court's judgments cannot invalidate legislation or undo a British judicial decision. It can only make declaratory statements. Furthermore the European Court could become increasingly reluctant to disagree with British judicial decisions based on a full consideration of the Convention. If national judges are going to have such increased powers to rewrite private law, arrangements would have to be made to ensure certainty, coherence and consistency in their judgments in the private law field. This might mean the creation of specialized bodies and instances to deal with Convention cases. Given that the Bill of Rights takes the form of an interpretation act, it would seem appropriate to state explicitly that the Convention should inform all judicial interpretation of the law even in the sphere of relations between individuals.[217] In the absence of such an injunction, the judiciary may feel that they have to deny the application of the Convention in the private sphere, thus reinforcing the abuses that occur there and denying judicial protection to some victims.

The third issue is the creation of a national Human Rights Commission. Most commentators and activists advocate a Human Rights Commission, although they favour different emphases.[218] Among the functions that such a Commission should perform are the need to canvass in the courts some of the policy implications of different interpretations of the Convention. The national Commission may have to present information and policy arguments which represent the interests of neither litigant before the Court. In so far as the Convention covers the private sphere, the Commission would have to have expertise in employment and discrimination matters as well as traditional civil liberties issues. It would also have to ensure that its promotional and advisory functions are aimed not only at the State sector but also at non-State actors. Perhaps one of the most important functions for any new Commission will be to tackle issues of social and economic rights which fall outside the European Convention. Even though these rights are not made justiciable under the new Act a national Commission could enhance the enjoyment of social and economic rights through studies, investigations and monitoring.

The South African Human Rights Commission is given a series of specific functions and powers in the new Constitution. Apart from promotional, educational, monitoring, and investigative functions, the Commission is given a separate imperative in the field of economic and social rights. According to Article 184(3) of the Constitution:

Each year, the Human Rights Commission must require relevant organs of state to provide the Commission with information on the measures that they have taken towards the realization of the rights in the Bill of Rights concerning housing, health care, food, water, social security, education, and the environment.

The United Kingdom has international obligations under the European Social Charter and the International Covenant on Economic, Social and

---

[217] The Canadian and American courts have declined to apply national constitutional rights in the absence of State action. In Ireland, constitutional rights have been used in inter-personal disputes 'not just as a shield but also as a sword': Butler, 'Constitutional Rights in Private Litigation: A Critique and Comparative Analysis' (1993) 22 *Anglo-American Law Review* 1–41 at 20.

[218] See Straw and Boateng, 'Bringing Rights Home' n. 194 above at 78; Spencer andBynoe, 'A Human Rights Commission for the United Kingdom—Some Options' (1997) *European Human Rights Law Review* 152–60; Amnesty International, *United Kingdom: An Agenda for Human Rights Protection,* AI Index: EUR 45/12/97, June 1997 at 3.

Cultural Rights. The drive to bring rights home should include the repatriation of economic, social and cultural rights as well. The Act leaves open the option of adding further international obligations and the Government has 'not closed its mind to the idea of a new Human Rights Commission at some stage in the future'.[219] The Government has stated that it sees the best way to involve Parliament in protecting rights as the establishment of a new Parliamentary Human Rights Committee. Paragraph 3.7 of the White Paper outlines what this new Committee might do:

The new Committee might conduct enquiries on a range of human rights issues relating to the Convention, and produce reports so as to assist the Government and parliament in deciding what action to take. It might also want to range more widely, and examine issues relating to the other international obligations of the United Kingdom such as proposals to accept new rights under other human rights treaties.

By way of a more broadly applicable conclusion in the context of a volume dealing with Bills of Rights generally, it is suggested that incorporation of human rights treaties such as the Convention needs to be carried out in such a way that complex policy issues can be discussed in the national context rather than by reference to a lowest common denominator of the states that make up the membership of the relevant treaty regime. To do this there needs to be a symbiotic relationship between the national judges and Parliament so that legislation is discussed with reference to the Convention before it is finalized, and so that legislation can be easily adapted should it come to impact in ways that violate human rights. If human rights are to retain some currency as a relevant and useful concept as part of the national culture, then it is desirable to avoid creating artificial boundaries between State and non-State action, and between civil rights and economic rights. The way in which human rights treaties are incorporated into national law will determine whether human rights are indeed brought home and seen as part of domestic affairs rather than seen as something that takes place abroad and periodically divined by foreign judges. Incorporation means more than avoiding foreign censure; it should mean creating a national system capable of responding to new challenges to the enjoyment of human rights; it must mean that procedures are created to ensure a full debate where legislation is considered to possibly violate human rights. These procedures must ensure maximum participation by different sectors. Balancing policy and principle is too important and too complex to be determined by pretending that the final answer lies in a simple reading of a human rights treaty.

---

[219] White Paper, n. 194 above at para. 3.11.

5

Parliamentary Scrutiny of Human Rights: A Duty Neglected?

DAVID KINLEY*

This Chapter is divided into two parts: the first part concentrates on the reasons *why* there ought to be established an effective system of parliamentary scrutiny of legislation for human rights compliance in countries such as Australia, and the second is based upon an analysis of the mechanics of *how* such a scheme might be instituted.

The Need for Scrutiny

Article 2(1) of the International Covenant on Civil and Political Rights ('the Covenant') obliges every signatory State 'to respect and ensure to all individuals within its territory and subject to its jurisdiction the rights recognized in the present Covenant'.[1] It is, of course, trite to point out that of paramount importance for the successful or even adequate attainment of this goal is the existence of sufficient collective political acceptance and willingness to protect and further the noble sentiment of the rights 'guaranteed' by the Covenant. Any signatory country's professed adherence to the *form* of a human rights Covenant may constitute only a part of that will, for the interpretation of the form of words in any such Covenant remains a largely subjective exercise with the result that variances in domestic circumstance not infrequently lead to differences in the Covenant's implementation. Any discussion concerning the establishment and protection of human rights—particularly one in which the primary concern is with the *legal* means by which these ends might be furthered—has always to be conducted within the context of this undeniable determinant.

That much having been said and saving the Commonwealth's Human Rights and Equal Opportunities Commission which is discussed below, the only serious enterprise in Australia that has sought to comply more clearly with the spirit expressed in Article 2(1) has been the argument for the introduction of that quintessential legal instrument, a Bill of Rights. Controversial

* The author wishes to acknowledge the contributions, in thought and deed, made by Philip Alston, Stephen Argument, Peggy Dwyer, and Bronwen Morgan to the production of this essay.
[1] Australia signed the Covenant on 18 December 1972 and ratified it on 13 August 1980.

matters of its entrenchment and the 'politicizing' of the judiciary aside,[2] this particular initiative has failed due largely to political intransigence (both on the part of elected representatives—all three Commonwealth Bills of Rights have been defeated in Parliament,[3] and the Australian electorate when the 1988 'Mini Bill of Rights' proposal was so comprehensively rejected in a referendum), preventing it, to paraphrase the *Captain's Log* of the eponymous spacecraft, from boldly going where most other countries have gone before. This has led some to conclude, perhaps in exasperation more than conviction in the face of the conclusive referendum result, that Australia will likely never have a Bill of Rights.[4] In this Chapter I argue for a necessary supplement, or possibly alternative, to a Bill of Rights[5] as a means of giving fuller effect to the intention of Article 2(1). This might be achieved directly through the organ in which the theoretical synthesis of our collective political will is expressed: Parliament. The proposal that I outline is for the establishment of a Parliamentary scheme of pre-legislative scrutiny—both of primary and secondary legislation—for compliance with the provisions of the Covenant.

The rationale of the proposal stems not only from the pragmatic recognition of the apparent Bill of Rights impasse, but, more importantly, from the philosophical—that is democratic—justification of placing the greatest responsibility for the legal protection of human rights and civil liberties upon the elected legislators rather than the appointed judiciary. As this Chapter's examination of certain examples of controversial legislation illustrates, there exists within both the Australian Commonwealth Government and Parliament (and, doubtless, also within the corresponding State and Territory organs) attitudes of indifference to, or ignorance of, the demands of the Covenant. The implementation of the suggested scheme would necessarily contribute significantly to the protection and improvement of human rights and civil liberties in Australia by requiring stricter adherence to the provisions of the Covenant by legislation and legislative proposals. Thereby, it is suggested, in serving to heighten the awareness within executive and parliamentary offices of the scope and importance of the Covenant, the scrutiny scheme would provide a means by which legislative violations of the Covenant might

[2] Or as Sir Gerard Brennan has put it in the alternative, 'to judicialize questions of politics and morality'. See Brennan, ch. 12 below.

There was strong support in the submissions to the 1986 Constitutional Commission that as a necessary consequence of the constitutional entrenchment of rights '[t]he High Court of Australia would . . . find itself embroiled in political controversy to an extent previously unknown [in this country]': Constitutional Commission, *Final Report of the Constitutional Commission* (1988), para. 9.128; for a survey of this matter generally, see ibid. paras. 9.126–9.137.

[3] In 1973, 1984, and 1985; for a detailed account of these failures, see Galligan, 'Australia's Rejection of a Bill of Rights', 28 *Journal of Commonwealth and Comparative Politics* (1990) 344.

[4] Ibid. at 364. Professor Galligan is today less persuaded by that result in view of the political context in which the referendum took place: see Galligan, 'Australia's Political Culture and Institutional Design', in Alston ed., *Towards an Australian Bill of Rights* (1994), 55.

[5] The case for the scrutiny scheme would be at least as strong in the event of the Commonwealth Parliament legislating to incorporate the Covenant.

be anticipated rather than merely repaired or, worse, disregarded. 'There must be', in the words of Lord Scarman, 'a constitutional restraint placed upon the legislative power which is designed to protect the individual citizen from instant legislation, conceived in fear or prejudice and enacted in breach of human rights'.[6] Whilst Scarman's statement was made in support of the argument for the full incorporation of a Bill of Rights in the United Kingdom, the fact that it singles out the legislative power as being in need of restraint (which is not, of course, to deny that the Executive too must be similarly controlled) is testimony to the central importance of legislative potential to both the wider Bill of Rights debate and the narrower concern of this Chapter.

Even accepting the redundancy of the notion of Parliamentary Sovereignty in Australia—that is, in respect of its philosophical incoherence at least, (though at the level of practice it can be strongly argued that the orthodox, Diceyan expression of the notion has never applied in Australia if only because all Australian legislatures have been created by, and have been or are subject to, written constitutions)[7]—in no way detracts from the strength of the claim not only that it is *primarily* Parliament's duty to protect and advance our human rights, but equally that it is best placed to do so. It is argued that by way of the considerations that justify the nonetheless immense authority that Parliament wields—namely, 'legal certainty, institutional competence, the avoidance of intragovernmental conflict and above all the many principled and pragmatic grounds for representative democracy'[8]—there exists at least the potential for an effective preventive influence over Parliament by way of electoral pressure in respect of unacceptable legislation,[9] where the electorate is aware of such legislation and cognizant of its impact on human rights. The institution of a Bill of Rights, in this context, *may* aid this 'political' limitation on Parliament; it will, however, through the concomitant grant of guardianship of the Bill of Rights to the judiciary, produce a significant and controversial imbalance in authority within our system of government. Confirmation of this result comes from within the ranks of the judiciary itself: to wit, Sir Gerard Brennan's percipient observation that 'the effect of a Bill of Rights depends much more on the attitudes of the judges who interpret it than on the words themselves'.[10] Indeed this shift in the constitutional equilibrium might be the necessary price to pay if the above mooted *potential* of Parliament and the executive to adopt the mantle of human rights guardian

---

[6] Scarman, English Law—The New Dimension (1974), 20.

[7] See D. Kinley, 'Constitutional Brokerage in Australia: Constitutions and the Doctrines of Parliamentary Supremacy and the Rule of Law' (1994) 22 Federal Law Review, 194.

[8] Goldsworthy, 'The Constitutional Protection of Rights in Australia', in Craven ed., *Australian Federation, Towards the Second Century* (1991), 160.

[9] This potential was acknowledged by the Legal and Constitutional Committee of Victoria in its *Report on the Desirability or Otherwise of Legislation Defining and Protecting Human Rights* (1987), 27.

[10] Brennan, ch. 12 below.

remains, just that: 'potential' not actual. The scrutiny scheme here outlined, therefore, can be seen as means by which this potential might proceed towards fulfilment.

An obvious catalyst for the rejuvenation of the Bill of Rights debate and the relevance to Australians of the human rights guarantees in the Covenant in general has been Australia's accession to the Optional Protocol in September 1991 and its coming into force on Christmas Day of the same year. It is, naturally, difficult to predict what impact this initiative will have in Australia in the long term. There have been some signs of recognition of its potential in the establishment of a specialist Optional Protocol Unit in the Commonwealth Department of the Attorney-General (though its functions appear to be directed largely to events after a complaint has been made),[11] the formation of a national network of people concerned with the Optional Protocol, and Justice Brennan's observation in the *Mabo* case that Australia's endorsement of individual petition will bring to bear 'the powerful influence of the Covenant and the international standards it imports'.[12] The various decisions by the UN's Human Rights Committee in cases involving Australia have also demonstrated the considerable potential which the procedure presents.[13]

EXPERIENCES AND RESPONSES IN OTHER JURISDICTIONS

A general, but nonetheless useful, indication of additional consequences might be obtained from relevant experiences with human rights treaties in Australia's close constitutional and common law neighbours, Canada and the United Kingdom (I have excluded New Zealand at this stage principally because since it acceded to the Optional Protocol on 26 May 1989, it has had only one individual petition by a New Zealand resident declared admissible).[14] Canada acceded to the First Optional Protocol at the same time as it acceded to the Covenant itself, that is, 19 May 1976. From that date up to the beginning of 1990 there were 53 communications to the Human Rights Committee concerning allegations of violations of the Covenant by Canadian law.[15] Whilst it is true that of these only 6 were declared admissible, of which

[11] Thomson, 'Using the Optional Protocol: The Practical Issues', in *Internationalizing Human Rights: Australia's Accession to the First Optional Protocol* (1992), 22–4.

[12] *Mabo* v. *State of Queensland* (1992) 175 CLR 1.

[13] See *Toonen* v. *Australia* (31 March 1994) 1 (1994) No 3 Int'l Hum Rts Reports 97 (on which see generally W. Morgan 'Identifying Evil For What It Is: Tasmania, Sexual Perversity and the United Nations', (1994) 19 *Melbourne U.L. Rev* 740); and *A (name deleted)* v. *Australia* (3 April 1997), UN Doc. CCPR/C/59/D/560/1993.

[14] See P.T. Rishworth, 'Human Rights and the Bill of Rights' (1996) 3 New Zealand Law Review 298, 304–5.

[15] Turp, 'Les Communications concernant l'état Canadien au comité des droits de l'homme', 17 *CCIL Bulletin* 5 (1991) at 9–11. By the author's calculations, a further 12 communications had been made by June 1997, bringing the total to 65.

3 were found to constitute infringements of the Covenant,[16] the total of 53 complaints is not insubstantial.[17] For present purposes, what is perhaps a more revealing statistic is that more than twice the number of communications were lodged in the 6 years of Canada's ratification of the Covenant *before* the introduction of the Charter in 1982, than were lodged in the following 8 years to the beginning of 1990.[18] Clearly the advent of the Charter goes a long way towards explaining this disparity, but the facts that the number of communications during the pre-Charter period was considerable, at slightly over 6 per year, and that although dropping after 1982, remained notable at 2 per year, appears to indicate the scope for use of the right to individual petition under the Optional Protocol in a country as similar to Australia as Canada.

In the United Kingdom the analogues that one may elicit in relation to Australia are different from those based on Canada, but are perhaps more compelling. The United Kingdom, as a founding member of the Council of Europe and an original signatory of the European Convention on Human Rights ('the European Convention'), has not seen the need to ratify the first optional Protocol to the Covenant.[19] However, not only is there a substantive similarity between the two sets of rights, but since 1966 when the United Kingdom accepted the right of individual petition under Article 25 of the European Convention, its laws and actions have been subject to effectively the same procedural means of challenge on the basis of human rights as the laws and actions of Australia now are. Between 1975 (which marks the date of the United Kingdom's first violation) and the end of 1991, the United Kingdom was found by the European Court of Human Rights to have violated the Convention on 28 occasions, which is considerably more than any other signatory State. No less than 22 of these have involved infringements caused directly by domestic legislation.[20] What is more, in respect of the period up to the end of 1991, it has been estimated that if one also takes into account those cases which are ultimately found by the Court not to have established an infringement, or those which never reach beyond the European Commission to the Court, 'some 80 UK laws or regulations have been repealed or amended

[16] Turp, 'Les Communications concernant l'état Canadien au comité des droits de l'homme', 17 *CCIL Bulletin* 5 (1991) at at 9.

[17] Though a long way behind Uruguay, for example; see Bayefsky, *International Human Rights Law: Use in Canadian Charter of Rights and Freedoms Litigation* (1992), 619–68.

[18] The figures for the two periods are 37 and 16 respectively; see Turp n. 14 above. By the author's calculations 12 communications were lodged in the period 1990 to mid-1997.

[19] The United Kingdom ratified the ICCPR itself in 1976.

[20] Kinley, *The European Convention on Human Rights: Compliance Without Incorporation* (1993), 181–3 ('Table of all UK cases found by the European Court of Human Rights to constitute violations of the ECHR, including an indication where caused by legislative provisions'). See further, The Constitution Unit, *Human Rights Legislation* (1996), Appendix A, 'UK Cases Before the European Court of Human Rights', pp. 128–133. According to this table, in a further 12 cases between 1992 and 1996, UK laws were found by the Court to have breached the Convention.

as a result of proceedings under the European Convention'.[21] The issues affected by the established breaches alone are extremely diverse, including freedom of speech, fair trial, corporal punishment, trade unionism, prison rules, prevention of terrorism, homosexuality, child care, and mental health.[22]

This sort of analysis begs the obvious question of how the legislature of a State which has endorsed a human rights document such as the European Convention can pass legislation which, with such regularity, is found subsequently to violate certain of those protected rights.

Though apparent recognition of this potentially embarrassing anomaly within any of the executives and legislatures in the countries mentioned thus far is variable, as is the extent to which action has been taken to forestall such legislative breaches, in none is there established an substantially effective pre-legislative scrutiny scheme for compliance with relevant human rights instruments.[23] That is, fundamentally, a scheme, which whilst retaining the authority of Parliament to enact legislation (including authority for it to delegate such powers to the executive), all legislation is *both proposed and passed in the knowledge* of its likely impact (if any) on the guarantees provided in the relevant human rights instruments. Or, to put it more precisely, a scheme where the executive, by way of the direct or indirect influence of the legislature, is made politically aware of the human rights consequences of the legislation it introduces or plans to introduce.

In Canada, whilst there has never been any formal pre-legislative scrutiny for compliance with the Covenant, there today exist procedures for the express scrutiny of legislative proposals for compliance with both the 1982 Charter and the 1960 Bill of Rights. This task is undertaken by the Department of Justice. Under legislative provisions relating to both documents, substantially the same requirement is made of the Minister of Justice that she/he 'examine every Bill introduced in or presented to the House of Commons by a Minister of the Crown . . . in order to determine whether any of the provisions thereof are inconsistent with the purposes and provisions of [either human rights statute]'.[24] In both cases, also, regulations are scrutinized for conformity by the Minister.[25] In cases where any inconsistency is found the Minister must submit a report to the House of Commons 'at the earliest convenient opportunity'.[26] Such a report notwithstanding, Parliament may still enact the

---

[21] Thornton, *Decade of Decline* (1989), 92. Note also that Liberty, in its discussion document entitled *A People's Charter* (1991), has emphasized the significance of changes in United Kingdom Government policy consequent on 'friendly settlements'; a number of examples are discussed in the document in illustration of the point, ibid. at 111–12.

[22] See Kinley, n. 18 above, and The Constitution Unit, n. 18 above..

[23] For a more detailed survey of the various pre-legislative scrutiny schemes in these and other countries, see The Constitution Unit, *Human Rights* Legislation (1996), chapter 4, and Kinley n. 19 above, ch. 5.

[24] The Canadian Bill of Rights Examination Regulations 1978, Section 3a; and the Canadian Charter of Rights and Freedoms Examination Regulations, PC 1985–2561, Section 3a.

[25] Ibid. Section 4a of both regulations.   [26] Ibid. Section 6 of both regulations.

impugned legislation subject to the qualification that the Bill must contain an explicit statement that the prospective Act is to operate despite the provisions of either the Bill of Rights or the Charter. Plainly, the decision to use such a device in order to persist with legislation likely otherwise to be in breach of domestic human rights obligations is politically unpalatable.[27] This is illustrative of the preventive effect that the Canadian Federal scrutiny scheme can bring to bear.

In 1986, the Ministry of Justice in New Zealand established the Legislation Advisory Committee.[28] Its terms of reference indicate that it is expected to scrutinize all Bills introduced to Parliament in respect of any legislation 'affecting public law or raising public law issues', and to report to the Minister of Justice or the Legislation Committee of Cabinet on those issues where either has referred legislative proposals to it.[29] It would appear—though this is not to be found in the Committee's terms of reference—that the primary concern in identifying these public law issues is one of financial constraint, that is, to try to cut the cost of translating policy into legislation by making more efficient and effective the stages of the 'development of policy, the Cabinet approval process, the law-drafting and approval stage, and the Parliamentary approval process'.[30] The Committee has always laid great emphasis on the preventive measures to help ensure that these goals are met. Rather than relying solely on its critical, ex post facto reports on legislative proposals to exert pressure on the departments, Parliamentary counsel and the Cabinet, the Committee has produced legislative guidelines (in 1987 and a fully revised version in 1991) for the aid of those involved in the preparation of legislation.[31] Two specific questions that the guidelines suggest must be asked by legislators are: does the prospective legislation comply with (a) the New Zealand Bill of Rights Act 1990, and (b) New Zealand's international obligations, including, of course, the Covenant. Though it is perhaps too early to obtain an indication as to the impact of the former on legislative procedure, in respect of the latter, the Committee has produced a rather remarkable statistic. It has estimated that 'about one quarter of the 600 or so public Acts which make up the New Zealand Statute book give effect to [or raise issues concerning] international obligations',[32] ranging from the Abolition of the Death Penalty Act 1989, through the Criminal Justice Act 1985 and the

---

[27] On the sparing use of the *non-obstante* clause under Section 33 of the Charter, see Beaudoin and Ratushny, *The Canadian Charter of Rights and Freedoms* (2nd edn,. 1989), 104–7 and R. Penner, 'The Canadian Experience with the Charter of Rights: Are there Lessons for the United Kingdom', [1996] Public Law 104, 109–10.

[28] Whilst the membership of the Committee is largely non-Government (7 out of 10), the members owe their appointments to the Committee to the Government.

[29] Legislation Advisory Committee, *Legislative Change, Guidelines on Process and Content*, Report No. 6 (1991), ii.

[30] Ibid. at v, Foreword by the Hon. Douglas Graham, the then Minister for Justice.

[31] Ibid.   [32] Ibid. at 81.

Ozone Layer Protection Act 1990, to the Treaty of Waitangi Act 1975.[33] Whilst there is no breakdown of these obligations in respect of individual treaties, for instance, it is very likely a substantial task to scrutinize legislation in respect of such a broadly-termed document as the Covenant. A perusal of the Committee's reports on specific legislative proposals reveals little call for it to have had to remark on conformity of Bills to the Covenant, which may itself be the best indication that its own guidelines are being heeded.[34] A reiteration of the importance placed on the compliance of domestic laws with international human rights treaties obligations in New Zealand may be inferred from the on-going 'Consistency 2000' project. This is a project which aims to review all domestic laws for compliance with international human rights provisions by the end of 1998, and for any identified inconsistencies to be corrected by 1 January 2000.[35] The review is being undertaken by the New Zealand Human Rights Commission.

In 1991 a referral system was established for the scrutiny of legislative proposals for compliance with New Zealand's Bill of Rights Act 1990. Section 7 of the Act requires the Attorney-General to report to Parliament on the introduction of any government Bill (and as soon as practicable thereafter in the case of non-government Bills) on 'any provision of the Bill that appears to be inconsistent with any of the rights and freedoms contained in th[e] Bill of Rights'. In practice, the Attorney-General is assisted in this task by both the Law Reform Division of the Department of Justice and the Crown Law Office. In an effort to promote an awareness of this responsibility, the Attorney-General has, in addition, issued a memorandum to all departments detailing the scrutiny procedures which have been established pursuant to Section 7 of the Act and urging the departments to consult the Department of Justice for 'information about the ambit of the . . . Bill of Rights'.[36] Since its inception only three such reports concerning government legislation have been tabled in Parliament.[37] In respect of all three bills the 'justifiable limitations' provision of section 5 of the Bill of Rights Act[38] has featured prominently in the reports of the Attorney-General and the deliberations of Parliament. In the case of the first two reported bills the limitations were considered to be reasonable and the bills were passed accordingly; in the case of the third bill, the

---

[33] For a list of those relevant Acts, see ibid. at 71–5.

[34] See, for example, Legislation Advisory Committe, *Report No. 5* (1990).

[35] See *Human Rights Act 1993*, sections 5(1); 151 & 152.

[36] The memorandum (dated 8 April 1991) is reproduced in Appendix A to Fitzgerald, 'Section 7 of the New Zealand Bill of Rights Act 1990: A Very Practical Power or a Well Intentioned Nonsense', 22 VUWLR (1992) 135 at 156.

[37] The Transport Safety Bill 1991, The Films, Videos and Publications Classifications Bill 1992, and, The Children, Young Persons and their Families Amendment Bill 1993. A further six Private Members' Bills have been subject to reports, as of June 1997.

[38] The operative part of which reads: '. . . the rights and freedoms contained in this Bill of Rights may be subject only to such reasonable limits prescribed by law as can be demonstrably justified in a free and democratic society.'

limitation appears to have been considered unjustified and was not proceeded with.[39]

There may be little doubt that both the Canadian and New Zealand forms of pre-legislative scrutiny in this regard do have some effect, but it remains the case that fin respect of the object of this chapter they provide only guidelines rather than blueprints. It will perhaps take a little longer to gauge properly the full capability of the New Zealand scheme in respect of the Covenant, and both the New Zealand Bill of Rights scheme and the Canadian model (for all the latter's relative longevity) nonetheless lack independence, since they entrust the task of the scrutiny of Government legislation to the government.[40] Whilst it must be acknowledged both that reports critical of government legislation may nonetheless be made,[41] and that there is no direct evidence of this self-regulatory arrangement being abused, one cannot help feeling uneasy at the prospect of political convenience trumping scrutinizing probity in certain, perhaps pressing, circumstances.[42] Indeed, it is not unreasonable to adopt an even more cynical stance: it has been asked rhetorically in respect of the New Zealand scheme (though it applies equally to the Canadian model), '[w]ould a Cabinet member ever say Cabinet's legislation is not "demonstrably justified in a free and democratic society?" '.[43]

Despite, or perhaps *in spite*, of its unenviable record before the adjudicative organs for the European Convention, the United Kingdom currently has no established system of pre-legislative scrutiny. It is true that in 1987 the Cabinet issued to all government departments a pair of circulars entitled 'Reducing the Risk of Legal Challenge', and 'The Judge over your Shoulder—Judicial Review of Administrative Decisions'.[44] The former indicates the need for those responsible for policy formulation and the drafting of legislative proposals to minimize the risk of future legal challenge to the legislation on the ground, inter alia, that it infringes the provisions of the European Convention. Those persons indicated are urged to 'consider the effect of European Convention jurisprudence on any proposed legislative or administrative measure, in consultation with their legal adviser', and that '[a]ll

[39] For discussion, see G. Huscroft and P. Rishworth (eds) *Rights and Freedoms* (1995), chap. 4; esp. pp. 141–46.

[40] In spite of the independence of most of its membership, the Legislation Advisory Committee in New Zealand effectively functions as part of the Government, in that it is responsible to the Minister of Justice.

[41] E.g. the three reports of the New Zealand Attorney-General as discussed above. In respect of the Canadian system, see n. 41 below.

[42] Here again Lord Scarman's caveat is relevant: see n. 6 above and accompanying text.

[43] Taylor, 'That Bill of Rights', 13 TCL (1990) 33/1, as quoted by Fitzgerald n. 34 above at 148. Indeed, it is apposite to note that no report to the House of Commons has ever been made by the Minister of Justice under the Canadian Scrutiny Scheme for legislative compliance with the Charter.

[44] The first is dated March 1987, and the second dated 6 July 1987. For a general commentary on these memoranda see Bradley, 'The Judge over your Shoulder', PL (1987) 485; and 'Protecting Government Decisions from Legal Challenge', PL (1988) 1.

Cabinet Committee memoranda on policy proposals and memoranda for Legislation Committee should include an assessment of the effect, if any, of European Convention jurisprudence on what is proposed'.[45] No further specialized assistance is offered to the departments in the execution of these tasks beyond the seeking of 'ad hoc guidance from the Foreign and Commonwealth Office'.[46] The informality of this process (if it can be called such), and the scope for its inconsistent exercise throughout the departments are factors that have hardly aided its effectiveness. Indeed, there is irony in the fact that the same year in which these Cabinet Circulars were published also marked a sharp increase in the rate at which the European Court has found against the United Kingdom. Whereas 13 violations can be attributed to the 11-year period 1975–86, judgments against the United Kingdom were handed down by the Court on 27 occasions in the 9 years between 1987 and 1996. In light of these statistics, one might note with regret, that the fact that the second edition (published in 1994) of the 'Judge over your Shoulder' Memorandum omitted to mention the ECHR at all may make little difference as the Memorandum's original exhortation to ensure compliance appears to have had minimal effect.

In an effort to construct an effective scrutiny scheme in the United Kingdom I have argued elsewhere that the only viable option is to establish it as part of the Parliamentary legislative process (that is, crucially, beyond the sole control of the Executive).[47] Though there indeed exist within the United Kingdom's present legislative procedure some structural elements upon which to base such a scrutiny scheme, my argument in this respect has been strongly influenced by the Australian Senate Scrutiny of Bills, and Regulations and Ordinances Committees, which offer the greatest potential for development for the present purpose.[48] This, therefore, demonstrates what promising foundations for an Australian Commonwealth pre-legislative scrutiny model already exist, though it cannot be over-emphasized that this potential has yet to be acted upon.

---

[45] Paras. 4(1) and (2).

[46] Ibid. Annex. II, para. 6. For the position with respect to the tendering of general legal advice to departments, see HC Debates, vol. 124 (6th) (18 December 1987) at col. 781(w).

[47] Kinley n. 18 above, ch. 6. See also Liberty *A Peoples' Charter* (1991) at 95–9 and The Constitution Unit n. 18 above, ch. 4 for further discussion and M.T. Ryle, 'Pre-legislative scrutiny: a prophylactic approach to protection of human rights' [1994] Public Law 192, for a summary of constructive proposals to establish such scrutiny mechanisms.

[48] Indeed the House of Lords' Select Committee on the Scrutiny of Delegated Powers (see HL Debates, vol. 549 (10 November 1993) at column 9, avowedly recognized the heavy debt, in terms of inspiration, it owed to the Senate's Scrutiny of Bills Committee; see House of Lords Select Committee on the Scrutiny of Delegated Powers, *Report from the Select Committee on the Committee Work of the House* (1992), 35–I, 63–8. Its terms of reference, however, reflect only those aspects of the Senate Committee's terms that relate to the inappropriateness of using delegated legislation where the matter ought to be the subject of primary legislation. Conspicuously absent from the Lords Committee's current terms, therefore, is any power to inquire into the impact of proposed legislation on 'personal rights and liberties'.

In fact, a feature of the new United Kingdom Labour Government's commitment to incorporate the ECHR, it is anticipated, is the establishment of a scheme for pre-legislative scrutiny for compliance with the Convention.

PRE-LEGISLATIVE SCRUTINY FOR HUMAN RIGHTS CONFORMITY IN AUSTRALIA

I should first make a brief but necessary reference under this heading to the Federal dimension of Parliamentary scrutiny of human rights in Australia. It must be recognized, of course, that a substantial proportion of legislative competence in areas where it can be supposed human rights concerns might be raised lies with the States exclusively, or concomitantly with the Commonwealth—for example, criminal law and laws relating to industrial disputes, marriage, Indigenous people, and electoral franchise. However, as the principal concern of this Chapter is to identify a need for pre-legislative scrutiny and to suggest how we might go about meeting that need, I have chosen not to examine in detail either relevant State legislation that might be in violation of Australia's human rights commitments (notable examples of which are the persistence of Tasmanian legislation criminalizing homosexual acts;[49] Western Australia's former Crime (Serious and Repeat Offenders) Sentencing Act 1992 and its corollary, the Criminal Code Amendment Act (No. 2) 1996, both of which impose mandatory sentences on repeat offenders;[50] the extraordinary *ad hominen* provisions of Victoria's *Community*

---

[49] Criminal Code 1924 (Tas), Section 123. In 1987 the Criminal Code Amendment (Sex Offences) Bill was introduced in Parliament, but without any provision seeking to repeal Section 123 (an unsuccessful attempt to introduce an amendment to do so was made during Committee; see Legislative Council Debates (Tas), No. 11 (29 July 1987) at 1683–95). Throughout the parliamentary debates on the Bill there was no recognition, let alone discussion, of the impact of the relevant provisions on the rights guaranteed under the International Covenant on Civil and Political Rights (see second readings, House of Assembly Debates (Tas), No. 7 (14–16 April 1987) at 1584–6, 1601–22 and Legislative Council Debates (Tas), No. 10 (21–23 July 1987) at 1487–93, 1516–34); and that was, despite the prominence of the subject of homosexuality during the debates in both Chambers and the uncompromising, and in some cases unguarded, views of some members. (For example, the then leader for the Government in the Legislative Council, Mr Fletcher—who was, amongst others, concerned with the related issue of public health—declared that 'no matter what is said about this campaign about condoms being safe, I will not wear that at all'; Legislative Council Debates (Tas), No. 10 (23 July 1987) at 1607). This legislation was the cause of the first petition originating from Australia to be lodged with the Human Rights Committee under the Optional Protocol procedure. The Committee found the legislation to be in breach of Article 17 of the Covenant (right to privacy). UN Doc. CCPR/C/50/D/488/1992, Final Views of 31 March 1994. Though the legislation yet remains Tasmanian law, its authority has been directly annulled by the enactment by the Commonwealth Parliament of the *Human Rights (Homosexual Conduct) Act* 1995, which, by operation of s.109 of the Commonwealth Constitution, has primacy over the Tasmanian provision.

[50] It is argued, for instance, that provisions of these Acts infringe the rights of individuals to have the lawfulness of their detention determined by a Court (Article 9(4) of the Covenant), and to be presumed innocent until proved guilty (Article 14(2) of the Covenant). See Wilkie, 'Crime (Serious and Repeat Offenders) Sentencing Act 1992: A Human Rights Perspective', 22 *Western*

Protection Act 1990 and New South Wales' *Community Protection Act 1994*;[51] and both Queensland's Electricity (Continuity of Supply) Act 1985, and New South Wales' Essential Services Act 1988[52]), or the potential for the development of peculiarly State scrutiny schemes to prevent such occurrences. In any case, from an institutional and constitutional viewpoint, there is nothing to stop the States from following the Commonwealth model here suggested. Indeed, in respect of secondary legislation, all States currently have scrutiny committees working under broadly similar terms of reference[53] which could be appropriately adapted to incorporate specific scrutiny for compliance with the provisions of the Covenant. Even in respect of the scrutiny of primary legislation there now exists scrutiny schemes in Queensland and Victoria, as well as the Australian Capital Territory. In Queensland the former Electoral and Administrative Review Commission ('EARC') recommended that there be established a Scrutiny of Legislation Committee with responsibility for the examination of all legislative proposals (both primary and delegated) to

Australian Law Review (1992) 1 and, submission of the Aboriginal Legal Service of Western Australia in response to the Australian Law Reform Commission's Inquiry into Children and the Legal Process (Submission no. 78, 14 Aug. 1997), in respect of the Criminal Code Amendment Act (No. 2) 1996.

[51] The Victorian Act, which under Section 16 expired after one year, provided for the preventive detention of an individual who had a history of violent psychiatric disorder by way of a process that circumvented normal curial review. Though the Bill was roundly criticized during its passage through Parliament for its infringement of the rights and liberties of the person concerned (see second readings, Legislative Assembly Debates (Vic), vol. 397 (3 April 1990) at 644, and Legislative Council Debates (Vic), vol. 397 (11 April 1990) at 701), a second Bill intended to have general application was prepared by the Government in late 1991 as a draft proposal for consultation. This Bill—the Community Protection (Violent Offenders) Bill—has been heavily criticized by the Parliamentary Committee on Social Development in its *Inquiry into Mental Disturbance and Community Safety, Second Report* (1992).

The New South Wales statute, which was similar in effect to the Victorian Act, was successfully challenged before the High Court as being contrary to the restrictions on the exercise of judicial power under Chapter III of the Commonwealth Constitution (*Kable* v. *Director of Public Prosecutions* (NSW) (1996) 138 ALR 577). In particular, the provision for preventive detention without a crime being committed was considered to be contrary to the notion of the rule of law and a fair trial implicit in the exercise of judicial power under the Constitution. Such fairness is, of course, guaranteed under article 14 and 15 of the ICCPR.

[52] Provisions of both these Acts, it is argued, are in breach of Article 8 of the Covenant (as well as corresponding ILO guarantees), by effectively prohibiting relevant employees from taking any industrial action under certain circumstances.

[53] Importantly, included in all of their terms of reference is the requirement that they scrutinize secondary legislation to ensure that it does not 'trespass unduly on personal rights and liberties'—on which principle, see further, below. For a catalogue of the terms of reference of the Commonwealth's and the six State Committees see Appendix to the *Report and Transcript of Proceedings of the Second Conference of Australian Delegated Legislation Committees* (1989), 355–9; see also the comparative table of terms of reference in *Scrutiny of National Scheme Legislation and the Desirability of Uniform Scrutiny Principles*, Discussion Paper No. 1, published jointly by the Senate Standing Committees on Regulations and Ordinances and the Scrutiny of Bills; July 1995, pp. 26–7.

ensure, inter alia, that they do not 'trespass unduly on rights and liberties'.[54]
Whilst it was suggested that particular examples of provisions that would so
trespass ought to be provided (a number of which reflected rights protected by
the Covenant),[55] it was not the intention to require legislative compliance with
the Covenant in full. The Legislation Standards Act 1992 (Qld), however, did
not contain any of these suggestions, as the Government considered it prudent
not to establish any new Committee scheme until the completion of the a
review of the whole Parliamentary Committee system in Queensland.[56]
Subsequently, a Scrutiny of Legislation Committee was established in 1995
under the *Parliamentary Committees Act 1995* (Qld). A particular feature of
the Committee's terms of reference is the set of specified 'rights and liberties'
in respect of which the Committee must scrutinise both primary and secondary legislation for compliance.[57]

In Victoria, on the other hand, in 1987, the Legal and Constitutional
Committee made a specific and detailed recommendation to Parliament,
within its wider call for statutorily protected human rights, that the protection
of human rights in the State would be significantly aided by the institution of
a pre-legislative scrutiny system empowered to assess, amongst other issues,
compliance with the proposed Declaration of Rights and Freedoms Act.[58] It
was considered by the Committee that the 'failure of Parliament to rigorously
scrutinize proposed legislation which may unjustifiably impinge upon human
rights . . . directly results in the creation of serious anomalies in this area'.[59]
And whilst ex post facto redress may be obtained, it was in no doubt that 'the
best course is to ensure the proper functioning of a system which prevents
[these anomalies] coming into existence'.[60] The Committee suggested that
the terms of reference of the Legal and Constitutional Committee itself be

[54] See Part 4 of the Legislative Standards Bill 1991 (Qld); Electoral and Administrative Review
Commission, *Report on Review of the Office of Parliamentary Council* (1991), Appendix H.

[55] e.g. 'being inconsistent with principles of natural justice' (Articles 9, 14, and 15 of the
Covenant); 'conferring power to enter premises and search or seize documents or other property
without a warrant issued by a judge or other judicial officer' (Article 17); and 'failing to provide
appropriate protection against self-incrimination' (Article 14(g) in conjunction with Article 2(1));
see Part 4 of the suggested Bill (see n. 51 above).

[56] EARC published its *Review of Parliamentary Committees* in October 1992, and the
Parliamentary Committee for Electoral and Administrative Review tabled its report (on the
Commission's Review) in October 1993. Note, however, that the Office of Queensland
Parliamentary Counsel established under the 1992 Act is expressly charged with giving advice to
Ministers and public servants in respect of any of a number of fundamental legislative principles
(listed in Section 7(g)) that might be relevant to legislative proposals that they have formulated.
See Zifcak, 'Queensland, the Exemplar of Democracy', 18 *Alternative Law Journal* (1993) 260.

[57] These specified (though still broadly couched) rights are provided under s. 4(1) of the
Legislative Standards Act 1992.

[58] Legal and Constitutional Committee, *Report on the Desirability or Otherwise of Legislation
Defining and Protecting Human Rights* (1987).

[59] Legal and Constitutional Committee, *Report on the Desirability or Otherwise of Legislation
Defining and Protecting Human Rights* (1987) at 81.

[60] Ibid.

appropriately amended so that it might undertake the task of human rights scrutiny of both primary and secondary legislation.[61] The Committee would be charged with making 'findings' on legislative compliance with the proposed declaration which would not be binding but rather 'would operate to alert Parliament to what the [Scrutiny Committee] regarded as potential or actual breaches of human rights'.[62] Nonetheless, despite an eloquent and forceful summation of the benefits to be gained from such a system,[63] the recommendation was not acted upon by the Victorian Government at the time. The then Labor Government decided instead to introduce a Bill to establish the recommended Declaration of Rights and Freedoms, without any complementary Parliamentary 'watchdog'.[64] Subsequently, however, the then newly elected Liberal Government, ensured the passage of the Parliamentary Committees (Amendment) Act 1992 established the Joint Scrutiny of Acts and Regulations Committee. The Committee's terms of reference fall short of the Legal and Constitutional Committee's 1987 recommendations as they do not include any detailed set of human rights (such as the Covenant) against which to measure the compliance of Bills. Rather, they simply adopt the five broad principles used by the Commonwealth Senate's Scrutiny of Bills Committee (on which, see below).[65]

The current terms of reference of the Commonwealth Senate's Standing Committee for the Scrutiny of Bills[66] require it to report, inter alia, whether any Clauses of Bills introduced into the Senate 'trespass unduly on personal rights and liberties'. The same words are applied to the scrutiny of regulations

[61] See recommendations 4 and 5 of the Report, ibid. at 158–64.   [62] Ibid. at 105.

[63] 'Through such a process, Parliament would continually receive reports regarding the human rights implications of proposed legislation. Bills restricting human rights would thus not pass through Parliament unnoticed. An adverse report of a Scrutiny of Bills Committee would not only alert Parliament, and provide members with highly relevant material for use during debate on the Bill concerned, but would also generally publicize the fact that an issue of human rights was involved. A report in sufficiently adverse terms might well receive media attention, and would certainly attract the notice of the Opposition, and civil liberties groups. Parliament would be entirely free to decide that the limitation of human rights in question was justifiable, but the effect of a proper scrutiny of Bills would be to greatly increase the likelihood that this would only occur after appropriate consideration, full debate and exposure to the public': ibid. at 108.

[64] The Constitution (Declaration of Rights and Freedoms) Bill 1988 was introduced in May 1988; though it lapsed with the State election later that year, it was reintroduced after the election in November 1988; it proceeded no further than second reading in the Legislative Assembly, largely due to the opposition of the Liberal Party to the very absence of such a scheme of Parliamentary scrutiny: Legislative Assembly, Debates (Vic), vol. 393 (12 April 1989) at 652.

[65] This consequence may be traced to party political intransigence as the Liberal Party had consistently opposed the former Labor Government's Constitution (Declaration of Rights and Freedoms) Bill. See Legislative Council Debates (Vic), vol. 407 (3 June 1992) at 1237–42; see also n. 61 above.

[66] Senate Standing Order 24. In all, five principles are stated against which the Committee measures the Bills laid before it—that is (in addition to the principle mentioned), whether, by express words or otherwise, Clauses of Bills make rights, liberties or obligations unduly dependent upon insufficiently defined administrative powers; make rights, liberties, or obligations unduly dependent upon non-reviewable decisions; inappropriately delegate legislative powers; or insufficiently subject the exercise of legislative power to Parliamentary scrutiny.

in the terms of reference of the Senate Standing Committee on Regulations and Ordinances.[67] In relation to neither Committee is any elaboration on these stark instructions provided. Though it is true that this form of words is capable of being interpreted to include the 'rights and freedoms' enshrined in the Covenant (though such use is seldom made), it is important to note that the two Committees have always maintained that, as with all the criteria under which they operate, neither Committee forms a 'concluded view' in their reports to the Senate.[68]

The following example illustrates this point amply. In its *Report on the Political Broadcasts and Political Disclosures Bill 1991* ('the PBPD Bill') the Scrutiny Committee considered that the Bill's limitations on the opportunities to express 'political' views through the electronic media amounted to a prima facie interference with the above quoted 'rights and freedom' principle—specifically, the right to freedom of expression.[69] The stipulation that the legislative provision in question must 'trespass *unduly*' on such rights, however, was understood to permit certain limitations on these rights in a manner analogous to that which permits restrictions to the rights protected in the Covenant.[70] Thus, in respect of the right to freedom of expression, Article 19 of the Covenant recognizes that restrictions may be imposed:

but only . . . as are provided by law and are necessary:
(a) for the respect of the rights or reputations of others;
(b) for the protection of national security or of public order (*ordre public*), or of public health or morals.

As to addressing the task of establishing the necessity of a restriction on freedom of expression under one of these allotted categories in the case of the PBPD Bill, the Committee offered only that it 'has to be decided on the basis of what is justifiable in the particular circumstances', and that, '[u]ltimately, . . . is a matter of public policy . . . for decision by the Parliament'.[71]

---

[67] Senate Standing Order 23. In addition to this principle, the Senate Standing Committee scrutinizes delegated legislation to ensure that it is in accordance with the Statute; that it does not unduly make rights and liberties of citizens dependent upon administrative decisions which are not subject to review of their merits by a judicial or other independent tribunal; and that it does not contain matter more appropriate for Parliamentary enactment.

[68] Senator Michael Tate (a former Chairman of the Scrutiny of Bills Committee), 'The Operation of the Senate Standing Committee for the Scrutiny of Bills', paper presented to the Conference of the Australasian Study of Parliament Group on *The Legislative Process: How Relevant?* (1985), 57.

[69] 8/91 *Scrutiny of Bills Alert Digest* (15 May 1991), 14

[70] 8/91 *Scrutiny of Bills Alert Digest* (15 May 1991), at 15.

[71] Ibid. at 15–16. The Committee also acknowledged that as in the anticipated event of a legal challenge to the legislation the High Court might pronounce on its validity, it did not feel it necessary to communicate any additional views in its report: ibid. at 16. Indeed, the High Court subsequently declared the relevant sections of the PBPD Act invalid on the ground that the restrictions it imposed on the electronic media breached an implied constitutional right to freedom of communication: *Australian Capital Television Pty Ltd* v. *Commonwealth (No. 2)* (1992) 177 CLR 106.

Though it is accepted that under its present operational structure and staffing the Committee in this case would not have been expected to have provided much more than this, it is submitted, in the light of the subsequent Senate Select Committee appointed specifically to inquire into the PBPD Bill, that a more thorough assessment of the Bill's compliance with the International Covenant at the early stage of consideration by the Scrutiny of Bills Committee would have been most effective, particularly as the results of its deliberations would have been available to all Members of both chambers in advance of their respective second reading debates.[72] There existed then, and there exists now, no such process of human rights scrutiny within the Committee's current operation, so for such an exercise to be introduced it would be necessary to make appropriate modifications *both* to the Committee's terms of reference and its *modus operandi*. In respect of the former, this might be achieved by way of extending the 'rights and freedoms' principle so as expressly to include the provisions of the Covenant. In consequence, in respect of the latter, the Committee would have to be furnished with the additional power to appoint a specialist human rights adviser (perhaps on a permanent basis as with the current 'Specialist' Adviser to the Committee, who is in reality more a legal generalist) or alternatively to seek expert evidence on specific points of inquiry on human rights questions. These issues are developed in detail later in the Chapter.

As it was, in the case of the political advertising ban legislation, such specialist advice as to the likely adverse impact of the proposals on human rights had been earlier provided by Mr Brian Burdekin, the then Federal Human Rights Commissioner, not only to the Government,[73] but also to the Leader of the Opposition (at his request).[74] This was exceptional, however, as it is unusual for a Bill to attract so much attention both within and (as was particularly so in this case) without Parliament. Yet even conceding that concerns as to the Bill's impact on human rights had apparently reached a wider than usual audience, this fact did not itself ensure that the Parliamentary challenge to the Minister's assurance in his second reading speech that the Bill did comply with Australia's human rights obligations was any more effective.[75] The

---

[72] In the event the second reading in the House of Representatives immediately followed the Bill's introduction on 9 May, but was adjourned after the opening speech of the Minister responsible for the Bill until 30 May: House of Representatives Debates, vol 177 (9 May 1991) at 3483. The second reading debate in the Senate was split between 14 August 1991 (Senate Debates, vol. 147 at 251–71) and 4–5 December 1991 (Senate Debates, vol. 149 at 3859–79 and 4134–73 respectively).

[73] Mr Burdekin's advice was tendered principally in a letter to the then Attorney-General (Mr Duffy) dated 9 May 1991, though some additional observations were provided in letters to the Minister for Administrative Services (Senator Bolkus) dated 20 and 28 May 1991; the greater part of the second reading debate in the lower House took place on 30 May 1991.

[74] House of Representatives Debates, vol. 178 (28 May 1991) at 4038–9.

[75] See House of Representatives Debates, vol. 177 (9 May 1991) at 3477–83, for the speech of the responsible Minister (Mr Kim Beazley); for Mr Andrew Peacock's impassioned challenge of

reason for this, I believe, lies in the fact that in the absence of a formal stage[76] in the legislative process dedicated to scrutiny for compliance with the human rights obligations, the Government is little persuaded from seeking justifying advice for its legislative proposals from whatever sources it considers might be sympathetic, and then declaring itself satisfied that any countervailing advice offered to it may be legitimately rebutted. This is precisely what happened in the present case. Subsequent to the Human Rights Commissioner's substantial letter to the Attorney-General on 9 May 1991 projecting the Bill's likely contravention of Article 19 of the Covenant, and a letter to the Minister of Administrative Services on 20 May 1991 reiterating the Commissioner's concerns, the Government obtained advice from its own Office of International Law in the Attorney-General's Department that, whilst falling short of stating that the Bill if enacted would not transgress the Covenant, indicated that in the event of a legal challenge to the legislation on the basis of such a violation '[a]ny international body will be slow to question a national legislative decision that is taken in good faith'.[77] Though the reasoning behind this conclusion was subsequently heavily criticized,[78] perhaps the most disturbing aspect of the government's action was that this Office was chosen in preference to the acknowledged human rights experts within the department, the human rights specialists within the Department of Foreign Affairs and Trade, and indeed also, the statutorily appointed Federal Commissioner of Human Rights.[79]

This case illustrates clearly the inadequacies of any measure (one can hardly call the present position a 'system') that falls short of an appropriately appointed *intra-parliamentary* scheme in providing effective preventive scrutiny of legislative proposals for conformity to our human rights obligations. The current (independent) position established under Section 14 of the Human Rights and Equal Opportunities Act 1986 is plainly inadequate for the following reasons:

the Bill on the grounds of its violation of the Covenant, see House of Representatives Debates, vol. 178 (30 May 1991) at 4393–9. See also second reading in the Senate, n. 70 above.

[76] Commonwealth's *Legislation Handbook* (1988) indicates that departments should consult the Attorney-General's Department on proposed legislative provisions that may be inconsistent with, in particular, the Covenant, para. 5.22.

[77] At 2–3. It was also alleged that advice supporting the Government's view was also obtained from private counsel, though this was never publicly conceded by the Government.

[78] Peacock n. 73 above, at 4397; see also Professor Philip Alston—oral submission to the Senate Select Committee on Political Broadcasts and Political Disclosures, (26 September 1992), 78–80 and the Law Council of Australia—written submission to the Committee, *Submissions* (September 1991), vol. 1, 9–16

[79] In a response born of exasperation, Mr Peacock was moved to declare that to make such a request of the Attorney-General's Department was 'tantamount to asking it to advise on the breeding habits of a gnat': above n. 73 at 4397; see further criticism from Dr Hewson: n. 73 above at 4405.

(1) The Commission is not appropriately appointed in respect of all relevant resources to undertake the task.[80]
(2) The wording of the Section indicates that it is not meant to be exclusive[81] (illustrated by the fact that the only information offered to the then Human Rights Commissioner was the press release indicated above, despite Senator Bolkus's promises that more would come).[82] The Government may still seek or receive advice from elsewhere, as evidenced by the advice it obtained in the above example.[83]
(3) Clearly, also, the Government is under no obligation to adhere to the advice tendered to it by the specifically appointed expert office in the field.

Though it is possible for the shortcoming first identified to be rectified, in regard to the present concerns, any scrutiny role of the Human Rights Commissioner would nonetheless remain located outside the parliamentary legislative process. And as it is unrealistic to suppose that any government in the foreseeable future would consider removing the convenient facility of government discretion referred to in (2) and (3) above, the role played by the Human Rights Commission in any formal pre-legislative scrutiny process is destined to be supportive rather than instrumental.

A suitably modified Scrutiny of Bills Committee with the opportunity for a more constant, formal and *intra-parliamentary* system of reporting prima facie breaches of the Covenant (details of which are discussed below) would be much more effective in providing the means by which Parliament is better informed and better able to scrutinize legislation before lending its imprimatur to the proposals presented to it by the Government.

The informative and educative potential of such a scrutiny scheme is well illustrated by two further notable pieces of legislation which also contain unjustifiable limitations on the freedom of expression and which, the controversy they caused notwithstanding, were endorsed by the Commonwealth Parliament with little, or no comprehension of their effect on this fundamental human right. It might be pointed out at this stage that whilst the three examples detailed in this Chapter concern the right to freedom of expression, this ought to be seen as an indication of an especial lack of understanding of human rights culture in an area that one might suppose is perhaps most likely

---

[80] See Human Rights and Equal Opportunities Commission (HREOC), *Annual Report of the Human Rights and Equal Opportunities Commission* (1987–88), 8. This is even more apt of the HREOC's current circumstances in which Federal government funding has been cut by 43% over a three year period from 1 July 1996.

[81] This is explained in part by the pre-existence of a pair of Senate Committees charged with the specific task of pre-legislative scrutiny (albeit not expressly on grounds of compliance with human rights standards).

[82] See correspondence, 1, 19 (9 May 1991).

[83] To wit, the Office of International Law of the Attorney-General's Department, and private counsel: n. 76 above and accompanying text.

to be appreciated in the Australian system of Government,[84] rather than an absence of potential infringements by other pieces of legislation and proposed legislation.[85]

The first illustration is provided by Section 22 of the Bicentenary Authority Act 1980 (Cth) which made it an offence to use certain prescribed symbols and expressions 'in connection with a business, trade, profession or occupation', without the consent of the Bicentennial Authority.[86] Subsection (6)(d) provided that the term 'prescribed expression' was to include, inter alia, the words 'Bicentennial', '200 years', 'Australia', 'Sydney', and 'Melbourne' when used in conjunction with '1788', '1988' or '88'. Though the case resulting from the inevitable challenge to the validity of the Statute was on the basis of the

---

[84] See e.g. the Constitutional Commission's eloquent explanation of the crucial role played by the right to freedom of expression in 'the maintenance of a democratic system of government and the exercise of democratic rights'. See Constitutional Commission, n. 2 above at paras. 9.332–9.333.

[85] e.g. (1) 1992 amendments to the Migration Act 1958 (Cth) to curtail the rights of refugees entering Australia, including the detention of 'non-entrants'. These changes were instituted through the issuing of new ministerial guidelines and a set of three Migration Amendment Acts 1992 (Cth) (Nos. 24, 84, and 85 of 1992). See Mathew, 'Sovereignty and the Right to Seek Asylum: The Case of Cambodian Asylum-seekers', 15 *Australian Year Book of International Law (1995)*. The Attorney-General's Department was reportedly concerned that certain of the provisions, when used as a basis for 'unduly prolonged detention . . . could amount to a violation of Article 9(1)' of the Covenant; *Canberra Times* (31 August 1992), 4.

(2) The Broadcasting Services Act 1992 (Cth) ss. 4, 5, 158 which bestow upon the Australian Broadcasting Authority the power to make 'regulatory policy' (that is, quasi-legislation) over an extraordinarily broad range of issues, within the rubric of a concern over the influence that the various broadcasting services are able 'to exert in shaping community views'.

(3) The Parliamentary Privileges Act 1987 (Cth) s. 16 which, in severely limiting the use of words spoken in, or submissions made to, Parliament as evidence in Court proceedings, has been said to be inconsistent with Article 14(3)(e) of the Covenant which provides everyone with equal right to the examination of witnesses in criminal trials. Harders, 'Parliamentary Privilege, Parliament versus the Courts: Cross-Examination of Committee Witnesses', 67 ALJ (1993) 109 at 142–43.

(4) The Administrative Decisions (Effect of International Instruments) Bill 1997 (Cth) seeks to reverse the effect of the High Court's decision in *Minister of State for Immigration and Ethnic Affairs* v. *Ahtlin Teoh* (1995) 183 CLR 273, which established that ratification of an international treaty provides ground for the legitimate expectation that governmental decision-makers will endeavour to ensure that they comply with the treaty's obligations in making decisions. Prima facie, the bill contradicts the obligation under article 2(1) of the ICCPR that signatory states ensure the recognition of all rights provided by the Covenant to all individuals in their jurisdiction.

(5) The Native Title Amendment Bill 1997 (Cth) provides for the effective extinguishment of native title in most circumstances in which it has been established or could be established. As such title is peculiar to indigenous people in Australia, these provisions are clearly discriminatory. In particular, they are in breach of article 26 of the ICCPR and article 2(1) of the Convention on the Elimination of all Forms of Racial Discrimination. See further, S. Pritchard, 'Native Title from the Perspective of international standards', 18 *Australian Yearbook of International Law* (1997), 127.

[86] The Authority was an incorporated company. Clause 3 of its memorandum of association indicated that the '[p]rimary object for which the Authority is established is to formulate, to plan, to develop, to promote, to coordinate and to implement . . . a national program of celebrations and activities . . . to commemorate the bicentenary in 1988 of the first European settlement in Australia . . .'.

Commonwealth's lack of executive authority or an appropriate legislative head of power, rather than any claim of human rights violations, the High Court did have cause to make comments in respect of the latter issue in finding Section 22 of the Act to be invalid. The then Chief Justice, Sir Anthony Mason considered that this 'extraordinary power to regulate the use of expressions in everyday use in this country . . . is grossly disproportionate to the need to protect the commemoration and the Authority', and that it constituted an 'extraordinary intrusion into freedom of expression [that was] not reasonably and appropriately adapted to achieve the ends that lie within the limits of constitutional power'.[87] Crucially, however, the grounds for the expression of such views were hardly recognized, let alone properly addressed, during the formulation and enactment of the legislation.[88] Certainly Australia's obligations under the Covenant to protect the freedom of expression were not considered during the Parliamentary debates on the Bill.[89]

This example is illustrative also of the potential for secondary legislation to violate human rights provisions. Section 26 of the Act granted to the Governor-General the unusually broad power to make regulations 'prescribing all matters *required or permitted* by this Act to be prescribed, or *necessary or convenient* to be prescribed for carrying out or giving effect to this Act'. Under the combined authority of this Section and Section 22(6)(d)(ii), the Australian Bicentennial Authority Regulations were made in 1982.[90] This had the effect of introducing an additional set of words and figures to be included in the 'prescribed expression' provisions of Section 22.[91]

The second example concerns the statutory protection of the Australian Industrial Relations Commission against insult, interruption, improper influence and denigration, or the use of words *calculated* to produce these effects, under Section 299(1) of the Industrial Relations Act 1988 (Cth) (now Section 299(1) of the Workplace Relations Act 1996 (Cth))[92].[93] With one notable exception, the effect of this Section is to insulate the Commission (which is not

---

[87] *Davis* v. *Commonwealth* (1988) 82 ALR 633 at 645. Brennan J. was of a similar, if not more forthright, opinion, concluding that 'freedom of speech can hardly be an incidental casualty of an activity undertaken by the Executive Government to advance a nation which boasts of its freedom': ibid. at 657.

[88] There, of course, exists no Scrutiny of Bills report on the relevant bill as the Scrutiny of Bills Committee was not established until 1981.

[89] House of Representatives Debates, vol. 117 (20 March 1980) at 1026, and Senate Debates, vol. 85 (31 March 1980) at 1215.

[90] Statutory Rules 1982, No. 222.

[91] There was neither a report tabled by the Regulations and Ordinances Committee in respect of the rules, nor were they subject to any debate in either House.

[92] The new section 299 under the 1996 Act remains substantially the same. The only alteration has been to remove the offence of calculating to bring the Commission into disrepute. It remains an offence to calculate to influence a member of the Commission or a witness before it.

[93] Similar provisions exist in respect of the Coal Industry Tribunal, the Defence Force Disciplinary Appeals Tribunal, the Federal Police Arbitral Tribunal, and Local Coal Authorities.

considered to be a Court within the meaning of Chapter III of the Australian Constitution) in much the same manner as Chapter III Courts are protected by the common law rules of contempt. The difference in the statutory provision is that it preserves a common law principle of contempt based merely on intent (that is without actual harm resulting) that at common law (as is discussed below) is no longer in existence. The question of the proper interpretation of the word 'calculated' as used in Section 299(1)(d) has been held to turn on the context in which it is used, that is whether it is meant to indicate that improper influence is *likely* to be brought to bear on the Commission, or that it was *intended* that there be such an effect.[94] Though in two cases concerning the meaning of the word in the context of Section 229(1)(d) the former was preferred,[95] it is apparent that this interpretation requires no more than the merest *possibility* (rather than 'likelihood' which implies greater certainty) of interference resulting from the calculated use of words for contempt to be established. The defendant in this case, Mr Gallagher, was convicted on the basis that people who heard his remarks '*might* have been inclined to give some *slight* credence to the notion . . . [he] put forward', and despite the fact that in the Court's opinion 'nobody at all familiar with the workings of the Commission would have taken the defendant seriously . . . '.[96] The importance of the consequences of this statutory form of contempt in respect of this Chapter requires some explanation.

As has been amply demonstrated in respect of the uneasy relationship between the law in the United Kingdom in this area and the guarantees of the European Convention, the law of contempt can be exercised to curb the freedom of expression to a degree unwarranted in a democratic society—that is, contrary to the Convention. In 1991, in one of the cases in which the European Court has found legal provisions in the United Kingdom to be in violation of Article 10 of the Convention, it was concluded that the statutory requirement that intent alone is sufficient to found contempt—that is, *actual* prejudice to the 'administration of justice' need not follow the intention so to cause—constitutes an infringement of the Convention.[97] In fact, the impugned statutory provision preserved the strict interpretation of the

---

[94] *O'Sullivan* v. *Lunnon* (1986) 67 ALR 423 at 426 per Gibbs C.J. (which involved the use of the word in the context of another Act), and *Nationwide News Pty Ltd* v. *Wills* (1992) 177 CLR 1 at 2 per Mason C.J. Though it may now be unclear which interpretation is preferred, it remains the case that crucially neither interpretation requires there to be any actual effect resulting from the calculated use of words—see *Howard* v. *Gallagher* (1989) 85 ALR 495 at 497–8.

[95] Ibid.   [96] Ibid. at 501 (my emphasis).

[97] *Sunday Times (No. 1)* (the *Thalidomide* case), 30 ECHR ser. A (26 April 1979)—common law contempt was found to infringe; *The Guardian and The Observer*, 216 ECHR ser. A (26 November 1991)—injunction against publication infringed; *Sunday Times (No. 2)*, 217 ECHR ser. A (26 November 1991)—statutory provision used to extend the effect of an injunction beyond the parties against whom it was granted was found to infringe. Both of the second and third mentioned cases concerned the Government's attempts to prevent the publication of serialized excerpts of Peter Wright's book, *Spycatcher*.

common law liability 'for contempt of court in respect of conduct *intended* to impede or prejudice the administration of justice'.[98] Not long after the United Kingdom Parliament's statutory endorsement of this liability, the Supreme Court of New South Wales took the contrary view, by indicating that at common law it is insufficient merely to demonstrate intent to impede or interfere; rather it must be proven that there was *an actual tendency* (whether or not as a result of intent) to interfere with judicial proceedings.[99]

The relevance of the developing relationship of British and European human rights law is of assistance to Australia by analogy in respect not only of the shared common law heritage, but also the fact that the burgeoning jurisprudence of the European Court of Human Rights provides what is commonly considered to be the richest source of interpretative guidance as to the meaning of similarly styled human rights provisions in other jurisdictions, and in particular, those international human rights instruments (Covenant included) which lack a determinative Court from which such jurisprudence may stem.[100] This pertinence notwithstanding, Section 299 of the Industrial Relations Act 1988 (and the Workplace Relations Act following it) retained, with little amendment, the pre-existing provision that constituted Section 182 of the Conciliation and Arbitration Act 1904 (Cth) (which protected the Industrial Relations Commission's predecessor, the Conciliation and Arbitration Commission), in complete ignorance of its potential to infringe Article 19 of the Covenant.[101] For in terms of *form*, Section 299 of the Australian Acts is almost identical to Section 6(c) of the British Act, and whilst there appears to be some difference in their respective interpretations, in practice this has yielded little difference in implementation. *Pari passu*, the current Section 299(1)(d) & (e) provisioins of the Workplace Relations Act 1996, may also be found to curtail unjustifiably the right to free expression.[102]

---

[98] Contempt of Court Act 1981 (UK), s. 6(c) (my emphasis).

[99] *Prothonotary* v. *Collins* (1985) 2 NSWLR 549 at 567–72 per McHugh J.

[100] Merrills, *The Development of International Law by the European Court of Human Rights* (1988), 17–18. See further, Jones, 'Legal Protection for Fundamental Rights and Freedoms: European Lessons for Australia?' (1994) 22 Federal Law Review 57, and Kinley, 'Casting an Australian Eye to European Human Rights in the United Kingdom: The Political Dimensions of a Legal World' (1995) 2 Australian Journal of Human Rights 91.

[101] House of Representatives Debates, vol. 161 (28 April 1988) at 2339, and Senate Debates, vol. 128 (24 August 1988) at 188.

[102] In the *Nationwide* case, n. 91 above (which concerned the application of Section 299 to the proprietors of a newspaper company), the High Court determined (on constitutional grounds) that Section 229(1)(d)(ii) was invalid. Note Mason C.J.'s remark in obiter that '"likely" is the meaning of the word 'calculated' in the context in which it appears in Section 229(1)(d)': ibid. at 2.

The Mechanics of the Scrutiny Scheme

The practical consequence of my argument is the establishment of a scheme of pre-legislative scrutiny which is specifically but not exclusively directed towards obtaining legislative compliance with the Covenant. Notwithstanding the fact that some of the details of the proposed scheme have been foreshadowed, and as the scheme is to be based on the existing apparatus for the scrutiny of primary and secondary legislation in the Senate, it is perhaps most effective to approach this part of the Chapter in two steps. First, to review those aspects of the current Senate scrutiny schemes which are germane—both in form and substance—to human rights scrutiny to assess their suitability for this additional task; and second, to indicate what additions or modifications might be necessary, or desirable, to achieve this new goal.

In terms of structure, there is much to commend in the present committees. In respect specifically to the prospect of human rights scrutiny, the continued assignment of the two types of legislation to separate Committees would be both necessary and desirable. For not only does each type differ markedly in the manner by which it comes into being, the form and subject matter of instruments of delegated legislation are usually quite unlike those of Statutes. There is, in addition, the not inconsiderable matter of a division of workload (which could only increase with the added task of human rights scrutiny) that might otherwise swamp a single Committee. Still, both the Victorian and Queensland scrutiny committees review primary and secondary legislation.[103] As both committees are still very young, it is unclear the degree to which this workload stress adversely affects the quality of scrutiny. The Commonwealth's Scrutiny of Bills, and Regulations and Ordinances Committees share a number of characteristics which have contributed enormously to their respected and influential status within the parliamentary process, and which would advance the efficacy of the mooted scrutiny for compliance with human rights guarantees.[104] They invariably enjoy bipartisan relations amongst their membership; they are both aided and counselled by separate legal advisers who undertake the initial scrutiny of all legislative proposals and then advise accordingly; and both Committees have developed a degree of 'understanding' between themselves and the government departments by way of the formal process of requests for explanations from Ministers in respect of provisions over which the Committees have expressed some initial concern. A further dimension has been added to the last-

---

[103] See discussion above at pp. 13–14 for details of the two committees.

[104] See e.g. the assessment of the Constitutional Commission on the impact of the Scrutiny of Bills Committee, *Final Report* (1988) vol. 1, 449–50; and, in respect of the Regulations and Ordinances Committee, the observation of the then President of the Senate, Senator Kerry Sibraa, on the occasion of the opening of the Second Conference of Australian Delegated Legislation Committees, *Report and Proceedings of the Conference* (1989), 21.

mentioned point with the establishment in 1989 of the *Legislative Scrutiny Manual* which has been designed expressly for departmental consumption in an further effort to alert (if not to proselytize) those responsible for the translation of policy into legislation to the responsibilities and expectations of the two scrutiny Committees, and thereby, indirectly, to exert a degree of preventive control. This initiative is a continuation of the relative success that the Committees have achieved in effectively imposing a modest level of self-restraint on the Government.[105] Included in the *Manual* is a consolidated collection of guidelines on the Committees' application of their principles and statements of Committee 'policy' in respect of specific issues which were originally published in their annual reports.[106] These features of the present system would, in particular, greatly aid the object of ensuring Parliamentary observance of the provisions of the Covenant.

To fulfil the aims of the proposal in this Chapter, the two most obvious modifications (which were earlier alluded to) to the present scheme of pre-legislative scrutiny are that the terms of reference of both Committees be extended specifically to include scrutiny for conformity to the rights protected under the Covenant;[107] and that an additional adviser with expertise in the area of human rights law be assigned to each Committee. Ideally, therefore, the new adviser would be able to utilize the various, analagous human rights jurisprudence such as that of the Human Rights Committee (as provided in its Reports and Comments) and the voluminous body of law that has developed around the European Convention on Human Rights, and the burgeoning jurisprudence of the Canadian Charter of Human Rights and Fundamental Freedoms.[108]

[105] In regard to the Regulations and Ordinances Committee, see the impressive list of subjects and issues over which the Committee can claim to have had some influence—including the elimination or modification of strict criminal liability without proof of guilt; conferral on officials of unreviewable discretions; restriction of very broad powers of search and seizure, and reversals of the onus of proof: Whalan, 'Scrutiny of Delegated Legislation by the Australian Senate', 12 SLR (1991) 87 at 102–3.

In regard to the Scrutiny of Bills Committee, a former First Parliamentary Counsel, Ian Turnbull QC, has commented on the considerable influence that the Committee has had on his office and on Government departments: 'I think that it is safe to say that the provisions that get into Bills and come before the Scrutiny of Bills Committee are the tip of the iceberg. I think that a far greater number that would have offended have not been put in the Bills because we have advised the departments and the departments have had the sense to withdraw them. After all, when we say that the Scrutiny of Bills Committee does not like something, that is a very powerful weapon in our armoury': *Ten Years of Scrutiny*, proceedings of a seminar to mark the tenth anniversary of the Committee (1991), 62.

[106] New guidelines continue to be published by both Committees in their respective annual reports.

[107] This proposal has been endorsed by the Joint Standing Committee on Foreign Affairs, Defence and Trade, in its report entitled, *A Review of Australia's Efforts to Protect and Promote Human* Rights (Nov. 1994) paras 3.46–49.Such an additional principle would then have to be reflected in the guidelines contained in the above-mentioned *Legislative Scrutiny Manual*, or some similar memorandum.

[108] It is already clear that considerable use is made of relevant Canadian Charter cases by those responsible for the scrutiny of Bills under the New Zealand scheme: see, G. Huscroft & P. Rishworth, *Rights and Freedoms* (1995), pp. 136–51.

Perhaps the most radical alteration, however, is one born, not so much of direct necessity, but of the pragmatic view of how best to achieve the scheme's objectives. That is, to extend the membership of the Committees to include members of the House of Representatives by making them both Joint Committees. The logic of this suggestion in the present context accords almost exactly with that promulgated by the Senate Standing Committee on Constitutional and Legal Affairs in its 1978 report on the 'desirability and practicability' of establishing a scrutiny of Bills process, when it concluded that such a task should be undertaken by a Joint Committee:

a new Senate [only] Committee exercising this scrutiny function would not be able to provide a service to the Parliament as a whole. Members of the House of Representatives have the same obligations as Senators to ensure that legislative provisions do not unduly trespass on personal rights and liberties; that they do not make rights, liberties and obligations unduly dependent upon insufficiently defined administrative powers or non-reviewable administrative decisions; and that they do not inappropriately delegate legislative power or insufficiently subject its exercise to Parliamentary scrutiny. It is therefore appropriate that they should be assisted to fulfil their obligations in the same manner as Senators by having their attention drawn to these issues by the Scrutiny Committee. Only a Joint Committee reporting to both Houses of the Parliament could enable these obligations to be met.[109]

Furthermore, the Committee argued: '[c]ompared to a unicameral Committee a Joint Committee would generally have twice as long to consider Bills without imposing significant delays in the Government's legislative programme.'[110]

Despite the cogency of this argument the recommendation for a Joint Committee was not acted upon; the present model of a unicameral scrutiny Committee was preferred in its stead. The rationale of this choice, and the continued preferment of it over a Joint Committee model, is, however, less cogent. The Senate Scrutiny of Bills Committee itself (not undeniably an independent observer) offered the rather circular argument that its establishment largely obviated the need for a Joint Committee.[111] It added that there are certain problems of logistics—namely, the prospect of an increased number of members; the co-ordination of meetings, and the expedition of the scrutiny process if reports are to be made to both Chambers as early as possible in a Bill's passage.[112] None of these problems are insurmountable, however, and in any case they fall far short of countering the reasons cited by the Legal and Constitutional Committee for supporting the establishment of a bicameral scrutiny scheme.

[109] Senate Standing Committee on Constitutional and Legal Affairs, *Report on the Scrutiny of Bills* (1978), 18.
[110] Ibid. at 19.
[111] Senate Standing Committee for the Scrutiny of Bills, *Nineteenth Report* (1982), paras. 28–30.
[112] Senate Standing Committee for the Scrutiny of Bills, *Nineteenth Report* (1982), paras. 28–30.

As the above quotation of the Legal and Constitutional Committee makes clear, the impact of this initiative would apply to all of the principles against which the two Committees measure the legislative proposals before them; it would, however, be of especial significance for the scrutiny of such a broad-based, and politically sensitive area as human rights. Indeed, it is this reason above all that makes a Joint Committee, with its breadth of membership, the most appropriate vehicle for such scrutiny.

There are also arguments for at least two further, though less fundamental, alterations to be made to aid the efficiency and efficacy of the extended scrutiny scheme. The process, initiated by the Commonwealth Scrutiny of Bills Committee, of publishing weekly an 'Alert Digest' wherein the legal adviser indicates their opinion on the compliance of Bills introduced during the preceding week with the Committee's five principles, might be extended to the Commonwealth Regulations and Ordinances Committee and other State and Territory Scrutiny Committees.[113] As earlier stressed, the added dimension of human rights scrutiny necessitates the widest possible exposure within Parliament at least of any concerns of either scrutiny Committee over the compliance of a legislative proposal, if the object of preventing the enactment of legislation breaching the Covenant is to be attained. The Alert Digest is crucial in this regard as it 'enables the [scrutiny] Committee to place its preliminary comments before the Parliament at the earliest opportunity'.[114]

Finally, it would be appropriate, and perhaps necessary, to bolster the impact of the new Scrutiny of Bills Committee in respect of all issues within its purview by establishing some form of sanctioning power. The Regulations and Ordinances Committee is able to initiate a notice of a motion of disallowance[115] in the Senate where it is not satisfied with the responses of departments to its inquiries. Whilst this action may be taken infrequently, it is clear that the threat (implicit or explicit) of it exerts considerable preventive influence over Government departments.[116] Though such a procedure could not apply to Bills, a similar effect might be obtained by instituting a procedure whereby, for example, except under limited circumstances, no Bill would receive its third reading in the House in which it was introduced until the Scrutiny of Bills Committee had reported on the Bill.

As one can see, the suggested changes to the existing process of pre-legislative scrutiny to incorporate a human rights dimension are almost exclusively reformatory, rather than revolutionary. Not only does this reflect a

---

[113] The Victorian Scrutiny of Legislation Committee has established an 'Alert Digest' scheme similar to the one run by the Commonwealth Scrutiny of Bills Committee.

[114] Senate, *Legislative Scrutiny Manual* (1989), 22.

[115] The consequence of which is that, under the Acts Interpretation Act 1901 (Cth) s. 48(5), the impugned regulation will be disallowed unless the motion is withdrawn or otherwise disposed of within 15 sitting days of notice being given.

[116] See e.g. Senate Standing Committee on Regulations and Ordinances, *Eighty-third Report* (1988), para. 1.7.

desire to capitalize on the acknowledged benefits of the present system, but also the equally important, if pragmatic, desire to present a practicable as well as effective means of enhancing the role of the Legislature in the protection and advancement of human rights in Australia.

Concluding Remarks

To bring this Chapter round full circle: the *raison d'être* of Article 2(1) of the Covenant is that it be expressly declared that each signatory State is serious about the rights it has endorsed. For this to be anything other than a well-intended but forlorn hope, it is of paramount importance that we ensure that our legislators, both those in and out of government, are serious about the rights enshrined in the Covenant. And to do that they must first be alerted to the existence of such rights and educated as to their impact.

Whilst my concern throughout this Chapter has not been to seek to deprive or necessarily limit the executive's right or indeed duty to introduce into Parliament legislation it sees fit, it has been to suggest a means by which to ensure that in so doing the executive is made aware of the possible implications for the human rights it is obliged to protect. In the end, the key to the effective protection of human rights in countries such as Australia lies in the exertion of a sustained preventive influence over the executive; the parliamentary-based scrutiny scheme here outlined is designed to do precisely that.

III
Comparative Experiences with
Bills of Rights

6

The Kenyan Bill of Rights: Theory and Practice

YASH GHAI

Introduction: the Background to the Bill of Rights

I propose to examine the provisions of the Bill of Rights in the Kenyan Constitution and to assess its impact on policy and practice of the Government and other public authorities. The aim is to see how far the Bill has been instrumental in securing the rights and freedoms guaranteed under it. My conclusion is that the Bill has had almost no impact on the constitutional, legal and administrative systems. I then offer an explanation for the ineffectiveness of the Bill in terms of the specifics of the Bill as well as the political economy of the Kenyan state. I conclude by examining, through this review of the Kenyan experience, the role of formal legal and constitutional provisions in securing fundamental rights and freedoms in post-colonial African states.

Although many factors determine the acceptance and enforcement of rights and freedoms, this Chapter focuses on the role of legal institutions. The dominance of the Presidency and, until recently, the constitutionalization of one-party rule, the absence of supervisory institutions like an ombudsman or a human rights commission, and the relative weakness of civil society have meant that the courts have been a key determinant of the respect for human rights. In the conclusion I indicate the broad framework within which one must locate rights and freedoms in African states.

A brief word on the history of the introduction of the Bill may help to locate it in the general legal and political system of Kenya. During the colonial period, there were no restrictions, stemming from a fundamental law, on the legislative or executive power of the Government. The colonial administration established and maintained by means of the law a

* The research for this paper was facilitated by grants from the Ford Foundation (Eastern Africa Office) and the Committee on Research and Conference Grants of the University of Hong Kong. I am also grateful to Jennifer Van Dale for her research assistance.

My research on Kenya has been assisted in a number of ways by several Kenyan lawyers. I should like to acknowledge in particular the help I have received from Gitobu Imanyara, Gibson Kamau Kuria, John Khaminwa, Kiraitu Murungi, Pheroze Nowrojee, Sureta Chana, Paul Muite, Willy Mutunga and Stephen Mwanese. They are of course in no way responsible for views expressed in this Chapter.

governmental and social system characterised by authoritarianism, and racial discrimination in such vital fields as the administration of justice, the development of representative institutions, and agrarian administration.[1] Several features of this system may be mentioned. First, for a long time there was no local or popular participation in law-making. Laws were enacted either directly by the imperial authorities through a variety of prerogative instruments or by the fiat of the administrator/governor.[2] In the latter case there was in reality no difference between primary law and administrative regulations. Even when local inhabitants were appointed or elected to the legislature, their role was secondary to that of official members.[3]

Secondly, in general the law conferred wide discretion on officials. The law itself provided little guidance for the exercise of this discretion and the courts were, for the most part, reluctant to check the discretion. The result was that administrators, at all levels, became very powerful and for all effective purposes, beyond political or legal challenge. The powers that were given to administrators could certainly be used in ways that would violate the rights of the people. In many instances the powers as written in the law violated these rights.

Thirdly, there were at least two principal concerns of the law—to establish a privileged position for the white people and to maintain law and order. The first concern resulted in wide-scale discrimination, in law and practice, and the second in highly authoritarian rules.

In one of the first exercises of his legislative power—the Native Courts Regulations of 1897[4]—the Commissioner for the East Africa Protectorate armed himself with powers of preventative detention, and restriction of movement, in respect of any persons subject to the Regulations if it was shown to the satisfaction of the Commissioner, that the person was disaffected to the government, was about to commit an offence against the Regulations or was otherwise conducting himself so as to be dangerous to peace and good order in the Protectorate. There was no appeal against the Commissioner's exercise of this power, though he had to report on the same forthwith to the Foreign Secretary.

There are several interesting points about these provisions, paralleled in other colonial laws. First, they provide for special powers which have the effect of depriving a person of the basic rights of freedoms of the person, and of

---

[1] See Ghai and McAuslan, *Public Law and Political Change in Kenya* (1970) for copious illustrations.

[2] See ibid at ch. 1 for the legal basis of imperial authority to legislate for Kenya. The principal source of authority was the Foreign Jurisdiction Act 1890 (UK). A series of Orders in Council (applicable to Kenya) were made under it.

[3] It was only during the terminal stages of colonialism that the majority of official membership (i.e. members appointed to the legislature by virtue of their posts in the public service) was abandoned in favour of elected members.

[4] Regs. 77–79.

movement, and of recourse to the Courts. Similar deprivations appeared in the Vagrancy Regulations[5] which provided for the arrest and detention of any person found to be asking for alms or wandering about without any employment or visible means of subsistence; the Native Passes Regulations which enabled the Commissioner to make 'such general or local rules for controlling the movements of natives travelling into, or out of, or within the limits of the Protectorate as may from time to time appear to him to be necessary or desirable',[6] and laws empowering administrators to impose curfew or other restriction orders.[7] Under the Outlying Districts Ordinance,[8] the Commissioner or other officials to whom he delegated the power could declare districts 'closed', the effect of which was to confer power on the administration to restrict, by means of the issue of licences, persons other than natives of the area from entering the district.

Secondly, there was a complete absence of any provisions for appeal. This went further than some laws which at least provided for an appeal from one administrator to another, but it was by no means unique. In the regulations prohibiting *ngomas* or social activities there was no appeal from the order of the District Commissioner; and there was a similar absence of appeals in the Native Passes Regulations and the Outlying Districts Ordinance. The lack of adequate provisions for appeals was to some extent offset by the residual supervisory powers of the Colonial Office, its powers of disallowance of, or prior approval for, legislation, and the requirement that the action taken by local officials had to be reported to it in certain circumstances. It is very doubtful if in practice these provisions had a significant ameliorative effect, and in most cases non-compliance with them did not bring about invalidation.[9]

Thirdly, the powers of the Commissioner were discriminatory, for they were to be used only against those subject to the Native Courts Regulations—that is, Africans. Where laws were not expressly discriminatory, of which many examples have already been given,[10] administrators were given wide discretion, and in practice could and did exercise it in a discriminatory manner. In this they were generally supported by the courts, which seemed unwilling to extend their conceptions of justice from the administration of justice into other fields. The attitude of the courts may be illustrated by two decisions,

[5] Regulation 1898/2, replaced by 1900/3.

[6] Regulations 1900/12, repealed in 1961.

[7] Preservation of Order by Night Regulations 1901/15.

[8] Regulations 1899/31, replaced by Regulations 1902/25, now Cap. 104. A licensee who failed to comply with the terms of his licence was liable to have his building or crops seized or disposed of as considered fit by the District Commissioner; the offender, however, had a right to the residue of the proceeds—section 7 (2).

[9] *Attorney-General* v. *Kathenge* [1961] EA 348.

[10] See also Chanan Singh, 'The Republican Constitution of Kenya', (1965) 14 ICLQ 878, and McAuslan, 'Prolegomenon to the Rule of Law in East Africa', Proceedings of the EAISER (1963).

upholding the principle of racial discrimination, where in both cases the courts could have opted for different interpretations on the grounds that such discrimination was repugnant to public policy or the common law.[11]

The first concerned the power of the Commissioner of Lands to impose restrictions on who could bid at auctions for sales of Crown land, and their use thereafter.[12] The Commissioner had advertised the auction of town plots at which only Europeans were to be allowed to bid and purchase and had stipulated that during the terms of the grant the grantee should not permit the dwelling house or outbuilding thereon to be used for the residence of any Asiatic or African who was not a domestic servant employed by him. The Commissioner's powers to dispose of land were derived from the Crown Lands Ordinance of 1915. The Ordinance had made a distinction between the disposal of agricultural and urban land, and the power to impose racial restrictions or covenants was expressly granted only in the case of agricultural land. It was argued by the appellants that therefore there was no power to impose these restrictions on the disposal of lands in towns. The Judicial Committee of the Privy Council, saying they were concerned with law and not policy, found for the Commissioner, holding that prima facie the rights of the Crown and its servants to dispose of Crown property were analogous to those of the private owners. They had to observe the express terms of the statute, but apart from that they were free to impose what restrictions they chose. Their Lordships went on to argue that it would be valid to restrict the bidding to industrialists, or the trading community, in appropriate cases; so why not to racial groups?

The second decision concerned the validity of a curfew order whose application was restricted to Africans only.[13] It was made under the Public Order Ordinance 1950 (as amended), section 10 of which provided that the curfew orders may be applied to 'every member of any class of persons' specified therein. Without considering what might have been intended to be the proper purposes of this phraseology, the court held that it permitted racial discrimination. The court also stated its opinion that non-conformity with legislative procedures requiring the consent of the Secretary of State for specified kinds of legislation, contained in the Royal Instructions, was not an invalidating factor since it was not justiciable.

A further example of denial of human rights is contained in the laws allowing collective punishment to the disregard of individual guilt or responsibility, and the imposition of responsibility for the misconduct of others on one deemed to be in authority over them. Examples of the first are found in the

[11] See e.g. *Constantine* v. *Imperial Hotels* [1944] 2 All ER 171. But see *Koinage Mbiu* v. *R.* (1951) 24(2) KLR 130 where the High Court struck down discriminatory regulations as being ultra vires a statute.

[12] *The Commissioner for Local Government, Land and Settlement* v. *Kaderbhai* (1930) 12 KLR 12.

[13] *Attorney-General* v. *Kathenge* [1961] EA 348.

Special Districts (Administration Ordinance), and in the Stock and Produce Theft Ordinance, section 15 of which authorized a magistrate, though not necessarily acting in a judicial capacity, on a complaint of stock theft to order all or some members of a tribe or sub-tribe to pay compensation to the aggrieved party in specified proportions (to determine which, one of the factors to be considered was the ability to pay) if it was established that any member of that tribe or sub-tribe had been implicated in the theft.[14] An example of the second provision occurred in the Village Headmen Ordinance of 1902, under which a headman, appointed by the Commissioner, was required to keep order in areas adjacent to his village or villages, and an order against him in his official capacity was enforceable against all the inhabitants of his village or villages. If an 'outrage' (a term not defined) occurred in any area in which a headman was responsible for the preservation of order, and the perpetrator of such outrage could not be discovered, the Sub-Commissioner (later Provincial Commissioner) could in his discretion impose a fine upon such a headman unless he could prove to the satisfaction of the Sub-Commissioner that the outrage could not have been prevented by reasonable vigilance on his or his people's part.[15]

Examples of restrictions on rights may be given from some other laws which constituted centrepieces of colonial administration. A major instrument was (and is) the Chiefs' Authority Act (Cap. 128, first enacted in 1937). Government appointed chiefs have the duty to maintain order in their area, for which purpose they have been given wide powers. These powers are exercised in part through the issuing of orders, which may be made on the control of the manufacture or consumption of liquor, preventing the pollution of water, 'prohibiting any act or conduct which in the opinion of the chief might cause a riot or a disturbance or a breach of the peace', and 'prohibiting or restricting excessive dancing by persons or the public performance of any dance of indecent or immoral character or of such nature that it is likely to lead to immorality or a breach of the peace, and determining the hours within which, the place or places at which and the conditions under which any dance may be publicly performed' (sec. 10). They have extensive powers of arrest (which can be and have been used to harass the political opponents of the government or the local parliamentarian).

The freedom of association was tightly controlled through the Societies

[14] Ordinance No. 18 of 1933, now Cap. 355. (The first such law was passed in 1913, Ordinance No. 8.) The Judicial Committee has accepted collective punishment as an emergency measure: *Ross-Clunis* v. *Papadopoulos* [1958] 1 WLR 546 (Cyprus). However in *Mahuri* v. *Attorney-General* (Crown Case 1021/1964, unreported), the court had to determine the validity of an order for compensation made under the Stock and Produce Theft Act s. 15. It was held that it amounted to deprivation of property, and since it was not an 'order of the court in proceedings for the determination of civil rights or obligations' (Constitution s. 75 (6) (IV)) it was unconstitutional. After this decision such provisions for collective punishment as still exist in the law must now be regarded as void.

[15] Ordinance No. 22.

Ordinance, which provided that every society had to be first approved by an official before it could exist legally. The administration had a wide discretion as to the refusal to register a society (including that a person or official of it has previously been associated with a society which was banned or refused registration). The administration had wide powers to de-register a society. Many of the rules of evidence established for the purpose of the Ordinance placed the onus of proof on the accused; thus, for example, when the lawfulness of a society was an issue, the defence had to prove that it was lawful, not the prosecution that it was unlawful, and where any books or papers of a society were found in the possession of any person, it was presumed that he was a member of the society, whose existence was similarly presumed from the existence of the books and papers. There was no provision for appeals to courts, and in some, but not all, instances it was possible to appeal to a higher official.

It was also particularly hard to convene meetings or express political opposition to the administration. The Public Order Ordinance gave administrators wide powers of control. No public meeting or procession could be held without the prior permission of the District Commissioner, who could impose conditions on his permission. Permission could be refused if an applicant had contravened the provisions of the Ordinance or *any other written law* or any condition attached to a permission (my emphasis). Wide powers of cancellation were also given to the police.

There were many restrictions on the freedom of expression (and of the press). Particularly potent was the law on sedition. As is well known, the colonial law of sedition is notoriously broad and vague. A seditious intention is defined as an intention to overthrow the government by unlawful means, to bring into hatred or contempt or to excite disaffection against the government, to excite the people to attempt to procure the alteration, otherwise than by lawful means, of any matter or thing in Kenya as by law established, to bring into hatred or contempt or to excite disaffection against the administration of justice, to raise discontent or disaffection amongst the inhabitants of Kenya, or to promote feelings of ill-will or hostility between different sections or classes of the population. Although fair criticism of the government is excluded,[16] in practice that has been no real barriers to arrests or prosecutions. Serious consequences follow a conviction for sedition or attempted sedition—imprisonment up to 10 years; the confiscation of printing presses used to produce a seditious publication; ban on further publications for up to a year. A person found in possession of a seditious publication can be sentenced up to 7 years.[17] The law of sedition had (and continues to have) the most deleterious consequences for political debate and political participation, the

---

[16] Section 56 of the Penal Code, Cap. 63.   [17] Section 57 of the Penal Code, Cap. 63.

threat of prosecution under it being sufficient to discourage people from the exercise of their other rights as well.[18]

I have dwelt at considerable length on the nature of the colonial laws and administration. This is not because of any antiquarian interest, but because they had fashioned official attitudes and behaviour and the submissiveness of the people to authority. Not only have these attitudes and behaviour continued, but so have most of the laws I have discussed. The result of these laws and practices was the growth of a powerful administration which had scant regard for the rights of the people. The laws themselves provided limited protection. There was little tradition of challenge to administrative practice, while the legislation itself was immune to legal scrutiny. The interests of the Europeans were protected in this system through formal and informal consultations and pressures. Some urban groups might have had some limited access to the courts for redress, but rural people were completely subject to the whims of administrators (the local courts being largely an extension of the administration).[19] Thus there grew, from early days of British administration, a kind of duality of legal system and process, between urban and rural areas. It was and is exceedingly hard to ensure justice for malice, corruption and maladministration in the rural areas, the harder as one travelled further from the capital city.

However, European settler and commercial communities could not face with equanimity the prospects of such a legal and administrative system continuing into the era of African rule, and consequently as it became clear in the early 1960s that independence could not be staved off, they began the agitation for a liberal, decentralised and law-regulated regime. Under their pressure, Britain agreed upon a fundamental reversal of policy. This involved political and administrative decentralization (*majimbo*) of the country into seven units, creating a federation out of a highly centralised government on the eve of independence.[20] This would not only break up the powers of the national government, but create alternative centres of power and authority, based on

---

[18] See Scotton, 'Judicial Independence and Political Expression in East Africa—Two Colonial Legacies', (1970) 6 EALJ 1 and Shaloff, 'Press Controls and Sedition Proceedings in the Gold Coast, 1933–39', (1972) 71 *African Affairs* 241.

[19] On this see Ghai and McAuslan n. 1 above at ch. IV.

[20] The allocation of powers between the centre and the regions was provided for in great detail—greater than in any other Commonwealth Constitution. This was partly a consequence of the lack of consensus as well as lack of careful thinking and conceptualisation as to the functions appropriate to each level of government. The division of powers was complex, elaborate and confusing. The first schedule set out the division of legislative and executive powers. In Part I were listed matters which were within the exclusive executive competence of Regional Assemblies; Part II contained matters within the concurrent competencies of both Governments; and Part III matters within the legislative competence of the central legislature but the executive authority of regions. The complexity and detail—hardly appropriate to a constitutional instrument—is another manifestation of the failure of British draftspeople to understand the nature of a constitution (or the level of administrative, legal and financial resources in Kenya).

The specific legislative powers of the regions included agriculture, education up to the

different ethnic and racial coalitions. This would serve to establish a kind of political pluralism that Kenya had not experienced (or been allowed) in its colonial history.

The second aspect of the strategy—another fundamental break from the past—was the inclusion of a Bill of Rights in the Constitution for independence. Britain had in fact extended the European Convention on Human Rights ('ECHR') to Kenya in 1953, but it was not incorporated in local laws and therefore had little impact in the country.[21] Nor had Britain then signed the Optional Protocol, so that individual access to the European Commission or Court of Human Rights was not possible. Furthermore, on two occasions Britain invoked its right to derogate from its obligations under the Convention in relation to Kenya, when it declared emergencies in 1954 and 1960.

Equally ineffective was the first domestic Bill of Rights which made its appearance in 1960. It is not possible to trace a single case in which the Bill was successfully invoked. It was succeeded by another one in the self-governing constitution of 1963, which with minor modifications, was entrenched in the independence Constitution (December 1963). The 1960 Bill was closely modelled on the ECHR, although for subsequent Bills inspiration was drawn from the Nigerian and Ugandan constitutions. This made little difference since the latter two countries had drawn upon the ECHR (or rather the Colonial Office had drawn on it for them).

It should be stated that the decision to include the Bill of Rights was that of Britain.[22] By this time it was becoming normal (but by no means universal, as proved by Tanganyika's independence Constitution) for a colony to adopt a Bill of Rights on independence, but the need to protect Kenya's minorities, particularly the white settlers, was uppermost in the decision. There is no evidence of any enthusiasm on the part of African parties for the Bill (although it would have been hard for them to oppose it, given their anti-colonial stance). A perusal of such files on constitutional development as have recently become available (under the '30 year' rule) show that there was no detailed discussion on the nature and format of the Bill, which were effectively worked out in correspondence between the drafters in the Colonial Office and officials in the Kenyan Attorney-General's office. However, where special interests of the

tertiary level, housing, medical facilities and institutions, common minerals, barbers and disorderly houses.

[21] Article 63 of the ECHR enables a Member State to extend the application of the Convention to 'any territory for whose international relations a State is responsible'. However, the Convention is to be applied 'with due regard to local requirements' (Article 63(3)). This allows for the modification of the provisions of the Convention in the application in dependent territories, admitting perhaps the possibility of differential standards which is contrary to current notions of universal rights. Not many cases have arisen on this point, but it is likely that the European Court would not be sympathetic to deviations from the norms as applied in Europe.

[22] In 1960 the British Government declared its 'firm view' that Kenya needed 'the judicial protection of human rights'. Cmnd. 960 (1960), 9.

European settlers were concerned, these were vigorously pursued and carefully incorporated in the Bill. The protection given to property is one of the
most extensive anywhere in the world, and the freedom to leave Kenya was
preserved. Furthermore, most rights are guaranteed to 'everyone' in Kenya, as
many settlers were uncertain whether to opt for Kenyan citizenship.

The Bill of Rights was part of a new constitutional order. The constitution
was a repudiation of the colonial, bureaucratic system of administration in
which there were minimal protection of human rights, and the overriding concern was the use of the coercive status apparatus to keep a subject population
under control. Its ideology was that of 'white man's' burden, with its contradiction of domination and liberty, but in which wide discretion in officials was
the bedrock of the system. Now, with a liberal democratic constitution providing the framework for competitive politics, protection of human rights
through limitations on public power, the sharing of power among a plethora
of public bodies, and an independent civil service and judiciary, the Rule of
Law emerged as the ruling ideology. Kenya was therefore bequeathed two con-
tradictory legacies: that of the well established centralised and bureaucratic
state, with wide powers to control civil society, and the newly established
rechtstaat. (Constitutional arrangements continued in force the old laws but
made them subject to the Constitution).[23] The Bill of Rights was a centrepiece
of the latter legacy, for it had the potential to restrict and regulate this wide
discretion. In that sense it was even more important than the democratic rules
and institutions which the Constitution introduced (which in themselves were
consistent with discriminatory and restrictive legislation, and might indeed
tend towards it, as with Africanization policies referred to below).

The Bill of Rights

The principal source of the protection of rights in the Kenyan Constitution is
Chapter V, entitled *Protection of Fundamental Rights and Freedoms of the
Individual*, called here the Bill of Rights (it used to be Chapter II, the alteration suggesting a subtle downgrading of rights). However there are at least
two additional sources which are seen to protect rights. The first is that the
underlying law is the common law.[24] The common law is generally regarded as
a great safeguard of individual liberty, but it will be obvious from the preceding discussion that it did not prove so in the colonial period in Kenya, where
it was subordinated to the imperial imperatives of control. However, the

---

[23] The Kenya Independence Order in Council (SI 1963/1968), s. 4. Section 3 of the present
Constitution says that if any other law is inconsistent with it, 'this Constitution shall prevail and
the other law shall, to the extent of the inconsistency, be void'.

[24] The law as at independence was continued in force after independence by the Order in
Council containing the Constitution (SI 1963/1968, s. 4).

constitution, and in particular the Bill of Rights, would henceforth provide the context for the common law, guiding it in the direction of greater protection of rights and freedoms. The common law has been developed in England, Australia, India and New Zealand in recent decades to increase public accountability and to ensure a more rational and fair exercise of executive discretion (although the impact of these developments in Kenya has been minimal).

The second exception is that important political rights are not provided there but elsewhere in the Constitution. The right to vote was, curiously, not provided in the text of the independence constitution, but in a schedule. Apart from citizenship and age, residential qualifications had to be satisfied.[25] The right to stand for elections, although tied to registration as a voter, was secured in the Constitution (sections 41–2).[26] The present version of the Constitution protects the right to register as a voter as well as to stand for elections (sections 43 and 34 respectively). From 1982[27] until the 1991 constitutional amendments,[28] a person could be a parliamentary candidate only if he or she was a member of the Kenya African National Union and was duly nominated by it.

THE STRUCTURE OF THE BILL OF RIGHTS

The influence of the ECHR is evident both on the content and structure of the Bill of Rights. The rights covered are civil and political, and even then are limited, reflecting the early stages of the ECHR, which then claimed that it was the 'first steps' towards the protection of human rights in Europe.[29] The Kenyan Bill of Rights reflects only the rights and freedoms guaranteed in the original Convention (and even that incompletely, since it does not protect the right to marry and found a family, as in Article 12 of the Convention, omits gender as a prohibited basis for discrimination, Article 14, and has a narrower conception of privacy). Consequently there are no constitutional provisions for econopmic, social or cultural rights. However, the Kenyan Bill was in advance of the Convention in protecting the right of movement and residence and the protection of property (two special concerns of the white community

[25] A person otherwise eligible would be disqualified if (a) adjudged to be of unsound mind; or (b) was an undischarged bankrupt; or (c) was under a sentence of death; or (d) a sentence of imprisonment of or more than 12 months; or (e) had a conviction in connection with an electoral offence (Sch. 5).

[26] Since before independence, constitutions have required a knowledge of English as a pre-condition for Parliamentary candidacy, and since the 1971 constitutional amendment, a knowledge of Swahili is also required.

[27] The Constitution of Kenya (Amendment) Act 7 of 1982.

[28] The Constitution of Kenya (Amendment) Act 12 of 1991.

[29] These words occur in the Preamble of the Convention. Since the original Convention was adopted, the list of rights has expanded through successive Protocols.

in Kenya). The Convention has since incorporated these rights through Protocols. The Protocols have added others rights which are not present in Kenya—particularly the right to education (First Protocol), prohibition of deprivation of liberty for inability to fulfil a contractual obligation (Fourth Protocol), prohibition of collective expulsion of aliens (Fourth Protocol), prohibition of the death penalty (Sixth Protocol), right to compensation for miscarriage of justice (Seventh Protocol), and the equality of rights and responsibilities between spouses (Seventh Protocol). Indeed it is of interest to note that while the European Convention has been expanding the list and scope of rights, its offspring, the Kenyan Bill, has been attenuated (especially with regard to the derogations of rights during emergencies,[30] removal of the right of movement from non-citizens lawfully resident in Kenya,[31] and of the right to form trade unions,[32] extension of the permissible periods of detention for arrest on charges of capital offences,[33] and the removal of the right to take compensation for compulsory acquisition of property out of the country).[34]

The Bill begins with a preambular statement, seeking to set out the scope of rights. It is followed by 12 sections each of which provides for one or more rights (sections 71–82). The remaining sections of the chapter deal with derogations from several of the rights during special periods (section 83); the enforcement of protective provisions through the High Court (section 84); the procedure for declaring special periods when rights may be derogated from (section 85); and interpretations, which serve also to provide further exceptions to rights (section 86). The order, either of the substantive or procedural sections, is not very tidy.[35] The substantive rights are not sub-divided into categories, although seen the preambular section lists them into three classes: (a) life, security and protection of the law; (b) conscience, expression, assembly and association; and (c) privacy and property. Each of the rights has its own provisions for restrictions and limitations, so that there are no general standards or criteria for limitations on rights.

The drafting style of the Bill is prolix, with a large list of exceptions to the rights (the list of exceptions is longer than in the ECHR), giving the document the character more of a statute than a constitution. The impression one gets is that rights are struggling to stay afloat in the sea of exceptions (and alas not always succeeding!). There is the danger that the style may not encourage legislators, administrators or judges to take the rights seriously, and provide them with easy rationalization for restricting them.

---

[30] The changes are discussed below at p. 162ff.
[31] The Constitution of Kenya (Amendment) Act No. 14 of 1965.
[32] The Constitution of Kenya (Amendment) Act No. 16 of 1966.
[33] The Constitution of Kenya (Amendment) Act No. 4 of 1988.
[34] The Constitution of Kenya (Amendment) Act No. 13 of 1977.
[35] Thus 'personal rights' appear in sections 71, 72, 73, 74, 76, 77, and 81, separated by civil and property rights. Similarly the two provisions for derogation are separated by the provision for enforcement of rights.

The Kenya Constitution was evidently drafted by rather melancholy drafts-men in London, who had little concept of the political or legal dimensions of a constitution. For them it was another statute, to be written in the same turgid and boring language as the rest of legislation. In this aim they suc-ceeded remarkably well, making the Constitution long, verbose, complex and confusing.[36] No preamble bears witness to the onset of a new dawn or records promises of democracy and social justice. Curiously, the Bill of Rights does start with a mini-preamble of its own. A preamble might have been expected to set the tenor for the approach to the Bill, to extol the virtues of human rights and to mandate an expansive approach to their interpretation.[37] Since such an approach would undoubtedly embarrass an English draftsperson, we have a rather matter of fact statement of the rights granted and the limitations on them.

The Preamble

The preamble appears as section 70 of the current edition of the Constitution and says:

Whereas every person in Kenya is entitled to the fundamental rights and freedoms of the individual, that is to say, the right, whatever his race, tribe, place of origin or resi-dence or other local connexion, political opinions, colour, creed or sex, but subject to the respect for the rights and freedoms of others and for the public interest, to each and all of the following, namely—
(a) life, liberty, security of the person and the protection of the law;
(b) freedom of conscience, of expression and of assembly and association; and
(c) protection for the privacy of his home and other property and from deprivation of
       property without compensation,
the provisions of this Chapter shall have effect for the purpose of affording protection to those rights and freedoms subject to such limitations of that protection as are con-tained in those provisions, being limitations designed to ensure that the enjoyment of those rights and freedoms by any individual does not prejudice the rights and freedoms of others or the public interest.

This is a lot of words to say that the rights people are entitled to are subject to some limitations and that these limitations stem from the competing rights of others as well as the public interest. One could stretch the preambular state-ment a bit and say that it acknowledges a higher source of human rights than

---

[36] A *Times* leader, commenting on the Constitution—'a formidable instrument of Government'—remarked that the first requirement was a skilled corps of lawyers and clerks in the centre and the regions to explain to legislators what they were required, permitted, or forbidden to do under scores of legally-worded clauses. Quoted in Odinga, *Not Yet Uhuru* (1967), 233.

[37] Lest any one accuse me of naivety, I should declare that I do not think that resounding or flowery statements of this kind would have turned the fortune of human rights and freedoms, any more than they have done in countries where the draftspersons have allowed themselves to be car-ried away. Unlike academics, governments and judges are hard-headed.

the Constitution (it certainly does not employ the revolutionary language of 'inherent rights') and that the Constitution merely gives effect to them.[38] However, 'entitled' is the language of the law, not theology. In so far as it seeks to reflect the scope of rights guaranteed by the Constitution, the preamble is not entirely accurate. Not every one enjoys equal rights; non-citizens may be discriminated against (section 82(4)(a)), and the prohibited grounds of discrimination exclude sex (section 82(3)).[39] Nor is privacy as such protected, although aspects of it would be covered by the protection against arbitrary search and entry (section 76). The rights of property would seem to be more extensive in the preamble than in the substantive section dealing with it (section 75). The restrictions on rights mentioned in the preamble could be construed to cover all rights whereas some rights are indeed absolute (e.g. to bail, or the prohibition on slavery or servitude, for which see below).

Since there are these discrepancies between the declaratory or preambular statement and the substantive provisions, the precise status and effect of the statement is a matter of some importance. It should be noted that the Constitution envisages substantive rights under it, since section 84 (dealing with remedies) enables a person to go to the High Court if he/she alleges that any of the relevant sections, including 70, have been contravened in relation to him or her, and authorises a subordinate court 'when a question arises as to the contravention of any of the provisions of sections 70 to 83 (inclusive)' to refer it to the High Court. However, there is no consensus, either in Kenya or elsewhere where similar provisions exist, on its effect.

Section 70 was cited in *Wadhawa* v. *City Council of Nairobi* (see below),[40] but the case did not turn on it and the court not consider the point. Likewise the provisions in it for non-discrimination were raised by the plaintiff, allegedly the victim of racial discrimination in the allocation of licenses, in *Shah Vershi* v. *Transport Licensing Board*.[41] The argument was considered at some length by Chanan Singh J. who concluded that 'Although given a separate number, this section is quite clearly in the nature of a preamble . . . the section itself creates no rights: it merely gives a list of the rights and freedoms which are protected by other sections of the Constitution'.[42] However, the case was decided in favour of the plaintiff on the basis of section 82, which prohibits discrimination among citizens or discrimination against non-citizens without authority of law (Simpson J. also concurred in this result although for somewhat different reasons, and did not even consider section 70

---

[38] This interpretation would not appeal to either of the Presidents Kenya has had, who claimed that the law (or sometimes that they themselves) have given the people their rights. The Constitution itself avoids the terminology of 'human rights'—which has also become something of a taboo with the government.

[39] The exemption of large parts of customary law from the application of the principle of non-discrimination has similar effect.

[40] [1968] EA 406. [41] [1971] EA 289. [42] Ibid. at 298.

arguments).[43] Therefore on this point the views of Singh J. may be regarded as *obiter*, but he also ruled that the 'protection of the law' referred to in section 70 could only bear the meaning given to it in section 77 (which deals with criminal trials).

Section 70 may be invoked not only to claim rights, but also to justify restrictions on them. *Ngui* v. *Republic*[44] concerned the validity of legislation which restricted the competence of the court to grant bail on charges of murder or robbery with violence in apparent contravention of section 72(5), which gives an accused the right to bail if the trial is not held within a reasonable time. The Government argued that, although apparently unfettered, the right to bail had to be read subject to the limitations mentioned in section 70, namely the rights and freedoms of others and the public interest. The court rejected this argument on the basis that the limitations mentioned in section 70 referred to the limitations in the substantive sections. However, in a subsequent case, Sachdeva J., in a perfunctory judgment, used the limitations mentioned in section 70 (and the gravity of the charges against the accused) as a reason for restricting the right to bail.[45]

Foreign precedents on comparable provisions are similarly unhelpful. On an appeal from Malta on the restrictions on the freedom of expression, the Privy Council made some comments on the scheme of the Bill of Rights which follows largely the order in Kenya. Referring to the opening word in the preambular section, namely 'Whereas', it said that 'Though the section must be given such declaratory force as it independently possesses, it would appear in the main to be of the nature of a preamble. It is an introduction to and in the sense a prefatory or explanatory note in regard to the sections which follow'. It was clear that the rights and the limitations on them were to be found in the substantive provisions, for the preamble itself states that the rights and the limitations are such 'as are contained in those provisions'.[46] However the status or effect of the preambular section was not an issue in the case, and appears not to have been adverted to by either party.

On the other hand, the section was relied upon in the Uganda case of *Shah* v. *Attorney-General* (No. 2),[47] where the government had abrogated a contract with the plaintiff. Since there was some doubt whether the section on the protection of property covered the situation, the reference to property right in the preambular section was invoked.[48] The government does not appear to have

[43] While Chanan Singh J. held that the subsidiary legislation authorising the Board to discriminate against non-citizens was ultra vires the parent Act, Simpson J. held it valid. However the discrimination practised by the Board was as among different classes of citizens, and this even the Constitution did not permit.

[44] [1986] LRC (Const) 308.

[45] *Mutunga* v. *Republic*, reported in 16 *Nairobi Law Monthly* 33.

[46] *Olivier* v. *Buttigieg* [1967] AC 115 at 128–9.   [47] [1970] EA 523.

[48] The substantive section on property protected against compulsory acquisition, while the preambular section refers to 'deprivation' of property.

contested the binding effect of the section, and two judges in the Court of
Appeal gave judgment for the plaintiff on the basis of the violation of that section. But the third judge, Wambuzi J., took a different view of the preambular
section, his view being substantially similar to that enunciated by the Privy
Council. He held that no provision of the preambular section 'can be said to
have been infringed unless it is shown that a corresponding provision defining
and limiting the right or freedom has been infringed'.[49]

The Supreme Court of Nauru has held that the preambular section gives no
rights by itself,[50] while in Mauritius, where the issue has arisen more than
once, the courts have been divided.[51] However, if section 70 cannot be used to
expand rights, nor can it be used to limit rights beyond what is substantively
provided in succeeding sections.[52]

Even though it may not be possible to use the preamble to bring in rights
not explicitly provided for in the Chapter, with some courage and imagination

[49] *Shah* n. 47 above at 538.

[50] *In re Dagabe Jeremiah* (Miscellaneous Cause No. 2, unreported). Nauru law prohibits
Nauruan women from marrying non-Nauruan men without official permission (in an attempt
undoubtedly to keep the phosphate fortunes within the community), although no parallel restriction applied to Nauruan men wishing to marry foreigners. Since the substantive right to non-discrimination did not cover 'sex' (any more, as we shall see, does it in Kenya), the plaintiff sought
(unsuccessfully) to rely on a reference in the preamble to 'respect for his private and family life'.

[51] In *Societe United Docks* v. *Government of Mauritius*, in an interlocutory judgment delivered
on 7 December 1981, the Supreme Court held (disregarding an earlier decision of the same court)
that the declaratory or preambular section had substantive consequences. The issue was whether
the reference in that section to the 'deprivation of property' (which the plaintiffs claimed had been
done to them) could be read as supplementing the protection given to property in section 8, which
mentions only compulsorily 'taking' or 'acquiring'. Rault C.J., was certainly able to read poetry
into the prose (and prosaic text) of the preambular section (section 3). 'One should remember in
what spirit the Constitution was framed. Those who thought of independence as a dangerous
gamble as much as those who looked upon it as an inspiring adventure were agreed on one point:
before embarking on such an enterprise we had to equip ourselves adequately for it . . . And it was
accepted by all that an indispensable safeguard was a Constitution enshrining those reasons to
live which are more precious than life itself. Now some of the other sections in Chapter II no
doubt sounded highly technical to non-lawyers, but to all who care for human rights and liberty,
section 3 spoke loud and clear. It set out the essence of the pact between the people and
Government on the eve of independence. If the other sections are severed from their common origin in section 3, they will lose their fundamentality at the same time as their foundation. They will
be left over as unlinked fragments which may for a time protect bits and pieces of liberty, but fail
to give comprehensive cover to liberty against those who seek to curtail and mutilate it.'
    The Chief Justice's eloquence was inspired by a desire to 'protect' two major companies the
gravamen of whose complaint against the Government was that its Sugar Corporation, by taking
advantage of new technology, had effectively put them out of business! At the hearing on merits,
another bench of the same court held there had been no violation of the plaintiff's rights (even
taking into account section 3). (I am indebted to a case note by James Read for this information,
[1982] *Journal of African Law* 177).

[52] An attempt (unsuccessful as it turned out) to do so was however, made by the Government
in *Ngui* v. *Republic* [1961] LRC (Const) 308, which concerned the power of the court to grant
applications for bail. The Constitution requires that if an arrested person is not tried within
a reasonable time, then he or she shall be released conditionally or unconditionally pending
the trial. A law was passed in 1978 which restricted the power of the court to grant bail if
the charge was one of murder or robbery with violence. When this law was challenged as unconstitutional, the government argued that although apparently unfettered, the right to bail had to

it could be used to establish the priority of rights and freedoms in the constitutional order and to determine the proper balance between them and their restrictions. The preamble is emphatic about the entitlement of the people to rights and freedoms, and permits limitations on them for narrow and specific purposes. The primary responsibility of public authorities (including the judiciary) is therefore to facilitate, not obstruct, the enjoyment of rights and freedoms. It can also be seen as an invitation to the judges to engage in the discourse on the value of rights and the justifications for limitations (which has rarely been taken up by them, in contrast to other senior judiciaries in the Commonwealth and elsewhere).

BENEFICIARIES OF RIGHTS AND FREEDOMS

In general the rights granted by the Constitution are available to all persons in Kenya. However, non-citizens have no guarantee of freedom of movement, which is defined as the right to live in any part of Kenya or move freely within it (section 81(1)). Likewise non-citizens do not have any protection against discriminatory legislation (section 82(4) (a)). But they are protected against discriminatory acts or policies which cannot be justified under a law. This became clear when various authorities began to implement Africanization policies soon after independence. In *Madhawa*, the Nairobi City Council passed a resolution to evict non-African stall holders from the municipal market and to transfer their licences to Africans. When a number of Asians, then not citizens, challenged the decision, the High Court upheld their case as it fell more properly under subsection (2) of section 82 which protects every person against discriminatory treatment 'by a person acting by virtue of any written law or in the performance of the functions of a public office or a public authority'.[53]

Another 'Africanization' case helped to clarify the concept of 'person' for the purposes of the Constitution. The Transport Licensing Board denied licences for carriage to a company which was substantially owned by Asians. It is not clear from the judgment whether all or some of them were citizens. The Board's decision was based on the fact that they were *not* citizens of

be read subject to the limitations mentioned in section 70, namely the rights and freedoms of others and the public interest. However in a subsequent case, Sachdeva J., (in the *Mutunga* bail case) used the restrictions mentioned in section 70 as a reason for restricting the right to bail, which is unqualified otherwise. Report in 16 *Nairobi Law Monthly* 33.

[53] *Madhwa* v. *City Council of Nairobi* [1968] EA 406. A similar decision was reached in *Fernandes* v. *Kericho Liquor Licensing Court* [1968] EA 640, where the renewal of the liquor licence held by the plaintiff was refused because he was not a citizen. The relevant legislation had set out six grounds for disqualification to hold a licence; being a non-citizen was not one of them. The case therefore did not strictly raise a constitutional issue (which was not argued), and Chanan Singh J. disposed of it on administrative law grounds.

African origin. The court found for the company, but it is not clear on what basis. At one point Simpson J. argued that 'person' included a company, as defined in the interpretation clause of the Constitution,[54] and any discrimination against it was invalid. But he also took into account that most of its shareholders were members of one race, and that was the basis of discrimination, contrary to section 82. But then he also argued that the Board had no lawful authority to make a distinction 'between different classes of citizens'[55]. One may therefore surmise that what Simpson J. meant was that a company may be a person for the purposes of the enjoyment of rights and freedoms, but when a right could be confined to a citizen, whether a company was so qualified depended on the nature of its shareholding. But he provides no guidance on whether he would require all or only a majority of its shareholders to be citizens. He reached his decision without any discussion of policy or comparative case law.[56]

Another group of persons whose rights are less than others is women, especially African women. The basis for this is twofold: the non-discrimination provision does not prohibit unequal treatment on grounds of gender (and since the principal bias of the law is in favour of males, women are disadvantaged); and it also excludes from its application a large body of law, especially customary or personal laws, under which women tend to be placed in an inferior position to males. The prohibition against discrimination does not apply to laws 'with respect to adoption, marriage, divorce, burial, devolution of property on death or other matters of personal law' (section 82(4)(b)). It is also provided that the prohibition against discrimination shall not apply to any law which makes provision 'for the application in the case of members of a particular race or tribe of customary law with respect to any matter to the exclusion of any law with respect to that matter which is applicable in the case of other persons' (section 82(4)(c)). The result of these provisions is to validate the continued application of different regimes of customary laws to different ethnic groups as well as to preserve inequalities in these laws.[57]

A third group excluded from several rights is members of disciplinary

[54] Section 123—'person' includes a body of persons corporate or unincorporate.

[55] *Shah Vershi Devshi* v. *The Transport Licensing Board* [1971] EA 289. After this decision, cases on racial discrimination seem to have ceased. The reason is not that this and the preceding cases had clarified the law and thus dissuaded public authorities from carrying out Africanization as opposed to Kenyanization policies. No, the reason is not the triumph of the Rule of Law but a certain weariness on the part of Asian citizens, and the devising of ways, legal and illegal, around official restrictions.

[56] The other judge, Chanan Singh J., provided clearer guidance when he said that a company is a person and would be entitled to all the rights and freedoms given to a 'person' which it is capable of enjoying. But he likewise does not provide any guidance as to how to establish if a company is a 'citizen'.

[57] For discussions of the position of women under customary law, see Armstrong and Ncube eds., *Women and Law in Southern Africa* (1992); Cotran ed., *Casebook on Kenya Customary Law* (1987); and Armstrong et al., *Uncovering Reality: Excavating Women's Rights in African Family Law* (1992).

forces. A disciplinary force is defined as (a) any of the armed forces; (b) a police force; (c) a prison service; or (d) the National Youth Service (section 88). Most of the fundamental rights of a member of a disciplinary force are vulnerable to a disciplinary law, which is defined as 'a law regulating the discipline of a disciplined force'. It therefore deals with matters of commands etc. within the force, and these exemptions would not extend to the general law in its application to members of a disciplinary force. A disciplinary law cannot be challenged for the violation of any right except for three: the rights to (a) life (section 71); (b) protection from slavery and forced labour (section 73)[58] and (c) protection from torture or inhuman treatment (section 74). These cut a broad swathe into the rights of members of the disciplined forces. It is hard to justify such a broad exclusion of rights, for it cannot all be related to the proper discharge of their duties. Undoubtedly some restrictions on their rights may be necessary for reasons of security and internal discipline, but these ought to be justified as such, and not covered under a blanket exemption.

Finally there are a miscellany of people whose entitlement to some rights are less equal than of others. The right of public officers or members of a disciplined force to move freely within or to leave Kenya may be restricted (section 81(3)(e). A person under 18 years may have her personal liberty restricted for the purpose of her education or welfare (section 72(1)(g)), as may vagrants or those addicted to alcohol or drugs, either for their own good or the good of the community (section 72(1)(h)).

RIGHTS AND FREEDOMS: INTRODUCTION

There are many ways in which human rights can be classified. Even disregarding controversies between economic, social and cultural rights on one hand and civil and political rights on the other, the latter themselves can be further classified. Departing somewhat from the scheme in section 70, we may divide the rights and freedoms under the Constitution into five categories: (a) personal rights and freedoms; (b) civil rights; (c) protection of the law; (d) right of property; and (e) the general right of non-discrimination. The justification for this categorization is that personal rights speak to the security of life and the dignity of the individual, while civil rights pertain to her participation in the community and the political affairs of the state. Sometimes a distinction is made between civil and political rights. The distinction is hard to sustain for many civil rights have as one of their purposes the pursuit of political goals. Explicitly political rights like that of the franchise and the ability to stand for public office were, in Kenya, dealt with under a separate Chapter of the

---

[58] But section 73(3) expressly provides an exception to the protection against forced labour in the case of 'labour required of a member of a disciplined force in pursuance of his duties as such . . .'.

Constitution. At independence, as I have mentioned, Kenya was guaranteed a multi-party parliamentary political system, and the right to register as a voter was granted to all citizens who had reached the age of 21, barring some exceptions for reasons of public policy. The right to stand for parliamentary seats was restricted to members of the Kenya National African Union when Kenya was made a one-party state, but the old rights were reinstated in 1982.

The general right of non-discrimination is an important attribute of citizenship, and it applies to matters of personal as well as public life. It is a right which protects the inherent equality and dignity of an individual, but also that of the group and the community to which he or she belongs. Although Kenya is a multi-racial and multi-ethnic state, the Constitution does not explicitly provide for rights of minorities (although the federal arrangements were devised for this purpose) and therefore the importance of non-discrimination is obvious.

The right of property is treated separately for the reason that it is somewhat special, not falling easily in other categories. It used to be regarded as part of personal liberty, since it was assumed that one's possessions were acquired through one's labour. Today this rationale can no longer be maintained (especially given the reasons for its presence and precise format in the Kenyan Constitution), since the reason for protection are economic, although of course property serves many functions, including the security of a person, physically and politically.

The protection of the law is not strictly speaking a right (or a set of rights). It does not speak to any specific need of an individual. In one sense, these rights should be encapsulated in the preceding substantive rights, and thus the right to bail should be an aspect of the right to liberty, etc. Nevertheless, the provisions which define a citizen's relationship to the legal system have become so important that they are now regarded as among the most basic of 'rights'. The reason for their importance is of course the growing power and scope of activities of, and regulation by, the state. Human rights have become essentially a function of the relationship of the individual to the apparatus of the state. The legal system is meant to provide a particular mode of the articulation as well as the mediation of this relationship which would enhance the security and dignity of the individual. Legal rights (or the protection of the law) are central to this articulation.

Personal Rights and Freedoms

The first, and the most important, personal right is the right to life itself (section 71). The second personal right is the right to be free, which could be said to comprise of two entitlements. The first is that of personal liberty, i.e. the right not to be incarcerated or detained (and this is secured by section 72). The other element is not to be a slave or in servitude; or to perform forced labour (section 73). Closely connected with these personal freedoms is the right against searches of person or property (section 76). This is the closest the Bill comes to protecting privacy which is mentioned in section 70. In many countries privacy has become the most personal and intimate of rights, enabling an individual to organise his or her private and sexual life as he or she wishes. Another provision protects the privacy of correspondence (section 79(1)). The Kenyan provisions are nowhere so extensive, but do seek to provide some space for an individual.

A further personal right is that of movement, which is defined as the 'right to move freely throughout Kenya, the right to reside in any part of Kenya, the right to enter Kenya and immunity from expulsion from Kenya' (section 81).

Civil Rights

The Bill protects four kinds of civil rights. The first of these is the freedom of conscience, which is defined as 'the freedom of thought and of religion, freedom to change his religion or belief, and freedom, either alone or in community with others, and both in public and private, to manifest and propagate his religion or belief in worship, teaching, practice and observance' (section 78). Every religious community may establish places of education and manage them if they are maintained wholly out of its own funds, and in these places it may offer religious instruction for persons of that community (section 78(2)). No person attending an educational institution may be forced to receive religious instruction or to take part in or attend a religious ceremony or observance if that instruction, ceremony or observance relates to a religion other than his (section 78(3)—but does it mean that he or she can be so forced if the instruction, etc. relate to his or her religion?). Finally, no person shall be compelled to take an oath which is contrary to his religion or belief (section 73(4)).

The Bill protects the freedom of expression, defined as 'freedom to hold opinions without interference, freedom to receive ideas and information without interference, freedom to communicate ideas and information without interference (whether communication to the public generally or to any person or class of persons) and freedom from interference with his correspondence' (section 79).

The remaining rights are those of assembly and association—an individual's rights to assemble freely and associate with other persons and in particular to form or belong to trade unions or other associations for the protection of his or interests (section 80(1)).

Protection of the Law and the Legal Process

The bulk of these rights are connected with the criminal law process. Various pre-trial rights are dealt with in section 72. Any person who is arrested or detained has to be informed as soon as reasonably practicable, in a language that he or she understands, of the reasons for his/her arrest or detention. He or she should be brought before a court as soon as practicably possible, normally within 24 hours of arrest (except where the alleged offence carries a death penalty in which case within 14 days). Otherwise the burden is on the prosecuting authority to establish that the accused was brought before the court as soon as it was practicable. Once a person has been brought before a court, his/her further detention can be permitted only by an order of the court. If he/she is not tried within a reasonable time, then he/she shall be released either unconditionally or upon reasonable conditions to ensure his/her appearance at the trial.

Rights at trial are governed by section 77. No person can be convicted of a criminal offence unless that offence (except for contempt of court) is defined and the penalty prescribed in a written law. Neither criminal liability nor penalties can be applied retroactively. The Penal Code of Kenya had codified most common law offences, but as mentioned above, Africans were frequently punished for vague offences under customary law.[59] Although this provision appeared in the independence Constitution, it was not to come into effect until 1 June 1966. The intention appears to be to allow time for the incorporation into written law of such customary offences as it was considered should be continued in force. A report on customary offences and recommendations on those which should have statutory force was prepared by Dr. Eugene Cotran, but no action was taken on it, and these offences must therefore be deemed to have lapsed.[60] The rationale for this provision is of course to ensure the certainty of the law and to prevent its capricious use, although it has not been achieved since so many statutory offences remain broad and vague.

The second general principle is that every accused shall be afforded a fair hearing within a reasonable time by an independent and impartial court established by law. Thirdly, every person charged with a criminal offence shall be presumed to be innocent until he or she is proved or has pleaded guilty. He or she has to be informed in a language that he/she understands and in detail

[59] In his *Report on Native Tribunals in Kenya* (1944), Arthur Phillips criticized the administration of customary criminal law. What it amounted to was either 'the application of non-indigenous penal sanctions to infringements of native law which were formally settled by the payment of compensation' (ibid. at para. 794) or 'a sort of 'contingencies vote' on which a tribunal can always fall back to justify a conviction in circumstances which were not foreseen or provided for by any other law' (ibid. at para. 799).

[60] However, Attorney-General Njonjo announced in Parliament that he had instructed African Courts that where formerly there would have been criminal liability, they should now treat it as a case of civil liability. The authority for this transformation is not apparent. See Ghai and McAusla, n. 1 above at 425.

of the nature of the charge; be given adequate time and facilities for the preparation of the defence; be permitted to defend himself/herself before the court either in person or through a legal representative of his/her choice; be afforded facilities to examine in person or by the legal representative witnesses called by the prosecution and to call his/her own witnesses; and to have the use of an interpreter if necessary. The trial must take place in his/her presence unless the accused's conduct makes that impracticable. He/she has a right to the transcript of the trial (on payment of fees). An accused cannot be compelled to give evidence at the trial. Once a person has been convicted or acquitted of an offence, he/she cannot be tried again for it (except as part of a review or appeal procedure). Nor can he/she be tried for an offence for which a pardon has been given.

The third set of legal rights concern civil proceedings. A court or other adjudicating authority prescribed by law for the determination or extent of a civil right or obligation has to be established by law and shall be independent and impartial. The case shall be given a fair hearing within a reasonable time. The hearings shall be in public (except with the agreement of all the parties). (Incidentally there is no requirement of a public hearing in criminal cases, although of course that is mandatory under the common law) (section 77(9) and (10)). The scope of this provision has been little explored or litigated in Kenya. It comes from Article 6(1) of the ECHR, where it has given rise to a great deal of both case law and controversy. No consensus has yet emerged on whether it concerns purely 'private' law rights/obligations; on whether it affects relations between an individual and a public authorities, and if so, what specific kinds or sources of relationship.[61] Its potential for the development of administrative law is obvious, for it is now accepted that relations between a state and an individual, particularly in his/her status as a citizen, are covered.[62] There are also implications for the structure and procedures of administrative bodies charged with adjudication and appeals.[63]

---

[61] The issues are usefully canvassed in van Dijk and van Hoof, *Theory and Practice of the European Convention of Human Rights* (2nd edn., 1990), 295–312.

[62] Ibid. at 302–3, list the following matters as having been determined by the European Court or Commission of Human Rights to fall within this section:
  (a) procedures concerning a permission or another act of a public authority which forms a condition for the legality of a contract to be concluded with a private party;
  (b) procedures which may lead to the cancellation or suspension by the public authorities of the qualification for practising a particular profession or carrying on an economic activity;
  (c) procedures concerning the grant or revocation of a licence by the public authorities which is required for practising a particular profession or carrying out certain economic activities in that particular place;
  (d) procedures in which a decision is taken on claims to a sickness benefit on account of industrial disability;
  (e) procedures in which a decision is taken on claims to a retirement pension in virtue of a compulsory insurance against accidents.

[63] For example the procedures for compulsory compensation ordered collectively under the Stock and Produce Theft Act, for it was not the duty of the magistrate to fix any individual with

Protection of Property

This is perhaps the most comprehensively protected of the rights. It is provided that 'No property of any description shall be compulsorily taken possession of, and no interest in or right over property of any description shall be compulsorily acquired' unless the taking or acquisition is necessary in the interests of defence, public safety, etc. and the necessity is such as to afford reasonable justification for the hardship to the person whose property is thus affected. Even then the taking of property is not lawful unless 'provision is made by a law applicable to that taking of possession or acquisition for the prompt payment of full compensation' (section 75). I have already mentioned the protection accorded to the owner of property from unauthorized entry by others on his/her property (section 76).

Protection from Discrimination

This right protects a person or community from discrimination which is based wholly or mainly on his or its race, tribe, place of origin or residence or other local connexion, political opinions, colour or creed. The omission of sex or gender is striking. It is included in Article 14 of the ECHR (from which this section is drawn) and its omission in Kenya can perhaps be explained by the fact that its Bill was drawn directly from Nigeria (which with its influential, conservative Muslim majority was not ready for gender equality). Given, as I show later, that section 82 exempts personal laws from the application of non-discrimination, gender equality could have been provided without any great threat to social or tribal order.

Discrimination is defined as being 'subjected to disabilities or restrictions to which persons of one such description are not made subject or are accorded privileges or advantages which are not accorded to persons of another such description' (section 82(3)). The Constitution protects from discrimination in two ways—first against the enactment of any law which is discriminatory expressly or in its effect; and secondly, against discriminatory action by persons acting under written law or in the performance of the functions of a public office or a public authority. While the purpose of the Bill is to protect against abuse of rights by the Government and its agents, limited protection is guaranteed against private discrimination for it is provided that no person shall be treated in a discriminatory manner in respect of access to shops, hotels, lodging houses, public restaurants, eating houses or places of public entertainment (section (82(7)).

The protection against official and private discrimination in a country in which during its colonial period the administration was based on racism and

responsibility but to place liability upon a group or class of persons once one or more members are shown to have been involved in the theft. Ghai and McAuslan n. 1 above at 426.

racial discrimination and which after its independence was threatened by tribal animosities, scarcely needs emphasis. The independence Constitution had various mechanisms to deal with these problem, particularly the emerging one of tribal tensions (*majimbo*, a regionally based Senate, and local control of land transactions). With the abolition of most of these shortly after independence, the burden on section 82 has increased (but it is doubtful if it has been discharged).

RESTRICTIONS ON RIGHTS AND FREEDOMS

There are different ways in which Bills of Rights provide for restrictions on and derogations from human rights. The criteria are rather broad.[64] The Kenya Bill follows the somewhat older tradition where each of the rights has its own, and often very detailed, list of restrictions; and it is hard to trace an underlying philosophical basis (although as we have seen, section 70 makes some attempt at a broad formulation).

Most formulations of human rights represent a balance between the interests of the individual (or a group) and the community or the public (although there are a few rights, like that against torture or degrading treatment that should be and are frequently protected without limitations). The language of most human rights instruments and the manner in which reservations are expressed proceed from the assumption that rights are inherent in the individual and are for the most part absolute. But even schools of thought given to this view recognise that rights are only relevant in a community and in relation to the community. The technical language of limitations conceals bitterly contested debates about the origin, nature and purpose of human rights.

'Limitations' are thus a major way to strike a balance between the

---

[64] The Canadian Charter of Rights and Freedoms (which came into effect in 1984) merely says in Article 1 that the Charter 'guarantees the rights and freedoms set out in it subject only to such reasonable limitations prescribed by law as can be demonstrably justified in a free and democratic society'.

New Zealand has followed a similar policy. Section 4 of the New Zealand Bill of Rights says, 'the rights and freedoms contained in the Bill of Rights may be subject only to such reasonable limits prescribed by law as can be demonstrably justified in a free and democratic society'.

In the American Constitution, rights are unqualified, and it has been left to the Courts on their own to establish the grounds for and extent of restrictions.

The Constitution of South Africa (1996) has a general provision for limitations. Part of the relevant section, reads as follows:

36. (1) The rights in the Bill of Rights may be limited only in terms of law of general application to the extent that the limitation is reasonable and justifiable in an open and democratic society based on human dignity, equality and freedom, taking into account all relevant factors, including—

(a) the nature of the right;
(b) the importance of the purpose of the limitation;
(c) the nature and extent of the limitation;
(d) the relation between the limitation and its purpose; and
(e) less restrictive means to achieve the purpose.

individual and the community, or more accurately, to provide the framework in which the balance can be struck in particular instances. It is also usual to provide for the derogation or suspension of all or some rights in certain, specified circumstances, on the basis that the higher goals of public order or national security can only be maintained through a stricter regime of authority than would be possible if these rights were absolute. The justification for such derogations also attests to the inter-dependence of the individual and the community, that human rights cannot be realised if the community itself is under threat. Unfortunately all too often the community is conflated with the state, and the threats to the political supremacy of certain office holders in the apparatus of the state are equated with threats to social stability and national security. These, frequently discredited, office holders are also the authorities who decide what restrictions to place on rights, or rights of particular individuals or communities. In this way 'limitations' are used for perverse purposes, and lead to the denial of legitimate rights. It is therefore specially important to establish the permissible scope of limitations and derogations, and the proper approach to their interpretation. That becomes, in these circumstances, largely the responsibility of the judiciary; and hence the need for both independent and competent judges. Both the limiting provisions of the Kenyan Bill of Rights and the judicial and executive approaches to them show how easy it is to negate rights (with an aura of plausibility).

The Bill follows the ECHR in providing separately for limitations on each of the rights, but the grounds for restrictions are more numerous and broader than in the latter. It is not proposed to delineate all the restrictions to the rights and freedoms,[65] but some impression is given of the scope and nature of restrictions by some examples. This is followed by a general discussion of the grounds and methods for restrictions (as well as the means of controlling the application of restrictions).

Some rights are indeed absolute. The protection against slavery and servitude is absolute (section 73), but not apparently against torture or inhuman treatment to the extent that provisions in law for punishment in existence at the time of independence may violate the protection (section 74(2)). Otherwise all the absolute rights are connected with the protection of the law—no retroactivity of criminal liability or punishment; no double jeopardy (except for members of the armed forces); the right to bail; no detention without court order once an accused has been brought before a court; fair hearing by an independent court; access to interpretation; and the presumption of innocence (although the Bill is not unambiguous on the burden of proof).[66] However, how absolute some of these rights turn out to be depends on the courts; for example the right to be told reasons for one's arrest as soon as

[65] For a detailed analysis see Ghai and McAuslan n. 1 above at ch. XI.

[66] Section 77(12)(a) qualifies the presumption 'to the extent that the law in question imposes upon a person charged with a criminal offence the burden of proving particular facts'.

'reasonably practicable' can be rather illusory (as practice has shown), just like the right to bail which depends on the trial not proceeding within a 'reasonable time' (the courts not having interpreted these in a manner likely to enhance the rights).

The scope of restrictions is summarised in the two tables below. Table 1 indicates the grounds on which limitations may be imposed and Table 2 provides a guide to the control on the use of the limitations.

The most common grounds are public morality; public order and safety; public interest; public health; defence; and protection of the rights or interests of others (or even of the person restricted a measure of paternalism). Illustrations of the kinds of restrictions on rights that are authorised may be given from one personal right and one civil right. Personal liberty may be limited for one of nine reasons, including execution of a court order (whether of a criminal or civil nature), upon reasonable suspicion of a person having or about to commit a crime, for a person under 18, for his/her education or welfare, for drug or alcohol addicts, for their treatment or the protection of the community, and for various purposes connected with extradition. The freedom of assembly and association may be qualified if 'reasonably required' in the interests of defence, public safety, public order, public morality or public health, or protecting the rights and freedoms of others; for imposing restrictions upon public officers, members of a disciplined force, or persons in the service of a local government; and for restrictions on (including refusal for) the registration of trade unions or associations of trade unions if another union or association is sufficiently representative of the interests seeking the new registration.

Techniques for Imposing Restrictions

One technique is to exclude particular sections of the people from a right e.g. non-citizens from the protection against discriminatory laws or the right of movement, or vagrants, drug addicts or children from the full enjoyment of their personal liberty, or members of disciplined forces from various rights. Another technique is to put particular parts of the law beyond the reach of the Bill: punishments in force before independence continue to apply regardless of their compatibility with protection against torture or inhuman or degrading treatment or punishment; the continued validity of the Outlying Districts Act or the Special Districts (Administration) Act (or any laws amending them) as in operation in May 1963 despite inconsistency with the freedom of movement; and the regime of personal laws and other customary laws from the protection against discriminatory laws. Some rights may also be restricted on a geographical basis, as with the Outlying or Special Districts mentioned above. Another technique is 'definitional', whereby it is expressly provided that

Table 1: *Grounds on which Limitations on Rights may be Imposed*

Rights	Main Grounds for Limitations							
	public morality	public order/safety	public interest/benefit	public health	defence	protection/promotion of others' rights	paternalism	misc.
Life	72(2)(c)	72(2)(c)	70(a)		71(2)(a)	70(a)		
Personal liberty	72(g)	72(g)	72(1)(g)				72(1)(h)(f) vagrancy & children	72(1–4)[a]
Slavery/ servitude			73(3)(d–e)	73(3)(b)				
Torture								
Property	75(1)(a)	75(1)(a)	75(1)(a) 70(c) 75(6)(a)vii	75(1)(a) 75(6)(a)v	75(1)(a)	70(c)	75(6)(b)(ii) unsound mind & children	
Arbitrary search	76(2)(a)	76(2)(a)	76(2)(a)	76(2)(a)	76(2)(a)	76(2)(b)		
Protection of law	77(11)(a)	77(11)(b)			77(11)(b)	70(a) 77(11)b	77(2) trial in	see [b]

[a] Restrictions are permitted with regard to enforcement of the law.
[b] Section 77(12)(c) allows double jeopardy in the case of members of disciplined forces. Section 77(13) deprives those held in lawful detention of the following rights in relation to their trials for a criminal offence under the law regulating the discipline of persons held in lawful detention: the choice of a legal representative; the right to examine witnesses; the right of access to a record of the proceedings; the right to trial within a reasonable time before an impartial Court.

Table 1: cont.

Rights Main Grounds for Limitations

Rights							
Freedom of conscience/religion	78(5)(a)	78(5)(a)	78(5)(a) 70(b)	78(5)(a)	78(5)(a)	78(5)(b) 70(b)	absentia
Freedom of expression	79(2)(a)	79(2)(a)	79(2)(a)	79(2)(a)	79(2)(a)	79(2)(b)	see [c]
Assembly and association	80(2)(a)	80(2)(a)	80(2)(a)	80(2)(a)	80(2)(a)	80(2)(b)	see [d]
Movement	81(3)(b)	81(3)(b)	81(3)(b)	81(3)(a), (b)	81(3)(b)	81(3)(b) control of nomadic people and 82(6)(b) controlling transactions in agricultural land	see [e]
Discrimination						82(5)	qualifications for public office [f]

[c] Section 79(2)(c) makes exception for those laws which restrict public officers while doing their job.

[d] Section 80(2)(c) allows restrictions on members of the disciplined forces, public officers and those in the service of a local government. Section 80(2)(d) allows reasonable conditions to be placed on trade unions.

[e] Section 82(6) does not permit conflict with the Outlying Districts Act or the Special Districts (Administrative) Act. Only Kenyan citizens are protected. Restrictions are permitted for members of a disciplined force or for public officers.

[f] Only Kenyan citizens are protected. Sex is not included in the list of grounds for the avoidance of discrimination.

Table 2: Controls on the Limitations on Rights

Rights	Controls on Limitations		
	derogation must be reasonably justified in a democratic society	by law	misc
Life		71(1) 72(2)(b)(d)	
Personal liberty		72(1), (a)–(g) 72(4)	
Slavery/servitude	73(3)(d)		
Torture		74(2)	
Property	75(6)(a)	75(6) 75(1)(b)–(c) 75(1)(b)g 75(2) 75(7)	
Arbitrary search	76(2)	76(2)(c), (d)	
Protection of law		77(11)(a) 83(3)	
Freedom of conscience/religion	78(5)	78(5)	
Freedom of expression	79(2)(c)	79(2)	
Assembly and association	80(2)	80(2)	
Movement	81(3)(b), (g)	81(2) 81(3)(c),(f),(g) 81(5) 72(1)(i)–(j)	81(6)h
Discrimination	82(4)(d)	82(4)(b),(c) (customary and personal law) 82(6)	

g Hardship to any person having an interest or right in the property must be reasonably justified.

h Restrictions cannot be greater than those in force on 31 May 1963 and cannot apply to areas other than those where such a restriction was in force on 31 May 1963.

certain practices are deemed not to constitute the protected right, for example as to what constitutes 'forced labour'[67] or what factors are comprehended in the notion of 'discrimination' (e.g. the exclusion of gender).

Some restrictions are specific (for example the protection against the taking of property does not apply 'for so long only as may be necessary for the purposes of an examination, investigation, trial or inquiry, or in the case of land, for the purposes of carrying out thereon of work of soil conservation or the conservation of other natural resources . . .' (section 75(6)(a)(vii)). Others use a broad standard (the typical being the formula which allows derogations from different rights in the 'interests of defence, public safety, public order, public morality or public health'). The other reasons for restrictions are the protection of the rights and freedoms of others; and in a few cases, due to a form of paternalism (for the welfare of those denied rights).

The Bill tries to regulate the use of the authority to impose restrictions on rights. One way is by specifying the purpose for which the restrictions may be imposed (e.g. public safety or public interest, etc). It is frequently specified that the restrictions must be 'reasonable' and in one case 'necessary' (for property protection) to secure these purposes. In most instances it is also provided that the restrictions should be such as are 'reasonably justifiable in a democratic society',[68] the exceptions being 'legal rights' which are theoretically supposed to be absolute, and the right to personal liberty. Another safeguard is that the restrictions must be sanctioned under the provisions of a 'law'.

There are special safeguards in relation to certain rights. When a person is deprived of his liberty for the purpose of bringing him or her before a court in execution of the order of a court or upon reasonable suspicion of his having committed or about to commit a crime, he or she has to be brought before a court as soon as reasonably practicable, and if this is not done within 24 hours (or in the case of detention in connection with a capital offence, within 14 days), the prosecution has to prove that the delay is reasonable (Section 72(3)). The provisions for bail, already mentioned, could also be regarded as a safeguard for the protection of personal liberty. Another instance relates to the compulsory acquisition of property; in addition to other safeguards, it has to be proved that the necessity for the acquisition is such as to 'afford reasonable justification for the causing of hardship' to the owner (Section 75(1)(b)).

---

[67] Section 73 provides that the following are *not* forced labour: (a) labour required by a Court order; (b) labour required of a detainee for purposes of hygiene or maintaining the place where he/she is detained; (c) labour required of a member of a disciplined force in pursuance of his/her duties or that required from a conscientious objector; (d) labour that might be required during an emergency; and (e) 'labour reasonably required as part of reasonable and normal communal or other civil obligations'.

[68] Under the ECHR, restrictions must be 'necessary' rather than reasonable. Thus the Kenyan Constitution requires a lower degree of justification for the restrictions.

INTERPRETATIONS OF RESTRICTIVE CLAUSES

How effective these safeguards are depends on the interpretation put on them (this emphasises again the important role of the courts). Unfortunately in Kenya there has been relatively little discussion of what is the scope of the restrictions or what are the implications of the controlling formulas. What for example is the scope of the restriction based on 'the rights and freedoms of others'? What is meant by 'reasonably justifiable in a democratic society'? What is defence or public safety? What does it mean to say that restrictions must be provided under 'law'? etc.

To show that these are not simple matters (as the Kenyan courts seem to have assumed) but require the most careful consideration of competing values we can turn, for illustrative purposes, to some interpretations of some of these terms elsewhere (especially by the European Court and Commission of Human Rights since the ECHR was the basis of the Kenyan Bill). On 'democracy' the European Court of Human Rights has said that its essential qualities are pluralism, tolerance, and broadmindedness.[69] Although individual interests must on occasion be subordinated to those of a group, democracy does not simply mean that the views of the majority must always prevail: a balance has to be achieved that ensures the fair and proper treatment of minorities and avoids any abuse of a dominant position.[70]

'Reasonably justifiable' must mean that there should be a rational connection with a permitted ground for limitation and that every formality, condition, restriction or penalty must be proportionate to the legitimate aim pursued.[71] As the Court said in the *Sunday Times Case*,[72] the test is whether the interference complained of corresponds to a 'pressing social need'; is it proportionate to the legitimate aim pursued;[73] are the reasons given by national authorities to justify it relevant and sufficient?

The principle of proportionality is also implicit in the concept of 'law'. Courts have sometimes referred to this requirement as the principle of legality or the Rule of Law, and thus incorporated formal and substantive principles under it. A provision to be 'law' must have a basis in law, must be accessible to the public and must be clear so those affected by it can guide their conduct by it. These are formal requirements. However, 'accessible' has been interpreted to mean additionally that a law which is broad, general or vague may fail the test. If arbitrary and discriminatory laws are to be avoided, laws

---

[69] *Handyside* v. *United Kingdom* (1976) 1 EHRR 737.
[70] *Young James and Webster* v. *United Kingdom* (1982) 4 EHRR 38.
[71] The *Handyside* case n. 69 above at para. 49.
[72] *Sunday Times* v. *United Kingdom* (1979) 2 EHRR 245.
[73] Under this criterion, the provisions of the Societies Act under which an association may be denied registration if one of its officers or members has a prior conviction of any kind (discussed above) would be invalid (both for the reason that the conviction may have nothing to do with the purposes or management of the society, and because there cannot be such general penalties for past conviction). See *De Becker* v. *Belgium* (1962) 2 ECHR ser. B, 127.

must provide explicit standards for those who apply them. A law which gives too much discretion to an official may also fail the test of clarity, for it does not enable the public to know the purposes for which the law may be used.[74] It may also mean that the discretion could be used for an improper purpose. The law must be fair and reasonable in the sense of procedural due process. It must also bear some proportion to its objectives.[75]

DEROGATIONS FROM RIGHTS AND FREEDOMS

The provisions for derogation from rights have changed considerably from the independence Constitution, in favour of greater powers for the executive.[76] Controls over the continuation in force of the special regulations have been greatly reduced (they are now in force indefinitely, unless revoked by the President or an *absolute* majority of Parliament). During an emergency the only special powers which became available were to enact, or take executive action under, legislation which derogated from the freedom of personal liberty and the protection from discrimination, but only to the extent reasonably justifiable for dealing with the actual situation. In 1966 the provisions for special powers were established on a new basis, through the amendment of sections 83 and 85 and the revamping of the old colonial ordinance, the Preservation of Public Security Act (Cap. 57). No part of the original Bill of Rights has been as emasculated as the safeguards against the extent or abuse of emergency powers, and the Kenya law on this subject is now well below the minimally accepted international standards.[77]

Special powers are available either when Kenya is at war or the President has made an Order under section 85 (published in the Kenya Gazette) bringing into operation generally or in any part of Kenya all or part of the provisions of Part III of the Preservation of Public Security Act (section 83). No criteria are specified for the guidance of or control over the President for invoking the Act (nor in the Act itself, although the bringing into operation of the less drastic Part II depends on it appearing to the President that 'it is necessary for the preservation of public security' (section 3(1) of the Act). The Presidential Order has to be approved by a simple majority of the legislature within 28 days of its commencement, and once approved it continues in force

---

[74] *Sunday Times* n. 72 above; *Barthhold* v. *Germany* (1984) 4 EHRR 82 (Commission) and (1985) 7 EHRR 383 (Court); *Malone* v. *United Kingdom* (1985) 7 EHHR 14 and *Kruslin* v. *France* (1990) 12 EHRR 547.

[75] *Ong Ah Chua* v. *Public Prosecutor* [1981] AC 648 (Singapore) and *Maneka Gandhi* v. *Union of India Air* [1978] SC 597.

[76] For special emergency powers as provided under the independence constitution, see Ghai and McAuslan n. 1 above at 430–3.

[77] Chowdhury, *The Rule of Law in a State of* Emergency (1989) and Oraa, *Human Rights in States of Emergency in International Law* (1992).

unless the President revokes it or it is revoked by an absolute majority of the legislature.

During these periods nothing contained in or done under the authority of an Act or any provision of Part III of the Preservation of Public Security Act would be regarded as violations of the right to liberty (section 72), protection against arbitrary search or entry (section 76), freedom of expression (section 79), freedom of association and assembly (section 80), the freedom of movement (section 81) and the protection against discrimination (section 82). In other words, these rights may lawfully be suspended or derogated from, and it is no longer necessary to prove that any suspension of or derogation from the rights is reasonably justifiable in the circumstances of the situation.

It is unnecessary to go into the details of the confusing and difficult Preservation of Public Security Act.[78] The Act distinguishes between public security and special public security measures; the former are available under Part II and are brought into operation by a declaration of the President which does not require the approval of the legislature, and the latter, under Part III, by an Order under section 85 (as mentioned above). The 'preservation of public security' is widely defined and covers situations of political instability or subversion, the breakdown of the economic order, and natural disasters. The primary effect of bringing in Part II or Part III is to enable the President to make law by regulations. Regulations can be made for any of the purposes specified in section 4(2). These purposes are extensive and include the detention or the compulsory movement of persons, censorship or the prohibition of communications, control or prohibition of meetings and processions, compulsory acquisition of property, forced labour, control of trade and prices, and the modification of any law. Although it would appear that the specified purposes are wide enough to comprehend any regulations, there is a residual provision which permits regulations on any matter not expressly specified which is necessary or expedient for the preservation of public security (section 4(2)(m)).

Although a common list of purposes is provided for regulations under Part II and Part III, it is clear that regulations under Part II cannot derogate from any provisions of the Constitution or written law. However, under Part III, as we have seen, the derogations may be quite extensive. The only safeguard on the exercise of the power to make regulations that the Act provides is that regulations under it must be laid before Parliament as soon as may be after they are made, and empowers it to annul them within the period of 20 days commencing on the day on which it first sits after they were so laid (section 6(1)).[79]

The other safeguard, provided in the Constitution itself, is specific to the deprivation of liberty. The detainee must be provided with reasons for detention, in a language that he/she understands, as soon as reasonably practicable

[78] A detailed discussion is contained in Ghai and McAuslan n. 1 above at 434–40.
[79] This safeguard has never been effective under Kenyan law.

(but no later than 5 days). An announcement of the detention must be made in the Gazette within 14 days, and within one month (and thereafter every 6 months) his/her case has to be reviewed by an independent and impartial tribunal chaired by a presidential nominee qualified for the High Court.

For much of its independent life, Kenya has been under various forms of special regulations (some of which had been authorised under the constitutional instruments for its independence).[80] As far as Part III is concerned, it has been brought into operation only for the purposes specified in section 4(2)(a) and (b)—respectively authorising the detention of persons; the registration, restriction of movement (into, out of or within Kenya) and compulsory movement of persons, including the imposition of curfews.

PROVISIONS FOR THE ENFORCEMENT OF RIGHTS AND FREEDOMS

The principal responsibility for the enforcement of rights and freedoms is vested in the High Court. The primary provision (section 84) enables any person who considers that his or her rights have been violated to apply to the High Court, without prejudice to any other remedy that may be open to him/her.[81] If in proceedings in a subordinate court a question of the violation of rights arises, the judge may refer it to the High Court, but must do so if requested by any party to the proceedings. The High Court has wide powers to ' make such orders, issue such writs and give such directions as it may consider appropriate for the purpose of enforcing or securing the enforcement of any of the provisions of sections 70 to 83 (inclusive)' (section 83(2)).

[80] The Kenya Independence Order in Council providing for various matters in connection with independence had authorised the Governor-General to make regulations as appeared to him to be necessary or expedient for ensuring effective government in or in relation to the North-Eastern Province (even if they were inconsistent with the Constitution or other law). (See SI 1963/1968 s. 19(1)). These powers were taken over into section 127 of the Constitution and extended to contiguous districts, and a large number of regulations giving the administration extensive powers to derogate from people's rights and freedom were made. See Ghai and McAuslan n. 1 above at 430–3.

[81] Although it is provided that another person may apply on behalf of a person who is in detention, the phraseology of the section suggests a narrow basis for standing to challenge a violation of human rights. Courts in several Commonwealth countries, particularly India and New Zealand (and the USA) have broadened the basis of standing so that NGOs, the press and other interest groups can raise allegations of the violations of human rights. See contributions by a former Chief Justice of India, Bhagwati 'The Role of the Judiciary in Plural Societies', in Tiruchelvam and Coomaraswamy eds., *The Role of the Judiciary in Plural Societies* (1987), 20; Baxi, 'Taking Suffering Seriously: Social Action Litigation', in Tiruchelvam and Coomaraswamy ibid., 32; Cottrell, 'Social Action Litigation' in Adelman and Paliwala eds., *Law and Crisis in the Third World* (1993).
The Constitution of South Africa has constitutionalized this broader basis of standing. section 38 provides for the following to move the Court for a remedy: (a) Anyone acting in their own interest; (b) anyone acting on behalf of another person who cannot act in their own name; (c) anyone acting as a member of, or in the interest of, a group or class of persons; (d) anyone acting in the public interest; and (e) an association acting in the interest of its members.

Parliament is authorised to confer such additional powers on it as may appear to be necessary or desirable to enable it to exercise this jurisdiction more effectively (section 83(5), but so far no steps have been taken towards it).

This is not the only procedure for the enforcement of rights. The High Court has unlimited original jurisdiction in civil and criminal matters (section 60(1)), as well as special responsibility for the interpretation of the Constitution (section 67), providing for references to it from a subordinate court on a substantial question of law concerning the Constitution. Unless a party or the court has already invoked the reference mechanism under Section 84(3), a party may appeal to the High Court against a decision of a subordinate court or court-martial on a question of the interpretation of the Constitution. The section dealing with the protection of property provides specifically for access to the High Court for the determination of an owner's right or interest or the legality of the acquisition, or the amount of compensation, as well as for obtaining the prompt payment of the compensation (section 75(2)).

There is thus some choice for a person who considers that his or her rights have been violated. Additionally, of course, rights can be invoked in the form of a defence, as part of the ordinary court procedure. Due to certain interpretations by the courts, the choice may be a matter of considerable consequence. The Court of Appeal has held (by majority) that it has no jurisdiction to hear an appeal from a decision of the High Court given under section 84(2)(a), on the ground that the Court of Appeal has only such jurisdiction as is expressly conferred by law (section 64(1)), and no statute has provided for an appeal from a decision of the High Court under section 84(2)(a).[82] Whatever the legal merits of the decision (it is perhaps the most closely analysed, and lengthy, constitutional decision of any Kenyan court), it produces the strange result that under the procedure envisaged by the Constitution as the most usual and normal for the enforcement of rights (as indeed is also the practice), the highest court in the land is prevented from deciding the constitutional issue.

It is also worthy noting that for a while the courts (under the leadership of Miller C.J.) denied access to courts under Section 84.[83] His argument, subsequently espoused vigorously by Dugdale J., was that section 84 remained inoperative until Parliament and the Chief Justice had made rules regarding

[82] *Anarita Karimi Njeru* v. *Republic* [1979] KLR 102. The majority opinion is that of Wicks C.J. and Miller Ag.J.A. Law J.A. dissented, holding that there was a general common law rule (which applied in Kenya) that an appeal lies from a decision of the High Court made in the exercise of its original jurisdiction. He also pointed to the incongruity that if a person sought an application under section 84(3) (i.e. on a reference from a subordinate court) he or she would still have the right to appeal to the Court on conviction and then a second appeal to the Court of Appeal, but if the approach was direct to the High Court under section 84(1), there is no further appeal. The majority considered that the expression 'law' in section 66(1) meant statute, while Law considered that it also covered common law and equity.

[83] The issue has been extensively explored by Vazquez, 'Is the Kenyan Bill of Rights Enforceable After 4th July 1989?' (1990) 2 *Nairobi Law Monthly* 7–18.

the procedure for the exercise of the jurisdiction under the section. Section 84(6), to which the first subsection is made subject, says that the Chief Justice may make rules with respect to the procedure and practice of the High Court in this regard. Section 84(5) says that Parliament may confer additional powers on the High Court for the more effective discharge of its functions under the section. Neither subsection requires the Chief Justice or Parliament to make additional rules. Moreover Kenyan courts had previously accepted jurisdiction in a number of cases under the section (adopting a Privy Council decision on a Guyanese case on an identical issue).[84]

Another restriction on access to the court has been placed by the judges through their interpretation of the reference in section 84(1) to the availability of complaint to the High Court 'without prejudice to any other action with respect to the same matter which is lawfully available'. The High Court held in the *Njeru* case that if a person has invoked another remedy, he or she is subsequently barred from the use of section 84—not perhaps the most natural interpretation of the phrase.[85]

It is hard to resist the conclusion that Miller's and Dugdale's interpretations were inspired by a wish to deny the plaintiffs the opportunity to assert their rights and to avoid embarrassment to the government. The first case raised the legality of the government's confiscation of the passport of Gibson Kamau Kuria, the best known of Kenya's human rights lawyers, in violation of his right to free movement.[86] The second case, arising out of charges of creating a disturbance likely to cause a breach of the peace (under section 95 of the Penal Code), involved the plaintiffs' right to the freedom of expression (since the charge was based on their press release alleging election rigging).[87] The

---

[84] *Jaundo* v. *Attorney-General of Guyana* [1971] AC 972. The statement by the Privy Council that the failure of a rule-making authority to make rules to enforce rights does not defeat those rights which can be raised or enforced by any procedure available had been adopted in Kenya in *Raila Odinga* v. *Attorney General and Detainees Review Board* (Mis. Applic. 104 of 1986).

Miller C.J. was a member of the Court of Appeal in the *Njeru* case (see n. 82 above), which had upheld the jurisdiction of the High Court under section 84 notwithstanding that no rules had been made under either subsection. In any case it ill became Miller C.J. to adopt this argument since as Chief Justice he was responsible for making the rules. Under his own interpretation, by his failure to do so he was undermining the Constitution—a somewhat inappropriate role for a Chief Justice.

[85] This decision has been used to bar the access of many litigants seeking to enforce their constitutional rights. The High Court criticised and refused to follow the decision in *Harun Thungu Wakaba* v. *Republic* (High Court Misc. Criminal case 34 of 1992, unreported) so that its precise status is unclear until a three bench court rules on it. For a discussion of the case law, see M'Inoti, 'Enforcement of Fundamental Rights in Kenya: Righting Some of the Initial Wrongs', 42 *Nairobi Law Monthly* (April/May 1992).

[86] *Kamau Kuria* v. *Attorney-General*, High Court, Mis. Civil Appl. 550 of 1988, reported in 15 *Nairobi Law Monthly* 33 (March/April 1989).

[87] *Maina Mbacha* v. *Attorney-General*, High Court, Mis. Civil Appl. 356 of 1989, reported in 17 *Nairobi Law Monthly* (July/August 1989) 38.

In this case the plaintiffs had based their application on Section 60, in addition to section 84. Dugdale J. dismissed the case at the stage of mention, with the help of a pre-typed ruling, without giving counsel the opportunity of argument. He made no mention of section 60.

confiscation of passports and charges for breach of peace have been the principal instruments of the government to harass and silence its opponents.[88] The
procedure adopted meant that these issues could not be litigated, and the government was free to carry on with its previous practice.[89] As for remedies, the
High Court has a wide discretion. As has already been mentioned, the High
Court under a section 84 reference or application 'may make such orders,
issue such writs and give such directions as it may consider appropriate for the
purpose of enforcing or securing' the rights and freedoms guaranteed under
Chapter V. Although most of the orders would be one or more of traditional
judicial remedies, they are not so confined. Traditional common law and equitable remedies (like the prerogative orders and injunctions and declarations)
are available to the courts both under the common law and statute.[90] The
Criminal Procedure Code contains a remedy known as directions in the nature
of habeas corpus, but the powers of the High Court in issuing such a direction
and the procedure to be followed in applying for it are similar to those pertaining to the writ.[91] The Bill of Rights provides for a specific remedy for
unlawful arrest or detention—that of compensation (section 72(6)). There is no
reason to believe however that compensation cannot be given for denials of
other rights, as has been done in other jurisdictions.

The importance of legal remedies is emphasized by the guarantee of access
to a lawyer. A person charged with a criminal offence has the right to representation by a lawyer (section 77(2)(d),(e)), and a person held in detention
under special powers has to be afforded 'reasonable facilities' to consult a
legal representative of his own choice to present his case to the review tribunal
(section 83(2)(d)). It is, however, made clear in both instances that the person
is responsible for the costs of such representation. But in 1992, the
Constitution was amended to require Parliament to make provision for financial assistance to any indigent citizen 'where his right has been infringed or
with a view to enabling him to engage the services of an advocate to prosecute
his claim' provided that 'the allegations of infringement are substantial and
the requirement or need for financial or legal aid is real'.[92]

It is clear that much store was set by the efficacy of the legal process in
securing rights and freedoms. Although, as I have mentioned, the independence Constitution also established a massive decentralisation of power, guar-

---

[88] See Africa Watch, *Kenya: Taking Liberties* (1991) particularly chs. 8 and 11 and Appendix
C.

[89] The Courts have also blocked the review of the procedures of the then sole political party,
KANU (which involve both the electoral process and the expulsion of members), so failing to
ensure the fairness of the political processes (see below). They have also refused to review the powers of the executive in the exercise of administrative detentions (so enabling dissent to be easily
crushed). *Raila Odinga* v. *Republic* (see n. 84 above).

[90] Law Reform (Mis. Provisions) Act (1956).   [91] Penal Code

[92] Act 6 of 1992, section 10; it now appears as section 84(5)(b).

anteed a multi-party political system, instituted an upper house with important supervisory and veto powers, and created many neutral and independent centres of authority (e.g. the civil service), it cannot seriously have been expected that the political or administrative process would provide much protection. Indeed the length and complexity of the Constitution owes itself to the distrust of democratic politics. And indeed the length and complexity indicates that lawyers were expected to be the first and last line of defence. However, as I show below, lawyers and the legal system were ill-suited for this responsibility. But before then, I examine briefly the fortunes of the Bill of Rights and the effectiveness of the constitutional processes.

The Effectiveness of The Bill of Rights

THE CONTEXT

This Chapter is concerned with the legal and judicial enforcement of the Bill of Rights. It is, however, not easy to understand its success or failure without an appreciation of the political context within which the Bill of Rights has operated. The account in the following paragraphs attempts to sketch in the broad framework within which questions of the enforcement of human rights were determined. It does not examine other mechanisms, political, administrative and social, for the enforcement of rights. But the availability and use of these other mechanisms influence the possibilities and scope of judicial enforcement. After the context is established, the Chapter examines specifically the role of the Government and private legal practitioners and the judiciary in relation to the Bill of Rights.

Despite its shortcomings, the Bill of Rights represented a major advance for the cause of democracy, political participation and human rights. Its implications were quite transformative. Numerous aspects of law and administration would have had to be abandoned or modified to conform to the Bill. As is now clear, the promise of the Bill was not fulfilled, and Kenya has become, if that is possible, an even more repressive state than before. From the very beginning of independence, it was clear that the new government (or indeed any significant politician) had no genuine commitment to democracy, human rights or the rule of law. The European settlers (and the British government) quickly made their peace with Kenyatta, and their new found enthusiasm for human rights turned out to be rather short-lived. Their interests, after all, were not threatened by the Kenyatta government.

The government did little to prepare itself for a democratic and human rights constitution. It had no (and never has had any) human rights lawyer on its staff. It did not organize any training programme for its staff on the implications of the Constitution for law, administration or policy, nor did it engage in any general educational programme in the new Constitution. In fact it embarked almost from the start of its new life with strong attacks on the Constitution, and set about dismantling its key elements. The rule of law and constitutionalism had no place in its ideology; indeed developmentalism and Africanization, which were the principal features of its ideology, to a large extent ran counter to them.[93]

It is not surprising therefore that the Government took no steps to review its laws and practices to establish conformity with new standards required by the Bill of Rights, with the exception of discriminatory laws. By this time many discriminatory laws had been abolished, but a few remained and these were repealed or modified to apply to all races, following the review.[94] Otherwise the government's attention was focused on 'streamlining' the Constitution, which it did with remarkable success and speed. The first casualty was effectively the parliamentary system, with the establishment of an executive presidential system.[95] In due course it led to such a dominance of the political and administrative system by the President that it became hard to exercise many of the rights in the face of presidential displeasure. The other major development was the establishment of a de facto (and subsequently de jure) one-party system, which closed remaining channels of dissent and debate, and brought about enormous restrictions on rights and freedoms. (Elsewhere too executive presidentialism and one-party rule have been the bane of Africa). But before the goal of one party was reached, *majimbo* or federalism, and its accompanying safeguard, the Senate, were put away.[96] Meanwhile the central government (or effectively the President) was assuming greater powers, including wide powers of detention of its opponents without trial. The independence of the judiciary was emasculated, typically for Kenya, through both administrative practice and legal amendments (as is examined below). Legislation weakened trade unions and co-operatives. Government bought the obedience of many as the scope of its patronage increased with the diminution of the Public Service Commission, and the establishment of state commercial and industrial corporations.

It is not surprising in these circumstances that whatever opposition there was to the government was harshly dealt with. The government used all kinds of methods to harass its opponents—pressure through finance companies, dismissal from jobs, withdrawal of contracts, and administrative detentions,

[93] See Ghai, 'The Rule of Law, Legitimacy and Governance' (1986) 14 *International Journal of the Sociology of Law* 179–208.

[94] See Ghai and McAuslan n. 1 above at 441–2.

[95] The Constitution of Kenya (Amendment) Act of l964.

[96] That the regional governments would be still-born was ensured by the national government by administrative means—by the simple expedient of ignoring the fiscal and other entitlements of the regions. The first constitutional amendment took away their substantive powers, and by the second (Act 38 of l964) the provisions for the independent revenue of the regions were abolished. By the Amendment Act of l965 (Act 14) most of their remaining powers were taken away, and in a 1966 Amendment (Act 40), the Senate was abolished.

even torture and extra-judicial killings. There is no space to provide details or documents—but the violations of rights and freedoms are so notorious that even judges can take judicial notice of them.[97]

A peculiar feature of the government's violation of rights and freedoms has been the use of the legal process. People have been held in custody for long periods, ostensibly for trial, but released subsequently without charge. Others have been brought to court on trumped up charges, and pressure brought on the judges to secure a conviction. These tactics have caused a particular crisis for the law and the legal process. They have pointed to the value as well as the ineffectiveness of legal protection. The banning of opposition parties, the erosion of local autonomies, the destruction of independent trade unions, and the wide use of detention powers weakened the will of victims of human rights violations to use courts just as it weakened the resolve of the judges to provide justice to them.

THE ROLE OF THE ATTORNEY-GENERAL

The Attorney-General is the chief legal adviser to the Government. He was seen at independence as having a key responsibility for upholding the Rule of Law. This view was reflected in the provisions relating to his functions, appointment and dismissal.[98] He[99] was (and is) a public servant. He was to be appointed by the Governor-General acting in accordance with the advice of the Public Service Commission (who in turn had to consult the Prime Minister before presenting their nomination). The Attorney-General enjoyed great security of tenure. He could not be removed from office except for inability to exercise the functions of his office (whether arising from infirmity of body or mind or any other cause) or for misbehaviour. The question of his removal could be raised by the Prime Minister, Chairman of the Public Service Commission, or a regional President (which points to the need for the Attorney-General to be even-handed between the centre and regions), and if raised, it had to be referred to an independent tribunal consisting of senior Commonwealth judges, whose decision was binding on the Governor-General. This position did not last long for the very first constitutional amendment gave the President absolute discretion as to his appointment, although his tenure continued to be protected—but only until 1986, after

---

[97] There are numerous accounts of these violations. The most detailed general account is a report by Africa Watch n. 88 above. Amnesty has documented the use of torture in *Kenya: Torture, Political Detention and Unfair Trials* (1987). Issues of the *Nairobi Law Monthly* contain numerous analyses and accounts of violations.

[98] See Section 86 for his functions and Section 189 for his appointment and tenure.

[99] I use 'he' advisedly because all holders of this office have been males.

[100] The Constitution of Kenya (Amendment) Act of 1987.

which the President could remove him at will.[100] The office of the Attorney-General had become so political (equivalent almost to a Cabinet Minister) and its holders, for the most part, had so completely surrendered their independence, that in a way this mode of appointment or removal was not particularly anomalous.[101] Nevertheless, as part of the general return to more democratic and rule of law forms in 1990, his tenure was once again protected through the interposition of a tribunal (with no reference to Commonwealth judges).[102]

The Attorney-General's functions have not changed. All holders of the office have been able to centralise government legal advice in his office, as few departments are allowed their own counsel. In addition he has special responsibilities for prosecutions; he may institute prosecutions, take over prosecutions initiated by others, and may discontinue them before judgment. In this function he acts independently of direction or control of anyone else (Kenya having opted against having an independent Director of Public Prosecutions for this task). Since independence he has also been given the power to require the Commissioner of Police to investigate any matter which in his opinion relates to any offence, and its exercise too is a matter for his discretion.

In practice Attorneys-General have been very powerful and the post is much coveted (although no subsequent Attorney-General has enjoyed the status occupied by the first holder of this office). It is clear that the power of the office does not come from the functions prescribed in the Constitution, since, as will have become apparent, the government is not particularly concerned about legality, and until the present occupant, no Attorney-General has been distinguished by his grasp of the law. The powers of prosecution do vest the holder with considerable authority, but they only become a source of power if they are abused. His powers come from the closeness to the President and from his control over the legal system (including the investigatory process) (which has systematically been wrested away from the Chief Justice). Whatever the reasons, it is obvious that he has considerable capacity to further or damage the cause of rights and freedoms, particularly as they operate in the interstices of the legal system or are mediated through it.

Enough has been said in the preceding sections to suggest that no Attorney-General (until the present occupant) has shown any predilection for human rights.[103] No-one has taken any initiatives to improve the capacity for the bet-

[101] See the *Weekly Review* (Nairobi) (12 April 1991) for an account of the politics and performance of various Attorneys-General.

[102] The Constitution of Kenya (Amendment Act), No. 17 of 1990.

[103] On the other hand, the present occupant, Mr Amos Wako, is internationally well-known for his work in human rights, having been a United Nations Special Rapporteur on Arbitrary Execution from the early 1980s onwards, served on the United Nations Committee on Human Rights, and having acted as the Special Rapporteur of the United Nations Secretary-General on Disappearances in East Timor. Even he felt constrained to say in his maiden speech in Parliament that 'no man, save the President, is above the law'—which is patently not the legal or constitutional position (speech reported in 34 *Nairobi Law Monthly* (July 1991) 47). How he influences

ter fulfilment of constitutional human rights mandates. On the contrary, most of them have bent the legal process and system to arbitrary government purposes and for the harassment of political or personal opponents. The dominance of the Attorney-General has vested his subordinates with wide power as well, and this too has led to corruption. But it is the use of the criminal process to deal with persons deemed undesirable by the administration that has, for our purposes, led to the perversion of the law and its processes. Unlike its neighbour, Tanzania, the Kenyan Government has seldom been able to use the political party or the political process to control its supporters or opponents. Therefore considerable resort has been had to the criminal process.

At first the fact that important politicians could be hauled before the courts enhanced the image of the law as an impartial process and of the government for its commitment to the law.[104] Court processes were used to destroy reputations and careers. After some time, however, the selective nature of prosecutions became obvious. Politicians in grace got away with assault and damage to property and well-documented allegations of corruption went uninvestigated. Those out of grace were prosecuted for trifling offences. A particularly serious consequence for MPs of convictions in these trials was that if they were (as they regularly were) sentenced to more than 7 months imprisonment, they lost their seats (and it was widely believed that this was often the reason for prosecution). A pattern appeared to emerge so that a prosecution of an important person was assumed to be politically motivated.

It was not only this selective and political use of the legal process which served to discredit the law. The logic of the strategy led to a compromise with the fundamental principles of its process. Constitutional provision for an independent judiciary, access to counsel, public proceedings and reasoned decisions meant that the court process could not be as tightly controlled as the bureaucratic. It was necessary to undermine the open-endedness of the process, which it has been claimed, was achieved by the appointment of a few compliant magistrates and judges (especially expatriates on contract). It is significant that cases of this kind tend to be heard by a few judges, that bail is regularly refused, and severe punishments are inflicted. Numerous lawyers claim that these judges sought instructions from the executive before making their decisions (and this has now been corroborated by at least two judges who refused to toe the executive line).[105]

In order to ensure convictions, pressure was brought on defence lawyers.

the human rights' situation in Kenya is therefore of particular interest, and will tell us much about the triumph or otherwise of entrenched interests over good intentions.

[104] I have abstracted the following analysis from my paper, 'Law and Lawyers in Kenya and Tanzania: Some Political Economy Considerations' in Dias, Luckham, Lynch and Paul, *Lawyers in the Third World: Comparative and Developmental Perspectives* (1981) to which the reader is directed for references and authorities for statements in this section.

[105] Cotran and Schofield. See account in Africa Watch n. 88 above at 148–53.

Larger law firms were easier to control for they tended to depend on commercial work from the government and its corporations. Less subtle pressure was applied to other lawyers; one was deprived of his citizenship and deported; another was warned off for his work for trade unions and left practice for 2 years before being restored to grace. An extremely able defence lawyer who himself fell a victim to a prosecution, characterized his trial as follows, 'This prosecution is back to front. You choose the accused first. You look for an offence afterwards . . . It is not the first time that I have defended a case of this nature'. Lawyers who persisted in defence of politically marked accused despite these blandishments[106] suffered worse fates, including administrative detention and torture.

Growing militancy among a few lawyers and the determination to use constitutional and legal processes to secure justice for their clients led to major confrontations between them and the government which are mentioned in the next section. Suffice it to say by way of conclusion that, on the whole, Kenya has not been well served by its Attorneys-General, who have been more than accomplices in the conspiracies to destroy constitutional principles and the rule of law. They have failed again and again to live up to the time honoured traditions of chief law officers to maintain the coherence of legal principles and the integrity of the legal system.[107]

THE PRIVATE LEGAL PROFESSION

The record of the legal profession as defenders of human rights is mixed. In our study of the legal profession (principally during the colonial period) McAuslan and I concluded that the legal profession had never given a lead in the field of human rights and the Rule of Law since it acquired self-government in 1949. It acquiesced in the draconian regime of emergency laws before independence and since then had taken no stand against the extensive and harsh powers of preventive detention, the large amount of retrospective legislation introduced by the government, and the failure of the government to prosecute its supporters for breaking the law.[108] We were writing at a time when the profession was still dominated by Europeans and Asians, and it was easy to explain their lack of interest in human rights on the basis that they could not empathize with Africans who were the principal victims of the violations of rights. But there were undoubtedly structural problems as well;

[106] Men of courage like Dr. John Khaminwa, Gibson Kamau Kuria, Kiraitu Murungi, Gitobu Imanyara, Mirugi Kariuki, Rumba Kinuthia and Paul Muite.

[107] For a study of the trust vested in and responsibilities placed upon law officers, see Edwards, *The Law Officers of the Crown: a Study of the offices of Attorney General and Solicitor General of England with an Account of the office of the Director of Public Prosecutions of England* (1964) and *The Attorney General: Politics and the Public Interest* (1984).

[108] Ghai and McAuslan n. 1 above at 401–2.

financial rewards lay in commercial work. Moreover, Asian and European lawyers by now had little political clout, and were already beginning to feel vulnerable in changed political circumstances; safety was seen to lie in less spectacular work. Nor perhaps at this time was the potential in the Bill of Rights to challenge legislation or administrative policy and acts fully realized by the members of the profession who had been trained in England under the system of parliamentary supremacy.

Although some Asian lawyers participated in the defence of politically charged accused, it was not until the early 1980s that a significant challenge was advanced by a group of lawyers to repressive laws and practices. For the most part they were Africans, trained in East Africa where they had studied the Constitution. They had a strong academic background, having done graduate work, some research and in a few cases teaching. They were familiar with the jurisprudence of jurisdictions with fundamental rights and had a sense of the special nature of constitutional law. They became involved in challenges to the law on sedition and other restrictions on expression, arbitrary dismissals, administrative detentions, treason charges, and torture. Although there was a political dimension to most of these cases, at this time the nature of the involvement of the lawyers was non-political. Their primary commitment was to human rights and the rule of law. However, only a small number of cases were filed, and only a small number of lawyers were involved. The Law Society changed but little, and its affairs were dominated by professional matters and the cultivation of a positive image of lawyers—the usual functions of any law society. But these were high profile cases, and the lawyers involved in them became well known, both for the unusual nature of their challenge and for the harsh treatment meted out to them by the government. Despite their skills, dedication and courage, it cannot be said that they won many victories for human rights (not their fault—generally their arguments were excellent—more due to the timidity of the judiciary), except that they exposed, some times quite graphically, the extent and nature of violations of human rights.

It was not until the late 1980s that the involvement of lawyers in the matter of human rights changed. This time it was political, and while some lawyers continued to use the courts for legal challenges (including to the very legality of the one-party system), they now used many different fora and took to holding press conferences. They tackled a much broader set of issues, particularly those connected to electoral abuses and the suppression of political dissent and debate. Soon a multi-party democracy became their rallying cry. They sought alliances with other like-minded groups, especially among religious denominations, and made astute use of the media. Lawyers became the most active of the government's opponents. They made skilful use of the courts at a time when no forum was available to protest government policies (in the full knowledge that a coterie of judges would thwart their efforts to challenge violations of rights). They succeeded in raising public consciousness of the issues and of the oppressive practices of the Government. The *Nairobi Law Monthly* became the most radical and outspoken journal. The profession internationalized the issue of human rights in Kenya, and called for economic sanctions against the Government unless it undertook political reform. They succeeded in persuading the International Bar Association to cancel its large and prestigious bi-annual conference in 1990, as a rebuff to the Government for its human rights record.

That this was not action merely of a handful of lawyers is evidenced by the struggles for the control of the Law Society among its members (and the seriousness with which the government took them). When 'human rights lawyers' were detained in 1992, there was a most impressive show of solidarity by a large group of lawyers, who crowded the courts with their presence when habeas corpus applications were filed. In 1991 the 'radical' group[109] won control of the Law Society with the election of Paul Muite, who had been active in pro-multi-party democracy campaign, and was later to become the deputy leader of the new political party, FORD (the Forum for the Restoration of Democracy). The espousal by the Council of the Law Society of pro-democracy politics led the government to launch a concerted attack on the Society (and the increased harassment of its more active members). It succeeded in getting an injunction from the High Court to prevent its officials from making 'political' statements. Subsequently the chairman and other officials were charged with contempt for having violated the injunction.

There is little doubt that the political agitation by these lawyers played an important role in hastening the demise of the one-party system. And in subsequent campaigns and elections, lawyers were prominent. Although they used the rhetoric as well as the specific provisions of human rights, they did not succeed in persuading the courts to uphold rights and freedoms. In the inter-regnum between the declaration of multi-partyism and President Moi's re-election, it appeared as if the courts might become more sympathetic to their cause, but it was not long enough for useful precedents to emerge. Thus paradoxically we have to conclude that while a group of lawyers carried on a valiant fight for human rights in courts, their victories were few and generally insubstantial, while their more overtly political agitation was more effective. Nevertheless the framework for their political work was that of human rights (although it is hard to say whether the advocacy of human rights or some element of ethnic dissent was the decisive factor in their success).

---

[109] They were almost always referred to by the press (and their critics) as radicals, but they were radical only in a political sense, not economic. They seemed quite content with Kenya's market economy.

THE JUDICIARY

The independence Constitution recognised the key role of the judiciary in enforcing the Constitution. Consequently not only were judges made the final arbiters of its meaning, but their appointments were secured against political partisanship and their tenure was protected against political or executive interference.[110] The Chief Justice was to be appointed by the Governor-General on the advice of the Prime Minister. The Prime Minister was, however, to consult the Presidents of the regions and could not submit his nomination to the Governor-General unless Presidents of at least four regions (out of seven) endorsed it. Other judges were appointed on the nomination of an independent Judicial Service Commission. A judge could be removed only for inability to perform his/her job or for misconduct, the final judge of which was to be Privy Council.

The first constitutional amendment gave the President absolute powers of appointing the Chief Justice, eliminating any role for the regions. Judicial tenure was removed in 1988, so that it became dependent on the President,[111] but was restored in 1990 under considerable international and domestic pressure.[112] The Chief Justice plays a key role in the organization of the judicial work and in assigning responsibilities to different judges. It was pointed out in a preceding section that there has been a measure of collusion between some judges and the government, and the role of the Chief Justice can be crucial in that respect (particularly in ensuring that political cases are assigned to the 'right' judges, and if necessary, cajoling others).[113] It would seem that it is for that reason that particular care has been exercised in ensuring that an appointee to that office is likely to be sympathetic. One Chief Justice (Madan)

[110] Section 172 dealt with appointments and section 173 with tenure of judges of the Supreme Court.

[111] The Constitution of Kenya (Amendment) Act, No. 4 of 1988.

[112] The restoration of tenure may not be particularly significant unless administrative practices about the recruitment and posting of judges is made strictly within the constitutional framework. Despite a Judicial Commission, the influence of the government members on it is predominant. There is also the practice of doubtful constitutional propriety whereby judges are appointed on contract, not tenure. It would seem that this is true not only of expatriates (some of whom have been most vulnerable, and amenable, to official pressures) but also citizens. A few judges have resigned or refused renewal of their contracts because of these pressures or other forms of victimisation.

[113] See Africa Watch n. 88 above at ch. 9; interview with Schofield J. in the *Nairobi Law Monthly* (January 1988), who claimed to have resigned because of interference by Miller C.J., saying that 'any lawyer knows that he was not acting in accordance with the law. I cannot operate in a system where the law is so blatantly contravened by those who are supposed to be its supreme guardians'.

In a lengthy interview with me, former Justice Eugene Cotran outlined the numerous ways in which different Chief Justices had interfered with the course of justice to secure verdicts favourable to the Government.

See the report of the Robert Kennedy Centre for Human Rights, *Justice Enjoined*, which confirms these allegations.

who turned out to be more independent than was expected was suddenly relieved of his office (he had also objected to the removal of the jurisdiction of courts over land as the government had wanted, and had tried to raise the standards of probity among judges).[114]

Under the circumstances it is not surprising that the courts have not supported the cause of human rights. One must be careful not to generalise overmuch, for if no major political issue is involved, judges have frequently upheld the Constitution. It is thus possible to find judgments which have tried to ensure the provisions of fair trial, representation by advocates, and protection against double jeopardy. Courts have also secured the economic rights of litigants, either against discrimination or unlawful taking of property. In the only instance of the courts finding a statutory provision unconstitutional, a three member bench of the High Court held that Parliament could not restrict its right to give bail to accused charged with particular types of offences,[115] but in numerous cases judges have denied bail even though the trial has been long delayed and the actual offences have not been serious.[116] In a landmark case, the High Court has held that the discretion of the Attorney-General to prosecute can be judicially reviewed and that it is subject to the normal rules of the fair exercise of public authority and so must not be employed in an arbitrary or oppressive manner.[117]

However, decisions against upholding rights and freedoms are more numerous. The courts have regularly denied citizens the 'right' to a passport, although the constitutionally protected right to leave and enter Kenya cannot be exercised without it. They have preferred outdated notions of prerogative powers to the clear mandates of the Constitution.[118] Another area where the courts have failed abysmally is in the protection against arbitrary detentions

[114] See 18 *Nairobi Law Monthly* 16 for a history of Chief Justiceship in Kenya.

[115] *Ngui* v. *Republic* [1986] LRC (Const) 308.

[116] See Maina, 'Judicial Responses to Bail Applications: An Essay on Constitutionalism', 22 *The Nairobi Law Monthly* (1990) 31.

[117] *Githunguri* v. *Republic of Kenya* [1986] LRC (Const) 618.

[118] In *Re Application by Mwau*, High Court of Kenya at Nairobi *Misc. Civil Case No. 299 of 1983* (Reported in (1984) 10 *Commonwealth Law Bulletin*, July–October, at 1108–9), the Principal Immigration Officer withdrew the applicant's passport without giving any reason for so doing. The applicant brought suit seeking the return of his passport since the withdrawal constituted a violation of his freedom of movement under the Kenyan Constitution. He based his claim on s. 81(1) of the Constitution of Kenya which provides 'No citizen of Kenya shall be deprived of his freedom of movement, that is to say, the right to move freely throughout Kenya, *the right to enter Kenya, the right to leave Kenya* and immunity from expulsion from Kenya'.

The High Court held: (i) The issue and withdrawal of passports is the prerogative of the President and it is open to the minister responsible to decide on each application whether or not to grant a request in respect of the applicant. If the minister thinks it would not be in the best interests of the country to grant such a request it would be open to him to refuse to issue a passport. Subject to the directions of the President it is a matter entirely within the discretion of the minister *and being purely in the exercise of presidential prerogative, is not subject to judicial review*.

(ii) Although s. 81 of the Constitution recognizes that a citizen has a right to leave Kenya, the right is not absolute;

(iii) There is no statutory or legal duty laid upon the principal immigration officer to issue or

and long periods in police custody. The law on both these matters is reasonably clear, but the courts have chosen to disregard procedural safeguards and to believe the 'evidence' of the police. This failure has had monumental consequences for it effectively stifled debates and dissent, and the insecurity that the threat of detention (against which no judicial redress could be expected) meant that individuals as well groups were afraid to exercise their rights as citizens. It had the effect of negating most rights and freedoms.

Courts have provided no protection against torture and other inhuman and degrading treatment. They have done nothing to prevent massive abuses of the legal process—long remands in custody of accused against whom charges are frequently dropped, long detentions in custody without being charged or brought to court, the free use of 'confessions' so that important legal issues are not litigated, etc. They have shown little understanding of the nature or value of human rights, of the jurisprudence on these matters built up carefully and deliberately over years by international, regional and national courts. They have paid no regard to Kenya's international obligations regarding human rights.[119] They have made no attempt to establish a proper balance between a right or freedom and restrictions on it, and have forgotten that restrictions cannot be so extensive or broad that they extinguish the right or freedom. In many cases they have accorded a higher privilege to restrictions than the substantive right to which they are attached.[120] All this has involved them in great casuistry (as for example in deciding on the legal status of the

return passports, he acts in accordance with instructions given by the minister; and an order of mandamus does not lie against him.

This decision was affirmed by the Court of Appeal. See J.B. Ojwang and J.A. Otieno Odek, 'The Judiciary in Sensitive Areas of Public Law: Emerging Approaches to Human Rights Litigation in Kenya', (1988) XXXV *Netherlands International Law Review*, Issue 1 at 44.

See also 'The Extra-Ordinary Saga of a Citizen, John Harun Mwau's Request for a Passport Reveals Uncertainty in Kenya's Passport Law', *Nairobi Law Monthly*, December 1988 to January 1989 at 6–10.

[119] Kenya is signatory to the International Covenant on Civil and Political Rights, the International Covenant on Economic, Social and Cultural Rights, and the conventions on refugees, women and children, the ILO Convention No. 98 and the African Charter of Human and Peoples Rights. But as far as I can tell, judges have never referred to them to resolve ambiguities in the Constitution or other laws.

[120] This approach goes against the now well-established rule adopted by most international and Commonwealth courts that the provisions for human rights must be given an expansive meaning, avoiding 'the austerity of tabulated legalism', as warned by Lord Wilberforce in *Ministry of Home Affairs* v. *Fisher* [1989] AC 319 at 329.

The High Court decision in *Njeru* (above pp. 166–7) is a typical example of narrow formalism that courts now elsewhere uniformly deprecate. Trevelyan and Hancox JJ., rejecting the plaintiff's argument that 'without prejudice' meant 'apart from', said, 'but we prefer 'without derogating from', the Latin 'prae' meaning (for our purposes) before in point of time and 'judicium' meaning judgement, which leads us to the conclusion that you can apply under section 84(1) before but not after you have taken other action . . .'. Another argument they advanced was that the section says 'other action . . . is' available, not 'was' available! (Ibid. at 159–60). The judges made no attempt to discover what might have been the intention behind giving a special remedy under section 84 for the redress of the violation of rights and freedoms.

Law Society and the then sole party, KANU, for the purposes of its jurisdiction—not surprisingly, both cases came before the same judge, whose task was complicated by the fact that consistency would be inconvenient!).[121]

The courts have been particularly weak where they should have been most robust, the defence of legal process rights. The almost invariable refusal of bail in any case suspected to have a political angle, the sanctioning of long periods of detention, and the disregard of evidence pointing to ill-treatment and torture, and the bias in favour of prosecution 'evidence', has meant that various criminal charges are not litigated properly for by the time of the trial the accused has been coerced into a plea of guilty. This is particularly so in the cases of sedition and breaches of the peace.[122] The result is that no evidence is presented and there is no opportunity to argue the points of law. Consequently we do not have a reasonable judicial discussion of the elements of sedition or the reach of defences against it, or what action may properly constitute breach of the peace.[123] Yet these offences have been used extensively to

[121] A challenge was made to the rules enunciated by KANU for the nomination of candidates for Parliament and their implementation. Akiwumi J. held that the Court had no jurisdiction to entertain the suit, for although KANU could not be said to be 'a club in the ordinary sense of the word', all its members must be deemed to have consented to its rules, and in the absence of bad faith, the court would not interfere. The court thus ignored the fact that KANU was legally the sole political party, that it had a constitutional status, and that the effect of the regulations was that in many cases, this preliminary process decided the election of members of Parliament. It was well known that the 1988 elections (the subject of this litigation) were the most corrupt and rigged in the country's history. See *Kefa Wagara* v. *Anguka* (High Court, Civil Case 724 of 1988) reported in the *Nairobi Law Monthly* (March 1988) 12.

When Paul Muite was elected Chairman of the Law Society, a number of members of the Society sought to gag him in his public statements by seeking an injunction, and obtained from Dugdale J., an order barring Muite from presiding over meetings of the Council of the Society and making statements of a 'political nature'. The appeal was heard by Akiwumi J. who rejected the argument that the courts could not interfere in the internal affairs of a society. See Ross, 'Lawyers in Kenya' (1992) *Journal of Modern African Studies* 421.

[122] For copious illustrations, Africa Watch n. 88 above at ch. 8.

[123] The case of Rev. Ndege Imunde, a well known opponent of some of the harsher practices of the government, may serve as an example. He was arrested outside his hotel in Nairobi, and his diary and letters were confiscated. Nothing was heard of him until he managed to smuggle a letter to his wife from a police station. She filed a habeas corpus writ, but Imunde refused to see the lawyer (Kiraitu Murungi) she had briefed, although he had earlier notified his wife and the police of his wish to have counsel. On pleading guilty he was sentenced to 6 years imprisonment. It turned out that the police had threatened him with further reprisals if he engaged counsel, and promised him release if he did not. But the prosecution asked for and obtained this stiff sentence.

The evidence against him consisted of entries in his diary which were mildly critical of the government. The entries were not intended for publication and had not been communicated to anyone else, so that a crucial element of sedition was missing. He alleged that the police forced him to add further entries, including the comment, 'Can't someone or a group do something while he [President Moi] is away . . . to change our situation for prosperity?' (a sophisticated version of planting evidence, not unknown in Kenyan police practice).

On appeal, when these facts were alleged, the sentence was reduced, but the court refused to address the questions of whether the entries could be publication for the purposes of the offence of sedition or whether the confession of guilt was secured through duress.

This account is based on personal interviews as well as a report in Africa Watch n. 88 above at 138–42.

punish and silence opposition to the government or the ruling party, and have become the fulcrum for the destruction of many other rights and freedoms.

The attitudes of the courts have meant that recourse to courts for protection is rarely sought. There are no great judicial statements on human rights, on the relationship between citizens and the state, on the responsibilities of public office, etc. Most constitutional judgments are brief, involve no close examination of the relevant sections of the Constitution, dwell on the restrictions on rights but make no attempt to relate them to the circumstances of the case, and avoid foreign precedents when they are inconvenient.[124] This has greatly impoverished public and private debates in the country. The judiciary has failed to live up to its responsibilities, and has ensured the mockery of the Constitution.

Conclusion: The Reason for the Ineffectiveness of the Bill of Rights

Most African states adopted shortly before or at independence a Bill of Rights, very similar in form and content to that in Kenya. In the large majority of instances, the Bill of Rights was no more effective than in Kenya. How is one to explain the ineffectiveness of the Bill of Rights? This Chapter has suggested some specific Kenyan reasons.

Elsewhere, in an attempt to provide a theory of 'African constitutionalism', I have argued, drawing upon Weberian typologies, that there has been a major shift in African states in the systems of governance from the legal-rational to patrimonialism.[125] It is well known that the notion of the Rule of Law is associated with a mode of domination and legitimation, the rational-legal, which Weber regarded as central to the development and functioning of the modern state.[126] The authority of state actions is founded in the law, which also provides the basic framework for the institutions and operation of the state. No-one is above the law, which is itself purposive and rational, the product of human deliberation and consensus. The principal instrument of the state is the bureaucracy, recruited on the basis of merit and expertise. Its neutrality and impartiality are ensured through an independent method of recruitment and

---

[124] A typical judgment is that of Sachdeva J. in *Mutunga* v. *Republic* (a bail application reported in 16 *Nairobi Law Monthly* 33).

[125] 'The Theory of the State in the Third World and the Problematics of Constitutionalism' in Douglas, Greenberg et al. eds., *Constitutionalism and Democracy: Transitions in the Contemporary World* (1993) and 'Towards a Theory of African Constitutions: A Prolegomenon' in Adelman and Paliwala eds., *Law and Crisis in the Third World* (1993).

As I mention there, although my typologies are Weberian, my explanation is Marxian.

[126] The most accessible presentation of Weber's view on law and economy is Rheinstein ed., *Max Weber on Law in Economy and Society* (1954). A more complete collection is Ruth and Wittich eds., *Max Weber, Economy and Society* (1978).

promotion as well as fidelity to the law. Independent judges, helped by an independent legal profession, act in a general supervisory role over the constitutional and political system, subjecting it to the discipline of the law. The ideology and legitimation of such a state is the Rule of Law. The constitutions of most African states on independence conformed to this model.

Patrimonialism is a different mode of domination, characterized by the personal regime of a ruler. Power is centralized in him and the administration is based on his total power and unfettered discretion. The bureaucracy is an extension of his household, and to which he delegates his powers. Officials owe their appointments to his trust and goodwill. There is no clear separation of the public and the private spheres of the ruler. He is above the law (as are his officials so long as they are in his grace) and dispenses justice according to his whims; petitions to him for clemency and generosity substitute for legal writs. Opposition is not tolerated and is harshly treated. The ideological superstructure of such domination is the goodness, generosity and the concern of the ruler for his people. He is the 'father of his people', 'the father of his nation'.

It is possible to establish, through the successive amendments of the Constitution and laws, the shift in Kenya (and other African states) from the legal-rational to patrimonialism. Law is not the only (and often not the principal) instrument for this shift; much reliance is placed on extra- and illegal measures, in the expectation that no-one would dare to challenge them. An apparatus of coercion and oppression (again a mixture of the legal and the illegal) is established to deal with those who resist the exercise of arbitrary exercise of patrimonialism, while the resources of the state provide a ready source of patronage to keep others in line.

The explanation for this shift lies in the nature and purposes of the state in Africa. The state is an imposition, and stands in a relationship of antagonism to civil society (unlike in the West where it may be said, admittedly with some simplification, that the state grew out of and was reflective of civil society). I have already discussed the colonial state, which, with its mission of subjugation of indigenous society, bequeathed a legacy of authoritarianism and a corresponding apparatus of coercion to new African rulers (which has undoubtedly facilitated the shift from legal-rational to patrimonialism). Independence facilitated the access to state power of leaders who had only a weak hold in the economy (here again representing a contrast with the West where the state reflected underlying economic forces in society, arising out of the industrial-market revolutions and committed to the maintenance of social relationships that grew from the economy). The state therefore became the primary form for the accumulation of wealth for this new class. The market has to be tightly controlled, so that one economic group may be replaced by another, and the regime of rules, considered so functional to a market economy, has consequently no particular value. The use of state resources involved essentially what one may call primitive accumulation, which took the form primarily of exploitation of the peasantry and workers. Compulsory state marketing channels and other forms of state enterprise are frequently used for the former; serious restrictions on trade union rights are necessary for the latter. As the state is the primary instrument of accumulation, corruption is endemic, woven into the very fabric of the apparatus of the state. The pressures towards corruption arise not only from economic greed, but also from the imperatives of political survival, since the main basis of a politician's support is generally not the party or another political platform, but clientilism, sustained by regular favours to one's followers. Public control and accountability over that apparatus are unacceptable; resistance on the part of the exploited is met with coercion. The role of constitutions and laws becomes totally instrumental, unmediated by autonomous processes and procedures. Law itself becomes a commodity that only the state may mobilize and manipulate. The government thinks it dangerous to allow dominated groups any purchase on the law, except as part of careful stage management. In these circumstances it becomes impossible to secure the enforcement of rights and freedoms.

The domestic and international environment was not unpropitious to the centralization of power. The leitmotif of the time was 'nation building' and economic development, and African leaders managed to present the independence constitutions (with the diffusion of power and checks and balances) as obstacles to the achievement of these goals. Arguments were also presented as to the failure of the constitutions to reflect the 'African personality' and understandings of authority and power.[127] Thus from the very beginning the legitimacy of these Constitutions was undermined, the ideology of legality replaced by that of developmentalism. (The legal system was allowed to atrophy; law reports ceased to be published, law libraries were run down, the system of filing in courts became the victim of inefficiency and corruption). The fact that this was merely a cover for the aggrandisement and consolidation of personal power did not become obvious until later. There were few domestic groups with a genuine commitment to human rights (for the truth is that anti-colonialism was not about human rights but about black power). The European community which had been in the vanguard of the demands for a Bill of Rights, realising that its political clout had diminished with decolonisation, rapidly made its peace with the Kenyatta regime, and secure in the knowledge that its interests could be protected in other ways, lost interest in the Bill—such was its commitment to human rights! The situation was muddied by incipient ethnic competition for state and other resources, so that violations of human rights took on increasingly a tribal coloration and got interwoven (and disappeared) in ethnic politics.[128]

[127] See Ghai, 'Constitutions and the Political Order in East Africa' (1972) 21 ICLQ 403.
[128] Unfortunately Kenya is not the only country where ethnic differences, propagating a strong

Internationally, this was the time of the cold war, when western powers were keen to have protégés in Africa and establish conditions for western investments. It seemed easier to deal with a strong man and centralised administration than work one's way through a complex political process. Kenya's early commitment to the market (albeit controlled market) economy and willingness to have foreign troops stationed there quickly established it as the favourite of the United Kingdom and the USA, who were thenceforth willing to turn a blind eye to the violations of human rights (and whose military support in fact facilitated these violations). There was no talk of 'conditionality' then. The Organisation of African Unity was becoming increasingly a trade union of authoritarian rulers, and no support for human rights could be expected from that quarter.

In these circumstances it easy to understand that the Bill of Rights became largely irrelevant (and this explains why successive constitutions in Africa, erecting strong and unchallengeable presidencies, then one-party systems, and in some instances, military regimes, have retained the inherited Bill of Rights). Even if a judicial decision favourable for human rights can be secured, it seems to have little impact on administrative or police practice, or indeed on subsequent litigation. However, this assessment needs a qualification. The experience of the 1980s shows that the Bill is not without effect in other ways. The skilful use of it by a few lawyers tied the government in litigation of key political issues. Courts became the only venue where these issues could be aired. They exposed the inconsistencies and malpractices of the government and raised public consciousness of rights and politics (the *Nairobi Law Monthly*, using law as the medium of exposure, became the best-selling journal). The Bill established standards by which the conduct of the government and the courts could be judged. It inspired the establishment and work of some NGOs. It helped to produce a sense of solidarity among disparate persons working for social and political reform. For a time it provided the only alternative coherent ideology to that of tribalism and one-partyism of the government. It also enabled democratic struggles in Kenya to be linked to the growing international concern with rights and democracy, and being focused on rights which by now were proclaimed as universal rather than on specifics of local politics, it facilitated the engagement of foreign private and official institutions. These linkages were skilfully exploited. In reversals of previous policies, western powers imposed 'conditionalities' of democracy and rights.

The salience of the Bill of Rights from the mid 1980s resulted from a congruence of growing dissatisfaction with the government among key Kenyan communities and groups and foreign interest in democracy and rights in the wake of the ending of the cold war. They may represent a new conjuncture in which rights and freedoms would thrive and the Bill of Rights begin to come

sense of the 'other', have dulled the consciousnes or concern about human rights violations. The connections between ethnicity and human rights is an under-researched area.

to life. But it is important to remember that both these forces are fragile and unreliable. It is hard to assess how far the opposition to the Moi administration has been based on its violations of rights and how far it represents ethnic disenchantment with his tribal politics. Some of the political leaders now regarded as the advocates of human rights have in the past served happily under President Moi when government practices were no different. The results of recent general elections show support for and opposition to Moi was divided largely along ethnic lines (even after allowing for alleged electoral malpractices). So a change of guard may not inaugurate a happier era of human rights. International support for human rights is equally opportunistic. It is one of many elements that go to make up the foreign policy of a western state, the underlying basis of which is the national self-interest, as is amply demonstrated by the reversal of the USA policy on the link between trade and human rights in its relations with China.

Fortunately, ethnic dissatisfaction and foreign opportunism are not the only supports for human rights. The authoritarianism of African rulers and the bankruptcies of their policies have raised a consciousness of the value of human rights. A number of NGOs, with a commitment to human rights, have arisen. There is greater awareness of the procedures to secure human rights (and a growing number of lawyers willing to risk the use of them). The international environment is supportive. The role of the state is being down graded. There are growing demands for public accountability. Despite these promising circumstances, the task of securing human rights will remain formidable, unless the legacy of colonial bureaucratic and authoritarian structures is disowned and dismantled (and that unfortunately is not in sight).

7

The Canadian Charter of Rights and Freedoms: A Feminist Perspective

MARY EBERTS*

1992 was the tenth anniversary of the coming into force of the Constitution Act 1982, containing the Canadian Charter of Rights and Freedoms.[1] The Charter is not the first measure to provide entrenchment in the constitution of basic rights guarantees: the Constitution Act 1867 provided certain assurances of minority language and denominational school rights, as part of the constitutional bargain at Confederation.[2] However, the Charter guarantees a wide range of fundamental freedoms and political, language, mobility, legal, and equality rights, and thus is the most thoroughgoing venture in rights protection in Canadian history. Experience with interpretation and enforcement of these rights will be of interest, and possibly assistance, to other jurisdictions considering whether to entrench basic guarantees.

It being impracticable to comment on the full range of experience over the first decade, I offer here a narrower perspective. As a feminist advocate, I was involved in efforts to promote women's equality in the 'pre-Charter' era, and subsequently in the discussions and advocacy which shaped the nature of the Charter's equality guarantees. Since 1985, when these equality guarantees came into effect,[3] I have been engaged in litigation invoking them, both as a counsel and as a founder of Canada's only national organization dedicated to test case litigation to promote women's equality, the Women's Legal Education and Action Fund ('LEAF'). My observations, then, relate to the effectiveness of the Charter as a means of promoting the equality of disadvantaged or excluded groups. My particular vantage point means that I will concentrate on the Charter's effect on women's equality; and limitations of time and space require that I focus my analysis primarily on the work of the Supreme Court of Canada. It is also appropriate to note that this Chapter is

---

* I wish to thank Lucy McSweeney, B.Sc., LL.B., for her valuable assistance with the research for this Chapter while she was a summer student at Tory Tory DesLauriers & Binnington and thank the firm for making her time and mine available for this undertaking.

[1] Constitution Act 1982 Sch. B to Canada Act 1982 (UK) Clause 11.

[2] Constitution Act 1867 (UK) ss. 93, 133 (30 & 31 Victoria, Clause 3).

[3] Although the Constitution Act 1982 and Charter came into effect in 1982, the Charter provided in Section 32(2) that the equality guarantees found in Section 15 of the Charter would not come into effect for a further 3 years. They came into effect on 17 April 1985.

written from the perspective of an English-Canadian; experience suggests to me that women in Quebec may have a different perspective on the Charter and it would be presumptuous of me to claim any particular Canadian point of view. Similarly, as a white lawyer who practises in central Canada, I am aware that my view of women's experience with the Charter will not easily encompass the experience of poor women, of women with a disability, lesbians, women of colour, or Aboriginal women. This Chapter does not claim to be 'representative' and should not be taken as such. However, I hope that its one perspective will nonetheless prove illuminating for those considering how best to protect and advance rights in a jurisdiction that does not yet have an entrenched Bill of Rights.

In this Chapter, I first examine the background developments leading up to the coming into force of the Charter of Rights, and offer a brief outline of the Charter's guarantees, as a framework for the discussion to follow. Then I examine the experience of the Supreme Court in dealing with women's rights issues under the Charter. It is tempting simply to use a scorecard approach to this assessment, reporting on women's gains and losses in this first period of Charter interpretation. While my account will certainly enable the reader to discern my reading of the scorecard, I hope to do more than this. Entrenched Bills of Rights are often subject to the criticism that they give power to unelected judges, who are drawn from a narrow segment of the community and then work in a remote setting, where they are unaccountable for their actions. Accordingly, I think that it is important to review the Court's work with a view to discerning the extent to which it has been able to adopt the perspective of women in analysing the problems that come before it. Women have been excluded for centuries from the making of laws, and from their administration, only coming into the legal profession in any numbers in recent years. Women judges are rare. Making women's perspective (or perspectives) part of judicial decision-making, then, would be a real achievement, helping to contradict or unravel the assumption that judicial work, like other law-making, can be seen as gender neutral.

Following a survey of the Court's work from this vantage point, I then conclude with some observations about the factors that have contributed to the comparatively positive experience of Charter adjudication on women's issues, and point out some areas of concern for the future.

The Background to the Charter of Rights

By 1980, when the Federal proposals for what later became the Charter of Rights were put forward, a number of developments had taken place that were to be important to the achievement and later interpretation of the Charter's guarantees.

In 1960, the Federal Government of Progressive Conservative John Diefenbaker had passed the Canadian Bill of Rights.[4] Applying only to the Federal Government, it provided for certain guarantees of legal and equality rights, but gave courts no power to declare inoperative a Statute which offended the protections. The record of the Supreme Court of Canada in interpreting and applying these guarantees was disappointing: it refused to strike down the Criminal Code provisions limiting access to abortion,[5] it ruled that discrimination against pregnant women in the Unemployment Insurance Act was discrimination on the basis of nature, not law;[6] and it held that the Bill's equality before the law guarantees applied only to the administration and not the substance of legislation, declining to invalidate a provision which deprived Indian women (but not men) of status under the Indian Act upon marriage to non-Indians.[7]

By 1980, human rights legislation was in place in every jurisdiction in Canada, and its protections had expanded to include not only the initial prohibitions of racial and ethnic discrimination but also discrimination on the basis of sex, marital status, and handicap. In *Bhadauria* v. *Seneca College*,[8] the Supreme Court of Canada precluded tort actions for discrimination, holding that remedies for violations of human rights Code prohibitions were available only through the enforcement mechanisms provided for in the Codes themselves. This method involved initial investigation by a human rights Commission, and adjudication before independent, specialized, ad hoc Boards of Inquiry of cases which were deemed to warrant it. Courts became involved only at the stage of enforcement of the Board awards, or on appeal. As one observer has pointed out, this exclusive reliance on specialized human rights tribunals as 'Courts of first instance' meant that the legal doctrine of discrimination developed under the aegis of persons committed to the aims of the codes, and knowledgeable in the area, instead of in Courts which had had a disappointing record in the interpretation of the Canadian Bill of Rights.[9] By the 1980s a large and sophisticated body of jurisprudence had grown up around the human rights Codes, which later informed the interpretation of the Charter's guarantees.

Activism on the part of disadvantaged groups, such as women, the disabled, gays and lesbians, and members of racial and ethnic minorities, had played a role in the extension of the provisions of the human rights Codes which took place in the 1970s and 1980s, and in securing other key legislative reforms, for example, family property changes, protections for victims of sexual assault in

---

[4] Canadian Bill of Rights, 8–9 Eliz. II, Clause 44, assented to 10 August 1960.
[5] *Morgentaler* v. *R.* [1976] 1 SCR 616.
[6] *Bliss* v. *Attorney-General (Canada)* [1979] 1 SCR 183.
[7] *Re Lavell* v. *Attorney-General (Canada)* [1974] SCR 1349.   [8] [1981] 2 SCR 181.
[9] This point was made by Québec lawyer Béatrice Vizkelety at a conference sponsored by the Women's Legal Education and Action Fund (LEAF) in Ottawa, Canada: LEAF Equality Symposium, mid-February 1992.

the criminal process, and provisions in Federal law calling for equal pay for work of equal value. Aboriginal women had struggled throughout the years to secure removal of the Indian Act provision which effected their 'statutory excommunication' upon marriage to non-Indians. The activities of some of these groups were assisted by the policy of the Federal Government, Liberal in the 1970s and 1980s, to fund certain interest groups outside the Parliamentary structure. This measure was intended to facilitate input by the disadvantaged into policy-making processes in which they would not otherwise have a role (because of their absence from elected office and senior bureaucratic positions); it did not provide funding on a broad basis, or even a particularly generous one, but did enable some greater participation than might otherwise have been the case.

The intersection of these earlier examples of rights advocacy and the constitutional renewal process occurred in 1978, when Prime Minister Trudeau proposed to cede to the provinces Federal jurisdiction over marriage and divorce. Alarmed by what this might mean for enforcement and variation of support and custody orders in a Federal State, and at the prospect that some provinces might even return to their traditional opposition to divorce, grassroots activists (mostly women) mounted opposition to the proposal. Effective lobbyists as a result of years of family property law reform activities, these groups managed to stall the momentum of the Federal initiative. This episode served to alert women to the practical implications of a constitutional renewal process that had been proceeding sporadically for years without attracting their attention or interest.[10] The women of English Canada, in particular, were thus ready for the round of constitutional lobbying and advocacy which attended the Federal proposal for an entrenched Charter of Rights in the early 1980s.

The Federal Liberal Government intended that patriation of the Canadian Constitution would result from its initiatives in 1980; there is relatively widespread consensus that its sponsorship of entrenched rights guarantees ('the people package') was intended to rally public support for the measure, short-circuiting the opposition of the provinces.[11] The strategy was to a large extent successful: both patriation and entrenchment of rights guarantees were achieved. However, such success came at a high cost: almost 2 years of political manoeuvring to improve the Charter's equality guarantees and keep them from being rendered ineffective by the provision permitting legislative 'override' of Charter provisions left many advocacy groups suspicious of Government intentions and determined not to leave interpretation of the guarantees to courts staffed by Government lawyers and adjudicated by male

[10] See Eberts, 'Women and Constitutional Renewal', in Doer and Carrier eds., *Women and The Constitution in Canada* (1981), 3.

[11] Hôsek, 'Women and Constitutional Process', in Banting and Simeon eds., *And No One Cheered* (1983), 280.

decision-makers. Moreover, the patriation bargain was not accepted by Quebec, which for several years thereafter regularly used the override to exclude the Charter's application to provincial laws, and remained estranged from English Canada.

The public's allegiance to the goals of the Charter greatly surpassed the expectations of its Federal proponents in 1980 to 1982. The commitment has continued. During the three year postponement of the coming into effect of the Charter's equality guarantees, it was expected that Governments would make the legislative amendments necessary to ensure compliance with the Charter. They did little in furtherance of this objective. However, the delay had another result: the women's groups active in Charter lobbying took the opportunity to establish LEAF and begin the fundraising that would sponsor its test cases, the first of which were begun the day the equality guarantees came into effect.[12] Within a short time, other Charter litigation groups had come into existence: the Canadian Disability Rights Council, the Minority Advocacy Rights Council of the Canadian Ethnocultural Council, the Charter Committee on Poverty Issues, and L'Égale, an advocacy organization for gays and lesbians. These specialized litigation organizations joined others who used litigation as one of their strategies, for example the National Anti-Poverty Organization and the Canadian Abortion Rights Action League. The Federal Government provided a modest amount of funding for litigation dealing with equality and language rights through its Charter Challenges Program, administered by a non-governmental agency which screened and approved cases.

These litigation organizations have played an important role in informing the decision-making of the Supreme Court of Canada. The Court has recently declared that: 'Public interest organizations are, as they should be, frequently granted intervener status. The views and submissions of interveners on issues of public importance frequently provide great assistance to the Courts.'[13] The Supreme Court has granted intervener status in criminal appeals,[14] and in actions between individuals[15] as well as in what could be seen as more conventional cases: applications by individuals or groups for declaratory

---

[12] These were the cases of Suzanne Bertrand, in Yukon Territory, seeking the right to use her birth name although married, and of Brenda Horvath and Sheila Beaudette, Ontario women challenging the welfare administrators' rule that a woman in any sort of relationship with a man could not claim mother's allowance because the man, not the State, should support her children. All three women were successful, Ms Bertrand in an unreported decision of the Yukon Supreme Court, and the Ontario women as a result of a settlement arrived at with the Government that ushered in a change of the rule.

[13] *Canadian Council of Churches* v. *Canada* (1992) 88 DLR (4th) 193 at 207 per Cory J.

[14] In, for example, *R.* v. *Keegstra* [1990] 3 SCR 697; *R.* v. *Seaboyer* [1991] 2 SCR 577; *R.* v. *Swain* [1991] 1 SCR 933; *R.* v. *Sullivan* [1991] 1 SCR 489.

[15] See *Tremblay* v. *Daigle* [1989] 2 SCR 530; *Norberg* v. *Wynrib* [1992] 2 SCR 226; *K. M.* v. *H. M.* [1992] 3 SCR 6; *Moge* v. *Moge* (unreported, Supreme Court of Canada, No. 21979, 17 December 1992) per L'Heureux-Dubé J.

relief.[16] Particularly in cases where equality-promoting legislation is under attack, such interventions can increase public confidence in the process by ensuring that arguments in favour of upholding the Statute will reflect not just the perspective of Government (which frequently is simply balancing opposing interests) but also of those whose interests are protected by the legislation.

The Scheme of the Charter

The Charter contains a number of substantive guarantees, of fundamental freedoms, and of political, mobility, legal, language, and equality rights. For example, Section 7 provides that everyone has the right to life, liberty, and security of the person, and the right not to be deprived thereof except in accordance with the principles of fundamental justice. Section 15(1) guarantees that every individual is equal before and under the law and has the right to the equal protection and equal benefit of the law without discrimination and, in particular, without discrimination based on race, national or ethnic origin, religion, sex, age, or mental or physical disability. Although grounds such as citizenship and sexual orientation are not specifically mentioned in Section 15, they have been held to be protected.[17] The touchstone for whether any particular non-enumerated ground can serve as the basis for a Section 15 challenge seems to be whether the person advancing the claim is a member of a 'discrete and insular minority' which has suffered social, political, and legal disadvantage, as indicated by such signals as stereotyping, historical disadvantage, or vulnerability to political and social prejudice.[18] Subsection 15(2) specifically provides that the basic equality guarantee does not preclude any law, program, or activity that has as its object the amelioration of conditions of disadvantaged individuals or groups, including those disadvantaged because of the characteristics enumerated in subsection (1).

Section 28 of the Charter, added following a round of intense lobbying by women's groups in 1981, provides that notwithstanding anything in the Charter, the rights and freedoms referred to in it are guaranteed equally to male and female persons. This Section has not yet received an authoritative interpretation from the Supreme Court of Canada.

Rather than leave the fashioning of limits on Charter rights entirely to judicial discretion, the framers clearly stated such a limit in Section 1: the rights and freedoms guaranteed in the Charter are subject only to such reasonable limits prescribed by law as can be demonstrably justified in a free and democ-

---

[16] *Canadian Newspapers* v. *Canada* [1988] 2 SCR 122; *Andrews* v. *Law Society of British Columbia* [1989] 1 SCR 143; *Borowski* v. *Canada (Attorney-General)* [1989] 1 SCR 342; *Schacter* v. *Canada* [1992] 2 SCR 679.

[17] *Andrews* n. 16 above; *Haig and Birch* v. *The Queen in Right of Canada* (1992) 9 OR (3d) 495.

[18] *R.* v. *Turpin* [1989] 1 SCR 1296 at 1332–3 per Wilson J.

ratic society. A few guarantees are expressed in terms that carry with them internal or self-limits: for example, the rights of mobility guaranteed by Section 6 are subject to any laws or practices of general application in force in a province other than those that discriminate among persons primarily on the basis of province of present or previous residence. The other major source of limits on Charter rights is Section 33, the famous 'override' provision that overcame the opposition to the Charter of provincial Governments in English Canada. It provides that Parliament or the Legislature of a province may expressly declare that a statute shall operate notwithstanding the guarantees of freedom of conscience and religion, expression, peaceful assembly, and association found in Section 2, the legal rights in Sections 7–14, or the equality rights in Section 15. Political, language, and mobility rights are immune from the override, as is the Section 28 gender equality provision. The declaration permitted by Section 33 may remain in effect for up to 5 years and be re-enacted for additional 5-year periods.

The Court has often articulated the approach to be taken to an analysis of the position under Section 1 of the Charter. While emphasizing that the task is not to be performed in a mechanistic fashion, it sets out two parts of a balancing exercise. The starting point of the inquiry is an assessment of the objectives of the law to determine whether they are sufficiently important to warrant the limitation of the constitutional right. The objectives must be found to be 'pressing and substantial' following an analysis that tests them against the fundamental values of a democratic society. These have been held to include respect for the inherent dignity of the human person, commitment to social justice and equality, accommodation of a wide range of beliefs, respect for cultural and group identity, and faith in social and political institutions which enhance the participation of individuals and groups in society.[19] The challenged law is then subjected to a proportionality test in which the objective of the impugned law is balanced against the nature of the right, the extent of its infringement, and the degree to which the limitation furthers other rights or policies of importance in a free and democratic society.

The proportionality test which forms the second stage of the analysis normally has three aspects: the limiting measures must be carefully designed, or rationally connected, to the objective; they must impair the right as little as possible; and their effects must not so severely trench on individual or group rights that the legislative objective, albeit important, is nevertheless outweighed by the abridgment of rights.

Where the law in question represents an incursion by the State against the individual, the Court has indicated that it will normally accord very little leeway to the Government in the Section 1 analysis. Where, however, the impugned statute represents an attempt by the State to balance different

[19] *R. v. Oakes* [1986] 1 SCR 103 at 136, 138–9 per Dickson C.J.C.

interests, it would appear that more tolerance for legislative choice will be exhibited, particularly if those choices have been in favour of protecting a vulnerable group.[20]

Section 24 of the Charter provides that anyone whose rights or freedoms as guaranteed by the Charter have been infringed or denied may apply to a Court of competent jurisdiction to obtain such remedy as the Court considers appropriate and just in the circumstances. Section 52 of the Constitution Act 1982 provides that the Constitution of Canada is the supreme law of Canada, and any law that is inconsistent with it is, to the extent of the inconsistency, of no force or effect.

The Supreme Court has recently held in *Schachter* v. *Canada*[21] that a Court has flexibility in determining what course of action to take following a violation of the Charter which does not survive Section 1 scrutiny. Pursuant to Section 52, a Court may simply strike down a law, it may strike down and temporarily suspend the declaration of invalidity, or it may resort to the techniques of 'reading down' or 'reading in'. The Court has set out very intricate guidelines for determining which of these remedies will be appropriate. Remedies under Section 52 follow upon a finding of institutional invalidity; action under Section 24 presupposes the constitutionality of the Statute, and focuses on unconstitutional behaviour by Government. Rarely will an individual remedy under Section 24 be available in connection with action under Section 52. In choosing how to apply Section 52 or Section 24, a Court should refer to the nature of the violation and the context of the specific legislation under consideration.[22]

Human Rights and Charter Equality Rights: a Direct Inheritance

The 3-year hiatus in the coming into effect of the main equality guarantees of the Charter had an additional positive, if unintended, effect besides affording groups the opportunity to create litigation organizations. The interpretation of the new equality guarantees was recognized, even by equality advocates, as potentially troubling to the Court, because of the positive nature of the equality right.[23] The Court's record with the equality cases in the Bill of Rights had given further cause for concern; the debate on the prospect that the whole approach to the Charter could be weakened because of reservations by the Court about all, or some, of the equality rights was, in 1982, a lively one.

During the 3-year hiatus, however, the Courts could embark upon consideration of the Charter without having to come to grips with the additional

---

[20] *McKinney* v. *University of Guelph* [1990] 3 SCR 229 at 280–9 per LaForest J.
[21] [1992] 2 SCR 679.   [22] Ibid. at 719–20 per Lamer C.J.C.
[23] Eberts, 'Risks of Equality Litigation', in Martin and Mahoney eds., *Equality and Judicial Neutrality* (1987), 89.

challenges of interpreting positive equality guarantees. By the time the first case on the Section 15 guarantees had reached the Supreme Court in 1987 (and finally been decided in 1989) the Court confidently established that it would take a purposive approach to the Charter,[24] and that the party seeking to limit Charter rights had to meet a very high threshold of justifiability.[25] It had also continued to affirm, and develop, in a remarkable series of judgments, the importance and the outline of human rights guarantees.

The Court's first comprehensive judicial statement of the correct attitude toward the interpretation of human rights legislation can be found in *Insurance Corporation of British Columbia* v. *Heerspink*,[26] where Lamer J. emphasized that a Code is not to be treated as any other law of general application, but recognized for what it is, namely 'a fundamental law'. The principle was further articulated by McIntyre J. for a unanimous Court in *Winnipeg School Division No. 1* v. *Craton*.[27] He emphasized the 'special nature' of human rights law, noting that it 'may not be altered, amended or repealed, nor may exceptions be created to its provisions, save by clear legislative pronouncement'.[28] In *Craton*, the Court held that provisions of the Human Rights Act would prevail over a conflicting provision of a pension statute, even though there was no explicit primacy provision in the human rights legislation. In *Ontario Human Rights Commission* v. *Simpsons-Sears Ltd.*[29] McIntyre J., again for a unanimousCcourt, stated that: 'Legislation of this type is of a special nature, not quite constitutional but certainly more than the ordinary—and it is for the Courts to seek out its purpose and give it effect. The Code aims at the removal of discrimination.'[30]

In *Action Travail des Femmes* v. *C.N.R.*[31] Dickson C.J.C. identified two significant consequences of the commitment to a purposive approach to human rights legislation: the rejection of the necessity to prove intent in order to establish discrimination, and the unequivocal adoption of the idea of 'adverse effect' discrimination. Further, the Court acknowledged,[32] that systemic discrimination is a particular type of unintentional discrimination which can be reached by human rights legislation, defining it in the employment context as 'discrimination that results from the simple operation of established procedures of recruitment, hiring and promotion, none of which is necessarily designed to promote discrimination'. The Court pointed out that the discrimination is then reinforced by the very exclusion which fosters the belief, both within and outside the group, that the exclusion is the result of 'natural' forces.

In the *ATF* case, the Court accepted a human rights tribunal's imposition of affirmative action as a remedy for systemic discrimination in the hiring of women. The remedy, also known as employment equity, was seen by the Court

---

[24] *Oakes* n. 19 above. [25] Ibid. [26] [1982] 2 SCR 145 at 158.
[27] [1985] 2 SCR 150. [28] Ibid. at 156. [29] [1985] 2 SCR 536.
[30] Ibid. at 546–7. [31] [1987] 1 SCR 1114 at 1137 (the *ATF* case).
[32] Ibid. at 1139.

to function in three ways: it counters the cumulative effects of systemic discrimination and renders any future intentional discrimination ineffective to exclude the target group; it addresses the attitudinal problem of stereotyping by placing members of the excluded group in the workplace and allowing them to prove their ability on the job, and it creates a critical mass of women in the workplace to overcome the problems of tokenism and marginalization.[33]

In three other decisions in human rights matters, decided after the Charter's equality guarantees came into effect, the Court displayed a similar understanding of aspects of women's inequality and what is needed to promote equality. Two of these, *Robichaud* v. *Canada (Treasury Board)*[34] and *Janzen* v. *Platy Enterprises*,[35] dealt with sexual harassment in the workplace. The third, *Brooks* v. *Canada Safeway Ltd*,[36] dealt with a differentiation in employment benefits on the basis of pregnancy.

In *Janzen*, Dickson C.J.C. for a unanimous Court held that sexual harassment does constitute discrimination on the basis of sex, as prohibited by the Manitoba Human Rights Act. He described sexual harassment:

as unwelcome conduct of a sexual nature that detrimentally affects the work environment or leads to adverse job related consequences for the victims of the harassment. It is . . . an abuse of power. When sexual harassment occurs in the workplace, it is an abuse of both economic and sexual power. Sexual harassment is a demeaning practice, one that constitutes a profound affront to the dignity of the employees forced to endure it. By requiring an employee to contend with unwelcome sexual actions or explicit sexual demands, sexual harassment in the workplace attacks the dignity and self-respect of the victim both as an employee and as a human being.

Perpetrators of sexual harassment and victims of the conduct may be either male or female. However, in the present sex-stratified labour market, those with the power to harass sexually will predominantly be male and those facing the greatest risk of harassment will tend to be female.[37]

In *Robichaud*, the Court's purposive interpretation of the Canadian Human Rights Act caused it to hold that an employer is responsible for the discriminatory acts of its employees, including sexual harassment. LaForest J. stated[38] that if the Act is concerned with the effects of discrimination rather than its causes or motivations, it must be admitted that only the employer can provide the most important remedy, a healthy work environment. He saw the imposition of responsibility on the employer as 'placing responsibility for an organization on those who control it . . .'.[39]

In a decision which squarely overruled its holding on pregnancy discrimination under the Canadian Bill of Rights, the Court in *Brooks* held that discrimination on the ground of pregnancy is sex discrimination under

---

[33] Ibid. at 1144 per Dickson C.J.C.   [34] [1987] 2 SCR 84.
[35] [1989] 1 SCR 1252.   [36] [1989] 1 SCR 1219.
[37] *Janzen* n. 35 above at 1284.   [38] *Robichaud* n. 34 above at 94.   [39] Ibid. at 95.

applicable human rights legislation. The Chief Justice stated 'how could pregnancy discrimination be *anything other than* sex discrimination?',[40] going on to confirm that pregnancy discrimination is sex discrimination because of the basic biological fact that only women have the capacity to become pregnant. Commenting on the reasons for overruling the Court's earlier holding, he stated:

Combining paid work with motherhood and accommodating the childbearing needs of working women are ever-increasing imperatives. That those who bear children and benefit society as a whole thereby should not be economically or socially disadvantaged seems to bespeak the obvious. It is only women who bear children; no man can become pregnant. As I argued earlier, it is unfair to impose all of the costs of pregnancy upon one half of the population. It is difficult to conceive that distinctions or discriminations based upon pregnancy could ever be regarded as other than discrimination based upon sex, or that restrictive statutory conditions applicable only to pregnant women did not discriminate against them as women.[41]

In its first decision dealing with the equality guarantees of Section 15 of the Charter, the Supreme Court made it clear that it was specifically adopting the approach towards equality and anti-discrimination fashioned in human rights jurisprudence, and rejecting the Aristotelian formulation that 'things that are alike should be treated alike, while things that are unalike should be treated unalike in proportion to their unlikeness'.[42] Calling upon the Court's earlier Charter jurisprudence, McIntyre J. stated that the equality guarantees must be given a purposive interpretation, and noted that it is readily apparent that the language of Section 15 was deliberately chosen in order to remedy some of the perceived defects under the Canadian Bill of Rights.[43] He defined the purpose of the guarantees as 'to ensure equality in the formulation and application of the law,' and 'the promotion of equality . . . of a society in which all are secure in the knowledge that they are recognized at law as human beings equally deserving of concern, respect and consideration'.[44] He emphasized that the promotion of equality has a more specific goal than the mere elimination of distinctions, because 'for the accommodation of differences, which is the essence of true equality, it will frequently be necessary to make distinctions',[45] and 'identical treatment may frequently produce serious inequality'.[46]

The judgment of McIntyre J. draws on the pre-Charter human rights history to assist in the determination of when a distinction will violate Section 15 and when it will not. It will constitute a violation when it amounts to 'discrimination'; to that word used in the Charter, he gives a meaning drawn directly from human rights jurisprudence:

---

[40] *Brooks* n. 36 above at 1242.   [41] Ibid. at 1243–4.
[42] *Andrews* v. *Law Society of British Columbia* [1989] 1 SCR 143 at 166.
[43] Ibid. at 170.   [44] Ibid. at 171.   [45] Ibid. at 169.   [46] Ibid. at 171.

I would say then that discrimination may be described as a distinction, whether intentional or not but based on grounds relating to personal characteristics of the individual or group, which has the effect of imposing burdens, obligations or disadvantages
on such individual or group not imposed upon others, or which withholds or limits
access to opportunities, benefits, and advantages available to other members of society.
Distinctions based on personal characteristics attributed to an individual solely on the
basis of association with a group will rarely escape the charge of discrimination, while
those based on an individual's merits and capacities will rarely be so classed.

The Court in the case at bar must address the issue of discrimination as the term is
used in Section 15(1) of the Charter. In general, it may be said that the principles which
have been applied under the Human Rights Acts are equally applicable in considering
questions of discrimination under Section 15(1).[47]

Human rights legislation usually has no counterpart to Section 1 of the
Charter. The Court thus considered the relationship between Section 15 and
Section 1 without reference to any cognate jurisprudence in the human rights
area. Here, however, it could draw on its own prior Charter decisions interpreting and applying Section 1. The Court decided to require analytical separation between the determination of rights violations under Section 15 and
their attempted justification under Section 1 in just the same way as it did with
respect to other rights, overruling the decision of the Court of Appeal under
review, which had found numerous limitations on equality rights internal to
Section 15 itself. Similarly, this approach departed from the earlier analytical
method employed in connection with the Canadian Bill of Rights, where a test
had been developed within the concept of equality itself, to distinguish
between justified and unjustified legislative distinctions, in the absence of anything equivalent to the Section 1 limit.

The decision of the Supreme Court of Canada in *Andrews* was an important watershed in the development of the Charter. Up until this time, many of
the complaints of violation of Section 15 had come from corporations challenging the differential provisions of regulatory legislation. Had the Court not
stemmed the flood of these cases by making it clear that Section 15 was available only to those persons who suffer discrimination in the sense understood
by human rights Codes, the purpose of the guarantee would have been
obscured, and unfulfilled.

The importance of the *Andrews* ruling to women's Charter advocacy can be
appreciated with reference to a study of resort to the equality guarantees
which was performed prior to the Supreme Court decision by Shelagh Day
and Gwen Brodsky, who had been, respectively, the first President and first litigation director of LEAF. After a review of the 591 reported and unreported
decisions handed down by Courts at all levels during the first 3 years Section
15 was in effect, the authors concluded that women were initiating few cases,

---

[47] *Andrews* v. *Law Society of British Columbia* [1989] 1 SCR 143 at 174.

that cases involving challenges to the criminal law and to regulatory legislation were preoccupying the Courts' time and significantly influencing interpretations of the equality guarantees, that men were using the Charter to strike back at women's hard-won protections and benefits, and that the theories of equality and interpretive tests that had been developed to that point would not improve women's condition.[48]

In these circumstances, the authors concluded that there was some justification for the position that women and other disadvantaged groups would be wiser to put their efforts into the democratic system, trying to change conditions of disadvantage through political rather than legal means. They acknowledged that the findings of their study 'give reason for concern about the efficacy of seeking redress for equality problems in the Courts'.[49] Day and Brodsky proposed in their study an approach to Charter equality similar to that advocated by LEAF in its brief to the Court in *Andrews*, and not unlike that ultimately adopted by the Court.

If the Court had not decided as it did in *Andrews*, there is a strong likelihood that women and other disadvantaged groups would have rejected litigation as a means of addressing problems of equality. Because of the *Andrews* decision, litigation remained as a strategy: it now remains to judge its effectiveness.

Rights Adjudication under the Charter: the Pattern and the Experience

As has been observed by Wilson J.,[50] there has been almost no adjudication under the Charter at the level of the Supreme Court specifically implicating Charter guarantees in the area of family law. One case, relating to spousal support after divorce, has recently been argued, and is still under reserve.[51] A few early attempts by men to undermine the statutory framework of divorce or support law were not treated seriously by the Courts before which they were made.[52]

This is not to say that matters touching upon the family sphere have not figured in the Charter jurisprudence. In particular, issues relating to women's reproductive freedom, statutory benefit programs for mothers, and child sexual abuse have been considered within the Charter framework, and I shall deal with them below.

One of the most distinctive features to emerge with respect to those Charter cases affecting women's rights which have reached the Supreme Court of

[48] Brodsky and Day *Canadian Charter Equality Rights for Women: One Step Forward or Two Steps Back* (1989), 3.
[49] Ibid.
[50] The Hon. Bertha Wilson, 'Women, the Family, and the Constitutional Protection of Privacy', 17 *Queen's LJ* (1992) 5 at 10.

Canada is that most of them were brought at the instance of men, or involved Charter arguments raised by men in proceedings taken against them by the State. In the area of reproductive rights, for example, the major case of *R.* v. *Morgentaler*[53] arose out of a prosecution of well-known abortion rights advocate Dr Henry Morgentaler. *R.* v. *Borowski*[54] dealt with the application for a declaration of foetal rights by equally well-known right-to-life crusader Joseph Borowski. *Tremblay* v. *Daigle*[55] concerned the attempt by a man to use the Charter and civil proceedings to prevent his former girlfriend from obtaining an abortion, following the declaration in *Morgentaler* that the Criminal Code prohibition of abortion was unconstitutional; it was one of several such cases brought within the same period but the only one to reach the Supreme Court.[56] Only the decision in *R.* v. *Sullivan*[57] actually arose from the activity of women; two midwives were prosecuted for criminal negligence when a full-term foetus they were delivering died in the birth canal and the case involved whether the foetus was a 'person' within the relevant Criminal Code definition.

In the social welfare area, too, the leading Supreme Court of Canada decision is in a case brought by a father, Shalom Schachter, seeking benefits under the Unemployment Insurance Act for the period immediately after the birth of his son, so that he could stay at home with the baby.[58] In two other cases that reached the level of a provincial Court of Appeal, fathers initiated attacks on benefits restricted to women: *Shewchuk* v. *Ricard*[59] and *A.G.N.S.* v. *Phillips*.[60] Although the women's equality perspective was introduced into both *Shewchuk* and *Schachter* by means of LEAF interventions, a woman-originated case raising a Charter challenge to an under-inclusive statutory benefits program has yet to reach the Supreme Court of Canada.

In cases involving statutory limits on equality, women have been slightly more prominent as litigants, although the applicant in the Court's first equality decision, Mark Andrews, was an Oxford-trained male lawyer. Schoolgirl Justine Blainey successfully challenged a provision of the Ontario Human Rights Code allowing the Ontario Hockey Association to prevent her from playing competitive hockey on a boys' team: a ruling in Ms Blainey's favour was delivered by the Ontario Court of Appeal,[61] and leave to apply to the Supreme Court of Canada was refused. The main challenge to legislative pro-

---

[51] *Moge* v. *Moge* n. 15 above.
[52] See e.g. *Elgaard* v. *Elgaard* (1986) 2 BCLR (2d) 200 (British Columbia Supreme Court); *Hommel* v. *Hommel* (1985) 71 NSR (2d) 85 (Nova Scotia Supreme Court).
[53] [1988] 1 SCR 30.   [54] [1989] 1 SCR 342.   [55] [1989] 2 SCR 530.
[56] *Dehler* v. *Ottawa Civic Hospital* (1979) 101 DLR (3d) 686 (Ontario High Court); *Medhurst* v. *Medhurst* (1984) 9 DLR (4th) 252; *Diamond* v. *Hirsch* (unreported, Manitoba Queen's Bench, 6 July 1989); *Mock* v. *Brandanburg* (1988) 61 Alta. LR (2d) 235 (Queen's Bench).
[57] [1991] 1 SCR 489.   [58] *Schachter* v. *Canada* n. 16 above.
[59] (1986) 2 BCLR (2d) 324 9 (British Columbia Court of Appeal).
[60] (1986) 34 DLR (4th) 633 (Nova Scotia Supreme Court, Appeal Division).
[61] *Re Blainey* (1986) 26 DLR (4th) 728 (Ontario Court of Appeal) (1986) 54 OR (2d) 513.

visions that indirectly validated mandatory retirement at age 65, *McKinney* v. *University of Guelph*,[62] was brought by a group of male university professors, and the different employment patterns of women were commented upon only by one of the dissenting Justices in the Supreme Court.[63] However, a second challenge, brought by a woman, did result in legislative removal of the cap at age 65 on entitlement under the Unemployment Insurance Act.[64] Interestingly, the woman applicant in this second case exhibited the precarious economic circumstances, low pension, and need to work after age 65 which L'Heureux-Dubé J., in her dissent, had in *McKinney* identified as characteristic of women's particular economic circumstances.[65] In a case for which leave to appeal to the Supreme Court of Canada has been granted, a professional woman is challenging the limits on deductibility of child care expenses from her professional income.[66]

A large number of Supreme Court of Canada decisions with a significant bearing on the equality of women and other disadvantaged groups have arisen in the criminal law context: cases articulating the role of the criminal law in control of hate literature and violent pornography, and decisions affecting both procedural and substantive outcomes for victims of sexual assault and spousal violence. A large majority of these cases are decisions arising in cases involving men, and in particular attacks on Charter grounds by male accused against legislative protection of the vulnerable.

In one small but important area, initiatives by women seem to have played a significant role in the breaking of new legal ground, both with and without reliance on the Charter. This is the area of tort, in particular, of recovery in tort for sexual abuse or violence. In two significant cases, Charter arguments have been put forward by women to underscore their entitlement to recover damages, or maintain a cause of action. The first of these was *Doe* v. *Municipality of Metro Toronto*,[67] asserting a Charter right to sue for police failure to warn of the profile and activities of a rapist on the part of a woman who had been assaulted by him after the profile became known to the police.

In the second case,[68] Charter arguments were made, but not ultimately ruled on by the Court, in support of a patient's right to sue her doctor for damages arising from his provision of the drugs to which she was addicted in return for sexual activities. A third case, in which survivors of childhood incest challenged the Limitations Act provision barring their recovery in tort, has been argued before the Court but is still under reserve.[69] In the second of these three cases, *Norberg* v. *Wynrib*, the plaintiff was an Aboriginal woman. With

---

[62] [1990] 3 SCR 229.   [63] See reasons of L'Heureux-Dubé J. Ibid. at 433–4.
[64] *Tetrault-Gadowry* v. *Canada* [1991] 2 SCR 22.   [65] [1991] 2 SCR 22 at 29–30.
[66] *Doe* v. *Metropolitan Toronto (Municipality) Commissioners of Policy* (1990) 74 OR (2d) 225 (District Court).
[67] (1990) 72 DLR (4th) 580.   [68] *Norberg* v. *Wynrib* n. 15 above.
[69] *K.M.* v. *H.M.* n. 15 above. The Supreme Court of Canada held that the Limitations Act should not bar an action for damages by an adult survivor of childhood incest.

this exception, the absence of women of colour, disabled women, lesbians, and poor women from high profile Charter adjudication is noticeable.

It is clear on the basis of this experience that the hope of LEAF's founders to engage in systematic and orderly development of the case law on women's equality has not been realized.[70] Maintaining the presence before the Court of issues important to women has, after all, depended on the initiative of men, both those well disposed to women's interests and those opposed to them, on being flexible enough to react to these initiatives of others, and on the Court's welcome of interveners.

A necessarily brief review of the resulting jurisprudence will show the extent to which the Court has reflected the experience of women in its decisions.

Interpretation of the Charter

REPRODUCTIVE FREEDOM

At issue in *R. v. Morgentaler*[71] was the validity of Section 251 of the Criminal Code. It prohibited abortions, but provided that abortions performed under certain conditions would not attract criminal sanctions. The accused doctor performed an abortion in circumstances that were not within the exculpatory provisions of the Section. Though he was acquitted at trial, the Crown appealed: the physician argued that the provisions offended the Charter's guarantees of liberty, and equality, and the plurality of the Court agreed that the entire Section, prohibition and exculpation, violated the liberty guarantee. The reasoning of the Justices who arrived at this result shows some diversity in approach, but it is basically sympathetic to the perspective of the pregnant woman who is faced with a decision whether or not to terminate her pregnancy.

Dickson C.J.C. said, for himself and Lamer J.:

At most basic, physical and emotional level, every pregnant woman is told by the Section that she cannot submit to a generally safe medical procedure that might be of clear benefit to her unless she meets criteria entirely unrelated to her own priorities and aspirations. Not only does the removal of decision-making power threaten women in a physical sense; the indecision of knowing whether an abortion will be granted inflicts emotional stress. Section 251 clearly interferes with a woman's bodily integrity in both a physical and emotional sense. Forcing a woman, by threat of criminal sanction, to carry a foetus to term unless she meets certain criteria unrelated to her own priorities and aspirations, is a profound interference with a woman's body and thus a violation of security of the person.[72]

[70] The 'blueprint' for strategic use of the Courts by women was developed in Atcheson et al., *Women and Legal Action* (1984), 163–70.
[71] [1988] 1 SCR 30.
[72] [1988] 1 SCR 30 at 56–7.

The Chief Justice pointed out the potential physical harm to the woman resulting from delay in obtaining an abortion, and also the harm to 'the psychological integrity of women seeking abortions' caused by both the wait for the procedure and the uncertainty about whether it would be permitted.[73]

In assessing under Section 1 the justifiability of the limit the Chief Justice decided it was unnecessary to evaluate any claim to foetal rights as an independent constitutional value; rather he evaluated the balance struck in Section 251 'as it related to the priorities and aspirations of pregnant women and the Government's interest in the protection of the foetus'.[74] He found that the legislation failed to satisfy any of the tests for justifiability under Section 1. Beetz and Estey J.J., in reasons prepared by Beetz J., took a somewhat similar approach to the questions posed; in common with the Chief Justice and Lamer J., they showed a sympathetic, if somewhat objectified and distant, attitude toward the pregnant woman.

Alone of the Justices who would strike down the legislation, Wilson J. attempted to take a subjective view of the pregnant woman, one which identifies the right to make decisions as an essential element of the liberty guaranteed by the Charter and places the woman's decision to terminate her pregnancy within the realm of protected decisions. She said, of that decision:

This decision is one that will have profound psychological, economic and social consequences for the pregnant woman. The circumstances giving rise to it can be complex and varied and there may be, and usually are, powerful considerations militating in opposite directions. It is a decision that deeply reflects the way the woman thinks about herself and her relationship to others and to society at large. It is not just a medical decision; it is a profound social and ethical one as well. Her response to it will be the response of the whole person.[75]

Continuing, she then observed:

It is probably impossible for a man to respond, even imaginatively, to such a dilemma not just because it is outside the realm of his personal experience (although this is, of course, the case) but because he can relate to it only by objectifying it, thereby eliminating the subjective elements of the female psyche which are at the heart of the dilemma.[76]

Wilson J. then placed the legal protection of this decision in the context of the differing paths which men and women have pursued towards equality, saying:

the history of the struggle for human rights from the eighteenth century on has been the history of men struggling to assert their dignity and common humanity against an overbearing State apparatus. The more recent struggle for women's rights has been a struggle to eliminate discrimination, to achieve a place for women in a man's world, to

---

[73] Ibid. at 50–63.   [74] Ibid. at 74.   [75] Ibid. at 171.   [76] Ibid.

develop a set of legislative reforms in order to place women in the same position as men (pp. 81–82). It has *not* been a struggle to define the rights of women in relation to their special place in the societal structure and in relation to the biological distinction between the two sexes. Thus, women's needs and aspirations are only now being translated into protected rights. The right to reproduce or not to reproduce which is in issue in this case is one such right and is properly perceived as an integral part of modern woman's struggle to assert *her* dignity and worth as a human being.[77]

These remarks were the first time in Charter jurisprudence that a woman was seen as an independent moral agent, whose path to autonomy and realization of dignity could not simply be assumed to be the same as a man's, or as 'humankind's'. This moment was a vivid one for women equality-seekers; this subjective female perspective was to emerge at least once more in the cases dealing with reproductive freedom.

Tremblay v. *Daigle*, *Borowski*, and *Sullivan* were all cases where claims on behalf of the foetus to personhood, or a life and liberty interest under Section 7 of the Charter were advanced. In *Tremblay*, this supposed status of the foetus, combined with paternal rights, was advanced as the basis for permitting the father to interfere with the woman's abortion; in *Borowski*, a declaration of the legal status of the foetus under Section 7 was sought, and in *Sullivan* it was suggested that the accused midwives had committed criminal negligence causing death of a 'person' by reason of the death of a full-term foetus in the birth canal during delivery.

In all three cases, arguments of the rights of the foetus either proceeded on the basis that the mother's rights were immaterial, or tried to obscure the position of the mother. In its interventions in all three cases, LEAF tried to refocus attention on the mother as the appropriate centre of analysis. In *Borowski*, for example, LEAF argued that the appellant's snapshot of intra-uterine life requires a wider lens to reveal that the uterus belongs to a woman with constitutionally protected rights, and that medical technologies that can visualize the foetus *in utero* should not be used to deny the foetus' complete physical dependence on the pregnant woman.[78] In *Sullivan* LEAF argued that the women's equality rights under the Charter meant that focus should be not on the foetus, but on the woman: 'recognizing that the foetus is in the woman's body and central to her pregnancy reveals that harm to a full-term foetus in the process of birth is harm to the woman giving birth'.[79] In *Daigle*, refocusing on the mother instead of the foetus caused LEAF to argue that a woman's relation to the foetus is unique and inseparable: what happens to it happens to her, and the person who controls it, controls her. LEAF argued that the case

---

[77] [1988] 1 SCR 30 at 172.

[78] Factum of the Women's Legal Education and Action Fund in *R.* v. *Borowski* n. 54 above at 1 (para. 3) (on file with author).

[79] Factum of the Women's Legal Education and Action Fund in *R.* v. *Sullivan* n. 57 above at 1 (para. 50)(on file with the author); Smith, 'An Equality Approach to Reproductive Choice: *R.* v. *Sullivan*', 4 *Yale JL and Feminism* (1991) 93.

is not a conflict between the mother and the foetus but rather between a woman and a man over that woman's body, life, and relation to her foetus.[80]

In *Borowski*, the matter was resolved on the basis that since *Morgentaler*, the issue of the rights of a foetus vis-à-vis abortion legislation had become moot, and Mr Borowski had lost his standing to pursue the Charter arguments: the Court refused to hear his case in the absence of a real statutory provision to examine. In *Sullivan*, too, the Court determined that procedural problems lay in the path of the Crown's appeal from the ruling of the Court of Appeal acquitting the midwives. However, it also suggested that it would have reached the same result following the equality argument of LEAF.[81]

In *Daigle*, however, the Court's reasons specifically encompassed the experience of the woman, as a person who experienced violence from Tremblay during her pregnancy and decided for that reason to leave him and seek an abortion. After describing the violent attack which precipitated her departure, the Court set out her declaration that she did not wish to have a child at the present time in light of her age, social situation as a single person, and moral values, 'as I want to provide for a child in a serene stable family environment in which there is no violence'.[82] These details of violence against Ms Daigle had not been noted at all by the Court of Appeal in its decision upholding Tremblay's injunction. While not as extensive as Wilson J.'s comments in *Morgentaler*, the Court's account of Ms Daigle's circumstances shows its respect for her as a moral agent, making a decision in light of difficult conditions.

THE CRIMINAL LAW REASONABLENESS STANDARD

By far the clearest examples of the Court's ability to see things from the woman's perspective in the field of criminal law occur in cases that do not contain any Charter rulings.

Lynn Lavallée was charged with murder of her common law spouse. Her defence was based on a provision of the Criminal Code providing justification to persons unlawfully assaulted who cause death repelling the assault, as long as the death was caused under reasonable apprehension of death or grievous bodily harm from the original violence, and the accused believed on reasonable and probable grounds that he or she could not otherwise avoid death or grievous bodily harm. Ms Lavallée had frequently been the victim of physical abuse at the hands of the deceased, but had not left him. The night of his death, after a drinking party in their home, she shot him after he thrust a shotgun at her and challenged 'Either you kill me or I'll get you'. Expert evidence

---

[80] Factum of the Women's Legal Education and Action Fund in *Tremblay* v. *Daigle* n. 55 above at 11 (para. 37) (unofficial translation from the French, on file with the author).
[81] *R.* v. *Sullivan* n. 55 above at 503 per Lamer C.J.C.   [82] [1989] 2 SCR 530 at 537.

about the 'battered wife' syndrome had been adduced at trial. Her acquittal by the jury was later reversed by the Manitoba Court of Appeal, and at issue in the Supreme Court was the usefulness of the expert evidence in assisting a jury to understand a plea of self-defence by a battered wife.

In *R.* v. *Lavallée*,[83] Wilson J., on behalf of the Court, delivered a harsh criticism of the role of the law in entrenching domestic violence. She stated:

Far from protecting women from it the law historically sanctioned the abuse of women within marriage as an aspect of the husband's ownership of his wife and his 'right' to chastise her. One need only recall the centuries old law that a man is entitled to beat his wife with a stick 'no thicker than his thumb'.

Laws do not spring out of a social vacuum. The notion that a man has a right to 'discipline' his wife is deeply rooted in the history of our society. The woman's duty was to serve her husband and to stay in the marriage at all costs 'till death do us part' and to accept as her due any 'punishment' that was meted out for failing to please her husband. One consequence of this attitude was that 'wife battering' was rarely spoken of, rarely reported, rarely prosecuted, and even more rarely punished. Long after society abandoned its formal approval of spousal abuse tolerance of it continued and continues in some circles to this day.[84]

She referred to recent changes in official attitudes toward violence, and continued:

However, a woman who comes before a judge or jury with the claim that she has been battered and suggests that this may be a relevant factor in evaluating her subsequent actions still faces the prospect of being condemned by popular mythology about domestic violence. Either she was not as badly beaten as she claims or she would have left the man long ago. Or, if she was battered that severely, she must have stayed out of some masochistic enjoyment of it.[85]

She concluded that expert evidence about the 'battered wife' syndrome is relevant to two aspects of the self-defence plea, namely in deciding whether the accused was under reasonable apprehension of death, and in assessing the amount of force she used. Its value is to counteract the effect of stereotyped notions of battered women which might otherwise guide the 'common sense' deliberations of judges and juries. The legal standard used to evaluate both is that of 'the reasonable man', and Wilson J. stated:

If it strains credulity to imagine what the 'ordinary man' would do in the position of a battered spouse, it is probably because men do not typically find themselves in that situation. Some women do, however. The definition of what is reasonable must be adapted to circumstances which are, by and large, foreign to the world inhabited by the hypothetical 'reasonable man'.[86]

---

[83] [1990] 1 SCR 852.   [84] [1990] 1 SCR 852 at 872.
[85] Ibid.   [86] Ibid. at 874.

She found apposite the remarks of the Washington Supreme Court in *State* v. *Wanrow*,[87] which she quoted:

The respondent was entitled to have the jury consider her actions in the light of her own perceptions of the situation, including those perceptions which were the product of our nation's 'long and unfortunate history of sex discrimination.' Until such time as the effects of that history are eradicated, care must be taken to assure that our self-defense instructions afford women the right to have their conduct judged in light of the individual physical handicaps which are the product of sex discrimination. To fail to do so is to deny the right of the individual woman involved to trial by the same rules which are applicable to male defendants.[88]

In *R.* v. *McCraw*[89] the male accused was charged with three counts of threatening to cause serious bodily harm contrary to the Criminal Code. He had sent anonymous letters to three football cheerleaders detailing sex acts he wanted to perform upon them, each letter ending with a threat to have sex with the woman even if he had to rape her. The Court, in a unanimous judgment, examined the issue of whether a threat to rape constitutes a threat of serious bodily harm, defined as 'any hurt or injury, whether physical or psychological, that interferes in a substantial way with the physical or psychological integrity, health or well-being of the complainant'.[90]

Cory J., speaking for the Court, asked, 'How would that wonderful legal character the ordinary reasonable person understand the word rape, bearing in mind that at least 50 per cent of the ordinary reasonable people in our society are women?'[91] He defined violence as 'inherent in the act of rape', saying:

It seems to me that to argue that a woman who has been forced to have sexual intercourse has not necessarily suffered grave and serious violence is to ignore the perspective of women. For women rape under any circumstance must constitute a profound interference with their physical integrity. As well, by force or threat of force, it denies women the right to exercise freedom of choice as to their partner for sexual relations and the timing of those relations. These are choices of great importance that may have a substantial effect upon the life and health of every woman.[92]

It is clear from his reasons that the Court appreciates that rape is primarily an act of violence. Cory J. held that the element of sexuality aggravates the physical interference caused by an assault, so that sexual assault results in a greater impact upon the victim than a non-sexual assault. He continued:

It is difficult if not impossible to distinguish the sexual component of the act of rape from the context of violence in which it occurs. Rape throughout the ages has been synonymous with an act of forcibly imposing the will of the more powerful assailant upon the weaker victim. Necessarily implied in the act of rape is the imposition of the assailant's will on the victim through the use of force. Whether the victim is so overcome by fear that she submits or whether she struggles violently is of no consequence

---

[87] 559 P. 2d 548 (1977).   [88] *Lavallée* n. 83 above at 875.   [89] [1991] 3 SCR 80.
[90] Ibid. at 81.   [91] Ibid. at 85.   [92] Ibid. at 83.

in determining whether the rape has actually been committed; in both situations the victim has been forced to undergo the ultimate violation of personal privacy by unwanted sexual intercourse. The assailant has imposed his will on the victim by means of actual violence or the threat of violence.[93]

The Court concluded its assessment of the grievous bodily harm issue by emphasizing the 'dramatic, traumatic' psychological harm inflicted on women by rape, and confirmed that threats of rape are within the prohibition of the Section.

The Court's understanding of the power relations in rape is not surprising in light of the sensitivity it has shown to imbalances of power in areas of its Charter jurisprudence. In cases dealing with employment relations, for example, it has been attentive to the inherent imbalance of power between the employer and the employee, upholding legislation or administrative action aimed at protection of the employee.[94] In upholding higher sentences for murder committed in the course of certain offences, such as hijacking, kidnapping, and forcible confinement, or indecent assault (first degree murder), the Court has emphasized that these offences all involve the unlawful domination of people by other people. It has applied the principle that where someone is already abusing his power by illegally dominating another, the murder should be treated as an exceptionally serious crime.[95]

In its recent decision in *Norberg* v. *Wynrib*,[96] the Court held that a former patient could maintain an action in battery against her physician, who had provided prescription drugs to which she was addicted in return for sex. Speaking for three of the justices in the plurality, LaForest J. relied on the doctrine of relief from unconscionable transactions to negate the patient's consent, because 'the unequal power between the parties and the exploitive nature of the relationship removed the possibility of the appellant's providing meaningful consent to the sexual contact'.[97] McLachlin J., in reasons concurred in by L'Heureux-Dubé J., characterized the doctor-patient relationship as a fiduciary one, and would have awarded damages for its breach on a somewhat higher scale than that assessed by her colleagues. Both LaForest J. and McLachlin J., in concurring reasons, relied on the study of the Task Force on Sexual Abuse of Patients commissioned by the College of Physicians and Surgeons of Ontario. However, McLachlin J. specifically noted that female patients are disproportionably the targets of sexual exploitation by physicians. She cited the Task Force's conclusion that the power imbalance inherent in the physician–patient relationship:

[93] [1991] 3 SCR 80 at 84.

[94] See e.g. *R.* v. *Edwards Books and Art Ltd* [1986] 2 SCR 713 and *Slaight Communications Incorporated* v. *Davidson* [1989] 1 SCR 1038.

[95] *R.* v. *Paré* [1987] 2 SCR 618 at 633 per Wilson J. and *R.* v. *Arkell* [1990] 2 SCR 695 at 704 per Lamer C.J.C.

[96] [1992] 2 SCR 226.   [97] Ibid. at 261.

is exacerbated when the doctor/patient roles are combined with certain other factors relating to personal characteristics of the parties. For example, an adult doctor and a child patient have a relationship with an even greater element of vulnerability present. The same may be argued for other groups in society, such as the handicapped and visible minorities, etc. *Since the overwhelming majority of sexual abuse/impropriety cases involve female patients and male doctors, the gender dynamic cannot be ignored. Professor Kathleen Morgan has argued that the stereotypical norms of behaviour for males and females throughout society correlate to the paternalistic model of doctor/patient relationships.*[98]

PORNOGRAPHY AND HATE PROPAGANDA

In *R.* v. *Butler,*[99] the Court applied its understanding of power imbalances and sexual exploitation to the analysis of the obscenity provisions of the Criminal Code. At issue was Section 163(8) which defined as obscene (and thus subject to prohibition) 'any publication a dominant characteristic of which is the undue exploitation of sex, or of sex and any one of the following subjects, namely, crime, horror, cruelty and violence'. The accused, proprietor of an outlet which offered 'hard core' videos and magazines for sale and rent, challenged the provision as contrary to the freedom of expression guarantees in the Charter. Because of the Court's prior jurisprudence giving a wide ambit to the freedom of expression guarantee,[100] there was agreement before the Supreme Court that Section 163(8) constituted a violation of freedom of expression. The arguments focused on whether it was justified under Section 1.

Sopinka J., writing for the majority, accepted that the object of the legislation is the prevention of harm related to obscenity, and found that objective to be pressing and substantial. In doing so, he drew upon a considerable body of jurisprudence that had already considered the 'harm' approach to pornography. He stated:

In the words of Nemetz C.J.B.C. in *R.* v. *Red Hot Video Ltd.* (1985), 45 C.R. (3d) 36 (B.C.C.A.), there is a growing concern that the exploitation of women and children, depicted in publications and films can, in certain circumstances, lead to 'abject and servile victimization' (at pp. 43–4). As Anderson J.A. also noted in that same case, if true equality between male and female persons is to be achieved, we cannot ignore the threat to equality resulting from exposure to audiences of certain types of violent and degrading material. Materials portraying women as a class as objects for sexual exploitation and abuse have a negative impact on 'the individual's sense of self-worth and acceptance'.[101]

---

[98] Ibid. at 280 (emphasis added by McLachlin J.).   [99] [1992] 1 SCR 452.

[100] See e.g. the description of the right to freedom of expression given by Dickson C.J.C. in *R.* v. *Keegstra* [1990] 3 SCR 697 at 726–34.

[101] *Butler* n. 99 above at 496–7.

Indeed, he concluded that the harm rationale is the sole constitutionally acceptable basis for the legislation, because the objective of maintaining conventional standards of propriety, independently of any harm to society, is no longer justified in light of the values of individual liberty which underlie the Charter. He also observed that the burgeoning pornography industry renders the concern more pressing and substantial than when the impugned provisions were first enacted.

Sopinka J. arrived at his conclusion after having reviewed the 'community standards' test for determining whether exploitation of sex is undue. He specifically remarked, in the course of his analysis, on the role of the 'degrading and dehumanizing test' in making this determination:

Among other things, degrading or dehumanizing materials place women (and sometimes men) in positions of subordination, servile submission or humiliation. They run against the principles of equality and dignity of all human beings. In the appreciation of whether material is degrading or dehumanizing, the appearance of consent is not necessarily determinative. Consent cannot save materials that otherwise contain degrading or dehumanizing scenes. Sometimes the very appearance of consent makes the depicted acts even more degrading or dehumanizing.[102]

Sopinka J. concluded that such material would fail the community standards test 'not because it offends against morals, but because it is perceived by public opinion to be harmful to society, particularly to women'. In analysing this branch of the law, he drew upon a well-developed body of jurisprudence from several Canadian provinces, which reflects the influence of feminist antipornography advocacy groups in bringing the harm analysis before the Bench.

In performing the proportionality analysis required by Section 1, Sopinka J. was able to draw on a large body of published reports from Study Commissions on pornography, which had resulted from considerable antipornography activism, both in having the Study Commissions appointed and in making representations to them. After a review of the not entirely consistent conclusions of these reports, he concluded that parliament was entitled to have a ' "reasoned apprehension of harm" resulting from the desensitization of individuals exposed to materials which depict violence, cruelty and dehumanization in sexual relations'.[103] Accordingly, there was a rational connection between the object of the legislation and the criminal sanction 'which demonstrates our community's disapproval of the dissemination of materials which potentially victimize women and which restricts the negative influence which such materials may have on . . . attitudes and . . . behaviour'.[104]

Sopinka J. also concluded that the minimal impairment test was satisfied. Of arguments that satisfactory alternatives to the criminal prohibition include measures such as encouraging women to lay charges against their assailants,

---

[102] *Butler* n. 99 above at 479.   [103] Ibid. at 504.   [104] Ibid.

provision of shelters and counselling for battered women, and education of law enforcement agencies, he observed, 'given the gravity of the harm, and the threat to the values at stake, I do not believe that the measure chosen by Parliament is equalled by the alternatives which have been suggested'.[105] In balancing the restrictions on liberty against the importance of the objective, the third branch of the Section 1 test, he concluded:

The objective of the legislation, on the other hand, is of fundamental importance in a free and democratic society. It is aimed at avoiding harm, which Parliament has reasonably concluded will be caused directly or indirectly, to individuals, groups such as women and children, and consequently to society as a whole, by the distribution of these materials. It thus seeks to enhance respect for all members of society, and non-violence and equality in their relations with each other.[106]

In an earlier decision. *R.* v. *Keegstra*,[107] the Court had considered the constitutional validity of Section 319(2) of the Criminal Code, which prohibits promotion of hatred against an identifiable group. The accused, a teacher who had communicated anti-Semitic and Holocaust-denying statements to his students, argued that the prohibition violated his right to freedom of expression and that the parts of the Section providing the basis for defending against the charge offended the presumption of innocence. There was no doubt that the freedom of expression guarantee had been violated, and the Supreme Court of Canada was closely divided on the issue of the justifiability of the incursion. Dickson C.J.C., for the majority, canvassed very broadly the evidence and reports relating to hate propaganda, as well as the international instruments dealing with the topic. He also examined the other provisions of the Charter. In coming to his conclusion that the objective of the prohibition was pressing and substantial in a free and democratic society, in particular, he adopted LEAF's reasoning that the public and wilful promotion of group hatred is properly understood as a practice of inequality. He observed:

In light of the Charter commitment to equality, and the reflection of this commitment in the framework of Section 1, the objective of the impugned legislation is enhanced in so far as it seeks to ensure the equality of all individuals in Canadian society. The message of the expressive activity covered by Section 319(2) is that members of identifiable groups are not to be given equal standing in society, and are not human beings equally deserving of concern, respect and consideration. The harms caused by this message run directly counter to the values central to a free and democratic society, and in restricting the promotion of hatred Parliament is therefore seeking to bolster the notion of mutual respect necessary in a nation which venerates the equality of all persons.[108]

He also invoked the provisions of Section 27 of the Charter, which provides that it is to be interpreted in a manner consistent with the preservation and

---

[105] Ibid. at 508.   [106] Ibid. at 509.   [107] [1990] 3 SCR 697.   [108] Ibid. at 756.

enhancement of the multicultural heritage of Canadians. Of the weight to be given to these values, he observed:

The value expressed in Section 27 cannot be casually dismissed in assessing the validity of Section 319(2) under Section 1, and I am of the belief that Section 27 and the commitment to multicultural vision of our nation bear notice in emphasizing the acute importance of the objective of eradicating hate propaganda from society. Professor J. E. Magnet has dealt with some of the factors which may be used to inform the meaning of Section 27, and of these I expressly adopt the principal of non-discrimination and the need to prevent attacks on the individual's connection with his or her culture, and hence upon the process of self development . . . Indeed, the sense that an individual can be affected by treatment of a group to which he or she belongs is clearly evident in a number of other Charter provisions not yet mentioned, including Sections 16 to 23 (language rights), Section 25 (Aboriginal rights), Section 28 (gender equality) and Section 29 (denominational schools) . . .

Hate propaganda seriously threatens both the enthusiasm with which the value of equality is accepted and acted upon by society and the connection of target group members to their community . . .

When the prohibition of expressive activity that promotes hatred of groups identifiable on the basis of colour, race, religion, or ethnic origin is considered in light of Section 27, the legitimacy and substantial nature of the government objective is therefore considerably strengthened.[109]

His review led him to conclude that a 'powerfully convincing' legislative objective exists. In addressing himself to the connection between the objective and the means chosen, the Chief Justice analysed three rationales often given for freedom of expression: the need to ensure that truth and the common good are advanced, the provision to individuals of a means to self-fulfilment by developing and articulating ideas as they see fit, and ensuring that participation in the political process is open to all persons. He found that hate propaganda contributes little to any of these goals, and infringements on it may, therefore, be easier to justify than other infringements of freedom of expression; after a careful analysis, he concluded that all three elements of the proportionality analysis had been met.[110]

PROSTITUTION

A group of recent decisions has considered the constitutional validity of Criminal Code provisions prohibiting communication for the purpose of prostitution, the keeping of a common bawdy house, and living off the avails of prostitution: *Reference re Sections 193 and 195.1(1)(c) of the Criminal Code (Man.)*;[111] *R. v. Stagnitta*;[112] *R. v. Skinner*;[113] and *R. v. Downey*.[114] The

---

[109] [1990] 3 SCR 697 at 757–8.   [110] Ibid. at 786–7.   [111] [1990] 1 SCR 1123.
[112] [1990] 1 SCR 1226.   [113] [1990] 1 SCR 1235.   [114] [1992] 2 SCR 10.

result of the cases was to uphold the prohibition of communication for the purpose of soliciting, as a reasonable limit on the freedom of expression guarantee; the prohibition on keeping a common bawdy house, because it is not a violation of the freedom of expression guarantee, and the prohibition on living off the avails of prostitution as a reasonable limit on the presumption of innocence.

There was some difference in the Court about how to view prostitution and the women who are engaged in it. All justices in the *Reference* case, for example, saw communication for the purposes of prostitution as within the Charter's protection for freedom of commercial expression, but in assessing the justifiability of the limit, took different views of the menace that was aimed at by the legislation. Lamer J., as he then was, had perhaps the most alarmed view of the extent of the threat posed by prostitution. While acknowledging that the prohibition is aimed at the street nuisance caused by soliciting, he continued with an analysis drawn in part from the work of the Ontario Advisory Council on the Status of Women:

In this case however we are dealing with a particular form of activity that brings with it other associated criminal activity, and which, as the Ontario Advisory Council on the Status of Women states, is at its most basic level a form of slavery. In a brief prepared in 1984 entitled *Pornography and Prostitution*, the Advisory Council had the following to say in respect of prostitution:
'There is a real victim in prostitution—the prostitute herself. All women, children and adolescents are harmed by prostitution . . .

Prostitution functions as a form of violence against women and young persons. It is certainly a blatant form of exploitation and abuse of power . . . Prostitution is related to the traditional dominance of men over women. The various expressions of this dominance include a concept of women as property and the belief that the sexual needs of men are the only sexual desires to be given serious consideration. Prostitution is a symptom of the victimization and subordination of women and of their economic disadvantage.'

I note that while prostitution is an activity in which both men and women participate, the data indicates that women overwhelmingly outnumber men as sellers of sexual services.[115]

He thus identified the legislative objective as, in part, that of giving law-enforcement officials a way of controlling prostitution in the street.

Dickson C.J.C., writing for himself and LaForest and Sopinka J.J., did not conceive of the object of the legislation as broadly as did Lamer J., although he implicitly accepted the contention that prostitution is degrading to women. He stated: 'In prohibiting sales of sexual services in public, the legislation does not attempt, at least in any direct way to address the exploitation, degradation and subordination of women that are part of the contemporary reality of

---

[115] *Reference* case n. 111 above at 1193.

prostitution'.[116] L'Heureux-Dubé J. similarly observed of Lamer J.'s reasons: 'While I do not disagree with my colleague that prostitution is, for the reasons he gives, a degrading way for women to earn their living, I cannot agree with his conclusion that Section 195.1(1)(c) of the Code attempts to address the problem'.[117]

The picture of the prostitute which emerges from the reasons of Lamer J. in the *Reference* case is of a person, usually a woman, who is almost totally degraded. In *Downey*, the majority of the Court upheld the prohibition on living off the avails of prostitution, with its presumption that one habitually in the company of a prostitute is supported by her, as a justifiable limit on the Charter's guarantees of the presumption of innocence. Cory J. included in his reasons a review of several research reports documenting 'the cruel, pernicious and exploitative evil of the pimp',[118] and the difficulty in securing the testimony of prostitutes in prosecutions of pimps:

Strangely, despite the abusive and corrosive relationship that exists between the pimp and the prostitute, many prostitutes are strongly attached to their pimps and truly believe that they are in love with them . . . Whether pimps maintain control by the emotional dependence of prostitutes upon them or by physical violence, prostitutes have exhibited a marked reluctance to testify against their pimps.[119]

It is only in the dissenting reasons of McLachlin and Iacobucci J.J. that the bleak picture of the prostitute as degraded, terrorized, and deluded is relieved. McLachlin J. stated that the presumption in the provision does not survive scrutiny under Section 1 of the Charter. While it is a reasonable inference in some cases, but not all, that someone who is habitually in the company of a prostitute is parasitically living on the avails of prostitution, many others might live with or be in the company of a prostitute without doing so: spouses, lovers, friends, children, parents, room-mates, business associates, and providers of goods and services. She quoted a passage from the judgment in *R.* v. *Grilo*[120] of Arbour M.J.of the Ontario Court of Appeal, which clearly portrays the prostitute as a rounded human being with moral and other ties:

For example, when a prostitute financially supports a disabled parent or a dependent child, she clearly provides an unreciprocated benefit to the recipient. However, in light of her legal or moral obligations towards her parent or child, the recipient does not commit an offence by accepting that support. The prostitute does not give money to the dependent parent or child because she is a prostitute but because, like everybody else, she has personal needs and obligations. The true parasite whom Section 212(1)(j) [as the provision is now numbered] seeks to punish is someone the prostitute is not otherwise legally or morally obliged to support. Being a prostitute is not an offence, nor is marrying or living with a prostitute. A person may choose to marry or live with a prostitute without incurring criminal responsibility as a result of the financial benefits

---

[116] Ibid. at 1134–5.   [117] Ibid. at 1210.
[118] *Downey* n. 114 above at 32.   [119] Ibid. at 34.   [120] (1991) 64 CCC (3d) 53.

likely to be derived from the pooling of resources and the sharing of expenses and other benefits which would normally accrue to all persons in similar situations.[121]

These conflicting observations about whether a prostitute is a degraded victim or an independent moral agent may perhaps simply show that the Supreme Court of Canada has as much ambivalence on the topic as does the women's movement itself, or the general public.

In its Charter decisions in another area of the criminal law area, however, the Court clearly chooses other interests over those put forward by or on behalf of women. Specifically, the interests of the criminal accused take priority over those of the victims of sexual assault; the gendered nature of the decision emerges clearly when we note that the large majority of such assaults are committed by men upon women.

SEXUAL ASSAULT AND THE RIGHTS OF THE ACCUSED

At issue in *R. v. Seaboyer*; *R. v. Gayme*[122] were provisions of the Criminal Code prohibiting the introduction of certain evidence about the prior sexual history of the complainant in a sexual assault case. These provisions had been part of a set of reforms made in 1982 in response to criticisms of the treatment in Court of complainants; the package included abrogation of the rules of recent complaint, removal of corroboration requirements, redefinition of the offence of sexual assault so that a man might be convicted of raping his wife, and permitting a complainant to apply for an order prohibiting publication of her name or identifying details. The latter provision was upheld in a Charter challenge brought on behalf of a newspaper chain which asserted the freedom of the press interest in disclosure of the information. Although the Court did not offer elaborate reasons, it did confirm that the justifiability of the provision resides in its effect on encouraging women to lay charges against those who sexually assault them: *Canadian Newspapers* v. *Canada (Attorney-General)*.[123]

The main elements of the 1982 package under attack in *Seaboyer* and *Gayme* were the prohibition against using evidence to support or impeach the credibility of a complainant, and a prohibition against introduction by the accused of evidence of the sexual activity of the complainant with persons other than the accused unless it is for purposes of rebutting evidence adduced by the Crown, it establishes the identity of the person who had sexual contact with the complainant on the occasion set out in the charge, or it relates to consent.

All members of the nine-person Court readily agreed that the provision forbidding use of evidence of sexual reputation was demonstrably justifiable

---

[121] Ibid. at 61.   [122] (1991) 83 DLR (4th) 193.   [123] [1988] 2 SCR 122.

under Section 1, but a large majority of the Court found the bar on evidence of prior sexual conduct to be an unjustifiable violation of the accused's right to life, liberty, and security under Section 7 of the Charter. McLachlin J. prepared the reasons of herself and the Chief Justice and LaForest, Sopinka, Cory, Stevenson, and Iacobucci J.J. L'Heureux-Dubé J. prepared eloquent dissenting reasons, with which Gonthier J. concurred.

All members of the Court saw the purpose of the legislation in a similar way. The majority reasons saw the main purpose as being to abolish the old common law rules which permitted evidence of the complainant's sexual conduct which was of little probative value and calculated to mislead the jury.[124] In particular, the legislation was to rid the criminal law of the outmoded and illegitimate notions of myths that prior intercourse on the complainant's part made it more likely that she had consented to the alleged assault, and undermined her credibility generally. Three related purposes were also recognized by the majority: to eliminate evidence of prior sexual activity because it usually prejudices the judge or jury against the complainant, to encourage the reporting of crime, and to protect the privacy interests of the complainant.[125] While the Court found these objectives 'laudable', it held that the means chosen to implement them overreach themselves and violate the right of the accused to a fair trial, protected by Sections 7 and 11(d) of the Charter.

While the majority reasons deal with the objective of the legislation in, at most, two pages, the dissenting reasons present a detailed account of the legislative history and of the mischief aimed at by the provisions. L'Heureux-Dubé J. drew heavily on feminist legal analysis to describe the problem of stereotyping of the sexual assault victim; indeed, she made these stereotypes the focal point of her analysis by beginning her reasons with this description of the issue: 'These two appeals are about relevance, myths and stereotypes in the context of sexual assaults'.[126]

She pointed out certain salient features of the crime of sexual assault: in the vast majority of cases the target is a woman and the perpetrator is a man;[127] the prosecution and conviction rates for sexual assault are among the lowest for all violent crimes;[128] and women under-report incidents of sexual assault for a number of reasons including fear of reprisal from their attacker, and concern about the attitude of police and Courts to this type of offence.[129] Saying it is 'not like any other crime', L'Heureux-Dubé J. noted that the fear and constant reality of sexual assault affects how women conduct their lives and define their relationship to the larger society; the pervasive influence of assault in shaping women's lives is true not just for women who have been assaulted but for all women.[130]

---

[124] *Gayme* n. 122 above at 258.   [125] Ibid. at 259.   [126] Ibid. at 201.
[127] Ibid. at 205.   [128] Ibid. at 206.   [129] Ibid. at 206–7.
[130] Ibid. at 206, 212.

Of the role of stereotype in determining how complaints will be dealt with, she said:

The woman who comes to the attention of the authorities has her victimization measured against the current rape mythologies, i.e., who she should be in order to be recognized as having been, in the eyes of the law, raped: who her attacker must be in order to be recognized in the eyes of the law, as a potential rapist; and how injured she must be in order to be believed. If her victimization does not fit the myths, it is unlikely that an arrest will be made or a conviction obtained.[131]

She described some of the myths which, research shows, are widely held: that men who assault are not like normal men (the 'mad rapist' myth); that women often provoke or precipitate sexual assault; that women are assaulted by strangers; that women often agree to have sex but later complain of rape, and the related myth that men are often convicted on the false testimony of the complainant; that women are as likely to commit sexual assault as are men; and that when women say no they do not necessarily mean no.[132] Evidence of prior sexual history, combined with these stereotypes, has the result of transforming the guilt or innocence determination into an assessment of 'whether or not the complainant should be protected by the law of sexual assault'.[133]

L'Heureux-Dubé J. also argued that the Court should acknowledge the interests of the victims of sexual assault in performing its constitutional analysis. She noted that the majority of the Court had earlier, in *R. v. Askov*,[134] recognized that Section 11(b) of the Charter (guaranteeing a trial within a reasonable time) impliedly protects the societal interest by reassuring the community that 'serious crimes are investigated and . . . those implicated are brought to trial and dealt with according to the law'. She also invoked Section 28 of the Charter, which guarantees all its rights equally to men and women arguing that it 'would appear to mandate a constitutional inquiry that recognizes and accounts for the impact upon women of the narrow construction of Sections 7 and 11(d) advocated by the appellants'.[135]

The majority agreed that viewing Section 7 as concerned with the interest of complainants as a class to security of person and to equal benefit of the law as guaranteed by Sections 15 and 28 of the Charter would be consistent with the view that Section 7 reflects a variety of societal and individual interests. However, it did not propose balancing the two sets of interests in the manner suggested by L'Heureux-Dubé J., stating rather that 'all proponents in this case concede that a measure which denies the accused the right to present a full and fair defence would violate Section 7 in any event'.[136]

Just as there was agreement, if a difference of emphasis, on the purpose of the legislation, so was there agreement among the Justices that the right to a

---

131 Ibid. at 207.
133 Ibid. at 238.
135 *Gayme* n. 122 above at 242.

132 Ibid. at 213.
134 [1990] 2 SCR 1199.
136 Ibid. at 257.

fair trial, one which permits the trier of fact to get at the truth and fairly dispose of the case, is a principle of fundamental justice within the meaning of
Section 7 of the Charter.[137] The majority also held that the principles of fundamental justice include the rules of evidence which require admission of relevant evidence unless the potential prejudice to the trial process of admitting
the evidence clearly outweighed its value,[138] an idea that the dissenting
Justices did not disagree with. The major difference between the majority and
minority decisions is in determining whether the prior sexual conduct exclusion excludes evidence, the probative value of which is not substantially outweighed by its potential prejudice.[139]

The majority reasons gave several examples of the kind of relevant evidence
which might be excluded by the impugned provision: evidence going to establish the defence of honest, if mistaken, belief in consent to sexual relations;
evidence upon which the accused could attack the credibility of the complainant by alleging bias or motive to fabricate; evidence to explain physical
conditions on which the Crown seeks to rely in order to establish intercourse
or use of force, or to negative consent; evidence that would negative the contention that a young complainant's knowledge of a particular term or practice
could only have come from the offence alleged; and evidence showing a pattern of conduct on the part of the complainant that would support the defence
of consent. By excluding all this evidence, and not just that tendered for the
'irrelevant or misleading *purpose*' of suggesting that the complainant consented or was an unreliable witness, the majority held that the provision is dis-
proportionately broad and cannot meet the test in Section 1.[140]

While striking down the exclusion, the majority proposed that the trial
judge should exercise discretion as to whether any particular piece of evidence
should be admitted, within a set of guidelines it formulates. The guidelines
would, basically, allow the judge to admit evidence going to the kinds of
defences outlined above, while demonstrating a 'high degree of sensitivity'
about whether the evidence offered by the defence demonstrates a degree of
relevance which outweighs the damage and disadvantages it presents and taking 'special care' to ensure that, in the exceptional case where this evidence is
admitted, the jury is fully and properly instructed not to draw from the evidence inferences of a likelihood of consent or of lack of credibility.[141] The
majority contemplated that a *voir dire* may sometimes be necessary to determine admissibility. It was also confident that 'a sensitive and responsive exercise of discretion by the judiciary' would reduce, or even eliminate, the
concerns which provoked passage of the legislation it was ruling unconstitutional.[142]

---

[137] Ibid. at 261.
[139] *Gayme* n. 122 above at 264.
[142] Ibid. at 281.

[138] Ibid. at 264.
[140] Ibid. at 265–8.

[141] Ibid. at 280–1.

Although the Court was careful to structure the discretion it relied upon, by means of carefully drawn guidelines, its reliance on judicial discretion in these circumstances raises troubling questions in light of some of its other decisions. As L'Heureux-Dubé J. pointed out in her dissent, the Court found judicial discretion about whether a victim's name could be disclosed an inappropriate response to the problem of under-reporting of sexual assaults addressed by another aspect of the rape shield provision. In *Canadian Newspapers*,[143] Lamer J.[144] stated that since fear of publication is one of the factors that influences reporting of sexual assault, certainty with respect to non-publication at the time of deciding whether to report plays a vital role in that decision. A discretionary provision under which a judge retains the power to decide whether to grant or refuse the publication ban would be counter-productive. Presumably, early certainty about whether evidence of prior sexual conduct will be used at trial would also be a factor in deciding whether to report. The majority did not allude to the *Canadian Newspapers* decision in its reasons.

The majority also failed to mention in its reasons in *Seaboyer* its decision in *R. v. Swain*,[145] taken only 3 months previously. *Swain* was charged with assault and aggravated assault at his trial, the Crown obtained leave to introduce evidence of his insanity, and he was found not guilty by reason of insanity and confined on a warrant, at the pleasure of the Lieutenant-Governor in Council, for longer than he could have been gaoled had he been convicted. He challenged under the Charter both the Criminal Code provision permitting use of Lieutenant-Governor's warrants for those acquitted by reason of insanity, and also the common law rule which permitted the Crown to introduce evidence of the insanity of an accused.

The Crown argued that the right of an accused to control his or her own defence is adequately safeguarded by the exercise of judicial discretion, after the exercise of a *voir dire*, if necessary. It relied on standards developed by the Ontario Court of Appeal to guide the exercise of such discretion: namely, that there must be convincing evidence that the accused has committed the act alleged, that the trial judge should consider the nature and seriousness of the offence alleged and the extent to which the accused may be a danger to the public, and that the evidence of insanity at the time of commission of the act must be sufficiently substantial, and create such a grave question about whether the accused had the capacity to commit the offence that the interests of justice require it to be adduced. The Chief Justice, speaking for a plurality of himself, Cory and Sopinka J.J. (all of whom were in the majority in *Seaboyer*), stated that the discretion confided to the trial judge to decide on admissibility of evidence of insanity is not an adequate safeguard for the rights of the accused. It does interfere with the conduct of the defence.[146] In language strikingly reminiscent of l'Heureux-Dubé J.'s description of what

---

143 Above n. 123.
145 [1991] 1 SCR 933.

144 Quoted in (1991) 83 DLR (4th) 193 at 250.
146 Ibid. at 974–5.

happens when evidence of prior sexual history is introduced, he observed, 'While I have a very high regard for the intelligence and good faith of Canadian juries, it is nonetheless apparent that an accused's viability could be irreversibly damaged by the Crown's raising evidence of insanity',[147] in large measure because of the stigma that has been attached to persons with a mental disability.

Lamer C.J.C. refashioned the approach to admissibility of evidence of insanity, holding that the Crown should not be able to introduce such evidence until after the trier of fact has concluded that the accused is otherwise guilty, or unless (in the view of the trial judge) the accused's own defence has put his or her capacity for criminal action at issue. This second provision is not unlike the 'rebuttal of Crown evidence' provisions of the legislation impugned in *Seaboyer*.

The inconsistency between the Court's own prior decisions in *Canadian Newspapers* and *Swain* is not the only disturbing feature of the *Seaboyer* decision. L'Heureux-Dubé J. noted that regardless of the definition used, the content of any relevancy decision will be filled by the particular judge's experience, common sense, or logic, which are, in some areas, 'informed by stereotype and myth'.[148] Even more pointedly she concluded:

Parliament was faced with a historical record which demonstrated that this discretion was abused and exercised in a discriminatory fashion by trial judges and with overwhelming social science research that says things have not changed. In this context, the notion that Parliament could have, in the name of minimal impairment, awarded a discretion to trial judges, loses sight altogether of the objective that has been found to be pressing and substantial.[149]

Significantly, in two other decisions, the Court demonstrated an awareness of judicial frailty which runs directly counter to the touching confidence in sensitivity which is exhibited in *Seaboyer*: *R.* v. *Lavallée*,[150] and *Edmonton Newspapers*.[151] In *Edmonton Newspapers*, ruling that an Alberta statute prohibiting newspaper reports of family law proceedings violates freedom of the press, Cory J. wrote that one of the things prevented by the law would be the right of the public to scrutinize judicial comments on such matters as wife abuse.

The response of the women's community to *Seaboyer* was swift and dramatic. Almost immediately after the release of the decision, a large national coalition of groups began to lobby the Minister of Justice to enact replacement legislation that would address some of the underlying problems with the existing law on sexual assault (for example, the mistaken belief defence), as well as replace the 'rape shield' protections with a version more likely to sur-

---

[147] [1991] 1 SCR 933 at 974.
[148] *Gayme* n. 122 above at 228.   [149] Ibid. at 251.
[150] [1990] 1 SCR 852, discussed in nn. 83–88 above and accompanying text.
[151] *Edmonton Journal v Attorney-General (Alberta and Canada)* [1989] 2 SCR 1326.

vive constitutional scrutiny. At first proposing only to codify in law the principles enunciated in the majority judgment, the Justice Minister changed her position, embarking upon the most extensive consultations with women's groups ever conducted in connection with the drafting of Federal legislation. The result is the recently enacted Bill C-49,[152] replacing the old provisions and including strong language in its preamble outlining the evil of sexual abuse at which it is aimed, as well as a 'No means No' provision aimed directly at one of the stereotypes identified by L'Heureux-Dubé J.

In *R.* v. *Askov*[153] (referred to by L'Heureux-Dubé J. in *Seaboyer*), the Court considered whether a lengthy delay in bringing an accused to trial violated his right to be tried within a reasonable time as guaranteed by Sections 11(b) and 7 of the Charter. In the passage referred to by L'Heureux-Dubé J., Cory J., for the majority of the Court, identified not only an interest of the accused in these Sections, but also a societal interest, namely the collective interest in ensuring that those who transgress the law are brought to trial and dealt with according to law, and that those who are on trial are treated fairly and justly.[154] In the case, Cory J. set out a number of factors which the Court should consider before staying a prosecution for delay; applying them to the facts of the matter before him, he suggested that in the area of Ontario where the accused was to be tried, a delay of from 6 to 8 months between committal and trial might be deemed to be the outside limit of what is reasonable.[155] His reasons make it clear that the Court considers that where inordinate delays are caused by institutional factors, 'it is those who are responsible for the lack of facilities who should bear the public criticism that is bound to arise as a result of the staying of proceedings . . . '.[156]

There was overwhelming response to the *Askov* decision on the part of Crown attorneys and trial judges: thousands of charges were either dropped, or stayed, as those responsible for law enforcement seemed to take the Court's guideline of 6 to 8 months as an inflexible standard. Public criticism was indeed directed at the Ontario Government, but pressure to reconsider the 'guideline' was also felt by Courts, prompted in part by some judges who considered it rigid or unrealistic. The results of the public and judicial unease with *Askov* was reflected, in part, by the Supreme Court's decision to take an opportunity in a later case to clarify what it had meant in the previous decision.

In *R.* v. *Morin*[157] Sopinka J., for a large majority of the Court, specifically returned to the two interests to be served by the speedy trial provisions. The judgment re-emphasizes the social interest in bringing to justice those who are charged with crimes, and speaks strongly of the need not to subordinate this interest to the task of clearing the dockets. He stated:

---

[152] Criminal Code Amendment Act (sexual assault), S.C. 1992, cl. 38.
[153] [1990] 2 SCR 1199.   [154] Ibid. at 1219–29.   [155] Ibid. at 1240.
[156] Ibid. at 1225–6.   [157] [1992] 1 SCR 771.

There is, as well, a societal interest that is by its very nature adverse to the interests of the accused. In *Conway*, a majority of this Court recognized that the interests of the accused must be balanced by the interests of society in law enforcement. This theme was picked up in *Askov* in the reasons of Cory J. who referred to 'a collective interest in insuring that those who transgress the law are brought to trial and dealt with according to the law' (pp. 1219–20). As the seriousness of the offence increases so does the societal demand that the accused be brought to trial. The role of this interest is most evident and its influence most apparent when it is sought to absolve persons accused of serious crimes simply to clean up the docket.[158]

The majority specifically rejected the idea of applying as a mathematical formula the insights it gave into what length of delay would be unreasonable and said that the correct analytical approach is to balance 'the interests'.[159]

McLachlin J., for herself and Gonthier J. (concurring in the result), went even further. She described as 'a fundamental and important interest' the interest of society in bringing those accused of crimes to trial. In assessing what happens when that interest is not attended to, she specifically invoked the perspective of the victim of crime (overwhelmingly women in the case of sexual assault):

When those charged with criminal conduct are not called to account before the law, the administration of justice suffers. Victims conclude that justice has not been done and the public feels apprehension that the law may not be adequately discharging the most fundamental of its tasks.[160]

Describing a balancing procedure that goes further than that of the majority, she stated that the trial judge must 'balance the societal interest in seeing that persons charged with offences are brought to trial against the accused's interest in prompt adjudication'.[161] Before staying charges, he or she must be satisfied that the interest of the accused and society in a prompt trial outweigh the interest of society in bringing the accused to trial.

Taken with the reasons of L'Heureux-Dubé J. and of the majority in *Seaboyer*, these observations in *Askov* and *Morin* seem to hint at the creation of foundations for judicial recognition of the interests of the victim in the criminal process.

Not so the case of *R. v. Stinchcombe*,[162] which was decided in between *Askov* and *Morin*. In *Stinchcombe*, Sopinka J., for a unanimous seven-person court (which included L'Heureux-Dubé, Gonthier, and McLachlin J.J.), affirmed in strong terms the Crown's obligation of full disclosure in a criminal case. Declining to consider in this case whether, and to what extent, the accused may have disclosure obligations, the Court nonetheless suggestively distinguished the position of the Crown and the accused by pointing out that while the Crown must 'see that justice is done' rather than simply aim to

---

[158] [1992] 1 SCR 771 at 786–7. [159] Ibid. at 787. [160] Ibid. at 809–10.
[161] Ibid. at 810. [162] [1991] 3 SCR 326.

secure a conviction, the accused is entitled to assume a purely adversarial role toward the prosecution.[163] As L'Heureux-Dubé J. pointed out in *Seaboyer*, that will often include assuming a purely adversarial role toward the complainant in a sexual assault case, but this feature of the criminal process was not remarked upon in *Stinchcombe*.

The omission is an unfortunate one, for it is clear that the ruling will have a significant impact on the position of the complainant. Though that position is to some extent protected because of the restricted scope of relevance brought about by Bill C-49, the prospect of such a Bill was not before the Court in *Stinchcombe*: it was decided in November 1991, about 3 months after *Seaboyer* and before the passage of Bill C-49.

The Court held that the Crown must disclose all relevant evidence to the accused, whether or not the Crown plans to use the evidence, and whether it is exculpatory or inculpatory.[164] Clearly, this wide rule would encompass at least some of the material disclosed to the Crown by the complainant about her previous sexual conduct that the Court had held potentially relevant in *Seaboyer*. The combined result of *Seaboyer* and *Stinchcombe*, then, before the intervention of Bill C-49, was not only that the complainant could be cross-examined about her prior sexual history, but that she, through the Crown, had to provide the accused with the evidentiary basis for that cross-examination.

The only limit on the broad scope of *Stinchcombe* is the Court's reservation to the Crown of some discretion about disclosure touching on such matters as timing, protection of privilege, and relevance. Even here, the decisions are reviewable at the instigation of the accused, in a *voir dire* before the trial judge. In the months following the *Stinchcombe* decision, it appeared as if defence counsel had developed a practice aimed at positioning themselves to challenge Crown decisions on relevance in sexual assault matters. They began to (or to attempt to) subpoena workers in shelters and rape crisis centres to obtain evidence about what the complainant had told them upon seeking their assistance. Presumably, the prospect of discovering prior sexual history evidence, or material from which a motive to lie could be inferred, was the object; such discoveries could then be used in their own right for cross-examination of the complainant or to impugn the Crown's discretionary decisions on relevancy.

The combination of *Seaboyer* and *Stinchcombe*, both so warmly espoused by the Court, had the effect of almost totally undercutting the legislative statutory reforms on use of evidence in rape trials, and putting the complainant in a worse position with respect to use of prior sexual conduct evidence than she had been before the legislation was enacted in 1982, when the Crown's obligation to disclose what she had revealed about her life was not so strong.

---

[163] Ibid. at 333.   [164] Ibid. at 343.

The results in *Seaboyer* and *Stinchcombe* reflect quite clearly the superordinate value placed by this Court on the rights of the accused in criminal law.[165] Although there are some suggestions in *Askov* and *Morin* that communitarian interests in law enforcement and victims' confidence in the legal system may be emerging as countervailing values, they have not yet reached the point where they will impinge in any significant way on the liberty and trial interests of the accused. In areas of criminal activity that are as gendered as sexual assault, the need for an equality-based approach to the rights of the accused is, in my view, obvious. How otherwise can the rights of women, overwhelmingly the victims of sexual assault, be ensured the equal benefit of the law? Given its firm grasp on the imbalance of power inherent in sexual abuse, and the terrible ravages wrought by sexual assault, it is disappointing that the majority of the Court did not follow the analytical approach to Sections 7, 15, and 28 of the Charter adopted by L'Heureux-Dubé J. in *Seaboyer*.

Overview and Conclusion

In spite of the major disappointment of the *Stinchcombe* case, I believe, on balance, that the experience of the first years of the Charter has been a positive one, from the point of view of women. The Court has shown sensitivity towards the position and perspective of women, placing women, for the first time, in the central position in judicial reasoning. At times, the Court's appreciation of women's experience has had a ring of passionate conviction. At times, the insights derived from regarding the woman as actor, as central to the moral inquiry at hand, have been striking. What Courts say about facts is very authoritative: when this Court has acknowledged the harm done by pornography, the real dynamics of wife abuse, the value of the child-bearing role of women, the power imbalances inherent in sexual harassment, and the agonizing consequences to women of sexual assault, it has validated the experience of women, and the speech of women about that experience. For women long excluded from a role in the making of laws about them, this installation of our perspective in the process has a very high public value, a value that enhances the substantive achievements of cases such as *Andrews*, *Morgentaler*, and *Butler*.

Although the enterprise of constitutional adjudication has, so far, been rewarding, it has not been untroubled. I observed in an earlier essay, before embarking on the course of equality litigation, that this is a high risk venture

---

[165] Robert Harvie and Hamar Foster have concluded that in some significant areas, the Supreme Court of Canada has interpreted the interests of the accused more broadly than has the United States Supreme Court. See Harvie, R. and Foster, 'Ties that Bind? The Supreme Court of Canada, American Jurisprudence, and the Revisions of Canadian Criminal Law Under the Charter', 28 *Osgoode Hall LJ* (1990) 729.

for women: the consequences of a decision denying equality under an entrenched Constitution may be severe and long-term.[166] Several years and several successful outcomes later, I have not changed my view that Charter equality litigation is a risky enterprise. Decisions on Section 15 before *Andrews* were conflicting, but uniformly discouraging; only the breakthrough in *Andrews* made future progress under the Charter possible. In spite of the Court's ruling in *Schachter* that a Court invalidating an under-inclusive benefits program should invariably postpone the effect of its decision so that those entitled to benefits would not suffer in the interval before legislative attention to the deficiency, challenging under-inclusive benefits legislation is still a difficult choice; one cannot be assured that the Court will 'read up' the legislation as *Schachter* says it might. It might still send the whole issue to the Legislature; in the Canada of today, Legislatures will be under serious temptation to trim benefits, rather than enhance them, in order to achieve an 'equal' result.

The process of Charter litigation has been, and remains, risky. It is also very costly. Taking a case to the Supreme Court can absorb thousands of dollars in disbursements, even if the lawyers offer services on a *pro bono* basis. Disadvantaged individuals, on their own, do not have the resources to pursue litigation. Even collective action through litigation groups is difficult: in its Spring 1992 Budget, the Federal Government cancelled the Charter Challenges Program which had provided modest funding to selected Charter cases; the worsening economy and the need to compensate with voluntary efforts the cutbacks in social services to women mean that the always elusive charitable contribution is even more difficult to direct to advocacy activities. For a disadvantaged person, or even group, taking on a Government adversary (as one inevitably does in Charter litigation) is fraught with worry; moreover, where the ground of the challenge is one that still has the potential to attract opprobrium in our society—having been sexually harassed or abused, certain kinds of disability, sexual orientation—the public profile given Charter cases may put additional pressure on the plaintiff. Unfortunately, the Court in *Canadian Council of Churches* v. *Canada*[167] refused to broaden the standing rules governing applications to enforce Charter rights, to permit more direct origination of litigation by groups of, or on behalf of, disadvantaged individuals. A means of alleviating the burden of enforcing Charter equality rights has thus been lost to us. In such circumstances, it will continue to be necessary for the disadvantaged to seek definition and elaboration of their rights in reaction to the initiatives of those with greater resources, who bring cases with potentially serious anti-equality consequences.

It is likely that the risk and cost of Charter equality litigation will remain features of the Canadian landscape for some time. To balance these factors,

---

[166] Eberts n. 23 above.　　[167] (1992) 88 DLR (4th) 193.

however, are some of the features that have contributed to the positive outcomes that have occurred to this point.

A major feature, if not *the* major feature, is the quality of the Supreme
Court itself. In its early Charter jurisprudence, its bold commitment to equality and human dignity was nicely juxtaposed with its sense of the proper role
of a Court in enhancing democratic values and practice, and according to the
Legislature an appropriate degree of deference. The Court's close attention to
the language of the Charter itself, and its willingness to expose the course of
its reasoning in well-crafted judgments, created a climate of confidence that
reasoned and principled argument, rather than political or social orientation,
would be dispositive. That confidence is absolutely essential in encouraging
the disadvantaged to confide their rights to adjudication.

Throughout the early years of the Charter, there were sometimes three,
sometimes two, women Justices in the Court. As the extracts cited above
reveal, all three of the women jurists were willing and able to carry forward a
distinctively identifiable woman's perspective. Importantly, too, the male
Justices have shown themselves capable of appreciating the situation of
women and speaking convincingly about women's equality. This leadership
sends an important signal to male, and female, judges at other levels of the system, a signal that it is legitimate—indeed essential—that these judges should,
and women judges dare, include women's perspective in their approach to a
case.

It is also, I believe, critical to observe that the Charter itself provides a very
constructive framework for rights adjudication. The Section 15 equality guarantees when initially proposed, were modelled after the 14th amendment to
the United States Bill of Rights, the interpretation of which has been based on
the Aristotelian 'treat equals equally' idea. In a prolonged period of public
debate and discussion, several improvements in the scope of the guarantees
were secured by equality advocates, including inclusion of protection for disabled persons and language intended to prevent repetition of the interpretive
mistakes of the Canadian Bill of Rights. The inclusion of Sections 27 and 28
was also achieved during this period of open discussion. So, too, was the final
form of Section 1, the limitations Section which has played such a major role
in shaping the appropriate relationship between Legislature, individual, and
Court in the Charter era. This period of public debate was uncharacteristic of
the constitutional reform process up to then, which had featured closed-door
intergovernmental negotiation and elite accommodation. There is little doubt
that the participation of equality-seekers in the shaping of the Charter's guarantees played a role in the Court's judgment in *Andrews*; importantly, the
Court correctly discerned the equality-promoting purpose behind the Section.

A third factor which has figured in the outcome of Charter equality litigation so far is the participation in it of equality advocacy groups. It has been, I
believe, essential in informing the Court of a diversity of perspectives, which

will, one hopes, illuminate its work even in those cases where interveners do not actually appear. Linked to its open attitude towards interveners has been the Court's openness to receiving a wide array of evidence bearing on so-called constitutional facts. The two features are mutually reinforcing: interveners will often bring the Court studies and sources proceeding from the intervener's own knowledge of an area. These sources include the scholarship on women and minority groups which has been taking a foothold in the academy in the last 20 years or so. It also includes the reports of special purpose studies commissioned by Governments in matters such as abortion and pornography, often in response to public pressure. Both these new sources of authoritative information about women and legislation affecting them have enhanced the Court's deliberative process.

In assessing the role of interveners in constitutional litigation, it is, I believe, essential to observe that interveners themselves influence the Court's policy on interveners. To the extent that interveners are willing and able to observe the conventions of the adjudicatory system, they contribute to the survival of a generous policy towards interveners. Interveners who want the Court to engage in reasoned and principled reflection on Charter matters must themselves do so, and direct their interventions toward assisting the Court, rather than simply engaging in political discourse. To a large extent, the interveners participating in Charter litigation so far have observed these guidelines.

The fourth factor contributing to the overall positive outcomes of gender equality litigation so far is that it is not the exclusive means available for enhancement of rights. The human rights Codes and adjudication mechanisms exist in parallel to the Charter, and the *Andrews* decision has set up a resonance between the jurisprudence under the Codes and the Charter. To have two systems working on rights adjudication and elaboration in mutually reinforcing ways holds enormous potential for strengthening rights protection.

The other pre-Charter approach to securing equality rights which continues into the Charter era is that of political action. Women's groups did not abandon political action in order to bring Charter challenges; they added litigation to impressive grassroots and national lobbying activities. In at least two major cases since 1988, the parallel existence of the political approach has proved invaluable. Following the *Morgentaler* decision, the Federal Government tried to reintroduce a criminal prohibition on abortion. Women took political action and also made Charter arguments to the Parliamentary Committee studying the Bill, as to why it, too, would be found unconstitutional. The Bill was ultimately defeated in the Senate by a close vote; interestingly, in the process, Canada's few women Parliamentarians and Senators worked in a non-partisan way to defeat the Bill.

The other major political response to the Charter activity of the Court was the passage of Bill C-49, following *Seaboyer*. The mobilization of such a strong response is attributable, at least in part, to the fact that a number of grassroots women's groups involved in anti-sexual assault advocacy had been involved in the preparation of LEAF's interventions in both *Canadian Newspaper* and *Seaboyer*. As its experience with Charter litigation broadened, LEAF increasingly adopted consultation and coalition-building as preferred techniques for formulating its submissions. This kind of inclusive technique, practised not only by LEAF but by many other advocacy groups, has been identified by the Charter Challenges Program as one of the salient positive features of Charter litigation, one that compensates in some modest way for the exclusion of the disadvantaged from the political process.

Despite its many difficulties, their litigation under the Charter has proved to be an important way to give disadvantaged and excluded groups some sense of engagement with the governmental and constitutional processes. By contrast, such people have been almost completely excluded from the process of constitutional renewal underway in Canada since the mid-1980s with the recent and dramatic exception of the inclusion of several national Aboriginal groups in the current 'Canada Round' of discussions. What is seen as a return to closed-door constitution-making and elite accommodation, after the very public round of discussions which gave rise to the Charter itself and the involvement through litigation in articulation of constitutional principle, has caused considerable discontent in the equality-seeking community. On the whole, the sense of 'ownership' of the Constitution which underlies this discontent must be regarded as a positive force: however, it has been annoying to Governments wanting to get on with the constitutional agenda. For this reason, constitutional proposals recently tabled by the Federal Government and premiers outside Quebec de-emphasize or postpone justiciability of rights.

While the performance of the Supreme Court of Canada in interpreting the Charter's equality guarantees has been, to a large extent, a good one, it is not only the current round of constitutional negotiations which vividly illustrates the limits of rights adjudication in improving the position of the disadvantaged. While the Court has been accepting in a progressive fashion women's claims for dignity and equality, economic restructuring and the retreat from Canada's commitment to the social welfare net have produced wide-scale worsening in the conditions of women's lives.[168] At this time, it is questionable whether the disadvantaged can secure judicial redress for such retrenchment, or establish by means of legal action some irreducible minimum standard below which Government provision of basic wellbeing cannot go. Preserving the minimum, whether by means of litigation or political action is, unfortunately, the newest and most urgent item to be added to the equality agenda. It will prove to be the severest test of the Court's confidence in its own role and of the equality principles it has accepted.

---

[168] Excellent status reports on Canadian women are produced yearly by the National Action Committee on the Status of Women. See National Action Committee, *Review of the Situation of Women in Canada 1992* (1992).

8

The New Zealand Bill of Rights Experience

PHILIP A. JOSEPH*

Introduction

New Zealand enacted its Bill of Rights Act 1990 in lieu of a more ambitious reform under the Government White Paper, *A Bill of Rights for New Zealand* (1985).[1] The White Paper proposed a constitutionalised (entrenched) Bill of Rights modelled on the Canadian Charter of Rights and Freedoms. The Bill was tabled in Parliament and referred to its Justice and Law Reform Committee for examination, but the proposal lapsed when the Committee reported in 1988. It recommended in its wake the New Zealand Bill of Rights Act 1990 ('the Bill of Rights Act' or 'the Act') which the Lange–Palmer Government (1984–1990) enacted as an ordinary Act of Parliament. It was a partisan measure promoted without the support of the (then) National Opposition, or of most Government members, and with little public interest. The Opposition parodied the Bill, dismissing it as a futile reform.[2] But the Act proved not as weak and inconsequential as many had supposed.

Initial attitudes gave way to a cautious acknowledgment of the Act as lawyers began embracing it in criminal and drink-driving cases,[3] in evidential matters[4] and issues of statutory interpretation,[5] and as an overriding code controlling the exercise of administrative discretions.[6] 14 months on, a leading commentator observed signs that the Act would be pleaded 'a great deal' by counsel, that it would have a significant effect on the way Statutes are interpreted, and on the conduct of officials, and that it may even influence the

---

* This Chapter is a revised and expanded version of a chapter from the author's book, *Constitutional and Administrative Law in New Zealand* (1993), 847–74. For a further update see Joseph 'The New Zealand Bill of Rights' (1996) 7 *Public Law Review* 162.

[1] *A Bill of Rights for New Zealand* (1985), *Appendices to the Journals of the House of Representatives* ('*AJHR*') (1985) A. 6, presented to the House of Representatives by leave of the Minister of Justice, Hon. Geoffrey Palmer.

[2] See *New Zealand Parliamentary Debates* ('NZPD'), vol. 502 (1989) at 13043.

[3] See *Ministry of Transport* v. *Noort* [1992] 3 NZLR 260 (Court of Appeal).

[4] See *R.* v. *Kirifi* [1992] 2 NZLR 8 (Court of Appeal); *R.* v. *Butcher* [1992] 2 NZLR 257 (Court of Appeal).

[5] See *Flickinger* v. *Crown Colony of Hong Kong* [1991] 1 NZLR 439 (Court of Appeal).

[6] See *R.* v. *Butcher* [1992] 2 NZLR 257 at 266–7 per Cooke P. commenting on the jurisdiction to ensure fairness under the Bill of Rights Act s. 27.

development of common law principles.[7] One judge anticipated that 'the Courts will use it . . . as a significant factor in disputed matters before the Courts of any nature where it is not specifically or impliedly excluded by relevant statutory material'.[8] A suspect's right under the Act to be informed of the right to legal counsel garnered early publicity when prosecutions or convictions were dismissed or quashed for breach. The police campaigned for repeal of the right, but the Bolger Government (1990–1996) lacked any mandate for change. Now 3 years on, the Bill of Rights Act is continuing to make its mark, with enterprising counsel discovering new ways of applying it.

This Chapter examines the operational aspects (or methodology) of the Bill of Rights Act. The Act has, in the main, worked well, with the Courts called upon to consult more explicitly the values distinguishing the liberal democracy. But they have also encountered difficulties with its operational provisions, in particular Sections 4–6. The Courts have had to reconcile three guiding principles: that the Bill of Rights has 'ordinary Act' status and does not control Acts of Parliament; that the Courts must, wherever possible, construe and apply statutes consistently with the rights affirmed; and that the scope of the rights is circumscribed by the 'justified limits' Clause[9] which Parliament adopted from the Canadian Charter. The following section surveys New Zealand's Bill of Rights background, including three earlier proposals for guaranteeing rights.

The Bill of Rights Background

BRITISH SOVEREIGNTY DOCTRINE

New Zealand's institutions adhere to the doctrine of Parliamentary sovereignty but this doctrine is essentially antagonistic towards Bills of Rights. New Zealand embraced traditional sovereignty doctrine from 1947, when it acquired plenary powers of legislation.[10] New Zealand's adoption of the Statute of Westminster 1931 (UK) in 1947[11] did two things: it revoked the repugnancy limitation on the New Zealand Parliament (that no Statute be 'repugnant to the laws of England')[12] and it facilitated full powers of constitutional amendment. Under the British Statute's 'request and consent'

---

[7] See Burrows, *Statute Law in New Zealand* (1992), 321.
[8] *Noort* v. *Ministry of Transport* [1992] 1 NZLR 743 at 750 per Gallen J. (High Court).
[9] Notably the Bill of Rights Act s. 5.
[10] For New Zealand's accession to full legal independence, see Joseph, *Constitutional and Administrative Law in New Zealand* (1993), 339 et seq.
[11] See the Statute of Westminster Adoption Act 1947 (NZ).
[12] Proviso to New Zealand's original grant of law-making power—the New Zealand Constitution Act 1852 (UK) s. 53.

provision,[13] New Zealand requested,[14] and the Westminster Parliament granted,[15] power to amend all sections of the New Zealand Constitution Act 1852 (UK). New Zealand finally revoked this Imperial Statute when it passed the Constitution Act 1986 for updating and consolidating its statutory constitutional rules.[16]

The 1947 grant established a *sovereign* Legislature, with all the accoutrement. No Act of Parliament could be adjudged void and any attempted legislative limitation could be ignored, including 'fundamental' or 'entrenched' rights. An entrenched Bill of Rights would have yielded ex hypothesi to pro tanto implied repeal. In 1952, Parliament's Constitutional Reform Committee accepted that Parliament could not restrict its freedom of action through special procedures for constitutional amendment.[17] This view constrained New Zealand to experiment with single entrenchment under its Electoral Act 1956, for effecting a moral (but not legal) protection of the reserved Sections. Governments remained free to amend the entrenching Section (which was not entrenched), remove a reserved Section, then introduce the substantive amendment. Double entrenchment—where the entrenching Section was itself entrenched—would have been an unworkable fetter on Parliamentary power.[18] This conception of an illimitable and immutable legislative power provided the backdrop for two Bill of Rights proposals in the 1960's.

THE 1960S PROPOSALS

The Constitutional Society for the Promotion of Economic Freedom and Justice (NZ) was founded in 1957 for seeking reform of the Constitution. This body persuaded the New Zealand National Party to adopt manifesto promises for a Bill of Rights and a written Constitution. When National took office in 1960, it pledged to introduce a Bill of Rights 'similar to that recently adopted by the Canadian Parliament'. The Constitutional Society lobbied the Government with a draft Constitution for establishing the 'supreme law of New Zealand'. It contained 55 Articles, including a Section entitled 'Fundamental Rights' which listed the rights to life, liberty, and security of the person, the rights to a fair trial, certainty of the criminal law, and to security of property and monetary stability, and the rights to freedom of religion, speech, movement and assembly, and freedom from inhuman treatment and

---

[13] The Statute of Westminster 1931 (UK) s. 4.

[14] New Zealand Constitution Amendment (Request and Consent) Act 1947 (NZ).

[15] New Zealand Constitution (Amendment) Act 1947 (UK).

[16] See Joseph n. 10 above at 158–65.

[17] 'Report of the Constitutional Reform Committee', *AJHR* (1952), I. 18.

[18] See NZPD, vol. 319 (1956) at 2839 per the Attorney-General, Hon. John Marshall. For discussion, see Joseph n. 10 above at 118–19. On the efficacy of entrenchment, see Joseph n. 10, above ch. 15 ('Constitutional Entrenchment').

arbitrary discrimination. The Society presented its draft to Parliament as a petition and appeared before its Public Petitions Committee, but the Committee recommended no action and the proposal lapsed.[19]

New Zealand had a second attempt at a Bill of Rights in 1963. National honoured its election pledge and introduced a Bill similar to the Canadian Bill of Rights of 1960. The Bill was not entrenched but 'declaratory' for giving statutory recognition to rights and freedoms, without controlling legislative power. It was intended as an aid for interpreting Statutes and a source of inspiration and guidance to policy-makers. The rights would establish benchmarks against which Courts could 'read down' Statutes, albeit not where Parliament had made its intention clear. No self-imposed limitation could fetter Parliament's legislative sovereignty. The Constitutional Reform Committee examined the Bill and recommended that it, too, not proceed,[20] and the Bill of Rights issue lapsed until the White Paper proposal.

THE WHITE PAPER PROPOSAL

The White Paper proposed an entrenched Bill, as 'supreme law', controlling Parliamentary legislation through judicial review. Its authors accepted that the Courts 'would probably not' uphold an entrenched Bill enacted by simple majority of Government members in Parliament.[21] The Bill signalled a 'constitutional departure . . . of such major significance that [it would require] a general consensus amongst the public, both that it is needed and on its content'.[22] A consensus was needed for the Courts to legitimise the departure—such were the constraints of classical doctrine. The Bill stood referred to a peripatetic select committee for hearing submissions in the main centres, but a good many were antagonistic, and no consensus emerged.[23]

The White Paper documented the limited checks on Parliamentary and Executive power[24] and recited New Zealand's obligations under the International Covenant on Civil and Political Rights.[25] Supporters of the Bill considered it a vital check on Governmental power, but opposition centred on two features: first, the entrenchment provisions which declared the

---

[19] 'Report of Public Petitions M to Z Committee', *AJHR* (1961), 1.2–1.2A.
[20] *AJHR* (1964), I. 14. See also 'Evidence Presented to the Constitutional Reform Committee 1964 on the New Zealand Bill of Rights', *AJHR* (1965), I. 14.
[21] *A Bill of Rights for New Zealand* 1985, n. 1 above at para. 7.19.
[22] Ibid.
[23] See 'Interim Report of the Justice and Law Reform Select Committee', *Inquiry into the White Paper—A Bill of Rights for New Zealand, AJHR* (1987), I. 8A. The committee received 431 submissions. 243 actually opposed the Bill (disregarding a further 84 submissions opposing only the 'right to life' guarantee). 91 submissions supported it (with or without suggested amendments). The remaining submissions made no final decision, seeing some merit in the proposal but also expressing some reservations.
[24] *AJHR* at paras. 4.1–4.19, 4.24–4.28.   [25] Ibid. at paras 4.21–4.23.

Bill 'the supreme law of New Zealand' and, secondly, the inclusion of New Zealand's instrument of cession, the Treaty of Waitangi,[26] as supreme law.

The Bill would have sounded the end of Parliamentary sovereignty. The fact of legislative enactment would no longer have been conclusive, with the Courts having power to strike down repugnant legislation. Parliament could override the Bill only with a 75 per cent majority in the House (a bipartisan vote of Government and Opposition members) or a majority at a referendum. Many of the 431 submissions to the Justice and Law Reform Committee opposed the power of judicial invalidation of Statutes.[27] The arguments were familiar: Parliament was democratically elected whereas the judiciary was not, and it was undemocratic to confer a power of veto on judges who were neither accountable nor representative of society. The debate failed to rise to the intensely philosophical questions judicial review posed.

Opposition was also directed at entrenching New Zealand's Treaty of cession in 1840 between the British Crown and the 500 or so Maori chiefs who signed. For many Maori, this would have demeaned the document and exposed it to change through the Bill's amending procedure. No Statute was needed to vouchsafe what the Treaty already guaranteed Maoridom; the Treaty stood high above the law and legal formalism. It was also objected that Bills of Rights dealt with rights and values attaching to individual human personality (freedom of speech, thought, association etc.), not bilateral obligations between races. Only the former, it was claimed, were properly justiciable.[28] Yet this objection carried less force with hindsight. In several decisions from 1987, the New Zealand Courts have applied, in practical and meaningful ways, statutory covenants enjoining the Crown to act consistently with the principles of the Treaty.[29] These decisions suggest that the Treaty may legitimately furnish justiciable obligations, capable of common sense applications.

Opposition to the White Paper Bill was expressed on the following grounds also:

(a) A Bill of Rights was unnecessary as there were no threats to human rights in New Zealand.

(b) A Bill of Rights would freeze New Zealand's constitutional development and impede social change.

---

[26] There is continuing debate whether New Zealand's indigenous tribes (the Maori) were capable of exercizing rights of sovereignty and whether the Treaty was, in fact, a valid cession under international law. See Joseph n. 10 above at 36 et seq.

[27] See the 'Interim Report of the Justice and Law Reform Select Committee' n. 23 above.

[28] See Joseph, 'The Challenge of a Bill of Rights: A Commentary', *NZLJ* [1986] 416 at 422.

[29] See the litigation between *New Zealand Maori Council* v. *Attorney-General* [1987] 1 NZLR 641 (High Court and Court of Appeal); [1991] 2 NZLR 147 (Court of Appeal); [1992] 2 NZLR 576 (Court of Appeal); [1994] 1 NZLR 513 (Privy Council) (Lords Templeman, Mustill, Woolf and Lloyd of Berwick, and Sir Thomas Eichelbaum).

(c) It would be premature to adopt the Bill without closer study of the implications of a Bill of Rights.

(d) The Bill would cause undue uncertainty in the law since one could not readily predict which Acts of Parliament would be repugnant to it.

(e) The Bill would lead to increased litigation.

(f) The Bill emphasised individual and not collective rights.

(g) The Bill relied on judicial enforcement but people (particularly the poor) did not have equal access to the Courts.

(h) If more checks and balances were needed, there were better ones available, with 39 submissions supporting an Upper House.

By comparison, protagonists argued that:

(i) New Zealand lacked constitutional safeguards and a Bill of Rights would be a check on the Executive.

(ii) The Bill would protect minorities and disadvantaged groups, which ordinary democratic and electoral processes cannot protect.

(iii) The Bill would protect against an insidious or a casual erosion of rights.

(iv) The Bill would provide a focus for and raise awareness about human rights.

(v) The Bill would advance New Zealand's compliance with its international obligations to respect human rights, particularly under the International Covenant on Civil and Political Rights.

THE NEW ZEALAND BILL OF RIGHTS ACT 1990

When the Justice and Law Reform Committee reported in 1988,[30] the National Opposition had declared that it would vote against the White Paper Bill and this foreclosed any prospect of its enactment. The Bill lacked popular support, or what Sir Robin Cooke (now Lord Cooke of Thorndon) termed 'practical sanctity'.[31] The select committee recommended in lieu a declaratory Bill which was introduced and enacted as the New Zealand Bill of Rights Act 1990. This measure was similar to the White Paper draft Bill, with the Long Title reproducing its objectives '[t]o affirm, protect, and promote human rights and fundamental freedoms in New Zealand' and 'To affirm New Zealand's commitment to the International Covenant on Civil and Political Rights'. It differed in two respects: it was an ordinary rather than entrenched document, and it omitted reference to the Treaty of Waitangi. Otherwise it

[30] See Justice and Law Reform Committee, *Final Report on a White Paper: A Bill of Rights for New Zealand* (1988), *AJHR* (1987–1990), I.8C.

[31] Sir Robin Cooke, 'Practicalities of a Bill of Rights', F.S. Dethridge Memorial Address (1984), reprinted in 112 *Council Brief* (1984) 4.

affirmed a similar catalogue of civil and political rights as contained in the earlier draft Bill: for example, the rights to life and security of the person and to be free from torture or cruel or degrading punishment, the rights to freedom of thought, conscience, religion and belief, freedom of expression, non-discrimination and minority rights, the rights to peaceful assembly and association, and rights relating to arrest, detention and search and seizure, and minimum standards of criminal procedure, including a suspect's right to legal representation.

Attempts were made within the Government caucus to embellish the Act with economic and social rights as guaranteed by some international instruments, notably the Universal Declaration on Human Rights. Advocated were the rights to work and an adequate standard of living, and the rights to housing, education and State health care. The Justice and Law Reform Committee noted New Zealand's international obligations and also suggested the inclusion of key economic, social and cultural rights, such as education, housing and medical care.[32] However the Government rejected this recommendation since it was felt that such 'rights' were, by nature, non-justiciable. Social or State welfare benefits fell to political rather than judicial process, and would have made the legislation 'unmanageable'.[33]

The Operational Provisions

RIGHTS AFFIRMED—SECTION 2

Section 2 provides that '[t]he rights and freedoms contained in this Bill of Rights are affirmed'. This textual affirmation of rights risked inviting a 'frozen concepts' approach to interpretation. The former Canadian Bill of Rights 1960 provided that the rights therein 'have existed and shall continue to exist' and some Canadian Supreme Court judges suggested that the content of rights were to be ascertained by reference to their state as at 1960. The Supreme Court eventually rejected that approach,[34] and the New Zealand Courts, too, after some initial prevarication,[35] settled upon a purposive approach for interpreting and applying rights.

In the first case to reach the Court of Appeal,[36] Cooke P. spoke of the

---

[32] Civil and political rights are sometimes referred to as 'first generation' rights, economic, social and cultural rights as 'second generation'. The White Paper, *A Bill of Rights for New Zealand* n. 1 above, argued for the exclusion of the latter. The interim report of the select committee examining the White Paper adopted the same position but its final report proposed the inclusion of second generation rights, when recommending a Bill that would not be supreme law.

[33] See Palmer, *New Zealand's Constitution in Crisis* (1992), 57.

[34] See *Curr* v. *R.* [1972] SCR 889.

[35] For example, *R.* v. *Nikau* (1991) 7 CRNZ 214 (High Court); *Minto* v. *Police* (1991) 7 CRNZ 38 (High Court); *R.* v. *Butcher* [1992] 2 NZLR 257 per Gault J. (Court of Appeal), expressing preference for the 'frozen concepts' approach.

[36] *Flickinger* v. *Crown Colony of Hong Kong* [1991] 1 NZLR 439 (Court of Appeal).

'purpose or spirit of the New Zealand Bill of Rights Act'[37] and applied the right to habeas corpus under Section 25(1)(c) in a manner not limited by its pre-existing form. In *Re S*,[38] Barker J. observed that the Long Title to the Act supplies a context ('[t]o affirm, protect, and *promote*') which indicated that Parliament did not intend a frozen concepts approach. Cooke P. in *Ministry of Transport* v. *Noort*[39] cited Barker J.'s decision and stated that the Bill of Rights Act implies development of the law where necessary: 'Such a measure is not to be approached as if it did no more than preserve the status quo.' In an action against a television network for malicious falsehood and defamation,[40] the Court of Appeal upheld the novel jurisdiction to grant a mandatory injunction ordering corrective advertising. Through merger of common law and equity, the remedy was available whenever justice required. However the Court also stated[41] that the Bill of Rights Act would have supplied any omission in the law. Cooke P. thought it 'tenable' that the right to impart information under Section 14 founded a jurisdiction to compel publication of corrective statements for an actionable defamation.[42] Corrective advertising would have constituted a justified limit on freedom of expression under the Act's 'saving' provision, Section 5.

Furthermore, some rights the Act 'affirms' are new to the law, such as the rights to be secure against unreasonable search and seizure,[43] and for a person arrested or charged to be informed of the right to legal counsel[44] and to be tried without undue delay.[45] The Courts formerly recognised the interests underlying these rights in striking out prosecutions for delay or evidence unfairly obtained,[46] and in guarding against abuse of the Court's process generally.[47] But the Bill of Rights Act actually erected these interests into substantive rights, warranting the development of appropriate remedies where

---

[37] Ibid. at 441 per Cooke P. for the Court following *Minister of Home Affairs* v. *Fisher* [1980] AC 319 (Privy Council) per Lord Wilberforce commending a 'generous interpretation' of Bills of Rights.

[38] [1992] 1 NZLR 363 (High Court).   [39] [1992] 3 NZLR 260 at 270.

[40] *TV3 Network Ltd* v. *Eveready New Zealand Ltd* [1993] 3 NZLR 435.

[41] Ibid. per Cooke P. at 440–1. Gault and McKay J.J. did not address the point.

[42] Ibid.

[43] *R.* v. *Longtin* 147 DLR (3d) 604 at 608 per Blair J.A., approved in *Terekia* v. *Ministry of Transport*, unreported, High Court Auckland, 13 May 1991 per Barker J. at 13–14 of the transcript.

[44] Ibid. at 14–15 of the transcript ('the right . . . is something new conferred by the New Zealand Bill of Rights Act').

[45] *Jago* v. *District Court (NSW)* (1989) 168 CLR 23; *R.* v. *E.T.E.* (1990) 6 CRNZ 176 at 181 per Holland J. (no common law right to a speedy trial in either New South Wales or New Zealand).

[46] See e.g. *R.* v. *Alexander* [1989] 3 NZLR 395 (Court of Appeal) (evidence may be excluded through undue delay); *R.* v. *Webster* [1989] 2 NZLR 129 (Court of Appeal) (evidence may be excluded when access to a solicitor denied).

[47] *Moevao* v. *Department of Labour* [1980] 1 NZLR 464 (Court of Appeal), particularly at 482 per Richardson J.; *Department of Social Welfare (Russell)* v. *Stewart* (1988) 3 CRNZ 648 (High Court); *R.* v. *Webster* [1982] 2 NZLR 129 at 140 per Bisson J.

necessary.[48] It was for this reason that the Courts in Canada and New Zealand refused to give their Bill of Rights legislation retrospective application.[49]

APPLICATION OF THE ACT—SECTION 3

Where the Burden Falls

The burden of the Bill of Rights Act falls upon the Government and public entities, not private individuals. Section 3 describes those persons and entities to which it applies:

3. Application. This Bill of Rights applies only to acts done—
(a) By the legislative, executive, or judicial branches of the Government of New Zealand; or
(b) By any person or body in the performance of any public function, power, or duty conferred or imposed on that person or body by or pursuant to law.

Individuals enjoy the benefit of the rights and freedoms affirmed insofar as these may be exacted from the persons and entities described: that is, from 'Government' in all its manifestations. Private individuals inter se may not invoke the Act (except possibly in private common law actions).[50] Section 3 may be problematic in respects, as one High Court judge has observed:[51]

There are rights stated in the Act which are unlikely ever to arise in situations between a citizen and a branch of Government or an official exercising functions, powers or duties conferred on the official by or pursuant to law. I have difficulty in seeing how a purposive interpretation of the Section can be applied if the words used are held literally to mean what they say.

Seldom will individuals have cause to claim their right to freedom of expression[52] against the Government or some Governmental body, when the common law already recognises the right to free speech (subject to defamation, incitement to violence etc.). Freedoms of religious belief and worship,[53] and of minorities to practise their culture and use their language,[54] and the rights to freedom of association and movement,[55] may have less practical application against Government or public entities than against private individuals or associations, such as private employers or clubs. The Bill of Rights Act is no panacea for bigotry or human frailty.

[48] See e.g. *Terekia* n. 43 above.
[49] See *R.* v. *Lee* (1982) 142 DLR (3d) 574 (Saskatchewan Court of Appeal); *R.* v. *Longtin* 147 DLR (3d) 604 (Ontario Court of Appeal); *R.* v. *James* (1988) 40 CCC (3d) 576 (Ontario Court of Appeal), [1988] SCR 669; *Stevens* v. *R.* 51 DLR (4d) 394 (Supreme Court of Canada) followed in *Terekia*.
[50] See nn. 95–103 below and accompanying text.
[51] *Police* v. *Geiringer* [1991] 1 NZBORR 331 at 342 per Holland J.
[52] See the Bill of Rights Act s. 14.
[53] See ibid. ss. 13 and 15.
[54] See ibid. s. 20.
[55] See ibid. ss. 17–18.

'Acts Done' Includes Omissions

Section 3 is predicated on 'acts done' but these words also include omissions. Early case law involved the failure of police to inform an arrested person of the right to legal counsel.[56] It was simply assumed that the words 'acts done by' also included omissions. The 'due process' rights of persons arrested or charged impose obligations on the law enforcement authority (for example, to state promptly the reason for arrest and to inform of the right to counsel),[57] and to exclude omissions under Section 3 would negate these rights.

Acts Done by the Legislative Branch

Commentators, relying on Canadian authority, have suggested that the words 'acts done by the legislative branch' refer only to legislation passed by Parliament, including delegated legislation.[58] In *Retail Wholesale and Department Store Union* v. *Dolphin Delivery*,[59] McIntyre J. stated: 'It would seem that legislation is the only way in which a Legislature may infringe a guaranteed right or freedom.' But it is difficult to envisage why, when the Canadian and provincial Legislatures enjoy certain privileges and contempt powers and are expressly subject to the Charter. Their powers to commit, censure and fine may be as punitive and coercive as any State agency's. In *New Brunswick Broadcasting Co. Ltd.* v. *Donahoe*,[60] the Nova Scotia Supreme Court reflected that the Canadian Legislatures enjoyed the same privileges and powers as the British House of Commons and declared that the Charter, as supreme law, controlled their exercise. On appeal, the Supreme Court of Canada upheld the protection of Parliamentary privilege (as having excluded the Charter) but ruled that the Charter might apply to the Legislature in areas not covered by privilege, or where applying the Charter did not, in terms, abrogate or negate the privilege.[61] Thus, not only legislation might infringe the Charter.

The scheme of the Bill of Rights Act also excludes McIntyre J.'s suggested limitation. On his approach, reference to the legislative branch in Section 3 would have been superfluous since the Bill of Rights Act already specifically deals with the question of Statutes. Section 6 commands Courts wherever possible to interpret Statutes consistently with the rights affirmed, while Section

---

[56] See *R.* v. *Kirifi* [1992] 2 NZLR 8 (Court of Appeal); *R.* v. *Butcher* [1992] 2 NZLR 257 (Court of Appeal).

[57] See the Bill of Rights Act ss. 23–24.

[58] Rishworth, 'The New Zealand Bill of Rights Act 1990: The First Fifteen Months' in *Essays on the New Zealand Bill of Rights Act 1990* (1992), 7 at 15, citing *Retail Wholesale and Department Store Union* v. *Dolphin Delivery* (1987) 33 DLR (4th) 174 (Supreme Court of Canada).

[59] (1987) 33 DLR (4th) 174 at 195.   [60] (1990) 71 DLR (4th) 23.

[61] *New Brunswick Broadcasting Co.* v. *Nova Scotia (Speaker of the House of Assembly)* [1993] 1 SCR 319 by a 7:1 majority. Four judges ruled on the facts that the Charter did not apply, while Sopinka J. held that the Charter applied but that any infringement was justified.

4 preserves the validity and operation of legislation that cannot reasonably be reconciled. It is therefore pedantic to suggest that 'the legislative branch' may not refer to the House of Representatives in its corporate capacity, and then conclude that the House and its officers are not subject to the Bill of Rights Act.[62] When the Speaker issues a committal warrant for contempt of the House, it is the legislative branch *acting* and (subject to considerations of Parliamentary privilege) it is as controlled by the Act as any other public authority exercising coercive power. Thus the Serjeant-at-Arms must inform any person whom he or she arrests of the right to legal counsel,[63] and that person will be entitled to the Act's 'due process' protections, including the right to seek habeas corpus for challenging the committal.[64]

The Bill of Rights Act binds the House, notwithstanding Parliamentary privilege. The reasoning which excluded the Charter in the *New Brunswick Broadcasting* case[65] lacks relevance for New Zealand. There, the appellants unsuccessfully sought the right to televise the assembly's proceedings, claiming the Charter right to freedom of the press and media communication. However the Supreme Court held that the Charter could not prevail over the assembly's legislative privileges, including its exclusive right to be sole judge of its own proceedings. Parliamentary privilege was a constitutional protection and one part of the Constitution (the Charter) could not abrogate or negate another part (Parliamentary privilege).[66]

Parliamentary privilege in New Zealand lacks 'supreme law' status. The privileges of the House of Commons were adopted into New Zealand in 1865 from English common law[67] and apply subject to the Bill of Rights Act. The only reservations are whether the Courts would retreat behind their disclaimer of jurisdiction in *Bradlaugh* v. *Gossett*[68] (and leave the Bill of Rights Act to the House to administer in its application to it), and whether Parliament's privileges would be upheld as imposing justifiable limits on the rights affirmed. An exception must be made for Parliament's freedom of speech which is given statutory foundation under Article 9 of the Bill of Rights 1688 (UK).[69] Thus no-one could assert the rights to natural justice and judicial review under the

---

[62] Cf. *New Brunswick Broadcasting Co.* v. *Nova Scotia (Speaker of the House of Assembly)* [1993] 1 SCR 319 per Lamer C.J. holding that the term 'Legislature' referred to the body capable of enacting legislation and not to its component parts. None of the other judges adopted this reasoning. In New Zealand, Section 3 refers to the 'legislative branch', not the 'Legislature', which clearly includes the House of Representatives.

[63] See the Bill of Rights Act s. 23(1)(b).   [64] See ibid. s. 23(1)(c).

[65] *New Brunswick Broadcasting Co.* v. *Nova Scotia (Speaker of the House of Assembly)* [1993] 1 SCR 319.

[66] See also *Reference re An Act to Amend the Education Act (Ontario)* [1987] 1 SCR 1148 (the Charter does not apply to invalidate other provisions of the Constitution).

[67] By virtue of the Legislature Act 1908 (NZ) s. 242(1).   [68] (1884) 12 QBD 271.

[69] The Bill of Rights 1688 applied as law in New Zealand from the establishment of the Colony. See *Fitzgerald* v. *Muldoon* [1976] 2 NZLR 615 per Wild C.J. The inheritance of British laws is now governed by the Imperial Laws Application Act 1988 (NZ).

Bill of Rights Act[70] in respect of Parliamentary proceedings which are protected under Article 9. Under Section 4, limiting Statutes prevail.

Acts Done by the Executive Branch and Public Authorities

The application of the Act to the Executive branch begs closer examination in
the Courts. In two decisions, hospital doctors were held to be subject to the
Act when taking blood samples for determining the blood-alcohol levels of
motorists within their charge.[71] It was enough that medical practitioners were
invested with statutory powers and responsibilities under the Transport Act
1962 (NZ) establishing the blood-alcohol scheme. In another case,[72] a private
television station was bound because it was licensed under New Zealand's
broadcasting legislation and exercised '[c]ertain responsibilities, including
some relating to balance in controversial issues of public importance'.[73] In a
further case, involving review of the National Party's constitution and rules,
the judge did not rule whether political parties were bound but treated the Act
as 'relevant background'.[74] In none of those decisions did Section 3 claim the
Court's closer attention.

   The term 'Government' is the Canadian Charter equivalent of the New
Zealand wording, 'Executive branch'. For the Canadian Courts, 'what is
Government?' has proved a thorny question. 'Government' lacks obvious
boundaries, and its scope is constantly shifting as the State enters or with-
draws from particular fields or activities. The Canadian Courts have taken an
expansive approach, bringing within the Charter's sweep adjudicative and
administrative tribunals,[75] educational establishments,[76] labour law arbitra-
tors[77] and municipal Government.[78] However New Zealand Courts need not
replicate this approach owing to the separate 'public functions' limb under
Section 3(b) which has no counterpart under the Canadian Charter. Section 3
has two distinct applications—one involving a 'status' classification, the other
a 'functions' classification. Paragraph (a) embraces the State's central administrative apparatus, notably Government departments and State enforcement

---

   [70] Bill of Rights Act s. 27.
   [71] *R.* v. *Clarke* (1992) 8 CRNZ 528 (High Court); *Smith* v. *Ministry of Transport* (1992) 8
CRNZ 621 (High Court).
   [72] *TV3 Network Ltd* v. *Eveready New Zealand Ltd* [1993] 3 NZLR 435 (Court of Appeal).
   [73] Ibid. per Cooke P. at 441.
   [74] *Peters* v. *Collinge* [1993] 2 NZLR 554 at 565 per Fisher J. (High Court).
   [75] *Biscotti* v. *Ontario (Securities Commission)* (1991) 76 DLR (4th) 762, (1991) 1 OR (3d) 409
(Ontario Court of Appeal) (the Charter applied but no violation of a Charter right established).
   [76] *Douglas/Kwantlen Faculty Association* v. *Douglas College* [1990] 2 SCR 570. Cf. *McKinney*
v. *University of Guelph* (1990) 76 DLR (4th) 545; *Connell* v. *University of British Columbia* [1990]
3 SCR 451.
   [77] *Slaight Communications Inc.* v. *Davidson* [1989] 1 SCR 1038.
   [78] *Retail Wholesale and Department Store Union* v. *Dolphin Delivery Ltd* [1986] 2 SCR 573 at
602 (municipal by-laws 'possibly' constitute Government action).

agencies such as the police and customs, fisheries and immigration officers, while para. (b) embraces persons or bodies discharging functions of a public nature, whether or not they fall within the 'Executive branch' per se.[79]

Paragraph (a) ostensibly embraces the Executive in all its activities—public or private—but the scope of this limb may be narrower. In *McKinney* v. *University of Guelph*,[80] two Supreme Court judges thought that not all actions of a governmental body will attract Charter scrutiny. For Sopinka and L'Heureux-Dubé J.J., the 'public/private' divide applied to Government itself: '[N]ot all activities of an entity that is generally carrying on the functions of Government will be governmental in nature.'[81] Sopinka J. thought it important to identify two things: '[F]irst, that [the entity] is a governmental body and, second, that it is acting in that capacity in respect of the conduct sought to be subjected to Charter scrutiny.'[82] The seven member Court split over the status of a university, with the majority holding that universities were neither part of 'Government' nor engaged in 'governmental action'.[83] However Sopinka and L'Heureux-Dubé J.J. thought that a university might attract Charter scrutiny in respect of some functions, though not others. A university, for example, may perform the public function of education and be bound by the Charter, and discharge private functions as employer of its staff. This would entitle a student, but not an employee, to invoke the Charter.

This approach would confine Section 3 to *public* acts and would substantially restrict the reach of the Bill of Rights Act. The Act would control Government action under the Royal prerogative and the Crown's statutory (public) powers, but not the Crown's private acts carried out in concert with individuals. The Crown has legal personality[84] and enjoys all the freedoms and capacities of a natural person.[85] Thus the Crown may transact land, enter into contracts, engage employees and do whatever is not legally forbidden,

---

[79] See e.g. *Re 'Penthouse (U.S.)' Vol. 19, No. 5* (1991) 7 NZAR 289 (Indecent Publications Tribunal is subject to the Bill of Rights Act).

[80] (1990) 76 DLR (4th) 545.

[81] Ibid. at 697 per Sopinka J. See also L'Heureux-Dubé J. at 678. See further *Harrison* v. *University of British Columbia* (1988) 49 DLR (4th) at 695–6, 687 (British Columbia Court of Appeal).

[82] Ibid. But cf. *Lavigne* v. *Ontario Public Service Employees Union* [1991] 2 SCR 211 (the Charter applies so long as 'Government' is present, notwithstanding the quality of the activity).

[83] Per La Forest J. for the majority on this point; Wilson J. dissenting (Cory J. concurring on this issue).

[84] See *Adams* v. *Naylor* [1946] AC 543 at 555 (House of Lords); *Town Investments Ltd* v. *Department of the Environment* [1978] AC 359 at 400 (House of Lords), adopting Maitland's conception of the Crown as a corporation aggregate 'embracing the State in all its activities'; Maitland 'The Crown as Corporation' (1901) 17 LQR 131. See Joseph, 'The Crown as a Legal Concept—Part I', [1993] NZLJ 126.

[85] See e.g. *Malone* v. *Metropolitan Police Commissioner* [1979] Ch D 344 per Sir Robert Megarry V-C (the Crown may do whatever is not forbidden by law). See Joseph, 'The Crown as a Legal Concept—Part II' [1993] NZLJ 179.

without need of further justification or power.[86] In *R.* v. *Goodwin*,[87] the Court of Appeal foreshadowed Sopinka J.'s approach by stating that the Bill of Rights Act was limited to 'the public field' and does not apply 'in the field of purely private law'.

The para. (b) 'public-functions' limb avoids the need for a forced analysis of 'Government' or 'Executive branch'. But this limb also imports all the ambiguity that infects the public/private distinction. Private contractors, for instance, when working on Crown land, have been held entitled to the Crown's immunity from Statute.[88] Their interests were imputed to the Crown (in reality, the Government) since to have applied the Statute would have worked prejudice to the Crown. The difficult tests for determining whether public corporations may claim the Crown's immunities also apply by analogy under Section 3(b).

The State-owned enterprises were established in New Zealand for discharging essentially State functions,[89] but as independent commercial operations. Should these entities fall under the Act's umbrella?[90] And should hospitals or universities, which are likewise removed from normal notions of ministerial responsibility? The Courts must answer such questions as best they can, as they have had to do in Canada. In *McKinney*, Wilson J. laid down a three-fold test:[91]

(1) Does the Executive or administrative branch of Government exercise general control over the entity in question?

(2) Does the entity perform a traditional Government function or a function which, in modern times, is recognised as a responsibility of the State?

(3) Does the entity act pursuant to statutory authority granted for furthering an objective that Government seeks to promote in the broader public interest?

Affirmative answer(s) would indicate an entity that formed part of 'Government', but the response need not be conclusive. Wilson J.'s 'questions' were, she conceded, no more than 'practical guidelines'.[92]

---

[86] But subject to any overriding public responsibility by implication of Statute or at common law. See e.g. *Webster* v. *Auckland Harbour Board* [1983] NZLR 646 (Court of Appeal); *Minister of Energy* v. *Petrocorp Exploration Ltd* [1992] 3 NZLR 1 (Privy Council) (public bodies may be in a different position from private individuals when exercising contractual freedoms).

[87] (1992) 9 CRNZ 1 at 25 and 37 per Cooke P.

[88] See *Lower Hutt City* v. *Attorney-General* [1965] NZLR 65 (Court of Appeal).

[89] The State-owned enterprises were formerly Government departments or trading facilities but were reconstituted under the State Owned Enterprises Act 1986 (NZ) for increasing efficiency and cost-saving in the public sector.

[90] Compare *Federated Farmers of New Zealand (Inc.)* v. *New Zealand Post Ltd*, unreported, High Court Wellington, 1 December 1992 per McGechan J. holding that New Zealand Post (an S.O.E.) was bound by Section 14 of the Bill of Rights Act, affirming the right to impart and receive information.

[91] (1990) 76 DLR (4th) 545 at 592.   [92] Ibid. at 592–3.

Acts Done by the Judicial Branch

The Bill of Rights Act is binding on judges in the discharge of their functions. In *R.* v. *Chignal*,[93] the High Court cited freedom of expression under Section 14 in declining the Crown's request to prohibit publication of a witness's testimony. Robertson J. invoked the Bill of Rights Act as a reason why a contemplated judicial act—granting the order—was inappropriate. In *R.* v. *Shaw*,[94] the Court of Appeal referred to an accused's right to a defence lawyer in Section 24(c)(d) and quashed a conviction entered in the District Court. The judge had refused an adjournment to a defendant whose counsel had another engagement, and had convicted after hearing the case. Both *Shaw* and *Chignal* could have been dealt with on general principles—in *Chignal* because the order would have been a needless injunction against all the world, and in *Shaw* because the principles of fairness justified an adjournment. But in each case, the Bill of Rights Act identified the interests warranting protection and focused the judicial inquiry upon them.

There has been speculation whether the Bill of Rights Act might also reach into private common law litigation. Since the Courts are subject to the Act, it has been mooted whether they are at liberty to decide private actions in ways that contravene the rights affirmed.[95] There are two bases on which the Act might apply: first, a Court order for damages or an injunction or some other remedy is 'an act done by the judicial branch'. *Chignal* and *Shaw* are signal cases, although both authorities involved a 'public' element since it was the Crown prosecuting offences against the criminal law. In *Solicitor-General* v. *Radio New Zealand*,[96] the Bill of Rights Act was held applicable to contempt of court proceedings, 'as applying to acts done by the judicial branch under Section 3(a)'.[97] However this case also involved a public element since the superior Courts bear responsibility for punishing contempts and preserving the integrity of the justice system. The Courts are more intensely involved as participants, than in inter partes actions.

Secondly, the development and application of a common law principle amounts to 'an act done by the judicial branch'. The demise of the declaratory theory of common law entails acceptance that judges *make* the law. Lord Atkin's famous neighbour principle in *Donoghue* v. *Stevenson*,[98] for example, founded the modern law of negligence and signalled a new epoch for the common law. In *Solicitor-General* v. *Radio New Zealand*, the Full Court conceded the constant adjustment and development of common law principles, and the greater 'discretion' Courts exercise than when applying statutory provisions.[99]

---

[93] (1990) 6 CRNZ 476.   [94] [1992] 1 NZLR 652 (Court of Appeal).
[95] See Butler, 'The New Zealand Bill of Rights and Private Common Law Litigation', [1991] NZLJ 261; Burrows n. 7 above at 333–4.
[96] [1994] 1 NZLR 48 (Full ct., High Court).
[97] Ibid. at 58 per Eichelbaum C.J. and Greig J.
[98] [1932] AC 562 (House of Lords).   [99] *Radio New Zealand* n. 96 above at 63–64.

The Canadian Charter equivalent of Section 3 omits reference to acts of the judicial branch. In the much-criticised *Dolphin Delivery* case,[100] the Supreme Court held that the Charter did not apply to private litigation, except when it involved Governmental action which is based on Statute or the common law. A Statute is an act of the legislative branch and always remained to be tested against the Charter. The Supreme Court also held that the Charter applied to private actions 'insofar as the common law is the basis of some Governmental action which, it is alleged, infringes a guaranteed right or freedom'.[101] The Charter did not apply to Court orders per se. A Court order was not 'Governmental action':[102] 'To regard a Court order as an element of Governmental intervention necessary to invoke the Charter would . . . widen the scope of the Charter application to virtually all private litigation.'

Whether New Zealand Courts will follow suit depends on how intrusive they think the Act should be in shaping private relations. There are three options: apply the Act to private actions; or confine it to actions where the Crown or some 'public' element is involved; or give it qualified application as in Canada. Reference to the 'judicial branch' in Section 3(a) may not assist. In *Dolphin Delivery*, the Supreme Court accepted that the Canadian Courts are bound by the Charter, 'as they are bound by all law', but that they act 'as neutral arbiters, not as contending parties involved in a dispute'.[103] Hence a Court order did not constitute a Governmental (or *semble* judicial) *act*. There would also be less scope for challenge under the New Zealand Act. When a judicial order involves public acts based on Statute, the order may contravene the Bill of Rights Act with impunity because this instrument must yield to contrary Statutes. Only a judicial order based on the common law or involving a judicial discretion would support a challenge.

OTHER ENACTMENTS NOT AFFECTED—SECTION 4

Impermissible Judicial Responses

Section 4 avoids any argument that the Act controls Parliamentary power. It catalogues three impermissible judicial responses to inconsistent legislation:

4. Other enactments not affected. No court shall, in relation to any enactment (whether passed or made before or after the commencement of this Bill of Rights)—
(a) Hold any provision of the enactment to be impliedly repealed or revoked, or to be in any way invalid or ineffective; or

---

[100] *Retail Wholesale and Department Store Union* v. *Dolphin Delivery Ltd* (1986) 33 DLR (4th) 147. For academic criticism, see the references and discussion in *McKinney* v. *University of Guelph* (1990) 76 DLR (4th) 545 at 588 et seq. per Wilson J.
[101] Ibid. at 195 per McIntyre J. speaking for the Court on this issue.
[102] Ibid. at 196.
[103] *McKinney* v. *University of Guelph* (1990) 76 DLR (4th) 545 at 588 et seq. per Wilson J.

(b) Decline to apply any provision of the enactment—
by reason only that the provision is inconsistent with any provision of this Bill of Rights.

The plaintiff's argument in *Mangawaro Enterprises Ltd* v. *Attorney-General*[104] was destined to fail. Counsel submitted that the word 'only' in Section 4 supported a judicial power to invalidate Statutes, or to declare them inoperative or of no effect, where the Statute was inconsistent, not only with the Bill of Rights Act, but also with some other enactment or rule of law. A Court would not then be invalidating legislation 'by reason only' that it was inconsistent with the Bill of Rights Act. This argument presupposed an already existing power to strike down legislation when there was none, or that the words 'by reason *only*' had miraculously created one.

The Interdependence of Section 4

Section 4 operates in concert with Sections 5–6 which read:

5. *Justified limitations.* Subject to Section 4 of this Bill of Rights, the rights and freedoms contained in this Bill of Rights may be subject only to such reasonable limits prescribed by law as can be demonstrably justified in a free and democratic society.

6. *Interpretation consistent with Bill of Rights to be preferred.* Wherever an enactment can be given a meaning that is consistent with the rights and freedoms contained in this Bill of Rights, that meaning shall be preferred to any other meaning.

These Sections, read together, are problematic, for they serve different ends. Despite the caselaw, their interrelationship remains unsettled. Section 5 was adapted from the Canadian Charter which controls legislation. Under its Canadian equivalent, not all intruding legislation is struck down but only those provisions which cannot be 'demonstrably justified' as 'reasonable' and 'prescribed by law'. Sections 4 and 6, however, are specifically for upholding legislation notwithstanding the Bill of Rights Act. In *Ministry of Transport* v. *Noort*,[105] the Court of Appeal disagreed over whether Section 4 should apply in isolation or in tandem with Section 5—the 'justified limits' Clause. Cooke P. and Gault J. held that Section 5 had no application, Richardson, McKay and Hardie Boys J.J. held that it did. In *Temese* v. *Police*,[106] the President cautioned that the 'last word' was 'far from having been said'.

Contesting Approaches

Section 4 safeguards inconsistent Statutes. The Richardson approach employs Section 5 for determining whether there is, in fact, inconsistency. Under

[104] [1994] 2 NZLR 451 (High Court).   [105] [1992] 3 NZLR 260.
[106] (1992) 9 CRNZ 425 at 427.

Section 6, enactments must, wherever possible, be given a meaning that does not infringe the Bill of Rights Act. If to read down a Statute could reasonably attain that result, then that is what the Court must do and no question of inconsistency arises. If the legislation cannot be so read, then the question arises whether it may be reconciled under Section 5. Since rights are not absolute but qualified, one ought to speak of an 'infringement' of the Bill of Rights Act only when a limiting Statute fails the Section 5 test, as being neither 'reasonable' nor 'demonstrably justified'. Richardson J. (with whom McKay J. agreed) thought the Section 5 inquiry should, in fact, precede the application of Section 6, 'as the statutory sequence would itself . . . indicate'.[107] It was first necessary to fix the scope and content of the right within the factual context and, for Richardson J., 'Section 5 sets out the criteria for placing limits . . . on the generality of the rights as defined'.[108] Hardie Boys J. also applied Section 5, albeit in rather more oblique fashion (discussed below).

Cooke P. and Gault J. rejected the Richardson approach. Part I of the Bill of Rights Act sets out the operational provisions (Sections 2–7), and Part II the rights and freedoms affirmed. These judges preferred that, once an enactment was found to be inconsistent with Part II, Section 4 applied to the exclusion of Section 5. Cooke P. identified the textual differences in Sections 4–7 and stated:[109]

Whereas Section 4 has the words 'inconsistent with any provision of this Bill of Rights', the three following Sections have the formula 'the rights and freedoms contained in this Bill of Rights'. This seems to indicate, for instance, that the question under Section 6 is whether a meaning consistent with those rights and freedoms is open, not whether a meaning consistent with the Bill of Rights as a whole is open.

Accordingly, Gault J. held that:[110] 'Where, on a proper interpretation of a New Zealand Statute, there is a limit imposed upon a fundamental right, it is no part of the function of the Courts to examine whether that limit can be justified. The limit must be given effect to as directed by Section 4.'

It is understandable why Cooke P. and Gault J. should want to short-circuit the Section 5 inquiry: a statutory limitation, once identified, will prevail over the Bill of Rights Act, whether or not it is 'reasonable' and 'justified'. But it could be argued that Section 5 reserves at least a formal role to the Courts to declare a case of serious or patent inconsistency—where the limit is neither reasonable nor justified—even though Section 4 precludes any further judicial response.[111] Section 5 provides an opportunity for comparing the objectives underlying the Bill's rights and freedoms with the objectives of

---

[107] [1992] 3 NZLR 260 at 282.   [108] Ibid.
[109] Ibid. at 273.   [110] Ibid. at 295.
[111] See Brookfield, 'Freedom: The New Zealand Bill of Rights Act', *Recent Law Review* [1992] 236 at 239.

other enactments, and striking a balance between the two.[112] Applying rights and freedoms in their unqualified, pristine state increases the risk of excluding them altogether for inconsistency under Section 4.[113]

If Section 5 plays no ameliorating role, justified limitations on rights and freedoms are cast as infringements of the Bill of Rights Act, with the Government unable to argue a justified limitation but required to bear the political consequences. In *Temese* v. *Police*[114], Cooke P. took issue with this criticism, terming it a 'drawback that, if the Court were to say that the limitation was unjustified yet overridden by the enactment, the Court could be seen to be gratuitously criticising Parliament by intruding an advisory opinion'. But it seems odd why Governments should be spared notice of offending legislation, when an entrenched Bill of Rights calls on Courts actually *to strike down* legislation, as being constitutionally repugnant. Causing offence to Executive sensibilities did not constrain Sir Edward Coke in *Prohibitions del Roy*,[115] or Lord Campden C.J. in *Entick* v. *Carrington*,[116] or Wild C.J. in *Fitzgerald* v. *Muldoon*,[117] from checking Executive abuse. A declaratory Bill calls upon Courts to consult openly the values it enshrines.

JUSTIFIED LIMITATIONS—SECTION 5

The Utilitarian Calculation

Guarantees in a Bill of Rights are statements of the on-going conflicts between the individual and the State; they are not, in terms, the resolution of them. Section 5, reproduced above, makes this explicit.

Most rights and freedoms under the Act are couched in unqualified language without regard to specific limitations. Some contain their own limiting language, such as the rights to be free from 'arbitrary' arrest and 'unreasonable' search and seizure, and the rights to be tried 'without undue delay' and to 'adequate' time and facilities to prepare a defence. However none of the rights is absolute. Section 5 recognizes that rights 'do not exist in a vacuum, that they may be modified in the public interest to take account of the rights of others and of the interests of the community.'[118] This provision reflects what is implicit in the judicial function, whether or not this entails a Bill of Rights, or a Bill of Rights with or without a justified limitations Clause. In an appeal against conviction for disorderly behaviour under New Zealand's former Police Offences Act 1927, the Court of Appeal stated:[119]

---

[112] See e.g. *Herewini* v. *Ministry of Transport* (1992) 9 CRNZ 307 at 321 per Fisher J.
[113] Ibid. at 321–2; *Ministry of Transport* v. *Noort* [1992] 3 NZLR 260 at 287.
[114] (1992) 9 CRNZ 425 at 427.   [115] (1607) 12 Co Rep 63.
[116] (1765) 19 St Tr 1030.   [117] [1976] 2 NZLR 615.
[118] *Ministry of Transport* v. *Noort* [1992] 3 NZLR 260 at 282–3 per Richardson J.
[119] *Melser* v. *Police* [1967] NZLR 437 (Supreme Court and Court of Appeal) at 445–6 per McCarthy J.

The task of the law is to define the limitations which our society, for its social health, puts on freedoms . . . [T]he Courts must lay down the boundaries themselves, bearing in mind that freedoms are of different qualities and values and that the higher and more important should not be unduly restricted in favour of lower or less important ones.

The Courts must fix the constitutional 'worth' of rights and freedoms within a hierarchy or scale of values implicit in our legal culture. In *Noort*, for example, Richardson J. devoted one and a half pages of the reports to the socio-legal value attributed to the right to legal counsel under Section 23—as being 'pivotal' and 'part of our basic legal inheritance'.[120] Under Section 5, the Courts must make a utilitarian calculation as to where the balance of public welfare lies—between unrestricted enjoyment of a particular right or freedom, and any limitations on it. Do the social costs of unrestricted enjoyment exceed its benefits? This question may necessitate a broadening of the judicial inquiry to accommodate the 'Brandeis brief'—the technique of bringing before the Court a raft of sociological evidence comprising statistical data, legislative practice and history, scientific discussion and departmental reports, the economic implications of decisions and expert evidence relevant to the inquiry. This brief took its name from Louis D. Brandeis, counsel before the American Supreme Court in *Muller* v. *Oregon* (and later Justice of the Supreme Court from 1916–1939),[121] who adduced copious evidence in defence of a State Statute that the right to sell one's labour under the Fourteenth Amendment could lawfully be subjected to restrictions for the public welfare.

The 'Brandeis brief' features more prominently under an entrenched Bill of Rights than a declaratory Bill which preserves the primacy of legislation. For Richardson and McKay J.J., the brief may be employed in fixing the scope of rights against which to test limiting Statutes for ascertaining whether they may be reconciled under Section 6. They would receive evidence bearing on the 'justified limits' question, and only if the limiting statute could not be reconciled would they apply Section 4. However Cooke P. and Gault J. would exclude all evidence of a justified limit when a prima facie infringement could not be reconciled under Section 6. They would short-circuit the constitutional argument through the mechanical application of Section 4.

The Application of Section 5

The Court of Appeal in *Noort*'s case failed to agree on the application of Section 5. Cooke P. and Gault J. rejected the view that, once a statutory meaning consistent with Part II of the Bill of Rights Act could not be found, one must then inquire whether the limit is nevertheless reasonable and justified.

---

[120] [1992] 3 NZLR 260 at 279–80.   [121] 203 US 412 (1908).

Section 4 applied and the limiting Statute prevailed. This makes Section 5 a problematic provision. The Section was modelled on Section 1 of the Canadian Charter which is an entrenched constitutional document. The provision first appeared in the White Paper draft Bill, which was also to have been entrenched, but was carried over when that proposal lapsed, with the super-added proviso '[s]ubject to Section 4 of this Bill of Rights . . .'. Under an entrenched document, the provision applies to and controls all laws (including legislation), but this is not the case under a declaratory Bill. A justified limit under Section 5 must be 'prescribed by law'. When that 'law' is *statutory* (as in most cases), Section 4 applies, the limiting statute prevails, and Section 5 is superfluous. For Cooke P. and Gault J., Section 5 had relevance in two situations only: when a common law limit impinged[122] and when the Attorney-General was required under Section 7 to report Bills which contravene the provisions of Part II.[123] Cooke P. did not think that the provision could lay down a rule for interpreting other enactments, for example, for 'reading down' a limiting Statute in order to uphold a limit as 'reasonable' and 'justified': 'Rather it reads as a provision of substance stating when the rights and freedoms contained in the Bill may acceptably be made subject to limits.'[124]

The majority in *Noort* embraced Section 5 with a more generous spirit. Richardson and McKay J.J. held that Section 5 mandated the Court to ascertain the application of rights in particular cases, as being limited in scope, and then determine whether there was inconsistency with a particular law. The Section 5 inquiry logically preceded the application of Section 6 and the interpretation of a limiting Statute.

The third judge in the majority, Hardie Boys J., also adopted an approach which ameliorated the numbing effect of Section 4. He observed that Section 6 'does not permit any limitation or qualification of the Bill's rights and freedoms [but] rather treats them as absolutes'.[125] To avoid the pervasive application of Section 4, Section 5 allows a limiting Statute to be given a meaning that is consistent with the right or freedom 'in a limited or abridged form'.[126] Hardie Boys J. was committed to the lesser of evils. He stated: 'It is obviously consistent with the spirit and the purpose of the Bill of Rights Act that such a meaning should be adopted rather than that Section 4 should apply so that the rights and freedoms are excluded altogether.'[127] Section 5 was given a reconciling or bridging role between Sections 4 and 6. This approach identifies with Richardson and McKay J.J.'s, but through different reasoning. Whereas Richardson J. articulated the Section 5 elements as justifying substantive lim-

---

[122] The Bill of Rights Act prevails over common law limits. See e.g. *Solicitor-General* v. *Radio New Zealand Ltd* [1994] 1 NZLR 48 (Full Court). (Contempt of court rules a justified limit on freedom of expression.)

[123] See nn. 194–5 below and accompanying text.

[124] [1992] 3 NZLR 260 at 273 per Cooke P.   [125] Ibid. at 287.   [126] Ibid.

[127] Ibid.

its on the rights, Hardie Boys J. saw the provision as discharging an interpretive role only: namely, how best to interpret rights and freedoms in order to preserve their application for softening the effects of limiting Statutes.

In *Herewini* v. *Ministry of Transport*,[128] the High Court adopted the Hardie Boys J. approach for reconciling Sections 4 and 6. 'The test for inconsistency in Section 6,' observed Fisher J., 'appears to be the direct obverse of the test for inconsistency in Section 4.'[129] The Section 4 determination was directed at the scope of the subject enactment, not at its effect on rights or freedoms. Section 6 pulled in the opposite direction. Once a right or freedom survived inconsistency under Section 4, then Section 6 accorded prominence to rights and freedoms without further consideration of the objectives underlying the subject enactment. Section 5 provided the bridge 'between these two extremes':[130]

Under Section 5, the scope of the right or freedom in question could be openly influenced both by revisiting the objectives underlying the other enactment (see the implications of 'prescribed by law') and by articulating other aspects of social policy ('reasonable limits . . . demonstrably justified in a free and democratic society').

Fisher J. held that the right to legal counsel for an intoxicated driver who had been hospitalized was compatible with the blood-alcohol provisions of the Transport Act 1962 (NZ) which authorised the taking of a blood sample.[131]

Reasonable Limits Demonstrably Justified in a Free and Democratic Society

Those seeking to rely on Section 5 bear the onus of satisfying its substantive requirements.[132] Namely, is the limit *reasonable, prescribed by law*, and *demonstrably justified in a free and democratic society*? The Canadian Courts have established the onus of proof on the civil standard of the balance of probabilities.[133] In New Zealand, the Courts have been quick to acknowledge the persuasive value of Canadian decisions, as having relevance for both the content of rights[134] and the Act's operational provisions.[135] *R.* v. *Oakes*[136] is the leading authority on the justified limits inquiry. The Supreme Court of

---

[128] (1992) 9 CRNZ 307.   [129] Ibid. at 321.   [130] Ibid.
  [131] But see the majority decision on appeal: *Police* v. *Smith and Herewini* [1994] 2 NZLR 306 (Cooke P. and Casey J. dissenting).
  [132] See *Ministry of Transport* v. *Noort* [1992] 3 NZLR 260 at 283 per Richardson J. See also *R.* v. *Butler* (1990) 59 CCC (3d) 97 (Manitoba Court of Queen's Bench).
  [133] See *R.* v. *Butler* (1990) 50 CCC (3d) 97.
  [134] See e.g. *R.* v. *Butcher* [1992] 2 NZLR 257 at 266–67, 268 per Cooke P. on the right to legal counsel, following the Canadian Supreme Court cases *De Bot* v. *R.* (1989) 73 CR (3d) 129 and *Black* v. *R.* (1989) 70 CR (3d) 97.
  [135] See e.g. *Ministry of Transport* v. *Noort* [1992] 2 NZLR 260 at 272 per Cooke P. (following *R.* v. *Thomsen* (1988) 63 CR (3d) 1 (Supreme Court of Canada))and 283 per Richardson J. (McKay J. agreeing).
  [136] (1986) 26 DLR (4th) 200 (Supreme Court of Canada).

Canada restated the *Oakes* test thus in *Re A Reference re Public Service Employee Relations Act*:[137]

The constituent elements of any Section [5] inquiry are as follows. First, the legislative objective, in pursuit of which the measures in question are implemented, must be sufficiently significant to warrant overriding a constitutionally guaranteed right: it must be related to 'concerns which are pressing and substantial in a free and democratic society'. Second, the means chosen to advance such an objective must be reasonable and demonstrably justified in a free and democratic society. This requirement of proportionality of means to ends normally has three aspects: (a) there must be a rational connection between the measures and the objective they are to serve; (b) the measures should impair as little as possible the right or freedom in question; and (c) the deleterious effects of the measures must be justifiable in light of the objective which they are to serve.

In *R. v. Butler*,[138] the Manitoba Court of Queen's Bench embellished the *Oakes* test in the following ways. First, the Section 5 elements should be applied vigorously and will generally (but not always) require supportive evidence that should be cogent and persuasive. Secondly, the limiting measures must be carefully designed or rationally connected to the objective (they must actually achieve the desired social policy or goal). Thirdly, their effects must not so severely trench on individual or group rights that the legislative objective, though important, is out-weighed by the restriction of the guaranteed right. In *Noort*,[139] Richardson J. affirmed the *Oakes* test and emphasised that an abridging inquiry under Section 5 will involve consideration of all economic, administrative and social implications, including:

(1) the significance in the particular case of the values underlying the Bill of Rights Act;
(2) the importance in the public interest of the intrusion on the particular right protected by the . . . Act;
(3) the limits sought to be placed on the application of the Act provision in the particular case;
(4) the effectiveness of the intrusion in protecting the interests put forward to justify those limits.

The first part of the *Oakes* test—a compelling legislative objective—must be modified to reflect the status of the New Zealand Act, as an ordinary Statute which does not control legislation. In Canada, this element imposes an onus which, in the ordinary case, is easily met. The Courts are naturally disinclined towards second guessing legislative policy, and they are reluctant to hold that

---

[137] [1987] 1 SCR 313 at 373–4, affirmed in *Noort* [1992] 3 NZLR 260 at 283 per Richardson J. The *Oakes* test was also restated in *R. v. Butler* (1990) 50 CCC (3d) 97 and *R. v. Chaulk* (1991) 2 CR (4th) 1 at 27–8 (Supreme Court of Canada).
[138] (1990) 50 CCC (3d) 97.
[139] *Ministry of Transport* v. *Noort* [1992] 3 NZLR 260 at 283–4.

the Legislature has acted irrationally or with no good reason. The Canadian Courts speak of the need for flexibility in applying the proportionality test; that they should allow for a 'margin of appreciation',[140] even if there may have been open a less intrusive legislative choice.

The Bill of Rights Act applies subject to Statute but not the common law. In *Solicitor-General* v. *Radio New Zealand Ltd*,[141] the High Court applied the Bill of Rights Act but upheld contempt of court as a justified (common law) limit on freedom of expression. Significantly the Canadian Courts have applied the Charter more rigorously when the Government or a public authority has invoked the common law as justification for action. The Supreme Court has distinguished legislation challenges and stated that no similar need for deference arises apropos common law limits. The *Oakes* test may be applied with rigour.[142] Here the Bill of Rights Act may find its niche in controlling public or governmental acts at common law or under the Royal prerogative, or acts otherwise not prohibited by law but intruding on legally-recognised interests. Its attendant role as a restraining influence on the interpretation of Statutes is discussed below.[143]

Prescribed by Law

Section 5 requires a justified limit to be 'prescribed by law'. Limits should be fixed and ascertainable in advance, rather than left arbitrary and uncertain. In *Re Ontario Film and Video Appreciation Society and Ontario Board of Censors*,[144] the Ontario Court of Appeal struck down film censorship legislation which did not supply standards to control the censor. The statutory limits on free speech were not 'prescribed' because of the vagueness and breadth of the Board's discretion. In *Noort*,[145] Richardson J. stated that limits on rights must be 'formulated with sufficient precision to enable citizens to regulate their conduct and to foresee the consequences which a given action may entail'. In the leading authority,[146] the European Court of Human Rights cautioned that those consequences need not be foreseeable 'with absolute certainty', as that may infect the law with excessive rigidity. The European Court tempered the requirement with considerations of *reasonable* foreseeability in the circumstances, 'if need be with appropriate advice'.

---

[140] The phrase derives from the leading international law authority *Sunday Times* v. *United Kingdom* (1979) 58 ILR 491 at 529–37 (European Court of Justice).
[141] [1994] 1 NZLR 48 (Full Court).
[142] *R.* v. *Swain* (1991) 63 CCC (3d) 481 (Supreme Court of Canada).
[143] See nn. 172–80 below and accompanying text.
[144] (1984) 41 OR (2d) 583; affirmed in *Re Ontario Film and Video Appreciation Society and Ontario Board of Censors* (1984) 45 OR (2d) 80.
[145] [1992] 3 NZLR 260 at 283.
[146] *Sunday Times* v. *United Kingdom* (1979) 58 ILR 491 at 524–7 (the *Thalidomide* case) followed by Cooke P. and Richardson J. in *Noort* n. 139 above at 272 and 283 respectively. See also *Attorney-General* v. *Ryan* [1980] AC 718 (Privy Council).

In *Noort*,[147] the Court of Appeal approved the Supreme Court of Canada in *R.* v. *Thomsen*[148] on the sweep of the term 'law'. Le Dain J. for the Supreme Court stated:[149] 'The limit will be prescribed by law . . . if it is expressly provided for by Statute or regulation, or results by necessary implication from the terms of a Statute or regulation *or from its operating requirements.*'

Cooke P. and Richardson J. saw Le Dain J.'s 'operating requirements' as the New Zealand equivalent of 'making the Statute work'—where the Courts have taken to interpreting Statutes robustly, sometimes 'filling the gaps' in the statutory framework.[150] In *Slaight Communications Inc.* v. *Davidson*,[151] a labour arbitrator's award infringed an employer's free speech by prohibiting him from answering inquiries about a former employee. The Supreme Court held that the limit which the arbitrator's award imposed was reasonable and *prescribed by law*. The limit arose from the operating requirements of the labour law Statute, or (to use Cooke P.'s expression) as 'a form of implication from the enactment necessary to make the enactment work'.[152] In *Federated Farmers of New Zealand (Inc.)* v. *New Zealand Post Ltd*,[153] McGechan J. held that 'limits' imposed on freedom to receive information under New Zealand Post's rural delivery charge were 'prescribed by law'. The State-Owned Enterprises Act 1986 (NZ) mandated the defendant to carry on a 'successful business' and this anticipated the need to impose commercial charges.

In Canada, the requirement 'prescribed by law' posed a special problem for administrative authorities. Where the law conferred an administrative discretion, it was not *the law* but *the exercise of the power* which infringed rights. The limit would not then be 'prescribed by law' and not even reasonable infringements could be saved under the 'justified limits' clause. In *Slaight Communications*, however, the Supreme Court checked the uncontrolled application of the Charter to administrative bodies. The Court held that a limit is 'prescribed' if the Statute supplies the power which authorizes the infringement. Since decision-makers may do only that which their Statute authorises, any limits imposed are legally prescribed:[154]

It is the legislative provision conferring discretion which limits the right or freedom, since it is what authorises the holder of such discretion to make an order the effect of which is to place limits on the rights and freedoms mentioned in the Charter.

---

[147] [1992] 3 NZLR 260 at 272 per Cooke P. Richardson J. at 283 approved the same definition from *R.* v. *Therens* (1985) 18 DLR (4th) 655 at 680.
[148] (1988) 63 CR (3d) 1.   [149] Ibid at 10.
[150] See e.g. *Northland Milk Vendors Association Inc.* v. *Northern Milk Ltd* [1988] 1 NZLR 580 (Court of Appeal); *Auckland City Council* v. *Minister of Transport* [1990] 1 NZLR 264 (Court of Appeal); *Petrocorp Exploration Ltd* v. *Minister of Energy* [1991] 1 NZLR 1 (Court of Appeal).
[151] [1989] 1 SCR. 1038; (1989) 59 DLR (4th) 416.   [152] [1992] 3 NZLR 260 at 272.
[153] Unreported, High Court Wellington, McGechan J., 1 December 1992.
[154] (1989) 59 DLR (4th) 416 at 446.

This approach greatly reduces the requirement 'prescribed by law' in the administrative context, leaving the focus on the reasonableness of the limit complained of.

A justifiable limit may also result from the application of a common law rule. In *Solicitor-General* v. *Radio New Zealand Ltd*,[155] the Full Court accepted that contempt of court was a common law fetter on free speech but upheld it as fundamental to the administration of justice. The law of contempt was 'prescribed', although it was not closely circumscribed and left a broad discretion to the Court. The common law invariably lacks the precision of Statute.

FAVOURING CONSISTENT INTERPRETATIONS—SECTION 6

An Important Section

The Court of Appeal in *R.* v. *Phillips*[156] described Section 6 as 'an important section'. Cooke P. in *Noort*[157] considered it 'one of the key features' of the legislation, 'comparable in importance to—perhaps of even greater importance than—Section 5(j) of the Acts Interpretation Act 1924'. The Section lays down a rule of interpretation for general Statutes but in fact contemplates two interpretive exercises: first, that the scope of the right in question be ascertained and, secondly, whether a potentially infringing Statute may be so construed as to avoid the numbing application of Section 4. It may be helpful to recall what Section 6 enacts:

6. Interpretation consistent with Bill of Rights to be preferred. Whenever an enactment can be given a meaning that is consistent with the rights and freedoms contained in this Bill of Rights, that meaning shall be preferred to any other meaning.

Interpreting the Bill of Rights Act

When construing the Act, the Courts apply the purposive approach to the interpretation of Statutes: '[T]he Bill of Rights is a piece of human rights legislation and . . . must be accorded a broad purposive interpretation that will give full effect to the spirit of the rights contained therein.'[158] Courts must look to 'the purpose of the guarantee'[159] to ascertain the interests it protects,

---

[155] [1994] 1 NZLR 48.   [156] [1991] 3 NZLR 175 at 176 per Cooke P. for the Court.
[157] [1992] 3 NZLR 260 at 272.

[158] See *Palmer* v. *Superintendent of Auckland Maximum Security Prison* [1991] 3 NZLR 315 at 321 per Wylie J. See also *R.* v. *Edwards* [1991] 3 NZLR 463 at 469 per Hillyer J.; *Flickinger* v. *Crown Colony of Hong Kong* [1991] 1 NZLR 439 (Court of Appeal); *Ministry of Transport* v. *Noort* [1992] 3 NZLR 260 (Court of Appeal). For discussion, see Burrows n. 7 above at 322–5.

[159] See *R.* v. *Big M. Drug Mart Ltd* (1985) 18 DLR (4th) 321 at 360 per Dickson J. (Supreme Court of Canada). For critical commentary on the purposive approach, see Mathieson,

and then apply the right 'generously', avoiding technical or arcane argument which may detract from the Parliamentary purpose. Cooke P. has affirmed that a Parliamentary declaration of human rights 'is not to be construed narrowly or technically'.[160] This approach accords with that of the Canadian Courts under their Charter, and also with the now immortal words of Lord Wilberforce in *Minister of Home Affairs* v. *Fisher*.[161] Bills of Rights, said Wilberforce, 'call for a generous interpretation avoiding what has been called 'the austerity of tabulated legalism,' suitable to give to individuals the full measure of the fundamental rights and freedoms referred to'.[162]

The purposive approach serves two ends. First, the general and unqualified language of the Bill of Rights Act does not lend itself to purely literal meanings. Its drafting typifies that of declarations of human rights, described by Wilberforce as 'a broad and ample style which lays down principles of width and generality'.[163] Richardson J. in *Noort*[164] emphasised the Act's 'broad and simple language', as acknowledging the importance Parliament attached to the rights and freedoms proclaimed. Secondly, a purposive interpretation precludes a 'frozen concepts' approach which would stultify the legislation.[165] Bills of Rights must evolve through changing judicial interpretations; in the prophetic words of the Marshall Court, they must 'adapt to the various crises of human affairs'.[166] In *Hunter* v. *Southam Inc.*,[167] the Canadian Supreme Court spoke of the need for 'growth and development over time to meet new social, political and historical realities often unimagined by [the] framers'. Viscount Sankey L.C. once likened a constitutional document to 'a living tree capable of growth and expansion within its natural limits'.[168] A purposive approach facilitates those objects and weakens the binding force of judicial precedent under a Bill of Rights.

The Solicitor-General in *Noort* argued against the purposive approach proclaimed in *Fisher*. There, it was the Bermuda Constitution which called for 'principles of interpretation of its own, suitable to its character . . . without necessary acceptance of all the presumptions that are relevant to legislation of private law'.[169] The Solicitor-General argued that the Bill of Rights Act, being an ordinary Statute, was to be distinguished from the constitutional

---

'Interpreting the Proposed Bill of Rights', [1986] NZLJ 129 at 160; Joseph, 'The Challenge of a Bill of Rights: A Commentary', [1986] NZLJ 416 at 421.

[160] *R.* v. *Butcher* [1992] 2 NZLR 257 at 264 (Court of Appeal).

[161] [1980] AC 319 (Privy Council).

[162] [1980] AC 319 at 328. See also *Attorney-General of the Gambia* v. *Momodou Jobe* [1984] AC 689 at 700 per Lord Diplock (Privy Council).

[163] *Minister of Home Affairs* v. *Fisher* [1980] AC 319 at 328.

[164] [1992] 3 NZLR 260 at 277.   [165] See pp. 236–238 above.

[166] See *McCulloch* v. *State of Maryland* 4 Wheat. 316 (1819).

[167] [1984] 2 SCR 145 at 155 per Dickson J., approved in *Ministry of Transport* v. *Noort* [1992] 3 NZLR 260 at 292 per Gault J.

[168] *Edwards* v. *Attorney-General (Canada)* [1930] AC 124 at 136 (Privy Council).

[169] [1980] AC 319 at 329.

instrument in issue in *Fisher*. Cooke P. thought the argument 'of minimal importance',[170] while Richardson J. applied the purposive approach mandated for all statutory interpretation by Section 5(j) of the Acts Interpretation Act 1924 (NZ).[171] The argument was destined to fail since the Bill of Rights Act *is* a constitutional instrument. That it is not entrenched has no relevance to statutory interpretation and the meaning of civil rights. All Bills of Rights serve the same ends, whether they be 'fundamental' or 'ordinary Act' instruments.

Interpreting Other Enactments

The Courts must prefer the meaning of a Statute that is consistent with the Bill of Rights Act. Section 25(c) guarantees the right to be presumed innocent. In *R.* v. *Rangi*,[172] the statutory offence of possessing a knife in a public place without reasonable excuse was silent on the burden of proof—on whom was the onus of proving reasonable excuse or the lack of it? The Court of Appeal held that, as the Statute was 'neutral', the Bill of Rights Act placed the burden on the prosecution. Of the two possible solutions, that in conformity with the Bill of Rights Act was preferred.

Section 6 presupposes that an enactment is capable of two meanings—one potentially infringing, the other not. However an infringing Statute that is clear and unambiguous must be given effect according to its tenor, and Section 6 has no application. Section 4 applies and the Statute prevails. The critical words of Section 6 are italicized thus: 'Whenever an enactment *can be given a meaning* that is consistent with . . . this Bill of Rights'.[173] These words do not countenance a strained and unnatural interpretation.[174] In *Knight* v. *Commissioner of Inland Revenue*,[175] Hardie Boys J. thought there had to be genuine ambiguity or uncertainty. In *Noort*, Cooke P. and Gault J. held that the section applies only when a Statute can 'reasonably' be given a meaning that is consistent with the rights proclaimed, without taking into account any limiting or modifying effect Section 5 may have on those rights.[176] For the other members of the Court (Richardson, Hardie Boys and McKay J.J.), Section 6 had greater potential for reconciling Statutes since the Section 5 exercise logically preceded the application of Section 6. It will be easier to reconcile Statutes when the rights and freedoms are circumscribed by reasonable limits.

---

[170] [1992] 3 NZLR 260 at 269.
[171] Ibid. at 278. See the discussion of Section 5(j) of the Acts Interpretation Act 1924 at p. 259 below.
[172] [1992] 1 NZLR 385 (Court of Appeal).   [173] Emphasis added.
[174] See *R.* v. *Phillips* [1991] 3 NZLR 175 at 177 per Cooke P. for the Court. See also *Ministry of Transport* v. *Noort* [1992] 3 NZLR 260 at 272 per Cooke P. and 294 per Gault J.
[175] [1991] 2 NZLR 30 at 43.
[176] *Ministry of Transport* v. *Noort* [1992] 3 NZLR 260.

The question ultimately is how far the Court is prepared to depart from the natural meaning of a Statute to achieve a reconciliation. 'Reading down' (or restricting the scope of) general words is a time-honoured technique of construction for Statutes trenching on individual or common law freedoms. Sometimes the Courts may give to statutory provisions a liberal and expansive interpretation, if this is what is required to achieve a reconciliation.[177] Much will depend on the statutory context, the 'value' of the right in question and judicial willingness to uphold the Bill of Rights Act.

The Relationship to Section 5(j) of the Acts Interpretation Act 1924

Section 6 raises questions of theoretical importance. Rules of statutory interpretation are most often presumptions which yield to contrary legislative meanings. However Section 6 establishes a rule of interpretation that is expressed in peremptory rather than presumptive language—as a command to the Courts. This raises potential conflict with Section 5(j) of the Acts Interpretation Act 1924 (NZ), which is similarly expressed in peremptory language, and has been described as New Zealand's 'cardinal rule' of statutory interpretation.[178] Section 5(j) requires Courts to adopt an interpretation which furthers the purpose of the legislation thus:

(j) Every Act . . . shall be deemed remedial, . . . and shall accordingly receive such fair, large, and liberal construction and interpretation as will best ensure the attainment of the object of the Act . . . according to its true intent, meaning, and spirit.

The two rules of interpretation were in conflict sub silentio in *Flickinger* v. *Crown Colony of Hong Kong*.[179] In a long line of cases, the Courts had held that Section 66 of the Judicature Act 1908 (NZ) did not confer a right of appeal in criminal cases which, they had held, included applications for habeas corpus. Without deciding the matter, the Court of Appeal signalled a reversal of the earlier decisions 'to give full measure' to the rights in Section 23(1)(c), affirming entitlement to the writ of habeas corpus.[180] Section 6 invited this decision, although the meaning for which Flickinger argued had been specifically rejected in the earlier cases, as not being the meaning Parliament intended.

There are two ways of reconciling these interpretation Sections, although neither may be entirely satisfactory. The first accords primacy to Section 6, the second to Section 5(j). Section 6 expresses no qualification for statutory context but is applicable to all potentially infringing Statutes which can reasonably bear a meaning that is consistent with the Bill of Rights Act. Section 5(j), by comparison, is expressed to apply subject to the particular statutory

---

[177] See e.g. *Flickinger* v. *Crown Colony of Hong Kong* [1991] 1 NZLR 439 (Court of Appeal).
[178] See *Police* v. *Christie* [1962] NZLR 1109 at 1112 per Henry J. (Supreme Court).
[179] [1991] 1 NZLR 439. [180] Ibid. at 440–1.

context. Here, 'context' may arguably include the Bill of Rights Act (including its interpretation Section) where a Statute threatens to encroach, thereby ousting Section 5(j) in preference for Section 6. Alternatively, it could be argued that Section 5(j) should prevail when a meaning that is consistent with the Bill of Rights Act bears no relation to the original Parliamentary intention. To jettison an established statutory meaning by reason of the Bill of Rights Act involves an admission that the Act pro tanto overrides the earlier enactment, contrary to Section 4 and the primacy of inconsistent legislation. *Flickinger* preferred the first approach (the primacy of Section 6), but without canvassing the arguments.

ATTORNEY-GENERAL TO CERTIFY INCONSISTENT BILLS—SECTION 7

Background to Section 7

Section 7 is shaping as a key feature of the legislation.[181] This provision exacts political accountability for Government legislation that would flout the rights and freedoms proclaimed. Part of the rationale of the White Paper Bill was the strong disincentive to the Government to promote legislation that could be struck down.[182] Section 7 was the quid pro quo for relinquishing judicial review of legislation.[183] This Section establishes an administrative mechanism for monitoring legislative proposals and maintaining some disincentives to overriding the protected rights and freedoms:

7. Attorney-General to report to Parliament where Bill appears to be inconsistent with Bill of Rights. Where any Bill is introduced into the House of Representatives, the Attorney-General shall—
(a) In the case of a Government Bill, on the introduction of that Bill; or
(b) In any other case, as soon as practicable after the introduction of the Bill—
bring to the attention of the House of Representatives any provision in the Bill that appears to be inconsistent with any of the rights and freedoms contained in this Bill of Rights.

The origin of Section 7 can be traced to Section 3 of the Canadian Bill of Rights 1960 which required the Minister of Justice to scrutinise Bills against

---

[181] For discussion, see McGrath, 'The Bill of Rights and the Legislative Process' in *The New Zealand Bill of Rights Act 1990* (1992), 98; Fitzgerald, 'Section 7 of the New Zealand Bill of Rights Act 1990: A Very Practical Power or a Well Intentioned Nonsense?', 22 VUWLR 135 (1992); Telfer, 'Section 7 of the Bill of Rights Act 1990', unpublished LL.B. Research Paper, University of Canterbury, 1992.

[182] See the White Paper n. 1 above at para. 6.6.

[183] See Justice and Law Reform Committee n. 30 above. The Justice and Law Reform Committee recommended establishing, in tandem with Section 7, a Bill of Rights select committee to which all Bills would be referred for examination and report. No such committee was in fact established. Standing Orders already permitted select committees to undertake this role, if they so wished.

the rights affirmed and to report any inconsistency to Canada's House of Commons.[184] Canada's former Bill of Rights enjoyed the same 'ordinary Act' status as New Zealand's Bill of Rights Act, but its reporting procedure was never allowed to impose. Only once in 22 years did the Minister report to Parliament under it.[185] Section 7, on the other hand, was effective on at least six occasions during the first 3 years—once when the Minister of Justice modified a legislative proposal rather than face an adverse report, and on five occasions when the Attorney-General reported Bills as raising inconsistencies. It was also used twice in 1992 for commenting on Government Bills as they passed the House.[186]

The Section 7 Procedure

In 1991, the Attorney-General issued a memorandum outlining the monitoring procedure under Section 7.[187] Cabinet's Legislation Committee makes the initial decision on Government Bills. A Minister who submits a legislative proposal must state whether it complies with the Bill of Rights Act. When drafting the proposal, Parliamentary Counsel must also identify any provision thought to infringe a right or freedom. The Department of Justice then examines Government Bills (except Bills promoted by the Minister of Justice which are referred to the Crown Law Office) for possible breaches of the Act. Imprest Supply and Appropriation Bills are exempt as these are standard-form Bills and have no bearing on rights and freedoms. Where a Government Bill appears to contravene the Bill of Rights Act, the examining officer must report to the Parliamentary Counsel in charge and to the Attorney-General, and the Attorney-General is then under a statutory obligation to report. It was hoped that this would have a salutary effect on Ministers promoting legislation. Any contraventions subsequently enacted will be the result of an informed and conscious choice by Parliament, not inadvertent oversight.

For Government Bills, the obligation to report arises at the outset, before the question that a Bill be introduced is put.[188] The Solicitor-General

---

[184] See Tarnopolsky, *The Canadian Bill of Rights* (2nd edn., 1975), 125–8. The Canadian Charter of Rights and Freedoms did not originally carry over the former Section 3 reporting function, but this was later provided for by statutory amendment in 1985. See Beaudoin and Ratushay, *The Canadian Charter of Rights and Freedoms* (2nd edn., 1989), 13.

[185] See Telfer n. 181 above at 10.   [186] See p. 262 below.

[187] Memorandum of Attorney-General Paul East to all Ministers and Chief Executives, *Monitoring Bills for Compliance with the New Zealand Bill of Rights Act*, 8 April 1991. The Memorandum is reproduced by Fitzgerald n. 181 above at 156–8. See also Iles, 'New Zealand Experience of Parliamentary Scrutiny of Legislation', 12 SLR (1991) 165 at 183–185.

[188] Standing Order 216(1)(a) of the *Standing Orders of the House of Representatives* (NZ) (1992). Local or private or private member's Bills are examined as soon as practicable after their introduction. Potential infringements must be reported to the Chief Parliamentary Counsel and, under Standing Order 216(1)(b), the Attorney-General must report no later than 12 sitting days after the Bill is introduced.

identified this as a potential weakness in the monitoring procedure.[189] A Minister may anticipate an infringement of the Bill of Rights Act, instruct Parliamentary Counsel to omit the offending provision, introduce the Bill, and have the provision introduced at select committee stage, or after second reading by Supplementary Order Paper. Section 7 does not encompass post-introduction changes. 'It would be a matter of concern,' said the Solicitor-General, 'if a practice emerged whereby changes relevant to the Bill of Rights Act protection were to be made at stages subsequent to introduction.'[190]

Those fears have not materialised under current practice. The Attorney-General has, in fact, assumed a broad monitoring brief. Twice in 1992, he reported to the House on Bill of Rights issues although no Section 7 report had been made. Once he reported that a Supplementary Order Paper infringed the Act and suggested an amendment that would make the limit a reasonable and justifiable one,[191] and the House adopted his suggestion. On another occasion, he informed the House of the reasons why a limit was jus-tifiable, and thus not reported under Section 7.[192] The Attorney-General termed this an 'unusual step' but 'in the interests of Parliament and in the wider public interest'.[193]

Section 7 In Operation

Initial doubts were expressed whether the reporting function under Section 7 should take account of the limiting effect of Section 5 on the rights and free-doms affirmed. From the outset, the Crown Law Office, Justice Department officials and the Attorney-General considered that prima facie infringements did not require the Attorney's report if the limit was justifiable under Section 5. However differing opinions were aired in *Ministry of Transport* v. *Noort*.[194] Cooke P. anticipated the need to report prima facie infringements, with or without reference to Section 5. He stated:[195]

[I]n drawing it to the attention of the House [the Attorney-General] may well wish to draw attention also to Section 5 and to the question whether the Bill, although appar-ently inconsistent with one or more of the rights and freedoms, nonetheless prescribes a reasonable limit demonstrably justified in a free and democratic society.

Richardson J., it will be recalled, integrated justifiable limits within the rights and freedoms themselves, so as to be inextricably part of that which the Act protects. Rights were never absolute but were limited. Thus the Attorney-General's reporting obligation arose only when it was determined that a prima facie infringement was not reasonable and justifiable under Section 5. This approach is preferred for pragmatic reasons. If the Attorney-General must

---

[189] McGrath n. 181 above at 104.   [190] Ibid.
[191] NZPD, vol. 531 (1992) at 12534–5.   [192] NZPD, vol. 528 (1992) at 10621–2.
[193] Ibid. at 10622.   [194] [1992] 3 NZLR 260.   [195] Ibid. at 271.

report whenever legislative proposals anticipate prima facie infringements, without regard to what is reasonable and justified, the House would be deluged with Section 7 reports, coupled with explanations why Section 5 excuses inconsistency. Section 7 would lose any deterrent effect. The following precedents endorse the Richardson approach.

The Early Precedents

In December 1990, the Minister of Justice was considering new legislative restrictions on bail.[196] His original proposal would have removed the element of judicial discretion by directing judges to refuse bail to persons charged with a violent crime who had had previous convictions for such offences. Section 24(b) of the Bill of Rights Act provides that everyone charged with an office: '(b) Shall be released on reasonable terms and conditions unless there is just cause for continued detention.' The Minister was advised that previous convictions could not, without more, constitute 'just cause for continued detention'. Nor could the restriction be justified, as it was a substantial one. Anticipating a Section 7 report, the Minister introduced a modified proposal under which a person with previous convictions was entitled to bail if he or she could satisfy the judge that no offence of violence would be committed. The House considered that the retention of a judicial discretion justified the reverse onus provision.

Two reports by the Attorney-General in 1991 caused the legislation (or parts of it) to be withdrawn.[197] The Bills, one local and the other a private Bill, were not of national moment. The Napier City Council (Control of Skateboards) Empowering Bill authorised by-laws for controlling or prohibiting use of skateboards which might have included their seizure or confiscation. The Attorney-General reported that the Bill infringed Section 21, affirming freedom against unreasonable seizure of property. The select committee recommended that the Bill not proceed.[198] The second report concerned the Kumeu District Agriculture and Horticultural Society Bill which reconstituted the Society, setting out its objects and by-law making powers. Clause 8 proposed that civil liability flow automatically for breach of the Society's by-laws. The Attorney-General informed the House that this unjustifiably infringed the Section 27(1) right to observance of natural justice. The select committee examining the Bill deleted the offending Clause.

The first Government measure to be reported was the Transport Safety Bill 1992. The offending provisions authorised random breath-testing of

---

[196] Discussed by McGrath n. 181 above at 103.

[197] *Formal Report under Section 7 of the New Zealand Bill of Rights Act 1990 In Relation to the Kumeu District Agricultural and Horticultural Society Bill*, 23 July 1991; *Formal Report under Section 7 of the New Zealand Bill of Rights Act 1990 In Relation to the Napier City Council (Control of Skateboards) Empowering Bill*, 15 August 1991.

[198] See NZPD, vol. 522 (1992) at 6589.

motorists without need for the police to suspect the consumption of alcohol. The Justice Department advised that this would unreasonably infringe Sections 21 and 22, affirming the rights to be secure against unreasonable search and seizure and not to be arrested or detained arbitrarily.[199] The Bill breached the principle of proportionality. The evidence concerning random breath-testing was inconclusive and failed to establish a rational connection between the legislative proposal and the road safety objective. The current law (the need to suspect) was considered to be an equally effective but less intrusive means of deterring the intoxicated motorist.[200] The House nevertheless passed the offending provisions into law.

The Attorney-General has reported two further Government measures. A Clause under the Films, Videos and Publications Classification Bill 1992 was considered to infringe Section 26(1) of the Act, proscribing retrospective criminal liability.[201] The Attorney-General suggested inserting a reverse onus defence for justifying the limit, but the House passed the legislation unchanged. The second report concerned a Clause under the Children, Young Persons, and Their Families Amendment Bill 1993, which imposed mandatory reporting of child abuse on 15 occupational groups.[202] This infringed the right to freedom of expression and could not be justified under Section 5; the evidence did not establish that mandatory (as distinct from voluntary) reporting increased detection of child abuse. The Attorney-General made three proposals for reconciling freedom of expression, but Parliament was dissolved with the Bill still before the select committee.

Constitutional Convention and Section 7

The above reports of the Attorney-General, Hon. Paul East, may establish a rule-constitutive precedent. When in Opposition, East was scathing of the reporting procedure, noting that there was no requirement that every Bill be certified as complying and no remedy if the Attorney-General reneged on the duty.[203] He now exhibits an unqualified acceptance of the obligation to report, and this acceptance may establish a constitutional convention equal to the independence of his office. Such a convention may obviate any need to speak of judicial review of the Attorney-General's function. Judicial review may prove a fruitless pursuit when pitted against Parliamentary privilege and the lack of a purposeful remedy.[204] The final say must remain with the House; to suggest that the House could not proceed because the Bill of Rights Act

---

[199] In the Canadian case *R.* v. *Holman* (1982) 28 CR 378, a demand for a breath sample was a 'search' and the taking of it a 'seizure' under the equivalent of the Bill of Rights Act s. 21.

[200] NZPD, vol. 521 (1992) at 6367–8 per Hon. Paul East.

[201] NZPD, vol. 532 (1992) at 12764–5.

[202] NZPD, vol. 537 (1993) at 17313–15 and 17327–8.

[203] NZPD, vol. 510 (1990) at 3762.

[204] See *Mangawaro Enterprises Ltd* v. *Attorney-General*, [1994] 2 NZLR 451 (High Court)

binds the legislative branch would give the Act an unprecedented role, contrary to the principle of Section 4. Hence both the Transport Safety and the Films, Videos, and Publications Classification Bills passed the House notwithstanding the Attorney-General's report. However a legislative proposal would have to assume some political significance for a Minister to flout the Attorney's report. The Minister would want to weigh carefully the merits of the legislation against any political cost in defending it.

Conclusion

'The Bill is not entrenched but it is not an ordinary Statute either.'[205] Therein the ambivalence and dualism of the New Zealand Bill of Rights Act. The Courts have confronted 'formidable textual difficulties' when applying the Act's operational sections.[206] These lump together disparate provisions from a constitutional Charter which circumscribes legislative power (Section 5) with ones that uphold Parliament's legislation (Section 4) but qualify its application (Section 6). Judges have had to apply the Act as best they can, and they have done so with surprising success. The Act has intensified the 'rights' inquiry and the contestability of constitutional values, and this has not eased the judicial burden.

The Bill of Rights Act signals a changed constitutional emphasis. The Act supplements the purely facilitative functions of the Courts when proclaiming common law freedoms with more activist regulation of the bureaucracy and public power. The question looming is whether New Zealand will grasp the nettle and adopt an entrenched Bill with judicial power to strike down legislation. Canada took this route in 1982 when it replaced its Bill of Rights 1960 with the Charter of Rights and Freedoms. In New Zealand, both the Act's framers and the Courts have been quick to acknowledge the Canadian experience. In *Terekia*,[207] for instance, the Court was confident that New Zealand was 'going the way of Canada' with its Bill of Rights legislation. The 1990 Act is engendering broad acceptance of constitutional rights among the citizenry and its 'practitioners'—the police, politicians, public servants, their legal advisers, judges and the legal profession, and the Academy—all of which points to more ambitious reform.

where Parliamentary privilege under Article 9 of the Bill of Rights 1688 (UK) was held to preclude judicial review under the Bill of Rights Act s. 7. Quaere whether a declaration under the Judicature Amendment Act 1972 (NZ) for review of a statutory power of decision—that the Attorney-General had failed to give proper consideration to reporting under Section 7—would be compatible with the statutory scheme of the Bill of Rights Act.

[205] *Herewini v. Ministry of Transport* (1992) 9 CRNZ 307 at 326 per Fisher J.
[206] Ibid.   [207] *Longtin* n. 43 above at 12 of the transcript.

9

And Some Have Bills of Rights Thrust Upon Them: The Experience of Hong Kong's Bill of Rights

ANDREW BYRNES[1]

Introduction

The brutal scenes of the suppression of the pro-democracy movement in China in early June 1989 were seen around the world, where they elicited shock and disappointment at the loss of what might have been. However, there was perhaps nowhere outside the People's Republic of China (PRC) itself where the impact was felt more intensely than in Hong Kong, the British Crown colony taken from Qing China in the Opium War of the 1840s and destined to revert to the PRC just 8 years after the events of the fateful summer of 1989. The inhabitants of Hong Kong, never given a genuine opportunity to express their views on the status of the colony when decisions on its future were being made,[2] saw in the events of 3–4 June 1989 the realization of their worst nightmares. Many Hong Kong people supported the pro-democracy activists in China (financially as well as in spirit) not only because they considered such developments as good for China, but also because they perceived that the movement of China towards a somewhat more liberal and open society would, in a very real sense, significantly affect the prospects for the continuing prosperity, stability, and autonomy of Hong Kong in the years ahead. The pro-democracy movement and the crackdown brought millions out on to the streets of Hong Kong for the first time in the colony's history. While the mass public demonstrations of concern have waned with time, the effects of the political galvanization that the harsh acts of repression brought about continue to be felt today (as does the additional impetus they gave to many middle-class Hong Kong people to emigrate).

[1] I am particularly grateful to my colleague Johannes Chan for his detailed and helpful comments on a draft of this chapter, as well as to Ian Deane for his helpful comments and to Ian Heffernan for his careful review of the draft. This chapter, the first draft of which was completed in 1992, has been fully revised to cover developments up until the change of sovereignty over Hong Kong. The research for this chapter was supported in part by the Committee on Research and Conference Grants of the University of Hong Kong and the Hong Kong Research Grants Council.
[2] See Jayawickrama, 'Hong Kong: The Gathering Storm', (1991) 22 *Bulletin of Peace Proposals* 157.

Hong Kong's Bill of Rights[3] was one direct result of the Beijing massacre. The British Government, spurred into action by the events in China and aware of the blow they represented to Hong Kong, recognized that energetic and visible steps were required to help restore confidence in Hong Kong. It announced a number of major initiatives which were intended as confidence-building measures: a scheme under which 50,000 Hong Kong families would be granted full British passports (as distinct from the British Dependent Territories Citizens passports to which many of the Hong Kong population were then entitled), an increased pace of democratization, and a Bill of Rights for Hong Kong.

The decision to introduce a Bill of Rights was announced in October 1990 by the then Governor of Hong Kong in his opening address to the 1990/91 session of the Legislative Council; the process of drafting and public consultation then began, culminating in the enactment of the Bill of Rights in June 1991.

A number of the circumstances which led to the Hong Kong Bill of Rights have had a marked influence on its form and subsequent implementation:

(a) the fact that the Bill of Rights was essentially imposed from above (by London) on the government which was responsible for enacting and implementing it (Hong Kong), and which was not strongly committed to human rights legislation as a matter of philosophy or practice;

(b) the fact that the content of the Bill of Rights was determined largely by external political considerations rather than regard for the substantive issues of greatest concern to Hong Kong people; and

(c) the perception of the Bill of Rights primarily as a bulwark against post-1997 violations of human rights (possibly on a large scale), rather than having any special relevance for the law and practice of the colonial administration.

China's response to the enactment of the Bill of Rights has been one of suspicion and hostility, and as a result of the 23 February 1997 decision of the Standing Committee of the National People's Congress that certain sections of the Bill of Rights Ordinance will not be adopted as laws of the Hong Kong Special Administrative Region on 1 July 1997,[4] the Bill of Rights will survive

---

[3] The Bill of Rights package consists of the Hong Kong Bill of Rights Ordinance (c. 383) ((1991) 30 *ILM* 1310) and Article VII(3) of the Hong Kong Letters Patent (now renumbered as Article VII(5) of the Letters Patent). These instruments are reproduced in Byrnes and Chan (eds.), *Public Law and Human Rights: A Hong Kong Sourcebook* (1993), 20–1, 215–29; Chan and Ghai (eds.), *The Hong Kong Bill of Rights: A Comparative Perspective* (1993), Appendixes 1 and 2, 525–40; and (1991) 1 HKPLR liv–lxviii.

[4] *Decision of the Standing Committee of the National People's Congress on Treatment of the Laws Previously in Force in Hong Kong in accordance with Article 160 of the Basic Law of the Hong Kong Special Administrative Region*, Annex 2: see BBC Summary of World Broadcasts, 25 February 1997 (English summary). The decision appears in the People's Daily, 24 February 1997 (in Chinese).

only in a truncated form. This chapter examines the impact that the Bill of Rights has had in what may prove to be a brief life, from its enactment in June 1991 until the transfer of sovereignty in mid-1997.

Hong Kong's Constitutional History

Hong Kong became a British colony in the early 1840s under a treaty of cession of parts of present-day Hong Kong (Hong Kong Island and Stonecutters Island),[5] subsequent areas being added by treaty of cession in the 1860s (Kowloon)[6] and by way of a 99-year lease in 1898 (the New Territories).[7] The People's Republic of China has always taken the view that these treaties were 'unequal treaties' and did not affect China's sovereignty over Hong Kong, although it was prepared to tolerate British administration of the territory pending eventual resolution of the status of Hong Kong.[8]

The issue of the future status of Hong Kong after the expiry of the lease of the New Territories in 1997 was raised by the British in the early 1980s; the result was the Sino-British Joint Declaration of 1984,[9] in which the United Kingdom and Chinese governments agreed that China would resume sovereignty over Hong Kong on 1 July 1997 (the date of expiry of the lease of the New Territories).

The Sino-British Joint Declaration embodies an agreement that for 50 years after 1997 Hong Kong will be a Special Administrative Region (SAR) of the People's Republic of China, that its capitalist economic system will remain basically unchanged, and that the region will enjoy a high degree of autonomy in many areas. The story of the events which led up to the Joint Declaration has been told by many (although the real diplomatic story is unlikely to be revealed for some decades), and there are numerous discussions of the Joint Declaration (although these have far from settled its meaning in many important respects, since this seems to be an everchanging matter). It is not my purpose to do that here.

---

[5] Treaty of Nanking 1842, in Parry (ed.), *The Consolidated Treaty Series*, vol. 93, 465 and reproduced in Byrnes and Chan, above n. 3 at 5. See generally Chen, 'From Colony to special Administrative Region: Hong Kong's Constitutional Journey', in Wacks (ed.), *The Future of the Law in Hong Kong* (1989), 76–126; Wesley-Smith, *Constitutional and Administrative Law in Hong Kong* (1994), 23–76.

[6] Convention of Peking 1860, in *Hertslet's Commercial Treaties*, vol. XI (1864), 112 and reproduced in Byrnes and Chan, above n. 3 at 8.

[7] Convention of Peking 1898, in Parry (ed.), *The Consolidated Treaty Series*, vol. 186, 310 and reproduced in Byrnes and Chan, above n. 3 at 12.

[8] See Dicks, 'Treaty, Grant, Usage or Sufferance? Some Legal Aspects of the Status of Hong Kong', (1983) 95 *China Quarterly* 427; Mushkat, 'The Transition from British to Chinese Rule in Hong Kong: A Discussion of Salient International Legal Issues', (1986) 14 *Denver Journal of International Law and Policy* 171.

[9] For the text see 1399 *UNTS* 36, (1984) 23 *ILM* 1366, and Byrnes and Chan, above n. 3 at 43.

Pursuant to the Joint Declaration, the Basic Law of the Hong Kong SAR was adopted by the National People's Congress in April 1990.[10] A PRC statute, the Basic Law lays down the basic structure of the SAR after 1997, including a guarantee of Hong Kong's capitalist way of life and the continuation of a common law system. Its Chapter III contains a catalogue of fundamental rights,[11] including Article 39 which provides for the two International Covenants to continue to apply to Hong Kong and to be implemented through the laws of the Hong Kong SAR.

Hong Kong's Economic and Political Development

The years since the end of the Second World War have seen Hong Kong develop from a small, relatively unimportant trading centre into one of the world's leading economies. While the initial expansion of the Hong Kong economy was largely concentrated in the manufacturing industry, it is now predominantly a service economy, the major trading outlet and source of foreign exchange and investment for China, as well as a leading international centre for business and finance. The population, slightly over 6 million as of 1996, is overwhelmingly ethnic Chinese, many of whom came to Hong Kong from the mainland in search of better economic opportunities, as refugees, or to join family members.[12]

The economic expansion of Hong Kong has brought with it a significant increase in the standard of living in the territory, including for those who number among the less well off. However, there are still striking disparities of wealth among the various groups in Hong Kong society and a lack of social services and social security measures compared with other countries that enjoy a similar level of material wealth.

Hong Kong's constitutional structure up until the early 1990s was essentially that seen in many British colonies of the nineteenth century, at least in the early stages of their constitutional development. Hong Kong's evolution towards representative self-government, a progression witnessed in so many other colonies, has been stunted—the colony was never encouraged or permitted to move towards the stage of representative self-government as were other British possessions.[13] Any possible future development in that direction

---

[10] For the text see (1990) 29 *ILM* 1511; Byrnes and Chan, above n. 3 at 81; and Chan and Ghai, above n. 3, Appendix 3, at 541–71. For the final text as well as the drafting history of the Basic Law see Clark and Chan, *The Hong Kong Basic Law: Blueprint for 'Stability and Prosperity' under Chinese Sovereignty?* (1991).

[11] For discussion and an extensive bibliography see Clark and Chan, above n. 10.

[12] According to the 1991 Census, 60% of Hong Kong's population of 5,822,500 were born in Hong Kong and 34% were born in China: *Hong Kong 1992* (1992), 365 (hereinafter *Hong Kong 1992*). See generally Chen, 'The Development of Immigration Law and Policy: The Hong Kong Experience', (1988) 33 *McGill Law Journal* 631.

[13] As one commentator has noted, '[W]hile Hong Kong's economic development proceeded apace, its political development was suspended with the institutions of government fixed within

has been truncated and directed into a channel carved out by the Joint Declaration and Basic Law, the latter of which holds out the prospect, though not the promise, of a legislature fully elected by universal suffrage after the year 2007. Hong Kong's constitutional development after 1997 has now been set for a different course by the Basic Law and the opportunities for any major initiatives towards a more democratic government outside that framework are severely constrained.[14]

Until the transfer of sovereignty in 1997 Hong Kong's system of government remained formally (and to a large extent in practice) a gubernatorial system, to be replaced in 1997 with a system based on a presidential model. The Governor, appointed by, and responsible to, the United Kingdom government, had the power to make laws by and with the advice and consent of the Legislative Council. The Governor was advised by an Executive Council, all of whose members were appointed by him; they included members of the administration and members of the community.

Until 1985 all members of the Legislative Council were appointed by the Governor. They consisted of official members (members of the administration such as the Chief Secretary, the Financial Secretary, and the Attorney-General) and unofficial members. In 1985, for the first time, a number of Legislative Councillors were elected, not by universal and equal suffrage, but under a peculiar Hong Kong system of indirect election by 'functional constituencies'. While these functional constituencies included social workers (whose organizations voted) and teachers (who voted as individuals), they still consisted primarily of business and professional groupings. The inclusion of these groups in the political franchise reflects a pattern in the political development of Hong Kong which a number of commentators have identified: the co-option of newly emerging groups in society with economic power into the formal structures of government.[15]

---

their nineteenth century colonial constitutional framework': England, *Industrial Relations and the Law in Hong Kong*, 2nd edn. (1989), 8.

[14] For a review of recent developments and disagreements between the United Kingdom and China on constitutional developments in Hong Kong, see Chan, 'Constitutional Development in Hong Kong: 1989–1993', in Chan (ed.), *United Kingdom: British Dependent Territories—Hong Kong* (Booklet 4) in Blaustein (ed.), *Constitutions of Dependencies and Special Sovereignties* (1993), 1–180; Chan, 'A Constitution in Transition: Ten Years from the Sino-British Joint Declaration', paper presented at a conference on 'China's Constitutional Systems: Convergence or Divergence', Columbia University, School of International Affairs, April 1994; Mirsky, 'The Battle for Hong Kong', *New York Review of Books*, 7 April 1994, 16. For the two Governments' versions see *Representative Government in Hong Kong*, White Paper presented to the United Kingdom Parliament by the Secretary of State for Foreign and Commonwealth Affairs on 24 February 1994; Foreign Ministry of the PRC, *Facts About a Few Important Aspects of Sino-British Talks on 1994/95 Electoral Arrangements in Hong Kong*, February 1994, in English in *South China Morning Post*, 1 March 1994, 12–14. See also Foreign Affairs Committee, *First Report on Relations Between the United Kingdom and China in the Period Up To and Beyond 1997*, vols. 1 and 2 (1994).

[15] Scott, *Political Change and the Crisis of Legitimacy in Hong Kong* (1989).

It was only in 1991 that Hong Kong saw direct elections to the Legislative Council. In those elections 18 seats were directly elected by the people. However, there were still 21 members elected by the functional constituencies, 17 appointed unofficial members and 3 official members (plus the Governor as President) making up the total of 60 members of the Legislative Council.[16] The Council that met after the September 1991 elections differed from previous ones as, for the first time, the majority of members had been 'elected'. However, the fact that both the functional constituencies and the majority of the unofficial members appointed by the Governor represented business or conservative interests, while liberals were overwhelmingly returned in the direct elections, demonstrated that functional constituency 'elections' are no substitute for direct elections across the board if the aim is to ensure representation of the views of the populace at large.

The 1995 elections to the Legislative Council were conducted on the basis of reforms proposed by Governor Patten shortly after taking up office in 1992. Those reforms increased the number of directly elected seats to 20 and, while retaining functional constituencies, raised the number of constituencies and the number of electors entitled to vote in those constituencies. Although Patten fashioned these changes in a manner that was intended to conform to the electoral system proposed under the Basic Law, the Chinese authorities strongly objected to them on the grounds that they were inconsistent with the Joint Declaration and the Basic Law, and that they violated agreements between the two Governments. They decided, accordingly, that neither the Legislative Council nor any of its members would ride a constitutional through-train to the first legislature of the Hong Kong Special Administrative Region. Instead, the Chinese Government decided to establish a provisional legislature, whose main task would be to prepare for the election of the 'first' legislature of the SAR as foreseen by the Basic Law.

The predominant ideological and operational basis of the Hong Kong Government's approach to governing has been that of *laissez-faire* capitalism, an approach encapsulated in the slogan of 'positive non-interference' in the regulation of economic activity and, to a lesser extent, social affairs.[17] While this rhetoric of non-interference is invoked selectively in opposition to proposals for various 'progressive' social reforms and is less true than it may once have been, nevertheless the level of governmental regulation in many areas is far lower than in many other societies at a similar level of development. One consequence of the *laissez-faire* pro-business approach (and of the low tax

---

[16] On the 1991 elections (with figures for the composition of the Legislative Council and the breakdown of voter eligibility and turnout) see generally Kwok, 'The 1991 Legislative Council Elections in Hong Kong—Constrained Reforms to Representative Government', 30 *Representation* (No. 112), 68–71.

[17] For descriptions and discussions of this approach see Miners, *Government and Politics in Hong Kong*, 5th edn. (1991), 43–9; Scott, above n. 15 at 257–9. For a recent statement see *Hong Kong 1992*, above n. 12 at 59.

rates which accompany it and reflect concern about maintaining the competitiveness of the Hong Kong economy against the backdrop of a huge pool of cheap labour across the border in China and in other regional competitors) is the relatively low level of social assistance measures, although in a number of areas, such as housing and education, the Government has implemented ambitious programmes. More recent developments suggest that the Hong Kong Government has realized the desirability of extending the scope of social welfare services, and social welfare spending has increased significantly in recent years.

The stance of 'positive non-interference' has permitted those in possession of economic power within Hong Kong society a large measure of freedom to exercise that power, largely unhindered by 'excessive' government regulation. The access to, and involvement in, government of the economically better off and business groups has meant that business interests have had preferential access to the process of political decision-making. While it may not be accurate to claim that the Hong Kong Government is the pawn of business interests and never takes steps that may provoke their opposition, nonetheless, business interests have a considerable influence on the policy-making of the Hong Kong Government.[18] By contrast, the power of organized labour and its ability to influence policy-making in Hong Kong has been relatively limited.[19] The policy of 'non-intervention' has resulted not only in a large measure of economic success, but in a society characterized by gross disparities of wealth between the very rich and very poor, and in an environment which suffers from such extreme levels of pollution that it will require the expenditure of billions of dollars for even minimal cleaning-up to be achieved.[20]

Protection of Human Rights in Hong Kong Before the Bill of Rights

Until recently, the protection of human rights in Hong Kong had largely been left to the common law and statute,[21] with all the limitations that

---

[18] Leung, 'Power and Politics: A Critical Analysis', in Leung (ed.), *Social Issues in Hong Kong* (1990), 13 at 20.

[19] England, above n. 13 at 9–20.

[20] For an indication that the Hong Kong Government may finally have the political will to address the problems of pollution energetically, see the undertakings made by the new Governor, Mr Christopher Patten in his first address to the Legislative Council: 'Our Next Five Years: The Agenda for Hong Kong', Address by the Governor, The Right Honourable Christopher Patten at the Opening of the 1992/93 Session of the Legislative Council, 7 October 1992, paras. 64–73. In this area, as in most which have financial implications after 1997, the Hong Kong Government was somewhat hamstrung in its decision-making due to the need for consultation with China.

[21] See Wesley-Smith, 'Protecting Human Rights in Hong Kong', in Wacks, above n. 2 at 17. For a more theoretical approach to the problematic of rights in Hong Kong see MacNeil, 'Righting and Difference', in Wacks, above n. 4 at 86.

such an approach entails. Extremely broad powers and largely unfettered discretions were conferred on officials of the colonial government; these permitted, in theory at least, gross infringements of human rights. On the whole, these powers have been exercised in a relatively restrained way, although there are areas of the law in which both the law on the books and the law in practice are inconsistent with applicable human rights standards.[22]

The increasing awareness of human rights standards and concern that after 1997 the authorities of the Hong Kong SAR might not exercise a similar level of self-restraint have led to calls for the reform of the law in many areas, so that the enjoyment of human rights would be guaranteed by the provisions of the laws themselves rather than dependent on the goodwill of those on whom the law conferred broad powers. The campaigns for the reform of laws claimed to be inconsistent with human rights have been conducted both in Hong Kong and internationally. Increasing use has been made of available international fora in order to put pressure on a government which for a variety of reasons is reluctant to embrace wholeheartedly an approach to human rights implementation that is consistent with the letter and spirit of the various treaties applying to Hong Kong. While the enactment of the Bill of Rights represents an important step forward in this respect, it is nonetheless only a limited one. There are still important areas in which extensive reform of legislation and policies is still required if the law and practice in Hong Kong is to be brought into conformity with international standards.

Hong Kong's Participation in International Human Rights Treaties and Supervisory Mechanisms

The enactment of the Bill of Rights has led to a significant increase in awareness of the international dimensions of human rights among many sectors of the Hong Kong community, although groups in Hong Kong have previously appealed to international human rights standards as part of campaigns for the reform of existing law and practice.[23]

Hong Kong, while a dependent territory of the United Kingdom, did not have the power to ratify treaties on its own behalf, although it participated in a separate capacity as a member of a number of international organizations.[24] Prior to 1997, human rights treaties applied to Hong Kong by

---

[22] See the chapters in Wacks, above n. 4.

[23] The hearing before the Human Rights Committee in 1988 also represents a significant juncture, but well before that there were a number of groups engaged in campaigns to bring about human rights reforms in Hong Kong, in particular the laws relating to public order and freedom of expression, as well as in the area of economic and social rights. See Chan and Lau, 'Some Reflections on the Human Rights Committee's Hearing of the United Kingdom Second Report on Dependent Territories, held November 4–5, 1988, Geneva', (1990), 20 *HKLJ* 150.

[24] See Mushkat, 'Hong Kong as an International Legal Person', (1992) 6 *Emory International Law Review* 105 at 107 n. 6.

virtue of the United Kingdom's ratification of the treaty in question (from 1984 on with the consent of the Chinese Government for international obligations that were to continue beyond 1997). A number of the major United Nations human rights treaties have been extended to Hong Kong:[25] they include the International Convention on the Elimination of All Forms of Racial Discrimination (1969), the International Covenant on Civil and Political Rights (ICCPR) (1976), the International Covenant on Economic, Social and Cultural Rights (ICESCR) (1976), the Convention against Torture (1992) and the Convention on the Rights of the Child (1994). Although the United Kingdom ratified the Convention on the Elimination of All Forms of Discrimination against Women in 1986 (as did China in 1980), it was not until October 1996 that this Convention was extended to Hong Kong, and the first report under it was not due until after the resumption of sovereignty by China.[26] In addition, a number of International Labour Organisation (ILO) conventions apply to Hong Kong,[27] including the Convention on Freedom of Association and Right to Organize and the Convention on the Right to Organize and Bargain Collectively.[28]

[25] For a list which also makes reference to other treaties dealing with human rights that have been applied to Hong Kong, see Jayawickrama, 'The International Protection of Human Rights', in Wacks, above n. 4, 119 at 123–5.

[26] The United Kingdom and Chinese Governments have agreed that the International Convention on the Elimination of All Forms of Racial Discrimination, the Convention on the Rights of the Child, the Convention against Torture and the Women's Convention (to all of which China is party) will continue to apply to Hong Kong after 1997, and it appears that China will continue to report in respect of Hong Kong as part of its reporting obligation under those treaties. While the two states agreed in the Joint Declaration that the two Covenants would continue to apply to Hong Kong after 1997, there is disagreement between the two states as to whether this obliges China to submit reports under the Covenants and, whether, if it purports to do so, the treaty bodies concerned have the jurisdiction to consider them. For a discussion of the issues see Byrnes, 'Hong Kong and the Continuation of International Obligations Relating to Human Rights after 1997', paper presented at the international conference on 'Hong Kong in Transition: Political Order, International Relations and Crisis Management' (Theme 1: Changing International Relations and Crisis Management in Hong Kong after 1997), 18–19 September 1996, Lingnan College, Hong Kong; Byrnes, 'Hong Kong and the International Covenant on Economic, Social and Cultural Rights—Past and Future', in Proceedings of the Seminar on Hong Kong and the Implementation of the International Covenant on Economic, Social and Cultural Rights, University of Hong Kong, 15 October 1994; Chan, 'State Succession to Human Rights Treaties: Continued Application of the Covenant on Civil and Political Rights to Hong Kong (1996) 45 ICLQ 928; Jayawickrama, 'Human Rights in Hong Kong—The Continued Applicability of the International Covenants', (1995) 25 HKLJ 171.

[27] Hong Kong will continue to take part in the activities of the ILO after 1997: see 'Participation of Hong Kong in the Activities of the International Labour Organisation: Communications from the Governments of the United Kingdom of Great Britain and Northern Ireland and of the People's Republic of China', (1990) LXXIII ILO Official Bulletin, Series A, No. 1, 25, reproduced in Byrnes and Chan, above n. 3 at 524–6. See Shin-ichi Ago, 'Application of ILO Conventions to Hong Kong After 1997', (1994) 17 Dalhousie Law Journal 612.

[28] Neither the Convention on Discrimination in Respect of Occupation and Employment 1958 (ILO No. 111), 362 UNTS 31,nor the Convention on Equal Remuneration for Work of Equal Value 1951 (ILO No. 100), 165 UNTS 303, has been extended to Hong Kong. The former has not been ratified by the United Kingdom at all; the second has. As of 31 December 1993, of the approximately 80 ILO conventions ratified by the United Kingdom (of which 10 had

Although over the years the United Kingdom extended the European Convention on Human Rights to a large number of its dependent territories (and former dependent territories) under Article 63 of the Convention and recognized the right of individual complaint in respect of some of those territories, Hong Kong was the significant omission.[29] When calls were made for the United Kingdom to accede to the First Optional Protocol to the ICCPR and to extend that accession to Hong Kong, the United Kingdom justified its refusal to accede by noting that it is subject to the individual complaint procedure under the European Convention, while making no mention of the inapplicability of that Convention to Hong Kong[30]—a response that can only be viewed as, at best, a negligent disregard of the position of Hong Kong or, at worst, as wilful refusal to address the substantive issue in relation to Hong Kong. (As a practical political matter, after 1984 any such accession would have required the agreement of the Chinese Government.)

The only 'individual' complaint procedures which applied to Hong Kong prior to 1997 were the procedures of the ILO. One of these is Article 24 of the ILO Constitution, which permits a workers' organization to complain to the ILO that a member of the ILO 'has failed to secure in any respect the effective observance within its jurisdiction of any Convention to which it is a party'.[31] Complaints alleging violations of trade union rights may also be brought to the ILO against any member of the ILO, regardless of whether that member has ratified any of the Conventions dealing with trade union rights.[32] As of mid-1996, there had been only four complaints lodged in respect of Hong Kong with the ILO, the most recent being a complaint in 1991 against threats by the Postmaster-General to use powers under the Letters Patent to dismiss postal employees who were undertaking industrial action.[33]

Despite the lack of individual complaint procedures, Hong Kong also comes under the scrutiny of the various ILO supervisory bodies and the treaty bodies which examine reports submitted under the United Nations human

subsequently been denounced), a total of 49 conventions had been applied to Hong Kong (31 without modification): Hong Kong Labour Department, *The International Labour Organisation and the Application of International Labour Standards to Hong Kong* (1994), 14.

[29] Jayawickrama, above n. 25 at 125–6. The inapplicability of the Convention to Hong Kong was confirmed by the European Commission of Human Rights when it rejected as inadmissible *ratione loci* an application lodged on behalf of a number of Vietnamese asylum-seekers detained in Hong Kong *Bui Van Thanh* v. *United Kingdom* (application no. 16137/90, decision on admissibility of 12 March 1990, (1990) 1 HKPLR 364). See Byrnes, 'Shut Out in Strasbourg', *Law Society Gazette (Hong Kong)*, 31–33 (July 1990).

[30] For a recent statement of this position see Jayawickrama, above n. 25 at 127.

[31] For the procedure see Articles 24 and 25 of the ILO Constitution. See also the procedure under Articles 26–34 of the ILO Constitution.

[32] ILO, *Procedure for the Examination of Complaints Alleging Infringements of Trade Union Rights* (June 1985).

[33] See *Case No. 1553* v. *United Kingdom (Hong Kong)*, complaint presented by the Hong Kong Union of Post Office Employees, 277th Report of the ILO Committee on Freedom of Association, ILO Doc. GB.249/8/14 (1991), 110–15, and 281st Report of the Committee on Freedom of Association, ILO Doc. GB.252/9/13 (1992), 10–13, reported in (1992) 2 HKPLR 577.

rights treaties applicable to Hong Kong. Until relatively recently, these procedures and the opportunities they offered for raising human rights issues at
the international level were virtually unknown to Hong Kong people (including many in government and human rights activists alike). However, starting
with the hearings before the Human Rights Committee in 1988 and 1991,
many in the Hong Kong community began to follow hearings before the treaty
bodies more closely. The relatively frequent submission of reports under various treaties in the period 1994–97 (Hong Kong was scheduled to be considered on its own or as part of the United Kingdom on no fewer than eight
occasions from late 1994 up to mid-1997) has kept international scrutiny in
the limelight and there has been a great deal of government and non-governmental activity organized around these hearings.

    However, only very recently has there been more than minimal awareness of
treaties other than the ICCPR. Until the mid-1990s, for example, few people
in government or in the community appeared to be aware that the Racial
Discrimination Convention had applied to Hong Kong since 1969, and that
there had been regular reports made to the Committee on the Elimination of
Racial Discrimination (CERD) in respect of Hong Kong. The twelfth periodic report submitted in 1992 contained assertions that there was no racial
discrimination in Hong Kong,[34] as had earlier reports. That report also suffered the fate of earlier ones, being given no publicity in Hong Kong at all by
the Government (which had been chastised in 1988 by the Human Rights
Committee for failing to give publicity to similar reports under the ICCPR).
The CERD hearings, at which reports on Hong Kong were considered in
April 1991 and August 1993,[35] passed unnoticed, it seems, by everyone in
Hong Kong, with the unfortunate result that there was no input from NGOs
into the work of the Committee. By the time the Government submitted its
thirteenth report in 1995,[36] however, things had changed, and there was considerable local discussion of the report, and a number of NGOs made submissions to CERD (apparently the first occasion on which the Committee had
received NGO input of this sort from the United Kingdom).[37]

    Nor had any attention been given to the reports submitted under the
International Covenant on Economic, Social and Cultural Rights or to the
hearings before the Committee on Economic, Social and Cultural Rights
prior to the submission in late 1993 of the second periodic report[38] in respect

[34] UN Doc. CERD/C/226/Add.4 (1992), reproduced in Byrnes and Chan, above n. 3 at 502.
[35] See UN Doc. CERD/C/SR.907–908 (1991) and UN Doc. CERD/C/SR.996–998 (1993).
[36] UN Doc. CERD/C/263/Add.7 (part II), reproduced in *Bill of Rights Bulletin*, vol. 3, No. 4,
Appendix G.
[37] See *Concluding Observations of the Committee on the Elimination of Racial Discrimination*,
UN Doc. CERD/C/304/Add.9 (1996), reproduced in *Bill of Rights Bulletin*, vol. 4, No. 1, June
1996, Appendix A. See generally ibid. at 8–14.
[38] The early reports consisted largely of references to reports submitted to the ILO under the
corresponding ILO conventions. These ILO reports are relatively unknown in Hong Kong

of Hong Kong under that covenant.[39] Increasing interest on the part of the public and the legislature in the international reporting process has led the Government to adopt the practice of laying reports before the Legislative Council; at the instigation of various non-governmental organizations the Legislative Council, in an unprecedented move, held hearings in May 1994 on the reports submitted under the ICESCR. Since that time the Council has held public hearings on each report submitted by the Government pursuant to the major human rights treaties, and has sent a delegation to the meetings of the Committees. Hong Kong's initial appearance before the Committee against Torture[40] and its third appearance before the Human Rights Committee[41] (both in late 1995) aroused similar interest from the public.

It seems that the increased publicity given to the reports on Hong Kong submitted under the ICCPR and the criticisms voiced by NGOs and the Human Rights Committee have brought about, or quickened, the pace of reform in a number of areas in which Hong Kong law and practice was in conflict with the Covenant.[42] Although human rights standards have certainly entered the public debate in recent years, it must be admitted that on a number of major issues, including the question of self-determination, they have made relatively little impact.

The Genesis of the Hong Kong Bill of Rights

THE POLITICAL AND CONSTITUTIONAL CONSTRAINTS ON THE DEVELOPMENT OF THE BILL OF RIGHTS

Once the decision had been taken to enact a Bill of Rights for Hong Kong, the primary responsibility for drafting the document lay with the Hong Kong Government. It was decided at a fairly early stage that the Bill of Rights

amongst the human rights and broader community and are given no publicity by the Government, although they are available for public inspection in Hong Kong. However, the most recent reports are more accessible and informative: see UN Doc. E/1986/4/Add.27 (1993) and UN Doc. E/1990/7/Add.16 (1993), reproduced in Byrnes and Chan, *Bill of Rights Bulletin*, vol. 2, No. 4, December 1993, Appendix C and vol. 3, No. 1, May 1994, Appendix A. The third periodic report, covering all articles of the Covenant was submitted in January 1996 and is even more detailed: see UN Doc. E/1994/104/Add.10 (1996).

[39] For a discussion of those hearings see Byrnes, 'Will the Government Put its Money Where its Mouth Is? The Verdict of the Un Committee on Economic, Social and Cultural Rights on Hong Kong's Human Rights Record', (1995) 25 *HKLJ* 156.

[40] See the discussion in *Bill of Rights Bulletin*, vol. 3, No. 4, December 1995, at 5–8 and the *Concluding Observations of the Committee against Torture* (UN Doc. A/51/44, paras. 58–65 (1996), reproduced in ibid. at Appendix F.

[41] See the *Concluding Observations of the Human Rights Committee* (UN Doc. CCPR/C/79/Add. 57 (1995)), reproduced in ibid. at Appendix E.

[42] Jayawickrama, above n. 25 at 138, identifies a number of reforms which the hearings before the Human Rights Committee motivated or to which they contributed.

should, so far as possible, be a direct incorporation of the ICCPR as applied to Hong Kong. This model appears to have been chosen out of a desire to minimize grounds for 'rational' objections the PRC might put forward to the form and content of the Bill.[43] It was thought that, since the PRC had agreed in the 1984 Joint Declaration that the ICCPR as applied to Hong Kong would remain in force, it could have no objection to that treaty being incorporated directly in Hong Kong law, particularly in light of Article 39 of the Basic Law.

The direct enactment of the terms of a human rights treaty is not, of course, required by most human rights treaties in order to carry out the obligations imposed by them;[44] indeed, merely doing this may not be either a sufficient nor a particularly effective way of legally guaranteeing the rights to be protected. There appear to be few countries which have directly incorporated the ICCPR as part of domestic law,[45] although many of the members of the Council of Europe have done so with the European Convention[46] and many Commonwealth countries have Bills of Rights derived from that Convention. Within most common law systems it is not usual to incorporate such treaties directly into domestic law. The argument has been, at least so far as the United Kingdom and other countries which do not have an entrenched Bill of Rights are concerned, that the rights under the ICCPR, for example, are protected by the combined effect of common law and statutory protections. Where there is

[43] This concern to avoid likely or imagined hostility of the PRC informed much of the Government's thinking about the Bill of Rights and affected its attitude to implementing it. A form of 'China paralysis' seemed to emerge, although in many cases one suspects that this was a convenient excuse for a failure to take steps which the Government did not want to take in any event. The change of Governor in the middle of 1992 appeared to herald a different approach in a number of areas, but it did not lead to any dramatic change in relation to human rights policy, although a number of significant initiatives were adopted.

[44] See in relation to the ICCPR, Schachter, 'The Obligation to Implement the Covenant in Domestic Laws', in Henkin (ed.), *The International Bill of Rights: The Covenant on Civil and Political Rights* (1981), 311 at 312–15; Jhabvala, 'Domestic Implementation of the Covenant on Civil and Political Rights', (1985) 22 *Netherlands International Law Review* 461 at 463–7.

[45] They include the Netherlands, Belgium, and Finland: see Schermers, 'Netherlands', in Jacobs and Roberts (eds.), *The Effect of Treaties in Domestic Law* (1987), 109; Maresceau, 'Belgium", in ibid., 1; and Scheinin, 'The Status of Human Rights Conventions in Finnish Domestic law', in Rosas (ed.), *International Human Rights Norms in Domestic law: Finnish and Polish Perspectives* (1990), 25–43. With the apparent exception of Cyprus (see *Pavlou* v. *Chief Returning Officer, Mayor of Nicosia* (1987) 86 ILR 109 (Supreme Court of Cyprus)) and Nepal, no common law jurisdiction other than Hong Kong appears to have directly incorporated the ICCPR: the New Zealand Bill of Rights Act 1990 is based on the Canadian Charter rather than the ICCPR, and the Australian Bill of Rights Bill 1985, which was essentially a domestic incorporation of the ICCPR, was never enacted. While the USA has ratified the ICCPR, it has declared its provisions to be non-self-executing. The effect of this declaration is that the provisions of the Covenant cannot be directly relied on as part of Federal law.

[46] One country to do so recently is Denmark: Hoffmann, '*Das dänische Gesetz vom 29. April 1992 zur innerstaatlichen Anwendbarkeit der EMRK*', (1992) 12 *Europäische Grundrechte-Zeitschrift* 253. See generally Drzemczewski, *European Human Rights Convention in Domestic Law: A Comparative Study* (1983). For a recent discussion see Polaciewicz and Jacob-Foltzer, 'The European Human Rights Convention in Domestic Law: The Impact of the strasbourg Case-Law in States where Direct Effect is Given to the Convention", (1991) 13 *Human Rights Law Journal* 65 (Part 1), 125 (Part 2).

a domestic Bill of Rights (often modelled on the European Convention), this argument can be further bolstered by reference to the existence of the domestic constitutional guarantees. As will be seen below, in most jurisdictions it is to be expected that a directly enacted treaty will provide protection supplementary to the protections already available under existing law. The importance of that supplement will depend on the substantive protections available under existing law, any procedural requirements that existing non-constitutional remedies first be exhausted, and the approach of the courts (whether as a matter of interpretation or inclination) to preferring general law protections to reliance on treaty provisions.

During the drafting of the Hong Kong Bill of Rights there was some criticism of the decision simply to incorporate the terms of the treaty without adapting it in a manner appropriate to domestic legislation.[47] Concern was expressed that reproducing the word 'shall' (which appears in a number of the provisions of the ICCPR, for example, 'shall be prohibited' or 'shall have the right') might mean that the courts would treat these articles as declarations of principle rather than as enforceable guarantees. To anyone familiar with the experience in countries which have incorporated the European Convention or the ICCPR in their domestic law, these fears appeared largely misplaced, as indeed they have proved to be in practice. However, in some cases, changes were made to the language of the Covenant on the ground that some provisions were not appropriate for inclusion in a domestic statute.[48]

Other criticisms of the reliance on the ICCPR were more fundamental. One influential critic, for example, attacked the first draft of the Bill as 'alien' in nature and concepts, some of its provisions as 'bizarre', and claimed that the Bill was unsuitable for Hong Kong's legal and social system, predicting unfortunate consequences if the Bill was enacted.[49] While many of the criticisms reflected a lack of familiarity with the international background to the Bill of

---

[47] The political reasons for adhering closely to the text of the ICCPR have been mentioned above. This decision also had the advantage that the authentic Chinese and English texts of the ICCPR were included in the equally authoritative Chinese and English versions of the Bill of Rights.

[48] For example, the words 'States Parties to the present Covenant shall take appropriate steps to ensure [equality of rights and responsibilities of spouses]' which appear in Article 23 of the ICCPR were replaced in Article 19 of the Bill of Rights by the words 'Spouses shall have [equal rights and responsibilities]'.

[49] Henry Litton Q.C. (now Litton V.P. of the Court of Appeal) described the first draft of the Bill as 'a law which aims not only at curbing current undesirable practices, but proceeds at one fell swoop to change much of the present system of law'. In relation to discrimination he suggested that the Bill 'not only irons out the creases but burns up much of the fabric as well': *South China Morning Post*, 3 April 1990, 29. He also criticized the inclusion of 'bizarre" provisions such as the prohibition against slavery (taken from Article 8 of the ICCPR) and terms 'expressed in bad French' (referring to the inclusion of the term *'ordre public'* in a number of the limitation clauses of the Bill of Rights): ibid. He subsequently further criticized the Bill for 'the importation of concepts and vocabulary alien to the [Hong Kong] legal system': *South China Morning Post*, 6 June 1990. For a rejoinder to Litton's arguments, see Clark and Byrnes, *South China Morning Post*, 18 May 1990, 9 June 1990.

Rights and the resources available to assist in its interpretation, they did raise a number of valid issues, and in their more moderate formulations represented the concerns of many lawyers in Hong Kong. For that reason they were significant, especially for the subsequent implementation of the Bill of Rights. It must also be recognized that one of the persistent concerns voiced (namely that the Bill of Rights contained many broadly-worded guarantees which would give rise to difficulties of interpretation and would introduce some new concepts) was accurate, though perceptions of the difficulties this would create and the dire predictions of its impact on the overall legal system were on the whole rather exaggerated.

Some commentators argued that in a number of areas covered by the Bill of Rights it would be preferable to enact detailed legislation, with the Bill of Rights providing only a back-up guarantee (for example, in the area of protection of privacy or laws against discrimination). However, while this approach had considerable merit, there seemed little real prospect, in the Hong Kong context at the time of enactment of the Bill of Rights, that detailed legislation in these areas was on the administration's agenda. Accordingly, the limited protection afforded by the Bill of Rights, while far from ideal, appeared likely to be the only protection provided by the law in these areas, at least in the short term. In fact, the enactment of the Bill of Rights appears to have had the effect of generating legislative proposals (both within and outside government) in some of the areas in which detailed protection was lacking.

DISCUSSION OF ECONOMIC, SOCIAL, AND CULTURAL RIGHTS

The determination that the Bill of Rights should be, so far as possible, a domestic copy of the ICCPR, and not diverge from its language, largely preempted any attempts to fashion a home-grown catalogue of civil and political rights guarantees. However, the need to adhere closely to the Joint Declaration and the Basic Law did not require that only civil and political rights be included in the Bill of Rights; it would have been possible to draw on the International Covenant on Economic, Social and Cultural Rights in order to have a more comprehensive Bill of Rights.

Although calls were made to include in the Bill of Rights at least some of the rights guaranteed in the ICESCR that were not already explicitly guaranteed in the ICCPR, in particular those which were generally accepted as being justiciable,[50] the Hong Kong Bill of Rights does not contain these rights.

[50] See, e.g., the draft Hong Kong Bill of Rights prepared by Nihal Jayawickrama on behalf of the *Hong Kong Standard* newspaper, which was based on the standard Commonwealth Bill of Rights model and the two International Covenants. This draft included guarantees of the right to education, the right to work, the right to social security, the right to participate in cultural life, and the right to property (none of which are included in the Hong Kong Bill of Rights) *Hong Kong Standard*, 7 July 1989.

There were various reasons for the failure to consider seriously the inclusion of economic, social, and cultural rights in the Bill of Rights. Time was obviously a factor, since it was necessary for the Bill of Rights to be enacted with a certain dispatch. Another factor was the Government's relative lack of expertise and sophistication in the area of international human rights. The Legal Department of the Hong Kong Government, for example, had to build up its collection of human rights documentation largely from scratch, and there were few people in the Department who had any significant background or expertise in international human rights law. So the learning curve was steep.

However, the articulated justification (which probably underlay the decision) was the fairly traditional, though now somewhat discredited, notion of economic, social, and cultural rights as non-justiciable rights involving positive obligations permitting progressive implementation.[51]

The end result of the (self-imposed) constraints was that the ICCPR (with some significant omissions covered by the United Kingdom's reservations) was essentially adopted *uno ictu*; there was relatively little opportunity for the people of Hong Kong to design their own Bill of Rights adapted to the particular concerns of Hong Kong, either as to substance or to enforcement procedures. Indeed, the Government was largely unreceptive to the many constructive proposals made by NGOs, academics, and members of the legislature in so far as they concerned important issues of substance; the notable exception was the Hong Kong Bank and allied commercial interests, which spearheaded a successful campaign to have so-called 'inter-citizen rights' omitted from the Bill of Rights.[52]

THE GOALS OF SURVIVAL AND ENTRENCHMENT

In drafting the Bill of Rights there were two overarching legal goals. The first was to ensure that the Bill of Rights enjoyed entrenched constitutional status,

[50] See, e.g., the draft Hong Kong Bill of Rights prepared by Nihal Jayawickrama on behalf of the *Hong Kong Standard* newspaper, which was based on the standard Commonwealth Bill of Rights model and the two International Covenants. This draft included guarantees of the right to education, the right to work, the right to social security, the right to participate in cultural life, and the right to property (none of which are included in the Hong Kong Bill of Rights) *Hong Kong Standard*, 7 July 1989.

[51] In the debate in the Legislative Council, the Chief Secretary stated (*Hong Kong Hansard*, 2338 (5 June 1991)): 'The rights enshrined in the ICCPR and those in the ICESCR are different in nature and it was in recognition of this difference that the rights were included in two separate Covenants. many of the rights in the Economic Covenant are not capable of precise legal definition and States Parties are obliged to realize the rights and freedoms contained in that Covenant progressively, according to available resources. That said, Sir, in Hong Kong many such rights have already been taken care of by our existing social service programmes and legislative measures. Furthermore, we are satisfied that many of the civil and political rights which are made justiciable in the Bill of Rights will indeed protect the ICESCR rights and freedoms, albeit indirectly. I agree . . . that selection of rights from the ICESCR to be included in the Bill of Rights would have entailed extensive consultation and prolonged debate about which rights should be included and which excluded and that this would have delayed significantly the enactment of this Bill'.

[52] See discussion at pp. 69–70 below.

so that its provisions could not simply be overridden by subsequent legislation passed by the Hong Kong legislature. The second goal was survival of the Bill of Rights beyond 1997.

So far as survival of the Bill of Rights after 1997 was concerned, account had to be taken of the provisions of the Basic Law which provided for the continuation of certain Hong Kong laws after 30 June 1997. Articles 8 and 160 of the Basic Law provide that the laws in force in Hong Kong prior to the entry into force of the Basic Law shall remain in force unless they are inconsistent with the Basic Law or have been repealed or amended by the legislature of the Hong Kong SAR. It was thought that a Bill of Rights Ordinance based on the ICCPR as applied to Hong Kong could reasonably be viewed as a law contemplated by Article 39 of the Basic Law (or at least falling within its scope)[53] and would therefore continue in effect past 30 June 1997. However, since an ordinary ordinance passed by the Hong Kong legislature could be repealed by that legislature before 30 June 1997, the problem of entrenchment still had to be addressed.

Various options for entrenchment were considered,[54] but it was decided that the most suitable and effective was to entrench the Bill by means of United Kingdom legislation, which would prevail over any Hong Kong legislation in conflict with it. The problem with this technique was that United Kingdom primary and delegated legislation applying of its own force in Hong Kong would cease to have effect in Hong Kong as of 1 July 1997. Thus, while entrenchment by this route would be effective until then, some other means had to be found for entrenching the guarantees after that date.

A possible solution appeared in Article 39 of the Basic Law. If a Bill of Rights Ordinance were to continue in force, then arguably any law which was inconsistent with the rights and freedoms guaranteed by it would be in conflict with Article 39 of the Basic Law, and therefore invalid. Thus, the Basic Law itself, in conjunction with the Bill of Rights Ordinance, would entrench the provisions of the Ordinance.

The solution finally adopted drew on these possibilities. The Bill of Rights package consisted in the first place of the Hong Kong Bill of Rights Ordinance 1991, an ordinary statute with no entrenched status which largely copied the provisions of the ICCPR as applied to Hong Kong. The second element of the package was a piece of United Kingdom prerogative legislation,

---

[53] Article 39 of the Basic Law provides: 'The provisions of the International Covenant on Civil and Political Rights and the International Covenant on Economic, Social and Cultural Rights, and international labour conventions as applied to Hong Kong shall remain in force and shall be implemented through the laws of the Hong Kong Special Administrative Region. The rights and freedoms enjoyed by Hong Kong residents shall not be restricted unless as prescribed by law. Such restrictions shall not contravene the provisions of the preceding paragraph of this article'.

[54] See Wesley-Smith, 'Entrenchment of the Bill of Rights', in Wacks (ed.), *Hong Kong's Bill of Rights: Problems and Prospects* (1990), 59–67; and Dykes 'Hong Kong Bill of Rights 1991: Its Origin, Content and Impact', in Chan and Ghai, above n. 3, 39 at 41–2.

the Hong Kong Letters Patent Amendment (No. 2) 1991, which amended Hong Kong's constitutional instrument (the Letters Patent) by inserting a new clause which provided that:

The provisions of the International Covenant on Civil and Political Rights, adopted by the General Assembly of the United Nations on 16 December 1966, as applied to Hong Kong, shall be implemented through the laws of Hong Kong. No law of Hong Kong shall be made after the coming into operation of the Hong Kong Letters Patent 1991 (No. 2) [8 June 1991] that restricts the rights and freedoms enjoyed in Hong Kong in a manner which is inconsistent with that Covenant as applied to Hong Kong.

The new article of the Letters Patent was modelled closely on Article 39 of the Basic Law. The thinking here was that case law developed under that article might influence subsequent interpretation of Article 39 by the courts of Hong Kong, which would in the first instance be responsible for interpreting the Basic Law (though they will not have the final say, which is reserved to the Standing Committee of the National People's Congress of the People's Republic of China[55]). However, whether Article 39 of the Basic Law will bear this load and whether, in view of the guarantees of human rights contained in Chapter III of the Basic Law (of which Article 39 forms a part), the provisions of the Bill of Rights Ordinance will be viewed as 'consistent' with the Basic Law are questions that have given rise to some disagreement.[56]

It should be noted that it was the ICCPR as applied to Hong Kong which was entrenched and which limited the power of the Hong Kong legislature to enact laws on or after 8 June 1991. The Bill of Rights Ordinance was, in a sense, backward-looking, operating on statutes in force as of 8 June 1991 (although its effect will be felt for long after that date) and provisions of the common law. It was expected that, as time progressed, more and more cases would focus on the provisions of the Covenant itself, which had now been entrenched as part of the law of Hong Kong.

THE PRC'S RESPONSE TO THE BILL OF RIGHTS[57]

The official response from China (and the 'unofficial' response from pro-China media in Hong Kong and other groups aligned with China) to the

---

[55] Basic Law, Article 158.

[56] This analysis assumes that the provisions of Article 39 of the Basic Law would be considered self-executing or justiciable, but there appears to be disagreement on this issue: see Keller, 'Freedom of the Press in Hong Kong: Liberal Values and Sovereign Interests', (1992) 27 *Texas International Law Journal* 371 at 396–7. See Jordan, 'The Bill of Rights Ordinance and Article 39 of the Basic Law of the Hong Kong Special Administrative Region', in Edwards and Byrnes (eds.), *Hong Kong's Bill of Rights: The Final Year?* (forthcoming 1997).

[57] For the views of the Hong Kong population on the Bill of Rights see Cullen, 'The Bill of Rights: Some New Perspectives', in Edwards and Byrnes (eds.), *Hong Kong's Bill of Rights: The First Year* (1992), 109.

drafting and enactment of the Bill of Rights was not favourable.[58] No doubt one of the factors which led to this negative response was that the Chinese authorities perceived, quite correctly, that a major purpose of the Bill of Rights was to protect the people of Hong Kong against abuses by public authorities after the change of sovereignty in 1997. Allegations of hypocrisy on the part of the colonial government were also expressed, to the effect that, if the protections of the common law and statutes had been sufficient for almost 150 years of British rule (a position adopted by the United Kingdom Government since the extension of the ICCPR to Hong Kong), then it seemed unnecessary to enact a Bill of Rights of this sort. Some also saw the Bill of Rights as an attempt by the United Kingdom Government to undermine the Basic Law, which was being drafted at the same time as the Bill of Rights[59] and which contained in Chapter III a number of guarantees of human rights.[60]

Although at the time of passage of the Bill of Rights Ordinance official Chinese reaction was limited to a statement that the PRC reserved the right to review the Ordinance for inconsistency with the Basic Law, the implications of what this might mean emerged in 1995 in the deliberations of the Legal Subgroup of the Preliminary Working Group. This was the body established by China following the wrangle arising from the Patten electoral reforms and the Chinese decision to disband the Legislative Council in order to prepare for the Preparatory Committee, the body foreseen in the Basic Law as carrying out necessary preparations for the establishment of the SAR.

The Legal Subgroup recommended that the Bill of Rights Ordinance be repealed and that a number of pieces of legislation that had been repealed, at least partly to bring them into line with the Bill of Rights Ordinance, should be revived.[61] This recommendation, which aroused considerable protest, was forwarded by the PWC to the Preliminary Committee for its consideration.[62]

The reasons for the decision were various, though political factors appear to have been more important than legal ones: first, the fact that the Ordinance was enacted in the wake of June 1989 and was viewed as expressing a lack of

[58] See Allan, 'A Bill of Rights for Hong Kong', [1991] *Public Law* 175 at 179.

[59] The first draft of the Basic Law was published in April 1988, the second draft in February 1989, and the final version in April 1990. The first draft of the Bill of Rights was published in March 1990, the second draft was introduced into the legislature in July 1990, and the Ordinance was enacted in June 1991.

[60] See Ghai, 'The Hong Kong Bill of Rights Ordinance and the Basic Law of the Hong Kong Special Administrative Region', (1995) 1 *Journal of Chinese and Comparative Law* 30, at 40–1. For a quasi-official statement of the Chinese position by two mainland members of the legal sub-group of the PWC, see *Window* magazine (10 November 1995) at 10–14.

[61] See the Statement of the Legal Subgroup of the Preliminary Working Committee on the Bill of Rights, 17 October 1995, in Chan (ed.), *United Kingdom: Hong Kong* (Booklet 7), in Blaustein (ed.), *Constitutions of Dependencies and Special Sovereignties* (1996). The statement is also reproduced in the *Bill of Rights Bulletin*, vol. 2, no. 4, December 1995, Appendix A.

[62] See *Summary of Recommendations of The Preliminary Working Committee on the Repeal and Amendment of Existing Laws*, in Chan, above n. 61.

confidence in China's commitment to the preservation of human rights in Hong Kong; secondly, the perception that the Bill of Rights Ordinance had led to the repeal of a number of provisions in fields relating to criminal law and security and/or which gave the government broad powers—this was seen as an attempt to undermine the powers available to the SAR Government, and; finally, a difference in legal approach to determining 'inconsistency' of a statute with a constitutional document seems to have played a role as well. The legal analysis that has been advanced to support the conclusion that the Bill of Rights Ordinance is inconsistent with the Basic Law is based on the provisions in the Ordinance which provide that all pre-existing legislation inconsistent with the Bill of Rights is repealed.[63] In what has become the orthodox analysis, this is seen as different from ordinary legislation, thus giving the Bill of Rights Ordinance a 'higher status' than ordinary legislation. This in itself is inconsistent with the Basic Law, which does not contemplate any law enjoying special status other than itself. Accordingly, the Bill of Rights Ordinance is inconsistent with the (spirit of) the Basic Law and therefore invalid to that extent. In addition, the argument has been made that, as Chapter III of the Basic Law already provides a catalogue of rights guarantees, the Bill of Rights Ordinance, to the extent that it goes beyond those, is 'inconsistent' with it.

Whatever the merits of these arguments, the facts of political power meant that the Bill of Rights Ordinance was effectively amended by the decision of the Standing Committee of the NPC that Sections 2(3), 3 and 4 of the Bill of Rights Ordinance will not form part of Hong Kong law after 30 June 1997. The effect of the amendments will be is unclear. Formally, the repeal effect of the Bill of Rights Ordinance is spent: it took effect on 8 June 1991 and when a court finds a statutory provision inconsistent with the Ordinance, it is only declaring what has already taken place as a matter of law. Repealing the repeal provisions of the Ordinance does not revive those ordinances which the Bill of Rights has already repealed. Whether this means that a court of the SAR will be unprepared to find that it still has the power to declare that a pre-1991 law was repealed with effect from 8 June 1991 (while still recognizing pre-1997 decisions declaring such repealed) is unclear. For future laws the Ordinance would presumably have little or no effect other than as a statement of values (or similar to the New Zealand Bill of Rights Act).[64]

---

[63] For a discussion of the issue of consistency between the Bill of Rights and the Basic Law, see Ghai, above n. 60.

[64] For a comparative discussion, see Cooke, 'Brass Tacks and Bill of Rights', (1995) 25 *HKLJ* 64.

The Scope and Operation of the Bill of Rights Package[65]

Thus, the effect of the instruments that made up the Hong Kong Bill of Rights regime was to entrench most of the provisions of the ICCPR[66] that apply to Hong Kong, at least until 1997 and perhaps beyond that date. For most purposes, the substantive protection afforded by both the Ordinance and the Letters Patent was the same.[67]

The Bill of Rights Ordinance consists of three parts.[68] Part I contains provisions relating to the Ordinance's commencement, interpretation, scope of application, effect, remedies and jurisdiction of the courts, and the conditions under which derogation from the rights guaranteed in the Ordinance is permitted (Sections 1–7). Part II contains the text of the Hong Kong Bill of Rights, which consists of 23 articles (Section 8). Part III contains limitations on the scope of the Bill (essentially the reservations entered by the United Kingdom) and provisions relating to the partial 'freeze' on the operation of the Ordinance.

The Ordinance operates differently in relation to pre-existing legislation and subsequent legislation. It requires that legislation enacted before 8 June 1991 be read consistently with the Bill if that is possible; if it is not, then the existing legislation will be repealed to the extent of the inconsistency (Section 3).[69]

In relation to legislation enacted on or after 8 June 1991, the Ordinance acts as an interpretation provision, requiring that such legislation be read as subject to the ICCPR to the extent that the legislation admits of such a construction. If the subsequent legislation does not admit of such a construction, then under general principles of statutory interpretation, it would normally prevail over the Bill of Rights Ordinance. However, the amendment to the Letters Patent meant that subsequent legislation inconsistent with the

---

[65] For an interesting, though occasionally idiosyncratic, discussion of a number of issues of construction of the Bill of Rights Ordinance, see Morris, 'Interpreting Hong Kong's Bill of Rights: Some Basic Questions—Part I', (1994) 15 *Statute Law Review* 126, 'Part II', (1995) 16 *Statute Law Review* 144–65, and 'Part III', (1995) 16 *Statute Law Review* 200.

[66] For a comparison of the provisions of the ICCPR and the Bill of Rights, see Lillich, 'Sources of Human Rights Law and The Hong Kong Bill of Rights', in Chan and Ghai, above n. 3 at 109, Appendixes 1 and 2, 134–9.

[67] One area in which there may be a difference is in relation to 'inter-citizen rights', held not to be included within the scope of the Ordinance by the Court of Appeal in *Tam Hing-yee* v. *Wu Tai-wai* (1991) 1 HKPLR 261; [1992] 1 HKLR 185, but arguably covered by the Letters Patent. See Byrnes, 'The Hong Kong Bill of Rights and Relations between Private Individuals', in Chan and Ghai, above n. 3, 71 at 102.

[68] References in the following discussion are to the original version of the Bill of Rights Ordinance, before its amendment as a result of the NPC's decision. For a review of the content of the Bill of Rights Ordinance see Jayawickrama, 'The Hong Kong Bill of Rights: A Critique', in Chan and Ghai, above n. 3 at 55.

[69] Six Ordinances were specifically exempted from the operation of the Ordinance for a one-year 'freeze' period. That period expired on 7 June 1992.

Ordinance was likely in most, if not all, cases also to be inconsistent with the ICCPR as applied to Hong Kong[70] and therefore invalidated by the Letters Patent as a superior, constitutional norm.

The Bill of Rights applies to administrative actions as well as to legislation. The effect of the Ordinance is that any discretion conferred by statute is read subject to the Bill of Rights and the Letters Patent, so that an exercise of statutory power which is not consistent with the Ordinance or the Letters Patent will be *ultra vires*. (If the statute requires the power to be exercised in such a manner, the enabling statute itself will have been repealed by the Bill of Rights Ordinance or invalidated by the Letters Patent.)

The combined result of the Letters Patent and the Ordinance was that:

(a) from 8 June 1991 until 30 June 1997, any new law that restricted rights and freedoms in a manner inconsistent with the Covenant was invalid because of its inconsistency with the Letters Patent;[71] and

(b) legislation already existing at the time of the Bill's commencement was to be construed in accordance with the Bill if such a construction was possible; where such a construction was not possible, the earlier legislation would, to the extent of the inconsistency, be repealed.

The Bill was also intended to supersede existing common law rules which are inconsistent with the rights and freedoms guaranteed by the Bill.[72] This is the result of the general position that a statute supersedes the common law where there is an inconsistency between the two. The Bill took effect in relation to common law rules from its commencement; there was no freeze period.

REMEDIES FOR BILL OF RIGHTS VIOLATIONS

Section 6 of the Bill of Rights Ordinance provides:

Remedies for contravention of Bill of Rights
6. (1) A court or tribunal—
    (a) in proceedings within its jurisdiction in an action for breach of this Ordinance; and
    (b) in other proceedings within its jurisdiction in which a violation or threatened violation of the Bill of Rights is relevant,
may grant such remedy or relief, or make such order, in respect of such a breach, violation or threatened violation as it has power to grant or make in those proceedings and as it considers appropriate and just in the circumstances.

---

[70] See *R.* v. *Kwong Kui Wing* (1996) 6 HKPLR 125 at 130, DCt (holding that authoritative pronouncements on Article 11(1) of the Bill of Rights were binding in the interpretation of Article 14(2) of the ICCPR).

[71] See *R.* v. *Lum Wai-ming* (1992) 2 HKPLR 182 (HCt) and *R.* v. *Chan Wai-ming (No. 2)* (1992) 2 HKPLR 231 (holding post-June 1991 legislation inconsistent with the Letters Patent and void to the extent of the inconsistency).

[72] At least so far as those rules govern legal relations between a private individual and the State, but not as between two private individuals.

An action to enforce a claim under the Bill of Rights may be brought before any court which has jurisdiction over the parties and the subject matter. In addition, the Bill of Rights can be raised 'as a shield' against actions brought in any court, for example, in criminal suits in the Magistrates' Courts or other courts exercising criminal jurisdiction, or against a party seeking to enforce a contract in the Labour Tribunal where the contract violates freedom of expression or some other right (provided that the party seeking enforcement is a 'public authority').

Section 6, while intended to ensure that any court or tribunal before which a Bill of Rights issue is raised could deal with it, was also apparently designed to ensure that the power of the courts to develop innovative or new remedies was severely constrained. The courts have, in general, interpreted the section as not permitting them to grant remedies which they cannot presently grant.[73]

In most cases the remedies available under the existing remedial powers of the courts are adequate to deal with violations of the Bill of Rights. For example, the remedies of a stay for undue delay or the exclusion of evidence where evidence has been obtained in violation of the Bill of Rights may be available. However, there may be some cases in which under present law there is a remedial gap (for example, where there is a violation of the right to trial without undue delay or to release and a defendant who has been held in custody for the duration of his or her trial is finally acquitted, the court does not appear to have the power to award damages or provide any other appropriate remedy, except perhaps if the defendant commences a civil suit). Although the Government rejected proposals that a general remedial power be conferred on the courts when the Bill of Rights was being drafted, there is much to be said for conferring such a power on the courts.

THE EFFECT OF A DECLARATION THAT A STATUTE HAS BEEN REPEALED

One of the remedies a court may grant is a declaration that a particular statutory provision has been repealed by virtue of Section 3(2) of the Bill of Rights Ordinance. In *R. v. Sin Yau-ming*[74] the Court of Appeal held that, as a result of its conclusion that various presumptions in Section 47 of the Dangerous Drugs Ordinance were inconsistent with the Bill of Rights, those presumptions had been repealed by the Bill of Rights Ordinance with effect from 8 June 1991. Although there had been an earlier decision of the District Court holding the presumptions to be inconsistent with the Bill of Rights,[75] since the District Court's decisions do not bind other courts, cases had

---

[73] *Re Sin Hoi* (1992) 2 HKPLR 18; [1992] 1 HKLR 408, CA; *R. v. Yu Yem-kin* (1994) 4 HKPLR 75, HCt; *R. v. Cheung Ka Fai* (1995) 5 HKPLR 407 at 416, [1995] 3 HKC 214, CA.

[74] (1991) 1 HKPLR 88, [1992] 1 HKCLR 127.

[75] *R. v. Ng Po-lam* (1991) 1 HKPLR 25; *R. v. Leung Ping-lam* (1991) 1 HKPLR 52.

continued to be brought relying on the presumptions. Where trials had concluded after 8 June 1991 but before the decision in *Sin Yau-ming* (30 September 1991), appeals were subsequently allowed on the ground that the presumptions relied on were no longer in existence at the time of the trial.[76]

The fact that declarations of inconsistency with the Bill of Rights in the future will relate back to 8 June 1991 has given rise to concern from two perspectives. From the perspective of orderly administration of justice, such a declaration years after 8 June 1991 may give rise to considerable difficulties. From the point of view of those concerned with civil liberties, there is concern that this very prospect may make the courts more reluctant to declare legislation repealed as time passes.[77]

Although the Court of Appeal has taken the view that the issue is straightforward, it may be that there are other ways of interpreting the Bill of Rights Ordinance so that a court could declare that a repeal took effect from the date of its judgment in relation to any case presently pending. A similar approach has been taken by the Supreme Court of Canada in an analogous, though not entirely parallel, situation.[78] If the Hong Kong courts feel that they do not presently possess such a remedial power, then it may be appropriate to amend the Ordinance to introduce one (assuming that such an amendment would be consistent with the Letters Patent). Proposals along these lines were made during the drafting of the Bill but, like many other useful proposals put forward at that time, they were not adopted by the Government.

WHO IS BOUND BY THE BILL OF RIGHTS ORDINANCE?

The original draft of the Bill of Rights provided that the Bill of Rights bound all persons, whether acting in a public or private capacity. This provision gave rise to strong criticism from a number of quarters due to concern over its potential implications. The end result of a fairly vigorous campaign against the provision by business interests led to its removal from the Ordinance. Unfortunately, the removal of 'inter-citizen rights' from the Bill of Rights Ordinance was subsequently interpreted by the Court of Appeal[79] as excluding from the scope of the Bill of Rights not just common law rules regulating legal relations between private individuals (essentially the position under the

---

[76] This approach was confirmed by the Privy Council in *Attorney General* v. *Lee Kwong-kut*. See the comments of Penlington in *R.* v. *Lee Kwong-ming* (1992) 2 HKPLR 91 at 93 on the proper approach to applications for leave to appeal out of time on the basis of *Sin Yau-ming*.

[77] McCoy, 'Problems in the Area of Litigation', in Edwards and Byrnes, above n. 57. For an earlier discussion of this problem see Chan, 'A Bill of Rights for Hong Kong?', in Wacks (ed.), *Civil Liberties in Hong Kong*, 72 at 93–5 (1988).

[78] *Reference re Language Rights under the Manitoba Act, 1870* [1985] 1 SCR 721; 19 DLR (4th) 1.

[79] *Tam Hing-yee* v. *Wu Tai-wai* (1991) 1 HLPLR 261; [1992] 1 HKLR 185.

Canadian Charter which embodies a similar public/private distinction),[80] but also legislation which creates rights of private individuals *inter se*.[81]

The Bill of Rights and the Hong Kong Administration

Under international law all organs of a state are responsible for implementing treaty obligations which fall within their competence. Underlying this formal legal proposition is the understanding (one perhaps especially appropriate in the case of human rights treaties) that, in order for a treaty to be given full effect, a passive approach which leaves to the courts the primary or exclusive role in implementing obligations by providing remedies for violations which are brought before them is only ever a partial and often unsatisfactory method of proceeding. It is equally, perhaps more, important that the national legislature and executive observe human rights standards in the enactment and administration of the laws.

The record of the Hong Kong administration has been rather mixed, with support for the goals of the Bill of Rights varying over time and among the different branches of the administration. Although the Government has been conservative and cautious in many of the amendments it has put forward (and intransigent in its refusal to make others), there is little doubt that the enactment of the Bill of Rights Ordinance has led to the reexamination of much legislation that was sorely in need of review and that the result has been many desirable amendments.

It is important to recall that the decision to enact a Bill of Rights was not that of the Hong Kong Government but rather of the Untied Kingdom Government, and it seems that support for the move at the highest levels of the Hong Kong administration has never been more than lukewarm (at least

[80] See generally Byrnes, above n. 67. In *L.* v. *C.* (1994) 4 HKPLR 388, the High Court suggested *obiter* that provisions of legislation which would prevent an illegitimate child making an application for financial provision from his father if his mother did not make a timely application would be inconsistent with the Bill of Rights and repealed. This appears to be in conflict with the Court of Appeal's decision in *Tam Hing-yee* v. *Wu Tai-wai* that the Bill of Rights does not apply to rights of citizens *inter se*. In a 1995 decision the Court of Appeal seemed to accept the correctness of *Tam Hing-yee* and went on to apply the provisions of Article 19 of the ICCPR as an aid to the development of the common law in relation to damages for defamation *Cheung Ng Sheong Steven* v. *Eastweek Publisher Ltd* (1995) 5 HKPLR 428.

[81] Byrnes, above n. 67 at 97–8. In a series of private members' bills introduced in the 1994–5 and 1995–6 sessions of the Legislative Council, attempts were made to reverse the effect of the decision in *Tam Hing-yee* and to restore the interpretation originally intended by the Government: see Equal Opportunities Bill 1994, cl. 242 (*Hong Kong Government Gazette*, 1 July 1994, *Legal Supplement No 3*, C991 at C1250), and Equal Opportunities (Family Responsibility, Sexuality and Age) Bill 1995, cl. 103 (*Hong Kong Government Gazette*, 28 June 1996, *Legal Supplement No 3*, C1791 at C1892). The administration opposed this and other aspects of these bills, suffering (it seems) from a bout of institutional amnesia, since the proposed amendment would have achieved exactly what the Government intended the section to mean and thought that it did at the time of its passage.

in so far as the Bill of Rights was to affect the position before 1997). This has had important implications for those engaged in policy-making within the bureaucracy; since there has not been insistent pressure from the top to ensure that the letter and spirit of the ICCPR and the Bill of Rights are embraced, policy-makers in the different areas have been relatively free to define their own approach to the Bill of Rights. The role played by the Attorney-General's Chambers and the relative lack of institutional power of the Attorney-General and his Department within the governmental structure seem to have meant that the weight given to a legal view on the merits of a human rights argument has been less than it would be in countries such as Australia or Canada. While no doubt the Legal Department has given sound advice (which may not always have been followed), the primary role of the Department has been to act as legal adviser to those who have responsibility for policy decisions. This has meant, among other things, taking on the task of formulating arguments to defend policy decisions that seem inconsistent with the spirit of the guarantees of the Bill of Rights and, in some cases, advancing positions clearly inconsistent with established international interpretations of those guarantees.

Ironically, activity within the administration and its public rhetoric in support of a broad interpretation of the Bill of Rights was perhaps most energetic and visible in the period before the Bill of Rights was enacted. Government promised to undertake a thorough review of Hong Kong's laws in the light of the Bill of Rights, the implication being that, once possible inconsistencies were found, appropriate legislative amendments would be made. Individual government departments, concerned at the prospect of legislation being struck down for inconsistency with the Bill of Rights, examined their legislation closely in order to see how it might be amended to survive possible challenges.

As time progressed, however, this attitude began to change, encouraged by indications that the appellate courts, while maintaining the rhetoric of a 'generous and purposive' interpretation of the Bill of Rights, were retreating from what some saw as an initial, expansive approach. The official approach to amending laws became that legislative amendments would only be made if it was 'almost certain' that the courts would find the legislation inconsistent with the Bill of Rights.[82] The Government's view of the requisite level of certainty became more stringent over time and now seems to require the

---

[82] See, e.g., the statements by the Independent Commissioner for Corruption in 1992 and 1993: Allan, 'Independent Commissioner Against Corruption', in Edwards and Byrnes, above n. 57, 11 at 13 (describing the strategy of the ICAC, viz. to propose amendments to legislation that was 'almost certainly inconsistent' with the Bill of Rights); de Speville, 'Law Enforcement and the Independent Commission against Corruption', in Fong, Byrnes and Edwards, *Hong Kong's Bill of Rights: Two Years On* (1994), 11 at 13 (describing the strategy of the ICAC in similar terms, viz. 'to repeal or amend those elements of our Ordinances which were by consensus manifestly contrary to the Bill, and stay with the rest until the matter could be decided by the courts either in decisions or in unequivocal guidance').

existence of a (preferably unanimous) judgment of the European Court of Human Rights on an analogous United Kingdom provision, or a decision of the Privy Council, the Supreme Court of Canada, or the Human Rights Committee on a substantially identical point. Not only does this standard hardly seem consonant with the liberal and generous interpretation which both the Privy Council and the Court of Appeal have declared was appropriate for the interpretation of the Bill of Rights, but even in some cases in which this stringent standard has been met, the Government has refused to take steps to amend the offending law or has delayed excessively in doing so.[83]

In some areas the Government's approach has also begun to be characterized by what is almost a reversal of the normal approach to the interpretation of human rights treaties, under which rights are to be construed broadly and permissible restrictions read narrowly.[84] On occasion, the Government has adopted (in public at any rate) quite niggardly interpretations of rights and advocated expansive readings of limitations clauses,[85] in some cases maintaining interpretations of the guarantees that are directly at odds with stances taken by the United Kingdom internationally.[86] This attitude has been reflected in many of the legislative amendments put forward by the Government to the ordinances which were exempted from the operation of the Bill of Rights

[83] The most striking example is the wide power to intercept telephonic communications. Under Section 33 of the Telecommunications Ordinance, the Governor is given an essentially unfettered discretion to order telephone tapping. Despite the decision of the European Court in *Malone* v. *United Kingdom* (1984) Series A, No. 82; 74 ILR 304; 7 EHRR 14, until 1997 the Government had steadfastly refused to introduce appropriate legislation or even to give general details of the circumstances in which telephones are tapped. The Government published a draft Bill in the form of a consultation paper in February 1997, but it was unclear whether this would be enacted by 30 June 1997.

[84] See generally Ghai, 'Derogations and Limitations in the Hong Kong Bill of Rights', in Chan and Ghai, above n. 3 at 161.

[85] One example is the 1993 banning of mobile billboards. The Government maintained that advertising printed on mobile billboards was not a form of expression covered by the right to freedom of expression since mobile billboards were not 'an independent medium of expression'. This attitude has also been reflected in the positions advanced by the Government in a number of court cases to which it has been a party. See, e.g., the argument advanced, contrary to fairly clear international case law to the contrary, in *R.* v. *Man Wai Keung (No 2)* (1992) 2 HKPLR 164 that the guarantee against non-discrimination in Article 10 of the Bill of Rights (Article 14(1) of the ICCPR) was limited to discrimination on the basis of the grounds mentioned in Articles 1 and 22 of the Bill of Rights, and that this did not cover distinctions between different classes of litigants (as this did not amount to distinction based on '[an]other status').

[86] For example, the Government has put forward the argument in a number of cases (and succeeded in persuading a number of courts) that the guarantee of freedom from arbitrary arrest and detention in Article 5(1) of the Bill of Rights (Article 9(1) of the ICCPR) does not permit substantive review of a law permitting detention, but is confined to procedural protection and the requirement that there be a law providing for detention: see Byrnes, 'Killing it Softly? The Hong Kong Courts and the Slow Demise of the Hong Kong Bill of Rights', in *Hong Kong and the Implementation of the International Covenant on Civil and Political Rights, Proceedings of a seminar organised by the Centre for Comparative and Public Law, University of Hong Kong, 30 September 1995* (hereinafter *ICCPR Proceedings*) (referring to *R.* v. *Hui Lan-chak* (1992) 2 HKPLR 423 (DCt), *R.* v. *Hui Kwok-fai* (1993) 3 HKPLR 752 (DCt) and *R.* v. *Chong Ka-man* (1993) 3 HKPLR 789 (Mag)).

Ordinance for a year. In a number of important cases the amendments were largely cosmetic and based on a narrow interpretation of the rights guaranteed by the Bill of Rights.[87] The Government's concern became not what it must do to give full effect to a generous interpretation of the Bill of Rights, but how little it had to do in order to be able to resist a challenge should one come before the courts. This attitude was encouraged by the developments in the courts, which have become less demanding in their scrutiny of Government's justifications of restrictions on guaranteed rights.

Concern about the reaction of the PRC authorities has also been a factor influencing the Government's approach to reform. As already noted, the PRC was suspicious of the motivation that led to the Bill of Rights and saw its potentially wide-ranging effect on other laws as a fundamental change in the legal system and therefore inconsistent with the stipulation in the Joint Declaration that the Hong Kong legal system should remain basically unchanged. An overt and energetic approach to law reform in the light of an expansive interpretation of the Bill of Rights would have further fanned these concerns. The political path of least resistance and the views of many sectors of government appear to have coincided in this respect.

While it is difficult to give an overall assessment of the impact of the Bill of Rights on policy-making in view of the closed nature of much of that process, it can be said that the Bill of Rights has prompted an examination of laws and policies in some areas which were long overdue for reform. Indeed, it has provided the occasion for a thoroughgoing review of some laws—a review which has gone beyond what might have been strictly required to bring these laws clearly into conformity with the Bill of Rights.[88] The impression one gains, however, is that in many cases Government has decided to make amendments to provisions which do not matter very much, in order to be able to portray itself as adopting a reasonable, compromising approach to bringing legislation into line with the Bill of Rights.[89]

Legislation affecting freedom of expression provides a good example of the impact that the Bill of Rights has had in creating or adding momentum to the amendment and reform of laws that in many cases are quite antiquated or which do not comply with modern standards of human rights. Under pressure from various NGOs and in the light of the Bill of Rights, the administration undertook in 1992 to review laws relating to freedom of expression, in

[87] See Chan, 'The Legal System', in Cheng *et al.* (eds.), *The Other Hong Kong Report 1992* (1992), 14.

[88] The Prison Rules are one example of legislation that has been extensively reworked in the light of the Bill of Rights. See Chan, 'Prison Administration', in Fong, Byrnes, and Edwards (eds.), above n. 82 at 45. Extensive amendments, intended to bring the Rules into line with the Bill of Rights, were finally made in 1996: Prison (Amendment) Rules 1996, L.N. 300 of 1996, *Hong Kong Government Gazette*, 5 July 1996, *Legal Supplement No 2*, C1288.

[89] For example, the attitude taken by the Independent Commission Against Corruption, referred to above n. 82.

particular those which had an impact on press freedom. Following this review the Government announced that it would amend 16 of those laws; the others were considered compatible with the Bill of Rights.[90] In the course of the next couple of years most of those amendments were made.[91]

However, although many of these amendments did respond to the concerns that had been expressed, the Government refused to take action on some laws and the amendment of a number of other important laws continued to be delayed. This latter group included official secrets legislation, laws relating to treason and sedition, and the provisions relating to interception of communications, all legislation which was politically sensitive (and in some cases required prior consultation with the Chinese Government) or provisions which the Hong Kong administration did not particularly wish to dilute.[92]

The Bill of Rights, and the attendant legislative, community, and international scrutiny, have meant that since 1991 adminsitrative policies and new legislation have had to be considered against the standards of the Bill of Rights. While on many occasions this vetting still seems to let through legislation whose consistency with the Bill of Rights is questionable, it also no doubt operates to screen out other proposals which would breach the guarantees. The Bill of Rights has thus meant the repeal or amendment of many of the more egregious instances of legislation inconsistent with the Bill of Rights and has presumably tempered the excesses of some new legislation, preventing them from seeing the light of day. Nevertheless, the overall tone of the administration's legislative responses has been cautious and conservative, even niggardly on many occasions. Yet it is undeniable that a number of significant changes have come about as a result of the Bill of Rights, or have been influenced by it.[93]

One important area where the Government's refusal to take legislative initiatives has meant the restriction of the enjoyment of rights guaranteed by the ICCPR is in relation to those areas covered by reservations. These include, in

[90] For an overview see the fourth periodic report of the United Kingdom in respect of Hong Kong under the ICCPR, submitted in July 1995: UN Doc. CCPR/C/95/Add.5, paras. 213–44 (1995). In June 1995 the administration compiled a list of provisions affecting freedom of expression, their position in relation to each of them and details of amendments enacted or proposed: Home Affairs Branch, *Review of legislation for BOR compatibility and Press Freedom*, June 1995.

[91] See ibid. The amendments included a reworking of the Public Order Ordinance, which liberalized the regime for regulation of public meetings and processions, the abolition of the requirement of a permit to use a loudhailer in public, the repeal of excessive registration requirements for newspapers, abolition of restrictions on the reporting of certain aspects of court proceedings, the abolition of the offence of defamatory libel, and the enactment of provisions defining the circumstances in which journalistic material could be seized for the purposes of a criminal investigation.

[92] For a critical review, see Lau, 'Freedom of Expression' in *ICCPR Proceedings*, above n. 86. Bills on these subjects were eventually introduced in the first part of 1997.

[93] For a description of some of the changes brought about in the conduct of criminal cases, see Bailey, 'Criminal Law and Procedure', in Edwards and Byrnes (eds.), *Hong Kong's Bill of Rights: 1991–1994 and Beyond* (1995), 39.

particular, the operation of many aspects of immigration law, and effectively immunize the administration from review of laws, policies, and actions which raise serious human rights issues, especially so far as the right to respect for family life is concerned. On the whole the courts have been more than willing to give the reservations a broader rather than a more restrictive reading.[94]

Another area where the Government has refused to take proactive steps to enhance the implementation and enforcement of the guarantees in the Bill of Rights is in relation to the provision of remedies for alleged violations. The administration's stance has been one which appeared calculated to limit significantly the opportunities that people with a grievance may have to obtain a remedy. While legal aid in criminal cases was greatly expanded following the enactment of the Bill of Rights (by virtue of legislative amendments largely prompted by the Bill of Rights), in the civil area access to the courts or to any other suitable remedy is still limited, a situation due partly to the cost of litigation.[95] There has been only a small number of Bill of Rights cases in the area of civil law, and many of these have involved challenges by large corporate interests. Nevertheless, there have been a number of important cases brought with the assistance of legal aid, although some of these have required arduous efforts to obtain a grant of legal aid.[96] The Government has refused to consider waiving the normal rules as to costs in Bill of Rights cases that raise issues of public interest, refused to establish a Human Rights Commission with conciliatory and adjudicative powers, and refused to establish an independent fund for litigation under the Bill of Rights. Although they

[94] *R. v. Director of Immigration, ex p Wong King-lung* (1993) 3 HKPLR 253, [1993] 1 HKC 461 (reservation relating to immigration); *R. v. Director of Immigration, ex p Hai Ho-tak* (1994) 4 HKPLR 324, CA (same); *Chim Shing Chung* v. *Commissioner of Correctional Services* (1996) 6 HKPLR 313, CA (reservation relating to prisoners). But see *Chieng A Lac* v. *Director of Immigration* [1997] HKLRD 271, Hct.

[95] A 1994 report by Amnesty International noted the difficulties of access to the courts and called for the establishment of a human rights commission, an independent legal aid agency, and a change in the usual rules relating to costs, so that persons bringing Bill of Rights cases will not be required to pay the other side's costs if they lose (provided the case was not frivolous): Amnesty International, *Hong Kong and Human Rights—Flaws in the system: A Call for Institutional Reform to Protect Human Rights*, April 1994, AI Index ASA/19/01/94. The Hong Kong administration refused in 1994 to permit legislator Anna Wu to introduce into the Legislative Council a private member's bill to establish a human rights commission. See Wu, 'Human Rights—Rumour Campaigns, Surveillance and Dirty Tricks and the Need for a Human Rights Commission' in Edwards and Byrnes (eds.), above n. 93, 73 at 76–80. For the text of Wu's draft *Human Rights and Equal Opportunities Commission Bill*, see ibid., Appendix at 83. Some of the functions which would have been performed by Wu's proposed commission in relation to anti-discrimination legislation are now to be performed by the Equal Opportunities Commission, which was established by the Sex Discrimination Ordinance (c. 480) (enacted in 1995) and which commenced its work in mid-1996.

[96] Although a challenge to the Hong Kong electoral system was eventually brought with the assistance of legal aid, the original application for legal aid was declined by the Director of Legal Aid on the ground that it would bring a 'trivial advantage' to the applicant. The applicant was successful in an appeal and the case was funded by legal aid: Li, 'The Non-Impact of the Bill of Rights in the Civil Area', in Edwards and Byrnes, above n. 93, 45 at 46–7.

must have realized that access to the courts in the civil area is severely restricted and that these measures would improve the situation, the Attorney-General and the Government continued to maintain that any person with a legitimate grievance under the Bill of Rights can enforce those rights through the courts.

The Bill of Rights and the Legislature

The Bill of Rights has also had an impact on the legislature. During the passage of the Bill of Rights, the legislature devoted considerable attention to its content and also to considering the laws which were likely to be affected by it. After the enactment of the Bill of Rights, the nature of the legislature's focus shifted somewhat. Its primary concern was now to ensure that its enactments were consistent with the Letters Patent, as well as to replace legislation declared repealed by the courts (where revival of the legislation is considered appropriate).

This function was a new one for the legislature and involved unfamiliar terrain. The scrutiny of bills from a Bill of Rights perspective became an established part of the passage of a bill through the Legislative Council (providing an additional lobbying opportunity for those who may be opposed to a bill for these or other reasons) and a number of important bills were substantially amended as a result of objections based on the ground of possible inconsistency with the ICCPR.[97]

Scrutiny of bills for consistency with Bill of Rights standards has become a regular feature of the work of the responsible bills committees, which have frequently raised Bill of Rights issues with the administration or received submissions from the public on these matters.[98] The need for independent input and advice is important, since the Attorney-General's role as adviser to the Government has meant that it fell to him to make the argument that bills put forward were consistent with the Bill of Rights, even if that argument was a

[97] For example, the Organised Crime Bill, introduced into the Legislative Council in 1991, was the subject of intense discussion from the human rights standpoint, and the bill, when finally passed in 1994, had the benefit of a full discussion of its human rights implications, even if the final form of the bill may not have fully reflected those concerns (see Organised and Serious Crime Ordinance (c. 455)). Amendments to tax legislation which conferred a power to prevent taxpayers from leaving Hong Kong under certain circumstances were substantially modified in the light of opposition based on Bill of rights grounds: see Au-Yeung, 'Taxation and the Bill of Rights', in Fong, Byrnes, and Edwards, above n. 82 at 21. Provisions of the Leveraged Foreign Exchange Trading Bill 1993 (*Hong Kong Government Gazette*, 2 July 1993, C1055) were amended as a result of concern expressed at the Bills Committee stage about the consistency with the Bill of Rights of the imposition of vicarious criminal liability by the Bill (see now Leveraged Foreign Exchange Trading Ordinance (c. 451)).

[98] For a comparative discussion from an Australian perspective of parliamentary review of bills in the light of human rights obligations see Kinley, 'Parliamentary Scrutiny of Human Rights: A Duty Neglected?', Chapter 5 above.

difficult one to make in a given case. Accordingly, the Attorney-General's stance was consistently that the bills put forward by the administration did not give rise to significant Bill of Rights problems or, alternatively, would survive any challenge. In the case of bills which did give rise to serious concerns, such an approach did no great service to the legislature and possibly prejudiced the chances of survival of an ordinance in the face of a subsequent Bill of Rights challenge if the legislature had not given full consideration to all the relevant issues.

Originally, it was thought that one important and new aspect of the role of the legislature would be the need to develop a strong legislative record which would, with a view to an eventual challenge, demonstrate that full consideration had been given to all relevant Bill of Rights issues. This would have given the legislation a greater chance of surviving a court challenge, since a court is much less likely to second-guess a legislative decision where the legislative record shows that all relevant Bill of Rights issues were considered and that the legislative decision is based on solid empirical or other sociological evidence. However, the courts have adopted a rather loose standard when scrutinizing legislative decisions—indeed, considerable deference to the legislature has emerged as the dominant approach—and there has been relatively little examination of the nature and extent of consideration given by the legislature to particular issues.

The Bill of Rights in the Courts

BRINGING THE INTERNATIONAL (BACK) HOME

For an international human rights lawyer working within a common law system which adheres to a dualist approach to the relationship between international law and national law, the incorporation of an international human rights treaty as part of domestic law appears a heaven-sent opportunity to realize the promise of the international system in the domestic context. Rather than being restricted to fulminations against the failure of the national legislature and government to observe their international obligations, or pleading with positivist and dualistically-minded domestic courts to incorporate applicable international norms indirectly into domestic law by means of any one of a number of strategies,[99] one is faced with the challenge of interpreting positive norms within the system; the 'entry' problem is, in part at least, solved.[100]

---

[99] For an overview of the various techniques and arguments see Jayawickrama, above n. 25 at 142–52. For a detailed discussion in the Canadian context see Bayefsky, *International Human Rights Law: Its Use in Canadian Charter of Rights and Freedoms Litigation* (1992).

[100] For the experience of Hong Kong prior to the Bill of Rights see Mushkat, 'International Human Rights Law and Domestic Hong Kong Law', in Wacks (ed.), above n. 54 at 25. It does

The challenges of working with a treaty enacted as part of domestic law are many and expose a number of limitations not just of common lawyers' training and conceptual framework, but also of the international materials themselves. Hong Kong has served in many respects as a common law testing ground in the case of the ICCPR.[101] The following discussion of the interpretation of the Bill of Rights touches on a number of issues in this context:

(a) the prism of the common law and its illuminating and potentially distorting effect in the interpretation of internationally derived standards;

(b) the problems faced by courts unused to judicial review of the constitutionality of legislation in undertaking that task;

(c) the willingness and ability of lawyers to put international and comparative material before the courts;

(d) the receptiveness of courts to international and comparative material; and

(e) the accessibility and utility of the international material and the difficulties of working with it in the domestic context.

THE RESPONSE OF THE LEGAL PROFESSION TO THE ENACTMENT OF THE BILL OF RIGHTS

Although the violations of rights that can be addressed by litigating the guarantees of a Bill of Rights through the courts are limited, even that utility depends on lawyers and judges being willing and able to use it in a constructive and energetic way. The enactment of the Hong Kong Bill of Rights posed a significant challenge to the Hong Kong legal profession, since it introduced at the one time meaningful constitutional review of legislation and a Bill of Rights with its accompanying international baggage. For a jurisdiction whose courts had been largely content to follow the lead of other jurisdictions (in particular England), the Bill of Rights required a realignment of judicial attitudes if it was to have any significant impact through the courts.

The legal profession responded positively to the proposal to enact a Bill of Rights and since its enactment has continued to support it and to use it. Both the Hong Kong Law Society and the Hong Kong Bar Association made detailed submissions on the draft Bill of Rights, putting forward a number of suggestions for improvement of the Bill. Unfortunately, however, few of them were taken up by the Government. Following the passage of the Bill of Rights, both professional associations organized seminars on various aspects of the Bill of Rights for their members, and have continued to make submissions on

not seem that the incorporation of the ICCPR into Hong Kong law has affected significantly the courts' attitude to other human rights treaties which have not been directly incorporated.

[101] This is not to underestimate the role that is being played by other Commonwealth courts in considering international law in the interpretation of their constitutional or statutory law. see below n. 171.

bills before the legislature which they believe raise issues under the Bill of Rights.[102]

Nor was the profession slow to raise Bill of Rights issues before the courts, despite some initial difficulties in gaining access to both local and international material.[103] To begin with, these challenges were concentrated on a small number of provisions, but over time many different provisions of the Bill of Rights have been invoked. Although many challenges have been brought, overwhelmingly in relation to criminal law and procedure, resort to the Bill of Rights has declined, as important issues have been resolved by the courts, offending legislation has been amended, and the appellate courts have expressed their indifference to the Bill of Rights and their disapproval of what they see as its inappropriate invocation by some practitioners. The rise and decline of Bill of Rights litigation (due at least in part to judicial attempts to discourage 'excessive' recourse to Bill of Rights arguments) can be seen from statistics compiled by Johannes Chan relating to Bill of Rights litigation since the enactment of the Ordinance.[104] These figures show a decline in the number of cases raising Bill of Rights issues after the first two and a half years of the Bill's existence. This is hardly surprising, since one would expect many of the important questions of practical importance to have been resolved in the first few years of the Bill's life. This has in fact been the case, but within the Bar there is also a feeling that the senior members of the judiciary do not wish to encourage the taking of Bill of Rights points and that they look with some disfavour on the Bill of Rights. This impression is based not just on anecdotal evidence but on the pronouncements of a number of prominent judges both in judgments and extracurially.[105]

THE ATTITUDE OF THE JUDICIARY TO THE BILL OF RIGHTS

The approach taken by the judiciary to any Bill of Rights is of critical importance. This is true not just in relation to the outcome of cases before the courts,

---

[102] In addition to the educational activities undertaken by the two professional bodies, seminars were also organized by a number of professional seminar organizers. The University of Hong Kong has held an annual seminar on the Bill of Rights since 1990, the most ambitious event being a major international conference held shortly after the passage of the Bill of Rights in June 1991. The conference papers appear in Chan and Ghai, above n. 3.

[103] See generally Byrnes, 'The Impact of the Hong Kong Bill of Rights on Litigation', in Sihombing (ed.), *Law Lectures for Practitioners 1992* (1992), 151 at 159–61.

[104] Chan notes that there were 46 cases in 1991 (6 months), 77 in 1992, 56 in 1993, 43 in 1994 and 25 in 1995: Chan, 'The Hong Kong Bill of Rights 1991–1995: A Statistical Overview', in Edwards and Chan (eds.), *Hong Kong's Bill of Rights: Two Years before 1997* (1996), 7 at 8–19, 38 (Table 1). The statistics are based on cases noted in the *Bill of Rights Bulletin* and, while not an exhaustive listing of all cases, are reliable as a general indication of trends. Up to the end of 1996 there were less than a dozen judgments dealing with Bill of Rights issues. Chan, above n. 104, at 18–9 notes that the rate of success on Bill of Rights arguments appears to be lower in the Court of Appeal than in other courts.

[105] See discussion immediately following.

but because the approach taken by the judiciary directly influences the attitudes and actions of the legislature, the executive, and other sectors of the community which have responsibility for ensuring that the guarantees embodied in the Bill of Rights are enjoyed in practice.

The Hong Kong judiciary's response to the Bill of Rights has been somewhat disappointing to those who had hoped that the courts would embrace an expansive interpretation of the Bill, drawing enthusiastically and liberally on international and comparative case law, and in so doing lay down a well-articulated theoretical framework for human rights protection that would stand Hong Kong in good stead in the years ahead. While there have been cases in which judges have sought to interpret the guarantees of the Bill of Rights generously and to give appropriate recognition to its international origin and to the relevant international jurisprudence, the dominant trend has been rather different. After an initial period of expansive rhetoric, reasonably generous interpretations of the Bill of Rights, and a preparedness on the part of the courts to subject legislative and executive decisions to substantive scrutiny, the trend has been towards a more conservative and parochial approach to interpretation of the Bill of Rights, with an increasing reluctance on the part of the courts to subject the legislature and executive to meaningful scrutiny against the standards of the Bill.

With the occasional exception, the prevalent effect of the approach taken by the Court of Appeal in particular has been to wind back the scope of the Bill of Rights, to dampen expectations that it goes much beyond existing common law guarantees, and to look with indifference and occasionally irritation on attempts to invoke international jurisprudence. Given a lead such as this, it seems that many judges in Hong Kong have breathed a collective sigh of judicial relief and have made it clear that they too consider that the Bill of Rights has only a very limited role to play in supplementing existing common law guarantees, thus ensuring that practitioners will need to be cautious about raising Bill of Rights arguments.

It is difficult to obtain an overall assessment of the attitudes of individual judges, since only anecdotal evidence is available, supplemented by comments in cases and in extracurial statements. However, there appear to be relatively few judges strongly in favour of the Bill of Rights, while a large number are less than enthusiastic, with attitudes ranging from perplexity and irritation to hostility. A number of senior judges, including the former Chief Justice, have gone on record as having grave doubts about the desirability and impact of the Bill of Rights,[106]

---

[106] For the former Chief Justice's views see *Bill of Rights Bulletin*, vol. 3, No. 4, December 1995, Appendix B. Liu J.A. expressed similar doubts: Ibid. Appendix D. Litton V.P., while still a member of the Bar, went on record with strong opposition to the proposed Bill of Rights (see above n. 49), but has not repeated such comments publicly since joining the bench. Nevertheless, although he has taken a reasonably generous view of provisions of the Bill of Rights in two or three judgments, Litton V.P. has played a major role in defining the new direction followed by the Court of Appeal following *Lee Kwong-kut*.

and others have expressed the view in judgments that the Bill of Rights has been used excessively and inappropriately.[107]

This is not to say that judges have not sought to give effect to the provisions of the Bill of Rights when cases come before them, but it can hardly be doubted that personal attitudes towards the benefits of a Bill of Rights, combined with a certain institutional resistance, have led to what is overall a fairly conservative interpretation of the Bill of Rights.

After an initial period during which many judges went to some effort to approach existing laws with a fresh perspective, following the decision of the Privy Council in *Attorney-General* v. *Le Kwong-kut*, the courts appeared to relapse into a somewhat parochial mode of endorsement of the status quo. As noted above, few Bill of Rights challenges are now being made, and even fewer succeed. The standard of analysis of Bill of Rights issues varies widely, but despite a number of significant exceptions, the courts' analysis of Bill of Rights issues (as reflected in their written judgments at any rate) has often been disappointingly superficial and conclusory,[108] and in some cases clearly erroneous or in conflict with the relevant international jurisprudence.[109]

---

[107] In June 1993 Godfrey J. (now of the Court of Appeal) was quoted as saying that 'There is a tendency among lawyers to take hold of some new development in the law and milk it for all that it's worth . . . There are signs that human rights is developing into that sort of industry. We must be realists and approach human rights with a sense of proportion and not let it get out of hand'. *Hong Kong Standard*, 6 June 1993. The judge made similar comments during argument in *Kwan Kong Company Ltd* v. *Town Planning Board* (1996) 6 HKPLR 237, when he was quoted as saying that the Bill of Rights was designed to protect human rights, 'not to allow lawyers to have a field day in he courts' and warning against bringing 'half-baked' cases and trivializing the legislation, which he considered that any 'well-educated child of nine could understand' when it should be applied: *South China Morning Post*, 10 July 1996. He further commented in the judgment (6 HKPLR at 259): 'For so long as the Bill of Rights remains on the statute book, it will in suitable cases enable the judges to protect the people of Hong Kong against the abuse of their civil and political rights by the legislature or (in the rare case where the common law does not already do so) by the executive. But its utility will be lessened, and its value cheapened, in direct proportion to the number of misguided attempts to invoke its provisions in situations with which it really has nothing to do. We are not really concerned, for example, in the instant case, with the protection of the appellant's civil and political rights at all; we are concerned only with an attempt by the owner of a piece of land in Hong Kong (aided and abetted by its professional advisers) to frustrate a law provided by the legislature (not before time) "with a view to the promotion of the health, safety, convenience and general welfare of the community": see s. 3(1) of the Ordinance'.

Leonard J. in *R.* v. *Town Planning Board, ex p Real Estate Developers Association* (1996) 6 HKPLR 179 at 214–5 commented: 'It is a matter for regret that it has become the fashion to prolong litigation, thereby causing unnecessary expense, by piling upon respectable common law arguments optimistic submissions based on the Bill of Rights . . . Once the common law arguments were disposed of, the Bill of Rights arguments were academic'.

[108] Recent decisions of the Court of Appeal have been particularly disappointing in their failure to explain in any detail the reasoning that leads to a conclusion on Bill of Rights issues and their apparent disregard of relevant international authorities: see, e.g., *R.* v. *Wong Yan-fuk* (1993) 3 HKPLR 341; *R.* v. *Ko Chi-yuen* (1994) 4 HKPLR 152; and *Attorney General* v. *Ming Pao Newspapers Ltd* (1995) 5 HKPLR 13. See Byrnes, above n. 86.

[109] See, e.g., *R.* v. *Yu Yem-kin* (1994) 4 HKPLR 75, in which the judge was under the misapprehension that the Bill of Rights was intended to incorporate the European Convention on Human Rights rather than the ICCPR and also held that the guarantee against 'unlawful or

There are a number of reasons for the approach of the judiciary. Many of Hong Kong's judges are United Kingdom nationals or trained and educated in the United Kingdom against the traditional background of parliamentary sovereignty. Accordingly, for many of them the Bill of Rights was new not only because it was rooted firmly in international human rights standards, but also because it involved a major conceptual reorientation, giving judges the power to declare legislation repealed by the Bill of Rights, a power they had not, as a practical matter, exercised before. Some judges no doubt found the notion of a Bill of Rights alien and unnecessary, since they are firm believers (some fiercely so) in the genius and adequacy of the common law (of England), and are slow to accept that international standards could have anything to add to that, an attitude which reflects the dominance of the United Kingdom's model of parliamentary sovereignty and the conservative side of debates about Bills of Rights in the United Kingdom and elsewhere.[110] This view has led in practice to the assumption that the international standards mean the same as the similar common law standards, an attitude which has tended to limit the impact of a number of guarantees in the Bill of Rights.[111] Yet others may have objected to the substantive content of the Bill of Rights, seeing in it an unnecessary tipping of the balance of the legal system towards those engaged in criminal activities which may threaten Hong Kong's stability in the transition period. Others may have considered that the appropriate judicial attitude was one of neutrality, and that the time to consider the Bill of Rights was when a case raising Bill of Rights issues came before them.

The transfer of power to the judiciary that a Bill of Rights necessarily entails may also have been a matter for concern among judges (interestingly, there was relatively little discussion of this important political dimension of a Bill of Rights during the drafting process). Ironically, this transfer of power to the judiciary came at a time when the Hong Kong legislature was finally becoming somewhat more accountable to the people of Hong Kong, a factor which may have caused unease in the minds of at least some judges. The conferral of a meaningful power of constitutional review gave rise to the possibility that the courts would have to consider materials which Hong Kong courts are generally not required to deal with, such as sociological and statistical evidence. As things have turned out, relatively little reference has been made to material of this sort.

arbitrary interference' with one's privacy (Article 14, Bill of Rights; Article 17, ICCPR) did not permit substantive review of the reasonableness of the legislation permitting interference.

[110] Although the Bill of Rights may be viewed as a good idea for post-1997 Hong Kong.

[111] See *R. v. Egan* (1993) 3 HKPLR 277 at 286; [1993] 2 HKCLR 284 and 290–1 (Article 10 of the Bill of Rights codifies the common law); *R. v. Deacon Chiu Te-ken* (1993) 3 HKPLR 483 at 496 (Bill of Rights contains independent guarantees which may be more extensive than the common law). However, even those judges who find that the Bill of Rights is, in theory, an independent guarantee not constrained by the common law, tend to find in practice that it adds nothing to the common law guarantees.

Most judges, like many common lawyers, have had little exposure to international law and sources on a regular basis, and may thus feel somewhat uneasy in dealing with them. This is also the case with human rights materials. While many other sectors of the community (Government, the Bar, the Law Society) went to considerable efforts to familiarize themselves with the basic material, it seems that at the official level judges were relatively slow to do so.[112] (Individual judges have, of course, made considerable efforts to do so.)

The Bill of Rights also conferred a new independence and responsibility on the courts of Hong Kong. Judicial attitudes and judicial creativity in Hong Kong have been significantly influenced by the colonial status of Hong Kong. The courts of Hong Kong manifest an excessive reliance on, and deference to, English decisions at almost every level; they tend to follow, almost automatically, developments in England and have considerably less time for developments elsewhere in the common law world. Part of this is no doubt due to the fact that until July 1997 the Privy Council was still the highest appellate court in the Hong Kong court hierarchy (and decisions of the House of Lords on questions of English law bound the Hong Kong courts[113]), as well as to the fact that a large proportion of the judiciary are themselves British, trained in England and/or have spent a considerable proportion of their professional life in British colonies.[114] To the extent that the Bill of Rights conferred rights which are different from or which go beyond the common law, the Hong Kong courts have had to look elsewhere to develop interpretations of the Bill of

[112] At an official level, the judiciary was relatively slow to prepare itself for the challenges of the Bill of Rights. In contrast to the steps taken by the legal profession, it appears that no steps were taken under the in-house education programme of the judiciary (the Judicial Studies Board) in preparation for the enactment of the Bill of Rights. Since the commencement of the Bill, the first (and so far only) organized measure as part of this programme was a visit by a former Canadian Chief Justice and an official from the Canadian Justice Department some 9 months after the enactment of the Bill of Rights. During the preparations for the 1991 conference referred to above, the proposal was made to the judiciary that a special judges-only day be organized for them. That invitation was declined. Although the members of the judiciary were invited to attend the conference, only a handful did so. It is significant that one of the judges who did so, Judge Bernard Downey of the District Court, delivered the first Bill of Rights judgment in *Tam Hing-yee* v. *Wu Tai-wai* (1991) 1 HKPLR 1, striking down legislation permitting judgment debtors to be prevented from leaving Hong Kong. When the case came before the Court of Appeal, that court reversed the lower court's judgment: *Tam Hing-yee* v. *Wu Tai-wai* (1991) 1 HKPLR 261; [1992] 1 HKLR 185. The judgment of the Court of Appeal was delivered by Sir Derek Cons V.P., who also delivered the keynote address at the 1991 conference in which he extolled the virtues of the common law as a protector of individual rights and appeared somewhat sceptical about the impact of the Bill of Rights: see Cons, 'The Hong Kong Bill of Rights: A Judicial Perspective', in Chan and Ghai, above n. 3, 51–4. Having delivered this address, he left the conference. Unfortunately, the Court of Appeal's judgment in this case reflects a narrow common law approach towards interpretation and shows no great sensitivity to the international experience.

[113] See generally Wesley-Smith, 'The Common Law of England in the SAR', in Wacks (ed.), *Hong Kong, China and 1997: Essays in Legal Theory* (1993).

[114] See Wesley-Smith, 'The Criminal Courts", in Traver (ed.), *The Criminal Justice System in Hong Kong* (1993), at 129–32.

Rights appropriate to Hong Kong when they have been prepared to go beyond existing common law doctrines.

The Substantive Impact of the Bill of Rights—an 'Entirely New Jurisprudential Approach'?[115]

ISSUES OF APPROACH AND METHODOLOGY

Interpretation—The General Approach

The experience under the Bill of Rights in the courts can be conveniently classified into two periods: (a) from 8 June 1991 to the end of May 1993; and (b) from May 1993 onwards. The highlight of the first period, and the case that set the tone for interpreting the Bill of Rights during that time, was the decision of the Court of Appeal in *R.* v. *Sin Yau-ming*, in which the court declared various presumptions in the Dangerous Drugs Ordinance inconsistent with the presumption of innocence. The second period was ushered in by the first decision of the Privy Council on the Bill of Rights, in *Attorney General* v. *Lee kwong-kut; Attorney General* v. *Lo Chak-man and another*. The period during which *Sin Yau-ming* was the leading authority was one in which the courts appeared more open to new ideas and to scrutinizing closely the justification for legislative measures, although this was done in a fairly restrained manner. However, the Privy Council's decision in *Lee Kwong-kut* sent a much more conservative message, stressing the need for 'realism', 'common sense', and the pre-eminent role of the legislature in formulating policy. As was predicted at the time, the impact of the Privy Council's judgment has been to make the courts even more restrained and cautious than they were prior to that case.

Perhaps the most disappointing (but not entirely unexpected) feature of the courts' engagement with the Bill of Rights has been their overall failure to develop an explicit and coherent theoretical framework for addressing Bill of Rights issues. In some areas (such as the right to trial without undue delay and the presumption of innocence), some effort has been made, although it must be said that in these areas the courts have relied heavily on overseas analyses. But on other issues, such as the right not to be subjected to arbitrary detention or the right to freedom of expression, the courts have largely failed to raise and explore a broader theoretical framework. Instead, they have for the most part been content, with the occasional exception, to reproduce the status quo, while paying (increasingly less) obeisance to international sources. On major questions, such as the appropriate relationship between the courts and the legislature in the Hong Kong context, the judgments are largely devoid of contextual theoretical analysis, taking refuge in the easy platitudes of deference to the legislature that come from the instincts of the judge trained

[115] Silke V.P. in *R.* v. *Sin Yau-ming* (1991) 1 HKPLR 88 at 104; [1992] 1 HKCLR 127 at 141.

in a system of parliamentary sovereignty. This would be less unfortunate were it not for the fact that one of the hopes of those who introduced the Bill of Rights was to give the courts the opportunity to build a sound theoretical and doctrinal basis for the years to come, a need not served by the pragmatic decision-making and conclusory results that one has seen too often in the judgments delivered by the appellate courts since *Lee Kwong-kut*.

In *Sin Yau-ming* one judge described the Bill of Rights as ushering in an 'entirely new jurisprudential approach'.[116] This was not merely because the guarantees of the ICCPR enjoyed an entrenched status, but also because of the international origin and nature of the standards the Bill of Rights embodied. Being the almost verbatim enactment of an international treaty expressed in broad and general language, the Bill of Rights Ordinance was different from most domestic statutes; the Letters Patent incorporated the treaty itself as part of Hong Kong law as the standard to be applied in scrutinizing future Hong Kong legislation.

In *Sin Yau-ming* the court recognized the distinctive character of the Bill of Rights, in particular its international origin and its constitutional status. The court held that the Bill of Rights Ordinance, viewed in the light of the accompanying amendment to the Letters Patent, was a constitutional instrument and that its *sui generis* nature should be recognized by interpreting it in a broad and generous manner.[117] This liberal and purposive approach to the interpretation of the Bill of Rights was endorsed by the Privy Council and has been repeatedly invoked by the courts at every level since that case, although the results in at least some of those cases, while not perhaps reflecting the 'austerity of tabulated legalism' deprecated by Lord Wilberforce in *Ministry of Home Affairs* v. *Fisher*,[118] do appear to fall short of the broad and generous approach to interpretation which looms so large rhetorically.

Although a broad and purposive approach to interpretation was also endorsed by the Privy Council itself in *Lee Kwong-kut*, in that case the Board went on to say:[119]

While the Hong Kong judiciary should be zealous in upholding an individual's rights under the Hong Kong Bill, it is also necessary to ensure that disputes as to the effect of the Bill are not allowed to get out of hand. The issues involving the Hong Kong Bill should be approached with realism and good sense, and kept in proportion. If this is not done the Bill will become a source of injustice rather than justice and it will be debased in the eyes of the public. In order to maintain the balance between the individual and the society as a whole, rigid and inflexible standards should not be imposed on the legislature's attempts to resolve the difficult and intransigent problems with which society is faced when seeking to deal with serious crime. It must be remembered that questions of policy remain primarily the responsibility of the legislature.

[116] Silke V.P. in *R.* v. *Sin Yau-ming* (1991) 1 HKPLR 88 at 104, 107; [1992] 1 HKCLR 127 at 138, 141.

[117] *R.* v. *Sin Yau-ming* (1991) 1 HKPLR 88; [1992] 1 HKCLR 127.

[118] [1989] AC 319 at 329.   [119] (1993) 3 HKPLR at 100; [1993] AC 951 at 975.

Unfortunately, this passage and the analysis adopted by the Privy Council in the rest of its judgment represented a significant step backwards from the tone set by *Sin Yau-ming*.[120] The Court of Appeal in *R. v. Sin Yau-ming* in September 1991 had expressed a willingness to look afresh, though the 'glass provided by the Covenant', at established laws and practices, seeking to evaluate them against contemporary standards of human rights as embodied in the Bill of Rights. In so doing, it had endorsed the approach adopted by the Canadian courts under the Canadian Charter, although the Canadian tests were applied in Hong Kong with less vigour than they then were by the Canadian courts.

The Canadian approach (developed in the context of the presumption of innocence but subsequently applied to other rights) emerged from the line of cases starting with *R. v. Oakes*.[121] It involves first a determination whether there has been a *prima facie* infringement of the right concerned; if this is found, the infringement may then be justified under Section 1 of the Charter. Once there is a *prima facie* violation of a protected right, under Section 1 of the Charter the Crown bears the burden of justifying the breach by showing that (a) the impugned provisions pursue a sufficiently important objective which is related to pressing and substantial concerns in a free and democratic society; (b) there is a rational connection between the objective and the means chosen; (c) the means adopted causes minimal impairment to the right or freedom in question; and (d) the effects on the limitation of rights and freedoms are proportional to the objective.

The Privy Council's decision in *Lee Kwong-kut* heralded a retreat from that approach. The Board deprecated the approach adopted by the Canadian courts as unnecessarily complex and disapproved of it as a model to be emulated by the Hong Kong courts (except perhaps in a few exceptional cases). In *Lee Kwong-kut* the Privy Council suggested that the fact that the Canadian courts tend to reach the same result in the end as other courts which do not follow the same analytical framework was a reason for not adopting a similar framework. Such an approach is likely to lead to a replication of the status quo, and fails to ensure one of the major benefits of a Bill of Rights, namely the examination of laws and practices which may have been in existence for decades or even centuries in the light of current (sometimes new) standards and values. While the Canadian courts may perhaps have gone to excessive lengths in this process, it is a more satisfactory approach in many

---

[120] This unfavourable assessment of the Privy Council's decision is by no means shared by everyone, the judgment being welcomed by many, including government officials and judges. Whatever the merits of the approach of the Privy Council, those who welcomed it recognized only too clearly that the result of the decision was that the level of scrutiny given to legislation and administrative action under *Lee Kwong-kut* was less stringent than under *Sin Yau-ming*.

[121] [1986] 1 SCR 103, 26 DLR (4th) 200, 24 CCC (3d) 321. In the context of the presumption of innocence the leading case, in addition to *Oakes* was *R. v. Whyte* [1988] 2 SCR 3, 51 DLR (4th) 481, 42 CCC (3d) 97.

respects than that adopted by the Privy Council. Longevity is no guarantee of consistency with contemporary human rights standards. To start from the assumption that it is will very likely be a self-fulfilling prophecy.

The decision discouraged the attitude that a Bill of Rights requires a structured and analytical re-examination of established and long-accepted laws and practices to ensure their consistency with contemporary human rights values. As a result, it threatened to undermine the development of a constructive and meaningful role for the judiciary in reviewing legislative choices. At the same time, it encouraged both the legislative and executive arms of government to be less attentive to rights considerations, since the prospect of having legislative or executive decisions overturned was considerably reduced by a judicial attitude of deference. In short, it was predicted that the effect of *Lee Kwong-kut* would be a much higher level of judicial deference to legislative judgments, moving Hong Kong courts from a situation in which an approach analogous to the fairly demanding Canadian approach was endorsed as a matter of rhetoric but applied in practice in a relatively undemanding fashion (the reality was that Canadian tests were applied with Hong Kong pragmatism[122]), to a situation in which a formal standard of a fairly low level of scrutiny of legislative judgments was likely to be interpreted in practice as meaning virtually none. This did indeed prove to be the case.

Taking their cue from the Privy Council, subsequent decisions have continued the retreat from the approach set out in *Sin Yau-ming*, both in terms of judicial rhetoric and the outcomes of cases.[123] Although *Sin Yau-ming* and *Lee Kwong-kut* dealt with the presumption of innocence and evidentiary presumptions, their general approach has been carried across to other issues. The Court of Appeal, in particular, has moved towards a fairly deferential attitude in its review of legislative and executive decisions (indeed almost to the stage of requiring *Wednesbury* unreasonableness before a decision can be impugned under the Bill of Rights),[124] an approach the Privy Council left in place in its decision in the *Ming Pao* case.[125]

The Relevance and Use of International and Comparative Authorities

In *Sin Yau-ming* the Court of Appeal also addressed the relevance and utility of international and comparative material in interpreting the Bill of Rights.

---

[122] See Byrnes, 'Introduction', in Fong, Byrnes and Edwards, above n. 82 at 1.

[123] Many courts continued to employ the *Sin Yau-ming* analysis in relation to evidentiary presumptions. For a reformulation of the rules post-*Lee Kwong-kut*, see *R.* v. *Kwong Kui-wing* (1996) 6 HKPLR 125 at 136–7.

[124] See, in particular, the decisions of the Court of Appeal in *Attorney General* v. *Hui Kin Hong* (1995) 5 HKPLR 100, [1995] 1 HKCLR 227; *Lee Miu-ling* v. *Attorney General (No 2)* (1995) 5 HKPLR 585, [1996] 1 HKC 105 and *Attorney General* v. *Ming Pao Newspapers Ltd* (1995) 5 HKPLR 13.

[125] (1996) 6 HKPLR 103, [1996] 3 WLR 272. See Bruce, 'Criminal Law and the Bill of Rights: The Usual Suspects', in Edwards and Byrnes, above n. 56.

Section 2 (3) of the Ordinance provides:

[I]n interpreting and applying this Ordinance, regard shall be had to the fact that the purpose of this Ordinance is to provide for the incorporation into the law of Hong Kong of provisions of the International Covenant on Civil and Political Rights as applied to Hong Kong and for ancillary and connected matters.[126]

As Silke V.P. put it in *Sin Yau-ming*:[127]

[T]he glass through which we view the interpretation of the Hong Kong Bill is a glass provided by the Covenant. We are no longer guided by the ordinary canons of construction of statutes nor with the dicta of the common law inherent in our training. We must look, in our interpretation of the Hong Kong Bill, at the aims of the Covenant and give 'full recognition and effect' to the statement which commences that Covenant. From this stems the entirely new jurisprudential approach to which I have already referred.

The views of the Court of Appeal in *R.* v. *Sin Yau-ming* concerning the weight to be given to international and comparative materials have been summarized in the following term:[128]

In interpreting the Bill of Rights Ordinance considerable assistance can be gained from the decisions of common law jurisdictions with a constitutionally entrenched Bill of Rights (in particular Canada and the United States), from the general comments and decisions of the Human Rights Committee under the ICCPR and the Optional Protocol to the ICCPR, and from the jurisprudence under the European Convention on Human Rights. While none of these are binding, in so far as they reflect the interpretation of articles in the ICCPR and are directly related to Hong Kong legislation, these sources are of the greatest assistance and should be given considerable weight.[129]

Silke V.P., however, did recognize some of the limitations of the international material:[130]

In seeking guidance from the decisions and comments of the Committee and those of the Commission, and I accept this from Mr Fung, the Court should bear in mind that these are general comments and, in particular in respect of the Committee, that the

---

[126] In its initial form, the section provided: 'In interpreting and applying this Ordinance, the rules of interpretation applicable to other Ordinances may be disregarded and regard shall be had to—(a) the fact that the purpose of this Ordinance is to implement further the International Covenant on Civil and Political Rights as applied to Hong Kong; and (b) the international origin of that Covenant and the need for uniformity in interpretation of rights recognized in that Covenant and similar rights recognized in other international agreements'.

The provision was changed to its present form partly as a result of objections that the provision was part of an attempt to internationalize Hong Kong. The change has made no difference to the sources considered by the Hong Kong courts.

[127] (1991) 1 HKPLR at 107; [1992] 1 HKCLR at 141.

[128] This summary of the court's holding is taken from *Bill of Rights* vol. 1, No. 1, at 2.

[129] See also *R.* v. *Yiu Chi-fung* (1991) 1 HKPLR 167 (endorsing the approach in *Sin Yau-ming*, while noting that Hong Kong courts were not obliged to follow Canadian decisions). see generally Byrnes, 'Figuring Out the Bill', *The New Gazette*, 28, 30–1 (October 1991).

[130] (1991) 1 HKPLR 88, at 107–8; [1993] 1 HKCLR 127 at 141.

perspective adopted is to consider the international treaty obligations of State Parties. matters of principle are there stated in the widest and most general of terms so that all the individual State Parties, and there is a multiplicity of them with differing legal traditions and social aspirations, may interpret them more meaningfully. Further, the Committee, under the Optional Protocol, is normally concerned with individual petitions from citizens of the State Parties who are aggrieved by particular decisions of their domestic courts and who have exhausted all domestic judicial avenues of redress. The same applies in part to the Commission and the European Court in Strasbourg. They operate as supra-national tribunals empowered to scrutinize the conduct of different branches of the governments of the State Parties to the European Convention on Human Rights. They look to see whether the handling of a particular case in a complaint against the State Party in its domestic jurisdiction has infringed the rights of the complainant under that Convention.

The approach of those bodies differs from that of a domestic court whose task is to determine the constitutionality or otherwise of domestic legislation measured, as is the case in Hong Kong, against an entrenched instrument. So they are helpful but not always apposite.

The Privy Council in *Lee Kwong-kut* adopted a similar approach to that of Silke V.P. in *Sin Yau-ming*.[131] On the whole, the courts, taking their lead from the Court of Appeal in *Sin Yau-ming*, have been reasonably receptive to a wide range of material when counsel have placed such material before them, though they have not considered themselves bound to follow international case law.[132]

Interpreting the Bill of Rights in the Light of the Common Law—The Advantages and Dangers of Analogizing from the Common Law

In interpreting the broadly-worded guarantees of the Bill of Rights in the context of individual cases in Hong Kong, practitioners and judges have naturally enough taken the common law as their starting-point. This approach is both understandable and appropriate, since many of the guarantees in the ICCPR and Bill of Rights have their origin in the rich traditions of the common law, and common lawyers played an important role in the drafting of the Covenant. Furthermore, the Bill of Rights does not exist as an area of practice in splendid isolation from the general law; it is rather to be seen as an additional resource, supplementary to, but in many cases less sophisticated and useful than, existing common law doctrines.

This preference for working with familiar common law doctrines and interpreting the guarantees of the Bill of Rights as a 'constitutionalized' form of those doctrines has a number of practical advantages. As one commentator has noted:[133]

---

[131] (1993) 3 HKPLR at 90–1; [1993] AC at 966–7.

[132] For an early discussion of a number of decisions of the Court of Appeal see Jayawickrama, 'Interpreting the Hong Kong Bill of Rights', in Angus and Chan (eds.), *Canada–Hong Kong: Human Rights and Privacy Law Issues* (1994), 65.

[133] Dykes, 'The Law's Delay', paper presented at seminar on the Bill of Rights organized by Aberdare Consultants, 29 April 1992, p. 2.

I believe that some judges and magistrates and many practitioners can be put off by what is jurisprudentially unfamiliar. They may find arguments drawn directly from, say, a decision of the European Court of Human Rights virtually indigestible and difficult to apply pragmatically to a given fact situation in the context of the common law. The key to success in BOR cases will be, in my view, to try and keep things fairly simple and on home ground wherever possible. Do whatever you can to demonstrate that many, if not all of the rights and freedoms protected by the BOR are recognized in common law systems and that there may exist already legal devices and stratagems, some perhaps neglected, which can be used to secure the right in question.

However, too close an adherence to common law doctrines and to the rather narrow range of case law that is generally cited to and by Hong Kong courts can have its dangers. In a number of important instances, the guarantees of the Bill of Rights go beyond the doctrines of the common law; for example, the substantive guarantee of equal protection of the law in Article 22 of the Bill of Rights (Article 26 ICCPR) does not have a close common law analogy. Similarly, reference to relevant international and comparative material may persuade a court that a guarantee which looks identical to a similar common law doctrine should, in fact, be construed more broadly because of its international pedigree: the right to trial without undue delay under Article 11(2) (c) (Article 14(3) (c) ICCPR), for instance, arguably provides protection that the common law doctrine of abuse of process does not.[134] To rely on common law notions may be quite misleading in relation to some guarantees. For example, the guarantee of an '*independent* and impartial' tribunal under Article 14(1) of the ICCPR appears to be a broader guarantee than the right to an impartial tribunal that is guaranteed (subject to statutory exclusion) by the common law rules of natural justice.[135]

A related point may be made: the common law is not static and there may well be room for broadening the guarantees it offers. Reference to international and comparative jurisprudence as an appropriate standard may well catalyse courts to adopt a more expansive reading of common law guarantees

---

[134] Dykes, 'The Law's Delay', at 8. See *Attorney General* v. *Charles Cheung Wai-bun* (1993) 3 HKPLR 62, [1994] 1 AC 1, PC, and *R.* v. *William Hung* (1993) 3 HKLR 328, [1994] 1 HKCLR 47, CA.

[135] A distinction is frequently drawn between *independence*—which is seen as an 'objective' criterion, reflecting the institutional status of the tribunal *vis-à-vis* the parties—and *impartiality*—which is seen as a 'subjective' criterion, reflecting the individual attitudes and behavior of the members of the tribunal (or a reasonable observer's expectations of them). See *Piersack* v. *Belgium*, European Court of Human Rights, Judgment of 1 October 1982, Series A, No. 53, 68 ILR 128, 5 EHRR 169 and Harris, O'Boyle and Warbrick, *Law of the European Convention on Human Rights* (1995) at 230–9. There is some overlap, but it seems clear that the 'systemic bias' that may come from a close institutional connection between the tribunal and one of the parties may violate the guarantee in certain circumstances. The Hong Kong courts, while distinguishing between 'institutionalized' and 'operational' unfairness, have struggled with the notion of an 'independent' tribunal, and have tended to limit the scope of the guarantee to the types of bias covered by the rules of natural justice: see, e.g., *R.* v. *Lift Contractors' Disciplinary Board, ex parte Otis Elevator Company (HK) Limited* (1995) 5 HKPLR 78, CA; *Kwan Kong Co Ltd* v. *Town Planning Board* (1996) 6 HKPLR 237 at 258 (per Godfrey J.A.); and *Real Estate Developers Association* v. *Town Planning Board* (1996) 6 HKPLR 179 at 215, HCt.

than might otherwise be the case.[136] In some Hong Kong cases it seems that courts have done exactly this, rather than decide a case on a Bill of Rights point. Whether this is the result of the common lawyer's pride in the flexibility and modernity of our system (and a desire not to be bested by some decontextualized international treaty) or a stratagem to avoid having to address directly an unfamiliar jurisprudence, it is important to note that the Bill of Rights may have a 'grey area of operation'. The fact that the Bill of Rights does not form the explicit basis of decision or that the international material is not referred to in a judgment does not mean that these have not influenced the outcome of a case. The challenge is to encourage judges to 'blend' the old and the new,[137] to ensure that the common law enriches, but does not choke, the development of case law under the Bill of Rights (and vice versa[138]).

To neglect these (possible) 'enhancements'[139] of the common law by focusing too closely on (in particular) English authority—the United Kingdom being one of the few Commonwealth jurisdictions without a modern Bill of Rights as part of its national law—may have the effect of unduly and undesirably restricting the scope of the Bill of Rights. This is not to say that international material will invariably or even frequently prove decisive for the outcome of a case. The impact of international material will vary depending on the issue, since the available international case law is more detailed and helpful in some areas than in others. Furthermore, as Hong Kong case law itself has developed in particular areas, the role to be played by the use of international material has become less important.

Reference to International Sources[140]

Following the approval of resort to international material in *Sin Yau-ming* (and later in *Lee Kwong-kut*), counsel and the courts have referred on many

---

[136] See the Bangalore Principles, in Commonwealth Secretariat, *Developing Human Rights Jurisprudence: The Domestic Application of International Human Rights Norms* (1988), at ix; Kirby, 'The Australian Use of International Human Rights Norms: From Bangalore to Balliol— A View from the Antipodes', (1993) 16(2) *University of New South Wales Law Journal* 363. See also relating specifically to the human rights of women, the VIctoria Falls Declaration in Commonwealth Secretariat, *Report of the Commonwealth Judicial Colloquium on Promoting the Human Rights of Women*, Victoria Falls, Zimbabwe, 19–20 August 1994.

[137] Dykes, above n. 133, at 8.

[138] One of the problems which has been identified with the use of international case law is that it can easily become a 'ceiling' for national protection rather than a 'floor' below which national protection should not fall. See Clapham, 'The European Convention on Human Rights in the British Courts: Problems Associated with the Incorporation of International Human Rights' Chapter 3 above. This is particularly so in the case of the European Commission's summary procedure for rejecting complaints on admissibility grounds, since sometimes what seem to be arguable cases appear to be dismissed out of hand by the Commission. These decisions then acquire some persuasive force in argument sunder the Bill of Rights to support an argument that a claim is unfounded.

[139] Dykes, above n. 133 at 2.

[140] While there are quite a few counsel who have raised substantial Bill of Rights points in cases, there is a small core of some five or six counsel who have developed something of a speciality in the area. One important element in the materials placed before the court has been the

occasions to international sources in cases under the Bill of Rights. Assistance
has been sought from wherever it is to be found, with case law under the
European Convention on Human Rights being the most frequently cited
international source.

It is a well-established rule of statutory interpretation that, where a statute
is passed in order to implement a treaty, the statute should be interpreted in
such a way as to give effect to that treaty.[141] Since the Bill of Rights Ordinance
is clearly intended to implement the provisions of the ICCPR, where the
words of the Ordinance reproduce the words of the ICCPR, they should be
given the same meaning as they have in the ICCPR. Other provisions in the
Bill should also be interpreted in such a way as to ensure that the ICCPR is
given effect to so far as possible. This is despite the fact that, if the words in
the Bill of Rights Ordinance were construed without reference to the ICCPR,
they might be interpreted differently. This general principle is made explicit in
Section 2(3) of the Bill of Rights Ordinance, to which the courts have referred
in support of their reference to international materials.

Many Commonwealth courts have accepted that, in construing a statute
which gives effect to a treaty, it is appropriate to apply international methods
of treaty interpretation in order to ascertain what the relevant provision of the
treaty means and then to apply that meaning to similar or identical provisions
of the statute.[142] In particular, this means that it is appropriate to apply the
rules codified in the Vienna Convention on the Law of Treaties 1960.[143] While
the primary focus of interpretation is the terms of the treaty in their context
and in the light of the treaty's object and purpose,[144] reference to the drafting
history of a treaty (the *travaux préparatoires*) is also permissible under certain
circumstances.[145] Commonwealth courts have accepted that resort may be
had to the *travaux préparatoires* when interpreting a statute which implements
the treaty.[146]

In Hong Kong there has been little judicial discussion of the relevance of
the Vienna Convention's rules to the interpretation of the Covenant and the

academic input—it has been a small number of academics who have provided much of the international input into the cases decided at District Court level and above.

[141] See *Koowarta* v. *Bjelke-Petersen* (1982) 153 CLR 168, 265 per Brennan J. Cf. *Quazi* v. *Quazi*
[1980] AC 743, 808, HL and Bennion, *Statutory Interpretation* (1984), 534–41.

[142] See, e.g., *Fothergill* v. *Monarch Airlines Ltd* [1981] AC 251, 282; *Commonwealth* v. *Tasmania*
(1983) 158 CLR 1.

[143] 1155 UNTS 331.   [144] Article 31.

[145] Article 32 provides: 'Recourse may be had to supplementary means of interpretation,
including the preparatory work of the treaty and the circumstances of its conclusion, in order to
confirm the meaning resulting from the application of article 31, or to determine the meaning
when the interpretation according to article 31: (a) leaves the meaning ambiguous or obscure; or
(b) leads to a result which is manifestly absurd or unreasonable'.

[146] Lord Wilberforce, however, has suggested that this may only be done where the material is
public and accessible and indisputably points to a definite legislative intention (*Fothergill*, [1981]
AC 278); cf. *Gatoil International Inc* v. *Arkwright Boston Manufacturers Mutual Insurance Co.*
[1985] AC 255.

Ordinance,[147] or to the circumstances under which reference may be made to the *travaux préparatoires*. Nevertheless, the courts have been willing to draw on the international source material and to refer to the *travaux préparatoires*, both of the Covenant and of the European Convention, insofar as the latter sheds light on the interpretation of the ICCPR's provisions.[148]

The courts have also referred to the jurisprudence of the Human Rights Committee in the form of its general comments[149] and its decisions under the First Optional Protocol. Although a number of general comments have been cited in argument and judgments, in general they have provided relatively little assistance in the resolution of disputed issues, since they tend to be stated in fairly general language rather than addressing the sometimes rather narrow points that fall for decision in domestic litigation. Nor has the Committee's case law under the Optional Protocol provided more than minimal assistance on most issues, since that body of case law is still fairly small, deals with few of the issues that have come up before the Hong Kong courts (or does not pronounce definitively on them), and in some cases provides only fairly conclusory reasoning to support the outcomes.[150] There has been no reference in the cases to the comments of the Human Rights Committee on the reports of the United Kingdom in respect of Hong Kong or of its concluding observations on those reports.[151]

[147] See *R. v. Town Planning Board, ex parte Auburntown Ltd* (1994) 4 HKPLR 194 at 227, [1994] 2 HKLR 272 (referring to Article 33 of the Vienna Convention in relation to the French text of Article 14(1) of the ICCPR and Article 6(1) of the European Convention); *R. v. Director of Immigration, ex parte Wong King-lung* (1993) 3 HKPLR 253, [1993] 1 HKC 461 (referring to Article 19 of the Vienna Convention in the context of discussion of the United Kingdom reservations to the ICCPR and holding that those relating to immigration legislation were consistent with the object and purpose of the Covenant); and *R. v. Town Planning Board, ex parte Kwan Kong Co Ltd* (1995) 5 HKPLR 261 at 303E, [1995] 3 HKC 254 (referring to the use of the Vienna Convention by the European Court in *Golder* in construing Article 6(1) of the European Convention).

[148] See, e.g., *R. v. Yu Yem-kin* (1994) 4 HKPLR 75 (ICCPR, Article 14(1)); *Lau San Ching v. Apollonia Liu* (1995) 5 HKPLR 23 (ICCPR, Article 25(b)); *R. v. Wong Lai-shing* (1993) 3 HKPLR 766 (European Convention, Article 5(1); ICCPR, Article 9(1)); *R. v. Town Planning Board, ex parte Kwan Kong Co Ltd* (1995) 5 HKPLR 261, [1995] 3 HKC 254 (ICCPR, Article 14(1); European Convention, Article 6(1)). See also *R. v. Chan Chi-hung* (1995) 5 HKPLR 1, [1995] 3 WLR 742 and *R. v. Allen, ex parte Ronald Tse Chu-fai* (1992) 2 HKPLR 266; [1993] 2 HKLR 453 (ICCPR, Article 9(1)).

[149] The 25 general comments adopted as of mid-1996 by the Committee appear in UN Docs. HRI/GEN/1/Rev.2 (1996) and CCPR/C/21/Rev.1/Add.7 and are reproduced in Byrnes and Chan, above, n. 3 at 351–83 and (1993) 3 HKPLR at 323, (1994) 4 HKPLR at 727, and (1996) 6 HKPLR. The general comments that have been referred to in argument and judgments are general comment 8(16) (protection against arbitrary detention, etc), general comment 13(21) (Article 14, ICCPR), and general comment 18(37) (non-discrimination).

[150] There has been no reference made to the decisions of national courts in jurisdictions in which the ICCPR or the European Convention forms part of national law. This is largely the result of inaccessibility of useful material.

[151] The only reference to hearings before the Human Rights Committee is one to the consideration of the report of Canada in 1990: see *Sin Yau-ming* (1991) 1 HKPLR 88 at 99. Although the Committee expressed the view that the Hong Kong system of functional constituencies was inconsistent with Article 25 of the Covenant (CCPR/C/79/Add.57, para. 19 (3 November 1995))

There has been more extensive reference to and use of the case law of the Strasbourg organs under the European Convention on Human Rights.[152] Since many provisions of the European Convention correspond closely to provisions of the ICCPR, and the development of the Covenant and the Convention (and its Protocols) overlapped in time, as a matter of formal interpretative technique these decisions are obviously of considerable persuasive value in interpreting the ICCPR (and the Bill of Rights). These cases are frequently helpful, but on many occasions the nature of the review carried out by the Strasbourg organs, the fact that they may be examining the very different law and process of a civil law jurisdiction, and the *ex cathedra* and formulaic character of conclusions in a number of cases can make them difficult to use in the domestic context.[153]

There has been virtually no reference in either argument or judgments to the so-called 'soft law' of international human rights,[154] that is the extensive corpus of instruments which, though not binding in form, may themselves either form part of customary international law or provide a useful standard for making more explicit the very general guarantees of the Bill of Rights.

The 'Autonomous' Interpretation of Terms in the Bill of Rights

The challenge of giving an 'international' interpretation to the Bill of Rights has emerged most clearly when the courts have been faced with the question of whether provisions of the Bill should be given an 'autonomous' meaning; that is, a meaning which they would not bear were they construed in the light of ordinary common law principles without reference to the international source material. The justification for giving terms contained in the Bill of Rights an autonomous meaning lies in the rules of statutory interpretation referred to earlier. The courts have accepted that the Bill of Rights Ordinance is not to be construed as an ordinary statute in view of its international origin and quasi-constitutional status. They have also accepted that terms in the Bill of Rights may bear an autonomous meaning, although whether particular terms should bear the meaning established by the international (mainly European) case law has been the subject of debate.

The record of the courts in giving to terms of the Bill an autonomous meaning different from the meaning they bear under domestic law has varied. In

prior to the Court of Appeal's consideration of this issue in *Lee Miu-ling* (1995) 5 HKPLR 585, no reference was made to those comments by counsel or the court.

[152] As of May 1997 there had been only one reference in a case (in argument and the judgment) to decisions of the Inter-American Commission or Court of Human Rights: *R.* v. *Director of Immigration, ex parte Wong King-lung and others* (1993) 3 HKPLR 253.

[153] Cf. Silke V.P. in *R.* v. *Sin Yau-ming* (1991) 1 HKPLR 88 at 107; [1992] 1 HKCLR 127 at 141.

[154] For a listing of the most important instruments see Lillich, above n. 66 at 130–3. See *Chieng A Lac* v. *Director of Immigration* [1997] HKLRD 271, HCt (referring to the UN Standard Minimum Rules for the Treatment of Prisoners). The Siracusa Principles on the Limitation and Derogation Provisions in the ICCPR (1985) 7 *Human Rights Quarterly* 3 have been referred to in a number of cases.

some cases a broader notion has been accepted. The courts have consistently accepted that the reference to 'law' in the guarantee of the right to be presumed innocent until proved guilty according to law in Article 11(1) is not confined to national legislation but imports a substantive standard of a 'universal concept of justice' (apparently involving considerations of rationality and proportionality) that any law restricting this right must satisfy.[155] Similar views have been expressed in relation to the right to be free from 'unlawful' interference with privacy in Articles 14 and 15, although some doubts have been expressed in this context.[156] Similarly, in determining the extent of the right of a person 'detained on a criminal charge' to be tried within a reasonable time or the right of a person 'charged with a criminal offence' to a trial without undue delay, the courts have taken the view that the term 'criminal charge' should not be narrowly construed to mean the formal filing of a charge but should be construed in the autonomous international sense.[157] In relation to guarantees against 'arbitrary' arrest and detention, a number of judges have taken the view that 'arbitrariness' is a substantive standard that permits review of the content of the law permitting detention and is not confined to ensuring that the law is properly applied.[158]

In other cases there has been a reluctance to stray too far from accepted meanings of those terms under national law. Sometimes this has limited the scope of protection available to persons relying on the Bill of Rights, as for example with the refusal by the courts to consider fixed penalty traffic offences[159] as 'criminal', or to hold that the confiscation of the proceeds of drug trafficking[160] or the imposition of treble damages penalties in insider

---

[155] *R. v. Sin Yau-ming* (1991) 1 HKPLR at 129; [1992[1 HKCLR at 159; *R. v. Lam Wan-kow* (1992) 2 HKPLR 26 at 32–3; [1992] 1 HKCLR 272 at 276–7; and *R. v. Mak Chuen Hing and others* [1996] HKLD H26.

[156] In *R. v. Securities and Futures Commission, ex parte Lee Kwok-hung* (1993) 3 HKPLR 39 at 55–6, Cons V.P. expressed doubt as to whether the term 'law' in Articles 14(2) and 15 of the Bill of Rights (Articles 17(2) and 18 of the Covenant) should be interpreted as involving a substantive notion of law. Litton J.A. (at 50) held that Article 14 at least should be so interpreted.

[157] See, e.g., *R. v. Lam Tak-ming* (1991) 1 HKPLR 222, *R. v. Tung Chi-hung* (1991) 1 HKPLR 282, and *R. v. Charles Cheung Wai-bun* (1992) 2 HKPLR 123.

[158] *R. v. Wong Lai-shing* (1993) 3 HKPLR 766, but see *R. v. Allen, ex parte Ronald Tse Chu-fai* (1992) 2 HKPLR 266, which appears ambivalent on this issue. In a number of cases the courts have held that Article 5(1) does not permit substantive review, though the Court of Appeal in *Attorney General v. Fong Chin Yue* (1994) 4 HKPLR 430, [1995] 1 HKC 21 appears to leave that possibility open, an approach confirmed by the court in *R. v. Mak Chuen Hing and others* [1996] HKLD H26.

[159] *R. v. Wan Kit-man* (1992) 2 HKPLR 728; [1992] 1 HKCLR 224; *R. v. Crawley* (1994) 4 HKPLR 62.

[160] *R. v. Ko Chi-yuen* (1994) 4 HKPLR 152. The High Court and District Court had reached contrary conclusions (though these arguments were not referred to in the Court of Appeal's judgment): *R. v. Ko Chi-yuen* (1992) 2 HKPLR 310 at 321–2, HCt (confiscation proceedings under the Drug Trafficking (Recovery of Proceeds) Ordinance are not 'criminal' within the meaning of Article 11 of the Bill of Rights); *R. v. Wong Ma-tai* (1992) 2 HKPLR 490 at 506, DCt (such proceedings are criminal within the meaning of Article 11 of the Bill of Rights). Nor did the Court of Appeal refer to the decision of the European Commission of Human Rights on this issue in the

dealing cases[161] involve the imposition of a 'criminal penalty', despite European or other authority that suggest that they should be so considered. In yet other cases, the courts have failed to adopt the clearly established autonomous meaning of terms under international law.[162]

Perhaps the most difficult issue that the courts have faced in this context has been in relation to the right to a court, which is arguably guaranteed by Article 10 of the Bill of Rights. While the courts have accepted that the right to a fair hearing in the 'determination . . . of [one's] rights and obligations in a suit at law' goes further than merely guaranteeing a fair hearing in an action before a court, they have been split on whether the right is as extensive as the European Court has held it to be under Article 6(1) of the European Convention.[163]

Constitutional Jurisprudence from Other Jurisdictions

Not surprisingly, the courts have felt particularly comfortable in dealing with decisions under the Canadian Charter,[164] since these are the decisions of

context of Article 7 of the European Convention, which divided the Commission: *Welch* v. *United Kingdom*, Application No. 17440/90, Report of the Commission of 15 October 1993. The European Court subsequently held that the proceedings involved the imposition of a criminal penalty: *Welch* v. *United Kingdom*, Judgment of 9 February 1995, Series A, No. 307–A, 20 EHRR 247. *Welch* was applied by the District Court in *R.* v. *Chan Suen-hay* (1995) 5 HKPLR 345, [1995] 1 HKC 847, in holding that a disqualification order imposed on a company director involved the imposition of a 'penalty' within the meaning of Article 12(1) of the Bill of Rights.

[161] *R.* v. *Securities and Futures Commission, ex parte Lee Kwok-hung* (1993) 3 HKPLR 1. Jones J., while accepting that the term 'criminal proceedings' under Article 11 of the Bill of Rights had to be given an autonomous interpretation, concluded that provisions of insider trading legislation which permitted a tribunal to impose a financial penalty of up to three times the amount of profit made by the person concerned were not 'criminal'. In so finding, he placed considerable emphasis on the legislature's intention to avoid having insider dealing made a criminal offence under Hong Kong law: (1993) 3 HKPLR at 28. One may compare this result with *Schemmer* v. *Property Resources Ltd* [1975] 1 Ch 273, in which the English High Court held that the American Securities and Exchange Act 1934 was a 'penal' statute for the purposes of conflict of laws classification, and the decision to similar effect of the District Court of Hong Kong in *Nanus Asia Co Ltd* v. *Standard Chartered Bank* [1988] HKC 377. See also *Société Stenuit* v. *France*, European Commission of Human Rights, Application No. 11598/85, Report of 30 May 1991, 15 EHRR 509.

[162] The term 'arbitrary' under Article 5 of the Bill of Rights (Article 9, ICCPR) and Article 14 of the Bill of Rights (Article 17, ICCPR) is a particular example, which a number of courts holding that it does not permit substantive review of legislation on grounds of reasonableness and proportionality: in these cases the courts have not referred to the clear jurisprudence under the ICCPR on this point: *R.* v. *Hui Kwok-fai* (1993) 3 HKPLR 752; *R.* v. *Hui Lan-chak* (1992) 2 HKPLR 423 (DCt); *R.* v. *Yu Yem-kin* (1994) 4 HKPLR 75. In these cases the courts have rejected assistance from the case law under Section 7 of the Canadian Charter, essentially on the ground that its wording is different, without an exploration of whether the underlying goals of the provisions are similar. This approach seems to embody the very 'austerity of tabulated legalism' that the courts have foresworn. An interpretation more in keeping with the meaning of the ICCPR has been adopted in a number of Magistrates' Court decisions (see, e.g., *R.* v. *Wong Lai-shing* (1993) 3 HKPLR 766 (reviewing *travaux préparatoires*) and now the Court of Appeal (see *R.* v. *Mak Chuen Hing and others* [1996] HKLD H26). See generally *Bill of Rights Bulletin*, vol. 2, No. 4, at 12–14.

[163] For further discussion see, below, pp. 70–74.

[164] See generally on the relationship between the Canadian Charter case law and the development of Hong Kong's Bill of Rights case law Cullen, 'Bills of Rights: Canada Leads, Hong Kong Follows?', in Angus and Chan (eds.), *Canada and Hong Kong: Some Human Rights and Privacy Issues* (1994), 34.

national courts in a common law system under a relatively modern Bill of Rights with many similarities in wording to Hong Kong's Bill of Rights. The decisions of the Canadian courts are also readily accessible in Hong Kong, and counsel themselves have little difficulty in working with them. There has been less reference to United States authorities, the result no doubt of the unfamiliarity of many lawyers and judges with United States constitutional law, the differences of approach adopted in United States jurisprudence and the more limited availability in Hong Kong of United States case law and secondary sources.

There have been few references made to decisions from Commonwealth jurisdictions other than Canada and the United Kingdom (with the exception of Privy Council decisions on appeal from other Commonwealth jurisdictions).[165] This is a striking omission in view of the fact that many Commonwealth countries have constitutions which are derived from the European Convention (as well as those countries such as India which have developed home-grown models with a rich jurisprudence). The reasons for this are apparently once again the lack of familiarity with these sources and their limited availability in Hong Kong,[166] as well as the apparent unwillingness of judges to refer to such decisions in their judgments even when they are cited to them[167] (a factor which hardly encourages counsel to cite them). It may also be that Canada is seen as a more appropriate model for a modern, developed country such as Hong Kong than developing nations in Africa, Asia, or the Caribbean.[168]

---

[165] The Privy Council has a variable record in human rights appeals from Commonwealth jurisdictions and some of its decisions have been the subject of strong criticism (for an extremely critical review see Ewing, 'A Bill of Rights: Lessons from the Privy Council', in Finnie et al. (eds.), *Edinburgh Essays in Public law* (1991), 231–49). In recent years the Judicial Committee has delivered a number of decisions which strongly endorse fundamental human rights principles: see, e.g., *Hector* v. *Attorney-General of Antigua and Barbuda* [1990] 2 AC 312; *Ali* v. *R.* [1992] 2 WLR 357 (Mauritius); *Phillip* v. *DPP* [1992] 2 WLR 211 (Trinidad and Tobago). Nevertheless, there are some which appear to fall short of international standards, including a number of decisions in which the Judicial Committee has interpreted the provisions of the Jamaican Constitution in a manner which has been held to give rise to violations of similarly worded guarantees in the ICCPR: see, e.g., *Robinson* v. *Jamaica*, Human Rights Committee, Communication No. 223/1987, UN Doc. A/44/40, Annex X.H, p. 241 (the judgment of the Privy Council is reported as *Robinson* v. *R.* [1985] AC 956). While the constitutional provisions in question were worded differently to the ICCPR, nonetheless it would have been possible for the Privy Council to read them in a manner consistent with the Covenant, as did indeed the minority in one such case. The Privy Council has responded to the international scrutiny of its work: *Pratt and Morgan* v. *Attorney General for Jamaica* [1993] 4 All ER 769, the sequel to *Pratt and Morgan* v. *Jamaica*, Human Rights Committee, Communication Nos. 210/1986 and 225/1987, views adopted on 6 April 1989, in *Report of the Human Rights Committee in 1989*, UN Doc. A/44/40, 222.

[166] For most practical purposes the only way of accessing these decisions (unless they go to the Privy Council) is through the series *Law Reports of the Commonwealth*.

[167] Cases cited to the courts in Bill of Rights or international human rights cases but not referred to in the judgments include cases on the guarantee of equal protection of the laws under the Indian Constitution (*R.* v. *Man Wai-keung (No 2)* (1992) 2 HKPLR 164; [1992] 2 HKCLR 207).

[168] See, e.g., the comments of Duffy J. in *R.* v. *William Hung* (1992) 2 HKPLR 49 at 57; [1992] 2 HKCLR 90 at 94 who held that, in determining whether there is undue delay in criminal proceedings, Hong Kong should not be compared with Jamaica or Mauritius where long delays may

This reluctance to research Commonwealth cases may also be partly due to a perception that these cases—particularly some of the older decisions—are not likely to be as helpful for those seeking to challenge the validity of laws or practices under the Hong Kong Bill of Rights as are decisions from Canada.[169] There may be an element of truth in this perception,[170] yet it neglects quite a number of important decisions in which human rights standards have been strongly endorsed and given effect to in such jurisdictions.[171]

There has also been considerable reference to English decisions as a source of common law from which analogies might be drawn for interpreting the guarantees of the Bill of Rights. However, as noted above, there is a danger that hewing too closely to the common law position may lead to a less generous interpretation of the Bill of Rights that might be justified by reference to international and comparative authorities.

THE MOST IMPORTANT DEVELOPMENTS TO DATE[172]

By the end of July 1996, there had been more than 250 cases in which written judgments dealing with Bill of Rights issues had been delivered (this figure

be readily excusable, since the administration in Hong Kong has at its disposal the means to provide adequate resources to ensure the proper, efficient, and timely disposal of its criminal proceedings.

One should also heed the sensible warning given by Lester that it is only prudent to put before a court hearing a case the authorities which are likely to have the most persuasive impact on that particular tribunal: Lester, 'Human Rights Advocacy in Practice', in Chan and Ghai, above n. 3, 208 at 208–10.

[169] See, e.g., the limiting interpretations of the right to trial within a reasonable time or to release taken by a number of African courts (and the Privy Council on appeal from these courts): Byrnes, 'The Bill of Rights and Remand in Custody Pending Trial: A Warning SHot?', (1991) 21(3) *HKLJ* 362 at 364 n. 5.

[170] e.g., in a freedom of assembly case one would hardly want to rely on the decision of the Privy Council in *Francis* v. *Chief of Police* [1973] AC 671 as compared to the decision of the Supreme Court of Canada in *Committee for the Commonwealth of Canada* v. *Canada* (1991) 77 DLR (4th) 335. Nor might one wish to rely on the decision of the Supreme Court of Nigeria in *Merchants Bank Ltd* v. *Federal Minister of Finance* [1961] NSCC 264 when arguing that the right to carry on banking business was a 'right or obligation in a suit at law' under Article 10 of the Bill of Rights.

[171] See, e.g., the Zimbabwean cases referred to by Lillich, above n. 66 at 116–20. See also *Ephraim* v. *Pastory* (1990) 87 ILR 106 (High Court of Tanzania) (differential rights of men and women under customary law relating to land violates constitutional and international standards of equality and non-discrimination); *Attorney-General* v. *Dow* [1992] LRC (Const) 623 (Court of Appeal of Botswana, on appeal from the decision of the High Court, reported at [1991] LRC (Const) 574 and reproduced at (1991) 13 *Human Rights Quarterly* 614) (differential treatment of male and female citizens in Botswana's nationality laws in ability to transmit citizenship to their children violates constitutional guarantee of equality); *S.* v. *D.*, 1992 (1) SA 513 (High Court of Namibia) (special cautionary rule relating to sexual assault cases as opposed to other types of cases had no rational foundation and had the effect of discriminating against women; it therefore violated Article 10 of the Namibian Constitution which guarantees equality of all persons before the law). See also Byre and Byfield (eds.), *International Human Rights Law in the Commonwealth Caribbean* (1991).

[172] For an overview of the operation of the Bill of Rights in its first year see Chan and Ghai, 'A Comparative Perspective on the Bill of Rights', in Chan and Ghai, above n. 3 at 1.

includes all courts). In the initial period of the operation of the Bill of Rights, the overwhelming majority of the cases involved criminal law and procedure; while there was an increase in cases in the civil field as time progressed criminal cases still predominate.[173]

Bill of Rights cases have involved both challenges to the validity of legislation and challenges to administrative actions, as well as applications to a court in the course of a criminal trial to exercise its discretion to remedy a violation (whether by the staying of proceedings, the exclusion of evidence, or similar orders). The courts have upheld Bill of Rights arguments in a significant number of cases, though these still constitute a substantial minority of the total number of challenges made. A large percentage of the successful challenges have involved challenges to statutory presumptions; there has been a much lower level of success when other statutes have been impugned.

Since the Bill of Rights was enacted, the courts have had the opportunity to grapple with a wide range of issues under the Bill of Rights, in some cases dealing with issues which do not seem to have been previously addressed elsewhere. The case law under the Bill of Rights offers interesting insights into how common law courts have attempted to come to terms with an international treaty, which contains both familiar and unfamiliar elements, and to mould it to what they have seen as the present needs of Hong Kong.

The following section gives a brief overview of some of the more important substantive developments under the Bill of Rights. It does not purport to be a comprehensive discussion of the substantive impact of the Bill,[174] but mentions the most significant developments, as well as attempting to illustrate some of the areas in which drawing on the available international human rights sources has brought benefits or given rise to difficulties.

CRIMINAL LAW AND PROCEDURE

The large number of criminal cases brought under the Bill of Rights have provided the courts with the opportunity to touch on virtually every guarantee contained in the ICCPR relating directly to criminal law and procedure.[175]

The most significant developments have been in relation to:

(a) the guarantee of the right to be presumed innocent until proved guilty according to law (Article 11(1) Bill of Rights; Article 14(2) ICCPR);

(b) the right to trial within a reasonable time or to release, and the right to trial without undue delay (Articles 5 and 11(2) (c) Bill of Rights; Articles 9 and 14(3) (c) ICCPR); and

---

[173] Chan, above n. 104 at 8, states that some 74% of cases to the end of 1995 were criminal cases.

[174] See generally Byrnes, above n. 103 at 154–63. For an overview of the issues which have been raised in cases before the Hong Kong courts, see Byrnes and Chan (eds.), *Bill of Rights Bulletin*.

[175] Chan, above n. 104, notes that, of 323 challenges, some 156 (48%) had been made under Article 11, 56 (17%) under Article 10 (largely criminal cases), and 30 (10%) under Article 5.

(c) the general guarantee of the right to a fair hearing (Article 10 Bill of Rights; Article 14(1) ICCPR).

The right to legal aid (Article 11(2) (d) Bill of Rights; Article 14(3) (d) ICCPR), and the right to privacy in the context of the power to enter premises and to demand information have been the subject of a number of decisions,[176] as has the right to the benefit of a lighter penalty where provision is made by law for a lesser penalty (Article 12(1) Bill of Rights; Article 15(1) ICCPR).

The Presumption of Innocence

The right to be presumed innocent until proved guilty according to law (Article 11(1) Bill of Rights; Article 14(2) ICCPR) has been the most frequently invoked provision of the Bill of Rights. This is due partly to the widespread existence in Hong Kong legislation of provisions which place an onus of some kind on a defendant in criminal cases,[177] although many of these have now been amended or repealed as the result of Bill of Rights challenges.[178] In construing the presumption of innocence the courts have derived most assistance from cases under the Canadian Charter, although reference has been made to decisions from other Commonwealth countries, United States case law, and relevant international jurisprudence. This guarantee illustrates one of the difficulties sometimes encountered in working with international case law. In the area of the presumption of innocence (so far as it concerns mandatory presumption of fact), the case law is relatively sparse and not particularly helpful.

For example, what is perhaps the leading decision of the European Court, *Salabiaku* v. *France*,[179] arguably does not concern mandatory presumptions at all and its very general comments about the acceptability of presumptions that are 'reasonable' do not provide a great deal of insight into how the underlying rationale of the presumption of innocence can be applied in concrete presumption cases. Another oft-cited decision of the European Commission[180] had particular relevance to Hong Kong because the Untied Kingdom statute considered there had a Hong Kong parallel. However, the decision, which

[176] *Re Hong Kong and Shanghai Banking Corporation* (1991) 1 HKPLR 59, [1992] HKDCLR 37; *Re Reid* (1991) 1 HKPLR 275; *R.* v. *Securities and Futures Commission, ex parte Lee Kwok-hung* (1993) 3 HKPLR 1, HCt; *R.* v. *Securities and Futures Commission, ex parte Lee Kwok-hung* (1993) 3 HKPLR 39, [1993] 2 HKCLR 51, CA; *R.* v. *Yu Yem-kin* (1994) 4 HKPLR 75.

[177] In *Lee Kwong-kut* the Crown produced a list of over 280 provisions in Hong Kong primary legislation which placed some type of onus on the defendant in criminal cases.

[178] For a detailed survey see Bailey, 'The Presumption of Innocence (Article 11(1)): Significant Authorities from June 1992 to May 1993', in Fong, Byrnes and Edwards, above n. 82, Appendix A, 129, and Bailey, 'Summary of Decisions Regarding Hong Kong Statutory Provisions Challenged under Article 11(1) of the Bill of Rights', in Edwards and Byrnes, above n. 57, Appendix A, 155; Chan, above n. 104 at 56 (Table 10).

[179] European Court of Human Rights, Series A, No 141–A, 13 EHRR 379.

[180] European Commission on Human Rights, application No. 5124/71, decision on admissibility of 19 July 1972, 42 Collection of Decisions 135; *Digest of Strasbourg Case Law*, vol. 2, 755.

rejected the complaint on admissibility grounds, is poorly reasoned and rather unhelpful,[181] particularly when compared with a recent decision of the Supreme Court of Canada on a similar provision.[182]

Until May 1993 the leading cases under Article 11(1) of the Bill of Rights were two decisions of the Court of Appeal: *R. v. Sin Yau-ming*[183] and *Attorney-General v. Lee Kwong-kut*.[184] In *R. v. Sin Yau-ming* a challenge was made to provisions of the Dangerous Drugs Ordinance which provided that upon proof of possession of a specified quantity of drugs, a presumption that a person possessed them for the purpose of trafficking was to be drawn unless the defendant proved the contrary on the balance of probabilities. The court, following *R. v. Oakes*,[185] held that a mandatory presumption of fact of this sort was a *prima facie* breach of the presumption of innocence, since it left open the possibility that the accused could be convicted despite the existence of a reasonable doubt as to the existence of a fact necessary to a verdict of guilt. However, the section could be 'saved' if the Crown showed that it was a rational or proportionate restriction of that right.

Justice Kempster formulated the following test:[186]

A mandatory presumption of fact may be compatible with s. 8 Article 11(1) of the Bill of Rights if it be shown by the Crown, due regard being paid to the enacted conclusion of the legislature, that the facts to be presumed rationally and realistically follow from that proved and also if the presumption is no more than proportionate to what is warranted by the nature of the evil against which society requires protection.

In *Attorney-General v. Lee Kwong-kut*, the Court of Appeal held that Section 30 of the Summary Offences Ordinance violated the presumption of innocence and had been repealed by the Bill of Rights. Section 30 provided that a person who was proved to be in possession of a thing reasonably suspected of being stolen or unlawfully obtained and who failed to provide a satisfactory explanation to a magistrate was guilty of an offence. In declaring the provision repealed, the court appeared to endorse the approach to the presumption of innocence espoused in the Supreme Court of Canada by Chief Justice Dickson in *R. v. Whyte*.[187]

In *Whyte* the Supreme Court of Canada had adopted the position that the characterization of the fact to be proved by the defendant did not affect the first

---

[181] e.g., the Commission makes no mention of the fact that in the case before the English courts there was actual evidence before the court so that the presumption did not need to be relied on; and the Commission's conclusion that the presumption that a person habitually seen in the company of prostitutes can be presumed to be living off their earnings is rational and reasonable seems rather difficult to accept. For the case in the English courts see *R. v. Pink* [1971] 1 QB 508.

[182] *R. v. Downey* [1992] 2 SCR 10; 90 DLR (4th) 449; 9 CRR (2d) 1.

[183] (1991) 1 HKPLR 88; [1992] 1 HKCLR 127.

[184] (1992) 2 HKPLR 94; [1992] 2 HKCLR 76.

[185] [1986] 1 SCR 103; (1986) 26 DLR (4th) 200.

[186] (1991) 1 HKPLR at 134; [1992] 1 HKCLR at 163.

[187] [1988] 2 SCR 3; (1988) 51 DLR (4th) 48 at 493.

stage of the inquiry; it did not matter whether the defendant was required to disprove an essential or important element of the offence or was required to prove
an excuse, qualification, or existence of a licence; the relevant question was
whether (s)he faced the possibility of conviction if (s)he failed to prove the fact.

The position established by these two Court of Appeal decisions, which had
drawn heavily on the Canadian Charter jurisprudence, was modified in
important respects by the Privy Council in *Lee Kwong-kut*.[188] On the substantive issue of how one should determine whether provisions imposing a
burden of proof on the defendant are inconsistent with the presumption of
innocence, the Privy Council eschews what it describes as the unnecessarily
complex Canadian approach, endorsing a broad, unified approach to determining whether such provisions are a reasonable limitation on the right to be
presumed innocent. The Privy Council suggests that a pragmatic, intuitive
approach is what is called for: by examining the substance of a statutory provision the court will be able to come to a firm conclusion as to whether there
is a breach of the presumption of innocence. Although the Privy Council
describes the Canadian approach as unnecessarily complex, what is most disappointing is what it offers as a substitute for that test. In his judgment, Lord
Woolf writes:[189]

Some exceptions [to the general rule that the prosecution must prove the defendant's
guilt beyond reasonable doubt] will be justifiable, others will not. Whether they are
justifiable will in the end depend upon whether it remains primarily the responsibility
of the prosecution to prove the guilt of an accused to the required standard and
whether the exception is reasonably imposed, notwithstanding the importance of
maintaining the principle which article 11(1) enshrines. The less significant departure
from the normal principle, the simpler it will be to justify an exception. If the prosecution retains responsibility for proving the essential elements of the offence, the less
likely it is that an exception will be regarded as unacceptable. In deciding what are the
essential ingredients, the language of the relevant statutory provision will be important. However what will be decisive will be the substance and reality of the language creating the offence rather than its form. If the exception requires certain matters to be
presumed until the contrary is shown, then it will be difficult to justify that presumption unless, as was pointed out by the United States Supreme Court in *Leary* v. *United
States*, 395 US 6 at 36 23 L Ed 2d 57 at 82 (1969), 'it can at least be said with substantial assurance that the presumed fact is more likely than not to flow from the proved
fact on which it is made to depend'.

And in a later passage he comments:[190]

[I]t is their Lordships' opinion that, in applying the Hong Kong Bill, it is not necessary,
at least in the vast majority of cases, to follow the somewhat complex process now

[188] For a discussion see Nardell, 'Presumed Innocence, Proportionality and the Privy Council',
(1994) 110 *LQR* 223; Hor, 'The Presumption of Innocence—A Constitutional Discourse for
Singapore', [1995] *Singapore Journal of Legal Studies* 365, at 389–403.
[189] (1993) 3 HKPLR at 94; [1993] AC at 969–70.
[190] (1993) 3 HKPLR at 97; [1993] AC at 972.

established in Canada in order to assess whether an exception to the general rule that the burden of proof should rest upon the prosecution throughout a trial is justified. Normally, by examining the substance of the statutory provision which is alleged to have been repealed by the Hong Kong Bill, it will be possible to come to a firm conclusion as to wether the provision has been repealed or not without too much difficulty and without going through the Canadian process of reasoning . . . The court can ask itself whether, under the provision in question, the prosecution is required to prove the important elements of the offence; while the defendant is reasonably given the burden of establishing a provision or an exemption or the like of the type indicated by Lawton LJ [in *R.* v. *Edwards* [1975] QB 27]. If this is the situation article 11(1) is not contravened.

In a case where there is real difficulty, where the case is close to the borderline, regard can be had to the approach now developed by the Canadian courts in respect of 1 of their Charter. However in doing this the tests which have been identified in Canada do not need to be applied rigidly or cumulatively, nor need the results achieved be regarded as conclusive. They should be treated as providing useful general guidance in a case of difficulty.

In essence, the Privy Council has gone back to *Oakes*, drawing a distinction between essential or important elements of an offence; where proof of such matters is placed on the defendant, it is less likely that the provision will be consistent with the presumption of innocence. However, this distinction can be extremely difficult to draw, particularly in the case of new statutory offences.

These passages throw up a number of other issues and appear to muddy what were fairly clear waters until this decision. It is unclear, for example, whether a presumption will be held consistent with Article 11(1) once it is shown that there is a rational connection between the proved and presumed facts, or whether it is also necessary to satisfy tests of proportionality and minimal impairment (as endorsed in *Sin Yau-ming* on the basis of Canadian authority), or some other test (if so, what test?)[191] Apart from a reference to the case of licences and the difficulty the prosecution might have in establishing that a defendant has a licence, and to the case of insanity, Lord Woolf gives us little guidance as to the sorts of factors that should be considered when deciding whether a departure from the normal principle is justifiable.

Another issue on which the decision gives rise to uncertainty is in relation to evidential burdens. Towards the end of his judgment Lord Woolf remarks that there would not be any question of incompatibility with the Bill of Rights if Section 25(4) of the Drug Trafficking (Recovery of Proceeds) Ordinance were construed to impose an evidential, as opposed to a legal, burden of proof on the defendant. However, it is not clear whether this is because Lord Woolf

---

[191] For subsequent decisions of the Court of Appeal see *R.* v. *Li Tat* (1993) 3 HKPLR 171, [1993] 2 HKCLR 203; *R.* v. *Chan Chak-fan* (1994) 4 HKPLR 115, [1994] 2 HKCLR 17, [1994] HKC 145, CA; *R.* v. *Iu Tsz Ning* (1995) 5 HKPLR 94; *Attorney General* v. *Hui Kin Hong* (1995) 5 HKPLR 100, [1995] 1 HKCLR 227.

considered that an evidential burden is reasonable in this particular case, or because he considered that the imposition of an evidential burden could never infringe Article 11(1). If the former, we once again have no criteria by which to judge the reasonableness of evidential burdens; if the latter, there is no authority or discussion to support this conclusion.[192]

There have been dozens of cases challenging presumptions, leading to the striking down of a significant number of presumptions of fact which placed the onus on a defendant to disprove the facts presumed.[193] The initial wave of decisions invalidating such provisions has been followed by relatively few cases challenging presumptions (of which even fewer have been successful). This is partly because most of the vulnerable provisions have been challenged and/or amended, but also because the courts began to be less demanding in the standard they apply to testing the reasonableness of these presumptions,[194] and have been more than ready to uphold provisions which impose only an evidential burden on the defendant.

Article 11(1) has also been invoked, sometimes in conjunction with Article 5(1), to challenge the imposition of substantive criminal liability in other forms. While the courts appear to accept that the imposition of criminal liability without at least a minimal *mens rea* may in some cases violate the Bill of Rights,[195] they have held that strict liability offences are not *per se* inconsistent with the Bill of Rights, in particular where the imposition of strict liability is the result of interpreting the statute in accordance with the criteria laid down in the Privy Council's decision in *Gammon (Hong Kong) Ltd* v. *Attorney-General*.[196]

The Right to Trial within a Reasonable Time or to Release

Right to bail—more than the common law? While courts have stated on a number of occasions that Article 5(1) of the Bill of Rights (Article 9(1) ICCPR) essentially restates the common law position, the police and some lawyers

---

[192] The Court of Appeal had held in *R.* v. *Wong Hiu-chor* (1992) 2 HKPLR 288; [1993] 1 HKCLR 107 that the imposition of an evidential burden is a *prima facie* infringement of Article 11(1) that must be justified.

[193] Chan, above n. 104 at 51 (Table 8B) notes that of the 72 challenges under Article 11(1), some 29 have been successful.

[194] See, e.g., *R.* v. *Choi Kai-on* (1994) 4 HKPLR 105.

[195] *Attorney General* v. *Fong Chin Yue* (1994) 4 HKPLR 430, [1995] 1 HKC 21. It is not clear whether the right violated would be the presumption of innocence or the right to not be subject to arbitrary detention. See also *R.* v. *Mak Chuen Hing and others* [1996] HKLD H26. In *R.* v. *Wong Yan-fuk* (1993) 3 HKPLR 341, [1994] 2 HKCLR 139 the Court of Appeal held that the imposition of an increased penalty on a defendant convicted of an offence in relation to an unlicensed massage establishment where there had been a previous conviction in relation to the premises was a violation of Article 11(1). For other cases discussing whether Article 5(1) permits substantive review of laws see above n. 158.

[196] [1985] AC 1, in *Attorney General* v. *Fong Chin Yue* (1994) 4 HKPLR 430, [1995] 1 HKC 21. See also *Attorney General* v. *China State Construction Engineering Corp* (1995) 5 HKPLR 421, [1996] 1 HKC 53.

noted a greater willingness by the courts to grant bail following the enactment of the Bill of Rights and also a higher level of absconding by defendants released on bail; however, it is difficult to verify whether, in fact, this has been the case.

In the interpretation of Article 5(3) (Article 9(3) ICCPR), the European authorities, in particular, have been of considerable assistance (see above n. 169), since Article 5(3) of the European Convention is worded in similar terms. (There is also no closely analogous provision in the Canadian Charter.) In fact, the courts have essentially adopted the approach of the European Court, although they expressed the view that the factors required to be considered under Article 5(3) and the common law relating to bail are basically the same. Nevertheless, it is clear that the quite extensive European jurisprudence has been an important influence on the Hong Kong courts' interpretation of this provision. Periods of 15 months' detention in trials before the High Court have been held to be excessive.[197]

The Right to Trial without Undue Delay[198]

There have been over a dozen major cases in the District Court and High Court, in which permanent stays of proceeding shave been sought on the ground of undue delay relying on abuse of process under common law and Article 11(2) (c) of the Bill of Rights.[199] A significant number of these have been successful.

While the courts have drawn a close analogy with the common law powers of a court to stay proceedings for abuse of process resulting from delay, they have accepted (in theory at least) that there may be some differences and that the right under Article 11(2) (c) may be more generous to defendants in a number of respects.[200] The courts have drawn on common law abuse of process doctrine, particularly the English cases, but also including *Jago* v. *District Court of New South Wales*.[201] They have also relied heavily on the leading United States and Canadian cases, in particular *Barker* v. *Wingo*[202] and *R.* v. *Askov*.[203] The European cases have played a role, in particular, by

---

[197] *R.* v. *Lau Kwok-hung (No 1)* (1991) 1 HKPLR 19 (15 months' delay unacceptable) and *R.* v. *Lau Kwok-hung (No 2)* (1992) 2 HKPLR 261; [1992] 2 HKCLR 241 (defendant released on bail); *R.* v. *William Hung* (1992) 2 HKPLR 49; [1992] 2 HKCLR 90 (delay of 526 days from arrest to trial on serious drug trafficking charges held to be a violation of Article 5(3)).

[198] See generally Chan, 'Undue Delay and the Bill of Rights', (1992) 22 *HKLJ* 2 and Chan, 'The Right to Speedy Trial', (1993) 2(1) *Asia Pacific Law Review* 13.

[199] See generally Chan and Wilkinson, 'Abuse of the Criminal Process', in Heilbronn (ed.), *Modern Trends in Litigation* (1995), 31.

[200] *Attorney General* v. *Charles Cheung Wai-bun* (1993) 3 HKPLR 62, [1993] 1 HKCLR 249, [1994] 1 AC 1; *R.* v. *William Hung* (1993) 3 HKPLR 328, CA.

[201] (1989) 168 CLR 23.

[202] 407 US 514 (1972).

[203] [1990] 2 SCR 1199, 74 DLR (4th) 355, 59 CCC (3d) 449.

supporting an expanded notion of when a person is 'charged' with an offence.[204]

The factors identified by various Hong Kong courts as appropriate to be taken into account in determining whether delay is 'undue' are fairly similar to those that have been examined in cases under the common law and constitutional and human rights guarantees.[205]

The relevant period for the purpose of Article 11(2) (c) certainly begins to run with arrest or the formal laying of a charge. However, the courts have held that the period may commence earlier, viz. when an individual is officially advised by a competent authority that he or she is suspected of having committed a criminal offence (and may include time which elapsed before the commencement of the Bill of Rights Ordinance).

The periods which have been held to be acceptable have been extremely variable. For trials in the District and High Courts, 15 months and upwards seems to be the starting-point for looking closely at a case, although periods considerably in excess of 15 months have been held to be consistent with Article 11(2) (d), particularly where complex commercial cases are concerned.[206] One effect of the enactment of the Bill of Rights has been concerted

---

[204] See *R.* v. *Lam Tak-ming* (1991) 1 HKPLR 222 at 232–3; *R.* v. *Charles Cheung Wai-bun* (1992) 2 HKPLR 123 at 143; [1993] 2 HKCLR 189 at 203; *R.* v. *Deacon Chiu Te-ken* (1993) 2 HKPLR 483 at 500–1.

[205] They include:
 (a) the length of the delay;
 (b) the reasons for the delay:
   (i) delays attributable to the Crown;
   (ii) systemic or institutional delays;
   (iii) delays attributable to the defendant;
 (c) the existence of waiver by the defendant;
 (d) prejudice to the defendant both as to the conduct of his or her defence but also more generally;
 (e) the public interest in bringing offenders to trial and in having criminal proceedings conducted in an efficient and fair manner; and also
 (f) the fact that part of the delay occurred before the entry into force of the Bill of Rights; and
 (g) the need for the Government to have a limited 'transitional' period to take steps to ensure that the present situation involving lengthy delays be brought into conformity with the Bill of Rights.

[206] *R.* v. *Charles Cheung Wai-bun* (1992) 2 HKPLR 123 (presumption of prejudice arising from delay of 10 years between events and trial, 5½ years between beginning of investigation and trial, and 3 years and 9 months between arrest and trial and evidence of actual prejudice made it appropriate in light of circumstances of case to stay proceedings), affirmed on appeal by the Privy Council on common law grounds ((1993) 3 HKPLR 62; [1993] 1 HKCLR 249; [1994] 1 AC 1); *R.* v. *Wong Chi-yuen* (1992) 2 HKPLR 323 (third trial after two aborted trials stayed, since 2 and a half years had elapsed from arrest to commencement of third trial); *R.* v. *William Hung* (1992) 2 HKPLR 49; [1992] 2 HKCLR 90, affirmed by the Court of Appeal (1993) 3 HKPLR 328 (delay of 526 days from arrest to trial on serious drug trafficking charges *prima facie* excessive, but in the circumstances not undue delay; detention for this period held to be a violation of Article 5(3) and defendant's sentence was reduced by the time he spent in custody); *R.* v. *Lam Tak-ming* (1991) 1 HKPLR 222 (delay between arrest and charge of 2 years and 9 months and further delay of 7 months from charge to commencement of trial not 'undue delay' in the circumstances of this case which involved a complex investigation involving a considerable amount of documents);

efforts on the part of the judiciary to cut the delays in hearing criminal cases, efforts which have considerably reduced waiting times and thereby limited the occasions on which such delay can form the basis for a Bill of Rights application.

Legal Aid

The enactment of the Bill of Rights Ordinance led to a considerable expansion of the availability of legal aid (Article 11(2) (d) Bill of Rights; Article 14(3) (d) ICCPR) in criminal matters as the result of legislative amendments in 1991 and 1992 designed to bring the position in Hong Kong into line with the Bill of Rights. In particular, legal aid was made more widely available in the Magistrates' Courts. However, entitlement to legal aid under the statutory legal aid scheme has been held not to be an exhaustive statement of a person's entitlement to legal aid; Article 11(2) (d) goes beyond those entitlements and requires that a person be provided with legal aid both at trial and on appeal, if the interests of justice so require. In the interpretation of this guarantee the courts have drawn on both Canadian and European authority, as well as looking to English statutory provisions governing legal aid.

While accepting that a means test is appropriate and that an administrative scheme for determining eligibility for legal aid is proper and desirable, the courts have nonetheless affirmed the power (and the duty) of the courts to undertake an independent inquiry into the means of the applicant and the interests of justice in a particular case.[207]

Right to Examine and Have Examined Witnesses

The right to call witnesses and to cross-examine witnesses against one has given rise to a significant number of cases, often in conjunction with the general right to a fair hearing guaranteed by Article 10. In cases involving witnesses who have died or are otherwise unavailable, the courts have accepted that there may be a difference between the common law and the Bill of Rights,[208] although this does not seem to have been of any particular practical importance.[209] Attempts to invoke the guarantees of the Bill of Rights to

R. v. *Fung Shu-sing* (1992) 2 HKPLR 383 (delay of 3 years and 9 months from arrest in May 1987 to trial *prima facie* excessive, but not undue delay since investigation was complex, discovery of facts leading to charge occurred only in April 1990, and no evidence of prejudice); R. v. *Kwan Kwok-wah* (1992) 2 HKPLR 353 (delay of 2 years and 9 months from commencement of ICAC investigations in a complex commercial conspiracy case not undue delay). Three further stays had been granted up to the end of September 1993: R. v. *Chan Chak-fan* (1993) 3 HKPLR 456; R. v. *Deacon Chiu Te-ken* (1993) 3 HKPLR 483; and R. v. *Flickinger* (1993) 3 HKPLR 677.

[207] R. v. *Alick Au Shui-yuen* (1991) 1 HKPLR 71; R. v. *Wong Cheung-bun* (1992) 2 HKPLR 82; [1992] 1 HKCLR 240.

[208] R. v. *Fung Shu-sing* (1992) 2 HKPLR 383.

[209] See, e.g., R. v. *Chan Chak-fan* (1993) 3 HKPLR 456; R. v. *Kwan Kwok-wah* (1992) 2 HKPLR 353; R. v. *Ng Ming* (1994) 4 HKPLR 907, [1994] 3 HKC 320, [1995] 1 HKCLR 305; R. v. *Lam Tat Chung Paul* (1994) 6 HKPLR 147; R. v. *Pannu (No 1)* (1996) 6 HKPLR 217.

challenge the introduction of affidavit evidence or computer-generated evidence where the witness is not tendered for cross-examination,[210] and to argue that these rights apply in extradition proceedings[211] have, however, largely been unsuccessful.[212]

Right to the Benefit of a Lesser Penalty

Article 12(1) of the Bill of Rights (Article 15(1) ICCPR) provides not only that a person convicted of a criminal offence cannot be subjected to a *heavier* penalty than that which applied at the time of commission of the offence, but that the person is also entitled to the benefit of a *lighter* penalty, if the law is changed after the commission of the offence. In a series of cases, the Court of Appeal grappled with the implications of this guarantee in the case of an offence which was split into two offences, one a more serious version of the offence with a penalty equal to the penalty for the earlier version of the offence and a less serious version with a considerably lower penalty. Following a considerable divergence of views in the Court of Appeal on this issue[213] (on which there appears to be little or no direct common law authority or international case law), the Privy Council eventually resolved the matter, holding that, if the conduct of the accused had permitted the prosecution to charge him or her with the more serious version of the amended offence, then the law had not provided for a lighter penalty for that offence, and accordingly the accused did not benefit from the guarantee.[214]

Remedies

As has already been noted, the courts have taken the view that the Bill of Rights Ordinance adds little to the existing remedial powers of the courts in criminal cases. In most cases the power of the judge to order a stay of proceedings, a witness to attend for cross-examination, or an adjournment[215] have been adequate to remedy violations. Particularly disappointing, however, has been the refusal of the higher courts to move away from the traditional common law position relating to the exclusion of unlawfully obtained

---

[210] See, e.g., *R.* v. *Purkayasatha* (1992) 2 HKPLR 371 (upholding the validity of banker's books evidence provisions, but requiring affiants to appear for cross-examination).

[211] See, e.g., *Re Ng Hung-yiu and United States of America* (1992) 2 HKPLR 209; [1992] 2 HKLR 383; *Re Suthipong Smittachartch and the United States of America* (1992) 2 HKPLR 249; [1993] 1 HKLR 93; *Thanat Paktiphat* v. *Chief Superintendent of Lai Chi Kok Reception Centre* (1995) 5 HKPLR 73.

[212] See, however, *R.* v. *Wong Wai* (1994) 4 HKPLR 245.

[213] There were 10 decisions of the Court of Appeal on Article 12(1) in 1993–4, with a number of different approaches to the interpretation of the guarantee. The leading cases were *R.* v. *Lai Kai-ming* (1993) 3 HKPLR 58, *R.* v. *Faisal* (1993) 3 HKPLR 220 and *R.* v. *Wan Siu-kei* (1993) 3 HKPLR 228.

[214] See *R.* v. *Chan Chi Hung* (1995) 5 HKPLR 1, [1995] 2 HKC 721, [1996] 1 AC 442.

[215] *Attorney General* v *Tang Yuen-lin* (1994) 4 HKPLR 631, [1995] 1 HKC 209.

evidence, where that evidence has been obtained in violation of the Bill of Rights.[216]

CIVIL AND POLITICAL RIGHTS[217]

Freedom of Expression and Assembly

There have been relatively few cases raising issues of freedom of expression and association. The courts have rejected challenges to various provisions of the laws regulating public assemblies and processions (though these were subsequently amended by the legislature to introduce a more liberal regime).[218] In the field of freedom of speech, challenges to the laws regulating the publication of obscene and indecent articles,[219] those limiting the extent to which the press can report on a corruption investigation in its early stages,[220] and those restricting access by prisoners to horse racing information contained in newspapers to which they subscribed[221] have all been held to be permissible restrictions on the right to freedom of speech and the freedom to seek, impart, and receive information. Unfortunately, no particularly well-articulated framework of analysis has emerged in the decisions—in essence the Court of Appeal has been prepared, with little substantive scrutiny, to accept not only that the objectives pursued by such legislation are legitimate (they clearly are) but that the measures chosen are reasonable and proportionate to the achievement of those goals.[222]

Right to Equality and Non-Discrimination

The guarantees of equality in the Bill of Rights have been the subject of only

[216] See *R.* v. *Cheung Ka Fai* (1995) 5 HKPLR 407 at 416, [1995] 3 HKC 214 at 223, CA, in which Litton V.P. rejected an argument that evidence obtained in an allegedly unlawful manner should be excluded by the court. He considered that it would be 'an extraordinary thing if, by applying the normal rules of evidence and procedure, a piece of evidence is admissible and yet, by the operation of s 6(1) of the Bill of Rights Ordinance, it should be inadmissible'.

[217] For a review of developments in the civil field see Chan, 'Recent Developments of the Bill of Rights in the Non-Criminal Context', in Edwards and Byrnes, above n. 56.

[218] *R.* v. *To Kwan-hang and Tsoi Yiu-cheong* (1994) 4 HKPLR 356, [1994] 2 HKC 293; *R.* v. *Chan Sau-sum* (1993) 3 HKPLR 308.

[219] *R.* v. *Obscene Articles Tribunal, ex parte Loui Wai-po and Ming Pao Holdings Ltd* (1994) 4 HKPLR 5.

[220] *Attorney General* v. *Ming Pao Newspapers Ltd* (1995) 5 HKPLR 13, CA; (1996) 6 HKPLR 103, [1996] 3 WLR 272, PC.

[221] *Chim Shing Chung* v. *Commissioner of Correctional Services* (1996) 6 HKPLR 313, CA, reversing *Chim Shing CHung* v. *Commissioner of Correctional Services* (1995) 5 HKPLR 570, HCt.

[222] A more positive development is to be seen in the Court of Appeal's decision in *Cheung Ng Sheong, Steven* v. *Eastweek Publisher Ltd and another* (1995) 5 HKPLR 428; [1995] 3 HKC 601, in which the court held that it could have reference not to the Bill of Rights, but to Article 19 of the ICCPR in developing the common law in a defamation case. But Cp. the court of Appeal's reversal of the High Court decision in *Hong Kong Polytechnic University* v. *Next Magazine (No 2)* (1996) 7 HKPLR 41: Civ App 28 of 1997.

a small number of cases, ranging from challenges to rather obscure provisions of criminal procedure law to challenges to fundamental aspects of Hong Kong's political system. In analysing the equality guarantees of the Bill of Rights, the courts have drawn on both international and Canadian jurisprudence. They have treated the guarantees contained in Articles 1, 10, and 22 of the Bill of Rights as covering the same types of discrimination, and have accepted that the bases of discrimination are not limited to those explicitly mentioned in the guarantees.[223] Some courts have taken the view that discrimination must be by reference to a 'status' and that there are differences which do not constitute differentiation by reference to a status,[224] though this analysis has its problems.[225]

The critical issue in the application of a guarantee of equality is the stringency of the test that is applied to justify differential treatment. The starting-point has become the formulation of Bokhary J. in *R.* v. *Man Wai-keung (No 2)*:[226]

Clearly, there is no requirement of literal equality in the sense of unrelentingly identical treatment always. For such rigidity would subvert rather than promote true even-handedness. So that, in certain circumstances, a departure from literal equality would be a legitimate course and, indeed, the only legitimate course. But the starting point is identical treatment. And any departure therefrom must be justified. To justify such a departure it must be shown: one, that sensible and fair-minded people would recognize a genuine need for some difference of treatment, two, that the difference embodied in the particular departure selected to meet that need is itself rational; and, three, that such departure is proportionate to such need.

In that case the court held that a provision of the Criminal Procedure Ordinance which denied it the discretion to consider an award of costs to a successful appellant if a case was sent back for a retrial while other successful appellants were eligible for an award was inconsistent with the guarantee of equality before the law.

[223] *R.* v. *Man Wai-keung (No 2)* (1992) 2 HKPLR 164; [1992] 2 HKCLR 207.

[224] See, e.g., *Building Authority* v. *Business Rights Ltd* (1993) 3 HKPLR 609 (differentiation by reference to geographical location apparently not a status); *Commissioner of Inland Revenue* v. *Eekon Enterprises Ltd* (1995) 5 HKPLR 322 (impecuniosity not a prohibited ground of discrimination). These cases are arguably wrongly decided on this point in view of the international case law. The courts have accepted that the following fall within the scope of the guarantee: differential treatment of government and private car owners (*R.* v. *Crawly* (1994) 4 HKPLR 62), of successful criminal defendants whose cases are sent back for retrial and those whose are not (*R.* v. *Man Wai-keung (No 2)* (1992) 2 HKPLR 164; [1992] 2 HKCLR 207), between voters who are entitled to vote in both geographical and functional constituencies and those who are not (*Lee Miu-ling* v. *Attorney-General (No 2)* (1995) 5 HKPLR 181, HCt; (1995) 5 HKPLR 585, [1996] 1 HKC 105, CA), and between civil servants on local terms and those on overseas terms (*R.* v. *Secretary for the Civil Service, ex parte Association of Expatriate Civil Servants of Hong Kong* (1995) 5 HKPLR 490 and (1996) 6 HKPLR 333).

[225] The Human Rights Committee has also adopted such a position , though exactly how one defines a 'status' is somewhat unclear: see Byrnes, 'Equality and Non-discrimination', in Wacks (ed.), *Human Rights in Hong Kong* (1992), 225 at 237–8.

[226] (1992) 2 HKPLR 164 at 179, [1992] 2 HKCLR 207 at 217.

The only other case to reach the Court of Appeal[227] by mid-1996 involved a challenge to Hong Kong's electoral system, under which some permanent residents were entitled to a vote in both a geographical constituency and a 'functional constituency' (defined by reference to professional or industry affiliation), while others were entitled to a vote only in a geographical constituency. This system was challenged on various grounds, including that it violated the right to universal and equal suffrage in Article 21 of the Bill of Rights. While the case was, perhaps inevitably, lost on the ground that the Letters Patent had been amended to permit such functional constituencies and to immunize them against a Bill of Rights challenge, the judge at first instance noted that the right of equal suffrage 'requires each permanent resident of Hong Kong to have the same voting power and to be accorded votes of equal weight in such elections'. While noting that constituencies did not necessarily have to be the same size, he stated that:

the concept of equal voting power can only be satisfied by a system which accords to each voter the same number of votes—the 'one person, one vote' principle. Moreover a restriction on the right of all voters to have the same number of votes cannot be regarded as reasonable if the system which accords more votes to some voters than to others does so by reference to distinctions based on their status.[228]

On appeal the Court of Appeal also held that the claim based on the different numbers of votes for different permanent residents could not succeed because of the Letters Patent. However, in addressing a second argument that the huge variations in size among functional constituencies were discriminatory and unreasonable, Bokhary J.A. reiterated his earlier test in *Man Wai-keung*, but seemed to dilute it by suggesting that such differences would only be discriminatory if 'sensible and fair-minded people [would] condemn that arrangement as irrational or disproportionate',[229] a far less stringent standard for reviewing differential treatment.[230]

---

[227] There have been a number of lower court decisions. In *R*. v. *Crawley* (1994) 4 HKPLR 62 the court held that a difference in treatment under traffic laws between government and private cars was not discriminatory. In *L*. v. *C.* (1994) 4 HKPLR 388, [1994] 2 HKLR 93 the court expressed the view (*obiter*) that a 12-month limitation period for the mother of an illegitimate child to apply for maintenance from the father was discriminatory.

[228] (1995) 5 HKPLR at 189. Cf. Human Rights Committee, *General comment 25(57)*, UN Doc. CCPR/C/21/Rev. 1/Add. 7, para. 21 (1996).

[229] (1995) 5 HKPLR at 592. Yash Ghai comments: '[T]he test of "sensible and fair minded persons" is much looser than traditionally employed in most other places to govern departures from equal treatment, and the court arrived at its view of what such persons would accept in an exceedingly cursory way': Ghai, 'Sentinels of Liberty or Sheep in Woolf's Clothing? The Judicial Politics of the Hong Kong Bill of Rights', paper presented at Commonwealth Law Conference, Vancouver, August 1996, 18.

[230] This may be compared with the more demanding scrutiny by Cheung J. in *Lau San Ching* v. *Apollonia Lu* (1995) 5 HKPLR 23, where the court expressed the view (*obiter*) that a 10-year residence requirement in order to be eligible to stand for election to a district board was an 'unreasonable' restriction on the right to stand for election under Article 21(b) of the Bill of Rights. A similar level of scrutiny was applied by Keith J. in *R*. v. *Secretary for the Civil Service, ex parte*

PRIVATE LAW AND THE BILL OF RIGHTS: 'INTER-CITIZEN RIGHTS'

In the second case it heard under the Bill of Rights, *Tam Hing-yee* v. *Wu Tai-wai*,[231] the Court of Appeal held that the Bill of Rights Ordinance had no application to litigation between private individuals (even where the rights of private individuals have been defined by legislation).

The case involved a challenge to provisions of the District Court Ordinance which permitted a judgment creditor to obtain from a court an order preventing a judgment debtor from leaving Hong Kong. The provisions were challenged as violating the guarantee of liberty of movement in Article 8 of the Bill of Rights (Article 12 ICCPR). The court held that the Bill of Rights was not applicable, and that, in any event, the provision was a permissible restriction on the enjoyment of liberty of movement.

The decision is poorly reasoned[232] and was handed down after a hearing in which the court neither sought nor was provided with submissions which would have strongly supported the opposite conclusion.[233] But it has not been challenged by other litigants, and the Court of Appeal has shown no inclination to reopen the question. As a result, the Court of Appeal has drastically limited the impact that the Bill of Rights should have had in relation to legal relations between private parties. Nonetheless, the Ordinance still applies to litigation between private individuals and government or public authorities.[234]

It should also be noted that the holding in *Tam Hing-yee* v. *Wu Tai-wai* applies only to the scope of the Bill of Rights Ordinance, being based on the language of Section 7 of the Ordinance. It does not preclude the possibility that legislation passed on or after 8 June 1991 and affecting private legal relations could be attacked under the Letters Patent, although the courts may be reluctant to move away from *Tam Hing-yee*. Since the standard for post-June 1991 legislation is the ICCPR, to the extent that such legislation restricts a

---

Association of Expatriate Civil Servants of Hong Kong (1995) 5 HKPLR 490, in reviewing various civil service policies relating to differential treatment of local and overseas offers (though the judge in that case appeared to accept perhaps too readily that likely industrial opposition by others might be sufficient justification for *prima facie* discriminatory treatment: at 549). See the decision of the Court of Appeal: (1996) 6 HKPLR 333.

[231] (1991) 1 HKPLR 261; [1992] 1 HKLR 185; [1992] LRC (Const) 596.

[232] See *Bill of Rights Bulletin*, vol. 1, No. 2, at 1–4. See also Chan and Ghai, above n. 3 at 23–6. Others have expressed the view that, in fact, the Court of Appeal was correct in its conclusions, e.g., Oderberg, 'The Bill of Rights and Criminal Proceedings', paper presented at CLE seminar, 'Litigating the Bill of Rights Ordinance', Hong Kong, May 1992, p. 2.

[233] See generally Byrnes, above n. 67 at 71–107; Byrnes, ' "Recalcitrant Debtors" in a Town "Pollinated by Gold": Hong Kong's First Bill of Rights Judgment', (1991) 21 *HKLJ* 377.

[234] There has so far been little consideration of the term 'public authorities'. In *R.* v. *Hong Kong Polytechnic, ex parte Jenny Chua Yee-yen* (1992) 2 HKPLR 34, Mayo J. held that the Hong Kong Polytechnic was a 'public authority' for the purposes of the Bill of Rights Ordinance. For a more detailed discussion of the test to be applied see *Hong Kong Polytechnic University* v. *Next Magazine Ltd* (1996) 6 HKPLR 117.

person's rights by making it lawful for another private individual to infringe them, it can be tested against the guarantees of the ICCPR (which requires the state to protect a person against violations by other private individuals in certain circumstances, and certainly not to legalize them).[235]

THE RIGHT TO A COURT

One of the inevitable consequences of the negotiation of international agreements by parties from different legal systems is that the final text may include terms or concepts which originate in the particular experience of one culture or legal system and which may not be readily translatable to another context. In the case of the ICCPR, while there is a high level of congruity between the concepts contained in the Covenant and common law systems, there are nevertheless examples of terminology and concepts taken from the civil law system which may not fit so neatly into common law concepts.

An important example, which has given rise to particular difficulties in Hong Kong, is the right of access to a court, arguably guaranteed by Article 14(1) of the ICCPR and Article 10 of the Bill of Rights (which are in identical terms). In conceptual terms, this guarantee is one of the most difficult to give effect to in the common law context; despite the criticism in the public debate of the 'alien' concepts that were to be introduced into Hong Kong's legal system by the Bill of Rights, the implications of Article 14(1) passed largely unnoticed.

The relevant part of Article 14(1) (and Article 10) provides:

All persons shall be equal before the courts and tribunals. In the determination of any criminal charge against him, or of his rights and obligations in a suit at law, everyone shall be entitled to a fair and public hearing by a competent, independent and impartial tribunal established by law . . .[236]

On its face, Article 14(1) of the ICCPR (in its English version) looks unexceptionable, a guarantee of due process or natural justice and the open administration of justice, principles which are well entrenched in common law systems. However, Article 14(1) guarantees more than this, at least if the case

---

[235] For example, if the legislature were to enact an ordinance which permitted employers to search employees' correspondence or lockers, then that statute could be tested against the guarantee of privacy in Article 17 of the ICCPR, whereas similar provisions in any existing law could not be tested against the identical guarantee in the Bill of Rights.

[236] The corresponding provision of the European Convention, Article 6(1), provides: 'In the determination of his civil rights and obligations or of any criminal charge against him, everyone is entitled to a fair and public hearing within a reasonable time by an independent and impartial tribunal established by law'.

Note that, while the English versions of the ICCPR (and Bill of Rights) and the European Convention differ (ICCPR: 'determination of . . . rights and obligations in a suit at law'), the French texts of both treaties use the same language ('contestations sur ses droits et obligations *de caractère civil*') (emphasis added).

law under the corresponding provision of the European Convention is any guide.[237] It embodies the so-called 'right of access to court',[238] *not* just a right to fair and unbiased procedures in criminal or civil proceedings already before a court or tribunal. This means that, where there is a dispute between government and a private party over the existence of a 'right of obligation in a suit at law' (or a 'civil right and obligation'), the article requires that all issues of fact and law which are decisive for the existence of that right can be determined by a tribunal which satisfies the criteria of Article 14. Article 14 requires that at some stage in the process, the administrative decision affecting the right be:[239]

amenable to a properly constituted tribunal with power to give full consideration to issues of law, fact and merits, whether as initial decision-maker or subsequently on appeal.

While recent European Court case law suggests that a full review of facts and law on the merits by an independent and impartial tribunal may not be required in every case (and that the availability of judicial review may suffice, even if there is a dispute over facts), the article nevertheless guarantees a level of review of administrative action that goes beyond the general availability of judicial review.

[237] The Human Rights Committee has not examined this aspect of Article 14 in any great detail. Such indications as there are, however, suggest that it adopts an approach similar to that of the Strasbourg organs. See, in particular, *Y. L.* v. *Canada*, Communication No. 112/1981, *Selected Decisions*, vol. 2, (1986), 28, which involved a dispute over the denial of a disability pension to a person who had been dismissed from the Canadian army. The Committee commented:

'9.1 . . . the latter expression [suit at law] is formulated differently in the various language texts of the Covenant and each and very one of those texts is, under Article 53, equally authentic.
9.2 The *travaux préparatoires* do not resolve the apparent discrepancy in the various language texts. In the view of the Committee, the concept of a "suit at law" or its equivalent in the other language texts is based on the nature of the right in question rather than on the status of one of the parties (governmental, parastatal or autonomous statutory entities), or else on the particular forum in which individual legal systems may provide that the right in question is to be adjudicated upon, especially in common law systems where there is no inherent difference between public law and private law, and where the courts normally exercise control over the proceedings either at first instance or on appeal specifically provided by statute or else by way of judicial review. In this regard, each communication must be examined in the light of its particular features'.

[238] *Golder* v. *United Kingdom* (European Court of Human Rights) (1975) Series A, No. 18; 57 ILR 200; 1 EHRR 524 (prisoner entitled to access to a court to bring action for defamation under Article 6(1)). The guarantee also has implications for legal aid in civil proceedings: *Airey* v. *Ireland* (European Court of Human Rights) (1979) Series A, No. 32; 58 ILR 624; 2 EHRR 305 (lack of availability of legal aid in judicial separation proceedings, violation of the right of access to a court).

[239] Boyle, 'Administrative Justice, Judicial Review and the Right to a Fair Hearing under the European Convention on Human Rights', [1984] *Public Law*, 89 at 105. See generally Harris, 'The Application of Article 6(1) of the European Convention on Human Rights to Administrative Law', (1974–5) 47 *British Yearbook of International Law* 157; Newman, 'Natural Justice, Due Process and the New International Covenants on Human Rights: Prospectus', [1967] *Public Law* 274; Van Dijk, 'The Interpretation of "Civil Rights and Obligations" by the European Court of Human Rights—One More Step to Take', in Matscher and Petzold (eds.), *Protecting Human Rights: The European Dimension*, (1988), 131.

The guarantee only applies to a process involving the 'determination' of 'rights or obligations in a suit at law' under the ICCPR, or of 'civil rights or obligations' under the European Convention. The notion of 'civil rights or obligations' is a term of art derived from civil law systems with their traditional classification of law into civil, criminal, and administrative law; it does not encompass everything that we would understand as a civil action. However, it has been held to include the right to engage in development of one's land[240] and the right to engage in private commercial activity of many sorts,[241] even where these activities are subject to regulatory controls.

The guarantee gives rise to particular problems for common law jurisdictions[242] which do not distinguish in the same way between civil law and public/administrative law and under which judicial review by the courts of almost all administrative decisions is normally available as a matter of principle. Attempting to apply this model derived from civil law systems to the common law system is a difficult task.

Potentially, however, the impact of the right to a court could be far-reaching in a common law system such as Hong Kong, which does not have a developed system of independent review of administrative decisions on the merits but relies on internal review and/or judicial review.

The importance of Article 10's guarantee in the Hong Kong context is that persons affected by many administrative decisions have essentially only two avenues of 'appeal' open to them. One avenue is that of a full appeal on all issues to a body internal to the administration (in many cases with a final appeal to the Governor-in-Council) or to a body on which the administration has a nominee. Such a body would probably not satisfy the requirements of independence and impartiality required by Article 10. The other avenue is to seek judicial review of the decision in the courts, which are clearly Article 10 tribunals. However, the courts do not have the power on an application for judicial review to reconsider the merits of the decision, but are confined to a review of its legality. If there is a dispute over a question of law, then the availability of judicial review will satisfy Article 10. However, if there is a factual dispute between the person affected and the decision-maker with respect to

---

[240] *Skärby* v. *Sweden* (European Court of Human Rights) (1990) Series A, No. 180–B; 13 EHRR 90 (challenge to public authority's restrictions on building on land designated as a nature park a dispute over civil rights and obligations).

[241] *Kaplan* v. *United Kingdom* (European Commission of Human Rights), Report of 17 July 1980, 21 D & R. 5 (right to conduct insurance business was considered to be a civil right or obligation); *Tre Traktörer Aktiebolag* v. *Sweden* (European Court of Human Rights) (1989) Series A, No. 159; 13 EHRR 309 (revocation of licence to serve alcoholic beverages involved determination of civil rights and obligations).

[242] The guarantee has not been unproblematic for civil law jurisdictions, since the scope of the guarantee in the evolving European jurisprudence has been interpreted to include many activities subject to government regulation which were considered within national systems to be matters of public law. See, e.g., Oehlinger, 'Austria and Article 6 of the European Convention on Human Rights', (1990) 1 *European Journal of International Law* 286.

the merits of the decision, then judicial review may not be sufficient to satisfy Article 10's guarantee of a right to a court.[243] In such a case, there will be a violation of Article 10, and some or all of the relevant regulatory statute may fall.

In cases invoking Article 10, the Hong Kong courts have spent much time examining its international origin and the relevant European Convention case law. The courts have come to different conclusions on fundamental questions, in particular whether Article 10 embodies the right to a court in the European sense, and, if so, what the implications of this right are. The prospect that an interpretation following the European case law might bring down elaborate statutory schemes in areas such as town planning wholesale is a daunting one that has concerned the courts and militated against a broad reading of the right.[244]

Despite consideration of the guarantee in about a dozen decisions (the most significant of which have involved challenges to Hong Kong's town planning legislation made by developers objecting to re-zoning), the scope of the guarantee and its implications are still far from settled. The courts appear to have:

(a) accepted that the guarantee contained in Article 10 is not confined to proceedings before a traditional court, but may also apply to quasi-judicial proceedings;[245]

(b) accepted that the guarantee of an 'independent and impartial' tribunal embodies the protections of the common law against a biased tribunal (and accordingly overrides a statutory provision which mandates or permits this), but appear not to consider that the notion of 'independence' accepted internationally should be adopted in its full plenitude;[246]

(c) accepted that the guarantee is engaged only if the decision or process challenged involves a 'determination' of relevant rights or obligations (following the European case law in this respect);[247]

(d) accepted that the term 'rights and obligations in a suit at law' encompasses at least those rights accepted as falling within the term 'civil rights

---

[243] Cf. *O, W, B and R* v. *United Kingdom* (European Court of Human Rights) (1987) Series A, Nos. 120 and 121; 10 EHRR 29 (availability of judicial review or wardship proceedings insufficient to satisfy guarantee as did not permit review of the merits).

[244] See, e.g., Litton V.P. in *Kwan Kong Co. Ltd* v. *Town Planning Board* (1996) 6 HKPLR 237 at 252.

[245] *Kwan Kong Co. Ltd* v. *Town Planning Board* (1996) 6 HKPLR 237, CA (overruling Waung J. in *R.* v. *Town Planning Board, ex parte Kwan Kong Co. Ltd* (1995) 5 HKPLR 261); *Real Estate Developers Association* v. *Town Planning Board* (1996) 6 HKPLR 179, HCt.

[246] *Kwan Kong Co. Ltd* v. *Town Planning Board* (1996) 6 HKPLR 237, CA; *Business Rights Ltd* v. *Building Authority* (1994) 4 HKPLR 43, [1994] 2 HKLR 341, CA; *R.* v. *Lift Contractors' Disciplinary Board, ex parte Otis Elevator Company (HK) Limited* (1995) 5 HKPLR 78, CA.

[247] *R.* v. *Town Planning Authority, ex parte Auburntown Ltd* (1994) 4 HKPLR 194, HCt; *R.* v. *Town Planning Board, ex parte Kwan Kong Co. Ltd* (1995) 5 HKPLR 261 (HCt), *Kwan Kong Co. Ltd* v. *Town Planning Board* (1996) 6 HKPLR 237, CA; *Real Estate Developers Association* v. *Town Planning Board* (1996) 6 HKPLR 179, HCt; *R.* v. *Obscene Articles Tribunal, ex parte Ming Pao Holdings Ltd* (1994) 4 HKPLR 5, HCt.

and obligations' under the European Convention (but that it may also include other rights that are the subject of civil proceedings);[248]

(e) not finally decided whether Article 10 provides a right to be able to challenge an administrative action involving a determination of protected rights if such a challenge cannot already be made under existing law (the right to a court in its broad sense);[249] and

(f) to the extent that they accept that the article guarantees the right to a court, left open whether that right always requires a full review of facts and law by an independent body, or whether judicial review will suffice in some cases.[250]

As of early 1997, only one case depended for its outcome on a finding that there was a right of access to court in order to challenge a decision affecting rights;[251] most of the cases in which the issue has been raised have been decided either on the basis that the decision challenged did not involve a 'determination' of rights, that the body which made the decision was 'independent and impartial', or that there was a full review of the challenged decision available. Time may eventually bring a resolution of the issue. The complexity of the issue, the apparent civil law ancestry of the guarantee, and the likely consequences for Hong Kong administrative law of adopting a broad view probably mean that the Hong Kong courts will eventually take a restrictive view of the guarantee, and will view it as little more than a restatement of the basic principles of fairness embodied in the existing rules of natural justice.

Conclusion

The enactment of Hong Kong's Bill of Rights was the result of a fortuitous combination of historical circumstances and the tragic dashing of hopes. Its

---

[248] Only Judge Cheung in *Commissioner for Inland Revenue* v. *Lee Lai-ping* (1993) 3 HKPLR 141 has applied the full rigour of the European distinction between a 'civil right' and an 'administrative' matter, following European case law in deciding that the assessment of liability to tax did not involve the determination of a civil right.

[249] Cases in which the right has been explicitly accepted, or explicitly or implicitly formed the basis of reasoning include: *Commissioner for Inland Revenue* v. *Lee Lai-ping*, DCt, *R.* v. *Town Planning Authority, ex parte Auburntown Ltd*, HCt; *R.* v. *Lift Contractors' Disciplinary Board, ex parte Otis Elevator Company (HK) Limited*, HCt and CA, and *Building Authority* v. *Business Rights Ltd* (1993) 3 HKPLR 609, DCt. Cases which have rejected the broad interpretation are: *R.* v. *Town Planning Board, ex parte Kwan Kong Co. Ltd*, HCt; *Commissioner of Inland Revenue* v. *Eekon Enterprises Ltd* (1995) 5 HKPLR 322, DCt, and *Real Estate Developers Association* v. *Town Planning Board*, HCt. Cases in which a clear position has not been taken include: *Kwan Kong Co. Ltd* v. *Town Planning Board*, and *Business Rights Ltd* v. *Building Authority* (1994) 4 HKPLR 43, [1994] 2 HKLR 341, CA.

[250] see *Real Estate Developers Association* v. *Town Planning Board* (1996) 6 HKPLR 179 at 215.

[251] *Commissioner for Inland Revenue* v. *Lee Lai--ping* (1993) 3 HKPLR 141 (failure to permit District Court to review stop order applied for by Commissioner a violation of Article 10).

future, and quite possibly its demise, will be determined by the obverse of those political forces that brought it into existence.

There is no doubt that the Bill of Rights has significant limitations: its limitation to the sphere of activities of government and public authorities (by the courts, but now with executive and legislative acquiescence) falls short of the obligations accepted by the United Kingdom under the ICCPR and limits the impact of the Bill. The lack of a human rights commission, the high cost of litigation, and the difficulties that have sometimes kept legal aid outside people's reach all limit access for many Hong Kong residents to a mechanism for the effective enforcement of the rights which the Bill guarantees. The attitude of the courts, now predominantly conservative and parochial and displaying a high level of deference to executive and legislative decisions, also means that its impact is further limited, the more so because of the flow-on effect of judicial attitudes on the legislative and executive branches of government. Finally, the amendment of Ordinance as a result of the NPC Standing Committee's decision of 23 February 1997 suggests that the Bill of Rights has probably already had most of the impact it will ever have.

Despite these negative features of the Bill's operation (and some would see cause in them for praise rather than criticism), the enactment of the Bill of Rights brought with it many positive contributions to the rule of law in Hong Kong. There is no doubt that it has had a catalyzing effect for the review of a great deal of legislation that was in sore need of revamping and modernizing, and has focused attention on and generated legislative proposals in areas where previously there was little or no protection of the rights it guarantees. It has contributed to a greater awareness among all branches of government of international standards and of the assistance that can sometimes be derived from international law. While a 'rights culture' may not have taken root deeply, the Bill of Rights has helped to stimulate public discussion of human rights issues, to frame much of that discussion, and to provide a standard of critique of new policies and laws in the political arena.

Finally, the Bill of Rights has provided an important opportunity for bringing together international standards and the rich body of the common law. In the meeting of the two, many of the advantages and shortcomings of each have been revealed; international law can supplement and enrich the common law, but in many areas the experience of the common law is far more subtle and developed than the international standards.

It has been suggested (cynically but perhaps with an element of accuracy) that the best chance for the Bill of Rights to survive 1997 was for it to have little or no impact before that date. Whatever the accuracy of that assessment, it seems that with the advent of the Basic Law and the amendment of the Bill of Rights Ordinance from 1 July 1997, the legacy of the Bill of Rights to the legal system of the Hong Kong Special Administrative Region may be the body of case law that already exists and the fruits of the reexamination of existing laws and policies that has been carried out during the brief period since the Bill's enactment. Whether that legacy will be a valuable one in helping to preserve the rule of law and develop the constitutional protection of human rights under the Basic Law remains to be seen.

10

A Post-Calvinist Catechism or a Post-Communist Manifesto? Intersecting Narratives in the South African Bill of Rights Debate

MARTIN CHANOCK*

Historical Paradoxes

In Wajda's film *Danton* we are shown Robespierre's son, a small boy in his bathtub, learning the new Declaration of the Rights of Man by rote. Each time the young boy falters in his recitation, he is punished. The ironies in these images come to mind when the nature of South African legal discourse over the past decade is considered. A remarkable consensus has developed, and a new orthodoxy has been established. In the place of lawyers' debates about the 'rule of law', which in past decades had accompanied the decay of legality, the disintegration and collapse of legalism during the 1980s sparked an intense interest in human rights and Bills of Rights. And as the prospect of the end of apartheid appeared on the horizon, English-speaking liberal lawyers lost their monopoly. Afrikaner intellectuals, both legal and religious, announced their conversion, and Marxists in the liberation movements joined the choir. In making sense of the unfolding debates about a Bill of Rights we must begin by noting that, though rights discourses have little internal history on either right or left, they came to assume the position of the *obvious* in political and constitutional discussions. Given both the power of human rights ideology, and rights jurisprudence, internationally, and the context of the need to construct new constitutional arrangements, the importance in constitutional debates of a Bill of Rights was not surprising. But in the setting of South African history it contained a fundamental paradox. A form of liberalism, which has failed

* I am grateful to Kathy Albertyn, Hugh Corder, Dennis Davis and Lorraine Gordon for assistance with sources, and to La Trobe University for financial assistance. The first part of this paper was written before the drafting of the South African Interim Constitution; the latter part after the Interim Constitution came into effect, but before the Constitutional Court had ruled on any matter relating to the Bill of Rights. It must be read, therefore, as a commentary on the pathways towards a Bill of Rights. It takes no accounts of later developments such as the extended controversies over the form of the final Constitution, or of the final wording of the Bill of Rights in that Constitution. Nor does it consider any of the cases in the Constitutional Court involving interpretation of the Bill of Rights, nor any of the recent literature regarding them.

over the whole of the period of the South African State to attract significant support from any segment of the population, found its political philosophy entrenched in the heart of a new Constitution.

Though there was agreement on the need for a Bill of Rights, there was deep division about what should be in it. Every Bill of Rights has its own story. Comparative discussions of rights declarations in Constitutions tend to focus on words and forms. For it is these that in international law form the basis of what is common, and are the currency of international law. But as soon as we think about each separate national context we can see that, in their own historical and political setting, each declaration has its own meaning and significance, which may often be obscured by its formulaic content. In South Africa, while groups formerly completely opposed politically and ideologically gather around the new symbol, they do not all do so for the same reasons. This Chapter looks at the differences in rights tactics, strategies, and meanings.[1] A number of different historical narratives lie behind the Bill of Rights debate in South Africa and only sensitivity to these can make the debate fully comprehensible. The specifics of the history of each Bill of Rights is not just a matter of recounting events past. We must be aware of the importance of the construction of narratives in ordering the logic of arguments, of action, of proposals for the future. A narrative, as Ricoeur has written, has a plot in which 'goals, causes and chance are brought together'[2]. The plot of a narrative 'grasps together and integrates into one whole and complete story multiple and scattered events, thereby schematising the intelligible signification attached to the narrative taken as a whole'.[3] Narrating and predicting are closely linked. '*Expectation is . . . the analogue to memory. It consists of an image that already exists . . .*'.[4]

It is with a sensitivity to the importance of the role of the many different narratives involved, including those that Cover has called the 'exiled narratives'[5] which have come home to South Africa like the political exiles, that we must approach recent South African political debates. Cover has written that: 'No set of legal institutions or prescriptions exists apart from the narratives that locate it and give it meaning. For every Constitution there is an epic, for each decalogue a scripture.'[6] As the wording implies, these are not simply stories, but moral stories. The 'communal character' of the narratives provides the content of normative behaviour.[7] But it may prove to have been far easier

---

[1] It does not attempt to describe the full contents of the rights instruments proposed. These can be found in the appendixes to the South African Law Commission's Reports on *Group and Human Rights* (1989 and 1991); in the African National Congress' *A Bill of Rights for a New South Africa* (1990), and in other documents referred to in the text. A sense of the development of the rights debate in South Africa from the lawyers' point of view can best be gleaned from *The South African Journal on Human Rights*.

[2] Ricoeur, *Time and Narrative* (1984), vol. 1, ix.   [3] Ibid. at x.

[4] Ibid. at 11 (emphasis added).

[5] Cover, '*Nomos* and the Narrative', 97 *Harvard Law Review* (1983) 4 at 19.

[6] Ibid. at 4.   [7] Ibid. at 10.

to make deals about the content of a new Constitution, than to bring together the narratives that ought to give it meaning.

I shall begin with what appears to have been the dominant tone of much of the new debate which was characterized by anxiety about the supposed effects of the Nationalist Government's abuse of law. A prominent advocate, Sydney Kentridge, gave what Dennis Davis called the 'chilling warning'[8] at the beginning of the decade that:

one day there will be change in South Africa. Those who then come to rule may have seen the process of law in their country not as a protection against power but as no more than its convenient instrument . . . It would not be surprising then if they failed to appreciate the value of an independent judiciary and of due process of law.

The lawlessness of the late 1970s and the 1980s, in the streets, in the prison cells, and in the Courts, has led not only to legal outrage but to legal fear. To re-establish legalism, a powerful new symbol of adherence both to rights and due process, such as a Bill of Rights, had enormous appeal. The crisis in legitimacy, not of white rule, but for the idea of rule according to law, appeared frequently as a focus of concern. In Dugard's view the Nationalist Government did 'incalculable harm' to South African legal institutions by using the law as an instrument of oppression, and it thereby 'destroyed respect' for law among the majority. One of the major tasks facing a post-apartheid South Africa would be 'the restoration of respect' for law.[9] One of the strands of the Bill of Rights debate, then, is concerned with these fundamental intangibles in which anxiety was fused with an analysis of legality built around legitimacy. A Bill of Rights was crucial not only to legitimacy in this sense, but to the whole question of legitimacy of a post-apartheid regime. For its powerful symbolism would establish an arena not just for law, but would also be a definition of what is, and is not, legitimate in politics.

While the lawyers perceived a legitimacy crisis for law during the 1980s, the Government finally saw one for the apartheid regime as a whole. As part of its search for legitimacy it amended the Constitution in 1983, and extended the franchise to Indian and coloured South Africans for separate Houses of Parliament. It is important to note that when making this change it specifically rejected calls from the Parliamentary opposition for a Bill of Rights and a constitutional court to accompany the constitutional changes. Only 3 years later the game had changed. The strategy of 1983 had been destroyed by overwhelming popular rejection organized by the extra-Parliamentary opposition, and by international financial sanctions. In the changed context it made sense for the Government to buy into the Bill of Rights debate in a renewed search for political legitimacy. Could it insert its agenda into the rights discourses dominated so far by opponents of the regime? But as the wolf struggled into

---

[8] Quoted in Davis, *Post Apartheid South Africa: What Future for a Legal System?* (1988), 220.
[9] Dugard, *Human Rights and the South African Legal Order* (1978), 258.

its sheep's clothing sharp divisions appeared in the flock. A liberal legal rights discourse, developed and deployed by the opposition when there was no countervailing political power to use against the Government, was, so far as radical lawyers were concerned, far less attractive as the prospect of real political power loomed larger.[10] The suddenness of the political collapse of the international Left, however, left only the possibility of retreat into the rights fold. In any case the apparent willingness of the Government to be converted to the idea of a Bill of Rights brought to the fore the ways in which such an instrument could be used to perpetuate the positions, and possessions, of white privilege. In a short time the politics of the debate had changed remarkably. After decades of hostility, liberals and Nationalists found themselves engaged in mutual rights-speak. Radicals were filled with sullen suspicion, co-opted into the Bill of Rights debate by the collapse of communism, and the liberation movement's new strategy of negotiation.

Some Constitutional History

The Bill of Rights debate coincides with that about a new Constitution and is not intelligible unless set against the varying stories of South Africa's constitutional development. In 1910 the former British Colonies of Natal and the Cape of Good Hope, and the conquered Afrikaner republics of the Transvaal and Orange Free State, were put together in an imperially created Union.[11] The processes of the formation of this Union have often been described. We are concerned here with the resulting legends, in particular the liberal legends of the 'Lost Opportunity' and the 'Great Mistake'. The first refers to the failure to nurture, and to extend, the weak and limited Cape tradition of non-racial liberalism to the rest of the new Union. The Union of 1910 had rested on a political compromise in which the non-white franchise at the Cape was preserved, but not extended to the former Republics. The second, which was to assume greater prominence in the 1950s, was the rejection of federalism and judicial review in framing the Union Constitution in favour of a Union in which the central Parliament was supreme. The Act of Union (passed by the Parliament in Westminster as the South Africa Act in 1909) did provide for certain protections against a majority in the sovereign Parliament in South Africa, by providing that the provisions related to the franchise and the official languages could only be altered by a two-thirds majority of both Houses of Parliament sitting together. Before the Statute of Westminster Act in 1931

---

[10] Sachs remarked that 'South Africa must be the only country in the world in which sections of the oppressed actually constituted an anti-Bill of Rights Committee': Sachs, *Protecting Human Rights in a New South Africa* (1990), 6.

[11] See Chanock, *Unconsummated Union: Britain, Rhodesia and South Africa 1900–1945* (1977), and Thompson, *The Unification of South Africa* (1960).

these provisions could not be altered by the South African Parliament which did not have the constitutional power to override an Imperial Act. But when South Africa became fully independent the constitutional protections logically appeared to have been swept away. Or so it seemed.

The stage was set for another vital part of the liberal legend, the 'Glorious Moment' of the 1950s, when the Appellate Division of the Supreme Court appeared to be successful in brandishing the law against the power of the Nationalist Government. In 1936 African voters in the Cape had been removed from the common roll by a Parliamentary majority well in excess of two-thirds. In 1950 the new Nationalist Government, embarking upon its apartheid program, purported to disenfranchise the Cape coloured community by a simple majority in Parliament. With considerable judicial artifice, however, the Appellate Division persuaded itself that the South African Parliament remained bound by the Act of Union, in spite of the change in the constitutional position in 1931.[12] After a prolonged confrontation in which the composition of both Parliament and Court were enlarged by the Government, the Court had to acquiesce. A constitutional amendment in 1956 subsequently ruled out any challenge by any Court to the validity of an Act of Parliament. A great 'If Only' was added to the liberal legend. 'If Only' there had been a 'real' Constitution in 1910, with a Bill of Rights, and judicial review of the validity of legislation in the light of such a Bill, the good judges would have had a real weapon with which to strike down the evil laws of apartheid. The contemporaneity of the passing of a battery of oppressive laws during the 1950s and early 1960s, and the impotence of the South African Supreme Court judges, with the liberal judicial activism of the Warren Court in the USA, in particular its use of the Bill of Rights to defeat segregatory laws, was of considerable importance also in the making of this legend. It seemed to some plain what the 'Missing Key' to a good constitutional order in South Africa was.

Without a knowledge of this history it is virtually impossible to understand the shape of current South African legal debates. I have referred to this version of events as a legend not out of a lack of sympathy but because it thrived, despite the obvious absence of any evidence for it. Perhaps this is unfair, as evidence of what did not happen is hard to produce. But on the face of the record there is very little to encourage the belief that South African judges appointed by the National Party Government, even had they been armed with a perfect Constitution with a Bill of Rights and right of review, would have been any more sympathetic to opponents of the Government, or treated them substantially differently.

---

[12] There is a large amount of literature on this episode. See Forsyth, *In Danger for Their Talents* (1985), and the references cited therein.

From Rule of Law to Bill of Rights

Until recently liberal legal commentators focused on 'the Rule of Law' rather than on a Bill of Rights. This was because the South African constitutional structure (until 1983) was a Westminster system, and because legal models of practice and rhetoric were drawn from Britain where the facts of Parliamentary sovereignty combined with Executive dominance have long been surrounded by a cloud of ideas about limited Government and the liberty of the subject. A reading of the recent Bill of Rights debate in South Africa must take place against the background of the shift in liberal symbolism which has displaced the Diceyan notions of the 'Rule of Law', which looked to the protection of civil rights by the operation of the ordinary law in the ordinary Courts, rather than by a special statement of principles and special tribunals. From the 1950s to the 1970s, as the weight of oppressive apartheid Statutes grew, liberal lawyers and their opponents, who intellectualized a defence of Government policies, were locked in debate about the meaning of the 'Rule of Law'. The liberals had huge political resources with which to conduct the debate, but only shadowy legal resources. They could win easily in the realm of what ought to be done in the way of respect by the Government for the basic liberties of the subject, freedom of speech, person, association, no penalty without law, the right to a hearing and so on. But these things, though they might be a part of the usual political practice of the British Constitution, which was the model against which liberal South Africans judged, were mostly not legally guaranteed. It was all too easy for Afrikaner lawyers to respond by pointing this out, and by showing that South African practice scrupulously followed the law of the Constitution. There were no arbitrary and extra-legal actions: the actions of the Government were authorized by the appropriate Statutes, and if they were not, the Courts were able to say so. This, the liberals claimed, was rule *by* law, not the rule *of* law. Legally, said their opponents, there can be no difference, and, therefore, the Rule of Law is a political notion. The more intellectually adventurous of these Afrikaner positivists were able to reject the idea of the Rule of Law in its English form as alien to the civil law tradition of the Roman-Dutch law, and to posit variants based on ideas ranging from scientific positivism, to natural law, to the *rechtstaat*. There was also a broader and more fundamental difference based upon a Calvinist rejection of liberalism and humanism (see below) in which the position was taken that the sovereignty of God, and the authority of the State he had ordained, and the primacy of national groups, took priority over individuals and their supposed rights. The rhetoric was heated and the ground disputed: it would have been hard to anticipate the current degree of unanimity.

To appreciate the degree of the shift in the debate it is worth examining the way in which it was presented in the leading (and representative) text of the period.[13] The Rule of Law was presented as an 'obvious'[14] and foundational feature of free societies. It is linked to a second, and more significant, feature of South African legal liberalism, its insistence on the separation of the Rule of Law doctrine from substantive politics.

The identification of human rights or of a particular philosophy . . . with the Rule of Law is here rejected as unscientific . . . theories [which] are inevitably contentious and unstable; and to identify the Rule of Law with any one of them is to make it . . . a weapon in the war of political and moral ideas. The essence of the approach in the ensuing study of the Rule of Law lies in the assumption that a notion bearing its name is, or ought to be, juridical in its character . . . [Its] internal, scientific principles are stable and permanent elements in the law . . . The theory of the Rule of Law adopted in this work focuses on the notion of *law* as the only fixed star in a shifting firmament.[15]

As the ensuing arguments show this was not just tactical realism, but it should be said that 20 years ago there was little point in standing on a substantive terrain, the only space open for opposition lawyers was for a claim to be more formally legalistic than that of the Government's.

Mathews' notion of the Rule of Law was built upon Dicey's. Individual rights, in this view, should be protected and developed by the workings of the ordinary system of common law precedent through individual cases, 'whereas under many foreign constitutions the security (such as it is) given to the rights of individuals results, or appears to result, from the general principles of the Constitution'.[16] Mathews specifically rejected both Jennings' view that Dicey's concept was 'Whig politics'[17] and also the realism of Schreiner J., the Appellate Division's most important liberal judge in the crises of the 1950s, who observed that '[t]he charge that the Rule of Law has been infringed is a political charge . . .'.[18] It was also important to Mathews, even while granting that the Diceyan notion of the Rule of Law was inherently connected to a nineteenth century notion of basic individual liberties, that it be prised apart from substantive notions of rights. In this approach he was in tune with many of the contemporary English commentators.[19]

In this context the importance of the international debates must be stressed. There were several factors at work here. One was the set of 'lessons' drawn

---

[13] Mathews, *Law, Order and Liberty in South Africa* (1971).   [14] Ibid. at 1.
[15] Ibid. at 1–2.
[16] Dicey quoted by Mathews, ibid. at 24.   [17] Ibid. at 18.
[18] Ibid. at 11. As Dugard n. 9 above at 45 remarked '[b]oth friend and foe of the Rule of Law in South Africa have been influenced by legal positivism and therefore see the Rule of Law as a political standard, rather than as a juridical concept'. He quotes Snyman J., to the effect that the Rule of Law 'is very much a tool of the politician and the politically-minded lawyer'. Ibid.
[19] Cf. Goodhart: 'It is therefore of the utmost importance to keep entirely separate the idea of basic rights and the idea of government under law because the former is bound to be vague and uncertain while the latter is clear and definite': quoted in Mathews n. 13 above at 20.

from the experience of the Nazi regime which was often characterized (not entirely accurately) as Government without law.[20] Another was the movement, in the context of the cold war, of large numbers of former Colonies towards independence. The transfer of power, and the writing of Westminster model independence Constitutions for new members of the British Commonwealth, was accompanied by a zealous attempt to export and invest an ideological version of free Government under the Rule of Law. The formalistic, liberal English version soon ran into problems in the Third World where there were demands for substance, preferably in the form of 'human rights'. As Mathews complained, for example, the 1959 international congress of the International Commission of Jurists which was held in New Delhi 'consciously transformed the Rule of Law into an instrument of political, social and economic justice'. This 'sweeping extension and transformation of the Rule of Law into an ideology is a development calling for lament.'

These developments were paralleled in the new dimensions of human rights thinking, and the development of a political and ideological cold war struggle to control the content of international rights discourse. This produced the elaboration of concepts of rights, which added social and economic—the so-called second generation rights—to the civil rights expounded by the West. As Western policies proclaimed adherence to first generation rights, the response from the Communist and Third World was that these could not be achieved without second generation rights, which had to be produced by determined, and sweeping, Government actions which might need to override the luxuries of civil liberties available to rich countries. But substantive content was simply not on the Rule of Law agenda in South Africa in the 1960s and 1970s. In Mathews' account the substantive economic questions, for example, are raised only in the form of a discussion in a footnote about the place of the Rule of Law in administering planning and in some mistrusting remarks on equality.[21] His remarks on transition to a new political dispensation were also remote from current circumstances. Warning that 'nowhere in the world has a free society sprung Athena-like from conditions of despotism or anarchy', he envisaged a managed process of change in which political equality would be introduced at the end, and in which a security law regime would probably have to continue: 'the immediate or even rapid introduction of the whole panoply of democratic rights and liberties, even if accompanied by constitutionally

---

[20] By the 1980s it was becoming not unusual to compare South Africa's judges to those of Nazi Germany and to criticize them for the opposite offence of paying attention only to positive law and not to morality.

[21] See Matthews n. 13 above at 27–8, 22 (n. 20). 'When we proceed beyond the rule of political equality to social equality we have truly entered the thicket. Social equality today implies governmental power and intervention; and positive State actions aimed at equality inevitably result in less freedom. Acton's famous words are apposite here: "The passion for equality made vain the hope for freedom." Moreover, a policy aimed at achieving a levelling out implies that some people will be treated unequally!': Mathews, ibid. at 280.

guaranteed minority and individual rights, is unlikely to lead to the successful establishment of a free and stable system.'[22]

The developments in debate were reflected towards the end of the 1970s by John Dugard. The ever increasing volume of apartheid legislation, and the cooperation of the Supreme Court judges in its administration, produced a liberal analysis with less faith in the ordinary workings of law in the ordinary Courts, and one with more attention to the substantive content of alternatives.[23] Procedural safeguards, as Dugard pointed out, were increasingly seen to be insufficient, as was shown by the world-wide growth of the human rights movement, and of rights declarations.

The emphasis is everywhere upon substantive freedoms and civil liberties. The time is ripe for South African civil libertarians positively to assert their demands for a Bill of Rights and, negatively to measure their losses by the new standards of liberty of the world community, rather than by the limited, largely procedural, standards of Dicey.[24]

There was also another aspect to Dugard's argument which focused on the failure of the judges themselves to make the choices about the enforcement of Statutes which the Roman-Dutch common law, in Dugard's view, allowed them to make.[25] The judges, he argued, should abandon their posture of elaborate subordination to legislative will and their 'myth of judicial impotence' and recognize that they had a law-making function. The problem, in Dugard's view, was the dominance of legal positivism, a baneful result of the dominance of English legal influences. The Roman-Dutch law, on the other hand, was not only closer to a natural law tradition, but was pregnant with 'obvious guiding principles' of freedom, which were 'part of the *legal tradition*' in South Africa.[26] The argument that the Roman-Dutch law was a source of rights, which has a suspiciously Diceyan ring, was a well-intentioned but unconvincing attempt to assert an indigenous rights tradition in the Roman-Dutch law, and to encourage the exercise of liberal choices by judges of conscience on the South African bench.

There were a number of reasons why the ground shifted. One was the simple failure of the idea of the Rule of Law in the South African context. Not only was the Government hostile to it, but its advocates significantly failed to persuade the judges that it meant anything other than rule *by* law. The ordinary law and the ordinary Courts failed to fulfil their assigned Diceyan tasks. Whether these tasks could be fulfilled was a matter of fierce legal controversy, as we shall see. The second was the retreat of the idea of the 'Rule of Law' in the face, not of its conventional Calvinist and Statist enemies, but of criticism

[22] See Matthews n. 13 above at 303, 309.
[23] Dugard n. 9 above at 41 wrote: 'There are several objections to the use of the Diceyan concept of the Rule of Law as a standard by which to judge South African legislation. First, it is too closely identified with English traditions; second it is too uncertain in its content; third, it is unacceptable to legal positivists; and fourth, it is too narrow in its scope.'
[24] Ibid. at 47.   [25] Ibid. at ch. 11.   [26] Ibid. at 371, 382–3.

from the Left. As the academic legal Left in South Africa has grown in critical strength and activity it has, as elsewhere, simultaneously, and confusingly,
exposed the limitations of law and made expanded demands for the rights
which it should advance and protect. Both directions cast doubt on the adequacy of the liberal 'Rule of Law'—not real in one direction, too limited in
another. The idea of a Bill of Rights also appeared to offer appropriate remedies for failures in the administrative law area, and a way of strengthening and
extending the 'Rule of Law' agenda. The directions which the liberal versus
Marxist debate took was also circumscribed by the fact that both sides were
allied in the immediate political struggle against apartheid. The differences
were to become plainer when projections about the content of a future Bill of
Rights came to be considered. We must also remember the change in the
nature of the Constitution in 1983, which put an end to the Westminster-style
Constitution and created an Executive presidency. The 'Rule of Law' stands
for an idealized version of a Westminster Parliamentary system; a Bill of
Rights for an idealization of a Presidential system.

Another crucial impetus in the change of direction was the complete failure
of the Courts to develop an administrative law which would protect people
from the abuses of power by officials empowered with huge discretions under
the apartheid Statutes. The apartheid regime depended on a statutory law
which gave vast powers over the person and property of South Africans.
Judged overall, the Appellate Division appeared willing to adopt a view which
favoured the purposes and perspectives of Government, rather than the rights
and liberties of the citizen. This was one of the most significant legal failures
of the apartheid period. It was one of the most important factors in pushing
reformist lawyers of all sorts towards a sharp break with reliance on 'Rule of
Law' ideas. At best, the Appellate Division could probably have offered no
more than a means by which a more rigid procedural accountability was
imposed by Courts on officials exercising discretions under apartheid
Statutes, and it could have contributed little of a substantive nature. But it
might, nonetheless, have changed the perception that the Courts were little
more than agencies of the Executive.[27]

The Bill of Rights debate must, then, be set against the long-running saga
of the role of the judiciary in the apartheid system; against the other parts of
the story of constitutional change; against the international spread of the
rights gospel; and above all, within the context of the political struggle which
brought an end to apartheid.

The recent political and constitutional history of South Africa had been
one in which both the policies and methods of Government moved further
away from the possibility of a rights-based political order and practice rather

---

[27] There is no space here to pursue this question in the detail it deserves. See the discussions in
Forsyth, *In Danger for their Talents* (1985); Davis ed., *Law Under Stress* (1988); and the *South
African Journal on Human Rights.*

than closer to one. Ever since 1948 the aim had been to exclude completely the possibility of a black majority exercising power over an undivided South African State. For the last three decades it was apparent that the Afrikaners (or even the whites as a whole) could not govern without assistance and support from allies co-opted from the subject population. The creation of the independent black States, Transkei, Bophututswana, Venda and the Ciskei, and the accompanying fiction that black South Africans were all citizens of a 'homeland', were one part of the strategy of division and co-option. Another part was developed in the 1983 amendments to the Constitution, designed to provide a form of political representation to Asian and coloured South Africans. But the narrowness of the political base and the huge popular resistance to these policies meant that the 'era of reform' of P.W. Botha was in reality one of intensified oppression. So our story is not one of a reform process building incrementally towards a rights-oriented Constitution, but one of a sharp change of political direction. With this in mind, and with so little to build upon in existing political or legal practice, the attraction, and uses, of a grand new statement like a Bill of Rights appears obvious.

Another part of the context was the fundamental shift in the economic policies of the South African State. The era of apartheid was characterized by the building-up of large State-run corporations which controlled huge sectors of the South African economy. In addition the vast administrative ambitions and needs of apartheid required a swollen bureaucracy. But the fiscal crises of the 1980s, intensified by financial sanctions against South Africa, as well as the swing towards economic policies in the rest of the world based on privatization and the priority of markets, had a decisive effect on the nature of the South African State. The privatization of major areas of State-run economic endeavour, and the reduction in the size of the bureaucracy, were clearly in one sense policies which were driven by the same ideological and economic imperatives as similar policies elsewhere in the capitalist world. But in South Africa it is impossible to ignore the drive to 'diminish the State' as a preparation for a new political dispensation.[28] It is clear that it was envisaged that a handover to black rule would be less painful and dangerous if the power of the central State could be reduced by both limiting the reach of central Government and minimizing its economic activities. A Bill of Rights as a part of a Constitution in which the central State was limited in power, and in a privatized economy in which property rights were protected, was a most powerful lure in the conversion of whites to liberalism. It might well save some of the purposes of abandoned plans for partition. Another part of this design was the aim of negotiating a Constitution which emphasized regional autonomy and in which minorities were to be given significant veto powers.

An ironic effect of the intensified oppression since the revolts of the late

---

[28] See the discussion in Greenberg, *Legitimating the Illegitimate. State, Markets and Resistance in South Africa* (1987).

1970s and the recurring crises which led to the passing of the Internal Security Act in 1982, and to the subsequent prolonged reliance on a State of Emergency by the Government of P.W. Botha, was that much greater attention was focused on the Courts as areas in which political battles could be fought. With no access to Parliament, and under strict conditions of censorship and restrictions on political organization and demonstrations, the Courts offered a rare oppositional space. The attempts made by the Government through the use of emergency powers and the Internal Security Act to exclude resort to judicial power, and to close off the legal spaces, sharpened the struggle for those spaces. This strengthened the impression that a judiciary which was not hampered by this kind of legislation, and which had the appropriate 'rights' tools, would be able to give a legitimate sympathy to oppositional political practices. The opposition's use of the Courts opened up a fierce debate about the role of, and responsibilities of, judges, which was connected to the Bill of Rights debate because that was also premised on an important and activist political role for judges. By closing off other avenues the Government succeeded in politicizing the Courts and the legal processes after years of insisting that these had nothing to do with politics.

It had always been a part of the defence of South Africa's judges that they had, in fact, given judgments that the Government has not wanted,[29] and this has been a feature of the 1980s.[30] It was precisely this small possibility of victories that led to the use of the Courts, and the fact that in the large majority of cases the judges gave no relief served to intensify criticism of them.

The De Klerk Era of Reform and the Bill of Rights

The manifest failure of the ordinary law to protect rights of political activists during the State of Emergency, and the increasing momentum towards political reform, contributed further towards the emergence of the Bill of Rights as the flagship of legal and constitutional reformers. After the fall of the Botha Government, and the beginning of that of F.W. de Klerk, a new policy of reform was proclaimed. In the first phases, discussion of a Bill of Rights had the advantages of avoiding actually discussing the transfer of power while focussing on the protective aspects of law.

In April 1986 the P.W. Botha Government's Minister of Justice had asked the South African Law Commission, the State's law reform body, to 'investigate and make recommendations on the definition and protection of group rights in the context of the South African constitutional set-up' and also to

---

[29] The most vigorous recent defence is in van Blerk, *Judge and be Judged* (1988).

[30] See e.g. the decisions giving residential rights to some urban blacks, which went against Government policies, especially *Oos-Randse Administrasie Raad* v. *Rikhoto* 1983 (3) SA 595 which had results of substance for nearly 26,000 people.

consider the possible extension of existing protection of individual rights, and the role the Courts might play.[31] The setting of the request was central to politics. As the National Party groped its way towards admitting black participation in the power of the central State, it searched simultaneously for ways of limiting majority domination. In the context of its philosophy, which had long justified its policies by insisting on the differentiation of national groups and their rights to develop differently, it was natural that it would seek to appropriate the constitutional and rights debates in this direction. In turning towards Afrikaner intellectuals who had previously been the major resource for justification of policies, the Government could not have expected to find that, in this area at least, international rights discourse had burst through the barriers of group differentiation. The Law Commission, in true South African legal fashion, noted that the question was 'controversial', and observed that they had tried to approach it 'as objectively as possible, from a practical legal point of view'. It was by a mass of objective legalism that they sought to effect what would, if acted on, be a fundamental change in political direction.

The first and most striking point about the Report was its size. More than 500 pages long, it contained huge and sweeping overall accounts of theories of human rights starting with Socrates; substantial country by country analyses of the protection of rights in legal and constitutional orders; a global 51 page analytical chart of rights protection in world constitutions; a lengthy presentation and analysis of every side of the South African debate; and it also printed numbers of Bills and Charters of rights. The great weight and scope of the presentation was directly indicative of its task, which was to persuade the Government that its policies related to rights were misconceived, and, by sheer weight of positivist argument, to effect a reversal in State policies.

In its long rehearsal of theories of rights the Law Commission was able to connect their line of argument to a form of Afrikaner nationalist legalism. Natural law thinking, they showed, had dominated the European tradition for centuries, while legal positivism in its nineteenth century form had been introduced to South Africa because of the pervasive effect of English law. The ideas of the 'Rule of Law'[32] and of rights protection were presented not as political practice but as part of a legal tradition. 'In our own legal history,' they write, 'there is much that testifies to the recognition of universal human rights', and Voet and Grotius, 'two of our greatest Roman-Dutch writers played a special role in this regard.'[33] They reviewed the history of the principle of Parliamentary sovereignty in South African law, and compared it unfavourably with the alternate tradition of rights protection which they found embodied in

---

[31] South African Law Commission, *Group and Human Rights* (1989).
[32] The Law Commission, ibid. at 20 notes: 'The expression "rule of law" . . . has been left untranslated in the Afrikaans version of this paper . . .', a startling admission of the inconceivable, but also a point about its specifically foreign and English nature.
[33] Ibid. at 46.

the 1854 Constitution of the Orange Free State, with its Bill of Rights and judicial review. They came to the conclusion, astonishing except in the context of painting the picture of the virtuous Roman-Dutch common law with its own rights ideology, that '[t]he idea of unbridled Parliamentary sovereignty is foreign to our common law.'[34] They also developed Dugard's argument which distinguished between the way the Courts had developed the Roman-Dutch law, and the way they had interpreted Statutes: 'As far as common law questions are concerned, our Courts have been consistently resourceful and creative. The best principles from the works of the old writers have been taken and adopted to the needs of the times.'[35]

While there was 'full recognition of and respect for the rights of the individual' in the common law,[36] the Courts have had to bow to the intention of the Legislature 'however unjust the result may be'.[37] The international community, they found, had given concrete shape to the idea of fundamental individual rights which needed protection, which 'has become a universal demand . . . It has become part of the international legal consciousness and of the contemporary law of nature'.[38]

After a substantial review of rights protection in Britain, the USA and West Germany, the Law Commission offered an assurance on two points of recurrent concern. The existence of a Bill of Rights in the USA, and the right of judges to test legislation against it, had not 'undermined the security of the State'.[39] And, they reported, it was possible to avoid an overtly ideological statement. In comparison with the American model, they wrote, the West German Bill of Rights 'is much more detailed and more modern, and is cast in the form of a legal document'.[40]

The Law Commission's report was based on an extensive range of views submitted to it and was of especial interest for its discussion of, and confrontation with, Calvinist-based Afrikaner ideological objections of the idea of human rights. There had long been, it noted 'outspoken repugnance' in 'church circles' to human rights, which were associated with the international campaign against apartheid and with 'liberal and humanist' thinking.[41] The concept of human rights, it was said:

was born in a climate alien to the Bible, that it belongs to a revolutionary atmosphere in which authority as instituted by God is rejected . . . [A] human being has no inherent rights to which he can appeal. All that he has and is he receives as unmerited gifts from the hand of God.[42]

---

[34] Ibid. at 181.   [35] Ibid. at 161.

[36] 'One of the oldest principles of natural law,' they wrote later, 'is that of equality before the law (Plato) which down the ages has remained the guiding star of Western civilisation. In our common law this ideal has been enunciated by Ulpian, at a time when slavery was still the order of the day': ibid. at 294.

[37] Ibid. at 169.   [38] Ibid. at 70–1.   [39] Ibid. at 97.

[40] South African Law Commission, *Group and Human Rights* (1989) at 106.

[41] Ibid. at 184.   [42] Ibid.

Rights which glorify the autonomy of individuals must, therefore, be rejected. However, the Law Commissioners found friendlier theologians. They quoted W.D. Jonker: 'The value which God sets on man is immeasurably high . . . The rights of man are as wide and inclusive as God's commandment itself', as he/she was created with a 'specific calling, responsibility and destiny.' While in relation to God, individuals have no rights, they do in relation to other individuals. 'The rights of man are the other side of God's commandment regarding our communion with one another.'[43] This is, in the South African context, a most important process of reasoning, for in it we see the juncture, after years of bitter opposition, of the internal Calvinist churches with their international counterparts, and with the other South African churches.[44] The General Synod of the Nederduitse Gereformeerde Kerk told the Law Commission that as 77 per cent of the total South African population were Christians, a Christian justification of human rights was more important than a:

clinically legal definition of those rights . . . In South Africa, where the First World and the Third World meet, there are grave dangers in adopting a particular classically liberal or socialist model of human rights . . . To make a success of human rights it is necessary to create a 'human rights culture'.

For this reason, the Synod told the Law Commission, the 'summary introduction of a Bill of Rights is not the correct approach', and they recommended instead an educative declaration of rights.[45] Thus, while joining in the chorus, they did so without any note of urgency.

Having navigated these difficult waters the Law Commission's report added to its persuasive weight by canvassing an extensive range of other Christian, other religious, and secular support for rights. In a powerful appeal to white South Africans who for generations had justified apartheid as the defence of Western civilization, the next section of the report was headed 'Western norms of civilisation as justification.'[46] Western thought on the subject, they advised, went back to Aristotle, and was 'woven into history like a golden thread'. The 'pinnacles' of Western thought 'may be seen whenever Western society has had to struggle against totalitarianism in any form'.[47] In the context of envisaging the South African future this definition of the 'pinnacles' has a special importance. J.L. Pretorious, the Professor of Constitutional Law and Legal Philosophy at the University of the Orange Free State, told the Law Commission that '[t]he recognition of human rights pre-supposes a choice in favour of a differentiated society where no societal form, including the State, dominates the others'.[48] And, the Law Commission reported, M.G. Erasmus,

---

[43] Ibid. at 185–6.

[44] It should be noted that the Nederduitse Hervormde Kerk still does not accept 'a metaphysical dream of universal man: every person and every group of persons are uniquely created in themselves': ibid. at 356. It continues to differ from the larger Nederduitse Gereformeerde Kerk's view that the 'Holy Spirit regards the human race as a unit': ibid. at 368.

[45] Ibid. at 193–4.   [46] Ibid. at 199.   [47] Ibid. at 200.   [48] Ibid.

Professor of Public Law at the University of Stellenbosch, 'shows in his sub-mission that the idea of a limited State authority is so essential to a democra-tic order that it is developed further into constitutional mechanisms that are in fact a feature of democracy'.[49]

A picture of a constitutional law, drawn from religious justification, and the 'golden thread' of the West's secular tradition, and suited also to the position of a white minority without ruling power, emerged: a limited State, rights as a justification for differentiation. A new constitutional law for South Africa had to emerge in which there was a curtailment of Parliamentary sovereignty, because without this 'minorities are at the mercy of the majority'.[50] Finally, urged the Law Commission 'everyone must eventually realize that the strug-gle between white and non-white is one that cannot be won outright by either side. An endless conflict is foreseeable . . .'. To avoid this there needed to be a negotiated settlement with a Parliamentary structure which 'may place a curb on absolute power'.[51] Prior to its all important discussion of the concept of group rights the Law Commission embarked upon a discussion of indigenous Bills of Rights, ranging from the Orange Free State Constitution of 1854, to the Freedom Charter adopted by the liberation movement in 1956, to odd outcroppings of the Constitution-making exercises of the 1980s: the Bophutatswana Bill of Rights; the South West African one; and the model produced by the Kwazulu/Natal Indaba. That the South African political and constitutional landscape was already littered with examples of rights instru-ments points to the compelling need felt for a magic constitutional key. In the case of Bophutatswana and South West Africa the Bills were introduced for cosmetic reasons. The negotiated Natal Bill, which was intended to provide a model as to how the rest of the country might find its way out of its difficul-ties, provided a group veto for both English and Afrikaner 'groups' of whites over matters affecting their interests. Even so, it had been criticized by Afrikaners on the grounds that while a group could block legislation, it could not implement and further its own wishes without the consent of other groups.[52]

When it turned its attention to group rights the Law Commission adopted the same global and comprehensive strategy, and the return to first principles that marked its approach to other areas. A vast historical canvass was unfurled: the history of the world was the history of group conflicts. Internal measures of group protection were dated from Article 19 of the Austrian Constitution of 1867.[53] After a full analysis of United Nations and other Conventions protecting the rights of minorities the Law Commission con-cluded that there was an 'international conviction' that minorities should be protected.[54] But how was it to be done? They looked at the concept of

[49] Ibid. at 202.   [50] Ibid. at 206–7.   [51] Ibid. at 209.
[52] South African Law Commission, *Group and Human Rights* (1989) at 247, 256–7.
[53] Ibid. at 324, 328.   [54] Ibid. at 338.

'confiliation' in which each group had a sort of ethnic autonomy, controlling matters such as family laws and schools, with central Government having a sphere limited to foreign affairs, defence and currency management.[55] The Law Commission discussed the protection of Canadian Indian and Maori rights and considered the unpromising lessons of group rights in relation to political power sharing in Cyprus, The Lebanon and Fiji. While dismissing these two approaches the Law Commission concluded that internationally, group rights were recognized in the form of the protection of minorities.

On this promising basis they examined the huge number of submissions received from inside South Africa favouring the group right concept. The Nederduitse Hervormde Kerk took its stand on the view which had been central to Afrikaner ideology that only group rights were possible. The Argus Company argued on the basis of Lancaster House model of transition, advising the reservation of Parliamentary seats for whites for a long period in order to ensure economic stability. Group rights, they said, would have to be recognized for the purposes of practical political negotiation, as it was the only way whites would accept majority rule.[56] The Federated Chamber of Industries contended that accommodation of Afrikaner ethnic nationalism was 'essential', and argued more widely that '[e]thnicity is at present deliberately being understated by urban black leaders'.[57] A large body of white opinion, both Afrikaner and non-Afrikaner made submissions in favour of the group right principle. One might quote G.C. Cloete in summing up. The only way to settle ethnic conflict in a plural society, he argued, was by the de jure recognition of de facto ethnic groups as the basis of society, and 'the institutionalization of ethnicity in the constitutional structures of the State in a non-discriminatory manner'.[58]

Here the Law Commission might have stopped, having argued the need for recognition of human rights, and demonstrated the international recognition of minority rights. Had they done this they would have been true to the ideal level of argument on which much of South African legalism has thrived. But they did not. There was instead a short plunge into realism. They quoted the acerbic remark in a submission from L. Blaauw that the rationale of the international law of protection of minorities did not apply in South Africa where those who sought the protections were the most advantaged group in the society.[59] This was supported by Professor L.M. du Plessis, of the Law Faculty in the University of Stellenbosch, who suggested that proponents of group rights were simply trying to continue privilege. But too much realism was not the Law Commission's style. It had, after all, already observed that 'Today there are few who deny that the system of apartheid *was* extremely unjust in many respects,'[60] as if the changes in official rhetoric had already changed the world. Instead the Law Commission chose to trump the notion of group rights with

55 Ibid. at 343.   56 Ibid. at 356.   57 Ibid. at 362.   58 Ibid. at 371–2.
59 Ibid. at 365.   60 Ibid. at 204.

an argument based on formal legalism, to take it onto a plane on which, to a lawyer, the arguments would be uncontestable and politically neutral. Legalism, so long invoked in service of white power, was suddenly deployed against the concept of group rights.

Groups, Professor du Plessis maintained, were not recognised as legal subjects in Roman-Dutch law, had no locus standi, and therefore could have no rights.[61] An ethnic group was a 'collectivity and in essence juridically undefinable'. The only way group rights could be protected 'in a juridical sense' was as rights of the individual. Ethnic group needs could be legally satisfied by endorsing individual rights of association and the cultural rights of individuals.[62] The Law Commission adopted the language of jurisprudence with apparent delight. The 'fundamental legal problem [was] the legal identification of the possessor of the rights'. From a legal point of view, 'before there is an enforceable right in respect of any person, there must also be a legal subject, a *persona juris* to whom that right belongs . . . After all, this is obvious'.[63] But Roman-Dutch law had no 'historical or juridical base' for group or minority rights. Even class actions were not possible.[64]

A season of revolution is one of disturbing uncertainty, perhaps especially to those who live intellectually and materially by regular processes and enforceable rules. A desire builds for the uncertainty to end, and for order to be re-established. One of the aspects of a Bill of Rights strategy was that it was part of the search for a strong Constitution, a strategy of order. In supporting the concept, and in putting forward its *Business Charter of Social, Economic and Political Rights* in January 1986, the South African Federated Chamber of Industries referred to the danger of 'chaos and revolution' unless action was taken.[65] In 1986 when the National Party appeared to change its views in relation to a Bill of Rights, and announced that such a Bill was justified on the basis of equity, the principle of the Rule of Law, and the Christian faith, the language of order continued to break through. The Minister of Justice in August 1986 referred to a Bill of Rights as a stabilizing feature, and envisaged that access to the Courts would be given only on the basis that 'it is not abused and does not in itself become an instrument of the anarchist aimed at destroying the State, including that very legal system'.[66] As the Law Commission said, such a Bill 'need . . . not impede the pursuit of public safety or state security, but is far rather an additional and equivalent means'. As they pointed out, 134 out of 165 sovereign countries had one, and they did not need to

---

[61] Ibid. at 376.   [62] Ibid.   [63] Ibid. at 383.

[64] They quoted *Director of Education, Transvaal* v. *McCagie and Others* [1918] AD 616 at 624 where Innes C.J. said that the *actio populares* of Roman law had become obsolete. 'The principle in our law is that a private individual can only sue on his own behalf, not on behalf of the public.' The right must be available to an individual personally and the injury sustained by an individual.

[65] South African Law Commission n. 31 above at 204.   [66] Ibid. at 265.

underline the obvious, that in very few cases did it operate as a constraint on Government or protect the rights apparently enshrined.

The Liberation Movement and the Bill of Rights Debate

There were, as we have seen, many reasons for the involvement of the Government in the Bill of Rights debate. But why, at this point, were they engaged by major elements of the opposition? Liberals, Marxists and Nationalists had for years been talking past each other in different languages. Yet at this point in history their discourses appeared to intersect. There were obvious traps set for the opposition, of which they were well aware. Our story began with the making of the 1910 Constitution, and the subsequent liberal fables of the 'Lost Opportunity' and the 'Great Mistake'. But that constitutional beginning is also recognized in liberal historical legend as the occasion of the 'Great Trade'. Imperial protection of the political rights of Africans was traded for the loyalty of Afrikaner political leadership to the Empire. It is to be expected that a constitutional settlement between bitterly contending sides will contain fundamental bargains. Whatever other compromises were to be reached in relation to other constitutional issues, it was clear that the lineaments of another 'Great Trade' appeared in the Bill of Rights proposed by the Law Commission which elaborately protected property rights. Whites would recognize black political rights, if blacks recognized white property rights. In 1910 the two parties agreed at the expense of a third. The dangers of repeating this process at the expense of the dispossessed were obvious. The acceptance of a 'Great Trade' also determined the question of the timing of the introduction of a Bill of Rights. A Bill of Rights which was constructed after a political transition could reflect the standards and ambitions of a new era in history and politics. One embodied in a Trade could contain a defence of the older order against the new.

We can come now to those 'exiled narratives' which are returning to provide different beginnings, middles and endings to the South African constitutional story. The analyses internal to the legal system of white South Africa which I have outlined above may soon appear as irrelevant as alchemy. For the returning narratives, the theme that arises out of the Constitution of 1910 is not that focused around the 'Great Mistake' of failing to federate with judicial review, but rather the 'Great Exclusion', the acceptance of the colour bar in the Act of Union.[67] The attendant and consequential foundational theme is that of

[67] The first page of the African National Congress' Constitutional Committee's *A Bill of Rights for a New South Africa* (1990) reads: 'The 1910 Constitution of South Africa gave no rights to the majority of the people.' The ANC's *What is a Constitution?* opens with Oliver Tambo's words: 'The South African Constitution excludes the blacks.' Cf. also Sachs n. 10 above at 194: 'At the centre of apartheid lies the destruction of African independence and the usurpation of African land'.

the 'Great Dispossession', the Land Act of 1913, which reserved most of the land in the Union for whites. A story based on the themes of the 'Great Exclusion' and the 'Great Dispossession' must be different from one based on the 'Great Mistake' and the 'Lost Opportunity'. Its continuation into the future must involve not just tinkering with judicial mechanisms, but the establishing of an entirely new legitimacy. For the different narratives ordain quite distinct sources of legal rights. In one, legitimate rights derive from the existing system of law, and must be defended by law. For the other, legitimate rights lie outside the existing legal system, (in the words of the *Freedom Charter*, 'our people have been robbed of their birthright to land, liberty and peace by a form of Government founded on injustice and inequality'), and can only be restored by going beyond it. In addition, the consummate feature of the story of the 1950s is quite different. It is not one of the Appellate Division's 'Glorious Moment', but that of the *Freedom Charter*, seen as the foundational declaration of rights.

There were also some quite different overarching political narratives. One is that of the continuing anti-Colonial revolution and in this narrative South Africa was the last country in Africa in which national liberation was yet to be achieved. The other is that of the 'Revolution', by which the fabulous mutant dragon capitalism/apartheid is slain. Recently the rhetoric of the latter narrative trajectory has been muted, especially in international fora, but it remains an important part of the ideology of elements of the leadership of the African National Congress ('ANC'), and still forms a major part of the popular politics and rhetoric of the liberation movement.

The ANC's *Working Document*, published in 1990, therefore presented a different sourcing of rights and a different purpose for a Bill of Rights. Rights were not found to be inherent in South African common law or European natural law, and nor were definitions simply available to be borrowed from existing formulations, such as that of the Federal Republic of Germany. A democratic Constitution, said the ANC's *What is a Constitution?* 'is a product of struggle'.[68] The specific nature and content of the South African struggle had to, therefore, result in a specific document, rather than the borrowing of a universal one. Nevertheless, universality was acknowledged as one of the sources, though the point was made that this source had hitherto been specifically rejected by South African law.[69] The Bill of Rights, said *What is a Constitution?*, 'will be a means of incorporating these universal rights and freedoms into the law of South Africa . . . They should be adapted to the South African situation with a view to dealing with the special forms of

[68] ANC, *What is a Constitution?* at 5.

[69] *What is a Constitution?* noted that South Africa refused to accept the Universal Declaration of Human Rights of 1948, and has not ratified other international instruments. Other external sources acknowledged were the International Covenant on Civil and Political Rights, and on Economic, Social and Cultural Rights (1966); the European Convention of Human Rights; and the African Charter of Human and People's Rights: ANC, *Working Document* (1990), iii–iv.

oppression [of] apartheid . . .'.[70] Or, in the words of the *Working Document*, 'a Bill of Rights becomes the fundamental anti-apartheid document'.[71] Coming from outside of South African law such rights could not be normalized within the South African system by the same Courts and the same judges that had ignored them.

There was also a vital local source of rights but it was not the Roman-Dutch law but the *Freedom Charter*, hitherto censored and suppressed, and in no way a part of the existing legal tradition. '*The Freedom Charter* . . . is the great source of any Bill of Rights in our country.'[72] The history of the adoption of the Charter was linked with the emphasis on political struggle as a part of the creation of the Bill of Rights. 'It is not the Constitution which creates the rights . . . the rights . . . have been gained in struggle, struggle by the people of South Africa and struggle by people the world over.'[73]

The Government's Law Commission had aimed at the least politicized and the most legalistic model of a Bill of Rights. They were not attracted to the inspirational style and wide open wording of the American Bill of Rights, favouring the detailed and closely worded German model. The Law Commission had envisaged that such a document would be construed accord-ing to the usual (literal and constrictive) rules of statutory interpretation by the ordinary Supreme Court. The ANC's preference, however, was for the most politicized solution. First, they favoured a widely worded document:

We have aimed at open and accessible language. This is in the tradition of the first great modern Bill of Rights, namely that contained in the Amendments to the American Constitution . . . in our view, a Bill of Rights should set out general principles . . . Moreover, it terms should be such that any person can understand them.[74]

But in spite of, or perhaps because of, its apparent clarity, interpretation could not be left to an ordinary Court. The ANC's solution was to choose nei-ther the American combination of an openly worded document interpreted by the ordinary Courts; nor the German solution of the closely worded docu-ment, interpreted by a special constitutional Court. They proposed the highly politicized combination of an openly worded document, and a special Court, as well as a Human Rights Commission to promote observance; monitor leg-islation; receive complaints; and bring cases.[75] While the Law Commission had worked hard to produce proposals for a Bill of Rights which would be a legal shield behind which white South Africa would be protected from politi-cal change, the ANC's response was to conceive of the Bill as a political weapon.

Both the Law Commission's and the ANC's proposals were attempts to write an indefeasible policy strategy into an immutable rights document, in an effort to place the fundamental directions of policy beyond political

[70] Ibid. at 9.   [71] Ibid. at iii.   [72] Ibid. at iv.   [73] Ibid. at iii.
[74] Ibid. at vi.   [75] Ibid. at vi, 34–5.

questioning. The *Working Document* rejected the Law Commission's legalist view that social, economic and educational rights should not appear in a Bill of Rights since they were not enforceable against the State by the Courts.

Our approach has been to identify certain needs as being so basic as to constitute the foundation of human rights claims, namely, the rights to nutrition, education, health, shelter, employment, and a minimum income . . . responding to the social indignities and inequalities created as a direct result of State policies under apartheid. The strategy proposed for achieving the realisation of these rights is to acknowledge them as basic human rights, and require the State to devote maximum available resources to their progressive materialisation.

In particular the document envisages the State establishing a minimum of enforceable statutory rights in relation to each area. Thus, with regard to nutrition, there can be the compulsory furnishing of a minimum diet to children; in the case of education for all, free and compulsory primary education, and a duty on local authorities to provide access to literacy classes; in respect of shelter there could be the duty to furnish electricity or other forms of energy and as well access to clean water for every home . . .[76]

These concerns were far from the world of the Law Commission, whose referents were natural law, Calvinism, State security, property rights, and comparative constitutions.

Article 10 of the ANC's proposal, which dealt with social, educational, economic and welfare rights, directed the State to use its resources to achieve these rights with a 'progressively expanding floor of enforceable minimum rights guaranteed by law'. And it was envisaged that the Bill of Rights would provide a foundational legal authorization for the ironing out of differences between white areas and others. 'In order to achieve a common floor of rights for the whole country, resources may be directed from the richer to the poorer areas . . .'.[77] This principle of enshrining the right to restitution was pursued in other Articles. Article 11 on the economy, land and property read: 'The State may by legislation take steps to overcome the effects of past statutory discrimination in relation to the enjoyment of property rights'. Persons could be deprived of property on the grounds of public interest 'including the achievement of the objectives of the Constitution'. Compensation would take into account 'the need to establish an equitable balance between the public interest and the interest of those affected'.[78]

Article 13 on 'Affirmative Action' was yet more sweeping.

1. Nothing in the Constitution shall prevent the enactment of legislation, or the adoption by any public or private body of special measures of a positive kind designed to procure the advancement and the opening up of opportunities, including access to education, skills, employment and land, and the general advancement in social, economic

---

[76] ANC, *Working Document* (1990), iii–iv at ix–x.   [77] Ibid. at 10(4).
[78] Ibid. at 11(5), (7), (9).

and cultural spheres, of men and women who in the past have been disadvantaged by discrimination.
2. No provision in the Bill of Rights shall be construed as derogating from or limiting in any way the provisions of this article.

On the ANC side there was sensitivity to the question of the placing of a political agenda in the Bill of Rights. Such a Bill, wrote Sachs, a leading ANC constitutional lawyer, could not resolve in advance all the fundamental political problems of the country, and it was:

certainly not the function of a Bill of Rights to foreclose public discussion and choice in relation to major social and economic issues . . . It is, thus, important to distinguish constitutional from electoral issues . . . the redress of structural inequalities resulting from past discrimination are constitutional, not electoral, questions, whereas the debate on . . . privatisation or nationalisation, are electoral and not constitutional ones.[79]

The Law Commission's Bill of Rights proposals, however, reversed these categories: to them affirmative action was an electoral matter; while property rights were fundamental to the Constitution.

Further Versions: A Widening Gap

In August of 1991 the Government's Law Commission produced a second huge volume, in which it responded to public debate and comments on its first report, and produced another version of its Bill of Rights.[80] It committed itself firmly to a different indigenous narrative origin for a Bill of Rights, which it continued to source in the natural law tradition of South African common law, the Free State Constitution of 1854, the *Freedom Charter*, and the homeland constitutions. Its continuing preoccupation with these questions indicates that the Law Commission was still largely addressing the divisions within the Afrikaner elite and reassuring them about a constitutional leap into the dark. For this audience they had a new narrative to emphasize which reversed the justification for apartheid, and placed the Bill of Rights debate into the whole story of human existence. In the old Afrikaner story the struggle for apartheid had been represented as the struggle of a 2000-year-old European civilization against the forces of barbarism. Western civilization, religion, and traditions used to be avidly ransacked for justifications of apartheid. In the new narrative all of civilization itself evolved towards the refinement of the human rights ideal. The theme was still civilization versus barbarism and chaos, but now civilization was represented by a definition of rights. This kind of story-telling again enabled the Law Commission to ignore

[79] Sachs n. 10 above at 33.
[80] South African Law Commission, *Group and Human Rights* (1991).

completely the recent history of political struggle in South Africa, and to place the rights debate outside of the struggle between one political order and another. This was a sharp reaction to the tone and content of the ANC's proposals, the language and content of which reflected, as we have seen, the struggle for and achievement of a sharp political change.[81] The Law Commission, on the other hand, sought to present rights in terms of an international moral, scientific and legal discourse, positivized and a-political. Human rights, the Law Commission asserted, in a brusque reaction to the ANC's view, must not be confused with human needs. Needs did not automatically or inherently become rights.[82] Rights did not exist outside of State law, but were actualized by it. This meant that the State decided what were rights and what were not.[83]

The tone of the Law Commission's second report was one of caustic criticism of both the general approach and the specifics of the ANC's draft. There was a clear difference in approach between the view that a Bill of Rights was an instrument which limited State power, and one which saw it as a document which mandated a series of actions which the State had to pursue. The Law Commission invoked the warning of a leading 'liberal' judge, Didcott J., that a Bill of Rights was 'not a political manifesto' and that it said what could not be done, not what should be done.[84] There were belligerent dissents on the questions of affirmative action and property rights. The Law Commission cautioned that experience of affirmative action world-wide had shown that 'it often gave rise to deep divisions within society'. More pointedly they criticized the ANC's document for aiming at reverse discrimination and the redistribution of wealth. They warned, in language markedly different from that which had characterized the debate so far, that attempts to lend juridical respectability to nationalization and redistribution under the banner of affirmative action 'will in all probability be opposed with force'.[85] They noted also that the ANC left very little scope for private education. 'If this is the intention, serious resistance and unrest can be expected.'[86]

The language reflected the change in the Law Commission's position. No longer was it the brave forerunner, introducing the concept of rights to white South Africa, and making noble concessions to the majority. By the time of the second report it was the defender of a concept of rights which had been sharply challenged. The pace of political change had quickened; violence in the country had increased; innocence about transition to a 'New Society' had

---

[81] The need for such a strategy becomes clearer when one remembers that the dominant Afrikaner narrative has long been that of the struggle for, and achievement of, national independence. This national story will now have to be submerged, as the Afrikaner nation becomes a national minority without a right of secession. To present the story of the new Constitution in terms of struggle, the Afrikaner intellectuals would have to write the story of their own defeat.

[82] South African Law Commission, *Group and Human Rights* (1991) at 30–1.

[83] Ibid. at 33. 'The Commission must emphasise that all needs and aspirations are negotiable, for the very reason that if needs and aspirations are to become enforceable rights must be legitimised by society and positivised by the legislature.' Ibid.

[84] Ibid. at 133.   [85] Ibid. at 302–3.   [86] Ibid. at 345.

dissipated; and political relationships between the negotiating partners had deteriorated. Broad agreement about the concept of a Bill of Rights was no longer at the centre of national debate as differences about the nature of the 'New Society' came into sharp focus. As the tide of accomodatory verbiage retreated, the original reefs were exposed. The Law Commission's first draft had enshrined the 'capacity to establish and maintain commercial undertakings, to procure property and means of production, to offer services against remuneration and to make a profit'. This had attracted harsh criticism from the Left on the grounds that no human right was involved, but rather a political entrenchment of capitalism for the future. This, responded the Law Commission, was not so. The proposed Article merely embodied common law rights and freedoms 'and it is purely coincidental if they are characteristic of a capitalist structure'.[87] The Law Commission castigated instead the provisions of the ANC's Bill on protection of property, compensation and mineral rights.[88] 'It will immediately be noted,' they wrote, 'that although lip service is paid to the concept of private property, this concept is undermined rather than respected.'[89] The ANC's Bill 'hardly disguises' the aim of nationalization without 'objectively testable norms for compensation'.[90] The ANC, the Law Commission asserted, wanted 'naked and arbitrary nationalization of private property . . . [the Commission] finds these provisions totally unacceptable and feels obliged to sound a serious warning against the introduction of such provisions in any proposed Bill of Rights, law or Constitution'.[91]

There were also some attempts to respond to the ANC's draft. The Law Commission retreated slightly from their earlier view that a Bill of Rights be applied by the existing Courts. They repeated the objection to a political Court and proposed a constitutional Court that would be one of two chambers of the existing Appellate Division. As such, all existing laws and procedures would apply to it. The Chief Justice would decide, when a case reached the Appellate Division, whether constitutional issues were raised. They accepted that this chamber would not only be composed of the present judges, and would not necessarily be drawn, like them, from the ranks of senior counsel.[92] They also accepted the suggestion that a Human Rights Commission be established, though in their view it would have only an advisory function, no testing function, and have no right to bring cases to the Courts.[93]

But the differences continued to be underlined. Their discussion of the

---

[87] Ibid. at 355.   [88] The most recent versions of these are outlined below.
[89] *Group and Human Rights* n. 82 above at 360.   [90] Ibid. at 362.
[91] Ibid. at 364.
[92] Ibid. at 446, 669. Cf. the ANC's proposal for the judiciary as a whole. 'Without interfering with its independence, and with a view to ensuring that justice is manifestly seen to be done in a non-racial way and that the wisdom, experience and judicial skills of all South Africans are represented on the bench, the judiciary shall be transformed in such a way as to consist of men and women drawn from all sectors of South African society.'
[93] Ibid. at 596.

application of a Bill of Rights to relationships between individuals noted that in the USA such matters were dealt with in the Civil Rights Acts, and did not come under the Bill of Rights. In Germany, they pointed out, the Bill of Rights did not operate between individuals, apart from its application in labour relations law to the protection of freedom of association.[94] And they continued to insist that second generation rights were not justiciable. These would, they said, 'prove to be juridically futile, and may plunge the country into a serious political crisis'.[95] The State, they maintained, must use all of the rights in the Bill as directive, and not just consider the social and economic rights to be guidelines for future legislative and administrative programs.[96]

While there had been fervid reaction in legal and political debate to the Law Commission's first report, there was virtually none to its second. The principle of the Bill of Rights having been conceded, its content was now a matter for negotiation between the political players, and not a question for lawyers alone. During 1992 a new draft of the ANC's proposals was prepared for its national policy conference. The style contrasted with that of the first version, its language being far more technical and legal. The differences between the proposals, and those of the Law Commission, were re-emphasized. There was an extended section on workers' rights. Within the movement it had been argued that far simpler provisions were to be preferred, and that complex ones would favour a legalization of industrial relations which would not necessarily be to the benefit of workers. The detailed draft, however, not only gave unusually wide protection and powers to unions, but mandated legislation about working environments, 'reasonable' pay and leave, and equal pay for work of equal value.

There were far more detailed sections on land and property rights, and on the enforcement of social and economic rights. These presented a strategy even further from that of the Law Commission. The Bill of Rights was not to protect against State action, but to ensure it. 'Legislation,' said the draft, 'shall ensure the creation of a progressively expanding floor of minimum rights in the social, educational, and welfare spheres for all in the country' (Article 10). A goal for national education was specified: 'strengthening respect for human rights.' The State would also be directed to establish a comprehensive national health service; and a detailed list of other welfare provisions such as pensions, family income benefits, superannuation, workers' compensation for injury, and unemployment benefits.

Article 11 was designed to satisfy the long-standing commitment in liberation politics to assert control over the country's mineral wealth, and, therefore, to strike fear into the heart of the established order. It also made plain to

[94] Ibid. at 489 et seq.
[95] *Group and Human Rights* n. 82 above at 664.
[96] This could, of course, pit liberty against planning, and immobilize a constitutional Court which would have to reconcile irreconcilable objectives.

militants that a 'Great Trade' would not necessarily be struck on the Government's terms. It asserted a sweeping claim by 'the people' to 'all the natural assets' of the country. Only 'appropriate compensation' would be payable 'in the event of any interference with any existing title, mining right or concession'. The nature of that compensation, which can be gleaned from the provisions on land rights, would not have been reassuring to shareholders, foreign or domestic. The new draft of Article 11 enshrined the most important demand of liberation, the reversal of the 'Great Dispossession'. 'Legislation shall provide', it read, for the creation of a tribunal which could adjudicate on land claims 'made on legal or equitable grounds . . .'. It would have the power to order the restoration of land to 'people dispossessed by forced removals . . .'. It would also have the power to award land to such claimants 'where there are special circumstances arising out of the occupation, use or other similar grounds, which make it equitable for such an award to be made'. The worst nightmare scenario of white South Africa's landowners was unfolding. Legislation was also to provide for access to land, with due regard to the financial resources of the State, 'to those historically deprived of land and land rights, or deprived of access to land by past statutory discrimination'. Defences for holders of existing title were flimsy. Legislation, the draft read, shall be based on the principle of achieving an equitable balance between the public interest, including the above objectives, and the interests of those whose existing title might be affected.

Any redistribution of land or interest in land required to achieve the above objectives shall be subject to compensation which shall be determined according to the principle of equitable balance between public interest and the interest of those whose existing titles might be affected.

Not only was there no priority given to existing rights, but no tangible principle of compensation, and instead, an obscure 'equitable balance'. And it would not be the Courts which would hear disputes, but a special tribunal.[97]

These matters were returned to in a separate section on property. Article 12 guaranteed the right to: 'undisturbed enjoyment of personal possessions, and, individually, in association or through lawfully constituted bodies, be entitled to acquire, hold or dispose of property, to take part in economic life, and to be rewarded for their work and initiative'. While avoiding the words 'means of production' and 'profit', this seemed to guarantee life in a capitalist system much as the Law Commission's draft had done. But there were qualifications. The 'taking of property' was to be permissible 'in the public interest, which shall include the achievement of the objectives of the Constitution'. It would be subject to compensation on the basis of 'equitable balance'.

[97] Provision was made for appeal to the Courts, but as such appeals from tribunals have, in South African practice, not reconsidered the substance of the case, this would have effectively excluded them from anything but jurisdictional and procedural issues and interpretations of points of law.

The document noted that it was unusual for Constitutions to contain reference to the principles governing economic life. But, as in case of the Law Commission, there was a felt need to address the issue. Article 12(7) provided for guiding principles of legislation on economic matters, among which was 'reducing inequality'. With an eye on the huge concentrations of capital which dominate the economic life of South Africa, reference was made to 'regulating or curtailing cartels or monopolies'.

On affirmative action, the 1992 draft ignored the Law Commission and firmed the ANC's stance. Any such action, it now declared 'shall not be deemed to contradict the principle of equal rights for all South Africans . . .'. The provision for 'achieving speedily the balanced structuring in non-racial form of the public service, defence and police forces and the prison service', was stripped of the potential to delay by adding (in that order) 'according to the principles of representativity, competence, impartiality and accountability'. The objections of the Law Commission to extending provisions to private organizations were ignored by repeating the provision that legislation could require 'non-Governmental organizations and private bodies' to adopt affirmative action principles. There were extensions also to the pro-active mechanisms. The Human Rights Commission, the notes to the new draft noted, was conceived of as having functions similar to the agencies in other Western countries which were established to secure compliance with anti-discrimination laws. The draft envisaged a role in helping to enforce the right to non-discrimination, investigating patterns of violation, and 'attempting conciliation and bringing proceedings in court . . .'. It would also have a role in the legislative process, monitoring proposed legislation and reporting to Parliament on the 'potential' impact on the realization of rights. And there was a new suggestion—a Social Rights Commission. Far from being impressed by the Law Commission's strictures on the impossibility of ensuring second generation rights, new ways of facilitation were envisaged. This body, it was explained, would not, like the Human Rights Commission, look at discrimination as such, but 'at the materialisation of social rights . . .'. The draft Bill directed the Courts to 'pay due regard to social, educational and welfare rights when considering the interpretation of Statutes, the validity of subordinate legislation and the reasonableness of administrative actions'. In a final sweeping provision Article 16(12) required that: 'Where justice and the achievement of the objectives of the Bill of Rights so require, the State or any private body or individual may be restrained by the Courts from doing anything which interferes with or reduces enjoyment of these rights or impedes their realisation.'

The Bill of Rights in the New Constitution: Sword or Shield?

By the middle of 1992 the prominence of the 'rights' debate, which served an important role while immediate change was not imminent, had given way to real, and far more difficult bargaining about the nature of the Constitution and the structures of power. The most difficult issues in the negotiations were the questions of regional powers, and the size of majorities required to make constitutional changes, not inconsonant rights instruments. It also became clear that the original strategy conceived by the Government of a Bill of Rights as a bulwark against change, had partly mutated into a weapon in the hands of its opponents. Nonetheless one of the questions that was decided, as a by-product of negotiating strategies, was *when* the Bill of Rights was to be drafted, whether it was to be a gift from the old order, or a manifesto of the new. The ANC envisaged a popularly elected constituent assembly which would draft South Africa's new Constitution, while the National Party Government, reluctant to relinquish control over the drafting of a Constitution to an elected assembly, wanted a new Constitution in place before democratic elections took place. In the face of the rising political violence both sides took a step back from a perceived abyss. An agreement was reached on a two stage transition process. An 'interim' Constitution was to be adopted by the existing Parliament. It was envisioned that the new Parliament elected under its terms would sit for 5 years, and that it would act also as a constituent assembly which would draft the final Constitution.[98] Thus the Bill of Rights, like the new Constitution itself, was to be a part of the beginning of this 'interim' process, the product of a negotiation between apartheid and democracy. But there was a problem. A Bill of Rights of its very nature embodies claims to be something that is not 'interim' but fundamental. While the political leaderships gave their attention to the main negotiations about the political shape of the Constitution, the question of the wording of the rights instrument was handed over to a 'Technical Committee', with a brief to consider the rights provisions necessary for the period of transition, especially those needed to hold elections. Once they embarked on a statement of rights for the transitional period, it quickly grew into a long and detailed document, on the grounds that rights could not be limited and transitional. In this, to some extent, the work that had gone into the drafting of the policies of the two main sides was ignored, but in the main, like much of the Constitution itself, the outcome represented an attempt to cobble together conflicting positions.

In both the style of drafting and the modes of enforcing the Bill of Rights the compromises are immediately evident. Chapter 3 of the interim Constitution, which contains the Bill of Rights, reads like a conventional

---

[98] See Friedman, *The Long Journey: South Africa's Quest for a Negotiated Settlement* (1993) and the Constitution of the Republic of South Africa, Act No. 200 of 1993.

rights instrument, with the broad aspirational and prescriptive policy Sections of the earlier ANC drafts absent. Some have been displaced and appear elsewhere in the Constitution.[99] Section 98 of the Constitution creates a new constitutional Court, with a President and members serving for a non-renewable period of 7 years. The Court is to have jurisdiction over all alleged violations of the Bill of Rights, and has been given the power to enquire into 'the constitutionality of any law, including an Act of Parliament, irrespective of whether such law was passed or made before or after the commencement of this Constitution' (Section 98(2)(c)). Only four of the eleven judges of the new Court were to come from the existing Supreme Court bench.

The original National Party strategy of protecting group rights in a Bill of Rights had finally disappeared. Schedule 4 of the Constitution encodes a declaration of 'Constitutional Principles'. Among them is:

Xll Collective rights of self-determination in forming, joining, and maintaining organs of civil society, including linguistic, cultural and religious associations shall, on the basis of non-discrimination and free association, be recognised and protected.

The contentious and emotional question of education was provided for in Section 32(3) which gave the right: 'to establish, where practicable, educational institutions based on a common culture, language or religion, provided that there shall be no discrimination on the ground of race.'[100]

Inasmuch as the group right issue was one of major importance to the former Government, much can be learned from this shrunken provision. What had happened was that the attempt to provide for minority protection within majority rule had been transposed to the political arena, and fought primarily on the basis of regional autonomy for the provinces, special majorities for constitutional change, (and also through the creation of an interim Government of National Unity). On this issue it seems that there was a realization that the better protection lay in politics rather than in law.

In relation to the disputed entrenchment of capitalism, the agreed text contained a section on 'Economic activity' (Section 26). It read:

(1) Every person shall have the right freely to engage in economic activity and to pursue a livelihood anywhere in the national territory.
(2) Subsection (1) shall not preclude measures designed to promote the protection or improvement of the quality of life, economic growth, human development, social justice, basic conditions of employment, fair labour practices or equal opportunity for all,

[99] See especially Chapter 8, which provides for a Human Rights Commission, a Commission on Gender Equality and for the Restitution of Land Rights, and Schedule 4, the Declaration of Constitutional Principles.

[100] Ironically, given the argument of the first Law Commission report that a group right would be unenforceable at law because of lack of locus standi, the first section of the Bill of Rights, (Section 7(4)(b) of the Constitution), gives the right to apply for relief to associations, and to people acting as a member of a group or class, and to a person acting for others.

provided such measures are justified in an open and democratic society based on freedom and equality.

Specific mention of the 'right to profit' had disappeared, but so had the references to curtailing monopolies and cartels, and the specific mention of
reducing inequality. But, as the politics of transition had made increasingly
clear, an assault on capitalism was no longer a real or immediate part of
the political agenda. The pledges of fiscal and economic 'responsibility', made
for international consumption, underlined the understanding of both
Government and ANC leaderships that the socialist narrative was to be without an ending. Both property in general, and a market economy and the right
to profit were now offered real protection by the new South Africa's need for
international acceptance and approval by the world capitalist economy and its
controllers of loans and investments.

The text agreed on in relation to property, which was the very last on which
consensus was reached, finally read:

28 (1) Every person shall have the right to acquire and hold rights in property and, to
the extent that the nature of the rights permits, to dispose of such rights.
(2)   No deprivation of any rights in property shall be permitted otherwise than in
accordance with a law.
(3)   Where any rights in property are expropriated pursuant to a law referred to in
subsection (2), such expropriation shall be permissible for public purposes only and
shall be subject to the payment of agreed compensation or, failing agreement, to the
payment of such compensation and within such period as may be determined by a
Court of law as just and equitable, taking into account all relevant factors, including,
in the case of the determination of compensation, the use to which the property is
being put, the history of its acquisition, its market value, the value of investments in it
by those affected and the interests of those affected.[101]

The earlier versions had been focused on sharply differing versions of protection of economic rights and property, but the important elements of the
symbolic in these differences needs some comment. Only a small proportion
of white South Africans held land that was threatened. The 'property' held by
the National Party's main constituency was in jobs in the huge public service,
and in pension rights. These interests were protected in other parts of the
Constitution.[102] It may also be argued that return of the land, while

[101] There is no mention of market value, nor of protection from confiscatory taxation. A 'court
of law' is to determine compensation.
[102] See Chapter 13 'Public Service Commission and Public Service'. Under s. 212, the
Constitution provides for a public service 'broadly representative of the South African community'; see s. 212(2)(b). Appointments are to be made according to 'qualifications, level of training,
merit, efficiency and suitability' but these are not to preclude the objectives in the above subsection; see s. 212(4) and 212(5). These provision apply also to the Defence Forces. Continuity of
employment and conditions are provided for in ss. 236 and 237.
    The second section of the Bill of Rights (s. 8 of the interim Constitution) provides extensive
guarantees of equality and freedom from discrimination. Section 8(3)(a) reads: 'This section shall

immensely important to the reversal of the 'Great Dispossession', was not the main economic interest of the ANC's constituency whose aspirations centred around housing, employment and education rather than peasant farming. (The Pan Africanist Congress, which campaigned most strongly on the issue of the return of the land, was spectacularly unsuccessful in the election). Thus, as in the case of the right to economic activity, once the debates about a Bill of Rights were connected to the world of politics and economics, some of the differences seemed less irreconcilable.

The question of the restitution of land found its place not in the Bill of Rights itself but in a separate chapter of the interim Constitution (Sections 121–3). These mandate Parliament to pass an Act dealing with restitution for dispossession under any law inconsistent with the prohibition of racial discrimination, and, specifically refers to the 'Great Dispossession', by envisaging that restitution can take place if the dispossession took place under any law going back to the Land Act of 1913. Under Section 123(2) acquisition of land for restoration cannot take place unless it is just and equitable, taking into account 'the history of the dispossession, the hardship caused, the use to which the property is being put, the history of its acquisition by the owner, the interests of the owner and others affected by any expropriation, and the interests of the dispossessed'.

The original thinking of the National Party Government on a Bill of Rights assumed the continuation of the content and character of the common law. As such it was a limited program for legal change. The judicial use of a Bill of Rights would, in such conditions of continuity, be enmeshed with the authority of existing precedents. As the South African Law Commission remarked, if a Bill of Rights was 'law', it would operate 'within recognised, familiar, juridical norms'[103] tamed by the existing legal system.[104] While a myriad of complexities will present themselves to the judges, on the level of the text of the Bill of Rights this aspiration seems to have been defeated. Section 7(2) in the interim Constitution appears to aim at taming the common law and preventing a continuation of possibly inimical doctrines of Roman-Dutch law by apparently subjecting the common law to the Bill of Rights. 'This chapter shall apply to all law in force and all administrative decisions taken . . .'. Under Section 33 no rule of common law, as well as no Statute, can limit rights entrenched in the Bill of Rights. The attempt to thwart continuity of judge-made law goes further than the rights actually enunciated. Under Section 35(3) in both the interpretation of Statutes and the 'development of common law and customary law, a Court shall have due regard to the spirit, purport

not preclude measures designed to achieve the adequate protection and advancement of persons and groups or categories of persons disadvantaged by unfair discrimination, in order to enable their full and equal enjoyment of all rights and freedoms'.

[103] *Group and Human Rights* n. 82 above at 103.   [104] Ibid. at 384.

and objects' of the Bill of Rights. In relation to the interpretation of the rights instrument itself, Section 35(1) provides that Courts:

shall promote the values which underlie an open and democratic society based on freedom and equality and shall, where applicable, have regard to public international law applicable to the protection of the rights entrenched in this Chapter, and may have regard to comparable foreign case law.

If this injunction is part of the 'spirit, purport and objects' of the Bill of Rights, it opens the way for an extensive 'foreign' based development of South African common law. (In addition Section 115 of the Constitution establishes a Human Rights Commission which will monitor amongst other matters, whether proposed laws are in breach of the Bill of Rights, or of 'norms of international law').[105]

Finally the text of the Constitution indicates the birth of a new narrative, that of the 'Great Reconciliation'. Few observers have failed to be astonished at the apparent achievement of a peaceful transition after so many years of violence. This is recognised in the statement that appears after the last section of the Constitution which is headed 'National Unity and Reconciliation'. The past is repudiated with a sweeping and emotive firmness (in spite of the evident continuity of structures and personnel). The Section begins:

This Constitution provides a historic bridge between the past of a deeply divided society characterised by strife, conflict, untold suffering, and injustice, and a future founded on the recognition of human rights, democracy and peaceful co-existence and development of opportunities for all South Africans . . .
    The pursuit of national unity . . . require[s] reconciliation . . .

The past is characterized as one which:

generated gross violations of human rights, the transgression of humanitarian principles in violent conflicts and a legacy of hatred, fear guilt and revenge . . . [This] can now be addressed on the basis that there is a need for understanding but not for vengeance, a need for reparation but not for retaliation, a need for ubuntu[106] but not for victimisation . . .
    In order to advance such reconciliation . . . amnesty shall be granted in respect of acts, omissions and offences associated with political objectives and committed in the course of the conflicts of the past.

We might at this point raise again the opening questions. To return to Ricoeur, does the narrative of reconciliation constitute a plot in which goals

---

[105] An issue of major importance which the constitutional Court will have to decide is whether the Bill of Rights applies only to the public sector—to acts of Government and Government agencies or to the whole of the private sector as well.

[106] Humanity—it is of considerable symbolical importance that this word is not translated in the Constitution. However, one might note in this context that together with the Law Commission's choice not to translate the phrase 'rule of law', (see n. 32 above) it serves to remind us of the great difficulty which different groups in South Africa have in translating their most basic concepts to each other.

and causes are brought together? What is 'the image that already exists?' Can the narrative of reconciliation perform Cover's task of locating and giving meaning to the Constitution?[107]

While the language of the new narrative stresses the coming together of the opposing old ones in reconciliation, the institutional arrangements of the new Constitution reflect to a considerable degree the two sitting side by side. Quite legitimately, mutual mistrust is an underlying narrative of the new constitutional arrangements even if it is hard to affirm this in a ringing declaration. Indeed, though the Bill of Rights encodes a narrative of mistrust as much as one of reconciliation, it seems likely that, unlike the Constitution, the Bill of Rights will not be an interim one. Such an idea, especially as the new Court will be developing a new rights jurisprudence based on the 'interim' Bill, seems odd, as it would highlight the relative and transient nature of what was otherwise masquerading as a statement of rights fundamental to South Africa's, indeed humanity's, political arrangements.[108]

In Conclusion

In May 1994 South Africa held its first democratic elections, and it has, for the first time, a Government representative of the majority of its people, elected on a non-racial franchise. At the time of writing, the constitutional Court created by the Constitution has yet to be formed, and therefore, the text of the new Bill of Rights has accreted no meanings. A host of excited rights lawyers waits to scrutinize its interpretations which will quickly become a part of the world of political strife and dispute.[109]

The skills and the political will which produced the interim Constitution have been more than admirable. But there must be questions about how far a Bill of Rights addresses the human rights needs of the post-apartheid situation. In South Africa the agenda for real material redress of the millions in poverty is vast and urgent, social dislocation is profound, there are grave

---

[107] See the discussion on p. 343.

[108] The second of the constitutional principles in Schedule 4 provides that: 'Everyone shall enjoy all universally accepted fundamental rights, freedoms and civil liberties which shall be provided for and protected by entrenched and justiciable provisions of the Constitution, which shall be drafted after having given due consideration to inter alia the fundamental rights contained in Chapter 3 of this Constitution. Under Section 71 the new Constitution to be drafted must comply with the Constitutional Principles, and this compliance must be certified by the constitutional court. Amendment or repeal of the constitutional principles by the present parliament is absolutely forbidden under Section 74'.

[109] The preamble to of the interim Constitution affirms that 'there is a need to create a new order in . . . a . . . democratic constitutional state'. The extent to which the new democracy will be willing to accept the limitations which can be imposed by judicial review—to give primacy to constitutionalism—may be an underlying consideration. The lesson for the Appellate Division in the 1950s still remains. The constitutional Court may not be able to withstand a hostile Government. Its judges do not have judicial tenure.

threats to the political viability of the successor State, and severe economic limitations on transforming ambitions. Yet one does not criticize a flautist for failing to address the problem of the balance of payments. It is legitimate for lawyers to debate and to construct legal mechanisms. It is a feature of law in general, however, that the universality of its language in relation to any given area tends often to obscure the limitations of its reach, and its contingent and tangential effects on the realms of action it appears to control. This is even more the case with rights declarations which appear to bring under control, and within reach, the entire area of just Government, liberty, and fairness of distribution of resources, opportunities and powers. But they do not do this, even when often and creatively used and frequently invoked. This is not the beginning of an argument which claims that such declarations have little value. Some do, and some do not. Nor is it to argue that their chief value is symbolic, or that the issues purported to be dealt with are in any case outside of the legal realm. The points are raised in order to rescue some of the submerged parts of the story. If apartheid is to be undone by a centralized State with a determined Government working to a definite agenda, the bureaucracy will be large and energetic, with much power delegated to it and with many tasks to perform. One might well wonder what degree of protection can be derived in these circumstances from a Bill of Rights administered by an Appellate Court. South Africa will be restructured (as apartheid was made) by administrators. Few cases will be heard by the constitutional Court and its rulings will be remote from the myriad instances of exercise of power on the frontier between State and citizen. Real protection may depend more on reform of the administrative law which is of necessity more attuned to the details of administrative processes and discretionary decision-making. There is some recognition of this (and an echo of the appalling record of the apartheid bureaucracy) in Section 24 of the Bill of Rights, which provides for a right to 'lawful' and 'procedurally fair administrative action' and to reasons for administrative decisions.[110]

It is a striking feature of the Constitution-making process how much the negotiators drew on comparative and international law. The high input of such legal scholarship is a sign that the document is nobody's manifesto and that its wording does not emerge from the internal political struggles and experience or the national political culture in the way that the American Bill of Rights, or the Declaration of the Rights of Man can be said to have done.[111] On the other hand, given the proliferation of and globalization of rights instruments, it is becoming hard to conceive of distinctiveness in either wording or provision. The Bill of Rights, therefore, is unimaginable outside of the

[110] In addition Chapter 8 of the interim Constitution provides for the creation of an office of Public Protector who is empowered (s. 112) to investigate maladministration and abuse of power.

[111] The protection, for example, against discrimination on the basis of sexual orientation, has no roots in South African political struggles.

international human rights movement, from its rhetorical responses and mobilizations in the early cold war period, through its harnessing to a materialist agenda, and to its renaissance in the West in the era of the rise of the market and the retreat of the State. The current strength of rights jurisprudence in the Western world is connected to the weakening of the welfare State model. In place of a politics in which rights of substance were supposed to be delivered through the political process, rights jurisprudence is premised on the possibility of re-situating important allocatory decisions. No longer a part of the constant bargaining and struggle of the political arena, decisions about who is entitled to what are in the rights-governed future conceived not only as depoliticized, but rendered according to a set of principles which is virtually unchangeable.

While a demand for 'human rights' might well be a part of the political program of a revolutionary movement, a call for a Bill of Rights can also be attractive to those who would limit a human rights agenda. The shared diction can be a facade behind which there are sharply differing goals. One must also think about what the adoption of a Bill of Rights in South Africa signifies. Rarely can so wide a range of meanings have been offered to so many different audiences. To an international audience of capitalist States it would appear to tie the State which emerged from the South African nightmare to a politics which would be legitimate in terms of the international political economy. To the fearful internally, it would offer defences; to the liberals, civil liberties; to the revolutionary, an embodiment of aspirations. To state this is not to dismiss it cynically. It explains why it can be a legitimate symbolic focus in the current situation. But it also warns of the risks. In a long and conflict-ridden post-transition period Governments will fail, and will be seen to fail, to meet the categorical promises and standards in the Constitution, with consequent effects on legitimacy and international image. Nor will it solve the problem of the *rate* of substantial change.[112] South African lawyers have long professed fear of the perils of politicizing law. Politicians should be as alive to the dangers of legalizing politics.

Lawyers on both sides in South Africa also drew heavily on the formulations and juridical experiences of other countries with similar backgrounds in public law, in particular Britain, Canada, Australia and the USA. But while there are emotive divisions in these countries, and vehement litigation about rights, there are not the fundamental differences about the nature and direction of society, nor the prospect of years of contested legitimacy and political instability. The experience of other Western countries has little to tell us about the fate of a rights instrument introduced to mediate political transition in a revolutionary situation. Nor is the history of the attempts to develop a

---

[112] We need only recall the years of struggle and litigation which followed the phrase 'with all deliberate speed' used in the school desegregation case *Brown* v. *Board of Education* (*Brown II*), 349 US 294 (1954). See Kluger, *Simple Justice* (1976).

constitutional order in post-Colonial societies encouraging. One of the few areas of real consensus in the opposing versions was that both envisaged, and made provision for, the declaration of States of Emergency, and detention without trial, and these are contained in the enacted version.[113] It may be that the hypothesis of rights discourses, that law can be placed beyond politics, will be cruelly exposed in South Africa in the coming years. But it is also likely that the alignment of South African law with international rights discourses, and international rights instruments, will have significant effects on legal practice within the country. What is not clear is which vision of the future will benefit most from this.

Despite the final constitutional exhortation about reconciliation, *politics* seems likely to reproduce the narratives of the years prior to reconciliation. There will be increasing demand to tell more of the socialist story, and the recently submerged narratives of race and ethnicity will continue to be a part, officially or unofficially, of a highly racialized and ethnically conscious society. Maintaining order will be an overriding preoccupation. However the constitutional Court interprets the Bill of Rights, its liberal framework may not fit easily into what has so far been an a-liberal polity.

---

[113] See s. 34. The elaborate provisions for protection of rights in such eventualities are a powerful renunciation of the former Government's National Security Act. But they are also a sign that both sides expect that such powers might well be used.

IV
The Judiciary and Bills of Rights

11

The Impact of a Bill of Rights on the Role of the Judiciary: A Canadian Perspective

ROBERT J. SHARPE

Introduction

The amendment of the Canadian Constitution in 1982 to include the Charter of Rights and Freedoms brought about a fundamental change to Canadian law and politics. Many important public issues formerly within the exclusive preserve of legislative authority are now subject to judicial review. Constitutional litigation has become an important tool used by interest groups to advance their political ends. Canadian courts now play a central role in deciding how the law should deal with such intractable issues as abortion,[1] mandatory retirement,[2] the legitimacy of laws restricting pornography[3] and hate propaganda,[4] and the definition of what may properly constitute a criminal offence.[5] The questions put to the courts in Charter cases range far beyond what was seen as appropriate to the judicial function before 1982 and this addition to the Canadian Constitution has unquestionably had a profound impact upon the role of the judiciary. Before 1982, the Supreme Court of Canada was to most Canadians a remote institution that had little, if any, real impact upon their lives. Within 10 years it had been recognized as a seat of great power and influence and had become the subject of much public attention.

Media attention to legal issues has increased significantly and this is undoubtedly attributable in large part to the Charter. Decisions of the courts are routinely front page news. The Supreme Court of Canada has developed a media relations policy designed to ensure that its judgments are adequately reported and the Canadian Judicial Council has suggested that provincial superior and appellate courts do the same.[6] Some judges have taken the view that they should become more visible and vocal. Interviews and profiles of

---

[1] *R.* v. *Morgentaler* (1988) 44 DLR (4th) 385.
[2] *McKinney* v. *University of Guelph* (1990) 76 DLR (4th) 545; *Stoffman* v. *Vancouver General Hospital* [1990] 3 SCR 483, (1990) 76 DLR (4th) 700.
[3] *R.* v. *Butler* [1992] 1 SCR 452, (1992) 70 CCC (3d) 1.
[4] *R.* v. *Keegstra* [1990] 3 SCR 697, (1990) 61 CCC (3d) 1.
[5] *R.* v. *Vaillancourt* [1987] 2 SCR 636, (1987) 47 DLR (4th) 399.
[6] See Sharpe, 'The Role of a Media Spokesperson for the Courts—The Supreme Court of Canada Experience', 1 *MCLR* (1991) 271.

judges in the daily news media are not uncommon as reporters try to demys-
tify the judicial process and explain it in terms the ordinary citizen can understand. Judges also contribute to scholarly journals, discussing their changed
role under the Charter.[7]

Appointments to the Supreme Court are now followed closely. To date, the
procedure for appointing Supreme Court judges has not changed. These
appointments are made by the Prime Minister after informal and private consultation with the Minister of Justice, provincial Attorneys-General and leading members of the bench and bar. Despite a distaste for the unsavoury
aspects of the American confirmation process, there has been increasing pressure to make more public the entire judicial appointments process. This seems
inevitable given the significant powers accorded our judges.[8] Governments
have also come under increasing pressure to appoint more women and members of cultural and ethnic minorities to the bench. While partly caused by the
pressures created by changing demographics and social attitudes, there can be
little doubt that the enhanced power of the courts in the Charter era has been
an important influence in this development.

The Charter has, then, had a major impact upon the role and profile of the
judiciary in Canada. In this Chapter, I will attempt to provide a survey of the
manner in which the Canadian courts have come to terms with a constitutionally entrenched Bill of Rights. I will argue that while the Charter has
changed the role of the judiciary and the courts have not hesitated to wield the
power of judicial review in some areas, the judges have also been mindful of
the inherent limits of adjudication. I will also argue that the Canadian experience to date suggests that an entrenched Bill of Rights enhances rather that
detracts from fundamental democratic values.[9]

At the outset I will put the Charter in its historical context. Next, I will
examine the nature of the judicial role in interpreting its scope and the
rights and freedoms it guarantees. I will then describe the reconciliation or
balancing of Charter rights with the broader social interest through proportionality review under Section 1. Finally, I will provide an assessment of the

---

[7] Justice McLachlin, a former academic, has been particularly active in this regard. See e.g.
McLachlin, 'The Role of the Court in the Post-Charter Era: Policy-Maker of Adjudicator?', 39
UNBLJ (1990) 43; McLachlin, 'The Charter of Rights and Freedoms: A Judicial Perspective', 23
UBCLR (1989) 579; McLachlin, 'The Charter: A New Role for the Judiciary', 29 Alta. LR (1991)
540; McLachlin, 'The Canadian Charter and the Democratic Process', 18 MULR (1991) 350.

[8] Appointments to the provincial superior Courts are now made after candidates have been
privately reviewed by committees of senior judges and lawyers and in some provinces, appointments to the provincial Bench are made after a similar process which involves lay participation.
For discussion, see Ontario Law Reform Commission, *Appointing Judges: Philosophy, Politics
and Practice* (1991).

[9] In writing this Chapter, I have drawn upon my previous articles 'Judicial Development of
Principles in Applying the Charter', in Finkelstein and Rogers eds., *Charter Issues in Civil Cases*
(1988), ch. 1; 'A Comment on David Beatty's 'A Conservative's Court: The Politicization of Law'',
41 UTLJ (1991) 469; and a paper delivered at the University of Padua in 1991.

relationship between Charter review as elaborated by the Courts and fundamental democratic values.

Nature of the Pre-1982 Canadian Constitution

PARLIAMENTARY DEMOCRACY AND FEDERALISM

Before 1982, there were two central features of the Canadian Constitution. By
entrenching fundamental rights and freedoms, Canadians added a third. The
first essential feature of our Constitution is that Canada is founded upon the
principles of British Parliamentary democracy. These principles do not form
part of the written Constitution, but are to be found in conventions, traditions
and practices that evolved over time and which continue to govern the structure of Canadian Government.

The second fundamental element of the Canadian Constitution is federalism and the division of powers between the Parliament of Canada and the ten
provincial legislatures. This division of powers is contained in Canada's original Constitution, the British North America Act 1867, now known as the
Constitution Act 1867. Canada is geographically, culturally and linguistically
diverse and the division of legislative power between a central national
Parliament and ten provincial Legislatures represents an attempt to accommodate that diversity.

While Canada's pre-1982 written Constitution was silent on the matter of
judicial review, the courts have routinely acted as the referee in deciding
whether legislative matters fall within federal or provincial jurisdiction, and
have invalidated those laws enacted without a proper constitutional basis. In
this respect, the Canadian Constitution, like that of Australia, departs from
the principles of British Parliamentary democracy. Canadian judges have
exercised the power of judicial review for over 100 years and have struck down
a significant number of statutes, both federal and provincial, on the grounds
of ultra vires. However, before 1982, the scope for judicial review was essentially limited to questions of legislative jurisdiction as between the provinces
and the federal Parliament.[10] That changed dramatically in 1982 with the
introduction of the third central feature of the Canadian Constitution, the
Charter of Rights and Freedoms.

PRE-CHARTER CIVIL LIBERTIES

Civil liberties were always an important feature of Canadian law even
before this important constitutional change, and judicial decisions played an

[10] The 1867 Constitution did contain certain language (Section 133) and minority religion
education (Section 93) rights.

important role in the protection of fundamental rights.[11] Many of our most important civil rights, such as habeas corpus and trial by jury, were the creations of the common law tradition. The courts also paid heed to underlying values, such as freedom of expression, when interpreting and applying statutes. However, the pre-1982 Constitution offered little possibility for the courts to strike down laws which violated fundamental rights. While the Supreme Court of Canada was often able to protect civil liberties values indirectly through federalism review,[12] the suggestion that there was an 'unwritten bill of rights' in the 1867 Constitution[13] protecting fundamental freedoms garnered little support.

Human rights codes played an important role in the protection of human rights before the Charter and continue to do so today. Human rights legislation in all provinces[14] and at the Federal level,[15] establishes an administrative apparatus to combat discrimination in both the public and private sectors. Human rights commissions have played an important role in the struggle against racism, sexism, and other forms of discrimination,[16] and will continue to play a significant role in light of the Charter's limited application to private action. Moreover, when interpreting and applying the equality guarantee of the Charter, the Courts have paid close heed to the jurisprudence developed by human rights commissions.[17]

While human rights legislation has been a success, another pre-Charter experiment in the statutory protection of fundamental freedoms was a disappointment. The 1960 Canadian Bill of Rights, an ordinary Act of Parliament, declared a list of important civil rights to be fundamental and provided that all laws should 'be so construed and applied so as not to abrogate, abridge or infringe' any of the rights or freedoms so declared.[18] This instrument suffered from two fundamental defects. First, it applied only to federal laws and did not reach the laws of the provinces. Secondly, as it was an ordinary Act of Parliament and not entrenched in the Constitution, the mandate it conferred upon the Courts to strike down laws that infringed protected freedoms was suspect. While the Bill of Rights acquired 'quasi-constitutional' status in the view of Laskin J.,[19] with one notable exception,[20] the courts did not consider that this enactment of the Parliament of Canada conferred upon the judiciary

[11] See Laskin, 'An Inquiry into the Diefenbaker Bill of Rights', 37 Can. Bar Rev. (1959) 77.
[12] See e.g. *Reference Re Alberta Statutes* [1938] SCR 100, (1938) 2 DLR 81 (freedom of expression); *Saumur* v. *Quebec* [1953] SCR 299, (1953) 4 DLR 641 (freedom of religion).
[13] *Switzman* v. *Elbling and Attorney-General (Quebec)* (1957) 7 DLR (2d) 337 at 371.
[14] See e.g. Human Rights Code, R.S.O. 1990, c. H–19.
[15] Canadian Human Rights Act, R.S.C. 1985, c. H–6.
[16] See Tarnopolsky, *Discrimination and the Law* (1985).
[17] This point is discussed by Eberts, 'The Canadian Charter of Rights and Freedoms: A Feminist Perspective on the First 10 Years', ch. 7 above.
[18] Section 2.
[19] *Hogan* v. *R.* [1975] 2 SCR 574, (1975) 48 DLR (3d) 427.
[20] *R.* v. *Drybones* [1970] SCR 282, (1970) 9 DLR (3d) 473.

the authority to invalidate duly enacted laws, and the rights and freedoms it declared were interpreted in a disappointingly narrow fashion.

The Bill of Rights experience was very much in the minds of the political actors who enacted the Charter. The courts were given a deliberate push away from the cautious and highly deferential posture they exhibited in the Bill of Rights case law. As the Supreme Court of Canada has observed,[21] the judges of Canada did not seek a mandate for judicial review: that choice was consciously and deliberately made by the political actors of the day.

Interpretation of Charter Rights and Freedoms

NATURE OF CHARTER RIGHTS

The Canadian Charter identifies and enshrines six broad categories of rights:

(1) the so-called 'fundamental freedoms' of conscience, religion, thought, belief, opinion, expression, assembly, and association;[22]
(2) democratic rights, including the right to vote, the guarantee of regular elections, and Parliamentary sessions;[23]
(3) mobility rights to enter and leave the country and the right to reside in and gain a livelihood in any province;[24]
(4) legal rights, particularly those pertaining to the criminal process such as the right against unreasonable search and seizure, habeas corpus, the right to counsel, to a trial within a reasonable time, and to be presumed innocent until proven guilty;[25]
(5) the right to equality before and under the law and to the equal protection and equal benefit of the law;[26] and
(6) language rights.[27]

This catalogue of rights and freedoms is essentially liberal in nature, defining a zone of autonomy for the individual within which the state may not intrude. This feature of the Charter has been the cause for concern on the part of those who fear that its emphasis upon traditional liberal values will have an Americanizing influence on the Canadian legal and political culture. The Charter probably has had something of an Americanizing influence, although it does reflect a view more receptive than found in the American Constitution to affirmative state measures designed to advance certain collective interests. For instance, 'affirmative action' measures that have as their object the amelioration of conditions of disadvantaged individuals or groups, are explicitly protected from scrutiny as denials of equality,[28] and provinces

---

[21] *Reference re Section 94(2) of the Motor Vehicle Act (B.C.)* (1985) 24 DLR (4th) 536 at 545.
[22] Section 2.   [23] Sections 3–5.   [24] Section 6.   [25] Sections 7–14.
[26] Section 15.   [27] Sections 16–23.   [28] Section 15(2).

are constitutionally obliged to provide facilities for minority language educa-tion.[29] More generally, Section 1 of the Charter, the 'reasonable limits' clause discussed in greater detail below, has been interpreted to accommodate affir-mative legislative measures designed to enhance the values underlying funda-mental rights and freedoms. American jurisprudence is frequently cited in Charter judgments, and while relevant and often persuasive, it is certainly not governing, given the differences in the Canadian and American political and legal traditions.[30]

ELABORATION OF CHARTER RIGHTS

The Canadian courts have adopted a two-step process of interpretation and justification to give the general language of the Charter concrete meaning. First, the courts interpret the meaning of the right or freedom at issue to determine whether the matter complained of constitutes an infringement. For the most part, at this first stage, narrow definitional limitations on rights that take into account the general social interest have been avoided. It has been held, for example, that commercial advertising,[31] hate propaganda,[32] and pornography[33] are, prima facie, forms of expression protected by Section 2(b). But at the same time, it has been recognized that rights are not absolute, par-ticularly when given such a wide and generous interpretation, and that the interests of society at large will require that rights be limited. That is left to the second step of justification pursuant to Section 1 of the Charter which pro-vides that the rights and freedoms guaranteed are subject 'to such reasonable limits prescribed by law as can be demonstrably justified in a free and democ-ratic society'. I will discuss in this part the interpretive stage, and then exam-ine the limitation of rights in the section that follows.

THE PURPOSIVE METHOD

From the earliest Charter cases, the Supreme Court of Canada made it clear that it recognized that Charter adjudication was going to be different from the traditional work of adjudication. In *Law Society of Upper Canada* v. *Skapinker*,[34] the first Charter case to reach the Court, the judges indicated that they were prepared to assume responsibility for interpreting this 'new

[29] Section 23.
[30] See Cameron, 'The Motor Vehicle Reference and the Relevance of American Doctrine in Charter Adjudication', Sharpe ed., *Charter Litigation* (1987), ch. 4.
[31] *Irwin Toy Ltd.* v. *Attorney-General (Quebec)* (1989) 58 DLR (4th) 577.
[32] *R.* v. *Keegstra* n. 4 above.   [33] *R.* v. *Butler* n. 3 above.
[34] (1984) 9 DLR (4th) 161.

yardstick of reconciliation between the individual and the community and their respective rights'. Mindful that the 'Charter is designed and adopted to guide and serve the Canadian community for a long time', Estey J. added that 'narrow and technical interpretation' that could 'stunt the growth of the law and hence the community it serves'[35] would be avoided.

In another early case, *Hunter* v. *Southam*,[36] the Court distinguished the method of statutory construction from that of constitutional interpretation. Insisting that the Charter must 'be capable of growth and development over time to meet new social, political, and historical realities often unimagined by its framers', Dickson J. repeated Paul Freund's plea that Courts should not 'read the provisions of the Constitution like a last will and testament lest it become one'.[37] A similar note was struck by Beetz J. in *Attorney-General (Manitoba)* v. *Metropolitan Stores (MTS) Ltd*[38] when he dismissed the contention that the so-called presumption of constitutionality should be weighed in the scales of Charter adjudication: 'the innovative and evolutive character of the Canadian Charter of Rights and Freedoms conflicts with the idea that a legislative provision can be presumed to be consistent with the Charter'.[39] The rights and freedoms set out were not 'frozen' in content and had to 'remain susceptible to evolve in the future'.[40]

The Supreme Court of Canada subsequently held that the supposed 'original intent' of those who drafted the Charter will not be conclusive for two reasons.[41] First, statements of the intent of particular individuals are an unreliable guide to discerning the intent of many others who took an active role in the creation of the Charter, and it is doubtful that there was a single or identifiable intent shared by all. Secondly, adoption of a strict interpretivist approach would freeze the meaning of the Charter at a particular point in time 'with little or no possibility of growth, development and adjustment to changing social needs'.[42]

It was in *Hunter* v. *Southam* that the Court first enunciated and applied the 'purposive' method that has served as the standard model for the elaboration of Charter rights and freedoms. It is a complex, value-laden exercise that draws upon a range of sources in the innovative spirit that the Charter demands. It calls upon the judge to reflect upon the purpose of and rationale for the Charter right at issue in the light of the overall structure of the Charter, our legal and political tradition, our history, and the changing needs and demands of modern society.

Perhaps the most often cited passage describing the nature of this exercise of purposive interpretation is from the judgment of Dickson J. in *R.* v. *Big M Drug Mart Ltd*:[43]

---

[35] Ibid. at 168.
[36] (1984) 11 DLR (4th) 641.
[37] Ibid. at 649.
[38] (1987) 38 DLR (4th) 321.
[39] Ibid. at 330.
[40] Ibid.
[41] *Reference re Section 94(2)* n. 21 above at 554.
[42] Ibid. at 554 per Lamer J.
[43] (1985) 18 DLR (4th) 321 at 359–60.

In my view, this analysis is to be undertaken, and the purpose of the right or freedom in question is to be sought by reference to the character and larger objects of the Charter itself, to the language chosen to articulate the specific right or freedom, to the historical origins of the concepts enshrined, and where applicable, to the meaning and purpose of the other specific rights and freedoms with which it is associated within the text of the Charter. The interpretation should be, as the judgment in *Southam* emphasizes, a generous rather than a legalistic one, aimed at fulfilling the purpose of the guarantee and securing for individuals the full benefit of the Charter's protection. At the same time it is important not to overshoot the actual purpose of the right or freedom in question, but to recall that the Charter was not enacted in a vacuum, and must therefore, as this Court's decision in *Law Society of Upper Canada* v. *Skapinker* illustrates, be placed in its proper linguistic, philosophic and historical contexts.

The purposive method of interpretation is indicative of the most significant effect of the Charter upon the role of the judiciary. Charter adjudication is anything but the mechanical application of pre-established rules. The judges are called upon to delve deeply into the very foundations of our legal system and political culture to answer questions of the most fundamental nature. Many of these questions cannot be answered adequately by reference only to traditional legal sources.[44] There was, of course, some pre-Charter authority for an expansive judicial role in constitutional interpretation. In federalism review, the Canadian Courts were guided by the metaphor of the Constitution as a 'living tree capable of growth and expansion within its natural limits'.[45] But it is one thing to allow scope for judicial creativity in the context of federalism and quite another under the regime of a Charter. A decision that a law is beyond the powers of one level of government almost inevitably means that the other level is clothed with legislative jurisdiction to deal with the matter. This may cause inconvenience or inefficiency, but rarely will the judges be precluding all legislative initiatives. A Charter decision has far more serious repercussions. If a law is found to infringe a Charter right, then no government can enact the law.[46] Moreover, Charter interpretation is inherently more

---

[44] While the Court has avoided an overtly philosophical approach, many opinions are sprinkled with references to philosophical writings. In the first case to interpret the meaning of freedom of expression, reference was made to the writings of Milton and Mill in elaborating the meaning of freedom of expression: *Dolphin Delivery Ltd.* v. *Retail, Wholesale and Department Store Union, Local 580* (1986) 33 DLR (4th) 174 at 183. Mill has been cited with some frequency (see *Reference re Public Service Employee Relations Act* (1987) 38 DLR (4th) 174 at 197 per Dickson C.J.; *Jones* v. *R.* (1986) 31 DLR (4th) 569 at 582 per Wilson J.), as has Dworkin: *Edwards Books & Art Ltd.* v. *R.* (1986) 35 DLR (4th) 1 at 61 per Wilson J; *Operation Dismantle* v. *R.* (1985) 18 DLR (4th) at 517 per Wilson J.; *R.* v. *Therens* (1985) 18 DLR 655 at 675 per LeDain J. Wilson J.'s opinion in a case dealing with language rights under the Constitution Act 1867 s. 133, contains an extensive discussion of the views of various legal philosophers—Hohfeld, Austin, Hart, Stone, and Salmond—on the meaning of rights: *MacDonald* v. *City of Montreal* (1986) 27 DLR (4th) 321 at 363–7. Wilson J. also cited the writings of various philosophers when elaborating the meaning of 'liberty' in Section 7: *Morgentaler* n. 1 above at 484–5; *Jones* n. 44 above at 582; *Reference re Sections 193 and 195(1)(c) of the Criminal Code* (1990) 56 CCC (3d) 65 at 135.

[45] *Edwards* v. *Attorney-General (Canada)* [1930] AC 326 at 354.

[46] Subject to resort being had to the 'override' Clause, discussed below.

controversial that federalism review in that it deals so explicitly with seemingly open-ended questions of value.

There are many instances where the purposive approach has yielded generous interpretation of Charter guarantees. The interpretation of the Charter's procedural guarantees has had a major impact upon the enforcement of the criminal law in Canada. There is now a vast body of case law, far too extensive to review in this essay, interpreting Sections 8–14 of the Charter. Police powers are now closely scrutinized under the Charter, and significant procedural protections have been imposed. Canadian Courts have the power to exclude evidence obtained in violation of a protected right where to admit such evidence would bring the administration of justice into disrepute.[47] A Supreme Court of Canada interpretation of the right to be tried within a reasonable time[48] resulted in the staying of thousands of serious charges caught in a backlog caused by institutional delay.[49]

The Supreme Court has also given a very generous and expansive interpretation to the Charter's minority language education guarantee[50] and to aboriginal rights,[51] partially entrenched at the same time as the Charter's introduction. This corresponds with the generous interpretation given religious freedom,[51a] and the determination to make equality review meaningful, discussed below. Just as the Court has made something of the Charter's procedural protections, so too has it demonstrated a firm commitment to protecting minority groups who do not enjoy significant political or economic power.

LIMITING DEFINITIONS

While the purposive approach has tended to produce broad and generous definitions in the areas indicated, the Supreme Court has also imposed some significant limitations on the reach of the Charter. These limitations may be seen as self-imposed restraints upon judicial power. In my view, they evolved from the view of the judges that their new found powers conferred by the Charter had to be contained within the limits of the judicial function.

The first area in which the scope of judicial power has been limited is that of the Charter's application. In an early case, it was held that the Charter only applied to government and that private action was excluded.[52] More recently,

---

[47] Section 24(2).   [48] Section 11(b).

[49] *R. v. Askov* [1990] 2 SCR 1199, (1990) 74 DLR (4th) 355.

[50] *Mahe* v. *Alberta* [1990] 1 SCR 342, (1990) 68 DLR (4th) 69, interpreting s. 23.

[51] *R. v. Sparrow* [1990] 1 SCR 1075, (1990) 70 DLR (4th) 385, interpreting s. 35.

[51a] *R. v. Big M Drug Mart Ltd.* n. 43 above.

[52] *Dolphin Delivery Ltd.* v. *Retail, Wholesale and Department Store Union, Local 580* n. 44 above.

this principle was applied to public state-funded universities,[53] indicating that the Court intends to give 'government' a relatively narrow interpretation in this context. In adopting this limitation on the reach of the Charter, the Court did not consider that it was departing from the 'purposive' approach to Charter interpretation. The Court justified limiting the application of the Charter to government by focusing on what it perceived to be the very purpose of the Constitution, namely, the definition of the appropriate relationship between the individual and the state. The restriction of the application of the Charter to government action has, however, been strongly criticized by many who contend that the reach of the country's most fundamental law should be unlimited.[54] While one might quarrel with the precise manner in which the Supreme Court drew the line, I would argue that the decision to limit the reach of the Charter can be defended, particularly in view of the vigorous enforcement of human rights standards in the private sector by nonjudicial human rights commissions. It was an appropriately deferential posture to avoid constitutionalizing all law and all human interaction and to leave ample scope for the operation of this alternate model of human rights protection which has been carefully tailored to deal with private relationships.

The second important area in which the purposive approach has produced a narrow definition of Charter rights to contain the judicial function within what the courts deem to be appropriate limits is that of economic rights. The courts have been very unsympathetic to Charter claims which seek to vindicate purely economic rights. This view is the product of judicial deference to the judgment of the elected representatives of the people on distributional questions and general regulation of the economy. The right to strike was held not to fall within the ambit of the guarantee of freedom of association.[55] Corporations have been held not to be entitled to claim the protection of the broadly worded liberty guarantee in Section 7,[56] nor may a corporation claim equality rights under Section 15.[57] Property rights are not included in the text, and so far the courts have refused to read property rights into the Charter.[58] Similarly, the Supreme Court of Canada foreclosed the use of the guarantee of equality to challenge business regulation by limiting the Section to the protection of vulnerable groups.[59] While sometimes tempted to protect rights

[53] *McKinney* v. *University of Guelph* n. 2 above.

[54] See Beatty 'Constitutional Conceits: The Coercive Authority of Courts', 37 UTLJ (1987) 183; Elliot and Grant 'The Charter's Application in Private Litigation', 23 UBCLR (1989) 459.

[55] *Re Public Service Employee Relations Act* n. 44 above; *Public Service Alliance of Canada* v. *Attorney-General (Canada)* [1987] 1 SCR 424, (1987) 38 DLR (4th) 249; *RWDSU* v. *Saskatchewan* [1987] 1 SCR 450, (1987) 38 DLR (4th) 277.

[56] *Irwin Toy* n. 31 above.

[57] *Edmonton Journal* v. *Attorney-General (Alberta)* [1989] 2 SCR 1326, (1989) 64 DLR (4th) 577.

[58] *Irwin Toy* n. 31 above. Note, however, that in the current round of talks on constitutional reform, the Federal Government has proposed the entrenchment of property rights.

[59] *Andrews* v. *Law Society (B.C.)* (1989) 56 DLR (4th) 1, *R.* v. *Turpin and Siddiqui* [1989] 1 SCR 1296, 48 CCC (3d) 8.

with an economic element, such as the right to practise one's chosen profession,[60] the judges have attempted to distinguish these cases as involving matters of fundamental personal choice rather than mere economic rights.

At the other end of the spectrum are social welfare rights, very much a part of the Canadian political fabric, but not explicitly protected in the Charter. It has been argued that the right to a basic level of material wellbeing is implicit in the Section 7 guarantee of 'life, liberty and security of the person'.[61] The Supreme Court has deliberately avoided answering the question[62] but it seems unlikely that the Court will give an affirmative answer. While the Court will not be able to avoid social welfare issues entirely, in view of what it has said about economic rights, it seems unlikely that the Court would interpret the present language of the Charter to include social welfare entitlements. More recently there have been calls for the amendment of the Constitution to include a 'social charter'. Proposals to this effect have been advanced during the current round of negotiations aimed at further constitutional reform, but the most powerful voices have been mindful of the limits of the adjudicative process in this context, and have pushed instead for non-justiciable social rights.

The third way in which the extent of judicial power under the Charter has been limited lies in the interpretation of two broadly worded rights. While the Supreme Court has, for the most part, avoided definitional limitations on most Charter rights at the first stage, without some interpretive limitations on certain rights the reach of the Charter would, in my view, be too broad. The point is applicable to Sections 7 and 15. Section 7 provides: 'Everyone has the right to life, liberty and security of the person and the right not to be deprived thereof except in accordance with the principles of fundamental justice.'

The Supreme Court has yet to give a complete definition of this Section. I would argue, however, that some definitional limitation is required. If 'liberty' means nothing more specific than a right to be unconstrained by law then all laws would constitute a prima facie Charter violation and all laws would have to be justified pursuant to the stringent test of Section 1. This would impose an impossible burden on the Courts and would represent a massive reallocation of power away from the Legislatures.[63]

In an early case,[64] the Court held that 'the principles of fundamental justice' are not restricted to procedural values, but have substantive content as

---

[60] *Wilson* v. *British Columbia (Medical Services Commission)* (1988) 53 DLR (4th) 171 (British Columbia Court of Appeal) (leave to appeal refused: [1988] 2 SCR viii).

[61] See Johnstone, 'Section 7 of the Charter and Constitutionally Protected Welfare', 46 *UT Fac. L Rev.* (1988) 1; Jackman, 'The Protection of Welfare Rights under the Charter', 20 Ottawa LR (1988) 257.

[62] *Irwin Toy Ltd.* v. *Attorney-General (Quebec)* n. 31 above 633.

[63] This point is discussed in greater detail in Sharpe, 'A Comment on David Beatty's 'A Conservative's Court: The Politicization of Law'', n. 9 above.

[64] *Reference re Section 94(2) of the Motor Vehicle Act (B.C.)* n. 21 above.

well. In the Court's view, one such principle is the mens rea requirement, and
in subsequent cases, the Court dismantled the Criminal Code provisions
which obviated the need to prove intent to kill if death was caused in the commission of certain offences and in other specified circumstances.[65] Thus the
Court has read Section 7 of the Charter as mandating the substantive review
of laws. At the same time, however, the Court was at pains to impose some
restraints upon this sweeping power. Lamer J., writing the majority decision,
recognized at the outset of his opinion that the case raised 'fundamental questions of constitutional theory, including the nature and very legitimacy of constitutional adjudication under the Charter as well as the appropriateness of
various techniques of constitutional interpretation'.[66] Lamer J. imposed two
limitations upon the mandate of the Court under Section 7. First, he made it
clear that, despite the generous meaning given to 'the principles of fundamental justice', they are not a freestanding guarantee, but can be invoked only
when the rights of 'life, liberty or security of the person' are interfered with.
Secondly, the concept of fundamental justice was specifically tied by Lamer J.
to 'the basic tenets of our legal system' and the traditional 'domain of the judiciary as guardian of the justice system', rather than to 'the realm of general
public policy'.[67] He also made reference to 'the spectre of a judicial "super-
Legislature" ' and the need to give 'meaningful content' to Section 7 while
avoiding adjudication of policy matters, and the need for 'objective and man-
ageable standards'.[68] While this is admittedly imprecise, it does reflect a keen
judicial awareness of the need to limit the powers of judicial review to matters
upon which the Courts have institutional competence and expertise. In subsequent decisions, Lamer C.J. and Wilson J. engaged in a debate as to the scope
of the meaning of 'liberty'. Wilson J. sees the word as encompassing all fundamental personal decisions, most notably, the decision of a pregnant woman
whether or not to carry her foetus to full term.[69] Lamer C.J. takes a narrower
view and essentially would limit the scope of the Court's power to review laws
that infringe 'liberty' to the realm of criminal law.[70] While the issue has yet to
be conclusively settled, the view of Lamer C.J. has tended to attract stronger
judicial support. But even if the view of Wilson J. were to prevail, there would
be some definitional element to preclude 'liberty' from having an all-embrac-
ing meaning that would sweep within the reach of Section 7 virtually all laws.

A similar definitional issue has to be confronted under Section 15. If all differences in treatment were considered to be a violation of equality rights, virtually no legislative distinction will escape Charter scrutiny and all legislative
classifications would become the legitimate subject of judicial review.

The first Section 15 case[71] to reach the Supreme Court concerned a

---

[65] *R. v. Vaillancourt* n. 5 above.
[66] *Reference re Section 94(2) of the Motor Vehicle Act (B.C.)* n. 21 above at 543.
[67] Ibid. at 550.   [68] Ibid. at 546 and 550.   [69] *R. v. Morgentaler* n. 1 above.
[70] *Reference re Sections 193 and 195(1)(c) of the Criminal Code* n. 44 above.
[71] *Andrews* n. 59 above.

challenge to a provincial law, the British Columbia Barristers and Solicitors Act,[72] which imposed the requirement of citizenship for entry into the legal profession.[73] The plaintiff alleged that the citizenship requirement infringed his right to equality.[74] The key issue of interpretation was how to identify those classifications that offend the promise of equality and non-discrimination. The Supreme Court rejected the suggestion that Section 15 could be interpreted in a neutral or formal manner. The Court held that not all differences in treatment between individuals should be subject to Charter scrutiny under Section 15, but rather that 'consideration must be given to the content of the law, to its purpose, and its impact upon those to whom it applies, and also upon those whom it excludes from its application'.[75] In determining which distinctions or classifications would infringe upon the guarantee of equality, the Court held that one had to pay heed to the under-lying spirit and purpose of Section 15, 'the promotion of a society in which all are secure in the knowledge that they are recognized at law as human beings equally deserving of concern, respect and consideration'.[76] A central concept in Section 15 is discrimination, defined by the Court as follows:[77]

. . . discrimination may be described as a distinction, whether intentional or not but based on grounds relating to personal characteristics of the individual or group, which has the effect of imposing burdens, obligations, or disadvantages on such individual or group not imposed upon others, or which withholds or limits access to opportunities, benefits, and advantages available to other members of society. Distinctions based on personal characteristics attributed to an individual solely on the basis of association with a group will rarely escape the charge of discrimination, while those based on an individual's merits and capacities will rarely be so classed.

The Court held that while the enumerated grounds in Section 15 (race, national or ethnic origin, colour, religion, sex, age, or mental or physical dis-ability) were not exclusive, they did reflect the 'most common and probably the most destructive and historically practiced bases of discrimination,'[78] and that to qualify for consideration as a prohibited ground of discrimination, another category would have to be analogous in nature to one of the enumer-ated grounds. The Supreme Court clearly contemplated a substantive assess-ment of the law and its impact upon particular individuals or groups. However, only those differences based on historic patterns of discrimination

---

[72] RSBC 1979, c. 26, s. 42.

[73] For a more complete discussion of citizenship as a category in Canadian constitutional law, see Sharpe, 'Citizenship, The Constitution Act, 1867, and the Charter' in Kaplan ed., *Belonging: the Meaning and Future of Canadian Citizenship* (1993), 221.

[74] Section 15 provides as follows: 'Every individual is equal before and under the law and has the right to the equal protection and equal benefit of the law without discrimination and, in par-ticular, without discrimination based on race, national or ethnic origin, colour, religion, sex, age or mental or physical disability.

[75] *Andrews* n. 59 above at 13 per McIntyre J.   [76] Ibid. at 15 per McIntyre J.

[77] Ibid. at 18 per McIntyre J.   [78] *Andrews* n. 59 above at 13 per McIntyre J

or disadvantage, such as those listed in Section 15 itself, will constitute a denial of equality.

All judges agreed that denying the plaintiff entry into the legal profession because he was not a citizen constituted discrimination and a denial of Section 15 rights. The Legislature had adopted a classification that excluded the members of a group on the basis of a characteristic analogous to those set out in Section 15 and without regard to the qualifications or merits of the members of the group. Wilson J. emphasized that non-citizens were a disadvantaged group in that they lacked political power and were accordingly vulnerable to having their interests overlooked and the right to equal concern and respect violated:[79]

Non-citizens, to take only the most obvious example, do not have the right to vote. Their vulnerability to becoming a disadvantaged group in our society is captured by John Stuart Mill's observation in Book III of *On Liberty and Considerations of Representative Government* that 'in the absence of its natural defenders, the interests of the excluded is always in danger of being overlooked . . .'. I would conclude therefore that non-citizens fall into an analogous category to those specifically enumerated in Section 15.

Disadvantage is a guiding principle to the exercise of the power of judicial review under the Charter not only with respect to Section 15, but also in relation to the assessment of laws that infringe the rights of some to protect the rights or interests of others, a topic discussed in the following section. The clear message from the Court is that equality review will be substantive and stringent in cases dealing with discrimination on enumerated or analogous grounds, but that the Court is not prepared to second-guess the Legislature on all legislative distinctions.

Reconciliation of Rights with the General Social Interest

A central task in the interpretation of any instrument guaranteeing fundamental rights and freedoms is to reconcile the rights of the individual with the interests of the community at large. The effect of the Charter is to shift an important share of responsibility for this task from the elected representatives of the people to the judiciary. In the light of the generous definition of most enumerated rights through the purposive method of interpretation, it is unsurprising to find that heavy reliance is placed on the second stage of Charter adjudication. Charter rights are not absolute and the definition of the limitation of rights is achieved pursuant to Section 1 which, as noted above, provides that the rights and freedoms guaranteed are 'subject only to such

---

[79] Ibid. at 32 per Wilson J.

reasonable limits prescribed by law as can be justified in a free and democratic society'.

LIMITS PRESCRIBED BY LAW

The first requirement for a justifiable limit is that it be, in the words of Section 1, 'prescribed by law'. There must be some positive legal measure imposing a discernible standard sufficient to guide with reasonable clarity the individual whose rights are limited and the State officials responsible for enforcement. While measures that leave some room for judgment in application will be tolerated, laws that confer an open-ended or vaguely defined discretion to limit protected freedoms will not. Thus, for example, the Courts have struck down as too ill-defined a customs regulation that allowed officials to restrict from entry into Canada materials they considered to be 'immoral'.[80] Similarly, a scheme conferring the power of censorship on a film board without setting out the grounds or criteria by which such powers were to be exercised was struck down as a violation of freedom of expression which was not prescribed by law.[81]

PROPORTIONALITY REVIEW

The Charter itself says very little, if anything, about how limitations on rights are to be justified, but the Supreme Court of Canada, employing the purposive approach, established the basic framework for analysis in *R. v. Oakes*.[82] In that case, it was established that the initial burden of proving a violation of rights rests with the individual asserting a Charter claim. In light of the generous definition accorded Charter rights, in most cases this burden is relatively easy to discharge. It will, however, still be incumbent upon the challenger to establish the facts necessary to sustain the Charter claim. As soon as a prima facie violation is proved, the burden shifts to the party attempting to justify the infringement, usually the State. It is at the justification stage that the Court must consider the collective interest in limiting a right or freedom, and weigh that collective interest against the right of the individual. The reconciliation of the collective interest against individual rights is achieved through 'proportionality' review.

The proportionality test has three steps. First, it must be established that

---

[80] *Re Luscher and Deputy Minister Revenue Canada* (1985) 17 DLR (4th) 503 (Federal Court).

[81] *Re Ontario Film & Video Appreciation Society and Ontario Board of Censors* (1984) 5 DLR (4th) 766 (Ontario Court of Appeal).

[82] (1986) 26 DLR (4th) 200. For a good discussion of the evolution of Section 1, see Hogg, 'Section 1 Revisited', 1 NJCL 1 (1991).

there is an objective 'of sufficient importance to warrant overriding a constitutionally protected right or freedom'.[83] In *R.* v. *Oakes*, the Supreme Court of
Canada said that the objective must 'relate to concerns which are pressing and
substantial in a free and democratic society'.[84] While this language suggests a
stringent test, it is in practice rare for the proportionality inquiry to end at this
first stage. The Courts have been relatively deferential to legislative judgment
of the importance of the objective. The only notable exceptions have been
those cases where the Court considered the legislative objective constitutionally impermissible. In one case,[85] the Supreme Court held that Quebec legislation limiting the rights of English-speaking parents to have their children
attend English language schools constituted a direct attack on the very right
enshrined in Section 23 of the Charter, and hence the law was not motivated
by a proper objective. Similarly, in an Ontario case,[86] it was held that legislation requiring the recital of the Lord's prayer in non-denominational state
schools constituted an attempt to impose a form of religious observance and
that such an objective was not permitted by the guarantee of freedom of religion. These cases, however, are the exception rather than the rule, and in most
cases, the state is readily able to satisfy the Court that the law being challenged
is motivated by an objective of sufficient weight.

The next step in proportionality review is to ask whether there is a rational,
non-arbitrary, non-capricious connection between the objective and the law
that is challenged. Is the law carefully tailored to meet the objective? Once
again, the Courts have been deferential at this stage, and it is rare to find that
there is no rational connection between the legislative objective and the law
that is subject to scrutiny. In the *Oakes* case itself, the Supreme Court held that
there was no rational connection between the objective of curbing traffic in
drugs and a law that reversed the usual onus of proof in criminal cases and
required anyone found in possession of drugs to prove that he or she did not
have the intent to traffic in drugs. Most commentators suggest that the Court
might more readily have justified striking down the law under the minimal
impairment test, discussed below. In subsequent cases, the rational connection component of proportionality review has rarely been determinative.

The core element of proportionality review is the minimal impairment test,
or the principle of least intrusive means. Was there some other way for the
Legislature to satisfy the objective that would not impair the right or freedom
at issue, or that would have less impact on the right or freedom than does the
law under review? In one of the most notable Charter cases to be decided by
the Supreme Court, it was held that a Quebec law prohibiting the display of

[83] *R.* v. *Big M Drug Mart* n. 43 above at 366 per Dickson J.

[84] *Oakes* n. 82 above at 227 per Dickson C.J.

[85] *Attorney-General (Quebec)* v. *Quebec Association of Protestant School Boards* [1984] 2 SCR
66, (1984) 10 DLR (4th) 321 (Supreme Court of Canada).

[86] *Zylberberg* v. *Director of Sudbury Board of Education* (1988) 52 DLR (4th) 577 (Ontario
Court of Appeal).

commercial signs in English could not survive scrutiny under the minimal impairment test.[87] The Court was prepared to find that the preservation and enhancement of the French language was a sufficiently important objective in the province of Quebec to justify limiting the guarantee of freedom of expression, and that a law that required such signs to be in French and forbade signs in English was rationally connected to the objective. However, the Court found that the law went too far in prohibiting English altogether. The province could, in the Court's view, have satisfied the legitimate objective of preserving and enhancing French by requiring that commercial signs display a marked predominance of French. The Court was not persuaded that a total ban on English was necessary, and the law therefore failed as it was not the means least intrusive of freedom of expression capable of satisfying the objective.

The final step in proportionality review, in the words of *Oakes*, is that there 'must be proportionality between the effects of the measure which are responsible for limiting the Charter right or freedom, and the objective which has been identified as of "sufficient importance" '.[88] This final step applies where all other aspects of proportionality have been satisfied. It requires the Court to engage in a balancing exercise, weighing the significance of the infringement of the right against the importance of attaining the objective of the legislation. In the cases decided by the Supreme Court, this step has never been decisive. It appears highly unlikely that the Court would ever find that the objective was of sufficient importance to justify overriding a protected freedom, that the least intrusive means had been employed, and yet that on balance the effects on the right were disproportionate.

The result is that the central element in proportionality review is the principle of least intrusive means. It is this stage which is the focus of most litigation under the Charter, and this clearly is significant in assessing the impact of the Charter upon the role of the judiciary. Proportionality review requires the judges to weigh and assess the choices made by the Legislature and the other options that were available. This is not an exercise considered to fall within the realm of judicial competence in non-constitutional cases, and yet it is very often the central question in Charter litigation.

The key issue is really how strictly the principle of minimal impairment is applied. The decided cases indicate that the stringency of proportionality review, and in particular, of the application of the minimal impairment test is both controversial and variable. While the Supreme Court has yet to openly acknowledge that there are varying levels of scrutiny, it would seem that the standard of review is influenced by at least three factors.

First, the Supreme Court has demonstrated a marked tendency to defer to legislative judgment and apply a relatively relaxed standard of review in cases

---

[87] *Ford* v. *Attorney-General (Quebec)* [1988] 2 SCR 712, (1988) 54 DLR (4th) 577.
[88] *Oakes* n. 82 above at 227 per Dickson C.J.

involving broad issues of social and economic policy. This corresponds closely with the use of definitional limitations, noted above, to avoid subjecting to judicial scrutiny certain legislative decisions in the realm of property rights and business regulation. The most striking examples of a relaxed standard of Section 1 review are the cases dealing with mandatory retirement.[89] The Court found that mandatory retirement at age 65 violated the right conferred by Section 15 not to be discriminated against on grounds of age, but held that the legislation permitting this form of discrimination should be upheld under Section 1. In the view of the majority of the Court, the issue was 'whether the Government had a reasonable basis, on the evidence tendered, for concluding that the legislation interferes as little as possible with a guaranteed right, given the Government's pressing and substantial objectives'.[90] This is plainly a much more relaxed standard of review than that applied in cases dealing with those rights or freedoms which do not pose complex distributional questions.

Secondly, the Court has explicitly stated that a more relaxed standard of scrutiny is called for where the legislation challenged represents an attempt by the Legislature to reconcile competing claims or protect vulnerable groups. In a case dealing with a Sunday closing law,[91] the Court noted that the Legislature had been motivated by a secular purpose, namely, to provide workers with a common day of rest. The legislation did attempt to accommodate non-Sunday observers, but those exemptions were drafted with a view to protecting retail sales workers, a particularly vulnerable group, from being forced to work. The exemptions were less than perfect from the perspective of non-observers, but the majority held that in such circumstances, the Legislature had to be given a certain latitude to ensure that the Charter 'does not simply become an instrument of better situated individuals to roll back legislation that has as its object the improvement of the condition of less advantaged persons'.[92] This line of analysis was expanded in a later case where the Court indicated that a distinction should be drawn between cases where 'the Government is best characterized as the singular antagonist of the individual whose right has been infringed,' and those where the Government is 'mediating between the claims of competing groups' and attempting to strike a balance that will protect the vulnerable while impinging as little as possible upon protected freedoms 'without the benefit of absolute certainty concerning how that balance is best struck'.[93] In the former case, a rigorous standard of review should be applied under Section 1, while in the latter, the Legislature will not be held to such a strict test.

Thirdly, a definitional element has been introduced into proportionality review. As noted above, the Court has avoided definitional limitations and given most Charter rights a liberal and generous meaning. For example, both

---

[89] *McKinney* n. 2 above.
[90] Ibid. at 666 per LaForest J.
[91] *Edwards Books & Art Ltd* v. *R.* n. 44 above.
[92] Ibid. at 49 per Dickson C.J.
[93] *Irwin Toy* n. 31 above at 625, 626.

commercial expression and hate propaganda have been found to fall within the definition of 'expression' and accordingly are prima facie protected by Section 2(b).[94] Any limits imposed upon those forms of expression must undergo proportionality review to survive Charter scrutiny. However, definitional considerations definitely affect the strictness of proportionality review. The Court has spoken of a 'core' meaning of freedom of expression. Where a form of expression lies at or near that 'core', proportionality is strictly applied. But where the form of expression at issue is peripheral to the core, legislation imposing limitations is much more likely to survive. While neither commercial speech nor hate propaganda are excluded at the stage of defining Charter rights, it is equally the case that neither lie at or near the 'core' meaning of freedom of expression and a relatively relaxed level of Charter scrutiny is applied as a consequence. Again, the motivation here is to avoid an unduly burdensome standard of Charter review where the Legislature is acting to protect vulnerable groups. In the advertising case,[95] the law at issue was designed to protect children from exploitative commercial messages, while the hate propaganda law aimed to protect ethnic minorities,[96] and the pornography law was aimed at protecting the rights of women to equal respect.[97]

LEGISLATIVE OVERRIDE

While the Charter confers an important mandate upon the judiciary, there is another significant device in addition to the interpretive limitation provision in Section 1, whereby most Charter rights can be limited, which significantly qualifies the powers of the courts. Section 33, the so-called 'notwithstanding' or 'override' clause, permits Parliament or a Legislature to declare that a legislative provision shall operate notwithstanding a violation of Section 2 (freedom of expression, religion, association, and assembly) or Sections 7–15 (legal rights and equality). As might be expected, the propriety of the clause is a much debated question.[98]

Section 33 is limited in several ways. Certain rights are exempted altogether from the provision and may not be overridden. These are the democratic and political rights of Sections 3–5, mobility rights guaranteed by Section 6, and language rights found in Sections 16–23. Section 33(3) imposes another significant limit. It provides that a declaration ceases to have effect after 5 years. While such a declaration may be renewed, the enacting body will once again have to justify the provision to the electorate. Another limitation has been

---

[94] *Irwin Toy* n. 31 above; *R.* v. *Keegstra* n. 4 above. [95] *Irwin Toy* n. 31 above.
[96] *R.* v. *Keegstra* n. 4 above. [97] *R.* v. *Butler* n. 3 above.
[98] See Greshner and Norman, 'The Courts and Section 33', 12 Queen's LJ (1987) 155; Weinrib, 'Learning to Live with the Override', 35 McGill LJ (1990) 541.

imposed by judicial interpretation. It has been held by the Supreme Court of Canada that the override clause cannot be applied retrospectively.[99]

It has been argued that the Courts should control resort to Section 33 by interpreting the Section to implicitly impose certain other constraints on its use. The case[100] in which the issue was raised was one in which the extraordinary action of Quebec in 1982 was brought into question. The Government of the day was separatist and bitterly opposed to the 1982 constitutional amendments that not only introduced the Charter of Rights but also the formula to govern amendments to the Constitution. The Quebec National Assembly enacted an omnibus override provision, amending every Quebec Statute to include a generally-worded provision to the effect that all Quebec legislation should operate notwithstanding Sections 2 and 7–15 of the Canadian Charter.[101] It was argued that this constituted an improper use of Section 33, and that to be valid, an override provision had to specify precisely what right was being overridden. The Supreme Court refused, however, to impose any form of substantive review of use of the override clause, and held that so long as the formal requirements of the provision were respected, the courts should not look beyond the declaration nor impose any conditions for its exercise beyond those stated in the Section.

Despite this highly deferential judicial approach, with the important exception of Quebec's sign law, discussed below, there has been no rush by Parliament or the provinces to resort to the override power. Indeed, the present Federal Government has indicated that it is opposed to the existence of the override and will not use it. Perhaps the most significant constraint on use of the clause is political: as resort to the override provision is bound to be controversial, few Governments will risk the political price that might have to be paid.

Political forces will not, however, always serve as a constraint, as was demonstrated by the Quebec signs law. The Supreme Court decision that dealt with the general use of the override by Quebec arose in the Quebec signs case. This law, designed to enhance and encourage the use of French as the daily language of life and business, was strongly opposed by the English-language minority in Quebec. The Supreme Court held that the law violated freedom of expression, but upheld the power of the province to protect it from Charter scrutiny by use of Section 33. The law was overwhelmingly popular among the French-language majority in Quebec, and the Quebec National Assembly quickly moved to salvage the law by enacting another override provision, the original omnibus provision having expired in 1987, 5 years after its enactment. This action was strongly resented outside Quebec and produced an enormous

---

[99] *Ford* n. 87 above.   [100] Ibid.
[101] At the same time, Quebec enacted its own Charter of Human Rights and Freedoms (R.S.Q. ch. 12) which closely parallels the Canadian Charter.

controversy. Indeed, there can be little question but that the enactment of the override provision to save the sign law significantly undermined support for the 'Meech Lake' package of constitutional amendments so eagerly sought by the Quebec Government, plunging Canada into its present constitutional crisis.

Conclusion

The Charter of Rights and Freedoms has plainly had a major impact upon the role of the judiciary in Canada. Some Canadian critics decry what they see as the 'legalization of politics' and contend that the Charter represents an inappropriate shift of power from the elected representatives of the people to the unelected and allegedly elitist judiciary.[102] Others contend that the courts have been far too timid and unduly restrained and deferential to legislative judgment.[103] I would reject both views. Our highest court has been asked agonizingly difficult questions. So far the judges have been cautiously positive. While much can be achieved to enhance the protection of fundamental rights and freedoms through judicial review, it is appropriate to give careful consideration not only to what can be achieved, but also to the inherent limits of the judicial function. Those limits, the Canadian courts have started to develop and probe, both through the process of interpretation at the initial stage of Charter review, and through the development of standards of proportionality review that are responsive to the nature of the rights and regulation under scrutiny.

The Charter has had a major impact in the area of criminal procedure where the Courts have not hesitated to act. The courts have also demonstrated a commitment to the protection of minority rights, and the guarantee of equality has been given substantive content. A variable standard of review under Section 1 has been developed to accommodate affirmative legislative measures intended to benefit the disadvantaged and vulnerable groups. At the same time, the courts have refused to second-guess legislative judgment of economic issues or business regulation by excluding economic and property rights from Section 7 and by moulding proportionality review under Section 1.

In determining the reach of the Charter and the meaning of the rights and freedoms it guarantees, it seems to me that the courts have been strongly influenced by their assessment of the strengths and weaknesses of the judicial method. While the courts have proceeded with caution in areas where their institutional limitations are most evident, they have demonstrated a clear

---

[102] See Mandel, *The Charter of Rights and the Legalization of Politics in Canada* (1989); Hutchinson, 'Charter Litigation and Social Change: Legal Battles and Social Wars', in Sharpe ed., *Charter Litigation* (1987), ch. 13
[103] Beatty, *Talking Heads and the Supremes* (1990).

willingness to wield the power of judicial review in those areas of procedural and substantive justice most amenable to the judicial method.

I would argue that overall, the Charter has had a beneficial impact upon Canadian law and politics. Fundamental human rights are properly at the forefront of public debate, and the claims of those often forgotten in the cut and thrust of day-to-day politics can no longer be ignored. At the same time, the courts have avoided allowing the Charter to become an instrument whereby powerful interests are able to attack progressive social and economic measures. I believe that the Charter has the potential to strengthen our democratic tradition and our commitment to toleration and equal respect for all, and that judges have an appropriate role to play in that exercise. The Charter protects the bedrock principles essential for free and open democratic debate and which give a voice to many in our society who are effectively shut out of the political process. As interpreted by the courts to date, it neither precludes nor entrenches particular socio-economic outcomes, but has the potential to enrich the democratic process that determines social and economic policy.

The Charter permits judges to strike down measures enacted by the majority, and to many, the power of judicial review is offensive to democratic principles. I would suggest that the Canadian courts have been appropriately sensitive to this concern and have defined and limited the reach of the Charter accordingly. A true democracy is surely one in which the exercise of power by the many is conditional on respect for the rights of the few. Our history shows lamentable departures from respect for individual dignity and conscience. The Charter provides a check on such excesses and provides religious and other minorities with the voice denied to them in the political process. The same can be said of freedom of expression, the lifeblood of democracy. It is often tempting for the majority to shut out annoying and unpopular views. The 'haves' of our society do not really want to listen to the gripes and grievances of the dispossessed. Do we not want to check the inevitable but unworthy inclination of the majority to silence those who hold unconventional or unpopular views? Does history not suggest there is more to fear from the threat of unbridled majority rule than from the risk that judges will usurp the power of the elected representatives? The Charter really says nothing more than this: if those who exercise power choose to deny one of the bedrock values of our democratic tradition, they must be prepared to justify their action by evidence and reasoned argument. I would submit that the Canadian experience to date indicates that the judiciary is capable of exercising the powers of judicial review in a way that protects such fundamental rights as freedom of religion and expression without unduly inhibiting the capacity of the elected representatives to develop social policy.

The purpose of the Charter, as I see it, is to facilitate, not frustrate, genuine democracy. The Charter assigns to the courts the role of refereeing our democracy, providing a mechanism to ensure that the claims of those without political clout and influence must be listened to. Moreover, it should be remembered that the courts are not given the last word. Ultimately Canadian elected officials have the final say, for the Charter provides that most rights are subject to the legislative override provision.

It remains to be seen whether the courts are able to articulate a coherent vision of the Charter that protects fundamental rights and freedoms without undue interference with legislative judgment. While it is perhaps still too early to say whether this important Canadian experiment will succeed, my assessment of experience to date makes me cautiously optimistic.

12

The Impact of a Bill of Rights on the Role of the Judiciary: An Australian Perspective

SIR GERARD BRENNAN

Introduction

Since the abolition of the last avenues of appeal from the Australian Courts to the Privy Council, we have broadened our focus of interest in the laws and Courts of countries in the common law tradition. The heritage of the common law allows each country to draw on the experience of others, especially when their societies are similar in culture and their constitutional institutions are comparable. Australia therefore has a particular interest in the Canadian experience of the last decade or more, when the Courts of Canada have been administering the Canadian Charter of Rights and Freedoms. Not only is Canada a Federal democracy operating under a system of representative and responsible Government; it was, at the time when the Charter came into force, a society whose legal institutions operated in much the same way as do Australian legal institutions.

The Diceyan tenet of Parliamentary supremacy was accepted by Canadian courts then, as it is accepted by Australian Courts now, as a fundamental postulate of the legal system. Each country has a written Constitution which distributes legislative powers between central and provincial Legislatures. The Courts of each country are accustomed judicially to review the exercise of legislative and Executive power and to strike down any purported exercise which is beyond the power conferred upon the repository by the Constitution. But, most importantly, the Courts of Canada deferred, as Australian Courts defer, to the political judgment of the political branches of Government in the exercise of their respective powers. The Charter has introduced a massive constitutional change which, as Robert Sharpe has demonstrated, has evoked a corresponding change in judicial function and judicial method.[1]

If Sharpe is 'cautiously optimistic' about the prospects of judicial articulation of a coherent vision of the Charter that protects human rights and fundamental freedoms without undue interference with legislative judgment, then there are substantial grounds for optimism in considering a

[1] Sharpe, 'The Impact of a Bill of Rights on the Role of the Judiciary: A Canadian Perspective', ch. 11 above.

constitutionally entrenched Bill of Rights for Australia. If Canada and Canadian judges could cope with—indeed, revel in—the change, surely Australia and Australian judges might do the same. Moreover, the latest Bill of Rights exposed for public examination in Australia was that modelled on the Canadian Charter and proposed by the Constitutional Commission in 1988. If such a provision were entrenched in our Constitution, the judicial experience of Canada and the careful development of Canadian Charter jurisprudence would give to the Australian Courts an advantage which the Canadian Courts had to acquire by their own labours. We could introduce a Bill of Rights and have it administered by our existing Courts, but would Australians wish that to be done? The voting at the 1988 referendum suggests that the answer is resoundingly negative. However, non-party political interest in and discussion of the Constitution, in the last decade of this century, restores the question to the agenda. I do not propose an answer to the question, for reasons which I shall mention. The question is essentially political and should be answered by reference to the political needs that might be satisfied by an entrenched Bill of Rights and the burdens which might be imposed by its introduction.

The question should not be answered generally; it should be answered by reference to a specific proposal tailored to the particular political needs of the Australian people. But, in whatever terms an Australian Bill of Rights be cast, it would contain guarantees of rights which, though expressed in unqualified terms, would not be absolute. No individual rights can be pushed so far as to deny the rights of others: the right to life itself cannot be held to protect the murderous assailant against necessary self-defence by his victim. And liberty, if absolute, is the enemy of equality for it leaves the powerful free to oppress the weak. The scope of an entrenched right is necessarily left for definition in the administration of the entrenched provisions. In whatever terms a Bill of Rights be cast, it calls for what Sharpe describes as a weighing of the collective interest against the right of the individual and an adjustment of broadly expressed individual rights inter se.

This is a function which the Fathers of our Constitution, fully alive to the American Bill of Rights and the 14th Amendment, consciously left to the political branches of Government.[2] If the exercise of political power is to be subjected to a Bill of Rights, there is no institution to which the administration of those provisions can be entrusted save the Courts. The Courts, in supervising the exercise of political power, would be constrained to base their decisions on political considerations. This is foreign to our present conception of judicial function. In *Clunies-Ross* v. *Commonwealth* the High Court said:

[2] See the comments of Sir Owen Dixon, 'Two Constitutions Compared', speech to the American Bar Association in August 1944 reprinted in Dixon, *Jesting Pilate and Other Papers and Addresses* (1963), 102, quoted in Menzies, *Central Power in the Australian Constitution* (1967), 52–3.

It would be an abdication of the duty of this Court under the Constitution if we were to determine [this] important and general question of law . . . according to whether we personally agreed or disagreed with the political and social objectives which the Minister sought to achieve . . . As a matter of constitutional duty, [the] question must be considered objectively and answered in this Court as a question of law and not as a matter to be determined by reference to the political or social merits of the particular case.[3]

If the Courts are to decide issues on their political and social merits, the Courts will have to be given, as the Canadian Courts were given, 'a deliberate push away from the cautious and highly deferential posture they exhibited' in cases governed by Statute law.[4] Constitutional entrenchment is required to project the Courts onto the political stage. Hitherto, under the influence of Diceyan theory, the Courts have distanced themselves from the political branches of Government.

Potential Dangers to Human Rights and Fundamental Freedoms

Diceyan theory, which has informed much of the rhetoric about our democratic system, assumes that the legislative will expressed in statutory form expresses the permanent—or long-term—wishes of the electors.[5] The Courts then interpret and apply the legislative will. The theory is no longer tenable. The greater bulk of legislation today consists of statutory instruments which Parliamentary committees may endeavour to supervise, but which Parliament itself cannot hope to consider. Much legislation emanates from the permanent bureaucracy rather than from the elected representatives of the people. More importantly for present purposes, two factors have combined to expose human rights and fundamental freedoms to danger from an exercise of power by the political branches of Government. First, our society has become more diverse in its ethnic, cultural, religious, and economic composition. Or, to put it another way, there are more minority groups whose particular interests are liable to be overreached by the exercise of legislative or Executive power. The control of the political process by political parties favours the creation of poll-driven policies which will appeal to the majority of the electorate whether or not they unjustifiably discriminate against minority groups or against the weak. There is a consequent risk that factors which justify special consideration of the position of a minority or special support of the weak will be disregarded. A Bill of Rights is seen as a protection of minorities and the weak against a discriminatory exercise of power by the political branches of

---

[3] (1984) 155 CLR 193 at 204.   [4] Sharpe n. 1 above.
[5] Dicey, *Lectures Introductory to the Study of the Law of the Constitution* (1885), 77.

Government. Lord Scarman advances this as the chief political argument for a Bill of Rights in the United Kingdom:

. . . if you are going to protect people who will never have political power, at any rate in the foreseeable future (not only individuals but minority groups with their own treasured and properly treasured social customs, religion and ways of life), if they are going to be protected it won't be done in Parliament—they will never muster a majority. It's got to be done by the Courts and the Courts can only do it if they've got the proper guide-lines.[6]

A further danger to human rights and fundamental freedoms is posed by the dominance of the Executive Government, supported by its bureaucracy, over the Parliament. This dominance has undermined the theory that the Westminster model of responsible Government effectively guarantees democratic control of Executive power, to the extent that Lord Hailsham concluded that '[w]e live under an elective dictatorship, absolute in theory if hitherto thought tolerable in practice'.[7] A Bill of Rights is seen as a protection against the oppressive exercise of this enormous mass of power. As Sir Anthony Mason put it:

Human rights are seen as a countervailing force to the exercise of totalitarian, bureaucratic and institutional power—widely identified as the greatest threats to the liberty of the individual and democratic freedom in this century. One result has been the widespread entrenchment of fundamental rights in Constitutions throughout the world.[8]

A New Role for the Judiciary

If the exercise of political power is no longer subject to effective checks and balances which protect human rights and fundamental freedoms then, so the argument goes, new checks and balances are needed. A Bill of Rights, which exposes the exercise of legislative and Executive power to review, will bring a new and dominant force into the political process. If the risk of discriminatory exercise of power to the disadvantage of minorities and the weak and the risk of oppressive exercise of power by the political branches of Government are sufficiently grave, and if there is no other means available to avoid or diminish those risks, then a case can be made for casting on the Courts a supervisory role, albeit a role which is radically different from the role which courts have been accustomed to exercise. Over time, the function and significance of the third branch of Government will be substantially changed and the relationship between the Courts and the political branches of Government will be altered. Before Australia commits itself to a Bill of Rights, we should consider

---

[6] Lord Scarman, 'Britain and the Protection of Human Rights', [1984] NZLJ 175 at 177.
[7] 'Elective Dictatorship', Dimbleby Lecture (1976).
[8] 'A Bill of Rights for Australia', 5 *Australian Bar Review* (1989) 79 at 79–80.

the impact it would have on the role of the judiciary. After all, the very object of a Bill of Rights is to create a new role for the judiciary—by exercise of a new jurisdiction, the Courts are to protect human rights and fundamental freedoms. But what effect would a new jurisdiction have on the exercise of the jurisdiction now vested in the Courts?

If a Bill of Rights were entrenched in the Constitution, new judicial skills would be required. A Bill of Rights, drawn in open-textured terms, necessarily requires individual human rights to be defined with a content specific to the case in hand. In other words, the Court must define whether a particular right or immunity exists and ought to be protected by curial order. And, in so far as individual human rights are not always capable of simultaneous unqualified enjoyment, a Bill of Rights evokes a determination of a priority of rights or values by reference to which the human rights in competition with each other may be adjusted. Once the right is defined, the Court must weigh the collective interest against the right of the individual. This is the stuff of politics, but a Bill of Rights purports to convert political into legal debate, and to judicialize questions of politics and morality.

Decision-making under a Bill of Rights starts, no doubt, with a construction of the relevant provisions of the Bill. But a Bill of Rights is merely the key that opens the door of jurisdiction: once inside, the question is whether the law or the exercise of Executive power which would otherwise result in one verdict or order should be held obnoxious to the relevant provisions of the Bill of Rights so that another verdict should be returned or another order made. What would otherwise be enforced as legal rights and legal liabilities are qualified by the Bill of Rights, and are enforceable only to the extent that they are, and are held to be, consistent with its terms. Of course, a decision, once made, would have the value of a judicial precedent but, in cases where there is no binding precedent precisely applicable, the trial must expand to encompass the issues raised by the Bill of Rights. The major premiss of the syllogism which leads to judgment must be ascertained not merely by reference to legislation and the common law but also by reference to the diverse and difficult issues created by the Bill of Rights.

Practical Impact of a Bill of Rights

These issues—which I shall call human rights issues, though human rights issues may arise independently of a Bill of Rights—must be resolved by methods which are different from the methods used to resolve other issues in a case. In the first place, the ordinary procedure of adducing evidence simply will not do. The rules of evidence govern the proof of the facts of a particular case—the minor premiss in the judicial syllogism. They do not necessarily apply to the determination of the legal rule which is relevant to the case—the major premiss. The issues under an entrenched Bill of Rights are constitutional issues and the decision affects the powers of Government and the interests of all who live under the Constitution: such issues cannot be made to depend upon the choice or the capacity of the parties to adduce the evidence necessary for the making of an informed decision. The evidence may be quite complex, for the effect of striking down a law or an Executive act which has been passed or done in the collective interest must be ascertained. It is no light thing to strike down a law or an Executive act which one of the political branches of Government, armed with information and experience much wider than the Court can muster, has deemed to be justifiable.

COST OF LITIGATION

The advocacy of human rights issues must range over wider fields than advocacy of other issues. Political, sociological and ethical considerations which impact on the existing legal system can be handled only with an appreciation of both the law and those other considerations. Professor Ferguson, reflecting on the Canadian experience, observed that the Charter has had a dramatic and, for many lawyers, a very stimulating effect on their work. The enactment of the Charter has provided lawyers with a sumptuous smorgasbord of new arguments. One effect, of course, is that a lawyer's research and trial preparation time has increased, which ultimately raises the cost of litigation.[9]

The cost of litigation is a matter of no small moment. As constitutional issues and the powers of Government are necessarily involved, provisions must be made for Governments to intervene to uphold the validity of laws or Executive actions which are attacked as obnoxious to a provision of the Bill of Rights. Though the underlying purpose of a Bill of Rights is the protection of individual interests, few individuals could afford to fund the major litigation which would be launched by raising one of its provisions. If an individual litigant succeeded at first instance by relying on such a provision, the prospects of appeal would surely be substantial. Of course, corporate litigants may seek to rely on Bill of Rights provisions in order to achieve a commercial or other advantage unrelated to the interests protected by the Bill of Rights,[10] and interest groups may use litigation as a means of advancing their political, social or ethical objectives.[11] Individuals may take the benefit of decisions given in litigation funded by others, but civil litigation under a Bill of Rights is hardly a practicable means for an individual to protect his or her individual rights against overreaching by Government. However, Bill of Rights litigation

---

[9] Ferguson, 'The Impact of an Entrenched Bill of Rights—The Canadian Experience', 16 *Monash University Law Review* (1990) 211 at 219.
[10] As in the case of *R.* v. *Big M Drug Mart Ltd* [1985] 1 SCR 295, (1985) 18 DLR (4th) 321.
[11] As in *Operation Dismantle* v. *R.* (1985) 18 DLR (4th) 481.

may be frequently conducted in the criminal jurisdiction where the cost may be borne by public funds. By whomsoever the cost of Bill of Rights litigation is met, it is likely to be substantial.

COURT LIST CONGESTION

Nor should the effect of such litigation on Court lists be underestimated. Court congestion, particularly in the criminal lists, would be aggravated by such litigation. Delay in the delivery of judgments, if the Canadian experience is any guide, is likely to grow.[12] And, in the High Court, a flow of Bill of Rights litigation could be accommodated only by shedding a corresponding volume of non-constitutional civil and criminal cases. The Court would be confined substantially to constitutional cases. With such a fascinating diet, the Court would in time have a diminished appetite for the pedestrian issues of the law.

At the end of the litigating day, the translation of political, social and ethical values into legal principles must be articulated by the judge. He or she cannot avoid giving effect to his or her values in determining whether an impugned law or Executive act is obnoxious to a Bill of Rights and unjustifiable in the collective interest. What the judge can and, if required, will do is to expose the reasoning which leads to the conclusion and to articulate a legal rule which gives effect to the conclusion.

TRANSFER OF POLITICAL OBLOQUY

It is the very process of open consideration of the issue arising under a Bill of Rights, its formalized debate between adversaries in the cool dignity of the Courtroom, the exposure of reasons and the articulation of the applicable legal rule that commends the Courts as the repositories of a supervisory power over the political branches of Government. A new judicial role under a Bill of Rights has attractions not only for those who would challenge the actions of Government, but for Government itself. There are some issues which, in a pluralist and divided society, are the subject of such controversy that no political party wishes to take the responsibility of solving them. The political process may be paralysed. If Governments can create a situation where such issues are submitted to curial decision, political obloquy can be avoided by Governments, though it is sometimes transferred to the Courts, as the continuing controversy over *Roe* v. *Wade* illustrates.[13] However, the

---

[12] See Professor Ferguson n. 9 above at 218.
[13] 410 US 113 (1973); *see* in this respect the judgment of Scalia J. in *Webster* v. *Reproductive Health Services,* 492 US (1989) 490 at 535, and the conflicting opinions in *Planned Parenthood of Southeastern Pennsylvania* v. *Casey,* 60 USLW (1992) 4795.

judicial method commands a broader acceptance than the political process, and the Courts, in exercise of a jurisdiction under a Bill of Rights, can sometimes cut a political Gordian knot. The desegregation decisions of the Supreme Court of the USA provide the classic example.

Training and Selection of Judges

As the powers conferred on the Courts under a Bill of Rights are powers to make political, social and ethical decisions affecting the whole community, the training and selection of judges must be accommodated to the additional functions they perform. That is because the effect of a Bill of Rights depends much more on the attitudes of the judges who interpret it than on the words themselves. Sir Harry Gibbs pointed out:

It is because of this that some apprehend that the adoption of a bill of rights will cause some dangers for the judiciary. It is not unnatural for a Government to think that it is justifiable to appoint judges who will be sympathetic to its views. It is a short step to the appointment of judges who, the Government believes, will carry out its wishes. The danger of the appointment of judges on purely political grounds is the greater if the Government strongly holds a policy which may be advanced or frustrated depending on how the bill of rights is interpreted.[14]

The exposure to public gaze of judicial personalities and beliefs is to be expected, if not welcomed, if a Bill of Rights were introduced. The Canadian experience is described by McLachlin M.J.:

The advent of the Charter in Canada has elevated judges from a position where they once toiled in relative obscurity, to the level of media figures. Now, more than ever before, the contributions made by the Courts are seen to impact so directly and profoundly on the everyday life of the country that judgments of the Supreme Court on the Charter receive regular and extensive attention from the news media.[15]

Whether the Australian people wish to alter the role the judiciary now performs is a matter of speculation. It is clear that the Australian judiciary could not perform a role under a Bill of Rights unless the Australian people consciously casts that role upon them. And it is only if the Australian people are made aware that a Bill of Rights will involve changes in judicial modes of thought, in the function of the Courts, in the magnitude and cost of some classes of litigation and in the projection of the Courts into the political dynamic that an informed decision can be made as to the desirability of a Bill

---

[14] Sir Harry Gibbs, 'Eleventh Wilfred Fullagar Memorial Lecture: The Constitutional Protection of Human Rights', 9 *Monash University Law Review* (1982) 1 at 8.
[15] Southey Memorial Lecture, 'The Canadian Charter and the Democratic Process', 18 MULR (1991) 350 at 355.

of Rights and the terms in which it should be cast. It will be necessary to determine what rights need to be constitutionally entrenched in order to protect minorities and the weak from discrimination; what rights need to be constitutionally entrenched in order to prevent the oppressive exercise of legislative or Executive power. That calls for an assessment to be made of the present capacity of the political process to prevent the excesses against which protection is sought and an assessment of the extent to which the Courts are presently incapable of extending the needed protection, even if aided by Statute. An Act of Parliament may suffice, for example, to ensure that a person suspected of crime is protected in a particular respect—say, in respect of a failure to bring the suspect to trial within a reasonable time. The New Zealand Court of Appeal has recently accorded a substantial operation to a statutory Bill of Rights to enhance the rights of a suspect under interrogation.[16] Constitutional entrenchment is not necessary unless there is an apprehension that a law will be directed or will operate against a minority group or against the weak in a discriminatory fashion or will vest in the Executive Government powers which can be exercised oppressively without the possibility of adequate supervision by the ordinary processes of judicial review. Of course, where there is a real risk of legislative sanction of State oppression, incapable of effective remedy by the existing political processes, or where there is a real risk of State discrimination incapable of remedy by the existing legal processes, a Bill of Rights offers a solution. The magnitude of the risk is a matter for the informed judgment of the Australian people.

In a very real sense, it does not matter what the impact of a Bill of Rights will be on judges; what is important is the impact of a Bill of Rights on the role of the judiciary. If the role be limited to the role hitherto discharged by the judiciary, the impact of a Bill of Rights will be to impair the capacity of the judges to perform that role. On the other hand, human rights issues, however arising in litigation, give the Courts a new relevance to the society they serve. The reason why the Courts might be required to assume a new relevance was stated by Sir Anthony Mason:

. . . the nature of society and place of the individual within it has changed markedly over the last hundred years. The common law of the 19th century was directed primarily at governing the relationships between individuals. Landlord/tenant and contract law come to mind. The common law, a body of rules crafted by judges and susceptible to modification by Legislatures, was well suited to regulating these relationships. However, the emergence of the omnipresent welfare state throws up problems of a different complexion. Government is now a major source of wealth and it participates in nearly every facet of social and economic life.[17]

---

[16] *R.* v. *Kirifi* (1991) 7 CRNZ 42.
[17] 'A Bill of Rights for Australia' n. 8 above at 85–6.

A new jurisdiction would be unattractive to many judges; to others, the heady powers conferred by a Bill of Rights would present a welcome challenge and an opportunity to sweep aside legislative and Executive action which impedes the doing of justice in the instant case. To all judges, however, the introduction of a Bill of Rights would bring a burden of decision-making far heavier than the burden of applying the existing law.

Is a New Constitutional Weapon Necessary to Maintain a Democratic Society?

However, it would be a mistake to think that judges are wholly unfamiliar with considerations of policy and are not affected—albeit to a strictly limited extent—by political, social or ethical values in the decisions which they render under the existing constitutional regime. Other writers have canvassed the ways in which Courts may, without constitutional entrenchment, give effect to human rights and fundamental freedoms. In interpreting Statutes, in judicially reviewing administrative action, in ascertaining the connection between a law of the Commonwealth and a head of constitutional legislative power, and in declaring the common law the Courts do not operate in a valueless vacuum. The decisions of the Australian Courts during the last decade owe much to judicial appreciation of human rights and fundamental freedoms. It is likely that, particularly under the influence of the First Optional Protocol to the International Covenant on Civil and Political Rights, concepts drawn from the developing international law of human rights and fundamental freedoms will find a reflection in the municipal law of this country. That said, there remains the question whether the Courts should be more fully equipped to stand between the power of the modern State and individual rights and interests and should be required to assume a supervisory role of a particular kind over the exercise of political power. In short, the question is whether the arming of the Courts with an additional constitutional weapon is desirable to assist in the creation and maintenance of a free and just society.

The answer to this question does not depend on some simplistic or doctrinaire view about the respective roles of the three branches of Government. The answer must depend on a number of factors. The first is whether the political processes of this country leave open a risk of State discrimination against minority groups or against the weak or a risk of oppressive exercise of Executive power that cannot be adequately supervised by judicial or other independent review, for example, review by the Administrative Appeals Tribunal. The next factor for consideration is the capacity of Courts and tribunals, either in exercise of existing jurisdiction or in exercise of a jurisdiction that could be conferred satisfactorily by Statute, to reduce the risks to an acceptably low level. Then, having assessed the extent of the otherwise irremediable risk, the desirability of entrenching a Bill of Rights must be balanced against the inevitable change which such entrenchment would bring in the role of the judiciary.

The question of an entrenched Bill of Rights or no is a political question in the broadest sense, though the constitutional lawyer has a great deal to contribute to the debate. But, as the other Chapters in this book reveal, the question requires an assessment of the operation of our existing constitutional institutions and an examination of the way in which they protect or can be made to protect human rights and fundamental freedoms. We are benefited by the Canadian experience and I would hope that, if the Australian people should cast on Australian Courts the responsibility of administering a Bill of Rights in this country, the Courts may win the respect which the decisions of the Supreme Court of Canada have earned for that distinguished tribunal.[18]

[18] See, e.g. Alexander, 'The Supreme Court of Canada and the Canadian Charter of Rights and Freedoms', 40 UTLJ (1990) 1 at 40, cited by Professor Ferguson n. 9 above at 227.

13

Bills of Rights in Comparative Perspective

MAC DARROW AND PHILIP ALSTON

*A society where rights are not secured
or the separation of powers established
has no constitution at all.*[1]

Introduction

CONSTITUTIONS, CONSTITUTIONALISM AND BILLS OF RIGHTS

Constitution-making is an activity that has been especially high on the agenda of an unprecedented number of states during the final decade of the twentieth century. It is by now a truism that the adoption of a constitution does not, in and of itself, signal a state's commitment, even in theory, let alone in practice, to constitutionalism. While the latter has been the subject of a great many definitions, it will suffice for present purposes to accept the minimum ingredients noted by Louis Henkin:

(1) government according to the constitution;
(2) separation of powers;
(3) popular sovereignty and democratic governance;
(4) constitutional review;
(5) an independent judiciary;
(6) controlling the police;
(7) civilian control of the military;
(8) individual rights;
(9) suspension and derogation provisions; and
(10) provision for amendment.[2]

Drawing upon this type of approach, a bill of rights has often been considered to be a vital ingredient in the overall recipe that makes up the elusive notion of constitutionalism.[3] The importance attached to human rights will

---

[1] Article 16 of the Declaration of the Rights of Man and the Citizen 1789.

[2] Henkin, 'Elements of Constitutionalism', Occasional Paper Series, August 1994, Centre for the Study of Human Rights, Columbia University.

[3] Nowhere is the term authoritatively defined, although various commentators have argued that the concept enshrines respect for human worth and dignity as its central principle, fostering conditions for political participation and legitimating substantive restraints on governmental power, even in cases where government action purportedly mirrors the popular will. Murphy,

depend in part upon factors such as the perceived relationship between law and politics, [4] the relationship between the individual and the community, [5] and the preferred philosophical understandings which are considered to underpin notions of government, human rights,[6] and the rule of law. [7]

International relations theories popular in the aftermath of the Cold War have also given an impetus to efforts to link constitutionalist approaches and especially their human rights components to the quest for international peace. So-called 'democratic peace' theories underscore this linkage. In its broadest form, the argument is that governments which are not democratically accountable to their own people are more likely to commit abuses of human rights, both within and beyond their borders, than are democratically elected governments whose options are constrained by constitutional institutions and processes.[8] Thus to the extent that constitutions reflect and provide effective safeguards for the exercise of civil and political rights (such as the right to vote, and the rights to recognition and equality before the law, and the right to freedom of thought, expression and political association), they play a potentially important role in the protection of human rights internationally and not just domestically.

Despite the obvious appeal of such a link and the welcome vindication it provides to those who advocate bills of rights, causality can be difficult to demonstrate. The role of other factors such as population size, inequality, type

'Constitutions, Constitutionalism, and Democracy' in Greenberg, et al. (eds.), Constitutionalism and Democracy: Transitions in the Contemporary World (1993), 67.

[4] For example, Richard Bellamy argues that constitutionalism so rendered is deeply rooted in political and social structures, rather than 'pre-political legal norms.' Thus, the goals of constitutional government are broader than upholding the rule of law and rights against the arbitrary exercise of power, although it includes these concerns. With appropriate institutional design, this account also ensures that groups and interests within society are brought together into dialogue with each other, ensuring that the making of law reflects 'mutual concern and respect and a desire to promote the common welfare'. See Bellamy, 'The Political Form of the Constitution: the Separation of Powers, Rights and Representative Democracy' in Bellamy and Castiglione (eds.), Constitutionalism in Transformation: European and Theoretical Perspectives (1996), 44. Of course, none of this implies mutual exclusivity between law and politics—see e.g. MacCormick, 'Liberalism, Nationalism and the Post-sovereign State' in Bellamy and Castiglione (eds.) ibid. at 145.

[5] See e.g. Bellamy, n. 4 above, at 43-4.

[6] For a range of views see e.g. Waldron, 'A Right-Based Critique of Constitutional Rights', (1993) Oxford Journal of Legal Studies 12; Dworkin, Taking Rights Seriously (1977); Dworkin, 'Constitutionalism and Democracy', (1995) 3 European Journal of Philosophy 2 at 2–11; Rawls, 'The Law of Peoples' in Shute and Hurley (eds.), On Human Rights: The Oxford Amnesty Lectures 1993 (1993), 41 at 68–71.

[7] See Dicey, The Law of the Constitution (1915), 3–4: 'The principle of parliamentary sovereignty means neither more nor less than this, namely, that Parliament . . . has, under the English constitution, the right to make or unmake any law whatever; and, further, that no person or body is recognised by the law of England as having a right to override or set aside the legislation of Parliament'. These theories have come under heavy criticism. See e.g. Prosser, 'Understanding the British Constitution' in Bellamy and Castiglione (eds.), n. 4 above, at 63 (citations at n. 12).

[8] Gartzke, 'Kant We All Just Get Along?: Opportunity, Willingness, and the Origins of the Democratic Peace', (1998) 42 American Journal of Political Science 1.

of political regime, the extent to which the views of citizens can be effectively represented, and the extent to which the state is linked into international economic and trade networks will all need to be taken into account.[9] Moreover, there is evidence to show that the so-called 'democracies' are just as war-prone as others insofar as conflict with 'non-democracies' is concerned. It has been argued that the validity of the suggested relationship depends upon a *substantive* vision of democracy,[10] safeguarding not merely the bare civil and political rights, but embracing all guarantees required to make the exercise of those rights effective, including minority rights protections and economic and social rights guarantees.[11] Such approaches bring us back to the question of the appropriate place of rights in a theory of constitutionalism.

But the range of case studies contained in the present volume does not provide a definitive answer to the question as to whether a constitutionalist approach actually requires any particular type of relationship between the constitution and a bill of rights, however such a bill may be formulated. There continue to be states—although their numbers are dwindling—which meet all or most of the requirements of constitutionalism but which have not opted to have a bill of rights, or at least not one that is either constitutionally entrenched or proclaimed as a separately enforceable instrument.

Some commentators have disputed the assumption that there is a certain equilibrium between constitutionalism and human rights and have suggested that judicial review of a human rights framework is now 'the prime component of constitutionalism, providing a normative legal framework within which politics operates'.[12] This is not problematic *per se* but in this view, political mechanisms are relegated to playing no more than a secondary role; rights provide the constitutional substance while politics does little more than provide the means by which those goals can be achieved. '[C]onstitutionalism has come to mean nothing more than a system of legally entrenched rights that can override, where necessary, the ordinary political process.'[13] While this is a version of the relationship between rights and constitutionalism which would

[9] See generally Powell, *Contemporary Democracies: Participation, Stability and Violence* (1982); Gowa, 'Democratic States and International Disputes', (1995) 49 *International Organisation* 511; and Krain, 'Contemporary Democracies Revisited: Democracy, Political Violence, and Event Count Models', (1998) 31 *Comparative Political Studies* 139.

[10] One context in which a definition of constitutional democracy has been developed is in the work of the OSCE—the Organisation for Security and Cooperation in Europe—through texts such as the Copenhagen and Paris Declarations. The emerging concept involves the establishment of genuine, multi-party democracies, committed to the rule of law and the protection of individual and minority rights. See Pogany, 'Constitution Making or Constitutional Transformation in the Post-Communist Societies?' in Bellamy and Castiglione (eds.), n. 4 above, at 156.

[11] Prosser, n.7 above.   [12] Bellamy, n. 4 above, at 24.

[13] *Ibid.* See also Dworkin, n. 6 above, at 2; Ferrajoli, 'Democracy and the Constitution in Italy' in Bellamy and Castiglione (eds.), n. 4 above, at 52–3; and Rawls, n. 6 above, at 71, describing human rights as a 'necessary condition of a regime's legitimacy and of the decency of its legal order'.

be strongly contested by many commentators,[14] it draws some strength from developments at the international level. Thus, for example, Michael Reisman has suggested that '(w)e have unwittingly reached the point where international legal standards require states to have appropriate national constitutions. The Universal Declaration of Human Rights and the International Covenants necessarily imply a right to an appropriate constitution'.[15] He reaches this conclusion in part by discerning a causal connection between constitutional principles and economic performance and concluding that constitutional protection of economic and social rights is also necessary for the maintenance of a stable international order.[16]

This assertion goes well beyond the traditional position which is that a state must take whatever steps may be 'necessary to give effect to' its human rights undertakings, to use the terminology reflected in the International Covenant on Civil and Political Rights (Article 2(2)), but that it remains free to decide whether or not to give constitutional recognition to those rights.[17] Indeed international instruments have carefully avoided setting specific obligations in terms of the type of measures that are required. Article 4 of the Convention on the Rights of the Child contains the most comprehensive of the treaty formulations—requiring States Parties to undertake 'all appropriate legislative, administrative, and other measures' of implementation—but it still remains for the state concerned to determine what is 'appropriate'.[18] Some European commentators, however, have gone beyond this position. Thus, for example, a leading European Community lawyer, Pierre Pescatore, has asserted that the good faith implementation of treaty provisions protecting individual rights generally requires that the relevant provisions be made part of domestic law so that the individual can rely on the rights before domestic courts.[19] Similarly, Frowein, a former senior member of the European Commission on Human Rights, has observed that 'it is very regrettable indeed that the Convention should not be internally applicable in all European countries.'[20] Such arguments have not, however, previously been developed outside of the European context, despite the frustration clearly felt by the United Nations

---

[14] e.g. Sniderman et al., The Clash of Rights: Liberty, Equality, and Legitimacy in Pluralist Democracy (1996).

[15] Reisman, 'Introductory Remarks', (1994) 19 Yale Journal of International Law 189 at 190.

[16] Ibid.

[17] Schachter, 'The Obligation to Implement the Covenant in Domestic Law' in Henkin (ed.), The International Bill of Rights: The Covenant on Civil and Political Rights (1981), 311.

[18] The state party is, of course, expected to take account of any pertinent observations made by the Committee on the Rights of the Child when exercizing its supervisory functions under the Convention.

[19] Pescatore, 'Conclusion' in Jacobs (ed.), The Effect of Treaties in Domestic Law (1987), 273 at 282.

[20] Frowein, 'The European Convention on Human Rights as the Public Order of Europe', (1992) 1 (2) Collected Courses of the Academy of European Law 267, 294.

supervisory bodies as a result of the inadequacy of measures taken by some states to give effect to the relevant rights in domestic law.[21]

There are, of course, external pressures upon states to demonstrate their commitment to respect human rights. As Eric Stein has observed, '(e)ven the traditional rules of recognition of states and governments appear to be changing, in that observance of basic human rights is increasingly required as an additional precondition to recognition'.[22] In addition, the conditions set by the European Community to be met by those states which aspire to future membership, put a strong premium upon constitutionalization of rights.[23] So too, albeit in a more understated way, does the increasing pressure on states to demonstrate good governance practices as a prerequisite to attracting loans and foreign investment.

These trends do not go as far as the proposition put forward by Reisman. But while his statement might be interpreted as greatly raising the stakes, it also leaves open the interpretation of what constitutes an 'appropriate constitution'. Clearly, a constitution which violates or contains provisions which are obviously inconsistent with any of the norms contained in the international bill of rights could not be considered to be appropriate by this standard. But assuming that there is no such incompatibility, the question remains as to whether a state is actually required to include certain minimum provisions in its constitution. Are there substantive norms, specific international arrangements, or a particular relationship between constitutional norms and international human rights law, which must be reflected in a constitution, whether written or otherwise?

While it would be difficult to provide a very detailed affirmative response to that question, the approach which emerges from the contributions to this volume is that it is becoming increasingly difficult for a state to demonstrate that it has taken all appropriate measures in the absence of some kind of constitutional recognition of human rights standards. The most common ways of doing this are either directly through a bill of rights or indirectly through provisions which

[21] In somewhat understated fashion, Nowak has discerned 'a certain tendency [on the part of the Human Rights Committee] to promote the direct applicability of the' International Covenant on Civil and Political Rights. See Nowak, *U.N. Covenant on Civil and Political Rights: CCPR Commentary* (1993) 54, para. 50. Similarly, in its General Comment No. 9 (1998), the United Nations Committee on Economic, Social and Cultural Rights stated that '[i]n general, legally binding international human rights standards should operate directly and immediately within the domestic legal system'. While conceding that the 'Covenant itself does not stipulate the specific means by which its terms are to be implemented in the national legal order [and that] there is no provision obligating its comprehensive incorporation or requiring it to be accorded any specific type of status in national law', the Committee emphasized that 'the means used should be appropriate in the sense of producing results which are consistent with the full discharge of its obligations by the State Party': UN doc. E/CN.12/1998/24 (1998), paras. 4–5.

[22] Stein, 'International Law in Internal Law: Toward Internationalisation of Central-Eastern European Constitutions', (1994) 88 *AJIL* 427 at 448.

[23] See Alston and Weiler, 'An "Ever Closer Union" in Need of a Human Rights Policy', (1998) 9 *European Journal of International Law* 658.

ensure that international human rights treaty obligations as well as international customary law will prevail over inconsistent municipal laws.

This volume also shows that even where neither of these two steps has been taken, the international human rights regime is gradually starting to narrow the other options which are open to states. Those which have opted neither for a bill of rights nor the entrenchment or incorporation of treaty obligations are coming under increasing pressure to develop other techniques by which human rights can be vindicated. Ultimately, as has proven to be the case with the United Kingdom, the shortcoming of those techniques is such that a bill of rights becomes the preferred option.

THE LIMITATIONS OF COMPARATIVE ANALYSIS

Before embarking upon an attempt to compare some of the approaches reflected in the bills of rights examined in this volume, it is appropriate to acknowledge that there are significant limits to such comparative analysis. In the first place, it is apparent that bills of rights cannot be viewed as a separate or self-sufficient dimension of a state's constitutional apparatus. Rather, they must be seen as a central part of an overall constitutional process, looked at in its political, social, cultural and (importantly) institutional dimensions. The latter dimension includes their actual and potential relationships with political institutions, domestic courts and human rights institutions.[24] For the same reason, any simple comparison of different constitutional texts is of limited value. An exploration of text, in the absence of any deeper exploration or analysis of the prevailing system of government, of the role played by the legal system, and of the *de facto* significance attributed to constitutional norms, inevitably provides only a very limited, detached and potentially misleading view of the overall situation in any given country.

[24] For present purposes the term 'human rights institution' can be defined as independent entities which have been established by a government under the constitution or by a law and entrusted with specific responsibilities in terms of the promotion and protection of human rights—see Gallagher, 'Making Human Rights Treaty Obligations a Reality: Working with New Actors and Partners' in Alston and Crawford (eds.), *The Future of UN Human Rights Treaty Monitoring* (forthcoming). A sense of the diversity of these institutions can be gained from the following list of those that addressed the United Nations Commission on Human Rights in April 1999: Asia-Pacific Forum of National Human Rights Institutions; Observatoire national des droits de l'homme (Algeria); National Human Rights Commission of India; Defensor del Pueblo (Columbia); Northern Ireland Human Rights Commission; Uganda Human Rights Commission; South African Human Rights Commission; Conseil consultatif des droits de l'homme du Royaume du Maroc; Commission nationale des droits de l'homme (Togo); Human Rights and Equal Opportunity Commission of Australia; Canadian Human Rights Commission; National Commission of Mexico; National Commission on Human Rights and Freedom (Cameroon); Procuradoria para la defensa de los derechos humanos de El Salvador; Philippine Human Rights Commission; Commission supérieure des droits de l'homme et des libertés fondamentales de Tunisie; New Zealand Human Rights Commission; National Human Rights Commission (Nigeria); and Indonesian National Commission on Human Rights. See UN Press Release HR/CN/927, 22 April 1999, 1–2.

The second observation is that, in comparing bills of rights, much depends upon the consequences that attach to the recognition of a specific list of rights, especially in terms of the legal and administrative consequences that follow and the availability or otherwise of judicial remedies. Where such remedies are available, constitutional texts are likely to make rather sparing use of the terminology of rights. In other states, considerable political importance may be attached to the designation of a value as a 'human right' but the practical consequences thereof may not extend very far, or they may be hedged around with procedural obstacles which strongly limit the actual utility of any purported remedy. While there is no single authentic model in this regard, the question which arises is how far we can reasonably go in insisting upon something which resembles American-style judicial review as a prerequisite for endorsing the adequacy of a bill of rights. At the end of the day, while underlining the legitimacy of a range (albeit not one without limit) of normative models, we cannot avoid the fact that comparative constitutional analysis of rights (particularly on a world-wide basis) is inevitably an exercise involving not only apples and oranges, but something closer to a comparison of peas and donkeys.

The third observation, which goes potentially in the opposite direction to the second, is that bills of rights are much more difficult to locate on the relativist-universalist spectrum than most observers would assume. On the one hand, it is true, as many commentators have pointed out, that inappropriate foreign models will not succeed when artificially transplanted to different environments. One commentator has spoken disparagingly of a 'Third World' model, in which 'constitutions tend to be ideal-typical statements of what the world should be like and which frequently involve heavy borrowing of institutions from western countries, often with unsuccessful results'.[25] Yash Ghai warns, in the context of constitutional design, against the 'enormous imposition of western political and cultural values on many peoples living in economic and social circumstances that have fashioned a different ethic'.[26] Yet despite the strong appeal of this modified relativism in relation to constitutions and by extension to bills of rights, there are also strong universalist trends which are not only applying international pressure to move towards a more standardised model but are also facilitating and helping to reinforce such convergence.

[25] Banting and Simeon (eds.), *Redesigning the State: The Politics of Constitutional Change* (1985), 7.
[26] Ghai, 'Bills of Rights: Comparative Perspectives' in Wacks (ed.), *Hong Kong's Bill of Rights: Problems and Prospects* (1990), 15–16.

Informal Bills of Rights

While the focus of this volume is on the promotion of human rights through bills of rights, there is no indispensable direct link between the relevant bill of rights and the international standards that have come to be almost synonymous with the definition of human rights. Nevertheless, it is clear that international standards have come to play an increasingly important role even within those countries whose bills of rights are determinedly home-grown and the adoption of which precedes the acceptance of international treaty obligations on the part of the state concerned. In the survey that follows particular attention is given to the ways in which international standards relate to domestic bills of rights.

As we saw in the introduction to this volume, there is no single model, nor even a standard definition of what constitutes a bill of rights. Moreover, because instruments which so proclaim themselves can sometimes be less extensive or comprehensive in terms of the human rights protection they provide than can other techniques in use in some countries, it seems inappropriate to confine our inquiry to formally designated bills of rights. In the survey that follows, which draws directly upon the case studies presented above, account is therefore taken of what we have chosen to call informal bills of rights. These include the use of the common law to provide protection across a significant range of human rights issues and the use of other techniques such as pre-legislative scrutiny to ensure legislative conformity with human rights codes. In addition, a distinction is drawn between bills of rights which do not enjoy a superior status in comparison to other forms of legislation and those which are entrenched in some way in the sense that their amendment is somehow made more difficult and they are assumed in the normal course of events to override normal legislative enactments in the case of inconsistency.

THE COMMON LAW AS AN INFORMAL BILL OF RIGHTS

One way in which a state may informally adopt or develop a bill of rights is through the development of a corpus of common law rights. This is well illustrated by the analysis in this volume by Doyle and Wells,[27] who identify and discuss four ways in which the common law, conceived of in broad terms as judge-made law, can protect human rights. These are through:

(a) the development of common law rights;
(b) rules of statutory interpretation;
(c) reconstruction of express constitutional guarantees, and

---

[27] Doyle and Wells, 'How Far Can the Common Law Go Toward Protecting Human Rights', chapter 2 above.

(d) limitations on parliamentary power construed from constitutions in the form of 'implied rights'.

Doyle and Wells observe that the first method, the development of fundamental common law rights, is inherently limited in the sense that such rights are only residual in character, and can be overridden by parliament and thus readily extinguished. A further limiting factor is judicial willingness. Judicial conservatism, in the name of confining the judicial role to the application of the law, clearly has the potential to constrain the development of the common law in this field. [28] Similarly, Clapham is critical of what he perceives to be the lack of innovation shown by the English courts in human rights matters. Following a review of case law, he observes that although the European Convention on Human Rights (ECHR) has become an established point of reference in decisions of English courts determining the scope of the common law, British judges still have some way to go before the human rights in the ECHR will be vigorously protected as part of the common law.[29] On the present state of the common law, such conventions are likely to be used by courts to develop the law and interpret statutes only where the existing state of the law is unclear.[30] Another inherent limitation is that the development of the law is 'opportunistic', in the sense that legal progress depends upon human rights issues being raised on a case by case basis. This approach has the further effect of what Doyle and Wells call 'compartmentalism'—rights are not applied in a general or principled fashion, but differently according to the situation.[31]

Nevertheless, the High Court of Australia has shown that it is prepared to develop at least some rights, particularly in relation to issues which are not directly governed by statute or constitutional law. Doyle and Wells illustrate

---

[28] Doyle and Wells, *ibid.* at 47. See also Jones, 'Legal Protection for Fundamental Rights and Freedoms: European Lessons for Australia?', (1994) 22 *Federal Law Review* 57 at 60–61.

[29] Clapham, 'The European Convention on Human Rights in the British Courts: Problems Associated with the Incorporation of International Human Rights', chapter 4 above. For a different view see Lester, 'First Steps Towards A Constitutional Bill of Rights', (1997) 2 *European Human Rights Law Review* 124 at 124–6. Lord Lester (at 124–5) asserts that because the ECHR has not been incorporated into domestic law, it has been left to the judiciary and legal profession, unguided by legislation, to attempt to fill the gaps between Convention law and practice. In the face of 'parliamentary inertia', Lord Lester observes that British judges have become increasingly receptive to arguments based upon the ECHR, and have exhibited creativity and imagination in their use of the Convention to develop the common law and interpret legislation. His assessment (at 126) is that British judges are receptive to their anticipated role in interpreting a United Kingdom bill of rights, as long as it is not 'entrenched' (due to the strength of concerns about parliamentary sovereignty in the United Kingdom). See generally Beloff and Mountfield, 'Unconventional Behaviour? Judicial Uses of the European Convention in England and Wales', (1996) 1 *European Human Rights Law Review* 467.

[30] See in particular *R. v. Home Secretary, ex parte Brind* [1991] A.C. 696, HL, and also Doyle and Wells, n. 27 above, especially n. 219 and accompanying text, and Clapham, n. 29 above.

[31] Doyle and Wells, n. 27 above. See also Jones, n. 28 above at 62, noting that the European Court of Human Rights has in recent times concluded in a number of areas that the common law fails to provide the necessary protection for fundamental rights and freedoms.

this point by reference to the right to a fair trial and freedom of expression.[32] They observe an increasing willingness on the part of that court to use international standards to interpret and develop the common law, and a related willingness to take its own measure of what constitutes the 'prevailing social values' of Australia, on the basis that the common law must keep in step with those standards and values.[33]

In countries like Australia it has long been claimed by some observers that traditional common law rights, combined with parliamentary action, are sufficient to protect rights. This view can be based either on a conviction that the common law is well equipped for the task, or that parliamentary supremacy should not be impinged upon through the undemocratic route of closing off certain options to the representatives of the people and putting interpretative power in the hands of unelected judges.[34] Doyle and Wells point to the limitations of the common law which, at present, protects some civil and political rights such as the right to a fair trial, but not others such as freedom from torture, privacy, and minority rights, or economic, social and cultural rights. These limitations are also noted by other contributors to this volume. Chanock traces the failure of the apartheid-era South African courts to apply the concept of the rule of law in such a way as to protect rights, as well as their failure to develop close scrutiny of administrative decisions.[35] Ghai also describes the position of rights protection in Kenya under common law which was characterized by administrative discretion and law making of a very discriminatory nature, which the courts were reluctant to review.[36]

As for the second method of common law protection of human rights— statutory interpretation—Doyle and Wells argue that it can protect rights through interpreting value laden clauses such as those commonly included in obscenity laws. Interpretative presumptions, such as that parliament does not, unless expressly stated, intend to override common law rights, are also important in this regard. The Australian High Court has, subject to certain caveats, shown an inclination to give more weight to such presumptions than other factors, including even express statements in second reading speeches.[37] Finally in relation to statutory interpretation, Doyle and Wells point to the increasing use by judges in both Australian and English courts of inter-

---

[32] Doyle and Wells, n. 27 above. See also Jones, n. 28 above, at 75–83. Irrespective of how important these decisions are from a human rights perspective, the rights themselves still remain only 'residual' in nature.

[33] Doyle and Wells, n. 27 above. This is in stark contrast, for example, to judicial attitudes in Kenya, where the courts have shown little understanding of the nature and value of human rights and related international jurisprudence, and have paid no regard to Kenya's international human rights obligations. See Ghai, 'The Kenyan Bill of Rights: Theory and Practice', chapter 6 above.

[34] See Campbell, 'Human Rights: A Culture of Controversy', (1999) 26 *Journal of Law and Society* 6.

[35] See Chanock, 'A Post-Calvinist Catechism or a Post-Communist Manifesto? Intersecting Narratives in the South African Bill of Rights Debate', chapter 10 above.

[36] Ghai, n. 33 above.   [37] Doyle and Wells, n. 27 above.

national instruments to assist in resolving statutory ambiguities. They consider English courts to have now more or less accepted the ECHR as a legitimate, even obligatory, source and that Australian courts will turn increasingly to the principles in the Covenant on Civil and Political Rights, in particular, to resolve uncertainties in statute law.[38]

The third way that the common law can protect rights is through the reconstruction of express constitutional guarantees. Doyle and Wells note that there are few express provisions in the Australian constitution which, on their face, appear to offer a measure of protection to the civil and political rights of individuals and that the High Court has tended to put a narrow construction on such provisions. They speculate that, given recent trends exhibited by the Court to ensure that its decisions reflect contemporary values (including a greater respect for human rights and tolerance for the beliefs and practices of others) and give meaning to the object of constitutional provisions, the Court might be expected to take a wider view of express constitutional guarantees in the future.[39]

Implied rights are another potential source of constitutionally-derived limitations on legislative power. In Australia the concept of a 'democratic society' has been used in this way, although the extent of such implication is likely to be limited to matters which are considered to be essential to the preservation of the integrity of the constitutional structure. Doyle and Wells note a certain responsiveness on the part of the Australian High Court to challenges to the doctrine of parliamentary sovereignty, but they stop short of concluding that, as a matter of principle, the courts should be able to strike down legislation for contravening fundamental human rights. Their reluctance to do so is linked to the fact that there are no 'democratically sanctioned guidelines', such as a bill of rights, which would indicate to a court the rights that are to be protected in such a way.[40]

In trying to explain the recent trends in judicial attitudes in Australia, Doyle and Wells point to general 'rights consciousness' and a willingness to give effect to rights, and an increasing judicial awareness both of the contents of the Covenant on Civil and Political Rights and of the way in which rights are protected in other systems of law.[41] Other factors might include recognition of

---

[38] *Ibid.*   [39] *Ibid.*   [40] *Ibid.*, especially nn. 340–1 and accompanying text.
[41] It would seem that accession to the Optional Protocol of the ICCPR is also a factor likely to influence judicial attitudes towards recognition of human rights—see e.g. *Mabo* v. *Queensland* (No. 2) (1992) 175 CLR 1 at 42: 'The opening up of international remedies to individuals pursuant to the Optional Protocol to the International Covenant on Civil and Political Rights brings to bear on the common law the powerful influence of the Covenant and the international standards it imports. The common law does not necessarily conform with international law, but international law is a legitimate and important influence on the development of the common law, especially when international law declares the existence of universal human rights' (per Brennan J, Mason CJ and McHugh J agreeing). See generally Jones, n. 28 above, at 84–7, and Lester, n. 29 above, at 125, on the effect on British judges of the reviewability of their decisions by the European Court of Human Rights in Strasbourg, under the ECHR.

the extent to which the legislative branch of government in practice is dominated by the executive, and of the extent to which legislatures—even in ostensibly democratic societies—fail to protect the rights of all individuals.[42] The
overall situation in Australia is thus one in which the issue of the appropriate
role of the judiciary in relation to the legislature in the protection of human
rights requires considerably more reflection. But despite the general optimism
of some commentators, a more guarded assessment has recently been put forward by a former Australian Chief Justice. As he put it (judiciously): 'there are
grounds for apprehension that Australia is not as deeply committed to *judicial*
protection of human rights as a number of Western nations, including the
United States, the United Kingdom, Canada and New Zealand'.[43]

USE OF INTERNATIONAL STANDARDS AT THE NATIONAL LEVEL

A second means by which a bill of rights might evolve through informal
means is through a growing reliance, not just in a common law-type situation
but more generally, upon international human rights standards. The domestic
importation of such norms is by no means confined to the activities of the
judiciary. It can also occur through the activities of various other institutions,
whether or not they have a formal mandate in relation to human rights.
National human rights institutions are an obvious example.[44] But Ombudsman's offices, law commissions, specialized units of government departments,
and non-governmental organizations (NGO's) are also especially effective
conduits in this regard.[45]

In general, it has been observed that there has been a steady increase in the
extent to which judges and lawyers are prepared to accept the relevance of
international human rights standards within the domestic context.[46] This
phenomenon is not only of relevance in so-called 'dualistic' constitutional systems, in which international law *per se* exists separately from national law, and
requires enactment or 'transformation' in order to have legal effect at the
national level.[47] In fact, the extent to which international human rights law
has penetrated ostensibly 'dualistic' legal orders is difficult to explain solely by

[42] Doyle and Wells, n. 27 above.

[43] Mason, 'The Role of the Judiciary in Developing Human Rights in Australian Law' in
Kinley (ed.), *Human Rights in Australian Law: Principles, Practice and Potential* (1998), 26
(emphasis in original).

[44] See n. 24 above.

[45] See e.g. Mulgan, 'Implementing International Human Rights Norms in the Domestic
Context: The Role of a National Institution', (1993) 5 *Canterbury Law Review* 235 at 235–6.

[46] For a discussion see Agbakoba, 'The Role of Lawyers and the Observance of Human
Rights', (1995) 5(1) *Journal of Human Rights Law and Practice* 115 at 147–9. See also Kirby,
'From Bangalore to Balliol—A View from the Antipodes' (1993) *University of New South Wales
Law Journal* 363.

[47] See *Trendtex Trading Corp* v. *Central Bank of Nigeria* [1977] 1 All E.R. 881 per Lord
Denning.

reference to the old monism/dualism dichotomy, and indeed a clear understanding can only be arrived at on the basis of a considerably more sophisticated conceptual framework.[48]

In the English context, attention has been drawn to four ways in which the ECHR can and does influence domestic court proceedings. They are:

(1) when the courts are construing a statute enacted to implement an ECHR obligation;
(2) where the courts have a discretion;
(3) when the courts are called upon to decide what approach conforms to public policy; and
(4) where European Community law is relevant and account is taken of the role of the ECHR therein.[49]

But it is not only the English courts which have been moving in this direction. In addition to the case studies contained in this volume, the courts and other institutions in a great many other countries have also been making effective use of international human rights standards in their activities.[50] Two examples of cases from Africa must suffice by way of illustration. The first is a 1990 Tanzanian case, *Ephraim* v. *Pastory*.[51] The case concerned an interpretation of provisions of the Tanzanian Constitution which prohibited discrimination (but not on the ground of gender or sex), with a view to determining whether a prohibition in customary law on the alienation of clan land was unconstitutional.[52] In interpreting the anti-discrimination provisions of the Constitution, the High Court invoked Tanzania's ratification of major international

[48] See e.g. Conforti, *International Law and the Role of Domestic Legal Systems* (1993) at 13–14 and 26; Scheinin, 'Domestic Implementation of International Human Rights Treaties' in Alston and Crawford (eds.), *The Future of the United Nations Human Rights Treaty System* (forthcoming). As Conforti and Scheinin suggest, studying the written terms of the constitution may shed considerably less light on the role of international law in the municipal legal system, than a jurisprudential analysis of how judges apply international law in practice.

[49] Straw and Boateng, 'Bringing Rights Home: Labour's Plans to Incorporate the European Convention on Human Rights into UK Law', (1997) 1 *European Human Rights Law Review* 71 at 73–4. See also Jones, n. 28 above, at 68–72.

[50] By way of example see the useful discussion of the role of international human rights law in domestic law in Caribbean countries, see Demerieux, *Fundamental Rights in Commonwealth Caribbean Constitutions* (1992), 109–19. In surveying relevant cases, she notes the range of interpretative uses to which judges have put international human rights instruments, including in assisting to determine legislative policy, and concludes that recourse to international conventions and law to help determine the meaning of a provision in a West Indian bill of rights (fundamental rights are part of the Supreme Law of all Commonwealth Caribbean States) 'may well develop into a feature of litigation in the region' (*ibid.*, 115). On the incorporation of international human rights standards into constitutional arrangements in other parts of the world, including Africa, Asia and Central and Eastern Europe, see Neuman (ed.), 'Rights in New Constitutions', (1994) 26 *Columbia Human Rights Law Review* at 1–213.

[51] [1990] LRC (Const) 757. See discussion of the case in Pritchard, 'The Jurisprudence of Human Rights: Some Critical Thought and Developments in Practice', (1995) 2 *Australian Journal of Human Rights* 3 at 25–6.

[52] *Ibid.* at 25.

human rights instruments, including the United Nations Convention on the Elimination of All Forms of Discrimination Against Women, to support a modification of customary inheritance rules so that 'males and females now have equal rights to inherit and sell clan land'.[53]

The second is a 1992 case in which the High Court of Botswana used the 1981 African Charter on Human and Peoples' Rights and the 1967 United Nations Declaration on the Elimination of All Forms of Discrimination Against Women to find that a provision of the 1984 Botswana Citizenship Act which discriminated against women in the conferral of citizenship was *ultra vires* the Constitution.[54] Averring to the very real nature of international human rights obligations under relevant international instruments, the High Court noted that it is 'difficult if not impossible to accept that Botswana would deliberately discriminate against women in its legislation whilst at the same time internationally support non-discrimination against females or a section of them'. The Court of Appeal agreed: 'Botswana is a member of the community of civilised States which has undertaken to abide by certain standards of conduct, and, unless it is impossible to do otherwise, it would be wrong for its courts to interpret its legislation in a manner which conflicts with the international obligations Botswana has undertaken.'[55]

Many other such cases from other jurisdictions could be cited.[56] They demonstrate the potential of international law, properly applied by local judges, to help change long-standing social and cultural practices which are incompatible with human rights standards.

Administrative decision-makers are also able to use international standards to regulate the exercise of administrative discretion, although the viability of this approach can also depend upon judicial endorsement. In the United Kingdom, the courts have held that there is no obligation on decision-makers to consider international standards, although decision-makers can refer to them in exercising a discretion if they choose to do so.[57] In Australia, in the case of *Minister for Immigration and Ethnic Affairs* v. *Ah Hin Teoh*[58] (Teoh's

---

[53] [1990] LRC (Const) 757.

[54] *Dow* v. *Attorney-General* [1991] LRC (Const) 574; *Attorney-General* v. *Dow* [1992] LRC (Const) 623, discussed in Pritchard, n. 51 above, at 26–7.

[55] *Dow* v. *Attorney-General*, n. 54 above, at 586; and *Attorney-General* v. *Dow*, n. 54 above, at 657. See discussion in Pritchard, n. 51 above, at 26–7. See also Byrnes, 'And Some Have Bills of Rights Thrust Upon Them: The Experience of Hong Kong's Bill of Rights', chapter 9 above, especially nn. 99 and 171 and accompanying text.

[56] See Dugard, 'The Role of Treaty-Based Human Rights Standards in Domestic Law: The Southern African Experience' in Alston and Crawford (eds.), *The Future of UN Human Rights Treaty Monitoring* (forthcoming) (noting that in Namibia, South Africa and Zimbabwe, the courts have made frequent use of international human rights jurisprudence, most notably decisions of the European Court and Commission under the ECHR, but also jurisprudence under the ICCPR and other United Nations conventions).

[57] See Clapham, n. 29 above; and Lester, n. 29 above at 125, especially n. 5 and accompanying text.

[58] (1995) 128 ALR 353.

case), the High Court stated that the executive act of ratification of a treaty (in the instant case, the United Nations Convention on the Rights of the Child), without legislative incorporation of the treaty, created a legitimate expectation that the Commonwealth government would act in accordance with its terms:

[R]atification by Australia of an international convention is not to be dismissed as a merely platitudinous or ineffectual act, particularly when the instrument evidences international accepted standards to be applied by courts and administrative authorities in dealing with basic human rights affecting the family and children. Rather, ratification of a convention is a positive statement by the executive government of this country to the world and to the Australian peoples that the executive government and its agencies will act in accordance with the convention.[59]

This is hardly a remarkable decision from a legal point of view, although it gave rise to considerable controversy within Australia.[60] One would naturally expect that governments would not make administrative decisions in a manner contrary to the international obligations that they freely undertake. To do otherwise would be to reduce those obligations to mere 'window dressing'.[61]

Finally, no discussion of the domestic effects of international human rights law would be complete without at least a brief reference to the pervasive influence that international standards can bring to bear on shaping ideas and values within societies, fostering conditions at the national level which are conducive to the reception of new behavioural norms. The Convention on the Rights of the Child is an excellent example of this phenomenon.[62]

INFORMAL BILLS OF RIGHTS THROUGH PRE-LEGISLATIVE SCRUTINY

In the absence of a formal bill of rights another method of promoting compliance with international standards is to put in place a system of pre-legislative scrutiny which requires the examination of all legislation, both primary and subordinate, to check compliance with the principles set out in one or other of the international treaties. Kinley's chapter in this volume proposes such a system on the basis of the Covenant on Civil and Political Rights. Other commentators have suggested that such schemes need not be limited to

[59] Per Mason CJ and Deane J at 365. For an excellent commentary on this decision, see Allars, 'One Small Step for Legal Doctrine, One Giant Leap Towards Integrity in Government: Teoh's Case and the Internationalisation of Administrative Law', (1995) 17 *Sydney Law Review* 204.

[60] Successive Australian Governments indicated, in 1995 and 1997 respectively, that they would legislate to counter the *Teoh* case, with a view to removing any legitimate expectation that administrative decision-makers should act in accordance with Australia's international obligations. See generally Alston and Chiam (eds.), *Treaty-Making and Australia: Globalisation and Sovereignty* (1995).

[61] *Tavita* v. *Minister for Immigration* [1994] 2 NZLR 257.

[62] See L. Woll, *The Convention on the Rights of the Child Impact Study: A Study to Assess the Effect of the Convention on the Rights of the Child on the Institutions and Actors who Have the Responsibility and the Ability to Advance Children's Rights* (1999).

review of civil and political rights, but may be expanded to included other 'generations' of rights, including economic, social and cultural rights.[63]

Kinley focuses specifically on the way in which such an approach would work in relation to the Australian upper house, the Senate, and its Committees. He identifies the following steps:

(1) The terms of reference of each committee would include scrutiny of bills for conformity with the rights protected in the Covenant.
(2) A human rights expert would be appointed to advise each committee.
(3) Committee membership could be extended to include members of both houses of Parliament.
(4) The human rights adviser would provide the committee with a regular appraisal of the compliance of bills with the relevant standards.
(5) The committees would be given some form of sanctioning power, such as moving a motion of disallowance or a prohibition of proceeding to the final reading of a bill until it has been cleared by the Committee.[64]

Pre-legislative scrutiny can of course exist along side formal bills of rights, as it does (for example) in Canada and New Zealand. In New Zealand, the Attorney-General examines laws and reports to Parliament if a law breaches the New Zealand Bill of Rights Act 1990. In his chapter in the present volume, Joseph gives examples of when this procedure has been used. It appears that the procedure is relatively effective, subject to certain limitations, in particular, the fact that there is no obligation on Parliament to follow the Attorney-General's report, and there is no provision for sanctioning the Attorney-General should she or he fail to report.[65] Similar criticisms might be made of Kinley's proposal, but in societies with a strong tradition of parliamentary sovereignty it is doubtful that stronger enforcement provisions would be acceptable.

Other commentators have hailed the Swedish model of legislative scrutiny as providing 'a particularly good working example of democratic socialism in action',[66] and a means of review which is 'more sympathetic than is judicial review to the notion of political equality in the sense that the final decision remains vested in the elected representatives of the people'.[67] Chapter 2 of the Swedish Instrument of Government sets out a number of fundamental free-

[63] See e.g. Adjei, 'Human Rights Theory and the Bill of Rights Debate', (1995) 58 *The Modern Law Review* 17 at 35. Aspects of this question will be taken up later, in reviewing the effectiveness of bills of rights in safeguarding economic, social and cultural rights. See nn.169–204 below and accompanying text.

[64] See Kinley, 'Parliamentary Scrutiny of Human Rights: a Duty Neglected?', chapter 5 above.

[65] See Joseph, 'The New Zealand Bill of Rights Experience', chapter 8 above.

[66] Ewing and Gearty, 'Rocky Foundations for Labour's New Rights', (1997) 2 *European Human Rights Law Review* 146 at 150.

[67] Ewing, 'Human Rights, Social Democracy and Constitutional Reform' in Gearty and Tomkins (eds.), *Understanding Human Rights* (1996), 40 at 55.

doms. It is the responsibility of the Constitutional Committee of the Riksdag to determine whether any bill affects any of the listed freedoms. Thus, it is the primary responsibility of the legislature itself, rather than the judiciary, to review legislation for consistency with human rights standards. A limited 'judicial review' system does exist, in the form of a 'Law Council', a body of three senior judges whose task it is to scrutinize legislation to ensure consistency with the Constitution and the ECHR.[68] However the views of the Law Council, although influential, are not conclusive, and it is open to Parliament to ignore its advice.[69] This system functions side by side with a domestic bill of rights since Sweden's Constitution contains a range of entrenched rights.

Various pre-legislative scrutiny schemes were put forward in relation to the United Kingdom prior to the adoption of the Human Rights Act 1998. In the event, the Act contains a provision requiring the government minister in charge of a bill in either House of Parliament to make a statement prior to the second reading of the bill to the effect that either its provisions are compatible with the rights contained in the ECHR (to be known as 'a statement of compatibility') or that the Government proposes to proceed with the bill despite the absence of such a statement.[70]

Another means by which such scrutiny might be achieved is through the establishment of a national human rights institution which is given a role in advising the parliament as to compatibility.[71] While a properly constituted and independent Human Rights Commission may have a comparative advantage over a Parliamentary Committee in terms of its expertise and the time available to it, the fact remains that it will rarely be accorded an assured role in the legislative process and can thus be marginalized over time if its contribution to the process is not appreciated.

An assessment of the effectiveness of these different approaches, in the abstract, is not worth undertaking since so much will inevitably depend on the context in which any given institution or arrangement is permitted to function. Nevertheless, pre-legislative scrutiny schemes would seem to have much to recommend them, whether or not functioning in conjunction with a bill of rights.

---

[68] *Ibid.* The Swedish courts also have a limited power of judicial review (notwithstanding that the ECHR has been incorporated into domestic law in Sweden), enabling them to refuse to apply a statute only if the 'fault is manifest', a power which has rarely been exercised. See generally Cameron, 'The Swedish Experience of the European Convention on Human Rights since Incorporation', (1999) 48 *International and Comparative Law Quarterly* 20.

[69] Ewing, n. 67 above, at 55.　　　　　　　　　　　　　　　　　　　　　[70] Section 19.

[71] See Institute for Public Policy and Research, 'A Human Rights Commission for the UK: The Options', Consultation Paper, December 1996, at 10.

Legislated Bills of Rights

Legislated bills of rights may take the form of a discrete piece of legislation or a package of different statutes which, when brought together, may be treated as a bill of rights. The latter approach is exemplified by the Israeli approach, described in this volume by Kretzmer. The former approach is discussed above in relation to the statutory bills of rights in New Zealand and the various proposals which were put forward in the United Kingdom prior to the adoption of the Human Rights Act 1998, and their actual and potential institutional relationships with parliamentary scrutiny of bills committees and human rights institutions. The importance of the judicial role in the implementation of the various 'informal' bills of rights applies with equal force here. In his chapter, Joseph describes the numerous ways and contexts in which the New Zealand Bill of Rights Act 1990 has been applied domestically.[72] On the basis of experience to date, there is some reason to conclude that a progressive or purposive interpretation of such statutes is likely, at least in the common law world.[73]

There are several possible attractions of a legislated bill of rights, from both theoretical and practical points of view. For example, legislative measures might be appropriate either as a temporary or even medium-term means of accommodating strong traditions of parliamentary sovereignty, and thereby enhancing the likelihood of the bill's acceptance.[74] From a theoretical standpoint, it has been argued that a legislative rather than constitutional response might be preferable in view of the inherent and inevitable disagreement about underlying human rights theories, and the inevitable requirement for amendment of bills of rights in line with changing values.[75]

But there are also a number of drawbacks to legislated bills of rights. The most obvious is that such instruments cannot override directly inconsistent legislation, and are subject to being repealed by ordinary legislation.[76]

---

[72] Joseph, n. 65 above.

[73] *Ibid.* at 236–7. See also Sharpe, 'The Impact of a Bill of Rights on the Role of the Judiciary: A Canadian Perspective', Chapter 11 above, for a discussion of the purposive method of interpretation. On the rules for construction of human rights statutes in Australia, see the High Court decision in *Waters* v. *Public Transport Corporation* (1991) 173 CLR 349 at 359, 406–7. Cf. Clapham, n. 29 above; Byrnes, n. 55 above, in view of Hong Kong's particular circumstances, relating both to the strength of British parliamentary institutional inheritances, and the transition to Chinese sovereignty.

[74] See e.g. Lester, n. 29 above.

[75] See e.g. Adjei, n. 63 above. But as Sharpe observes, at n. 73 above, this is exactly the exercise that judges undertake in breathing life and relevance into an entrenched charter of rights, to ensure that it is not fixed in time.

[76] See e.g. Dworkin, *A Bill of Rights for Britain* (1990) at 39–40, and Joseph, n.65 above, at 246–8. This is of course not to say that such a piece of legislation cannot contribute significantly to the nature and pace of change, particularly in conjunction with an active and independent judiciary, and other institutional links of the nature we have discussed earlier—see e.g. Lester, n. 29 above. Indeed in some situations the boundary between 'statutory' and 'constitutional'

Further there is some force in the argument that legislative bills are more prone to being limited to reflect the concerns of the government of the day, than are constitutionally entrenched bills. [77] Moreover, especially in light of the experience with the 1960 Canadian Bill of Rights, it may be that constitutional entrenchment will influence the extent to which a bill of rights is actually given effect by the judiciary.[78] The value of the judicial role is an issue which will be taken up in more detail when looking at entrenched bills of rights, but at least in the New Zealand case it seems clear that it has been largely the attitudes of judges which has made the Bill of Rights Act work.[79] Other aspects of statutory bills of rights will be considered when looking at entrenchment. But as a final point, it is also worth noting the demonstrated potential of statutory bills of rights, as has been the case in New Zealand, to facilitate broad acceptance of constitutional rights, preparing the ground for entrenchment, should this eventually be deemed necessary and desirable.[80]

The second situation, the use of comprehensive legislation rather than a single statutory bill of rights, needs only brief consideration here. In considering the overall desirability of an entrenched bill of rights, one of the factors identified by Sir Gerard Brennan in this volume is 'the capacity of courts and tribunals, either in exercise of existing jurisdiction or in exercise of a jurisdiction that could be conferred satisfactorily by statute',[81] to reduce risk of human rights abuse. Australia is one example of a country which has no formal bill of rights, but only discrete pieces of anti-discrimination and other human rights-related legislation at federal, state, and territory levels. In the Hong Kong situation Byrnes assesses the impact of the bill of rights in conjunction with other legislative measures, and notes in particular the influence of the bill of rights in generating legislative proposals in areas where previously there was little or no human rights protection.[82] Eberts also supports the complementary use of legislation and a bill of rights in relation to the Canadian federal system. In her chapter, she attributes part of what she considers to be the Canadian success to the fact that the Canadian Charter of Rights and Freedoms operates alongside ordinary legislation—the Provincial human rights codes—in mutually reinforcing ways, establishing a resonance between code and Charter jurisprudence and strengthening rights protection.[83]

---

mechanisms is not at all clear. For example in the New Zealand context it has been remarked that '(t)he Bill is not entrenched but it is not an ordinary Statute either'—*Herewini* v. *Ministry of Transport* (1992) 9 CR NZ 307 at 326 per Fisher J, cited by Joseph, n. 65 above, at n. 205 and accompanying text.

[77] Dworkin, n. 76 above, at 39.   [78] See Sharpe, n. 73 above.

[79] Cooke, 'Brass Tacks and Bills of Rights', (1995) 25 *Hong Kong L.J.* 64 at 72–3 and 77.

[80] Joseph, n. 65 above.

[81] Brennan, 'The Impact of a Bill of Rights on the Role of the Judiciary: An Australian Perspective', chapter 12 above at 463.

[82] Byrnes, n. 55 above.

[83] Eberts, 'The Canadian Charter of Rights and Freedoms: A Feminist Perspective', chapter 7 above.

Therefore, while ordinary legislative means of human rights protection have various potential attractions, their principal benefits are to be seen in their mutually reinforcing interaction with other mechanisms and institutions. Taking a so-called 'comprehensive' legislative approach, a further significant and inherent drawback lies in its failure to ensure coverage of the broad range of internationally recognized human rights. While this applies equally in relation to the 'indirect' bills of rights discussed earlier, it is a criticism which applies with less force in relation to constitutionally entrenched bills of rights, to which we now turn.

Entrenched Bills of Rights

In historical terms, there are many reasons why different societies have come to embrace constitutional bills of rights. The incorporation of human rights guarantees into constitutional orders seems to have been largely a Western inheritance. Notably, largely at the insistence of the Americans, the defeated powers at the end of the Second World War—Japan, Germany and Italy—incorporated bills of rights into their new constitutions (although there had also been a rich history of rights provisions in a range of German state and federal constitutions well before that time).[84] Numerous other countries around the globe were simultaneously or shortly thereafter escaping colonial rule, and inherited constitutional bills of rights as part of their colonial legacy. More recently many newly emerged or transformed states of Central and Eastern Europe, from a desire to distinguish themselves from the arbitrariness that characterized colonial or communist rule as the case may be,[85] and for various political and economic reasons,[86] have adopted constitutional bills of rights of their own.[87]

---

[84] See Beatty (ed.), *Human Rights and Judicial Review: A Comparative Perspective* (1994), 2.

[85] *Ibid.* The need for the constitutionalization of human rights in East Central Europe after 1989 is discussed in Osiatynski, 'Rights in New Constitutions of East Central Europe' in Neuman (ed.), n. 50 above, at 112–15. Osiatynski comments that '(t)he constitutionalisation of human rights and other limitations on the government's powers could protect these societies from a relapse to old methods of exercising arbitrary power without any constraints' (*ibid.*, 115).

[86] Notably, to meet conditions of highly prized membership in the European Union, along with the general purpose of encouraging foreign investment. However in certain cases it has been suggested that the constitutionalization of human rights standards has occurred out of a cynical desire to avoid genuine transformation—Pogany, n. 10 above, at 177–9. Other motivations of a practical nature, relating particularly to the use or incorporation of international standards in municipal bills of rights, emerge from South Africa's constitutional drafting experience. As Dugard has remarked 'Great care is taken to ensure that the bill of rights complies with international norms. Although the rights are formulated in simpler language than that found in most human rights conventions, in pursuance of a deliberate policy to make the Constitution accessible to the people, the rights are broadly modelled on their international counterparts. In part this was done in order to facilitate South Africa's accession to international human rights treaties' Dugard, n. 56 above.

[87] Beatty, n. 84 above, at 3.

In considering whether to implement a constitutionally entrenched bill of rights, Sir Gerard Brennan suggests that three factors need to be taken into account. One of these, as already mentioned, is whether courts and tribunals in the exercise of their existing or extended jurisdiction, could play their part in reducing the risk of human rights abuse to acceptably low levels.[88] The other factors are:

(1) whether the political processes in a country leave open risks of human rights abuse that cannot be adequately supervised by judicial or other independent review; and
(2) the extent of change in the role of the judiciary which would be brought by entrenchment.[89]

The latter factor is central to much of the on-going debate on bills of rights. To the extent that objections to entrenched bills of rights assume a strictly positivist conception of the contemporary role of judges in the common law world—limited to the application of rules rather than the making of subjective decisions—they are increasingly out of touch with contemporary understandings.[90] The *desirability* of 'judicial activism' from a democratic point of view, however, is a separate issue on which views strongly differ, and we will return to it below.

Before considering the advantages of entrenched bills of rights from the point of view of ensuring respect (in particular, judicial respect) for the norms and protection from legislative amendment, it may be noted that it is not always easy to make a clear distinction between such bills and others with ordinary legislative force.[91] Depending upon such factors as the particular provisions of legislative bills of rights, and the political and judicial arrangements for their implementation, 'mere' legislated bill of rights may well effectively assume an 'entrenched' character.[92]

ARGUMENTS IN FAVOUR OF ADOPTING A CONSTITUTIONALLY ENTRENCHED BILL OF RIGHTS

In considering the arguments in favour of an entrenched bill of rights[93] it is necessary to bear in mind that any generalisations in this field are fraught with risk. Very much depends on the specific details of a given bill, on the legal, political and human rights cultures within which it is located and on a variety of other factors. Nevertheless, the case studies canvassed in this volume provide enough insights to enable us to identify at least some of the most

---

[88] Brennan, n. 81 above.   [89] *Ibid.*

[90] See e.g. Doyle and Wells, n. 27 above, especially nn. 23–5 and accompanying text. See also Mason, 'Future Directions in Australian Law', (1987) 13 *Monash University Law Review* 149.

[91] See e.g. Joseph, n. 65 above; Lester, n. 29 above at 127–8; Dworkin, n. 76 above, at 28; and Ewing and Gearty, n. 66 above, at 147-8.

[92] *Ibid.*   [93] Zander, *A Bill of Rights?* 4th ed. (1997), 40-69.

significant ways in which constitutionally entrenched bills of rights can work within an appropriate and supportive institutional framework.

Fostering a 'culture of liberty'

In contrast to statutory or implied bills of rights, the potentially valuable role of constitutional bills of rights in contributing to the overall 'culture of liberty' within any given society warrants emphasis.[94] Constitutions are not self-activating and one of the preconditions for effective constitutional human rights protection is the existence of a constitutional culture appropriate for ensuring that bills of rights are received and implemented in constructive ways.[95]

This is not to say that the constitutional culture must necessarily be nurtured over a prolonged period of time. The fractured post-apartheid society in South Africa, for example, required something quite drastic in terms of the constitution-building process, as is discussed in Chanock's chapter. Although the success of the South African Bill of Rights in striking a workable compromise looks likely,[96] Chanock comments that the South African story 'is not one of a reform process building incrementally towards a rights oriented Constitution, but one of a sharp change of political direction'. With this in mind, and with so little to build upon in terms of the prerequisites for a unifying constitutional culture, 'the attraction . . . of a grand new statement like a bill of rights [with legitimacy derived from its basis in international standards[97]] is obvious'.[98] Addressing the symbolic value imported by an entrenched bill of rights, he remarks that a ' bill of rights was crucial ... to the whole question of legitimacy of a post-apartheid regime. For its powerful symbolism would establish an arena not just for law, but would also be a definition of what is, and is not, legitimate in politics'.[99]

Canada's situation is particularly interesting in this respect, given the judiciary's relatively uninspiring record in interpreting the statutory bill of rights that preceded the 1982 Charter. Although a range of factors may have contributed to this, it is generally accepted that the record of the Supreme Court of Canada (prior to the Charter) in applying the statutory Canadian Bill of Rights varied from 'the dismal to the disastrous'.[100] Penner postulates that the Charter has brought a considerable enhancement of what Dworkin refers to

---

[94] See discussion in Dworkin, n. 76 above, at 10–11.

[95] See e.g. Okoth-Ogendo, 'Constitutions without Constitutionalism: Reflections on an African Political Paradox' in Greenburg *et al.* (eds.), n. 3 above, 65–82 at 79–80; Azzam, *Arab Constitutional Guarantees of Civil and Political Rights* (1996) especially at 111–14.

[96] See Ellman, 'The New South African Constitution and Ethnic Division' in Neuman (ed.) n. 50 above, 5 at 34–40 and 44; and Kentridge, 'Parliamentary Supremacy and the Judiciary Under a Bill of Rights: Some Lessons from the Commonwealth', [1997] *Public Law* 96 at 100–1.

[97] Chanock, n. 35 above, at 400.   [98] *Ibid.* at 402.   [99] *Ibid.* at 394.

[100] Penner, 'The Canadian Experience with the Charter of Rights', [1996] *Public Law* 104 at 114–15.

as 'the culture of liberty', and that this is reflected in many activities of federal and provincial government (notably, in amending statutes to ensure Charter compliance), as well as in academic writings, widespread publicity through the popular journals and mass electronic media (and commensurate wide-spread public receptiveness), affirmative action programs, pay equity legislation, and the expansion of judicial education programs to embrace issues of systemic discrimination, equality rights and judicial bias with respect to minority and disadvantaged groups.[101] Penner's view is that the 'undoubted strengthening of the "culture of liberty" has not come at the cost of electoral democracy in Canada',[102] notwithstanding the active judicial role in interpreting and applying a constitutional bill of rights. It is to that judicial role, contrasted with the protection of rights through parliamentary processes, to which we now turn.

Parliament protects only the 'loudest and most powerful voices'

In terms of the law-making role of the judiciary, the need for the courts to develop the law to respond to changes emanating from an increasingly pluralistic and rights-conscious society becomes clearer if we acknowledge the inevitable limitations of Parliament's capacity to protect the rights of all members of society. As Doyle and Wells note, 'the legislature reacts to those who raise their voices most loudly, and who apply the most insistent pressure . . . Many important causes are not "vote-winners" and are therefore neglected by the Executive, which has achieved an ascendancy over the Legislature'.[103] The growing power of the executive branch over the legislature, the dominance of party politics, the increasing influence of the bureaucracy, and the effects of these phenomena on responsible government and democracy have been widely recognized.[104] Further, the bureaucratic inertia that must be overcome to provoke government action on human rights issues—particularly from the point of view of politically marginalized minorities, where the desired action may well conflict with popular wishes—can be prohibitive. As Zander has put it: '(t)he vested interest of all government is to preserve the normal ways of doing things and to resist pressure for change. Government, of whatever political complexion, is usually moved to change things only when the pressure to do so becomes greater than the convenience of leaving things as they are'.[105]

Views differ quite markedly as to the appropriate response to this challenge. There is much evidence to support the view that, in line with the increasing diversity in society and the need to safeguard the rights and interests of minorities, an entrenched bill of rights represents a potentially valuable means

[101] *Ibid.*, 114–15.   [102] *Ibid.*, 115.
[103] Doyle and Wells, n. 27 above, at 21; see also Brennan, n. 81 above, especially nn. 7–8 and accompanying text.
[104] See e.g. Galligan, 'Parliamentary Responsible Government and the Protection of Rights', (1993) 4 *Public Law Review* 100 at 106–8 and 111–12.
[105] Zander, n. 93 above, at 65.

of checking the oppressive exercise of political power.[106] On this view, the role of a vigilant, active and independent judiciary is critical for ensuring that 'paper' rights in a constitution are interpreted purposively and applied fairly. This sort of judicial role may be unavoidable, irrespective of whether human rights are constitutionalized. As Sir Gerard Brennan remarks: '(H)uman rights issues, however arising in litigation, give the Courts a new relevance to the society they serve'.[107] The changing nature and increasing complexity of the relationships between society and government, and the fact that governments now participate 'in nearly every facet of social and economic life', may lead the courts forcibly towards acceptance of their new relevance.[108]

As for the need to overcome political or bureaucratic inertia, Zander remarks that: '(l)egitimate pressure can be generated through litigation under a bill of rights. Unlike the executive or legislature, a court cannot say that the time is unripe for a decision on the issue, or that it is politically awkward to alter existing rules or policy'.[109] He draws the conclusion that litigation may be easier to undertake than either legislative or executive action to enforce a bill of rights. But having a willing judiciary is not the complete answer. The value of a right of constitutional review of government action is little comfort in a practical sense if the means do not exist to assist disadvantaged and marginalized groups to have access to the courts, and to ensure that constitutional litigation is focused on areas of most need.[110]

Notwithstanding this, experience in Canada, the USA and other nations with entrenched bills of rights indicates that there would appear to be cause for healthy optimism at prospects for entrenched human rights standards to earn the respect of the judiciary and capture popular imagination, thus helping to empower those who lack the abilities or resources to compete in the political arena. Eberts, for example, lauds the effectiveness of the Canadian Charter of Rights and Freedoms in producing positive outcomes for women on gender equality issues, in conjunction with parallel political efforts, procedural innovations of the courts, and a range of other factors.[111] The relative lack of progress in the political struggle for equality rights, prior to the Charter, presents an interesting contrast.[112]

---

[106] See e.g. Joseph, n. 65 above.   [107] Brennan, n. 81 above, at 462.

[108] *Ibid.*, especially n. 17 and accompanying text.   [109] Zander, n. 93 above, at 65.

[110] See C. Harlow, 'Access to Justice as a Human Right. The European Convention and the European Union' in Alston with Bustelo and Heenan (eds.), *The EU and Human Rights* (1999), ch. 7.

[111] Eberts, n. 83 above. But for a different view, see Webber, 'Tales of the Unexpected: Intended and Unintended Consequences of the Canadian Charter of Rights and Freedoms', (1993) 5 *Canterbury Law Review* 207.

[112] This is not to suggest that legal and political avenues for the resolution of grievances need be pursued to the mutual exclusion of each other. As Eberts has noted (n. 83 above, at 281) in relation to equality litigation under the Canadian Charter, '(w)omen's groups did not abandon political action in order to bring Charter challenges; they added litigation to impressive grassroots and national lobbying activities' in order to further their overall goals of achieving equality.

An empirical study of the Charter cautiously supports the contention that it has influenced the Canadian Supreme Court's agenda, although its effects may be more limited than is generally suggested.[113] The data analysed in that study suggest that a number of the influences often attributed to the Charter itself in all likelihood resulted instead from what the author refers to as the 'support structure for legal mobilisation',[114] consisting of various resources that enable litigants to pursue rights claims in court. While the results of this unusual study are clearly of interest from the point of view of assessing the effectiveness of constitutional bills of rights, it is questionable whether the findings take sufficient account of the interrelatedness of the various factors under consideration, in particular, the symbolic potential for entrenched rights to constitute a rallying point around which the 'support structures for political mobilisation' can grow.[115]

Byrnes has pointed to an initial positive human rights response by the judiciary under the Hong Kong Bill of Rights, although subsequently this has given way to a more conservative and parochial attitude towards interpretation, under the difficult and rather unique political circumstances obtaining there.[116] The judiciary has, within certain limits,[117] responded positively in interpreting guarantees in the new constitutions of Poland and Hungary. Pogany has remarked that 'the general tenor of the political and constitutional process, in both Poland and Hungary, is democratic, pluralist, rooted in respect for the rule of law. The force and weight of these tendencies owes much to the countries' respective Constitutional Courts. In Hungary, the Court has played a particularly important role in ensuring observance by both government and the legislature of the country's revised, democratic Constitution. It has been said that the Hungarian Court, "has in a few years become one of the most important factors in safeguarding Hungary's transition to

---

[113] Epp, 'Do Bills of Rights Matter? The Canadian Charter of Rights and Freedoms', (1996) 90(4) *American Political Science Review* 765. Epp uses a quasi-experimental design known as 'triangulation'—a strategy commonly used in qualitative research whereby multiple sources of data and multiple indicators are used to verify causal inferences—to consider and test several alternative explanations of variations in judicial attention to civil liberties and civil rights. These are: (1) the presence or absence of a bill of rights; (2) the judges' policy preferences, conditioned by (3) the extent of judicial discretion over the docket.

[114] Critical elements in this 'support structure' are organized group support (such as that provided by rights advocacy organizations), financing and legal aid, and the diversification of the Canadian legal profession and growth of large law firms. Ibid., 767 and 776.

[115] See e.g. Penner, n. 100 above, at 114–15.   [116] Byrnes, n. 55 above.

[117] See generally, Pogany, n. 10 above, at 166. Although the Constitutional Courts have generally played a 'strong role' in the Eastern European region, the fact that the legislature is able to override decisions of the Constitutional Courts in certain states in that region (notably, in Romania and Poland) is a matter of some concern—Elster, 'The Role of Institutional Interest in Eastern European Constitution-Making', (1996) 5 *Eastern European Constitutional Review* 63 at 63–6. Moreover, the existence of a relatively robust and independent judiciary does not mean that new Constitutional human rights guarantees are implemented overnight—see e.g. Scheppele, 'Women's Rights in Eastern Europe', (1995) 4 *Eastern European Constitutional Review* 66.

democracy and constitutionalism." '.[118] In the Czech Republic, as well, the Constitutional Court has contributed significantly to the consolidation of the democratic process and to the recognition of new constitutional values.[119] The Nordic and Baltic countries provide further illustrations of rich and rapid growth of case law under entrenched bills of rights, much of it involving the application of international human rights principles,[120] and a significant amount has also been achieved through some of the decisions of the Israeli courts.[121]

Other notable achievements under entrenched bills of rights have been discussed earlier. One of the lessons to be learned from this experience is that, in interpreting and applying an entrenched bill of rights, the ability of the courts to provide a viable and effective alternative forum to parliament depends significantly upon the perceived relevance of the constitutional document (and particular formulation of rights) in the society concerned. The Kenyan experience illustrates this point rather well. As Ghai's chapter in this volume

[118] Pogany, n. 10 above, at 167, citing Venice Commission, *Bulletin on Constitutional Case-Law* (Strasbourg, Council of Europe, 1994), 35–7. The situation in certain other states in Eastern and Central Europe is not quite so positive, however—see Pogany, *ibid*. at 167–75. In states such as Slovakia 'there is a profound need for independent, tough-minded Constitutional Courts, willing and able to uphold the norms (and values) of the new, democratic Constitutions. The necessity of such Courts is all the greater where, as is often the case, the executive branch has gained effective control over a largely quiescent legislature' (*ibid*. at 169). Pogany also points to a number of factors in society explaining the discrepancy among the performance of constitutional courts in the Eastern and Central European region, such as levels of industrialization and literacy, type of political and constitutional structures, cultural factors and readiness for independent courts, and level of ethnic homogeneity.

[119] Pogany, *ibid*. at 164. For an account of constitutional rights protection in Poland (under the institutional auspices of its first ombudswoman) see Letowska, 'The Ombudsman and Basic Rights', (1995) 4 *Eastern European Constitutional Review* 63. See also Teitel, 'Post-Communist Constitutionalism: A Transitional Perspective' in Neuman (ed.), n. 50 above, at 170–82. Teitel's review of significant cases in Bulgaria, Albania, Hungary and former Czechoslovakia shows that 'when confronted with popular anti-communist measures implicating individual rights, political actors turned to the courts, and the new constitutional courts were able, to varying degrees, to draw a thin but bright line demarcating the rule of law. These precedents illuminate the potential of abstract judicial review for timely, principled resolution of political controversies and the protection of human rights in post-communist transitions' (*ibid*. at 182).

[120] See generally Scheinin n. 48 above. According to Scheinin, this is particularly so in the five Nordic states. Scheinin notes in particular the 'activist' or 'liberal' interpretation that the Finland Supreme Administrative Court has taken in the application of Article 8 of the ECHR (the right to respect for family and private life) in expulsion cases, in contrast to the relatively restrictive case law of the European Court of Human Rights. And even in Norway and Iceland, where the 'dualistic' nature of the constitution presents a formal barrier to the direct reception of international law, the Supreme Courts have shown their capability and willingness to allow human rights treaty provisions factual priority in relation to domestic law, achieving positive human rights outcomes.

[121] Although it is important in this context to note that Israel has no formal written constitution as such, but rather, human rights there have been protected almost exclusively by judge-made law. See Goldstein, 'Protection of Human Rights by Judges: The Israeli Experience' (1994) 38 *Saint Louis University Law Journal* 605. Note also the criticisms directed at the Court in relation to its 'tolerance' of torture in certain cases. For a nuanced but controversial defence of this approach see Benvenisti, 'The Role of National Courts in Preventing Torture of Suspected Terrorists', (1997) 8 *European Journal of International Law* 596.

relates, Kenya's neo-colonial Bill of Rights was drafted summarily by the British Colonial Office and officials in the Kenyan Attorney-General's office, without any consideration of Kenyan politics, culture or society. By contrast, where the special interests of the European settlers were concerned, these were 'vigorously pursued and carefully incorporated in the Bill'.[122] In the end, the ideology of the Bill of Rights became that of the 'white man's burden', with its 'contradiction of domination and liberty'.[123] The (ECHR-based) Bill reflected no understanding of African constitutionalism and Kenya's shift from legal-rational to patrimonial systems of governance.[124] Paradoxically, however, the very irrelevance of the Bill of Rights in this form was perhaps the factor which led to its being retained in successive constitutions and administrations in Kenya.[125] Thus, although favourable judicial decisions under the Bill of Rights (let alone their observance in administrative or police practice or subsequent litigation) were not possible, the Bill of Rights remained alive to be used successfully in the 1980s, obliging the government to respond to litigation, raising rights consciousness, inspiring a sense of solidarity and enlivening NGO activity, and enabling the democratic struggles in Kenya to be linked to universally proclaimed human rights.[126]

But facilitating an active judicial role in this way is not always appreciated, even by those sharing a commitment to human rights. From a 'democratic' perspective, a central point of contention relating to entrenched bills of rights is the empowerment of the (unelected) judicial arm of government at the expense of the political arms. Waldron, for instance, suggests that the entrenchment of rights in a constitutional document reflects a certain type of attitude towards one's fellow citizens which he sums up as 'a combination of self-assurance and mistrust: self-assurance in the proponent's conviction that what she is putting forward really *is* a matter of fundamental right ... and mistrust, implicit in her view that any alternative conception that might be concocted by elected legislators next year or the year after is so likely to be wrong-headed and ill-motivated that her own formulation is to be elevated immediately beyond the reach of ordinary legislative revision'.[127]

The question of how constitutions, at least in a practical sense, take account of theoretical disagreement is one to which we shall return. Whether the desire to entrench human rights is really a reflection of mistrust in one's fellow citizens, rather than a mistrust of institutions of government and their commitment to certain fundamental values (however expressed), is a matter of opinion. Whether such mistrust in political majorities is justified as a matter of fact is another interesting question. In a study in 1997, Gamble[128] surveyed a range of civil rights initiatives featuring on state and local ballots in the USA

---

[122] Ghai, n. 33 above, at 195.　　[123] *Ibid*.　　[124] *Ibid*. at 236–40.
[125] *Ibid*.　　[126] *Ibid*. at 239.　　[127] Waldron, n. 6 above, at 27.
[128] Gamble, 'Putting Civil Rights to a Popular Vote', (1997) 41 *American Journal of Political Science* 245.

between 1950 and 1993, focusing on the rights of racial, ethnic and linguistic minorities, gay men and lesbians and people with HIV/AIDS in connection with the enjoyment of the rights to employment, housing, education and public accommodation. On the basis of the review of three decades' worth of civil rights initiatives and referenda, Gamble concluded that not only have citizens in the political majority in the USA repeatedly used direct democracy to put the rights of political minorities to a popular vote, but that anti-civil rights initiatives have had an 'extraordinary record of success', with voters having approved 78 per cent of these initiatives, and endorsing only a third of all substitutive measures.[129] Gamble asserts that the results of this study show that 'American voters readily repeal existing civil rights protections and enthusiastically enact laws that bar their elected representatives from passing new ones. By repeatedly striking down the latter, the judicial system has vigilantly protected the rights of minorities to participate in the political process'.[130]

However Waldron, along with others such as Tom Campbell, criticize the 'disabling of representative institutions',[131] which they consider to follow from conferring jurisdiction on the judiciary to interpret an entrenched bill of rights. While acknowledging the practical failings of modern representative democratic institutions,[132] Waldron argues that the answer is to address those specific failings, and reform those institutions, rather than confer political (and effectively, legislative) power on an unrepresentative and unaccountable judiciary.[133]

But there can be no definitive solutions to these questions and opinions will inevitably differ greatly on such matters as:

(1) the relative need and prospects for reform of political and judicial institutions;
(2) whether 'mistrust' in other human beings and their behaviour in positions of power in government, to the extent that this motivates some to favour entrenchment of rights, can be reconciled with a respect for and belief in their equal fundamental human rights;
(3) whether mistrust in political majorities is justified as a matter of fact;

---

[129] *Ibid.* at 261.

[130] *Ibid.* at 262. She concludes that 'minorities suffer when direct democracy circumvents [the] system. Not only do they lose at the polls, the very act of putting civil rights to a popular vote increases the divisions that separate us as a people. Instead of fortifying our nation, direct legislation only weakens us'.

[131] Waldron, n. 6 above, at 28.

[132] Among the shortcomings to which he refers, in the United Kingdom context, are: the executive domination over the legislative branch; small or new parties being squeezed out by the plurality system; voters having to choose between whole packages of policies rather than being able to decide issue by issue; and the Prime Minister's Question-time and party political broadcasts' failure to permit meaningful participation. *Ibid.* at 45.

[133] Ibid. at 41–51, generally.

(4) the meaning of 'democracy' and 'sovereignty,' in the modern integrated world;[134]
(5) the nature and relative importance of the 'right to participate' and related 'democratic' rights, and their theoretical and functional relationships with other human rights, and
(6) the theoretical basis of human rights and how or whether, in a practical sense, constitutions can be crafted to take account of philosophical disagreements over matters as complex and fundamental as human rights.

Some of these issues will be taken up again shortly. Suffice it to say at this point that there are ample grounds, based on experience in countries with constitutional human rights protections, to suggest that entrenchment of bills of rights can contribute significantly to the empowerment of disadvantaged groups, providing a judicial forum in which they can be heard and seek redress, in circumstances where the political processes could not have been successfully mobilized to assist them.

Educative value

It is one thing for lawyers and judges to be fluent in rights talk, but it is considerably more difficult to ensure that the message is heard and understood more widely. As Harold Laski noted:

[V]igilance is essential in the realm of what Cromwell called fundamentals. Bills of rights are, quite undoubtedly, a check upon possible excess in the Government of the day. They warn us that certain popular powers have had to be fought for, and may have to be fought for again. The solemnity they embody serves to set the people on their guard. It acts as a rallying point in the State for all who care deeply for the ideals of freedom.[135]

While international standards and the formal acceptance of treaty obligations can provide the foundations upon which a human rights culture might be built, they will never be sufficient. Their educative value will inevitably be limited unless and until they are given adequate expression within the domestic legal order. While the assertion of individual rights can create a limited form of rights consciousness, a bill of rights or an international treaty which acts as one, can ensure that such consciousness is not atomistic in the sense so famously criticized by Karl Marx, but as part of an overall conception of a rights-based society. As Clapham observes in the context of domestic reception of the ECHR in the United Kingdom, rather than creating a culture of

---

[134] See e.g. Zander, n. 93 above, at 83. On the absence of democracy-based critiques of subjecting the United Kingdom to proceedings before the European Court of Human Rights in Strasbourg, Zander asks rhetorically: 'If it is undemocratic and therefore unacceptable to allow English judges to decide matters of consequence, why is it not even more undemocratic and therefore even more unacceptable to allow such matters to be decided by judges from a variety of European countries?'

[135] Laski, *Liberty and the Modern State* (1948), 75.

individualism the Convention is 'more likely to stimulate a democratic debate about the nature and purpose of the rights being claimed. Ignoring the Convention leaves the debate exclusively in the hands of lawyers who are the only ones entitled to "divine and define" ancient common law rights'.[136]

However, as experience has shown, if the language or particular conceptions of rights are alien to a particular society, there is a limited prospect that they will find acceptance or effective application there. That each situation needs to be looked at individually is well illustrated by the experience in much of Kenya's post-colonial history, as Ghai's chapter shows.[137] Hence, the involvement of society at large—not just lawyers and governing elites—is required to foster a sense of ownership of a bill of rights, and help assure its acceptance, relevance and effectiveness. The Canadian experience is a particularly apt illustration of this, as Eberts' chapter underlines. An entrenched bill of rights, reflecting internationally accepted standards as far as is practicable, constitutes a strong basis upon which educative efforts might proceed.

Other advantages

Other potential advantages of entrenched bills of rights include their capacity to consolidate a state's human rights commitment and to signal that fact to the international community, their inherent flexibility and adaptability (properly interpreted by an independent judiciary),[138] and their potential as 'higher' sources of law, in certain circumstances, to:

(1) assist in defusing political grievances by removing them to a legal setting;[139]

(2) assist governments effect needed reforms in circumstances that would otherwise prove politically difficult;[140] and to

(3) 'place the power of action where it belongs—with those who are aggrieved.'[141]

---

[136] Clapham, n. 29 above, at 122–3.   [137] Ghai, n. 33 above.

[138] Zander, n. 93 above, at 64-5.

[139] *Ibid.* at 66. See also Brennan, n. 81 above at 460: 'It is the very process of open consideration of the issue arising under a bill of rights, its formalized debate between adversaries in the cool dignity of the Courtroom, the exposure of reasons and the articulation of the applicable legal rule that commends the Courts as the repositories of a supervisory power over the political branches of Government. A new judicial role under a bill of rights has attractions not only for those who would challenge the actions of Government, but for Government itself. There are some issues which, in a pluralist and divided society, are the subject of such controversy that no political party wishes to take the responsibility of solving them. The political process may be paralysed. If Governments can create a situation where such issues are submitted to curial decision, political obliquity can be avoided by Governments . . . [T]he judicial method commands a broader acceptance than the political process'.

[140] Zander, n. 93 above, at 68.

[141] *Ibid.* For another list of advantages see Mason, 'A Bill of Rights for Australia?', (1989) 5 *Australian Bar Review* 79 at 88–9.

A great many of the arguments against bills of rights are directed at the key component that makes them effective. That is, the role of the judiciary in interpreting and applying entrenched bills of rights, including the capacity to strike down inconsistent legislation. Objections to this role are usually rooted in democratic theory and focus on the (undoubted) shift in power to the judiciary and away from the elected legislature. However whether such a shift actually results in a diminution or enhancement of democratic values and overall human rights protection is a separate question which warrants careful examination.

Matters of controversy and disagreement should not be constitutionally entrenched

The critique is often made that the contested and uncertain nature of human rights, themselves, mandates against entrenchment of one particular conception of rights. If it is accepted that disagreement as to the philosophical basis and nature of human rights is certain to continue, then it makes no sense to 'entrench' one particular conception of rights at the expense of others. Waldron, for example, argues that objections to entrenched bills of rights on democratic grounds are greatly strengthened by the extent to which there is room for good faith disagreement on rights-related issues:

Things might be different if principles of right were self-evident or if there were a philosophical elite who could be trusted to work out once and for all what rights we have and how they are to be balanced against other considerations. But the consensus of the philosophers is that these matters are not settled, that they are complex and controversial . . . [W]e should view the disagreements about rights that exist among citizens in exactly the same light, unless there is compelling evidence to the contrary.[142]

One response to this critique is the 'pre-commitment' thesis which posits that, in an attempt to reconcile entrenchment of one conception of human rights with competing theories of democratic or participatory rights, individuals may voluntarily agree to impose constraints on their future decision-making. The example of Ulysses instructing his crew not to release his bindings, no matter what he might say later, in order that he would not fall to the charms of the Sirens best illustrates the notion.[143] Waldron also rejects this approach, however, on the grounds that we must avoid simplistic analogies 'between the rational autonomy of individuals and the democratic governance of a community'.[144]

---

[142] Waldron, n. 6 above, at 49–50. See also Adjei, n. 63 above, at 18–22; and Allen, 'Bills of Rights and Judicial Power—A Liberal's Quandary', (1996) 16 *Oxford Journal of Legal Studies* 337 at 344–5.

[143] Waldron, n. 6 above, at 47.

[144] *Ibid.* at 48–9. For further criticism of the pre-commitment idea, see Allen, n. 142 above, at 350–1.

Indeed the pre-commitment approach is unpersuasive on a number of grounds. In the first place, individuals are not pre-committing only themselves but also future generations who will be given no say. Secondly, the more contested an issue is, the less desirable it is to lock in the predilections or preferences of a particular moment in history, especially when the matter will often have been determined with only a small majority in favour. Thirdly, the pre-commitment approach does not necessarily take account of the need to be able to respond to changing circumstances, even if we agree that changing values should not be accommodated.

Fortunately, however, a defence of bills of rights does not need to rest on a theory such as pre-commitment. The fundamental values entrenched in a bill of rights do not, or at least should not in normal circumstances, extend to issues in relation to which there are major and deep-rooted societal disagreements. It is unsurprising therefore that the issue of abortion is rarely addressed in human rights instruments and, that where it is, the application of the norm has generally been very reluctant and guarded. A strong case can be made that the irreconcilable differences that Waldron and others tend to base their analyses on very often do not go to the core values themselves but to the way in which they are interpreted or applied in particular instances. Thus, for example, norms against racial or gender-based discrimination are usually not in themselves controversial, although there may be significant community resentment at the result which obtains in relation to certain 'unpopular' groups. It remains true, nevertheless, that there will be some societies in which there is a numerically strong majority in favour of values which are incompatible with human rights, whether in terms of say harsh and inhumane treatment for criminal offenders or a determination to exclude racial, ethnic, or religious minorities from the exercise of various rights. In such cases, the principal justification for enshrining contrary norms in a bill of rights is simply one of values. In this respect, the human rights enterprise is unashamedly committed to eliminating certain options even from the reach of determined democratic majorities. Torture, for example, is branded as unacceptable, as is deliberate starvation. In this respect, democracy is not a unique fundamental value but rather one that must be understood in the light of a very limited list of other such values.

Other elements of the argument that human rights are anti-democratic also warrant closer scrutiny. The argument that pluralism and diversity are denied by the hegemony of rights needs to be seen in light of the general practice of formulating both the norms and the procedures for their implementation in a manner that takes account of diversity and of democratic inputs.

Just as disagreement is a vital part of reaching toward complicated philosophical truths, constitutionalism itself is all about acknowledging disagreement and accounting for it in the design of the constitution or the bill of rights. As Goodin has remarked, '(f)irst order disagreements over policy directions are the very stuff of politics . . . Coping with diversity at that level is precisely what the institutional designs of liberal democracy are all about. But beyond that surface disagreement must be a principled "agreement to disagree" ', or else collective decision-making would be impossible.[145]

At a practical level, bills of rights accommodate disagreement, uncertainty and diversity in a variety of ways, both explicitly and implicitly. Particularly trenchant or seemingly intractable issues, for example, might be reflected in a constitution's 'unwritten' dimensions. Foley describes this as a 'constitutional abeyance', or a 'form of tacit and instinctive agreement to condone, and even cultivate, constitutional ambiguity as an acceptable strategy for resolving conflict'.[146] The term is intended to accommodate practices such as intentional neglect, protective obfuscation, and complicity in non-exposure, all of which might be required to preserve the effectiveness of abeyances in keeping options open and avoiding rigidity.[147]

It might be argued that such deliberate omission or avoidance of vital and controversial issues is unprincipled or even unethical. However Foley stresses that 'the habitual willingness to defer indefinitely consideration of deep constitutional anomalies, for the sake of preserving the constitution from the severe conflict that would arise from attempts to remove them, represents the core of a constitutional culture'.[148] On this account, metaphysical and moral aspects of a constitution which cannot be known in any verifiable sense, and perhaps philosophical statements about the basis of human rights, are left in 'unwritten' form. For the overriding purpose of preserving the integrity of the constitution itself, these areas are left undefined and allowed to remain 'sufficiently obscure to allow them to retain an approximate appearance of internal coherence and clarity, while at the same time accommodating several potentially conflicting and quite unresolved points of issue'.[149]

Accommodation of diversity through the express written provisions of the constitution is also, of course, a common feature of constitutional design and of bills of rights. For example, there will invariably be provision for constitutional amendment, should the document (in its implementation) become seriously out of step with contemporary values, although necessarily, the practical requirements for amendment can be expected to be difficult to meet. Accommodating diversity can be seen in quite a striking way in the South African constitution, a compact struck in a society historically characterized by the deepest of political, ethnic and tribal rifts. Disagreement there was sought to be accommodated by means of various compromises, discussed by Chanock in his chapter.[150]

[145] Goodin, 'Designing Constitutions: the Political Constitution of a Mixed Commonwealth' in Bellamy and Castiglione (eds.), n. 4 above, 223 at 224–5.
[146] Foley, *The Silence of Constitutions: Gaps, 'Abeyances' and Political Temperament in the Maintenance of Government* (1989), xi.
[147] *Ibid.*   [148] *Ibid.* at 10.   [149] *Ibid.* at 9.
[150] Chanock, n. 35 above.

Of course, the gaps in the constitution—whether in its 'written' or 'unwritten' aspects—must be filled in at least to some degree over time, adding flesh to the bones, ensuring that the document responds to changing values and maintains its relevance and legitimacy (and hence, respect and support within the subject society). This is a role that the courts, rather than parliament, have increasingly played, going to the very heart of the 'democratic' objections. Accordingly it is this set of objections which it is now appropriate to consider.

Democratic objections

As suggested earlier, the cornerstone of objections based on democratic theory is that an entrenched bill of rights places power in the hands of an unelected, unaccountable, unrepresentative and elite group of people (i.e., judges), who are empowered to overturn Acts of Parliament, which reflect the values determined by the duly elected representatives of the people, to the extent that any inconsistency with the bill of rights is identified by the judge.[151] This argument is even more compelling in light of Legal Realist and Critical Legal Studies theories of the law, pursuant to which judicial discretion is seen to be generally unconstrained by the law, with the result that consequently judges decide cases based on their own subjective views.[152]

Critics note that there is a contradiction inherent in, on the one hand, entrenching (justiciable) norms which purport to declare and safeguard 'universal' human rights, while on the other disenfranchising and effectively denying people enjoyment of certain civil and political rights (and especially the right to participate in democratic processes).[153] These critics argue that the existence of defects in the system of representative government are a reason for the reform of political institutions, not for their abandonment, and that in any event parliament as the repository of constitutional power is still a far more representative and democratic body than the judiciary. Ewing and Gearty argued in 1991 that a justiciable bill of rights in Britain would threaten

[151] See e.g. Clapham, n. 29 above; Joseph, n. 65 above; Beatty, n. 84 above, at 3–7; and Waldron, as discussed in text accompanying nn. 127 and 131–3 above.

[152] Beatty, n. 84 above, at 5–7, constructs an interesting response to claims of subjectivity and indeterminacy of judicial decision-making. He characterizes the function of a bill of rights as being to entrench 'basic principles of rationality and proportionality—of necessity and consistency—into the framework of government'. He thus minimizes the court's interpretative function, and reduces its role to one of adjudicating on the 'rationality and proportionality' of governmental action. The result, in his view, is that the jurisprudence of human rights 'should be much less vulnerable to the charge of subjectivity and indeterminacy which has been so corrosive of the law'. See also Beatty, 'Law and Politics', (1996) 44 *American Journal of Comparative Law* 131 at 136–50. Suffice it to note that this attempt at conceptual accommodation is purchased at the expense of abandoning a number of the functions actually performed by constitutional courts, at least as their role is envisaged by most of the contributors to this volume.

[153] Waldron notes that: '(n)o one ever thought that the imperfection of existing representative institutions was a justification for not enfranchising women, or that in the United States it could be an argument to continue denying political rights to Americans of African descent'. See n. 6 above at 45.

what they regard as the three most fundamental elements of democracy—participation, representativeness and accountability:

In the first place it is properly assumed that a fundamental requirement of democracy is that every adult person should be entitled to participate in the system of government .... Secondly, the transfer of political power to the judges would undermine the principle that those who exercise political power should be representative of the community they serve .... Thirdly, the introduction of a Bill of Rights would violate the principle that those who wield political power should be accountable to the community on whose behalf they purport to act when they exercise this power.[154]

But such arguments do not take sufficient account of the role that appropriate constitutional design can play. The experiences in Canada and New Zealand are illustrative, where particular provisions (in the Canadian case, a 'notwithstanding' or parliamentary override clause, a common feature in national constitutions) plays a potentially important role in assisting to regulate the tension between the judicial and legislative branches of government, effectively permitting the government to 'veto' courts' decisions on human rights matters.[155] An alternative approach is that adopted in the United Kingdom Human Rights Act 1998 which, rather than empowering the courts to strike down legislation, enables them to make a declaration that legislation is incompatible with the ECHR. But the final decision as to whether the legislation will be revised accordingly rests with Parliament. Although it seems highly likely that in the great majority of cases the view of the courts will prevail, the option remains for electoral politics to override the courts. This compromise has been greeted by Ewing as preserving the sovereignty of Parliament both in principle and practice,[156] thus highlighting the role of creative and adaptive constitutional design in relation to human rights issues.

The 'democratic' objections have been criticized also as being based on 'simple majoritarianism'[157] or 'a crude statistical view of democracy'.[158] Dworkin's conception of democracy, for example, is well known as an attempt

[154] Ewing and Gearty, *Democracy or a Bill of Rights* (1991), 5–6.

[155] See McLachlin, 'The Canadian Charter and the Democratic Process', in Gearty and Tomkins (eds.), *Understanding Human Rights* (1996), 22, noting the limited number of times the Canadian override provision (s.33 of the Charter) has been invoked to date. Indeed a counter-argument, undermining the proposition that such provisions help to rectify the transfer of power to the judiciary and preserve power in the 'sovereign' parliament, is that the *limited* circumstances in which a government would be willing to invoke an 'override' provision effectively renders it useless.

[156] Ewing, 'The Human Rights Act and Parliamentary Democracy', (1999) 62 *Modern Law Review* 79 at 99.

[157] Russell, 'Standing Up for Notwithstanding', (1991) 29(2) *Alberta Law Review* 293 at 295. See also Freeman, 'Constitutional Democracy and the Legitimacy of Judicial Review', (1990) 9 *Law and Philosophy* 327 at 367. Cf: Waldron, 'Freeman's Defense of Judicial Review', (1994) 13 *Law and Philosophy* 27.

[158] Dworkin, n. 76 above, at 36. See also Prosser, n. 7 above, at 70, arguing that certain forms of rights are 'intrinsic to any conception of democracy beyond a crude view of democrary as the sovereign implementation of a unitary popular will'.

to bridge the gap between calls for democracy and respects for rights. For him, 'true democracy is not just statistical democracy, in which anything a majority or plurality wants is legitimate for that reason, but communal democracy, in which majority decision is legitimate only if it is a majority within a community of equals'. In his view that requires not only equal participation in the political process through voting and other means of expression, but also that 'political decisions must treat everyone with equal concern and respect, that each individual person must be guaranteed fundamental civil and political rights no combination of other citizens can take away, no matter how numerous they are or how much they despise his or her race or morals or way of life'.[159] A similar justification has been espoused by many of the judges who have been called upon to adjudicate bills of rights. As McLachlin has suggested, drawing on her experience gained in relation to the Canadian Charter:

If one accepts that democracy at its best reflects a tension between majoritarian will and individual rights . . . then it is far from evident that the transfer of a measure of power from the legislatures to the courts has weakened the Canadian democracy. Indeed, a case can be made that it has strengthened democracy by guaranteeing the fundamental values on which democracy rests and by enabling individuals and minorities to participate more fully in the democratic institutions of our society.[160]

This approach is also consistent with the recognition that there are significant shortcomings inherent in the actual operation of representative democracies today, as Gamble's survey of the anti-human rights bias of popular initiatives in the USA illustrates.[161] Some of these, such as the dominance of the executive over the legislative arms of government, and the machinations of party

[159] Dworkin, n. 76 above, at 35–6. Prosser, n. 7 above, at 71–2 argues that a more complex 'dualist' democracy has emerged in Britain, reflected in contemporary constitutional and institutional design (such as inter-governmental conferences for treaty amendment in Europe, and the role of national referenda), which cannot be explained by the traditional monist view of sovereignty. To similar effect see Sedley, 'Human Rights: A Twenty-First Century Agenda', [1995] *Public Law* 386 at 388–9, arguing that judicial assertiveness is consistent with democracy understood in a 'new and emerging constitutional paradigm' in which traditional notions of parliamentary sovereignty must be recast. See also Cooke, n. 79 above, at 66: 'The fact that democracy is an illusion without the security for minority rights provided by an independent judiciary is not an easy populist message. Nor is the fact that the power of the judiciary under an entrenched bill of rights is essentially one of check and balance, not of initiation of policy'. Cf: Waldron, n. 6 above, at 44–6, and Allen, n. 142 above, at 349–50. For a discussion in the European context, see Ackerman, 'The Political Case for Constitutional Courts' in Yack (ed.), *Liberalism Without Illusions: Essays on Liberal Theory and the Political Vision of Judith Shklar* (1996), 205–19.

[160] McLachlin, n. 155, above suggests (at 26) that from a liberal democratic perspective, 'the question whether the Charter has weakened or strengthened democracy in Canada is not answered by the assertion that the Charter confers a measure of power from the legislatures to the courts. In fact, this question misdirects the inquiry. We ought rather to be asking whether the Charter strikes the right balance between the power of the majority and the rights of the individual'. She notes (at 27) that if 'the deep conditions of democratic government include "political participation, equality, autonomy and personal liberty", then a vigorous and committed judicial approach which underscores these conditions of democracy is one of the strongest arguments in favour of the Charter'. To similar effect see Prosser n. 7 above at 70.

[161] See n. 128 above.

politics, have been referred to already. Indeed it is no sufficient counter-argument to say that judicial review exists predominantly for the rich and powerful, and to serve corporate interests, as some have charged.[162] While there is certainly much that could be done to enhance access to justice in human rights contexts,[163] litigation based on bills of rights has in fact has been successfully and widely used by hitherto marginalized persons or groups to counter injustice.[164] Furthermore it ignores the reality that access to government and the legislative processes, themselves, is more open to the rich and powerful than to the oppressed and downtrodden. As a result it may well be that in societies where fundamental rights are protected in a bill of rights—assuming the existence of an independent judiciary and a minimum level of essential supportive measures—the ordinary citizen has a much better chance of activating judicial processes, rather than the legislative agenda, in order to get his or her grievances addressed.

Further, the distinction between the judiciary and elected officials, in terms of their 'representativeness', is easily overstated. For the most part, judges are not representative of the community in the sense of being elected or reflecting the make-up of the community. In some countries, however, they are elected. On the other hand the process of electing representatives often seems to bear only a fleeting resemblance to full democracy. Members of parliament are elected by universal franchise but the electorate as a whole has a remarkably small say in the pre-selection process which is either confined to the party faithful in a given constituency, or heavily influenced by the central party machine. As Zander has noted, the electoral process 'tends to reflect national trends in regard to politics and the "feel-bad factor", rather than what the electorate thinks of the candidates either individually or in aggregate.' Nor, in the Westminster system, does the choice of Ministers from among those elected to Parliament involve any form of direct democracy or any assurance that the most qualified individual has been chosen. In the presidential system, cabinet-level officials are often not elected at all but are chosen by the President and, depending on the system, are subjected to a greater or lesser degree of parliamentary scrutiny. Zander has also emphasized the practical weaknesses in the 'accountability' criterion, noting the paucity of Ministerial dismissals or resignations in British political history, and querying the extent to which the requirement to face elections every several years really weighs on the minds of Ministers in day-to-day decision-making.[165]

---

[162] Ewing, n. 67 above, at 44–6.

[163] See generally de Schutter, *Fonction de juger et droits fondamentaux: transformation du contrôle juridictionnel dans les ordres juridiques américains et européens* (1999), ch. XI–XIV.

[164] See McLachlin, n. 155 above, at 28 on the creation of 'new insiders' (women and aboriginal people) within the Canadian political and constitutional order.

[165] Zander, n. 93 above, at 80. Indeed Jones (n. 28 above at 64) points to the growth in judicial review of administrative action as testimony to the failures of parliament.

An additional dilution of democracy comes from the inevitably very major role of non-elected civil servants in governmental decision-making, first highlighted in the United Kingdom by Lord Hewart's dramatically titled book *The New Despotism*,[166] and subsequently parodied with such insight in the television series *Yes Minister*. Yet civil servants are no more representative than judges, even though they are indirectly subject in principle if not often enough in practice, to democratic oversight.

Although judges are not elected, they are rarely oblivious to electoral politics nor are they immune to democratic influences, protestations to the contrary notwithstanding. Indeed, much although certainly not all of the criticism of the power of unaccountable judges seems to reflect an overly positivist or formalist view of the judicial function. Thus Sunstein has suggested that one of the most striking features of American law in the 1990s has been the extent to which a majority of the justices on the Supreme Court have sought to avoid taking a strong stand, especially on hotly contested issues, and instead have encouraged elected officials to take a stand on contentious issues and get voter feedback.[167] Of course, the insistence that judges are politically sensitive cuts both ways and will not reassure those who still believe that they should be wholly uninfluenced by such matters.

At the end of the day, the conclusions to be drawn from the debate over the 'democratic objections' to bills of rights is also heavily influenced by the frame of reference which the observer adopts. Arguing from particular conceptions of 'democracy'[168] is one possible starting point. But this usually results in a focus upon only a limited range of civil and political or 'democratic' rights. A broader framework which focuses on the goal of how best to ensure protection of all human rights promotes a wider scope of enquiry, although the distinction between the two positions diminishes as the relevant conception of democracy becomes more substantive. That brings us to the next major issue: whose conception of rights is being safeguarded?

Entrenchment of liberal ideology and only particular categories of rights

The principal issue that arises in this connection concerns the omission from a great many liberal formulations of those rights relating to livelihood and the individual's well-being. At the international level, the official policy position, reflected in all of the major international human rights instruments, is that the two sets of rights—civil and political, on the one hand, and economic, social and cultural, on the other—are indivisible, interdependent and interrelated. But this theoretical consensus evaporates, or at least shrinks dramatically and

---

[166] Hewart, *The New Despotism* (1945).

[167] Sunstein, *One Case at a Time: Judicial Minimalism on the Supreme Court* (1999).

[168] Cf: Waldron, n. 6 above, at 20, 36–8; Ewing and Gearty, n. 66 above, at 150. These authors do, however, acknowledge the mutually supportive nature of 'democratic' and 'participatory' rights, with other human rights (indeed, the point is central to Waldron's argument).

with remarkable speed, as soon as we move to the practical translation of these international standards into bills of rights. Where states have elected to establish a bill of rights by means of incorporation or entrenchment of international human rights instruments, the almost universal practice to date has been to incorporate instruments (such as the Covenant on Civil and Political Rights or the ECHR) which deal almost exclusively with civil and political rights, but not to go beyond that point to embrace economic, social and cultural rights. Where states have incorporated the Universal Declaration of Human Rights in its entirety so that it acts as an indirect bills of rights within the domestic legal order, the resulting inclusion of economic, social and cultural rights is usually undermined by the absence of meaningful enforcement provisions.[169] This overall neglect has led some commentators to argue that most modern bills of rights are deeply ideological documents which entrench liberalism and individualism over socialist or communitarian or other ideologies.[170]

There are, however, some precedents for the inclusion of at least some economic, social and cultural rights within bills of rights or constitutions. Leaving aside the pre-Second World War precedents such as the 1793 French, 1917 Mexican, 1936 Soviet and 1919 Weimar constitutions, the end of that War saw the adoption of constitutions in both Japan and Germany which contained important economic and social rights-related provisions.[171] More recently, there have been a number of important advances in the constitutional recognition of these rights. It must suffice to mention several from different regions. Finland, having previously incorporated the European Social Charter of 1961 into domestic law so that its provisions are applicable before domestic courts and administrative authorities, went even further in 1995. The Bill of Rights reform of that year included economic and social rights in Chapter Two of the Constitution Act, and in respect to some of the rights the formulation used suggests justiciability in courts of law.[172] The second

---

[169] The preamble to the Senegal Constitution, for example, provides: 'The people of Senegal solemnly proclaim their independence and their attachment to fundamental rights as they are defined in the Declaration of the Rights of Man and the Citizen of 1789 and in the Universal Declaration of December 10, 1948'. See Blaustein, 'Human Rights in the World's Constitutions' in Nowak, Steurer and Tretter (eds.), *Progress in the Spirit of Human Rights* (1988), 602.

[170] See e.g. Ewing and Gearty, n.66 above, at 150: 'Despite carefully fostered appearances to the contrary, the European Convention is a deeply ideological document. Incorporation would guarantee supremacy to its narrowly individualistic view of society and would then make it impossible or extremely difficult to undermine or overthrow this ideology through the ordinary democratic process. As such it represents a triumph of liberalism over socialism and as such fixes that triumph irrevocably into the constitution'. See also Ghai, n. 33 above, at 210, for a statement of the communitarian critique.

[171] In relation to Japan see Inoue, *MacArthur's Japanese Constitution: A Linguistic and Cultural Study of its Making* (1991), 91; and generally Rapaczynski, 'Bibliographical Essay: The Influence of U.S. Constitutionalism Abroad', in Henkin and Rosenthal (eds.), *Constitutionalism and Rights: The Influence of the United States Constitution Abroad* (1990), 405.

[172] See Parliament of Finland, Social Affairs Committee, Opinion No. 14 of 1990, cited by Scheinin who suggests that treaty provisions dealing with social and economic rights may become

example is the South African Constitution of 1996, chapter 2 of which (the Bill of Rights) recognises rights in relation to labour relations, environment, property, housing, health care, food, water, social security, education, language, culture and cultural, religious and linguistic communities. A third example, from Central Europe, is the Hungarian Constitution of 1989 which combines rights and duties along with a wide range of economic and social rights which are granted judicial protection. The Hungarian Constitutional Court has been relatively active in that regard since its creation in 1990.[173]

Nevertheless, these rights remain relatively neglected in bills of rights at the national level. In addition to the general issues that are commonly raised in relation to them, there are several objections which seem to have asserted particular influence in relation to bills of rights. Zander argues that economic, social and cultural rights have no place in such catalogues for two reasons. The first is that agreement on an appropriate list would be impossible. 'Thus where the Left wish to see the enactment of rights designed to enhance equality, the Right will press for recognition of the opposite (protection of the right to private education, private property, private medicine, etc.)'.[174] But this is clearly a flawed analysis. Economic and social rights do not insist upon equality as such, but on non-discrimination, a norm which is already accepted in relation to virtually all relevant issues. Moreover, the rights to private education, private property and private medicine were recognized long ago. The fact that the United Kingdom has been a party to the International Covenant on Economic, Social and Cultural rights since 1976, and to the European Social Charter, seems either to have escaped the author's attention or to have been dismissed as an irrelevancy.

The second reason cited by Zander is that these rights raise resource issues, the solutions to which should not be determined by the courts. 'The adjudicative process in courts of law dealing with disputes raised by litigants is not appropriate to determining the allocation of society's resources necessarily involved in deciding such issues'.[175] On this point, he is supported by many other commentators. Beatty, for example, argues that economic and social rights guarantees are inappropriate because their justiciability would infringe the separation of powers doctrine, which is central to democracy.[176] In his view, neither the strength of the human rights case in relation to those rights, 'nor the past jurisprudence of the courts warrants assigning the third branch

'self-executing' or directly applicable in Finland even against the actual intention of their framers. See n. 48 above.

[173] See Paczolay, 'The New Hungarian Constitutional State: Challenges and Perspectives' in Howard (ed.), *Constitution Making in Eastern Europe* (1993), 21–55; Sólyom, 'The Hungarian Constitutional Court and Social Change', (1994) 19 *Yale Journal of International Law* 223; and n. 118 above and accompanying text.

[174] Zander, n. 93 above, at 142.   [175] *Ibid.*, 143.

[176] Beatty, 'The Last Generation: When Rights Lose Their Meaning' in Beatty (ed.) n. 84 above, 321 at 350–1. Similarly, see Laws, 'The Constitution: Morals and Rights', [1996] *Public Law* 622, 630–5.

of government ultimate power over the purse'.[177] Further, when one examines exactly how courts have responded to social and economic claims, 'it is clear that guaranteeing people a right to "wholesome and cultured living" in a constitution will at best be a meaningless, empty gesture'.[178] For Beatty, the jurisprudential lessons are 'that the protection of people's social, economic and cultural well-being is neither dependant on nor furthered by their explicit recognition in the text of the constitution'.[179]

Sharpe, in his chapter in this volume, notes that when interpreting the Charter the Canadian Supreme Court has attempted to stay within its judicial role and not interfere in policy matters or issues of 'democracy' traditionally defined. This is said to be evident from the fact, amongst other things, the Court has been unresponsive to claims for economic, social and cultural rights.[180] He argues that the Charter has enhanced democracy by protecting such rights while not interfering greatly with policy choices of the legislature.[181] Blaustein, while supporting constitutional recognition of these rights calls upon constitutionalists to stop dwelling on the distinction between the two sets of rights and instead to classify all rights as either justiciable (and therefore enforceable by the judiciary) or non-justiciable (and therefore best reflected in guidelines for future executive, legislative and administrative action).[182] This approach is virtually identical to one put forward by Israel in 1952 when the International Human Rights Covenants were being drafted.[183]

There are many comments that could be made in response to these reasons for excluding economic, social and cultural rights from the proper purview of bills of rights. Perhaps the most authoritative rebuttal of such views has been made by the United Nations Committee on Economic, Social and Cultural Rights in two of its General Comments, the content of which is readily accessible and need not be recounted here.[184] It must suffice here to add several elements which respond directly to the comments cited above. First, we should be clear that we are speaking of minimum standards of a basic core of rights and not of anything as grandiose or vague as Beatty's right to 'wholesome and

---

[177] Beatty, n. 176 above, at 352.

[178] *Ibid.* at 325. Beatty observes that the guarantee to a 'wholesome and cultured living' is a phrase used in article 25 of the Japanese Constitution.

[179] *Ibid.*   [180] Sharpe, n. 73 above, at 12–13.

[181] *Ibid.* at 23–5: 'the Canadian experience to date indicates that the judiciary is capable of exercising the powers of judicial review in a way that protects such fundamental rights as freedom of religion and expression without unduly inhibiting the capacity of the elected representatives to develop social policy'. To similar effect, see McLachlin, n. 155 above, at 29–30; and Anderson, 'The Limits of Constitutional Law: The Canadian Charter of Rights and Freedoms and the Public-Private Divide' in Gearty and Tomkins (eds.) n. 67 above, 529 at 547–8.

[182] Blaustein, n. 169 above, at 602–3.   [183] UN doc. A/C.3/565 (1952), para. 9.

[184] General Comment 3 (Fifth session, 1990) on 'The nature of States parties obligations (art. 2, para. 1 of the Covenant)', UN doc. E/1991/23; and General Comment 9 (Nineteenth session, 1998) on 'The domestic application of the Covenant', UN doc. E/1999/23.

cultured living'.[185] Access to life-sustaining water, adequate housing to enable life to go on, a primary education, essential medical services, and food sufficient to make a right to life meaningful, are hardly so exotic or beyond the reach of the sort of societies in issue here as to make minimum guarantees unrealistic. Secondly, while justiciability is often important, it is by no means the only way in which a bill of rights might foresee the realization of these rights. Thirdly, the old distinctions between costly and cost-free rights or between positive and negative rights, which underpin so much of these critiques, have by now been shown to be too simplistic to be helpful, even in relation to American constitutional law.[186] Finally, courts have many options open to them in order to avoid getting too directly involved in budgetary matters. The role of the court would normally be limited to directing the executive to propose concrete but affordable measures which would address the problem identified.

But despite the extent of resistance to the inclusion of these rights in bills of rights, it is by no means monolithic. In recent years a number of calls have been made in favour of a more comprehensive reflection of international standards at the national level. As noted above, Reisman has made a strong case in favour of the proposition that constitutional protection of economic and social rights is essential and has buttressed his argument by insisting that it is also necessary for the maintenance of a stable international order.[187]

Blaustein predicted in 1988 that by 1990 more than three-quarters of the world's constitutions would have been promulgated since 1970 and that future constitutions would 'all encompass social, cultural and economic rights'. In retrospect, his first prediction has doubtless been vindicated but the second seems considerably overstated. In the case of Hong Kong, Byrnes has been strongly critical of the fact that the Bill of Rights did not protect economic, social and cultural rights.[188] At a more general level, other commentators have suggested that the constitutional incorporation of economic, social and cultural rights would be one possible solution to the problem posed by bills of rights being conceptualized solely in terms of restrictions on the exercise of government power.[189]

---

[185] As Inoue's work demonstrates, taking such a phrase out of its context in the Japanese Constitution is potentially quite misleading. See n. 171 above.

[186] For the most recent analysis along these lines see Holmes and Sunstein, *The Cost of Rights: Why Liberty Depends on Taxes* (1999).   [187] Reisman, n. 15 above, at 190.

[188] Byrnes (n. 55 above) attributes the failure of the United Kingdom properly to examine the feasibility of incorporating the Covenant on Economic, Social and Cultural Rights largely to the 'fairly traditional, but now somewhat discredited' view of the non-justiciability of those rights. For a discussion of the incorporation of economic and social rights in constitutions of developing nations, see Amankwah, 'Constitutions and Bills of Rights in Third World Nations: Issues of Form and Content', (1989) 12 *Adelaide Law Review* 1 at 9–17, and for a rejection of the 'non-enforceability' analysis of these rights, see Haysom, 'Constitutionalism, Majoritarian Democracy and Socio-Economic Rights', (1992) 8 *South African Journal on Human Rights* 451 at 456–8, and Mureinik, 'Beyond a Charter of Luxuries: Economic Rights in the Constitution', (1992) 8 *South African Journal on Human Rights* 464.

This approach has been taken up in the United Kingdom context by Ewing and Gearty who advocate inclusion of economic and social rights based on their view that recent years have seen serious violations of those rights.[190] They argue that government's failure to countenance incorporation of the Social Charter 'betrays a lack of understanding of the importance of rights, which lies not in the need to constrain the State . . . but to discipline private power to the language and practice of rights'.[191] They consider that '(t)here is no good reason why social and economic rights could not be constitutionally entrenched . . . The fact is that social and economic rights are constitutionally entrenched elsewhere in Europe and developments under EC law has (sic) shown that many give rise to justiciable issues which could be dealt with in the courts'.[192]

In practice, however, the reflection of these rights in recent constitutions has generally been in a form equivalent to what some older constitutions refer to as 'directive principles', in an effort to indicate that while they are indeed fundamental principles they are not enforceable as such. This is the case in relation to the recent wave of Eastern and Central European constitutionalism,[193] for example, where theoretical arguments for the inclusion of economic and social rights in new constitutions were set against perceived economic imperatives associated with the drive towards marketization. All such constitutions included social and economic rights but, for the most part, provided safeguards short of judicial enforcement.[194] The many proposals put forward in the United Kingdom prior to the 1998 Act also reflected a similar approach based on the assumption that 'it is not appropriate for courts of law to be determining the adequacy of levels of income maintenance, housing benefits and the like'.[195]

The directive principles terminology was first used in the constitution of Ireland which refers to 'Directive Principles of Social Policy'. The drafters of the Indian Constitution of 1947 subsequently followed this approach in a section entitled 'Directive Principles of State Policy'.[196] Later examples include the constitutions of Nigeria, Sri Lanka, Papua New Guinea and Bangladesh,

---

[189] Tushnet, 'Living With a Bill of Rights' in Gearty and Tomkins (eds.), n. 67 above, at 12–15.

[190] Ewing and Gearty, n. 66 above, at 151. [191] Ibid. [192] Ibid.

[193] See Council of Europe, The Rebirth of Democracy: 12 Constitutions of Central and Eastern Europe (1995).

[194] Osiatynski, n. 85 above, at 138–40. The Czech Constitution of 1992, for example, follows an American-style liberal model and specifically provides for 'the possibility for a statutory exclusion of judicial protection of social rights'. Ibid. at 166.

[195] Blackburn, 'A British Bill of Rights for the 21st Century' in Blackburn and Busuttil (eds.), Human Rights for the 21st Century (1987), 16 at 39.

[196] Article 37 of the Indian Constitution states that the Directive Principles contained in Part IV 'shall not be enforceable by any court, but the principles therein laid down are nevertheless fundamental in the governance of the country and it shall be the duty of the State to apply these principles in making laws'. See Sripati, 'Freedom from Torture and Cruel, Inhuman or Degrading Treatment or Punishment: The Role of the Supreme Court of India' in Gibney and Frankowski (eds.), Judicial Protection of Human Rights: Myth or Reality? (1999), 107.

reflecting the basis on which a compromise has been struck between the proponents of different emphases in development.[197] The Indian experience
shows that directive principles can be effective, especially if they are used in
conjunction with other rights whose justiciability is explicitly recognized.[198]
However it does not necessarily follow that this creative compromise resolves
the tensions that exists between the two sets of rights. These can be considerable. In the early years in India, legislation implementing the 'directives of
state policy' was repeatedly struck down by the Indian Supreme Court as violating political and civil rights. This in turn provoked constitutional amendment to safeguard implementation of the directive principles, and subsequent
litigation in the Supreme Court, where the amendments were eventually found
to be constitutional.[199] In two recent cases, the Court held that the right to life
under the Indian Constitution cannot be assured unless it is accompanied by
the right to education.[200]

Even in contexts in which civil and political rights have been assumed to
predominate there has been room to embrace some of the principles underlying social and economic rights. This is true in relation to the ECHR.[201]
Moreover, in the law of some states of the USA some economic and social
rights are characterised and enforced as civil and political rights, for example,
the right to choose one's occupation as a protected liberty, or the right to join
a trade union as an element of the right of association.[202] The right to education is also extensively recognized within the various American state constitutions. After canvassing case law from around the world, Beatty observes that
rights in the field of education, employment, financial security and even health
care are an important part of the protection which the 'traditional guarantees'
(of civil and political rights) have been able to provide.[203]

[197] Ghai, n. 33 above, at 210.
[198] See De Villiers, 'Directive Principles of State Policy and Fundamental Rights: The Indian
Experience', (1992) 8 *South African Journal on Human Rights* 29, and De Villiers, 'The Socio-
Economic Consequences of Directive Principles of State Policy; Limitations on Fundamental
Rights', (1992) 8 *South African Journal on Human Rights* 188 especially at 195–9.
[199] Ghai n. 33 above. For a theoretical account of the tension, see Laws, n. 176 above, at 630–5.
[200] *Mohini Jain* v. *State of Karnataka, JT* [1992] 4 S.C. 292 (India); *Unni Krishnan* v. *State of
Andhra Pradesh* [1993] 1 S.C.C. 645 (India). In *Mohini Jain*, the Indian Supreme Court upheld the
right to education of every citizen. It did so despite the fact that education is recognized not as a
right but as a directive principle. Its reasoning was that the rights to life and dignity, which the
Constitution does recognize (Article 21), could not be assured unless it was accompanied by the
right to education. The Court concluded that fundamental rights have to be interpreted against
the backdrop of the directive principles contained in the Constitution. See discussion in Gomez,
'Social and Economic Rights and Human Rights Commissions' (1995) 17(1) *Human Rights
Quarterly* 155 at 156–7.
[201] Robert, 'Constitutional and International Protection of Human Rights: Competing or
Complementary Systems?' (1994) 15(1–2) *Human Rights Law Journal* 1 at 9–10.
[202] *Ibid.*
[203] Beatty, n. 176 above, at 334. However he argues (at 352) that 'there is nothing in the way the
courts have protected economic and group rights so far which can be used as precedent for judges
taking over the job of fixing the levels of social welfare and cultural well-being which must be
guaranteed in any particular community'. To similar effect see Davis, 'The Case Against the

It is clear therefore that a great deal remains to be done in order to respond to the challenge of including economic, social and cultural rights within bills of rights, thus bringing them into conformity with the international human rights obligations that virtually every state in the world has accepted. No single model exists and there remains considerable scope for the development of creative approaches which can transcend the stale and unhelpful ideological point-scoring which has stifled much of the debate so far.[204]

The second major issue which demands attention at this point of our analysis is the extent to which bills of rights extend to actions involving only private parties. The debates over the vertical (government-individual) or horizontal (private-private) reach of human rights provisions is a very longstanding one which has not been resolved very clearly by international supervisory bodies applying the provisions of human rights treaties.[205] There has, however, been a rather active and instructive jurisprudence arising out of the application of the relevant provisions of various national bills of rights. Four such approaches have been identified.[206] The most straightforward is that adopted by the American courts which requires that there be some form of 'state action' involved before the constitutional protections contained in the Bill of Rights can be invoked. Various suggestions have been put forward for a more expansive approach such as the constitutionalization of economic and social rights or reconceptualization of the state action doctrine, so that the exercise of private power is seen as the exercise of a power delegated to individuals and corporations by the government and thus remains within an expanded conception of state action. However, it has been argued that such proposals reach too far into the core 'private' domain, where constitutions historically have feared to tread.[207] At the opposite end of the spectrum is the approach adopted in Ireland under which it is sufficient to show that a constitutional right has been breached and no significance is attached to the fact that the responsible party is a private one.[208]

The most extensive jurisprudence so far has been developed under the Canadian Charter but the conceptual picture that emerges has been subject to considerable criticism on virtually all sides. In interpreting Article 32(1) of the Charter,[209] the courts have adopted a reasonably broad interpretation which

---

Inclusion of Socio-Economic Demands in a Bill of Rights Except as Directive Principles' (1992) 8 *South African Journal on Human Rights* 475.

[204] Consider the potential role that might be played in this regard by national human rights institutions. See nn. 263–72 below and accompanying text.

[205] See generally Clapham, *Human Rights in the Private Sphere* (1993).

[206] An excellent survey is contained in Hunt, 'The "Horizontal Effect" of the Human Rights Act', [1998] *Public Law* 423.

[207] Tushnet, n. 189 above, at 15.   [208] Hunt, n. 206 above, at 428–9.

[209] Section 32(1) of the Charter provides that the Charter applies (a) to the Parliament and government of Canada in respect of all matters within the authority of Parliament including all matters relating to the Yukon Territory and Northwest Territory; and (b) to the legislature and government of each province in respect of all matters within the authority of the legislature of each province.

covers all executive and administrative action, both federal and provincial, but have stopped short of requiring that the provision be applied to the work of the courts themselves. For practical purposes, the result is that in the application of the common law in actions between private parties, the Charter does not apply. This amounts, in the view of some observers, to a judicial preference for a convenient and artificial interpretation which limits the Charter's reach, thereby ignoring the phenomenon of 'corporate governance' and the real extent of the judges' own law-making role and their role in private relations. In so doing, the courts have avoided tackling the economic and social implications of private constitutional disputes.[210] Even those critics who acknowledge both the challenges that the courts would face if they were to expand their jurisdiction in this way, and the inherent complexity of the debate about the extent of constitutional intervention necessary to achieve social justice, complain that these issues are merely avoided when the public/private debate is treated with such 'formal technicality'.[211] The South African Constitutional Court has also followed the Canadian approach by deciding that the Bill of Rights does not have 'general direct horizontal application'.[212]

There is, however, a less restrictive fourth alternative approach which is now emerging. The New Zealand Bill of Rights, for example, extends the jurisdiction of the courts only to acts done by the three branches of government or a body performing a public function.[213] Nevertheless, this formula seems to allow some scope for the operation of the Bill in private disputes, because it binds the judiciary.[214] In the South African case, a dissenting judgment in the principal case cited above, advocates such an indirect horizontal effect whereby relations between private parties would be covered to the extent that the law is involved in any way.[215] Such an approach has been advocated by various commentators in relation to the United Kingdom Human Rights Act.

In his chapter in this volume, Clapham traces various British approaches to this question, contrasting these to the approach taken by the European Court on Human Rights in interpreting the ECHR. He raises a number arguments about how individuals' rights can be affected by private actors, particularly in

---

[210] Anderson, n. 181 above, at 530–49. See also Webber, n. 111 above, at 218–21. Webber remarks (at 218 n. 55) that '(p)rivate action is rarely wholly private (on any definition of that term); it often receives power and structure from law'. He says (at 218) that '(t)he first structural bias afflicting charters of rights is the creation of an in-built privilege for private over state power. It is easy to fall prey to the fallacy that human rights are simply about curbing state power—that rights result, almost by definition, from restricting the state. Liberties can, however, be greatly undermined by private action . . . Far from limiting individual liberty and equality, the intervention of the state may advance precisely those interests that charters of rights are designed to protect'.

[211] Anderson, n. 181 above, at 549.

[212] *Du Plessis* v. *De Klerk*, 1996 (3) S.A. 850, 887.   [213] Joseph, n. 65 above.

[214] *Ibid.*

[215] Judgment of Kriegler J., discussed in detail by Hunt, n. 206 above, at 434–5.

an age of privatization, and expresses concern that a strict public/private split would encourage the courts to transform substantive questions into jurisdictional questions revolving around the appropriate boundaries between public and private action:[216]

Domestic violence, discrimination at work or in housing, and invasions of privacy are not primarily instigated by State agents. If a Bill of Rights is to have a really educative and preventive function, then everyone should feel bound by its norms—whether or not they perceive themselves as carrying out a public function. To create a culture of human rights means going beyond instructing officials that there are annoying limits on Government action. The challenge must be to allow everyone to feel that such principles and rules contribute to greater respect for people's dignity, and that it is respect for these rights which enables better participation in civil society and political decision-making.[217]

He supports the approach reflected in the New Zealand Bill of Rights, to the extent that that formulation binds the judiciary in its determination of disputes concerning private actors.[218] Hunt endorses a similar approach, arguing that the United Kingdom Human Rights Act should be interpreted as applying the ECHR to all law, including the common law as it applies in the context of private disputes. This approach falls short of full horizontal application because it would not confer a new cause of action where private parties are involved but would require the trigger of a pre-existing cause of action in relation to which the ECHR dimension could be raised.[219]

Entrenchment would politicize the judges

One of the principal objections to bills of rights, and one that is usually accorded particular prominence in discussions of both entrenching economic and social rights and applying bills of rights to the private sphere, is that the role of judges is thereby politicized. The resulting fears were colourfully expressed some years ago by Lord McCluskey:

Lawmaking should be left to lawmakers, policymaking to responsible policy-makers. [But a bill of rights] is inevitably a charter of enduring super-rights, rights written in delphic words but in indelible ink on an opaque surface. It turns judges into legislators and gives them a finality which our whole tradition has hitherto professed to withhold from them. It makes the mistake of dressing up policy choices as if they were legal choices. It asks those whose job it is to know and apply the law to create and reform the law.[220]

---

[216] Clapham, n. 29 above.   [217] *Ibid.* at 146.   [218] *Ibid.*

[219] Hunt, n. 206 above, at 435–43.

[220] McCluskey, 'Law, Justice and Democracy', Reith Lectures (1987), cited in Zander, n. 93 above, at 104. On the related question of whether an entrenched bill of rights should entail a different method of selection of judges, see Zander, n. 93 above, at 145–51. And see Beatty, n. 152 above, at 150 concerning the potential of politics to 'infect and undermine the legitimacy of the law'. Beatty argues that it is 'as much the personal and legal philosophy of the judge as the principles of rationality and proportionality, that determines how well human rights will be protected

There is no question that a bill of rights brings changes to the judicial *status quo*, affecting the range of functions entrusted to the courts, increasing workloads, raising new issues, demanding more attention to policy implications, and even affecting the balance of power within a democratic state. In turn judges are required to be more open in exercising their law-making functions, and judicial appointments assume more obvious political importance. But the real question is whether these developments should be seen either as radical innovations or merely as an acceleration of existing trends. The former assessment would seem to reflect an unduly positivist conception of the judicial role in the absence of a bill of rights and a refusal to accept the fact that judicial law-making is now a widely accepted reality. As Brennan has noted, in declaring the common law and in the discharge of their other functions, 'the Courts do not operate in a valueless vacuum'.[221] Even when they are ostensibly only applying the existing law, there is considerable scope for judges' own preferences to affect the way they marshal precedents, and assess the competing arguments, when deciding a disputed point of law.[222]

There are other reasons not to overstate the extent to which bills of rights introduce an additional political dimension into the work of the courts. First, at least in common law countries, judges have long chaired or participated in committees of inquiry dealing with highly political issues. The result has not been to tarnish the reputation of the judiciary as a whole, and in many instances it might be speculated that public appreciation of the useful and constructive role of judges has only been enhanced. Secondly, many critics tend to assume that what they consider to be the undesirable manifestations and consequences of the role of the judiciary in the USA in relation to the Bill of Rights can confidently be taken as marking the path down which any other country's judiciary will be pushed if a bill of rights is introduced. But as the contributions to this volume demonstrate persuasively, very much depends on other factors including the nature and scope of the bill of rights, its relationship to international standards, the procedures for its amendment, and the judicial ethos which exists in the relevant country.[223] Thirdly, as noted earlier,[224] the constitutional framework and the institutional design that it reflects will have a greater impact on the extent to which the judiciary is politicized than will the introduction of a bill of rights.

in any society', on which basis the judicial appointment system needs to ensure that candidates who are 'uncomfortable with or hostile to the role of the judiciary as guardian of the constitution (or treaty)' are screened out, and judges who are 'committed to the vigorous enforcement of the principles of rationality and proportionality in every case' are chosen.

[221] Brennan, n. 81 above, at 463. See also Jones, n. 28 above, at 74–5.

[222] Zander, n. 93 above.

[223] Writing about the USA, Tushnet notes with envy that 'people on the left elsewhere in the world have been able to articulate an agenda of advancing fundamental rights, including rights that aren't important parts of the U.S. Constitution, without becoming acolytes of judicial review': Tushnet, 'Is Judicial Review Good for the Left?', *Dissent*, Winter 1998, 65 at 70.

[224] See text accompanying nn. 145 and 159 above.

A fourth factor is the extent to which judiciaries have deferred to parliamentary preferences in interpreting bills of rights, at least to the extent that the outcome of a particular case does not seem to be clearly mandated by the Bill or by existing jurisprudence. In the view of some commentators, such deference has fostered relatively high levels of public respect for the judiciary.[225] A final factor, suggested by Russell, in his study of the effects of the Canadian Charter on Canadian politics, suggests that in any event courts only 'process' policy disputes; rarely do they settle them.[226] He concedes that 'in processing disputes, courts certainly influence the final outcome. A judicial decision is a very valuable resource for the winning side'.[227] However he contends that, 'like any other political resource—popularity, money, media access—a favourable judicial decision does not necessarily in itself deliver a complete and final political victory'.[228] Russell claims that a range of factors must be considered in an assessment of the effectiveness of judicial decisions, including the terms of the decision itself (which may leave openings for the losing side to recover some of its loss), the closeness of the vote in court, the status of the court, the state of public opinion, the losing side's resources, and the availability of provision for parliamentary override of judicial decisions.[229]

A closely related critique is that the entrenchment of bills of rights leads to the 'judicialization of politics'. This often manifests itself through high profile corporations fighting their policy wars in the courts, in the guise of human rights claimants. There is no doubt that corporations do increasingly seek to rely upon human rights provisions, but at the same time, there is an increasing trend towards seeking mechanisms by which to hold such private actors directly accountable for actions which are incompatible with human rights law. It would be odd if one side of this equation could proceed in the absence of the other. In any event it is clear that the use of courts to challenge government policy did not begin with the introduction of bills of rights, as Russell has noted in relation to the Canadian Charter. Much of Canadian administrative law in fact developed 'through court challenges brought by business organisations resisting the modern interventionist state', although it is true that the Charter did serve to expand such opportunities.[230] Further, Russell observes that the 'political losers' have greatly outnumbered the political winners in these matters, right across the political spectrum, and that in any event, these political battles represent the small minority of Charter cases. In fact, 75 per cent of Charter litigation is taken up with criminal cases, where the

---

[225] Russell, 'The Three Dimensions of Charter Politics' in Bickerton and Gagnon (eds.), *Canadian Politics* 2nd edn. (1994), 344 at 352. As Zander has observed, the experience in countries with bills of rights or written constitutions in general terms does not bear out the view that they necessarily result in unacceptable politicization of the judiciary: Zander, n. 93 above, at 108. See also Kentridge, n. 96 above, at 106–11, citing the experience of the courts in South Africa and Canada.

[226] Russell, n. 225 above, at 350.   [227] *Ibid.*   [228] *Ibid.*

[229] *Ibid.* at 350–51.   [230] *Ibid.* at 350.

Charter (through availability of legal aid) is most accessible to ordinary people.[231] While not necessarily relevant in all societies where bills of rights may
operate, these observations from the Canadian experience provide a useful
practical backdrop against which to evaluate criticisms of 'judicialized politics', subject to the existence of adequate support structures (including legal
aid) to assist ordinary rights claimants in getting access to the courts.

*Because judges are inherently conservative, entrenchment leads to regressive
outcomes*

It is frequently claimed that judges are inherently conservative, having regard
to their education and training, to their socio-economic background, and to
their institutional environment. It is further suggested that this conservatism
increases the likelihood of regressive human rights outcomes. The first claim
is difficult to contest in most societies, although its strength is probably also
easily overstated. There are many instances in which the judiciary in a great
many countries have in fact endorsed highly progressive outcomes and have
refused to give legitimacy to anti-human rights initiatives of governments.
While it may be productive for scholars of American constitutional law to
invest considerable energy into re-evaluating the role of the United States
Supreme Court in landmark cases such as *Brown* v. *Board of Education*[232]
(school desegregation), *Griswold* v. *Connecticut*[233] (overturning a ban on con-
traceptive use), or *Roe* v. *Wade*[234] (abortion), there are good reasons for questioning whether the record of that court is an appropriate basis upon which to
draw conclusions as to judicial conservatism or otherwise in human rights
matters which can usefully be generalized. The unique strength of the tradition of judicial review, the particular role accorded to the Supreme Court both
in American law and in the public imagination, the apparent inability of the
Congress to resolve many highly contested issues in any satisfactory way, the
virtual irrelevance of international norms within the judicial system, and various other factors all contribute to limiting significantly the transferability of
the American experience to other contexts. Whether in France, Germany,
Canada or Australia among developed countries or in a variety of Latin
American or African countries, highly significant examples can be found
which show the courts upholding the best human rights traditions.[235]

The inherent judicial conservatism argument can also be turned on its head
so that it becomes an argument in favour of the entrenchment of a bill of
rights. If the judiciary really is so conservative, then its capacity to promote
conservative goals to the extent that these can be equated with outcomes

---

[231] *Ibid.* at 347–8. See also Webber, n. 111 above, at 212–13, for a useful summary of the results
of Charter litigation during its first eleven years.

[232] 347 U.S. 483 (1954). [233] 381 U.S. 479 (1965).

[234] 410 U.S. 113 (1973).

[235] The best collection of current cases, albeit overwhelmingly from common law jurisdictions,
is contained in the *Commonwealth Human Rights Law Digest* published regularly since 1996.

which are hostile to human rights, is appropriately constrained by the adoption of a bill which constrains their options and makes it more likely that they will have to uphold respect for those rights. While a legal realist approach would dismiss any such purported constraints as illusory, the growing importance of international jurisprudence in this area adds another important element in making it difficult for a conservative judiciary to endorse outcomes which are radically at odds with those emerging from constitutional and other courts worldwide and being endorsed by international and regional courts and supervisory bodies.

The case studies in this volume are highly instructive on this issue. The Israeli case, described in this volume by Kretzmer,[236] illustrates the potentially highly progressive role which might be played by the judiciary, at least in relation to certain types of cases. In the United Kingdom, where judicial traditions are often seen as being especially conservative, ECHR standards and jurisprudence have often been well received and now constitute an important dimension of the human rights jurisprudence of the British courts. The judiciary in Britain, as a whole, seems to have taken reasonable cognisance of international human rights norms, even if only because of the threat of their judgments being reviewed by the European Court in Strasbourg. Moreover, some senior judges have been among the most prominent advocates of incorporation of the ECHR into domestic law. Of course, these facts need not *per se* contradict the inherent conservatism thesis, since it will be argued that the ECHR is itself an inherently conservative document which largely excludes social rights and seeks to lock in a liberal (in the conservative sense) vision of society. But this takes us back to a much broader debate over the nature of human rights which cannot usefully be developed further here.

The recent experience in New Zealand and Canada has been largely positive, as the case studies in this volume show. In the case of the latter, this has been attributed by some commentators to the nature and extent of public involvement and debate prior to the Charter's introduction. Thus the comments by a leading Canadian Supreme Court judge (Madam Justice McLachlin) that from the beginning the people of Canada took the Charter to heart and the judges gave it real substance, has been seen as a vindication of popular sentiment. As Penner notes:

[I]t seems to me she was saying in effect the judges gave it real substance because the people took it up. And this may well be the most important lesson to be learned from the Canadian experience. A minimalist Bill of Rights passed quietly, purely as a parliamentary measure without popular backing and substantial consensus, may not be given its full weight by a cautious judiciary.[237]

---

[236] Kretzmer, 'Basic Laws as a Surrogate Bill of Rights: The Case of Israel',Chapter 3 above.
[237] Penner, n. 100 above, at 107.

New Zealand's case was markedly different however, with a relatively muted period of debate and passage, and a clear majority of public submissions against the proposal. This certainly influenced the eventual form which the Bill of Rights Act of 1990 took, but did not prevent New Zealand judges from being prepared to give it teeth.[238] We have already seen the influence that international human rights law, and the existence of international obligations and individual complaint procedures, have exercised in domestic jurisprudence, including in New Zealand. With increasingly favourable reception of international norms and comparative jurisprudence within national law, one could expect this trend to continue, encouraging judges to warm more rapidly to their new expanded jurisdiction over human rights matters. Other factors, such as the increasing interaction between senior judges internationally, may help to consolidate this trend.[239]

Experience in relation to the countries reviewed in this volume is therefore mixed, but this serves to underscore the need to avoid sweeping generalizations which overlook the specificity of different situations. Thus account must be taken of factors such as the court involved, the composition of the court at a given time, the type of case, the broader community attitudes in relation to the issue, the strength of international precedents, and so on. Moreover, if the conservatism of the judiciary is seen as a major problem, it should not simply be treated as an unchangeable fact of life. As Tushnet has noted, 'it is not a Bill of Rights that is a bad idea for progressives; it is a badly interpreted Bill of Rights'.[240] Remedial measures should thus be explored in order to adapt either the method of choosing judges, the formal and informal criteria used in such choices, and the training given to them in relation to human rights matters. Other commentators have played down these concerns about inherent conservatism. In the extended debates leading up to the incorporation of the ECHR in the United Kingdom Dworkin concluded, after surveying both the American Bill of Rights jurisprudence and that relating to the ECHR, that '(t)he risk is ... inconsequential that after incorporation judges would be able to stop social and economic changes a future government of the left would actually want, and would otherwise be permitted to make'.[241] In particular he stressed the point that 'conservative or unimaginative judges who refused to exercise their power to check ministers and officials or to set aside Parliamentary statutes' based on their new ECHR-based mandate would simply be doing what they would have done anyway. Thus the situation would in

---

[238] See the comments by Justice Cartwright of the New Zealand High Court, suggesting that the Court of Appeal had seized the Human Rights Act, 'rescued it from imminent oblivion and emphasised its significance for the general body of New Zealand law'. It had done so despite the fact that 'this was not at all what was contemplated during the political debate which led to the enactment of the New Zealand Bill of Rights Act': Quoted by Zander, n. 93 above, at 99.

[239] Lester, 'The Georgetown Conclusions on the Effective Protection of Human Rights Through Law', [1996] *Public Law* 562.

[240] Tushnet, n. 189 above, at 17.   [241] Dworkin, n. 76 above, at 48.

no sense be worse than that prevailing prior to incorporation. The positive consequences would nevertheless be significant:

Some judges would exercise their new power well even if most did not, and the profession and the public would have a new basis for criticising and educating the laggards. Litigants who were denied their rights in decisions the profession criticised would be more likely to appeal to Strasbourg, and the European Court would hand down decisions that even the most conservative judges would then be obliged to follow in future cases.[242]

Bills of rights litigation is costly for applicants and would clog the courts

There is little doubt that the addition of a bill of rights has the potential to add significantly to the workload of the courts. But the extent to which this will occur in a given society depends on many factors and is thus not readily able to be predicted. In the Australian context, Brennan has identified a number of potential hazards including: the complexity of evidence required (given that constitutional matters affect the interests of all who live under the Constitution); the high costs of litigating constitutional matters; the need for changes to rules of procedure (concerning such matters as evidence and joinder of parties);[243] and court list congestion.[244] In relation to the last-mentioned factor, he notes that litigation triggered by a bill of rights could be accommodated by the Australian High Court only if it shed 'a corresponding volume of non-constitutional civil and criminal cases. The Court would be confined substantially to constitutional cases. With such a fascinating diet, the Court would in time have a diminished appetite for the pedestrian issues of the law'.[245]

Other commentators have acknowledged that the practical impact might be significant, but concluded that such a price is a small one to pay for the returns to society that will flow from the bill of rights.[246] As indicated previously,[247] much of the success of a bill of rights will depend upon the resources and support that are available to assist aggrieved persons to pursue their claims. Further, one feature of human rights litigation is that the subject of the claim is a question of principle, meaning that litigating the matters at issue to a final

---

[242] *Ibid.* at 51. To similar effect see Penner, n. 100 above, at 112.

[243] The requirement for flexible 'standing' rules is a factor noted particularly by Eberts (n. 83 above) in the context of equality litigation under the Canadian Charter, to encourage input from intervenors and facilitate the representation of people who would otherwise have limited prospects for accessing the judicial process.

[244] Brennan, n. 81 above.   [245] *Ibid.* at 460.

[246] Dworkin, for instance (n. 76 above at 42–4) claims that, even if the fear of judicial overwork were well-founded (and he gives a number of reasons for his belief that in the United Kingdom it is not), 'it would . . . be preposterous to complain that it would have been better to save judges the work than to ask them to help defend the fundamental rights of British citizens . . . So the argument that incorporation would overwork the judges is actually an argument based on stinginess, a particularly debased form of the bad idea that rights should be denied when it is expensive or otherwise inconvenient to recognise them'.

[247] See n. 114 above and accompanying text.

judicially determined outcome, rather than settling along the way, can be expected to be more common than in the ordinary run of cases.

But experience elsewhere, in particular in Canada, has shown that when required to do so, the courts can cope with the extra demands on their resources. In the early years of operation of a bill of rights one might expect a relatively high incidence of human rights litigation, including frivolous litigation, until such time as a reasonable body of case law develops to promote certainty in the law, and the courts are allowed to develop whatever procedures are necessary for the administration of their new jurisdiction. Moreover, groundless litigation would be discouraged by the normal practice that the loser must pay the winner's costs, along with the requirement, where applicable, to satisfy criteria for legal aid.[248] As McLachlin has noted, although the Canadian Charter has tended to lengthen the average length of criminal trials (especially by increasing the number of hearings necessary to determine whether evidence was taken in a way that breached the Charter), Charter work nevertheless comprises 'only a small portion' of trial justices' dockets.[249] Her view is that 'the evidence simply does not support the allegation that the Charter has opened the gates to floods of frivolous litigation, although it may have increased it somewhat'.[250]

Of course, not all situations will mirror the positive and receptive circumstances within which the Canadian Charter was brought into being, fostering the rights culture and support infrastructure so crucial for breathing life into abstract written human rights guarantees. But if the conditions are right, the Canadian experience does at least serve to illustrate that the extra practical demands brought by entrenchment of a bill of rights might not necessarily be as insurmountable or intractable as is sometimes feared. Indeed, within an appropriate constitutional culture, an entrenched bill of rights may enhance legislative-judicial cooperation to improve the law and promote respect for human rights.[251]

Excessive rights consciousness can be damaging

It is not uncommon today to hear laments about the excessive preoccupation of modern society with rights. Perhaps the best example is the proposal put to the United Nations General Assembly in 1998 that it should adopt a draft Universal Declaration of Human Responsibilities.[252] The draft was drawn up in September 1997 by the InterAction Council,[253] and modelled on the

---

[248] See Dworkin, n. 76 above, at 42.

[249] McLachlin, n. 155 above, at 32. Anderson, n. 181 above, at 547–8, suggests optimistically that courts always find ways of restricting their caseload through techniques such as mootness and *locus standi*.

[250] McLachlin, n. 155 above, at 32.   [251] *Ibid.* at 33.

[252] UN doc. A/C.3/53/L.5 (1998).

[253] A group of former government leaders, led by Helmut Schmidt of Germany and Malcolm Fraser of Australia.

Universal Declaration of Human Rights. It consists of nineteen articles stating 'norms of good behaviour, including honest dealing, speaking and acting truthfully, commends non-violence and generally showing respect to others' and its overriding emphasis is on duties and responsibilities. This is justified by a fear that 'the exclusive insistence on rights can result in conflict, division and endless dispute, and the neglect of human responsibilities can lead to lawlessness and chaos'. Without going into the merits and otherwise of a proposal to which the international human rights community has been understandably negative,[254] the point for present purposes is that there is a certain disenchantment with rights that needs to be taken into account in assessing proposals to proliferate bills of rights.

Much of this disenchantment stems from concern that rights tend to empower lawyers, to encourage the discussion of societal problems in terms of legal discourse, to promote legal resolution of a great range of matters which might best be dealt with in other ways. As Zander has put it, '(o)ne does not relish the thought of a society where citizens reach for a lawyer and a writ like a six-shooter in the Wild West'.[255] In a similar vein, Glendon's critique of the role of rights within American society has been widely cited. Apart from the fact that there will always be conflicts among rights which cannot easily be resolved through the simple insistence that a rights approach be applied, Glendon's preoccupation is with the particular brand of rights talk prevalent in the USA:

Our current American rights talk . . . is set apart from rights discourse in other liberal democracies by its starkness and simplicity, its prodigality in bestowing the rights label, its legalistic character, its exaggerated absoluteness, its hyperindividualism, its insularity, and its silence with respect to persona, civic and collective responsibilities.[256]

In her view, the rapidly expanding catalogue of rights in the USA 'not only multiplies the occasion for collisions, but it risks trivialising core democratic values'. In addition, insistence upon the use of a rights framework in inappropriate contexts 'impedes compromise, mutual understanding and the discovery of common ground.'[257] Her critique is an important one and draws heavily upon criticisms that have long been made by both the left and right in the USA and particularly by some critical legal scholars. The question in this context, however, is the extent to which it is applicable to the approach pursued in other countries and particularly those which have their own bills of

---

[254] See International Council on Human Rights Policy, *Taking Duties Seriously: Individual Duties in International Human Rights Law, A Commentary* (1999); and Amnesty International, 'Muddying the Waters. The Draft "Universal Declaration of Human Responsibilities": No Complement to Human Rights', Amnesty Report No. IOR 40/02/98, April 1998.

[255] Zander, n. 93 above, at 132.

[256] Glendon, *Rights Talk: The Impoverishment of Political Discourse* (1991), x.

[257] *Ibid.* at 307.

rights. For the most part, the contributors to this volume do not attach major importance to such issues in the different contexts that they analyse, although in countries like Australia and especially Canada some critics have taken up the cudgel in strong terms.[258]

For the most part, there would seem to be reason to discount the fear that the shortcomings of the American approach will inevitably come to afflict other societies which opt to go down the bill of rights path. In the first place, the principal problem in most such countries is a lack of respect for rights and a failure to reflect such values in everyday life. Rights saturation point would still seem to be a long way off. Secondly, the approach to rights which is reflected in the principal international instruments which have most heavily influenced national approaches (the ECHR, the Covenant on Civil and Political Rights, and the American Convention on Human Rights) differs quite significantly from that which has developed in over 200 years of American constitutionalism. These instruments reflect an awareness of the need to balance rights against one another, an acknowledgement that the application of rights must be undertaken within a broader community context, recognition of the legitimacy of taking account of relevant considerations within a democratic society, and provision for limitations and derogation where demonstrably and strictly necessary. This is evident in patterns of jurisprudence under the ECHR, with evaluations of 'necessity' and 'proportionality' often weighing heavily in the outcome in individual cases.[259] With the increasing reception of international human rights norms directly into national law, it is less likely that the American experience will simply be repeated elsewhere.[260] Rather, with the benefit of the influence of international norms (as fleshed out by international courts, treaty monitoring bodies and diverse national courts), it is reasonable to expect rights discourse to proceed in a more nuanced, balanced fashion, and to adapt to take appropriate account of the individual situations in particular societies.

---

[258] e.g. Hanks, 'Moving Towards the Legalisation of Politics', (1988) 6 *Law in Context* 80; Glasbeek and Mandel, 'The Legalisation of Politics in Advanced Capitalism: The Canadian Charter of Rights and Freedoms', (1984) 2 *Socialist Studies/Etudes socialistes* 84; and Mandel, *The Charter of Rights and the Legalization of Politics in Canada* (1989).

[259] See e.g. Beatty, n. 84 above, at 21–2.

[260] According to one commentator, prior to the adoption of the Canadian Charter, the country's judges 'had probably never heard of the [ECHR]. Now a typical Charter decision is imbued with a cosmopolitan rather than parochial perspective. If judges have not yet become internationalists, they have certainly become comparativists, particularly with respect to relying on United States law. [In the future] there may be a lessening in emphasis on American case law . . . There has been a tendency to use American case law selectively and eclectically . . . (T)here remains a suspicion of American law that does not extend to international law, particularly norms binding on Canada or deriving from European sources . . . A blend of comparative and international approaches will be vital in ensuring that the Charter is interpreted in a spirit commensurate with its pre-eminent role in Canada's legal system.' Claydon, 'The Use of International Human Rights Law to Interpret Canada's Charter of Rights and Freedoms', 2 *Connecticut Journal of International Law* (1987) 349 at 359.

Non-judicial Approaches to Implementing Bills of Rights

The foregoing analysis has focused heavily, although not exclusively, on the role of the courts in enforcing the provisions of a bill of rights. While appropriate, this emphasis should not be permitted to obscure the fact that a range of other actors play a vital part in promoting and upholding the values reflected in such a Bill. The role of the executive is obvious, and some aspects of the role that can be played by parliaments have been explored above.[261] Civil society also has a crucial role to play in almost every aspect of efforts to promote the understanding, acceptance, and appropriate application of a bill of rights, as well as in maintaining careful scrutiny of the approach adopted by the three branches of government.[262] But the focus of this final section is not on any of these actors. Instead it is necessary to draw attention to the increasingly prominent role which is being played in a diverse range of countries by what have become known in United Nations jargon as national human rights institutions.

While such institutions are proliferating at a surprising rate, there is no standard approach to defining their functions, the basis on which they are established, the status attributed to them, or the level of resources which should be available to them. In a recent 'General Comment' the United Nations Committee on Economic, Social and Cultural Rights sought to clarify the meaning of the concept in the following terms:

[National] institutions range from national human rights commissions through ombudsman offices, public interest or other human rights 'advocates', to *défenseurs du peuple* and *defensores del pueblo*. In many cases the institution has been established by the government, enjoys an important degree of autonomy from the executive and the legislature, takes full account of international human rights standards which are applicable to the country concerned, and is mandated to perform various activities designed to promote and protect human rights.[263]

The Committee's use of the phrase 'in many cases' was well advised, since there are also instances in which such institutions lack some of the features described: they lack autonomy, they attach little importance to international standards, and their mandate is extremely limited. It is precisely for these reasons that the United Nations has sought to develop a set of minimum

---

[261] See nn. 63–70 and accompanying text.

[262] See Epp, *The Rights Revolution: Lawyers, Activists and Supreme Courts in Comparative Perspective* (1998). Focusing on the courts in the USA, the United Kingdom, India and Canada, Epp highlights the extent to which the rights revolution in each country has been driven by the efforts of human rights activists.

[263] General Comment 10 (Nineteenth session, 1998) on 'The role of national human rights institutions in the protection of economic, social and cultural rights', UN doc. E/1999/23, para. 2.

standards to prescribe certain attributes and, in effect, proscribe others. [264] The following list gives an indication of the principal roles which might be performed by such institutions in relation to a national bill of rights:

(1) the performance of educative and promotional functions fostering a 'human rights culture';
(2) investigation and attempted resolution of complaints;
(3) involvement in the provision of legal aid;
(4) the conduct of bill of rights litigation (and particularly *strategic* litigation to maximize use of resources and ensure substantive outcomes of systemic relevance)[265] including, where rules of court permit, intervening in proceedings as *amicus curiae* to assist the court to resolve issues of particular importance;
(5) provision of advisory services to potential litigants and other services involved with the 'support structure for legal mobilization';
(6) review of legislation for compliance with relevant human rights principles;
(7) advising government generally in relation to its human rights obligations; and
(8) promoting the incorporation of international human rights norms into municipal systems.

National institutions can also perform a range of other functions which may contribute to building the constitutional culture required for the effective application of a bill of rights.[266] This should also involve an important potential role in relation to economic and social rights, although the United Nations Committee dealing with these issues recently observed that 'this role

---

[264] See 'Principles Relating to the Status of National Institutions', Commission on Human Rights resolution 1992/54 of 3 March 1992, Annex, UN doc. E/1992/22, chap. II, sect. A; General Assembly resolution 48/134 of 20 December 1993, Annex, ('the UN Principles') for agreed principles on the competence, responsibilities, composition, methods of operation, and guarantees of independence and pluralism relating to national human rights institutions.

[265] See e.g. Spencer and Bynoe, 'A Human Rights Commission for the United Kingdom— Some Options', [1997] 2 *European Human Rights Law Review* 152 at 155. The strategic litigation function is critical for addressing the 'opportunism' and 'compartmentalism' problems identified by Doyle and Wells (n. 27 above), as far as development of rights through the common law is concerned, and may assist in addressing other limitations inherent in the adversarial litigation process (such as the preference for simple over complex claims) suggested by Webber, n. 111 above, at 225–7.

[266] These include preparation of reports to government on human rights matters, encouraging ratification of and accession to international human rights instruments and ensuring their implementation, contributing to (but ideally not being responsible for) national reports pursuant to international reporting obligations, and cooperating with organizations within the United Nations system, regional institutions and other national human rights institutions in the promotion and protection of human rights. Others are mentioned in Gallagher (n. 24 above) focusing on their role in facilitating domestic reception of international law and their actual and potential interactions with the international human rights treaty system. See also Mulgan, n. 45 above at 238 and 246–7; Spencer and Bynoe, n. 265 above, and Gomez, n. 200 above, at 158–60.

has too often either not been accorded to the institution or has been neglected or given a low priority by it'.[267]

In recent years, a number of new constitutions have made explicit provision for the establishment of a national human rights commission. Examples include: Ethiopia, South Africa, Malawi, Uganda and the Philippines.[268] Mandating the creation of such an institution sends a strong symbolic message, gives bureaucratic clout to it, and accords a degree of protection from parliamentary or executive manipulation. While many such institutions will probably fail, at least in the short term, the record so far has been more encouraging than might have been anticipated. For example, both the Indonesian and Indian Human Rights Commissions have surprised many of their critics with their ability to take on a life of their own—to 'distance themselves from both the government and the mixed motivations that were behind their establishment', and provide a brake on abuse of executive power and a focal point for human rights advocacy.[269] However the structural weaknesses relating to the establishment of those two institutions in particular—most notably the fact that they were established and can be dismantled by Presidential Decree and legislation, respectively—justify concerns in relation to their longer-term viability.[270]

National institutions enjoy several advantages in comparison with the courts. Their involvement is not dependent upon the fortuitous emergence of appropriate and justiciable cases. They are more accessible, can use a wider range of techniques, have a much greater capacity for proactive and strategic action, can work in partnership with public or private actors, and can employ more culturally sensitive and flexible approaches to conflict resolution.[271] They can also develop international networks including international NGO links,[272] and act as a conduit for bringing home the benefits of normative developments at the international level or in other national jurisdictions in a timely and effective way. In terms of their relationship with the other branches of government, national human rights institutions can potentially add a valuable extra dimension to the overall system of checks and balances, engaging and interacting to draw attention to undesirable developments, elevating human rights discourse to new levels, and encouraging the development of constitutional human rights jurisprudence.

---

[267] General Comment 10, n. 263 above, at para. 3

[268] See Dugard, n. 56 above; Gallagher, n. 24 above.   [269] Gallagher, *ibid.*

[270] In Epp's terms (n. 113 at 766–7) entrenchment of institutional foundations would help get around the fact that bills of rights themselves are not 'self-activating'. In other words, it will succeed in tying 'individual interests to institutional resources', as part of the constitutional balance of power equation, in which circumstances 'self-activation' can in future be assured.

[271] See Marks, 'The New Cambodian Constitution: From Civil War to a Fragile Democracy' in Neuman, n. 50 above, 45 at 91–3. The comparative advantage of 'flexibility' is discussed by Gomez, n. 200 above, at 159.

[272] The importance of institutional networks and NGO links are emphasized in Mulgan, n. 45 above at 246–47.

Conclusion

This analysis has been sufficiently wide-ranging and synthetic in nature as to obviate any need for any overview of the main points which emerge. Indeed the entire chapter is a form of conclusion to the volume of essays as a whole. It can therefore suffice to draw attention to several of the key themes that have emerged. First, there is no single recipe for a successful bill of rights. Secondly, if a bill of rights is to be seen as a source of legitimacy for the constitutional order, it must possess a certain unity and an 'internal coherence',[273] and have come into being in accordance with 'right process'.[274] Thirdly, philosophical disagreement as to the basis for human rights protection is not necessarily a barrier to either constitutional entrenchment or the effective protection of human rights standards. Fourthly, it is desirable to tailor a bill of rights as far as possible (and permissible by applicable international norms) to reflect the specific needs of the society in question.[275] Finally, many of the concerns that have been expressed in the past in relation to the entrenchment of human rights norms and stronger reliance upon the courts, can be viewed in a significantly different light as a result of the rapidly growing internationalization of human rights norms and the spread of interpretative institutions at the international, regional and national levels.

An important research agenda for the future also emerges from the volume as a whole. First, there is a need for much more in-depth historical analysis with a view to seeking to discern some of the dynamics which are common to different situations in relation to bills of rights. Secondly, while acknowledging the complexity of comparative work in this field,[276] there is considerable space for more sophisticated comparative analyses of the jurisprudence emerging from the growing number of important decisions by constitutional and other courts around the world. Thirdly, there is a need to seek to develop a better understanding of the factors that facilitate, as well as those that impede, the success of bills of rights in different contexts. This also calls for efforts to come to grips with the potential contradiction between the extensive literature predicting the likely failure of 'legal transplants'[277] and other analyses that show the extent to which legal modelling has been effective in a wide range of contexts.[278]

---

[273] See discussion in Castiglione, 'The Political Theory of the Constitution' in Bellamy and Castiglione (eds.), n. 4 above, at 7–8.

[274] See Franck, 'Legitimacy in the International System', (1988) 82 *AJIL* 705 at 706.

[275] The South African Bill of Rights is a good example of a carefully crafted 'compromise' constitution. See Chanock, n. 35 above.

[276] See generally Grossfeld, *The Strength and Weakness of Comparative Law* (1990).

[277] e.g. Watson, *Legal Transplants: An Approach to Comparative Law* (1974).

[278] Braithwaite, 'A Sociology of Modelling and the Politics of Empowerment', (1994) 45 *British Journal of Sociology* 445–79.

Select Bibliography

1. General

ACKERMAN, B., 'The Political Case for Constitutional Courts', in Yack, B. (ed.), *Liberalism Without Illusions: Essays on Liberal Theory and the Political Vision of Judith N. Shklar* (1996), 205.

ADJEI, C., 'Human Rights Theory and the Bill of Rights Debate', (1995) 58 Modern Law Review 17–36.

ALLEN, J., 'Bills of Rights and Judicial Power—A Liberal's Quandary', (1996) 16 *Oxford Journal of Legal Studies* 337.

ALSTON, P. and CRAWFORD, J. (eds.), *The Future of U.N. Human Rights Treaty Monitoring* (forthcoming).

ANDREWS, J., 'The European Jurisprudence of Human Rights' (1984) 43 *Maryland Law Review* 463.

AZZAM, F., *Arab Constitutional Guarantees of Civil and Political Rights* (1996).

BANTING, K. and SIMEON, R. (eds.), *Redesigning the State: The Politics of Constitutional Change* (1985).

BEATTY, D., *Human Rights and Judicial Review: A Comparative Perspective* (1994).

——, 'Law and Politics', (1996) 44 *American Journal of Comparative Law* 131.

BELLAMY, R., 'The Political Form of the Constitution: the Separation of Powers, Rights and Representative Democracy' in Bellamy, R. and Castiglione, D. (eds.), *Constitutionalism in Transformation: European and Theoretical Perspectives* (1996), 24.

——, and CASTIGLIONE, D., *Constitutionalism in Transformation: European and Theoretical Perspectives* (1996).

BILLIAS, G., (ed.), *American Constitutionalism Abroad: Selected Essays in Comparative Constitutional History* (1990).

BLACKBURN, R., 'Parliamentary Opinion on a New Bill of Rights', (1989) 60 *Political Quarterly* 469.

BLAUSTEIN, A., 'Human Rights in the World's Constitutions', in Nowak, M., Steurer, D. and Tretter, H. (eds.), *Progress in the Spirit of Human Rights* (1988), 599.

BUERGENTHAL, T., 'The American and European Conventions on Human Rights: Similarities and Differences' (1981) 30 *American University Law Review* 155 at 155.

——, 'Modern Constitutions and Human Rights Treaties', (1997) 36 *Columbia Journal of Transnational Law* 211.

CAMPBELL, E., 'Papua New Guinea Government—Consideration of a Bill of Rights', (1971) 1 *Melanesian Law Journal* 44–59.

Canadian Bar Association and Cameroon Bar Council Committee Report, *Model Human Rights Charter for Developing Countries* (1989).

COHEN, R., HYDEN, G. and NAGAN, W. (eds.), *Human Rights and Governance in Africa* (1993).

'Comparative Constitutionalism: Symposium', (1991) 40 *Emory Law Journal* 723–942.

CONFORTI, B. and FRANCIONI, F. (eds.), *Enforcing International Human Rights in Domestic Courts* (1997).

DICKSON, B., *Human Rights and the European Community* (1997).

DOMINICK, M. F., 'Toward a Community Bill of Rights: the European Community Charter of Fundamental Social Rights', (1991) 14 *Fordham International Law Journal* 639.

DRZEMCZEWSKI, A., *European Human Rights Convention in Domestic Law: A Comparative Study* (1983).

DUGARD, J., 'The Application of Customary International Law Affecting Human Rights By National Tribunals', (1982) 76 *Proceedings of the American Society of International Law* 245.

DWORKIN, R., 'Constitutionalism and Democracy', (1995) 3 *European Journal of Philosophy* 2.

FALK, R., 'Taking Human Rights Seriously at Home', (1997) 68 *Political Quarterly* 179.

FINER, S., BOGDANOR, V. and RUDDEN, B., *Comparing Constitutions* (1995).

FINN, J., *Constitutions in Crisis: Political Violence and the Rule of Law* (1991).

FOLEY, M., *The Silence of Constitutions: Gaps, 'Abeyances' and Political Temperament in the Maintenance of Government* (1989).

FREEMAN, M., 'Measuring Equality: A Comparative Perspective on Women's Legal Capacity and Constitutional Rights in Five Commonwealth Countries', (1989–90) 5 *Berkeley Women's Law Journal* 110.

EPP, C., *The Rights Revolution: Lawyers, Activists and Supreme Courts in Comparative Perspective* (1998).

FABRE, C., 'Constitutionalising Social Rights', (1998) 6 *Journal of Political Philosophy* 263.

FREEMAN, M., 'Constitutional Democracy and the Legitimacy of Judicial Review', (1990) 9 *Law and Philosophy* 327.

FREEMAN, S., 'Constitutional Democracy and the Legitimacy of Judicial Review', (1990) 9 Law and Philosophy 327.

GAMBLE, K., 'Putting Civil Rights to a Popular Vote', (1997) 41 *American Journal of Political Science* 245.

GEARTY, C. A. and TOMKINS, A. (eds.), *Understanding Human Rights* (1996).

GHAI, Y., 'Constitutions and Political Order in East Africa', (1972) 21 *International and Comparative Law Quarterly* 403.

——, 'The Rule of Law, Legitimacy and Governance', (1986) 14 *International Journal of the Sociology of Law* 179.

——, 'Constitutions and Governance in Africa: A Prolegomenon', in Adelman, S. and Paliwala, A. (eds.), *Law and Crisis in the Third World* (1993), 51–75.

GLENDON, M., *Rights Talk: The Impoverishment of Political Discourse* (1991).

——, 'Rights in Twentieth-Century Constitutions' (1992) 59 *University of Chicago Law Review* 519.

GOLDWIN, R., 'What is a Bill of Rights and What is it Good For?', Licht, R. and de Villiers, B. (eds.), *South Africa's Crisis of Constitutional Democracy: Can the U.S. Constitution Help?* (1994), 143.

GOMEZ, M., 'Social and Economic Rights and Human Rights Commissions' (1995) 17 *Human Rights Quarterly* 155.

GOODIN, R.E., 'Designing Constitutions: the Political Constitution of a Mixed Commonwealth', in Bellamy, R. and Castiglione, D. (eds.), *Constitutionalism in Transformation: European and Theoretical Perspectives* (1996), 223.

GREENBERG, D., KATZ, S., OLIVIERO, M. and WHEATLEY, S. (eds.), *Constitutionalism and Democracy: Transitions in the Contemporary World* (1993).

GRIFITH, J., 'The Political Constitution' (1979) 42 *Modern Law Review* 1.

HARLOW, C., 'Access to Justice as a Human Right. The European Convention and the European Union', in Alston, P., with Bustelo, M. and Heenan, J. (eds.), *The EU and Human Rights* (1999), 187.

HASKELL, T., 'The Curious Persistence of Rights Talk in the "Age of Interpretation", (1987) 74 *Journal of American History* 984.

HENKIN, L., 'Elements of Constitutionalism', Occasional Paper Series, August 1994, Centre for the Study of Human Rights, Columbia University; reprinted in (1998) 60 *The Review of the International Commission of Jurists* 11.

HIMSWORTH, C., 'In a State No Longer: The End of Constitutionalism?', [1996] *Public Law* 639.

JACKSON, D. and TATE, C., *Comparative Judicial Review and Public Policy* (1992).

JANIS, M., 'The Declaration of Independence, the Declaration of the Rights of Man and Citizen, and the Bill of Rights', (1992) 14 *Human Rights Quarterly* 478.

——, KAY, R. and BRADLEY, A. (eds.), *European Human Rights Law: Text and Materials* (1995).

KENTRIDGE, S., 'Parliamentary Supremacy and the Judiciary Under a Bill of Rights: Some Lessons from the Commonwealth, [1997] *Public Law* 96.

KIRBY, M., 'The Role of the Judge in Advancing Human Rights by Reference to International Human Rights Norms', (1988) 62 *Australian Law Journal* 514.

——, 'The Bangalore Principles of Human Rights Law' (1989) 106 *South African Law Journal* 484, and (1989) 58 *Nordic Journal of International Law* 206.

——, 'The New World Order and Human Rights' (1991) 18 *Melbourne University Law Review* 209.

——, 'Human Rights: The Role of the Judge', in J. Chan and Y. Ghai (eds.), *The Hong Kong Bill of Rights: A Comparative Approach* (1993), ch. 10.

——, 'From Bangalore to Balliol—A View from the Antipodes' [1993] *University of New South Wales Law Journal* 363.

KRUGER, J. and CURIN, B., *Interpreting a Bill of Rights* (1994).

——, 'Towards a New Interpretive Theory', in Kruger, J. and Currin, B. (eds.), *Interpreting a Bill of Rights* (1994).

KOMMERS, D.P., 'Procedures for the Protection of Human Rights in Diffuse Systems of Judicial Review', in European Commission for Democracy through Law, *The Protection of Fundamental Rights by the Constitutional Court* (1996), 97.

LACEY, M. and HAAKONSSEN, K. (eds.), *A Culture of Rights—The Bill of Rights in Philosophy, Politics, and Law—1791 and 1991* (1991).

MAARSEVEEN, H. VAN, and TANG, G. VAN DER, *Written Constitutions: A Computerized Comparative Study* (1978).

MACKAY, W. 'Can Judges Change the Law?' (1987) LXXIII *Proceedings of the British Academy* 285.

MAHER, G., 'Human Rights in the Criminal Process' in Campbell, T. (ed.), *Human Rights: From Rhetoric to Reality* (1986), 197.

MANOHAR, S. V., 'The Indian Judiciary and Women's Rights' in (1996) *Indian Journal of International Law* 1–12.

MARKS, S., 'The New Cambodian Constitution: From Civil War to a Fragile Democracy', (1994) 26 *Columbia Human Rights Law Review* 45.

MASON, A., 'Future Directions in Australian Law', (1987) 13 *Monash University Law Review* 149.

McHUGH, M., 'The Law-making Function of the Judicial Process' (1988) 62 *Australian Law Journal* 15 and 116.

MINOGUE, K., 'What is Wrong with Rights' in Harlow, C. (ed.), *Public Law and Politics* (1986), ch 11.

MUELLER, D., *Constitutional Democracy* (1996).

MULGAN, M., 'Implementing International Human Rights Norms in the Domestic Context: The Role of a National Institution', [1993] 5 *Canterbury Law Review* 235.

MURPHY, W.F., 'Constitutions, Constitutionalism, and Democracy' in Greenberg, D. *et al* (eds.), *Constitutionalism and Democracy: Transitions in the Contemporary World* (1993), 3.

NEUMAN, G., 'Rights in New Constitutions—Introduction', (1994) 26 *Columbia Human Rights Law Review* 1–3.

O'BOYLE, M., 'Due process under the European Convention on Human Rights', in Kruger, J. and Currin, B. (eds.), *Interpreting a Bill of Rights* (1994).

OLSON, T. B., 'How Effective are Bills of Rights in protecting Individual freedoms?', (The Bill of Rights After 200 Years: The Tenth Annual National Federalist Society

Symposium on Law and Public Policy—1991) (1992) 15 *Harvard Journal of Law and Public Policy* 53–4.

OSIEL, J., 'Dialogue with Dictators: Judicial Resistance in Argentina and Brazil' (1995) 20 *Law and Social Inquiry* 481.

POHJOLAINEN, K. (ed.), *Constitutionalism in Finland: Reality and Perspectives* (1995).

PRITCHARD, S., 'The Jurisprudence of Human Rights: Some Critical Thought and Developments in Practice', (1995) 2 *Australian Journal of Human Rights* 3.

REID, LORD 'The Judge as Law Maker', (1972) 12 *Journal of Society of Public Teachers of Law* 22.

ROBERT, J., 'Constitutional and International Protection of Human Rights: Competing or Complementary Systems?' (1994) 15 *Human Rights Law Journal* 1.

RUZINDANA, A., 'Human Rights, the International Bill of Human Rights and the Ombudsman', (1992) 10 *Ombudsman Journal* 123.

SCHEININ, M., 'Domestic Implementation of International Human Rights Treaties: Nordic and Baltic Experiences', in Alston, P. and Crawford, J. (eds.), *The Future of the U.N. Human Rights Treaty Monitoring* (forthcoming).

SCHUTTER, O. de, *Fonction de juger et droits fondamentaux: transformation du contrôle juridictionnel dans les ordres juridiques américains et européens* (1999).

SEDLEY, S., 'Human Rights: A Twenty-First Century Agenda', [1995] *Public Law* 386.

SMOKE, S., *Bill of Rights and Responsibilities: A Book of Common Sense* (1996).

SORNARAJAH, M., 'Bills of Rights: The Commonwealth Debate', (1976) 9 *Comparative and International Law Journal of South Africa* 161.

STOTZKY, I., *Transition to Democracy in Latin America: The Role of the Judiciary* (1993).

STOVE, G., EPSTEIN, P. and SUNSTEIN, C. (eds.), *The Bill of Rights in the Modern State* (1992).

STURGESS G. and CHUBB P., *Judging the World: Law and Politics in the Worlds' Leading Courts* (1988).

SRIPATI, V., 'Freedom from Torture and Cruel, Inhuman or Degrading Treatment or Punishment: The Role of the Supreme Court of India', in Gibney, M. and Frankowski, S. (eds.), *Judicial Protection of Human Rights: Myth or Reality?* (1999), 107.

Symposium, 'Rights in New Constitutions', (1994) 26 *Columbia Human Rights Law Review* 1–213.

Symposium, 'The Protection of Human Rights in the Nordic Countries', (1975) 8 *Revue des droits de l'homme* 89–288.

TUSHNET, M., 'Is Judicial Review Good for the Left?', *Dissent* (Winter 1998), 65.

THOMPSON, K. and LUDWIKOWSKI, R., *Constitutional and Human Rights: American, Poland and France: a Bicentennial Colloquium at the Miller Center* (1991).

TUCKER, C., 'Regional Human Rights Models in Europe and Africa: A Comparison' (1983) 10 *Syracuse Journal of International Law and Commerce* 135.

WALDRON, J., 'A Right-Based Critique of Constitutional Rights' (1993) 13 *Oxford Journal Legal Studies* 18.

——, 'Freeman's Defense of Judicial Review', (1994) 13 *Law and Philosophy* 27–41 .

WATTS, D., *Securing Our Liberties : The Rights and Wrongs of the Bill of Rights* (1994).

WINTEMUTE, R., *Sexual Orientation and Human Rights: The United States Constitution, the European Convention, and the Canadian Charter* (1996).

2. Africa—General

AN-NA'IM, A., 'American and Islamic Constitutionalism: Prospects for Positive Interaction' in Thompson, K. W. (ed.), *The US Constitution and Constitutionalism in Africa* (1989), 55–76.

BAALI, A., 'The Algerian Constitution: A Constitution Based on the Separation of Powers and the Protection of Individual and Collective Freedoms', (1998) 60 *The Review of the International Commission of Jurists* 103.

BOIS DE GAUDUSSON, J. DU, CONAC, G. and DESOUCHES, C. (eds.), *Les Constitutions africaines publiés en langue française* (2 vols., 1998).

DUGARD, J., 'The Role of Treaty-Based Human Rights Standards in Domestic Law: The Southern African Experience' in Alston, P. and Crawford, J. (eds.), *The Future of UN Human Rights Treaty Monitoring* (forthcoming)

EL-MORR, A.M., *et al*, 'The Supreme Constitutional Court and its Role in the Egyptian Judicial System', (1998) 60 *The Review of the International Commission of Jurists* 113.

GAMBARI, I. A., 'Constitutionalism in Africa' in Thompson, K. W. (ed.), *The US Constitution and Constitutionalism in Africa* (1989), 27–54.

GONIDEC, P. F., 'Constitutionnalismes Africains' in *Revue Juridique et Politique* 23–50 (1996).

MAZRUI, A., 'The American Constitution and the Liberal Option in Africa: Myth and Reality' in Thompson, K. W. (ed.), *The US Constitution and Constitutionalism in Africa* (1989), 1–26.

MODERNE, F., 'Human Rights and Postcolonial Constitutions in Sub-Saharan Africa' in Henkin, L. and Rosenthal A. J. (eds.), *Constitutionalism and Rights. The Influence of the United States Constitution Abroad* (1990), 315.

NAHUM, F., 'Ethiopia: Constitution for a Nation of Nations', (1998) 60 *The Review of the International Commission of Jurists* 91.

NSEREKO, D., 'Religious Liberty and the Law in Botswana', (1992) 34 *Journal of Church and State* 843.

NYANG, S. S., 'The Impact of U.S. Constitutionalism in Africa: A Gambian Case Study' in Thompson, K. W. (ed.), *The US Constitution and Constitutionalism in Africa* (1989), 77.

OKOTH-OGENDO, H. W. O., 'Constitutions without Constitutionalism: Reflections on an African Political Paradox' in Greenberg, D. *et al* (eds.), *Constitutionalism and Democracy: Transitions in the Contemporary World* (1993), 65.

OULD-ABDALLAH, A., 'The Rule of Law and Political Liberalisation in Africa', (1998) 60 *The Review of the International Commission of Jurists* 29.

RAMCHARAN, B.G., 'Introduction, The Evolving African Constitutionalism: A Constitutionalism of Liberty and Human Rights', (1998) 60 *The Review of the International Commission of Jurists* 7.

ROSSANET, B DE, 'The Ghanaian Constitutionalism of Liberty', (1998) 60 *The Review of the International Commission of Jurists* 47.

SINJELA, J., 'Constitutionalism in Africa: Emerging Trends', (1998) 60 *The Review of the International Commission of Jurists* 23.

Special Issue: 'The Evolving African Constitutionalism', (1998) 60 *The Review of the International Commission of Jurists* 7–269.

3. Australia

ALLARS, M., 'One Small Step for Legal Doctrine, One Giant Leap Towards Integrity in Government: Teoh's Case and the Internationalisation of Administrative Law', (1995) 17 *Sydney Law Review* 204.

ALSTON, P., (ed.), *Towards an Australian Bill of Rights* (1994).

Attorney-General's Department (of the Australian Capital Territory), *Issues Paper— A Bill of Rights for the ACT?* (1993).

BAILEY, P. H., *Human Rights: Australia in an International Context* (1990).

——, ' "Righting" the Constitution Without a Bill of Rights', (1995) 23 *Federal Law Review* 1–36.

BURDEKIN, B., 'The Impact of a Bill of Rights on Those who Most Need Them', in Alston, P. (ed.), *Towards an Australian Bill of Rights* (1994), 147.

CALEO, C., 'Implications of Australia's Accession to the First Optional Protocol to the International Covenant on Civil and Political Rights' (1993) 4 *Public Law Review* 175.

CAMPBELL, E., 'Civil Rights and the Australian Constitutional Tradition' in C. Beck (ed.), *Law and Justice: Essays in Honour of Robert S Rankin* (1970), 295.

CASS, D. Z., 'Through the Looking Glass: The High Court and the Right to Speech', (1993) 4 *Public Law Review* 229.

CHARLESWORTH, H., 'Australia's Accession to the First International Covenant on Civil and Political Rights' (1992) 18 *Melbourne University Law Review* 428.

——, 'Individual Rights and the Australian High Court', (1986) 4 *Law in Context* 52.

——, 'The Australian Reluctance About Rights', (1993) 30 *Osgoode Hall Law Journal* 195.

——, 'Australia's Split Personality: Implementation of Human Rights Treaty Obligations in Australia', in Alston, P. and Chiam, M., *Treaty-Making and Australia: Globalisation versus Sovereignty* (1995), 129.

'Constitutional Rights for Australia? Symposium', (1994) 16 *The Sydney Law Review* 145.

DAVIDSON, A. and SPEGELE, R. D. (eds.), *Rights, Justice and Democracy in Australia* (1991).

Electoral and Administrative Review Commission (Queensland), *Report on Review of the Preservation and Enhancement of Individuals' Rights and Freedoms* (1993).

ENCEL, S., HORNE, D. and THOMPSON, E. (eds.), *Change the Rules! Towards a Democratic Constitution* (1977).

EVANS, G., 'An Australian Bill of Rights?', (1973) 45 *Australian Quarterly* 4.

——, 'Prospects and Problems for an Australian Bill of Rights', 1970–73 (1975), *Australian Yearbook of International Law* 1–18.

EWING, K., 'New Constitutional Constraints in Australia' [1993] *Public Law* 256.

FITZGERALD, B., 'International Human Rights and the High Court of Australia', (1994) 1 *James Cook University Law Review* 78.

GAGELER, S and GLASS, A., 'Constitutional Law and Human Rights', in Kinley, D., (ed.), *Human Rights in Australian Law: Principles, Practice and Potential* (1998), 47.

GALLIGAN, B., 'Australia's Rejection of a Bill of Rights' [1990] *Journal of Commonwealth and Comparative Politics* 344.

GALLIGAN, B., 'Parliamentary Responsible Government and the Protection of Rights', (1993) 4 *Public Law Review* 100.

GAZE, B. and Jones, M., *Law, Liberty and Australian Democracy* (1990).

GIBBS, H., 'The Constitutional Protection of Human Rights', (1982) 9 *Monash University Law Review* 1.

GOLDSWORTHY, J., 'The Constitutional Protection of Rights in Australia' in Craven, G. (ed.), *Australian Federation: Towards the Second Century* (1992), 151.

HANKS, P., 'Moving Towards the Legalisation of Politics', (1988) 6 *Law in Context* 80.

——, 'Constitutional Guarantees' in H. P. Lee and G. Winterton (eds.), *Australian Constitutional Perspectives* (1992), 92.

HUGHES, C., 'The Australian Bill of Rights: Some Key Issues', in Alston, P., (ed.), *Towards an Australian Bill of Rights* (1994), 165.

Joint Committee on Foreign Affairs, Defence and Trade (of the Australian Parliament), *A Review of Australia's Efforts to Promote and Protect Human Rights* (1992).

JONES, T., 'Legal Protection for Fundamental Rights and Freedoms: European Lessons for Australia?', (1994) 22 *Federal Law Review* 57.

KINLEY, D., 'Constitutional Brokerage in Australia: Constitutions and the Doctrines of Parliamentary Supremacy and the Rule of Law', (1994) 22 *Federal Law Review* 192.

—— (ed.), *Human Rights in Australian Law: Principles, Practice and Potential* (1998).

KIRBY, M., 'The Australian Use of International Human Rights Norms: From Bangalore to Balliol—A View from the Antipodes', (1993) 16 *University of New South Wales Law Journal* 363.

——, 'The Role of International Standards in Australian Courts', in Alston, P. and Chiam, M., *Treaty-Making and Australia: Globalisation versus Sovereignty* (1995), 81.

LEE, H., 'Reforming the Australian Constitution: The Frozen Continent Refuses to Thaw' [1988] *Public Law* 535.

——, 'The Australian High Court and Implied Fundamental Guarantees', [1993] *Public Law* 606.

MCHUGH, M., 'The Law-Making Function of the Judicial Process', (1988) 62 *Australian Law Journal* 15.

MCMILLAN, J. and WILLIAMS, N., 'Administrative Law and Human Rights', in Kinley, D. (ed.), *Human Rights in Australian Law: Principles, Practice and Potential* (1998), 63.

MASON, A., 'The Role of a Constitutional Court in a Federation: A Comparison of the Australian and the United States Experience', (1986) 16 *Federal Law Review* 1.

——, 'Future Directions in Australian Law', (1987) 13 *Melbourne University Law Review* 149.

——, 'A Bill of Rights for Australia?', (1989) 5 *Australian Bar Journal* 79.

——, 'The Role of the Judiciary in Developing Human Rights in Australian Law', in Kinley, D. (ed.), *Human Rights in Australian Law: Principles, Practice and Potential* (1998), 26.

MOFFAT, R., 'Philosophical Foundations of the Australian Constitutional Tradition', (1965) 5 *Sydney Law Review* 59.

MORAN, A., 'The Constitution (Declaration of Rights and Freedoms) Bill 1988

(Vic.)—a Doomed Legislative Proposal', (1990) 17 *Melbourne University Law Review* 418.

O'NEILL, N., 'A Never Ending Journey? A History of Human Rights in Australia', in L. Spender (ed.), *Human Rights—The Australian Debate* (1987), 7.

——, 'Constitutional Human Rights in Australia' (1987) 17 *Federal Law Review* 85.

——, 'The Australian Bill of Rights Bill 1985 and the Supremacy of Parliament', (1986) 60 *Australian Law Journal* 139.

O'NEILL, R., 'Freedom of Expression and Public Affairs in Australia and the United States: Does a Written Bill of Rights Really Matter?', (1994) 22 *Federal Law Review* 1–12.

PURCELL, T., 'Rights in the Constitution: the Bill of Rights Revisited?', (1988) 62 *Australian Law Journal* 268.

RUBINSTEIN, K., 'Towards 2001: An Assessment of the Possible Impact of a Bill of Rights on Administrative Law in Australia—Part I', (1993) 1 *Australian Journal of Administrative Law* 13–32; 'Part II', (1994) 1 *Australian Journal of Administrative Law* 59–79.

SAMUELS, G., 'A Bill of rights for Australia?', (1979) 51 *Australian Quarterly* 91.

SAWER, G., 'Protection of Human Rights in Australia', [1946] *Yearbook on Human Rights* 31.

Senate Legal and Constitutional References Committee, *Trick or Treaty?—Commonwealth Power to Make and Implement Treaties* (1995).

Senate Standing Committee on Constitutional and Legal Affairs, *A Bill of Rights for Australia? An Exposure Report for the Consideration of Senators* (1985).

SHEARER, I., 'The Implications of Non-Treaty Law-Making: Customary Law and Its Implications', in Alston, P. and Chiam, M., *Treaty-Making and Australia: Globalisation versus Sovereignty* (1995), 93.

SMALLBONE, D., 'Recent Suggestions of an Implied 'Bill of Rights' in the Constitution, Considered as Part of a General Trend in Constitutional Interpretation', (1993) 21 *Federal Law Review* 254.

SPENDER. L. (ed.), *Human Right—The Australian Debate* (1987).

STARKE, J. G., 'Durability of the Bill of Rights 1688 as Part of Australian Law', (1991) 65 *Australian Law Journal* 695.

THOMSON, J., 'An Australian Bill of Rights: Glorious Promises, Concealed Dangers', (1994) 19 *Melbourne University Law Review* 1020.

TRIGGS, G., 'Australia's Ratification of the International Covenant on Civil and Political Rights: Endorsement or Repudiation?', (1981) 31 *International and Comparative Law Quarterly* 278.

TOOHEY, J., 'A Government of Laws, and Not of Men?' (1993) 4 *Public Law Review* 158.

——, 'Towards an Australian Common Law', (1990) 6 *Australian Bar Journal* 185.

WILCOX, M. R., *An Australian Charter of Rights?* (1993).

——, 'The North American Experience: A Personal Reflection', in Alston, P., (ed.), *Towards an Australian Bill of Rights* (1994),187.

WILSON, R., 'The Domestic Impact of International Human Rights Law' (1992) 24 *Australian Journal of Forensic Science* 57.

WINTERTON, G., 'Extra-Constitutional Notions in Australian Constitutional Law', (1986) 16 *Federal Law Review* 223.

ZDENKOWSKI, G., 'Defending the Indigent Accused in Serious Cases: A Legal Right to Counsel?', [1994] *Criminal Law Journal* 135.

ZINES, L., 'A Judicially Created Bill of Rights?', (1994) 16 *The Sydney Law Review* 166.

——, *Constitutional Change in the Commonwealth* (1991).

4. Canada

ANDERSON, G. W., 'The Limits of Constitutional Law: The Canadian Charter of Rights and Freedoms and the Public-Private Divide' in Gearty, C. and Tomkins, A. (eds.), *Understanding Human Rights* (1996), 529.

BAKAN, J., 'Constitutional Interpretation and Social Change: You Can't Always Get What You Want (Nor What You Need)', (1991) 70 *Canadian Bar Review* 307.

BAYEFSKY, A. F., *International Human Rights Law: Use in the Canadian Charter of Rights and Freedoms Litigation* (1992).

BAYEFSKY, A., 'Mechanisms for Entrenchment and Protection of a Bill of Rights: The Canadian Experience', [1997] 5 *European Human Rights Law Review* 496.

BEAUDOIN, G. A. (ed.), *The Charter: Ten Years Later*, Proceedings of the April 1992 Colloquium of the Canadian Bar Association and the Department of Justice of Canada in Ottawa (1992).

——, and Ratushny, E. (eds.), *The Canadian Charter of Rights and Freedoms* 2nd edn. (1989).

BEATTY, D., 'Human Rights and Constitutional Review in Canada', (1992) 13(5–6) *Human Rights Law Journal* 185.

——, 'Labouring Outside the Charter', (1991) 29 *Osgoode Hall Law Journal* 839.

——, 'A Conservative's Court: The Politicization of Law', (1991) 41 *University of Toronto Law Journal* 147–67.

——, 'Protecting Constitutional Rights in Japan and Canada', (1993) 41 *American Journal of Comparative Law* 535.

——, *Talking Heads and the Supremes* (1990).

'Bibliography on the Canadian Charter of Rights and Freedoms', (1991–1992) *Canadian Human Rights Yearbook* 267.

'Canadian Constitution, 1982: A Symposium', (1982) 45 *Law and Contemporary Problems* 1–302.

CLAYDON, J., 'The Use of International Human Rights Law to Interpret Canada's Charter of Rights and Freedoms', [1987] 2 *Connecticut Journal of International Law* 349.

EBERTS, M., 'Risks of Equality Litigation', in Martin and Mahoney (eds.), *Equality and Judicial Neutrality* (1987), 89.

——, 'Women and Constitutional Renewal', in Doer and Carrier (eds.), *Women and the Constitution in Canada* (1981), 3.

EPP, C., 'Do Bills of Rights Matter? The Canadian Charter of Rights and Freedoms', (1996) 90 *American Political Science Review* 765.

ETHERINGTON, B., 'An Assessment of Judicial Reviews of Labour Laws Under the Charter of Realists, Romantics and Pragmatists', (1992) 24 *Ottawa Law Review* 685.

FERGUSON, G., 'The Impact of an Entrenched Bill of Rights: The Canadian Experience', (1990) 16 *Monash University Law Review* 211.

Fox, P. and White, G. (eds.), *Politics Canada* (1994).

Fraser, A., 'Beyond the Charter Debate: Republicanism., Rights and Civic Virtue in the Civil Constitution of Canadian Society', (1993) 1 *Review of Constitutional Studies* 27–74.

Glasbeek, H. J. and Mandel, M., 'The Legalisation of Politics in Advanced Capitalism: The Canadian Charter of Rights and Freedoms', (1984) 2 *Socialist Studies/Etudes Socialistes* 84.

Gibson, D., 'The Deferential Trojan Horse: A Decade of Charter Decisions', (1993) 72 *Canadian Bar Review* 417.

Hammond, R., 'The Bill of Rights and the Canadian Experience', [1987] *New Zealand Law Review* 132.

Harvie, R. and Foster, H., 'Different Drummers, Different Drums: The Supreme Court of Canada, American Jurisprudence and the Continuing Revision of Criminal Law Under the Charter', (1992) 24 *Ottawa Law Review* 39.

—— and ——, 'Ties that Bind? The Supreme Court of Canada, American Jurisprudence, and the Revisions of Canadian Criminal Law Under the Charter', (1990) 28 *Osgoode Hall Law Journal* 729.

Hucker, J., 'Antidiscrimination Laws in Canada: Human Rights Commissions and the Search for Equality', (1997) 19 *Human Rights Quarterly* 547–71.

Hutchinson, A. and Petter, A., 'Private Rights/Public Wrongs: The Liberal Lie of the Charter', (1988) 38 *University of Toronto Law Journal* 278.

Jackman, M., 'The Cabinet and the Constitution: Participatory Rights and Charter Interests', (1990) 35 *McGill Law Journal* 943.

——, 'Using the Charter to Support Social Welfare Claims', (1993) 19 *Queen's Law Journal* 65–94.

Knopf, R. and Morton, F. L., *Charter Politics* (1992).

Lysyk, K., 'The Canadian Charter of Rights and Freedoms: General Principles', (1994) 16 *Advocates Quarterly* 1–47.

McCullough, H., 'Parliamentary Supremacy and a Constitutional Grid: The Canadian Charter of Rights', (1992) 41 *International and Comparative Law Quarterly* 751.

McLachlin, B., 'The Charter: A New Role for the Judiciary', (1991) 29 *Alberta Law Review* 540.

——, 'Southey Memorial Lecture: The Canadian Charter and the Democratic Process', (1991) 18 *Melbourne University Law Review* 350.

——, 'The Charter of Rights and Freedoms: A Judicial Perspective', (1989) 23 *University of British Columbia Law Review* 579.

——, 'The Role of the Court in the Post-Charter Era: Policy-Maker or Adjudicator?', (1990) 39 *UNBLJ* 43.

——, 'The Canadian Charter and the Democratic Process', in Gearty, C. and Tomkins, A. (eds.), *Understanding Human Rights* (1996), 22.

Mahoney, K., 'A Charter of Rights: The Canadian Experience' in Papers on Parliament No. 23—*Parliaments and Constitutions Under Scrutiny* (Department of the Senate, Parliament House, Canberra, September 1994), 47–79.

Mandel, M., *The Charter of Rights and the Legalization of Politics in Canada* (1989).

Manfredi, C., *Judicial Power and the Charter: Canada and the Paradox of Liberal Constitutionalism* (1993).

MONAHAN, P. and FINKELSTEIN, M., 'The Charter of Rights and Public Policy in Canada', (1992) 30 *Osgoode Hall Law Journal* 501.

MORTON, F. L., RUSSELL, P. H. and WITHEY, M. J., 'The Supreme Court's First One Hundred Charter of Rights Decisions: A Statistical Analysis', (1989) 30 *Osgoode Hall Law Journal* 2–56.

PENNER, R., 'The Canadian Experience with the Charter of Rights: Are There Lessons for the United Kingdom?', [1996] *Public Law* 104.

RUSSELL, P., 'The Political Purposes of the Canadian Charter of Rights and Freedoms', (1983) 61 *Canadian Bar Review* 30.

——, 'The Political Purposes of the Charter: Have They Been Fulfilled? An Agnostic's Report Card' in Bryden, P., Davis, S. and Russell, J. (eds.), *Protecting Rights and Freedoms: Essays on the Charter's Public Lawace in Canada's Political, Legal and Intellectual Life* (1994), 33–43.

——, 'Standing Up for Notwithstanding', (1991) 29 *Alberta Law Review* 293.

——, 'The Three Dimensions of Charter Politics', in Bickerton, J. and Gagnon, A. (eds.), *Canadian Politics* (1994), 344.

SHARPE, R., 'A Comment on David Beatty's "A Conservative's Court: The Politicization of Law"', (1991) 41 *University of Toronto Law Journal* 469–83.

—— (ed.), *Charter Litigation* (1987).

SNIDERMAN, P. M., *et al.*, *The Clash of Rights: Liberty, Equality, and Legitimacy in Pluralist Democracy* (1996).

TRAKMAN, L. E., *Reasoning With the Charter* (1991).

WEBBER, J., 'Tales of the Unexpected: Intended and Unintended Consequences of the Canadian Charter of Rights and Freedoms', [1993] 5 *Canterbury Law Review* 207.

WILLIAMS, B., 'From Ottawa to Otorohanga: Reflections on a Bill of Rights: Perspectives from Canada in the Age of the Charter of Rights and Freedoms', [1988] *New Zealand Law Journal* 91–6.

WILSON, B., 'Constitutional Advocacy' (1992) 24 *Ottawa Law Review* 265.

5. The Caribbean

DEMERIEUX, M., *Fundamental Rights in Commonwealth Caribbean Constitutions* (1992).

FRANCIS, L. B. and RAMCHARAN, B. G. (eds.), *Caribbean Perspectives on International Law and Organisations* (1989).

GEORGE, T., 'The Protection of Human Rights Through Law in the Commonwealth Carribean', *Commonwealth Law Bulletin* (October 1992), 1286.

6. East and Central European Countries

BOWRING, B., 'Human Rights in Russia: Discourse of Emancipation or only a Mirage?', in Pogany, I. (ed.), *Human Rights in Eastern Europe* (1995), 87.

Council of Europe, *The Rebirth of Democracy: 12 Constitutions of Central and Eastern Europe* (1995).

DANILENKO, G., 'The New Russian Constitution and International Law', (1994) 88 *American Journal of International Law* 451.

ELSTER, J., 'The Role of Institutional Interest in Eastern European Constitution-Making' [1996] 5 *Eastern European Constitutional Review* 63.

European Commission for Democracy through Law, *The Protection of Fundamental Rights by the Constitutional Court—Proceedings of the UniDem Seminar, Brioni, Croatia, 23–25 September 1995* (1996).

FORSYTHE, D., (ed.), *Human Rights in the New Europe: Problems and Progress* (1994).

FRANKOWSKI, S. and STEPHAN, P. (eds.), *Legal Reform in Post-Communist Europe: The View from Within* (1995).

LETOWSKA, E., 'The Ombudsman and Basic Rights', [1995] 4 *Eastern European Constitutional Review* 63.

LETOWSKI, J., 'The Polish Supreme Court on the Rule of Law and Fundamental Civil Rights', (1996) 8 *European Review of Public Law* 283.

LUDWIKOWSKI, R., "Mixed" Constitutions – Product of an East-Central European Constitutional Melting Pot', (1998) 16 *Boston University International Law Journal* 1.

MAGGS, P., 'Enforcing the Bill of Rights in the Twilight of the Soviet Union', (1991) 199 *University of Illinois Law Review* 1049.

ODLE, R., JR. and ROSENBLATT, D. M., 'Does the State Make you Vomit? (Central European Countries Formulate Bills of Rights)' (1991) *Detroit College of Law Review* 1257.

OSIATYNSKI, W., 'Constitutionalism and Rights in the History of Poland' in Henkin, L. and Rosenthal A. J. (eds.), *Constitutionalism and Rights. The Influence of the United States Constitution Abroad* (1990), 284.

——, 'Rights in New Constitutions of East Central Europe', (1994) 26 *Columbia Human Rights Law Review* 111.

PACZOLAY, P., 'The New Hungarian Constitutional State: Challenges and Perspectives', in Howard, A.E. (ed.), *Constitution Making in Eastern Europe* (1993), 21.

POGANY, I., 'Constitution Making or Constitutional Transformation in the Post-Communist Societies?' in Bellamy, R. and Castiglione, D. (eds.), *Constitutionalism in Transformation: European and Theoretical Perspectives* (1996), 156.

ROTUNDA, R. D., 'Exporting the American Bill of Rights: the Lesson from Romania', (1991) 199 *University of Illinois Law Review* 1065.

SCHEPPELE, K., 'Women's Rights in Eastern Europe', [1995] 4 *Eastern European Constitutional Review* 66.

SCHWARTZ, H., 'The Bill of Rights in America and Central East Europe', (1992) 15 *Harvard Journal of Law and Public Policy* 93–8.

SCHWEISFURTH, T., and ALLEWELDT, R., 'The Position of International Law in the Domestic Legal Orders of Central and Eastern European Countries', in (1997) 40 *German Yearbook of International Law* 164.

SÓLYOM, L., 'The Hungarian Constitutional Court and Social Change', (1994) 19 *Yale Journal of International Law* 223.

STEIN, E., 'International Law in Internal Law: Toward Internationalisation of Central-Eastern European Constitutions', (1994) 88 *American Journal of International Law* 427.

TEITEL, R., 'Post-Communist Constitutionalism: A Transnational Perspective', (1994) 26 *Columbia Human Rights Law Review* 167.
VERDUSSEN, M. (ed.), *La Justice constitutionnelle en Europe centrale* (1997).

7. France

BOUTMY, E., 'La Déclaration des droits de l'homme et M. Jellinek', (1902) 17 *Annales des sciences politiques* 415.
CHINARD, G., *La Déclaration des droits de l'homme et du citoyen et ses antécédents américains* (1945).
FAURÉ, C., *Ce que déclarer des droits veut dire: histoires* (1997)
KLEY, D. VAN, (ed.) *The French Idea of Freedom: The Old Regime and the Declaration of Rights of 1789* (1994).
MARKS, S., 'From the "Single Confused Page" to the "Decalogue for Six Billion Persons": The Roots of the Universal Declaration of Human Rights in the French Revolution', (1998) 20 *Human Rights Quarterly* 459.
The French Declaration of the Rights of Man and the Citizen (1789) and its Influence on Constitutions. Japanese reports for the XIII International Congress of Comparative Law, Montreal, 19–25 August 1990, Tokyo: University of Tokyo (1991).
RIALS, S., *La déclaration des droits de l'homme et du citoyen* (1988).

8. Germany

BEER, L. W., 'American Constitutionalism and German Constitutional Development' in Henkin, L. and Rosenthal A. J. (eds.), *Constitutionalism and Rights. The Influence of the United States Constitution Abroad* (1990), 225.
GRIMM, D., 'Human Rights and Judicial Review in Germany', in Beatty, D. (ed.), *Human Rights and Judicial Review: A Comparative Perspective* (1994), 267.
KOMMERS, D. P., *The Constitutional Jurisprudence of the Federal Republic of Germany* (1989).
STEINBERGER, H., 'Judicial Protection of Human Rights at the National Level: Report on the Federal Republic of Germany' in Carpi, F. and Orlandi, C. (eds.), *General Reports—Judicial Protection of Human Rights at the National and International Level—International Congress on Procedural Law for the Ninth Centenary of the University of Bologna 22–24 September 1988* (1991), 135.
——, 'Historic Influences of American Constitutionalism upon German Constitutional Development: Federalism and Judicial Review', (1997) 36 *Columbia Journal of Transnational Law* 189.

9. Hong Kong

ALLAN, J., 'A Bill of Rights for Hong Kong', [1991] *Public Law* 175.
ARJUNAN, K. and Low-Chee-Keong, 'Self-incrimination, Statutory Restrictions and

the Hong Kong Bill of Rights', (1995) *Singapore Journal of Legal Studies (formerly Malaya Law Review)* 181.

BULLIER, A. J., 'Le Bill of Rights de Hong Kong (1991): Illustration d'une practique ou illusion d'une politique?', (1994) 71 *Revue de Droit International et de Droit comparé* 118.

BYRNES, A., 'The Hong Kong Bill of Rights and Relations Between Private Individuals' in Chan, J. and Ghai, Y. (eds.), *The Hong Kong Bill of Rights: A Comparative Perspective* (1993).

——, 'The Impact of the Hong Kong Bill of Rights on Litigation', in Sihombing, J. (ed.), *Law Lectures for Practitioners 1992*, (1992), 152.

CHAN, J., 'The Applicability of the Bill of Rights to a Body Corporate', (1992) 22 *Hong Kong Law Journal* 269.

CHAN, J., 'The Hong Kong Bill of Rights, 1991–1995: A Statistical Overview' in Edwards and Chan, J. (eds.), *Hong Kong's Bill of Rights: Two Years Before 1997* (1995).

——, 'Undue Delay in Criminal Trials and the Bill of Rights', (1992) 22 *Hong Kong Law Journal* 2–19.

——, and GHAI, Y. (eds.), *The Hong Kong Bill of Rights: A Comparative Approach* (1993).

CONS, D., 'The Hong Kong Bill of Rights: a Judicial Perspective' in Chan, J. and Ghai, Y. (eds.), *The Hong Kong Bill of Rights: A Comparative Perspective* (1993).

COOKE, R., 'Brass Tacks and Bills of Rights', (1995) 25 *Hong Kong Law Journal* 64.

CULLEN, R., 'Hong Kong's Bill of Rights', (1993) 6 *Law Institute Journal* 500.

DYKES, P., 'The Hong Kong Bill of Rights 1991: Its Origin, Content and Impact' in Chan, J. and Ghai, Y. (eds.), *The Hong Kong Bill of Rights: A Comparative Perspective* (1993).

FONG, W., BYRNES, A. and EDWARDS, G. (eds.), *Hong Kong's Bill of Rights: Two Years On* (1994).

GHAI, Y., 'Derogations and Limitations in the Hong Kong Bill of Rights', in J. Chan and Y. Ghai (eds.), *The Hong Kong Bill of Rights: A Comparative Approach* (1993), ch. 8.

——, 'Bills of Rights: Comparative Perspectives' in Wacks, R. (ed.), *Hong Kong's Bill of Rights: Problems and Prospects* (1990), 7–18.

——, *Hong Kong's New Constitutional Order: the Resumption of Chinese Sovereignty and the Basic Law* (1997).

JAMES, A., 'A Bill of Rights for Hong Kong', [1991] *Public Law* 175.

LILLICH, R., 'Sources of Human Rights Law and the Hong Kong Bill of Rights', (1990/91) 10 *Chinese Yearbook of International Law and Affairs* 27.

MORRIS, D., 'Interpreting Hong Kong's Bill of Rights: Some Basic Questions—Part I', (1994) 15 *Statute Law Review* 126.

SWEDE, R., 'One Territory—Three Systems? The Hong Kong Bill of Rights', (1995) 44 *The International and Comparative Law Quarterly* 358–78.

10. Israel

BARAK-EREZ, D., 'From an Unwritten to a Written Constitution: The Israeli Challenge in American Perspective' (1995) 27 *Columbia Human Rights Law Review* 309.

BENVENISTI, E., 'The Influence of International Human Rights Law on the Israeli Legal System: Present and Future', (1994) 28 *Israel Law Review* 136.

EDELMAN, M., *Courts, Politics, and Culture in Israel* (1994).

ELAZAR, D. J, (ed.), *Constitutionalism: The Israeli and American Experiences.* Jerusalem: The Jerusalem Center for Public Affairs, (1990).

GOLDSTEIN, S., 'Protection of Human Rights by Judges: The Israeli Experience', (1994) 38 *Saint Louis University Law Journal* 605.

GROSS, E., 'The Magna Carta of the Defendant According to the New Bill of Rights in Israel—A Comparative Study', 1 (1996) 8 *Pace International Law Review* 9.

JACOBSOHN, G., *Apple of Gold—Constitutionalism in Israel and the United States* (1993).

SEGAL, Z., 'A Constitution Without a Constitution: The Israeli Experience and the American Impact', (1992) 21 *Capital University Law Review* 1.

SPRINZAK, E. and DIAMOND, L., *Israeli Democracy Under Stress* (1993).

WEINRIB, L., 'The Canadian Charter as a Model for Israel's Basic Laws', (1993) 4 *Constitutional Forum* 85–7.

11. Japan

INOUE, K., *MacArthur's Japanese Constitution: A Linguistic and Cultural Study of its Making* (1991).

ITOH, H., 'Judicial Review and Judicial Activism in Japan', (1990) 53 *Law and Contemporary Problems* 169.

IWASAWA, Y., *International Law, Human Rights Law and Japanese Law: The Impact of International Law on Japanese Law* (1998).

PORT, K., 'The Japanese International Law "Revolution": International Human Rights Law and its Impact in Japan', (1991) 28 *Stanford Journal of International Law* 139.

RAMLOGAN, R., 'The Human Rights Revolution in Japan: A Story of New Wine in Old Skins?', (1994) 8 *Emory International Law Review* 129.

SONOBE, I., 'Human Rights and Constitutional Review in Japan', in Beatty, D. (ed.), *Human Rights and Judicial Review: A Comparative Perspective* (1994), 135.

12. Namibia

BJORNLUND, E. C., 'The Devil's Work? Judicial Review Under a Bill of Rights in South Africa and Namibia', (1990) 26 *Stanford Journal of International Law* 391.

ERASMUS, G., 'The Namibian Constitution and the Application of International Law', (1990) 15 *South African Yearbook of International Law* 81.

FOURIE, F., 'The Namibian Constitution and Economic Rights', (1990) 6 *South African Journal on Human Rights* 363.

KAHANOVITZ, C., 'The Namibian Bill of Rights: Implications for the Promotion of Procedural and Substantive Justice in Criminal Cases', (1992) 2 *Criminal Law Forum* 569.

NALDI, G., *Constitutional Rights in Namibia: A Comparative Analysis with International Human Rights* (1995).

STRYDOM, G. J. C., 'A Bill of Rights and "Value Judgments" vs. Positivism: the Namibian Experience', in Kruger, J. and Currin, B., (eds.), *Interpreting a Bill of Rights* (1994).

WELCH, C. E. Jr., *Protecting Human Rights in Africa: Strategies and Roles of Non-Governmental Organizations* (1995), 179.

13. New Zealand

ADAMS, G., 'Competing Conceptions of the Constitution: The New Zealand Bill of Rights Act 1990 and the Coole Court of Appeal', [1996] *New Zealand Law Review* 368.

AUSTIN, G., 'Righting a Child's Right to Refuse Medical Treatment; Section 11 of the New Zealand Bill of Rights Act and the Gillick Competent Child', (1993) 7 *Otago Law Review* 578.

BUTLER, A., 'The New Zealand Bill of Rights and Private Common Law Litigation', [1991] *New Zealand Law Journal* 261.

COOKE, LORD, 'Mechanisms for Entrenchment and Protection of a Bill of Rights: The New Zealand Experience' in [1997] 5 *European Human Rights Law Review* 490.

ELKIND, J., 'The Optional Protocol: a Bill of Rights for New Zealand', [1990] *New Zealand Law Journal* 96.

——, 'The Optional Protocol and the Covenant on Civil and Political Rights', [1991] *New Zealand Law Journal* 409.

——, 'Interpreting the Bill of Rights', [1991] *New Zealand Law Journal* 15–16.

——, 'New Zealand's Experience with a Non-Entrenched Bill of Rights', in Alston, P., (ed.), *Towards an Australian Bill of Rights* (1994), 235.

FITZGERALD, P., 'Section 7 of the New Zealand Bill of Rights Act 1990: A Very Practical Power or a Well-Intentioned Nonsense?', (1992) 22 *Victoria University of Wellington Law Review* 135.

HARRIS, B., 'Prerogative Powers and the New Zealand Bill of Rights Act 1990', (1993) 15 *New Zealand Universities Law Review* 323.

HASTINGS, W. K., 'The New Zealand Bill of Rights and Censorship', [1990] *New Zealand Law Journal* 384.

JOSEPH, P., 'The Challenge of a Bill of Rights: A Commentary', [1986] *New Zealand Law Journal* 416.

——, 'The New Zealand Bill of Rights', (1996) 7 *Public Law Review* 162.

KENYON, M. E., 'New Zealand Bill of Rights Act 1990', (1991) 6 *Auckland University Law Review* 610.

McGEE, D., 'The Application of Article 9 of the Bill of Rights 1688', [1990] *New Zealand Law Journal* 346.

NOVEMBER, J., 'Burdens of Proof and the New Zealand Bill of Rights Act s. 25(c)', [1991] *New Zealand Law Journal* 335.

PHILLIPS, C. and ENRIGHT, R., 'The Maori Magna Carta: New Zealand Law and the Treaty of Waitangi', (1992) 7 *Auckland University Law Review* 232.

PRINCIPE, M., 'The Demise of Parliamentary Supremacy? Canadian and American Influences upon the New Zealand Judiciary's Interpretations of the Bill of Rights Act of 1990', (1993) 16 *Loyola of Los Angeles International and Comparative Law Journal* 167.

——, 'The New Zealand Bill of Rights: a Step Towards the Canadian and American Examples or a Continuation of Parliamentary Supremacy?', (1990) 6 *Florida Journal of International Law* 135.

RISHWORTH, P. T., 'The Potential of the New Zealand Bill of Rights', [1990] *New Zealand Law Journal* 68–72.

——, 'Human Rights—From the Top', (1997) 68 *Political Quarterly* 171.

ROBERTSON, B., 'Confessions and the Bill of Rights', [1991] *New Zealand Law Journal* 398.

SHAW, A. and BUTLER, A., 'Arbitrary Arrest and Detention Under the New Zealand Bill of Rights: The New Zealand Courts Stumble in Applying the International Covenant', [1993] *New Zealand Law Journal* 139.

——, and ——, 'The New Zealand Bill of Rights Comes Alive (part I)', [1991] *New Zealand Law Journal* 400.

SMILLIE, J. A., '"Fundamental" rights, Parliamentary supremacy and the New Zealand Court of Appeal', (1995) 111 *The Law Quarterly Review* 209–17.

14. Nigeria

AGBAKOBA, O., 'The Role of Lawyers and the Observance of Human Rights' (1995) 5(1) *Journal of Human Rights Law and Practice* 115.

AJOMO, M. AYO and OWASANOYE, B. (eds.), *Individual Rights Under the 1989 Constitution* (1993).

Civil Liberties Organisation, *Justice for Sale: A Report of the Administration of Justice in the Magistrates and Customary Courts of Southern Nigeria* (1996).

EBEKU, K., 'Nigeria's New Constitution for the Third Republic: An Overview', (1993) 5 *African Journal of International and Comparative Law* 581.

IDIDAPO-OBE, A., 'Remedies for Breach of Fundamental Rights', in Ajomo, M. Ayo and Owasanoye, B. (eds.), *Individual Rights Under the 1989 Constitution* (1993), 84.

WELCH, C. E. Jr., *Protecting Human Rights in Africa: Strategies and Roles of Non-Governmental Organizations* (1995), 179.

15. South Africa

A Bill of Rights for a Democratic South Africa: Papers and Report of a Conference Convened by the ANC Constitutional Committee, May 1991 (Bellville: Centre for Development Studies, University of the Western Cape, 1992).

AMANKWAH, A. H., 'Constitutions and Bills of Rights in Third World Nations: Issues of Form and Content', (1988) 21 *Comparative and International Law Journal of South Africa* 190; and also in (1989) 12 *Adelaide Law Review* 1–22.

ANC Constitutional Committee, A Bill of Rights for a New South Africa: A Working Document. (Center for Development Studies, 1990).

ASMAL, K., 'Democracy and Human Rights, Developing a South African Human Rights Culture' (1992) 27 *New England Law Review* 287.

BEATTY, D., 'The Rule (and Role) of Law in a New South Africa: Some Lessons From Abroad', (1992) 109 *South African Law Journal* 408.

BERAT, L., 'A New South Africa?; Prospects for an Africanist Bill of Rights and a Transformed Judiciary', (1990) 13 *Loyola of Los Angeles International and Comparative Law Journal* 467.

BINDMAN, G., 'South Africa's Bill of Rights', (1991) 141 *New Law Journal* 997–8.

BJORNLUND, E. C., 'The Devil's Work? Judicial Review Under a Bill of Rights in South Africa and Namibia', (1990) 26 *Stanford Journal of International Law* 391.

BULLIER, A. J., 'Vers l'Introduction d'une Declaration des Droits "Bill of Rights" dans une Afrique du Sud Post-Apartheid', *Rev. Sci. Criminelle et Droit Penal Compare* (1992), 293.

CORDER, H., *A Charter for Social Justice: a Contribution to the South African Bill of Rights Debate* (Department of Public Law, University of the Western Cape Town: Legal Resources Centre, 1992).

——, 'Towards a South African Constitution', (1994) 57 *Modern Law Review* 491.

CURRIE, I. *et al.*, *The New Constitutional and Administrative Law* (1999).

CURRIN, B. and KRUGER, J., 'The Protection of Fundamental Rights in the Constitution of the Republic of South Africa, 1993: A Brief Contextualization' in Kruger, J. and Currin, B. (eds.), *Interpreting a Bill of Rights* (1994).

DAVIS, D., 'The Case Against the Inclusion of Socio-Economic Demands in a Bill of Rights Except as Directive Principles', (1992) 8 *South African Journal on Human Rights* 475.

——, *Post Apartheid South Africa: What Future for a Legal System?* (1988).

DE VILLIERS, B., 'Directive Principles of State Policy and Fundamental Rights: The Indian Experience' (1992) 8 *South African Journal on Human Rights* 29–49.

——, 'The Socio-Economic Consequences of Directive Principles of State Policy; Limitations on Fundamental Rights' (1992) 8 *South African Journal on Human Rights* 188.

DLAMINI, C. R. M., 'A Court-Enforced Bill of Rights for South Africa?', (1988) 7 *Journal of Contemporary African Studies* 81.

DU PLESSIS, L., 'The Interpretation of Bills of Rights in South Africa: Taking Stock', in Kruger, J. and Currin, B. (eds.), *Interpreting a Bill of Rights* (1994).

—— and CORDER, H., *Understanding South Africa's Transitional Bill of Rights* (1994).

DUGARD, J., 'A Bill of Rights for South Africa?', (1990) 23 *Cornell International Law Journal* 441.

——, 'Human Rights, Apartheid and Lawyers. Are there any Lessons for Lawyers from Common Law Countries?' (1992) 15 *University of New South Wales Law Journal* 439.

——, 'The Role of International Law in Interpreting the Bill of Rights', (1994) 10 *South African Journal on Human Rights* 208.

EISENBERG, A., '"Public Purpose" and Expropriation: Some Comparative Insights and the South African Bill of Rights', (1995) 11 *South African Journal on Human Rights* 207.

ELLMANN, S., 'Law and Legitimacy in South Africa', (1995) 20 *Law and Social Inquiry* 407.

——, 'The New South African Constitution and Ethnic Division', (1994) 26 *Columbia Human Rights Law Review* 5–44.

FORSYTH, C., 'Interpreting a Bill of Rights: The Future Task of a Reformed Judiciary?', (1991) 7 *South African Journal on Human Rights* 1.

GAUL, E., 'The Quest for a Constitution', (1993) 20 *Human Rights* 22.

HAYSOM, N., 'Democracy, Constitutionalism and the ANC's Bill of Rights for a New South Africa', (1991) 7 *South African Journal of Human Rights* 102; and also in (1991) 18 *Social Justice* 40–8.

——, 'Constitutionalism, Majoritarian Democracy and Socio-Economic Rights' (1992) 8 *South African Journal on Human Rights* 451.

'Human Rights in the Post-Apartheid South African Constitution: Special Issue', [1989] 21 *Columbia Human Rights Law Review* 1–251.

HUND, J., 'A Bill of Rights for South Africa', (1989) 34 *American Journal of Jurisprudence* 23–42.

JOZANA, M. C., 'Proposed South African Bill of Rights: a Prescription for Equality or Neo-apartheid?', (1991) 7 *American University Journal of International Law and Policy* 45–82; and also in (1990) 15 *West Indian Law Journal* 1–44.

KENTRIDGE, S., 'Bills of Rights—The South African Experiment' (1996) 112 *Law Quarterly Review* 237.

——, 'Lessons from South Africa', in Markesinis (ed.), *The Impact of the Human Rights Bill on English Law* (1998), 25.

KROEZE, I. J., 'The Impact of the Bill of Rights on Property Law', (1994) 9 *South African Public Law* 322.

LEVENBERG, P., 'South Africa's New Constitution: Will It Last?', (1995) 29 *The International Lawyer* 633.

LICHT, R. and DE VILLIERS, B. (eds.), *South Africa's Crisis of Consititutional Democracy: Can the US Constitution Help?* (1994).

LOURENS, J. and FRANTZEN, M., 'The South African Bill of Rights: Public, Private or Both—A Viewpoint on its Sphere of Application', (1994) 27 *Comparative and International Law Journal of Southern Africa* 340.

MUREINIK, E., 'A Bridge to Where? Introducing the Interim Bill of Rights', (1994) 10 *South African Journal on Human Rights* 31–48.

——, 'Beyond a Charter of Luxuries: Economic Rights in the Constitution', (1992) 8 *South African Journal on Human Rights* 464.

MURRAY, C., 'A Bill of Rights for a New South Africa', (1991) 3 *African Journal of International and Comparative Law* 589.

MYERSON, D., *Rights Limited: Freedom of Expression, Religion and the South African Constitution* (1997).

PATEL, E. (ed.), *Worker Rights: From Apartheid to Democracy—What Role for Organised Labour?* (1994).

SACHS, A., 'A Bill of Rights for South Africa: Areas of Agreement and Disagreement', (Special Issue: Human Rights in the Post-Apartheid South African Constitution) (1989) 21 *Columbia Human Rights Law Review* 13–44.

——, *Protecting Human Rights in a New South Africa* (1990).

——, 'Toward a Bill of Rights in a Democratic South Africa', (1990) 6 *South African Journal of Human Rights* 1–24.

——, 'Towards a Bill of Rights for a Democratic South Africa', (1988) 12 *Hastings International and Comparative Law Review* 289.

——, 'Towards a Bill of Rights for a Democratic South Africa', (1991) 35 *Journal of African Law* 21–43.

SARKIN, J., 'Innovations in the Interim and 1996 South African Constitutions', (1998) 60 *The Review of the International Commission of Jurists* 57.

SCHNEIDER, H. P., 'Value Judgments and the Spirit of the Constitution', in Kruger, J. and Currin, B. (eds.), *Interpreting a Bill of Rights* (1994).

SONNEKUS, J., 'South Africa's Transition to Democracy and the Rule of Law', (1995) 29 *The International Lawyer* 659.

STEENKAMP, A. J., 'The South African Constitution of 1993 and the Bill of Rights: An Evaluation in Light of International Human Rights Norms', (1995) 17 *Human Rights Quarterly* 101.

STROSSEN, N., 'Translating a Bill of Rights' Paper Guarantees into Meaningful Human Rights Protections', in Kruger, J. and Currin, B. (eds.), *Interpreting a Bill of Rights* (1994).

STYCHIN, C., 'Constituting Sexuality—The Struggle for Sexual Orientation in the South African Bill of Rights', (1996) 23 *Journal of Law and Society* 455.

TRAKMAN, L. E., 'Interpreting a Bill of Rights: Canada and South Africa Compared', in Kruger, J. and Currin, B. (eds.), *Interpreting a Bill of Rights* (1994).

VOS, P. DE, 'A Bill of Rights in a Post-apartheid South African Constitution: A Contextual International Human Rights Analysis', (1993) 24 *Columbia Human Rights Law Review* 277.

VYVER, J. D. VAN DER, 'Parliamentary Sovereignty, Fundamental Freedoms and a Bill of Rights', (1982) 99 *South African Law Journal* 557–88.

WESTHUIZEN, J. VAN DER and VILJOEN, H. (eds.), *A Bill of Rights for South Africa: Proceedings of Symposium held at the University of Pretoria on 1 and 2 May 1986* (1988).

WYK, D. VAN, 'The South African Bill of Rights: An Evaluation', (1994) 9 *South African Public Law* 278.

——, DUGARD, J., DE VILLIERS, B. and DAVIS, D. (eds.), *Rights and Constitutionalism: The New South African Legal Order* (1996).

16. Tanzania

LUBUVA, D., 'Reflections on Tanzania's Bill of Rights', (1988) 14 *Commonwealth Law Bulletin* 853.

MWAIKUSA, J., 'Genesis of the Bill of Rights in Tanzania', (1991) 3 *African Journal of International and Comparative Law* 680.

MWALUSANYA, J., 'The Protection of Human Rights in the Criminal Justice Proceedings—The Tanzanian Experience' in Bassiouini, M. and Motala, Z. (eds.), *The Protection of Human Rights in African Criminal Proceedings* (1995), 285.

PETER, C., *Human Rights in Africa: A Comparative Study of the African Human and Peoples' Rights Charter and the New Tanzanian Bill of Rights* (1990).

——, 'Respect for Fundamental Rights and Freedoms: A New Bill of Rights for Tanzania', (1989) 67 *Revue de Droit International, des Sciences Diplomatiques et Politiques* 255.

——, 'Five Years of the Bill of Rights in Tanzania', (1992) 4 *African Journal of International and Comparative Law* 131.

RWEZAURA, B., 'Tanzania: Family Law and the New Bill of Rights', (1991) 29 *Journal of Family Law* 453.

17. Uganda

SEKANDI, F. and GITTA C., 'Protection of Fundamental Rights in the Uganda Constitution', (1994) 26 *Columbia Human Rights Law Review* 191.

18. United Kingdom

ABERNATHY, M. G., 'Should the United Kingdom Adopt a Bill of Rights?', (1983) 31 *American Journal of Comparative Law* 431–79.

ALLAN, T. R. S., 'Constitutional Rights and Common Law', (1991) 11 *Oxford Journal of Legal Studies* 453.

ALSTON, P., 'Making Economic and Social Rights Count: A Strategy for the Future', (1997) 68 *Political Quarterly* 188.

ASHWORTH, A., 'The Impact on Criminal Justice', in Markesinis, B. S. (ed.), *The Impact of the Human Rights Bill on English Law* (1998), 141.

BELOFF, M. and MOUNTFIELD, H. 'Unconventional Behaviour? Judicial Uses of the European Convention in England and Wales' [1996] *European Human Rights Law Review* 467.

BINGHAM, T., 'The European Convention on Human Rights: Time to Incorporate', (1993) 109 *Law Quarterly Review* 390.

BIX, B. and TOMKINS, A., 'Unconventional Use of the Convention?', (1992) 55 *Modern Law Review* 721.

BLACKBURN, R., 'A British Bill of Rights for the 21st Century', in Blackburn, R. and Busuttil, J. (eds.), *Human Rights for the 21st Century* (1997), 16–59.

——, 'Legal and Political Arguments for a United Kingdom Bill of Rights', in Blackburn, R. and Taylor, J. (eds.), *Human Rights for the 1990s* (1991) 108.

——, 'Parliamentary Opinion on a New Bill of Rights', (1989) 60 *Political Quarterly* 469.

——, *The Bill of Rights Debate* (1996).

BLAKE, N., 'Judicial Review of Discretion in Human Rights Cases', [1997] 2 *European Human Rights Law Review* 391.

BOYLE, A., 'Freedom of Expression as a Public Interest in English Law', [1982] *Public Law* 574.

BRADLEY, A., 'The United Kingdom before the Strasbourg Court 1975–1990', in Finnie, W., Himsworth, C. and Walker, N. (eds.), *Edinburgh Essays in Public Law* (1991), 185.

BRAZIER, R., *Constitutional Reform: Re-shaping the British Political System*, (1991), ch 7.

BROWNE-WILKINSON, N., 'The Infiltration of a Bill of Rights', [1992] *Public Law* 397.

BROWNE-WILKINSON, LORD, 'The Impact on Judicial Reasoning', in Markesinis, B. S. (ed.), *The Impact of the Human Rights Bill on English Law* (1998), 21.

CAMPBELL, C. (ed.), *Do We Need a Bill of Rights?* (1980).

CAMPBELL, T., 'Human Rights: A Culture of Controversy', (1999) 26 *Journal of Law and Society* 6.

CHANDER, A., 'Sovereignty, Referenda, and the Entrenchment of a United Kingdom Bill of Rights', (1991) 101 *Yale Law Journal* 457.

CUMPER, P., 'A Path to a Bill of Rights' (1991) 141 *New Law Journal* 100.

DWORKIN, R. M., *A Bill of Rights for Britain* (1990).

EMMERSON, B., 'This Year's Model: The Options for Incorporation', [1997] 2 *European Human Rights Law Review* 313.

EWING, K., *A Bill of Rights for Britain?* (1990).

——, 'A Bill of Rights: Lessons from the Privy Council' in Finnie *et al* (eds.), *Edinburgh Essays in Public Law* (1991).

——, 'Human Rights, Social Democracy and Constitutional Reform', in Gearty, C. and Tomkins, A. (eds.), *Understanding Human Rights* (1996), 40.

——, 'The Human Rights Act and Parliamentary Democracy', (1999) 62 *Modern Law Review* 79.

——, and GEARTY, C. A., *Democracy or a Bill of Rights* (1991).

——, and ——, *Freedom Under Thatcher: Civil Liberties in Modern Britain* (1990).

——, and ——, 'Rocky Foundations for Labour's New Rights', [1997] 2 *European Human Rights Law Review* 146.

FINNIS, J., 'A Bill of Rights for Britain? The Moral of Contemporary Jurisprudence', (1985) LXXI *Proceedings of the British Academy* 303.

FOLEY, C., *Human Rights, Human Wrongs: The Alternative Report to the United Nations Human Rights Committee* (1995).

FREDMAN, S., 'Equality Issues', in Markesinis, B. S. (ed.), *The Impact of the Human Rights Bill on English Law* (1998), 111.

GEARTY, C. A., 'Democracy and a Bill of Rights: Some Lessons from Ireland', in Ewing, K. D., Gearty, C. A. and Hepple, B. A., *Human Rights and Labour Law: Essays for Paul O'Higgins* (1994), 188.

——, 'The European Court of Human Rights and the Protection of Civil Liberties: An Overview', (1993) 52 *Cambridge Law Journal* 89.

GORDON, R. and Wilmot-Smith R. (eds.), *Human Rights in the United Kingdom* (1996).

GRIEF, N., 'The Domestic Impact of the European Convention on Human Rights as Mediated Through Community Law', [1991] *Public Law* 555.

GRIFFITH, J., *The Politics of the Judiciary* (1985).

HAMPSON, F., 'The United Kingdom Before the European Court of Human Rights' (1990) 9 *Yearbook of European Law* 121.

HEPPLE, B., 'The Impact on Labour Law', in Markesinis, B. S. (ed.), *The Impact of the Human Rights Bill on English Law* (1998), 63.

HUNT, M., *Using Human Rights Law in English Courts* (1997).

——, 'The 'Horizontal Effect' of the Human Rights Act', [1998] *Public Law* 423.

——, 'The Effect on the Law of Obligations', in Markesinis, B. S. (ed.), *The Impact of the Human Rights Bill on English Law* (1998), 159.

Institute for Public Policy and Research, Consultation Paper 'A Human Rights Commission for the UK: The Options' (December 1996).

IRVINE, LORD, 'Constitutional Reform and a Bill of Rights' in [1997] 5 *European Human Rights Law Review* 483.

——, 'The Development of Human Rights in Britain under an Incorporated Convention on Human Rights', [1998] *Public Law* 221.

JACONELLI, J., *Enacting a Bill of Rights: The Legal Problems* (1980).

——, 'Incorporation of the European Human Rights Convention: Arguments and Misconceptions', [1997] 59 *Political Quarterly* 343 [1997].

——, 'The European Convention on Human Rights — The Text of a British Bill of Rights?', [1992] *Public Law* 226.

JONES, G. W., 'The British Bill of Rights', (1990) 43 *Parliamentary Affairs* 27–40.

JUSS, S. S., 'Silent Rights: the Time is Ripe for a New Bill of Rights to Protect Citizens from an Overbearing Executive', (1989) 139 *New Law Journal* 1069.

KERRIDGE, R., 'Incorporation of the European Convention on Human Rights into United Kingdom Domestic Law', in Furmston, M.P., Kerridge, R. and Sufrin, B.E. (eds.), *The Effect on English Domestic Law of Membership of the European Communities and of Ratification of the European Convention on Human Rights* (1983), 247.

KINLEY, D., 'Legislation, Discretionary Authority and the European Convention on Human Rights ', (1992) 13 *Statute Law Review* 63.

——, *The European Convention on Human Rights: Compliance Without Incorporation* (1993).

KLUG, F., 'A Bill of Rights for the United Kingdom: A Comparative Summary', in [1997] 5 *European Human Rights Law Review* 501.

——, *A People's Charter: Liberty's Bill of Rights* (1991).

——, 'Can Human Rights Fill Britain's Morality Gap?', (1997) 68 *Political Quarterly* 143.

——, STARMER, K. and WEIR, S., *The Three Pillars of Liberty: Political Rights and Freedoms in the United Kingdom* (1996).

KRÜGER, H. C., 'Current Topic: The Practicalities of a Bill of Rights' in [1997] 4 *European Human Rights Law Review* 353.

——, 'The Practicalities of a Bill of Rights', [1997] 2 *European Human Rights Law Review* 353.

LAWS, J., 'Is the High Court the Guardian of Fundamental Constitutional Rights?', [1993] *Public Law* 59.

——, 'The Constitution: Morals and Rights', [1996] *Public Law* 622.

LEE, S., 'Bicentennial Bork, Tercentennial Spycatcher: Do the British Need a Bill of Rights?', (1988) 49 *University of Pittsburgh Law Review* 777.

LESTER, A., 'Fundamental Rights: The United Kingdom Isolated', [1984] *Public Law* 46.

——, *A British Bill of Rights. Institute for Public Policy Research* (1990).

——, 'The Impact of Europe on the British Constitution' (1992) 3 *Public Law Review* 228.

——, 'English Judges as Law Makers' [1993] *Public Law* 269.

——, 'The Georgetown Conclusions on the Effective Protection of Human Rights Through Law', [1996] *Public Law* 562.

——, 'First Steps Towards A Constitutional Bill of Rights', [1997] 2 *European Human Rights Law Review* 124.

LLOYD, D., *A Bill of Rights and the U.K. Constitution: Conflict and Integration: Comparative Law in the World Today* (1989).

LOCK, G., 'The 1689 Bill of Rights', (1989) 37 *Political Studies* 540–61.

LYELL, N., 'Whither Strasbourg? Why Britain Should Think Long and Hard Before Incorporating the European Convention on Human Rights', [1997] 2 *European Human Rights Law Review* 132.

McCRUDDEN, C., 'The Impact on Freedom of Speech', in Markesinis, B. S. (ed.), *The Impact of the Human Rights Bill on English Law* (1998), 85.

MANN, F., 'Britain's Bill of Rights', (1978) *Law Quarterly Review* 512–33.

MARKESINIS, B. S. (ed.), *The Impact of the Human Rights Bill on English Law* (1998).

MARSHALL, G., 'On Constitutional Theory', in Markesinis, B. S. (ed.), *The Impact of the Human Rights Bill on English Law* (1998), 15.

MORRIS, D., 'The Scope for Constitutional Challenge of Westminster Legislation', (1991) 12 *Statute Law Review* 186.

MOYER, T., 'The Bill of Rights—its Origins and its Keepers', (1991) 75 *Judicature* 56–61.

MURDOCH, J., 'The European Convention on Human Rights in Scots Law', [1991] *Public Law* 40.

SCARMAN, L., 'Britain and the Protection of Human Rights', (1984) 15 *Cambrian Law Review* 5.

——, *English Law—The New Dimension* (1974).

——, 'Human Rights in an Unwritten Constitution' [1987] *Denning Law Journal* 129.

——, 'The Common Law Judge and the Twentieth Century' (1980) 7 *Monash University Law Review* 1.

SEDLEY, SIR S, 'Opinion: A Bill of Rights for Britain' in [1997] 5 *European Human Rights Law Review* 458.

SINGH, R., *The Future of Human Rights in the UK* (1997).

SKELLY WRIGHT, J., 'The Bill of Rights in Britain and America: A Not Quite Full Circle', (1981) 55 *Tulane Law Review* 291.

SPENCER, S. and BYNOE, I., 'A Human Rights Commission for the United Kingdom: Some Options', [1997] 2 *European Human Rights Law Review* 152.

STARMER, K. and WEIR, S., 'Strong Government and Weak Liberties: An Overview of Political Freedom in the UK', (1997) 68 *Political Quarterly* 135.

STRAW, J. and BOATENG, P., 'Bringing Rights Home: Labour's Plans to Incorporate the European Convention on Human Rights into UK Law', [1997] 2 *European Human Rights Law Review* 71.

WALLINGTON, P. and McBRIDIE, J., *Civil Liberties and a Bill of Rights* (1978).

WADHAM, J., 'Bringing Rights Half-way Home', [1997] 2 *European Human Rights Law Review* 141.

WARD, D., 'A Bill of Rights?', (1990) 134 *Solicitors Journal* 1375.

'What's Wrong With a Bill of Rights, (1990) 3(110) *New Statesman and Society* 12–14.

WINTEMUTE, R., 'Current Topic: Lesbian and Gay Britons, the Two Europes, and the Bill of Rights Debate' in [1997] 5 *European Human Rights Law Review* 466.

ZANDER, M., *A Bill of Rights?* 4th edn. (1997).

19. United States of America

ACKERMAN, B., *We the People*, Vol. 1: *Foundations* (1991); Vol. 2: *Transformations* (1998).

AMAR, A., 'The Bill of Rights as a Constitution', (1991) 100 *Yale Law Journal* 1131.

——, *The Bill of Rights: Creation and Construction* (1998).

BECKER, M., 'The Politics of Women's Wrongs and the Bill of "Rights": A Bicentennial Perspective', (1992) 59 *University of Chicago Law Review* 453.

BEER, L., (ed.), *Constitutionalism in Asia: Asian Views of the American Influence* (1979).

CAINE, B., GARRO, A. M., VAN POELGEEST, B. and ADAM, S., 'The Influence Abroad of the United States Constitution on Judicial Review and a Bill of Rights', (1988) 2 *Temple International and Comparative Law Journal* 59–78.

COGAN, N. H., *The Complete Bill of Rights: The Drafts, Debates, Sources, and Origins* (1997).

HENKIN, L., 'A Decent Respect to the Opinions of Mankind', (U.S. Bill of Rights, U.N. Universal Declaration of Human Rights) (A Symposium on Human Rights: 'A Decent Respect to the Opinions of Mankind'), (1992) 25 *John Marshall Law Review* 215.

——, 'Constitutionalism and Human Rights' in Henkin, L. and Rosenthal A. J. (eds.), *Constitutionalism and Rights. The Influence of the United States Constitution Abroad* (1990), 383.

——, and ROSENTHAL, A. (eds.), *Constitutionalism and Rights: the Influence of the United States Abroad* (1990).

HOLMES, S. and SUNSTEIN, C., *The Cost of Rights: Why Liberty Depends on Taxes* (1999).

LESTER, A., 'The Overseas Trade in the American Bill of Rights', (1988) 88 *Columbia Law Review* 537.

MARTIN, R. and GRIFFIN, S., 'Constitutional Rights and Democracy in the USA: The Issue of Judicial Review', (1995) 8 *Ratio Juris* 180.

RAPACZYNSKI, A., 'Bibliographical Essay: The Influence of U.S. Constitutionalism Abroad', in Henkin, L., and Rosenthal, A. (eds.), *Constitutionalism and Rights: The Influence of the United States Constitution Abroad* (1990), 405.

STRAUSS, D., 'The Role of a Bill of Rights', (1992) 59 *University of Chicago Law Review* 539.

STROSSEN, N., 'United States Ratification of the International Bill of Rights: A Fitting Celebration of the Bicentennial of the U.S. Bill of Rights', (1992) 24 *University of Toledo Law Review* 203.

SUNSTEIN, C., *One Case at a Time: Judicial Minimalism on the Supreme Court* (1999).

THOMPSON, K., (ed.), *The U.S. Constitution and the Constitutions of Asia* (1989).

—— (ed.), *The U.S. Constitution and the Constitutions of Latin America* (1991).

TRIBE, L., *American Constitutional Law*, 3rd ed. (2000).

WEISBURD, A., 'State Courts, Federal Courts, and International Cases', (1995) 20 *Yale Journal of International Law* 1–64.

WUNDER, J. R., *'Retained by the People': A History of American Indians and the Bill of Rights* (1994).

Index